[materialis[
[subjective[

THE ENDURING QUESTIONS

Melvin Rader

UNIVERSITY OF WASHINGTON

THE
ENDURING
QUESTIONS

MAIN PROBLEMS OF PHILOSOPHY

Henry Holt and Company · New York

Preface

THIS BOOK is designed for all adults who would like to know what philosophy is about. It is for the general reader, layman or student, not for the advanced scholar.

Philosophy, far from being dull, is exciting and provocative. The best way to demonstrate this fact is to allow the philosophers to speak for themselves. This book directly introduces the reader not only to the older philosophical masters, such as Plato, Aristotle, Descartes, Berkeley, and Hume, but also to more recent figures, such as Peirce, James, Dewey, Russell, and Santayana.

Original selections from the writings of leading philosophers are often difficult to understand. The present book, being both a guide *and* an anthology, not only includes ample reading from the classics but also attempts to give the reader assistance in understanding and integrating the selections. The editor's aim has been to supply background and supplementary material without dwelling upon what is obvious from the original texts. Except for the explanatory materials in Part One and the biographical sketches in the other Parts, the comments follow rather than precede the selections. They should be useful *after* a thorough study of the readings; they are not a substitute.

The critical remarks included in the comments are meant to be stimulative rather than authoritative. Altogether the reader is presented with many angles of vision; he may take his choice, keeping here and rejecting there; or he may gather ideas for some new synthesis of his own. The more he disagrees and questions, the more philosophy is probably taking hold.

The non-academic reader, who lacks the assistance of class room lectures and discussions, will appreciate the guidance of editorial comment, but students and teachers may be likewise appreciative. The teacher can take as his starting point the student's knowledge of the readings as illuminated by the comments, going on from there to higher-level discussions. There are many important issues that are touched upon but not treated in detail in the book—for example, the tests of a good hypothesis, the nature and status of universals, the relation between mind and body, the question of free will, the possibility of an after-life, the meaning of emergent evolution, the nature of moral obligation, the conflict between relativism and absolutism in ethics, the moral basis of national sovereignty, and the duty of a state to other states. In discussing such topics and in taking issue with the readings or with the editor's comments, the teacher will have ample scope to develop his own views.

The bulk of the book consists of original readings rather than interpretations. Any teacher who prefers to substitute his analyses and criticisms for the latter will be free to do so, since the readings alone constitute abundant material for the average course.

The chapters have been arranged in logical order, but this is not necessarily the order in which they should be read. There are some advantages in dealing with ethical or social questions before considering epistemological or metaphysical issues. The Parts are designed to be relatively independent and can be read in whatever order is preferred.

The readings have been selected on the basis of their clarity, profundity, and suitability for introductory study. Selections from some of the great thinkers, such as Leibniz, Spinoza, and Hegel, have been omitted because of the extreme difficulty of their style for lay readers and students in philosophy. Considerations of space have resulted in other omissions. It seemed better to include ample selections from relatively few authors than fragmentary selections from a large number. No choice of readings and commentary will suit everyone. It is hoped that the present book provides at least an abundance of material that will excite thought and discussion.

I wish to thank my colleagues Arthur Murphy, A. I. Melden, Arthur Smullyan, Leonard Miller and Marion Stanton for valuable suggestions; and Ellen Tallman and Dorothy Smullyan for preparation of the manuscript.

M. R.

February 1, 1956
Seattle, Washington

Contents

What Is Philosophy?

PART ONE

What Is Philosophy?

1

The Nature of Philosophy

The General Interpretation of Experience

If the philosopher can be called a "specialist," he is a specialist in the general. Socrates (in Plato's *Republic*) defines the philosopher as "the spectator of all time and all existence"; and William James declares that philosophy deals "with the principles of explanation that underlie all things without exception, the elements common to gods and men and animals and stones, the first *whence* and the last *whither* of the whole cosmic procession, the conditions of all knowing, and the most general rules of human conduct." [1]

C. D. Broad similarly characterizes philosophy in the following selection. He distinguishes between *critical* and *speculative* philosophy, both of which deal with what is general. The task of critical philosophy is to analyze and define our most fundamental and general concepts, such as "goodness," "truth," "reality," and "causation." The object of speculative philosophy is "to take over the results of the various sciences, to add to them the results of the religious and ethical experiences of mankind, and then to reflect upon the whole" in an attempt "to reach some general conclusions as to the nature of the Universe, and as to our position and prospects in it."

These characterizations seem to fit the problems that philosophers most often discuss: What is a good life? What is the relation between mind and body? Do we have free will? Is there a God? Shall we live forever? Is the world fundamentally material or spiritual? Can we know the ultimate nature of reality? These are basic questions involved in a general interpretation of the world. Accordingly, Herbert Spencer defines philosophy as "knowledge of the highest degree of generality." [2]

There are certain difficulties in this view. First, science also is sometimes *very* general. Newton's theory of gravitation, for example, characterizes the nearest and the most remote, the least and the greatest of objects—the pin

[1] *Some Problems of Philosophy* (Longmans, Green, 1911), p. 5.
[2] *First Principles* (New York: A. L. Burt, 1880), p. 111.

3

in one's bedroom as well as the most distant galaxy. Similarly, modern atomic physics is applicable to every material entity in the universe; and the theory of evolution, summarizing the whole history of life from the first germs in the primordial sea to the highest stages of human life, is also exceedingly wide in scope. Secondly, the synthesis of all the sciences, or the interpretation of the whole of reality, is a pretty big order. A person would need to be a kind of god, or at least a universal genius, to succeed at so prodigious an undertaking. But philosophy is not the peculiar business of the gods or of rare geniuses; it is everyman's business.

The Pursuit of Meaning

Such considerations have led many philosophers to define their field in a more restricted way. One of the most widely accepted definitions is that philosophy is the analysis, or systematic study, of meanings. This definition would in effect limit the field to what C. D. Broad calls critical philosophy.

Those who adopt this interpretation sometimes cite Socrates as an example of a philosopher. In employing his favorite conversational method of giving and receiving questions and answers, he is usually trying to analyse the meaning of some basic concept, such as "knowledge," "justice," "courage," "friendship," or "beauty."

One of the most influential philosophers of modern times, Moritz Schlick (1882–1936), has said:

> . . . Socrates' philosophy consists of what we may call "The Pursuit of Meaning." He tried to clarify thought by analyzing the meaning of our expressions and the real sense of our propositions. Here then we find a definite contrast between this philosophic method, which has for its object the discovery of meaning, and the method of the sciences, which have for their object the discovery of truth. . . . Science should be defined as the "pursuit of truth" and philosophy as the "pursuit of meaning." Socrates has set the example of the true philosophic method for all times.[3]

I do not believe that this is an adequate characterization of the method of Socrates or the nature of philosophy. Socrates was engaged not only in the pursuit of meaning but also in the pursuit of truth, and the former was largely instrumental to the latter. His definitions were intended not as arbitrary or merely verbal: they were what philosophers call "real" definitions—that is, they sought to characterize actually existent things. When Socrates asserted that justice or friendship or beauty was this or that, he implied that justice or friendship or beauty really existed and actually bore the character marked off and fixed in the definition. Consequently, he kept referring to the facts of experience so as to make his definitions truthful.

[3] "The Future of Philosophy," in D. J. Bronstein, Y. H. Krikorian, and P. P. Wiener (eds.), *Basic Problems of Philosophy* (Prentice-Hall, 1947), p. 739.

Also, he was interested in fitting together the various insights thus gained into a critical interpretation of man's nature, his destiny, and his values.

To define philosophy as the pursuit of meaning is at once too broad and too narrow. It is too broad because scientists as well as philosophers seek to clarify meanings. As C. J. Ducasse has said:

> To mention but a few, such concepts as salt, acid, gas, liquid, solid, water, air, iron, etc. are concepts the exact meaning of which is investigated and discovered not by metaphysicians, logicians, or mathematicians, but by chemists and physicists; and the same is true of such even more basic physical concepts as light, electricity, matter, mass, etc. Moreover, although physicists do give us precise accounts of the meaning of these and numerous other concepts, they do so in their capacity as natural scientists, *i.e.*, on the basis, ultimately, of observations and experiments. . . .[4]

In another sense, Schlick's definition of philosophy is too narrow. If Plato, Aristotle, Aquinas, Descartes, Spinoza, and Kant, for example, are to be considered philosophers—and no one has a better claim—it would appear that their field includes what Broad calls "speculative philosophy." Schlick seeks to dismiss the problems of speculative philosophy as either nonsensical or nonphilosophical. "Some of them will disappear by being shown to be mistakes and misunderstandings of our language," he declares, "and the others will be found to be ordinary scientific questions in disguise." [5] But it is unlikely that all the problems of speculative philosophy will either vanish when they are stated clearly or will turn out to be nonphilosophical problems, more appropriately treated by science. Moreover, the sharp distinction between the pursuit of meaning and the pursuit of truth is artificial, for the clarification of meaning and the discovery of truth go hand in hand. Broad rightly includes under "critical philosophy" not only the clarification of concepts but the resolute criticism of our fundamental beliefs. The proposal to restrict philosophy to the pursuit of meaning seems to me implausible and unattractive—implausible because the traditional problems of philosophy are of much wider scope, and unattractive because "philosophy," when confined in this way, becomes dry and dull.

The Cultivation of Wisdom

Philosophy, we conclude, involves both the analysis of meanings and the search for generic truths. To complete our definition, we need to distinguish the kinds of meanings and generic truths that are essentially philosophical from the kinds that are scientific.

It will help us to consider the original meaning of "philosophy." Etymologically, philosophy means "the love of wisdom" (from the Greek *"philein,"*

[4] *Philosophy as a Science* (New York: Oskar Piest, 1941), pp. 77–78.
[5] *Op. cit.,* p. 745.

to love, and *"sophia,"* wisdom). The word has ordinarily been used to designate an activity rather than an emotion—the activity of pursuing wisdom rather than the emotion motivating that pursuit. The essential question that we need to consider is what, exactly, is the wisdom that the philosopher seeks.

"Wisdom" has been used in two senses. First, it is contrasted with ignorance. The wise man is he who knows and therefore is not ignorant. This meaning, however, does not help us to distinguish philosophy from science, since the scientist also, of course, is trying to replace ignorance by knowledge. In the second sense, wisdom is contrasted with foolishness. The wise man is he who has good judgment and therefore is not foolish. The fool may have a great deal of knowledge about ordinary matters of fact, but he lacks the balance and maturity and ripe insight that make it possible not only to live but to live well.

If philosophy is the pursuit of wisdom as contrasted with foolishness, it *is* marked off from ordinary science. The subject matter of science is facts, and science attempts to discover verifiable laws—regularities—among these facts. These laws give a *description* of the facts. It is obvious that the physicist does not talk about wicked atoms or beneficent motions, and even the sociologist, in his purely scientific role, tries to *describe* rather than to *evaluate* the behavior of social groups. If philosophy, on the other hand, seeks wisdom as the opposite of foolishness, it must be a kind of critical activity concerned with appraisals. Matthew Arnold has defined poetry as "the criticism of life," but this definition fits philosophy better than poetry. It is similar to the definition of Ducasse, who maintains that "philosophy is the general theory of criticism," [6] and the definition of Dewey, who declares that "philosophy is inherently criticism, having its distinctive position among various modes of criticism in its generality: a criticism of criticisms, as it were." [7]

It is characteristic of criticism that it is yea-saying or nay-saying—a favoring or a disfavoring. The ways of saying "yea" or "nay" are quite various, and they correspond to different pairs of adjectives. In logic, for example, we speak of *valid* or *fallacious;* in epistemology, of *true* or *false;* in metaphysics, of *real* or *unreal;* in theology, of *holy* or *unholy;* in esthetics, of *beautiful* or *ugly;* in ethics, of *right* or *wrong.* In using these adjectives, we are making judgments. The function of philosophy is to provide the intellectual bases of sound judgments about the great issues of life.

Even when philosophy wears the garb of science, it is distinctive. For example, Lucretius was not primarily concerned with the hypotheses of atoms and evolution as scientific descriptions of the nature of things: he was con-

[6] *The Philosophy of Art* (Dial, 1929), p. 3.
[7] *Experience and Nature* (Chicago: Open Court, 1925), p. 398.

cerned with the right way to think and live in the sort of universe that he regarded as real. Metaphysics should not be interpreted—as it often is—as potential or generalized natural science; rather, it should be regarded as the attempt to achieve a true understanding of man and his place in the cosmos so that we can distinguish the deep and permanent from the superficial and temporary, the important from the unimportant. Thus to distinguish is to *judge,* and metaphysics, like other branches of philosophy, provides a basis for judgment.

Philosophy resembles science not so much in its aim as in its method. Both employ reason and evidence as means to the discovery of truth and the clarification of meaning. Both are forms of inquiry—science being an inquiry into the laws of nature; philosophy, into the norms of criticism. The faith of the philosopher, like that of the scientist, is that inquiry is worth while. In the *Apology,* Socrates expresses the fundamental conviction of all true philosophers: "The unexamined life," he declares, "is not worth living." Likewise, in the *Meno,* his faith rings out sharp and clear:

> Some things I have said of which I am not altogether confident. But that we shall be better and braver and less helpless if we think that we ought to inquire, than we should have been if we indulged in the idle fancy that there was no knowing and no use in seeking to know what we do not know;— that is a theme upon which I am ready to fight, in word and deed, to the utmost of my power.[8]

We can fully appreciate the brave words of Socrates only if we too engage in the quest for wisdom. The proof of the pudding is in the eating—we can best judge the value of philosophy after we have philosophized. Each person must himself taste of the pudding; no one can do it for him. Of course, it is immensely helpful to study the great thinkers, such as Plato, Aristotle, Hume, and Kant, or nearer to us, William James, Santayana, and Russell. As Descartes declares in the opening chapter of his *Discourse on Method,* "The reading of good books is, as it were, to engage in talk with their authors, the finest minds of past ages, artfully contrived talk in which they give us none but the best and most select of their thoughts." [9] But like all the very good things of life, wisdom is something that cannot be given and that each must attain for himself.

CHARLIE DUNBAR BROAD (1887–   )

Broad was born in London and educated at Dulwich and Trinity College, Cambridge, receiving there the M.A. degree and later the Litt.D. He has taught at St. Andrews, Dundee, Bristol, Dublin, and principally at Cam-

---

[8] *The Dialogues of Plato,* trans. by Benjamin Jowett (London: Oxford, 1924), II, p. 47.
[9] *Discourse on Method,* in *Descartes' Philosophical Writings* (London: Macmillan, 1952), p. 119.

bridge, where he became Professor of Moral Philosophy in 1933. During 1953–1954 he was a visiting professor at the University of Michigan and at the University of California at Los Angeles. His works include *Scientific Thought*, 1923; *Mind and Its Place in Nature*, 1925; *Five Types of Ethical Theory*, 1930; *Examination of McTaggart's Philosophy*, 1933, 1938; and *Ethics and the History of Philosophy*, 1952.

The Relation of Philosophy to the Sciences*

A very large number of scientists will begin such a book as this with the strong conviction that philosophy is mainly moonshine, and with the gravest doubts as to whether it has anything of the slightest importance to tell them. I do not think that this view of philosophy is true, or I should not waste my time and cheat my students by trying to teach it. But I do think that such a view is highly plausible, and that the proceedings of many philosophers have given the general public some excuse for its unfavorable opinion of philosophy. I shall therefore begin by stating the case against philosophy as strongly as I can, and shall then try to show that, in spite of all objections, it really is a definite science with a distinct subject-matter. I shall try to show that it really does advance and that it is related to the special sciences in such a way that the cooperation of philosophers and scientists is of the utmost benefit to the studies of both.

I think that an intelligent scientist would put his case against philosophy somewhat as follows. He would say: "Philosophers discuss such subjects as the ex-istence of God, the immortality of the soul, and the freedom of the will. They spin out of their minds fanciful theories, which can neither be supported nor refuted by experiment. No two philosophers agree, and no progress is made. Philosophers are still discussing with great heat the same questions that they discussed in Greece thousands of years ago. What a poor show does this make when compared with mathematics or any of the natural sciences! Here there is continual steady progress; the discoveries of one age are accepted by the next, and become the basis for further advances in knowledge. There is controversy indeed, but it is fruitful controversy which advances the science and ends in definite agreement; it is not the aimless wandering in a circle to which philosophy is condemned. Does this not very strongly suggest that philosophy is either a mere playing with words, or that, if it has a genuine subject-matter, this is beyond the reach of human intelligence?"

Our scientist might still further strengthen his case by reflecting on the past history of philosophy and on the

* From *Scientific Thought* (London: K. Paul, Trench, Trübner & Company, 1923; New York: Harcourt, Brace & Company, 1923; Humanities Press, 1949). Reprinted by permission.

method by which it is commonly taught to students. He will remind us that most of the present sciences started by being mixed up with philosophy, that so long as they kept this connection they remained misty and vague, and that as soon as their fundamental principles began to be discovered they cut their disreputable associate, wedded the experimental method, and settled down to the steady production of a strapping family of established truths. Mechanics is a case in point. So long as it was mixed up with philosophy it made no progress; when the true laws of motion were discovered by the experiments and reasoning of Galileo it ceased to be part of philosophy and began to develop into a separate science. Does this not suggest that the subject-matter of philosophy is just that ever-diminishing fragment of the universe in which the scientist has not yet discovered laws, and where we have therefore to put up with guesses? Are not such guesses the best that philosophy has to offer; and will they not be swept aside as soon as some man of genius, like Galileo or Dalton or Faraday, sets the subject on the sure path of science?

Should our scientist talk to students of philosophy and ask what happens at their lectures, his objections will most likely be strengthened. The answer may take the classical form: "He tells us what everyone knows in language that no one can understand." But, even if the answer be not so unfavorable as this, it is not unlikely to take the form: "We hear about the views of Plato and Kant and Berkeley on such subjects as the reality of the external world and the immortality of the soul." Now the scientist will at once contrast this with the method of teaching in his own subject, and will be inclined to say, if, e.g., he be a chemist: "We learn what are the laws of chemical combination and the

structure of the benzene nucleus, we do not worry our heads as to what exactly Dalton thought or Kekule said. If philosophers really know anything about the reality of the external world why do they not say straightforwardly that it is real or unreal, and prove it? The fact that they apparently prefer to discuss the divergent views of a collection of eminent 'backnumbers' on the question strongly suggests that they know that there is no means of answering it, and that nothing better than groundless personal opinions can be offered."

I have put these objections as strongly as I can, and I now propose to see just how much there is in them. First, as to the alleged unprogressive character of philosophy. This is, I think, an illusion; but it is a very natural one. Let us take the question of the reality of the external world as an example. Common-sense says that chairs and tables exist independently of whether anyone happens to perceive them or not. We study Berkeley and find him claiming to prove that such things can only exist so long as they are perceived by someone. Later on we read some modern realist, like Alexander, and we are told that Berkeley was wrong, and that chairs and tables can and do exist unperceived. We seem merely to have got back to where we started from, and to have wasted our time. But this is not really so, for two reasons.

(i) What we believe at the end of the process and what we believed at the beginning are by no means the same, although we express the two beliefs by the same form of words. The original belief of common-sense was vague, crude and unanalyzed. Berkeley's arguments have forced us to recognize a number of distinctions and to define much more clearly what we mean by the statement that chairs and tables exist unperceived. What we find is that the original crude belief of common-sense consisted of a number of different beliefs, mixed up with each other. Some of these may be true and others false. Berkeley's arguments really do refute or throw grave doubt on some of them, but they leave others standing. Now it may be that those which are left are enough to constitute a belief in the independent reality of external objects. If so this final belief in the reality of the external world is much clearer and subtler than the *verbally* similar belief with which we began. It has been purified of irrelevant factors, and is no longer a vague mass of different beliefs mixed up with each other.

(ii) Not only will our final belief differ in content from our original one, it will also differ in certainty. Our original belief was merely instinctive, and was at the mercy of any sceptical critic who chose to cast doubts on it. Berkeley has played this part. Our final belief is that part or that modification of our original one that has managed to survive his criticisms. This does not of course *prove* that it is true; there may be other objections to it. But, at any rate, a belief that has stood the criticisms of an acute and subtle thinker, like Berkeley, is much more likely to be true than a merely instinctive belief which has never been criticized by ourselves or anyone else. Thus the process which at first sight seemed to be merely circular has not really been so. And it has certainly not been useless; for it has enabled us to replace a vague belief by a clear and analyzed one, and a merely instinctive belief by one that has passed through the fire of criticism.

The above example will suggest to us a part at least of what philosophy is really about. Common-sense constantly makes use of a number of concepts, in terms of which it interprets its experience. It talks of *things* of various kinds; it says that they have *places* and *dates,* that they *change,* and

that changes in one *cause* changes in others, and so on. Thus it makes constant use of such concepts or categories as thinghood, space, time, change, cause, etc. Science takes over these concepts from common-sense with but slight modification, and uses them in its work. Now we can and do *use* concepts without having any very clear idea of their meaning or their mutual relations. I do not of course suggest that to the ordinary man the words *substance, cause, change,* etc., are mere meaningless noises, like *Jabberwock* or *Snark.* It is clear that we mean something, and something different in each case, by such words. If we did not we could not use them consistently, and it is obvious that on the whole we do consistently apply and withhold such names. But it is possible to apply concepts more or less successfully when one has only a very confused idea as to their meaning. No man confuses place with date, and for practical purposes any two men agree as a rule in the places that they assign to a given object. Nevertheless, if you ask them what exactly they mean by *place* and *date,* they will be puzzled to tell you.

Now, the most fundamental task of philosophy is to take the concepts that we daily use in common life and science, to analyze them, and thus to determine their precise meanings and their mutual relations. Evidently this is an important duty. In the first place, clear and accurate knowledge of anything is an advance on a mere hazy general familiarity with it. Moreover, in the absence of clear knowledge of the meanings and relations of the concepts that we use, we are certain sooner or later to apply them wrongly or to meet with exceptional cases where we are puzzled as to how to apply them at all. For instance, we all agree pretty well as to the place of a certain pin which we are looking at. But suppose we go on to ask: "Where is the image of that pin in a certain mirror; and is it in this place (whatever it may be) in precisely the sense in which the pin itself is in *its* place?" We shall find the question a very puzzling one, and there will be no hope of answering it until we have carefully analyzed what we mean by *being in a place*.

Again, this task of clearing up the meanings and determining the relations of fundamental concepts is not performed to any extent by any other science. Chemistry *uses* the notion of substance, geometry that of space, and mechanics that of motion. But they assume that you already know what is meant by *substance* and *space* and *motion*. So you do in a vague way; and it is not their business to enter, more than is necessary for their own special purposes, into the meaning and relations of these concepts as such. Of course the special sciences do in some measure clear up the meanings of the concepts that they use. A chemist, with his distinction between elements and compounds and his laws of combination, has a clearer idea of substance than an ordinary layman. But the special sciences only discuss the meanings of their concepts so far as this is needful for their own special purposes. Such discussion is incidental to them, whilst it is of the essence of philosophy, which deals with such questions for their own sake. Whenever a scientist begins to discuss the concepts of his science in this thorough and disinterested way we begin to say that he is studying, not so much chemistry or physics, as the *philosophy* of chemistry or physics. It will therefore perhaps be agreed that, in the above sense of philosophy, there is both room and need for such a study, and that there is no special reason to fear that it will be beyond the compass of human faculties.

At this point a criticism may be made which had better be met at once. It may be said: "By your own admission the task of philosophy is purely verbal; it consists entirely of discussions about the meanings of words." This criticism is of course absolutely wide of the mark. When we say that philosophy tries to clear up the meanings of concepts we do not mean that it is simply concerned to substitute some long phrase for some familiar word. Any analysis, when once it has been made, is naturally *expressed* in words; but so too is any other discovery. When Cantor gave his definition of continuity, the final result of his work was expressed by saying that you can substitute for the word "continuous" such and such a verbal phrase. But the essential part of the work was to find out exactly what properties are present in objects when we predicate continuity of them, and what properties are absent when we refuse to predicate continuity. This was evidently not a question of words but of things and their properties.

Philosophy has another and closely connected task. We not only make continual use of vague and unanalyzed concepts. We have also a number of uncriticized beliefs, which we constantly assume in ordinary life and in the sciences. We constantly assume, *e.g.*, that every event has a cause, that nature obeys uniform laws, that we live in a world of objects whose existence and behavior are independent of our knowledge of them, and so on. Now science takes over these beliefs without criticism from common-sense, and simply works with them. We know by experience, however, that beliefs which are very strongly held may be mere prejudices. [African] Negroes find it very hard to believe that water can become solid, because they have always lived in a warm climate. Is it not possible that we believe that nature as a whole will always act uniformly simply because the part of nature in which the human race has lived has happened to act so up to the present? All such beliefs then, however deeply rooted, call for criticism. The first duty of philosophy is to state them clearly; and this can only be done when we have analyzed and defined the concepts that they involve. Until you know exactly what you mean by *change* and *cause* you cannot know what is meant by the statement that *every change has a cause.* And not much weight can be attached to a person's most passionate beliefs if he does not know what precisely he is passionately believing. The next duty of philosophy is to test such beliefs; and this can only be done by resolutely and honestly exposing them to every objection that one can think of oneself or find in the writings of others. We ought only to go on believing a proposition if, at the end of this process, we still find it impossible to doubt it. Even then of course it may not be true, but we have at least done our best.

These two branches of philosophy—the analysis and definition of our fundamental concepts, and the clear statement and resolute criticism of our fundamental beliefs— I call *critical philosophy.* It is obviously a necessary and a possible task, and it is not performed by any other science. The other sciences *use* the concepts and *assume* the beliefs; critical philosophy tries to analyze the former and to criticize the latter. Thus, so long as science and critical philosophy keep to their own spheres, there is no possibility of conflict between them, since their subject-matter is quite different. Philosophy claims to analyze the general concepts of substance and cause, *e.g.;* it does not claim to tell us about particular substances, like gold, or about particular laws of causation, as that *aqua regia* dissolves gold. Chemistry, on the other hand, tells us a great deal about the various kinds of substances in the world, and how changes in one cause changes in another. But it does not profess to analyze the general concepts of substance or causation, or to consider what right we have to assume that every event has a cause.

It should now be clear why the method of philosophy is so different from that of the natural sciences. Experiments are not made, because they would be utterly useless. If you want to find out how one substance behaves in presence of another you naturally put the two together, vary the conditions, and note the results. But no experiment will clear up your ideas as to the meaning of *cause* in general or of *substance* in general. Again, all conclusions from experiments rest on some of those very assumptions which it is the business of philosophy to state clearly and to criticize. The experimenter assumes that nature obeys uniform laws, and that similar results will follow always and everywhere from sufficiently similar conditions. This is one of the assumptions that philosophy wants to consider critically. The method of philosophy thus resembles that of pure mathematics, at least in the respect that neither has any use for experiment.

There is, however, a very important difference. In pure mathematics we start either from axioms which no one questions, or from premises which are quite explicitly assumed merely as hypotheses; and our main interest is to deduce remote consequences. Now most of the tacit assumptions of ordinary life and of natural science claim to be true and not merely to be hypotheses, and at the same time they are found to be neither clear nor self-evident when critically reflected upon. Most mathematical axioms are very simple and clear, whilst most other propositions which men strongly believe are highly complex and confused. Philosophy is mainly concerned, not with remote conclusions, but with the analysis and appraisement of the original premises. For this purpose analytical power and a certain kind of insight are necessary, and the mathematical method is not of much use.

Now there is another kind of philosophy; and, as this is more exciting, it is what laymen generally understand by the name. This is what I call *speculative philosophy*. It has a different object, is pursued by a different method, and leads to results of a different degree of certainty from critical philosophy. Its object is to take over the results of the various sciences, to add to them the results of the religious and ethical experiences of mankind, and then to reflect upon the whole. The hope is that, by this means, we may be able to reach some general conclusions as to the nature of the Universe, and as to our position and prospects in it.

There are several points to be noted about speculative philosophy.

(i) If it is to be of the slightest use it must presuppose critical philosophy. It is useless to take over masses of uncriticized detail from the sciences and from the ethical and religious experiences of men. We do not know what they mean, or what degree of certainty they possess until they have been clarified and appraised by critical philosophy. It is thus quite possible that the time for speculative philosophy has not yet come; for critical philosophy may not have advanced far enough to supply it with a firm basis. In the past people have tended to rush on to speculative philosophy, because of its greater practical interest. The result has been the production of elaborate systems which may quite fairly be described as moonshine. The discredit which the general public quite rightly attaches to these hasty attempts at speculative philosophy is reflected back on critical philosophy, and philosophy as a whole thus falls into undeserved disrepute.

(ii) At the best speculative philosophy can only consist of more or less happy guesses, made on a very slender basis. There is no hope of its reaching the certainty which some parts of critical philosophy might quite well attain. Now speculative philosophers as a class have been the most dogmatic of men. They have been more certain of everything than they had a right to be of anything.

(iii) A man's final view of the universe as a whole, and of the position and prospects of himself and his fellows, is peculiarly liable to be biased by his hopes and fears, his likes and dislikes, and his judgments of value. One's speculative philosophy tends to be influenced to an altogether undue extent by the state of one's liver and the amount of one's bank-balance. No doubt livers and bank-balances have their place in the universe, and no view of it which fails to give them their due weight is ultimately satisfactory. But their due weight is considerably less than their influence on speculative philosophy might lead one to suspect. But, if we bear this in mind and try our hardest to be "ethically neutral," we are rather liable to go to the other extreme and entertain a theory of the universe which renders the existence of our judgments of value unintelligible.

A large part of critical philosophy is almost exempt from this source of error. Our analysis of truth and falsehood, or of the nature of judgment, is not very likely to be influenced by our hopes and fears. Yet even here there is a slight danger of intellectual dishonesty. We sometimes do our critical philosophy, with half an eye on our speculative philosophy, and accept or reject beliefs, or analyze concepts in a certain way, because we feel that this will fit in better than any alternative with the view of reality as a whole that we happen to like.

(iv) Nevertheless, if speculative philosophy remembers its limitations, it is of value to scientists, in its methods, if not in its results. The reason is this. In all the sciences except psychology we deal with objects and their changes, and leave out of account as far as possible the mind which observes them. In psychology, on the other hand, we deal with minds and their processes, and leave out of account as far as possible the objects that we get to know by means of them. A man who confines himself to either of these subjects is likely therefore to get a very one-sided view of the world. The pure natural scientist is liable to forget that minds exist, and that if it were not for them he could neither know nor act on physical objects. The pure psychologist is inclined to forget that the main business of minds is to know and act upon objects; that they are most intimately connected with certain portions of matter; and that they have apparently arisen gradually in a world which at one time contained nothing but matter. Materialism is the characteristic speculative philosophy of the pure natural scientist, and subjective idealism that of the pure psychologist. To the scientist subjective idealism seems a fairy tale, and to the psychologist materialism seems sheer lunacy. Both are right in their criticisms, but neither sees the weakness of his own position. The truth is that both these doctrines commit the fallacy of oversimplification; and we can hardly avoid falling into some form of this unless at some time we make a resolute attempt to think *synoptically* of all the facts. Our *results* may be trivial; but the *process* will at least remind us of the extreme complexity of the world, and teach us to reject any cheap and easy philosophical theory, such as popular materialism or popular theology.

2

The Socratic Mission

Socrates as a Type of Philosopher

We have been considering the meaning of philosophy and its relation to the sciences. But to understand the nature of philosophy we must have in mind more than a set of definitions and abstract distinctions. "Philosophy," as we have said, means literally the love of wisdom, and this is what philosophy at its best has always meant. As Thoreau put it, to be a philosopher means so to love wisdom as to live according to its dictates.

There is no better way in which to grasp the personal import of philosophy than to study the life and character of Socrates. More than anyone else in the history of thought, he represents the very type and ideal of the philosopher. His portrait, drawn by the genius of Plato, has for more than two thousand years been the standard by which all philosophy and philosophers have been measured. No one has loved wisdom more fervently than Socrates, and no one has lived more truly according to its dictates. In him, philosophy is not merely a way of thinking but a way of living.

Early Life and Character

Born about 470 B.C., Socrates grew up during the time of Athens' greatest power and achievement—the half century following the victories over the Persians—and he lived through the supreme crisis of Athenian history—the bitter, protracted, and catastrophic war with Sparta. He was a contemporary of many of the greatest figures in the history of culture, among them Sophocles, Herodotus, Phidias, and Pericles. Thus he knew the city both in the height of her glory and in the depths of her crisis and defeat.

His father was a sculptor or stone-mason and his mother a midwife. The family was apparently of good standing and aristocratic connections. Socrates, perhaps in jest, declared that the family pedigree could be traced back to Daedalus, a legendary maker of wooden images. Whatever his back-

15

ground, he moved with ease in the best and most select circles of Athenian society.

From an early age he exhibited psychic peculiarities and a strongly marked character. Even as a boy he had an inner "voice," which he called his "divine sign." Unlike the "voice" of Joan of Arc, Socrates' "divine sign" gave only negative commands. He was also subject to fits of abstraction, so that he would remain for hours lost in thought, completely insensible to what went on around him. In Plato's *Symposium* we are told that in the military camp at Poteidaia, when he was not quite forty years old, Socrates stood motionless from early morning on one day until sunrise of the next, buried in meditation. Impressed by Orphic and Pythagorean mystical teachings, he was a believer in the immortality of the soul at a time when most Athenians found the doctrine strange and unfamiliar. His conversations as reported by Plato are full of the language of love—a love that begins with the beauties of this world but mounts to the supersensual beauties of the intellectual and religious spheres.

These mystical characteristics did not prevent him from serving as a soldier and fighting with great bravery, or from exhibiting a great deal of shrewd common-sense. He realized that the traditional religious myths were creations of the human imagination, and he was sceptical of naive moral and political concepts. Although he was capable of great eloquence, he habitually used simple, homespun language. Humor, especially irony, was one of his most pronounced traits.

The contrast between the two sides of his nature, mysticism and common-sense, was paralleled by an equally striking contrast between the inner and the outer man. Externally, he was far from beautiful, with a heavy body, snub nose, protruding eyes, and shambling gait. Aristophanes compared his walk to the strut of a waterfowl, and poked fun at his manner of rolling his eyes; and Alcibiades, in Plato's *Symposium,* compared him to one of the Silenus-figures such as were found in sculptors' shops whose exteriors were ugly but from whose interior recesses golden images of the gods would gleam. Perhaps Plato heightened the picture to sharpen the contrast between the outer homeliness and the inward grace and beauty of his mentor.

Socrates' admirers lauded his moderation, but he did not carry this trait to the point of asceticism. Indeed, he heartily enjoyed good company, and could himself be very entertaining. In the all-night party described in the *Symposium,* he drank with self-control while most of the others, one after another, sank under the table; then at dawn he rose and went about his business unaffected. Similarly, at a feast described by Xenophon, he asked for small cups not from fear that he would overindulge but from a desire that the exhilaration might come upon him gradually and thus prove more enjoyable. No craver of luxury, he lived abstemiously and dressed simply, going barefoot save on special occasions. His moderate tastes reflected his virtually perfect mental freedom; he did not scorn pleasure and worldly goods, but held them to be much inferior to wisdom.

We know relatively little about the details of his daily life. Rather late in life, he married a woman named Xanthippe, by whom he had three sons, and who is portrayed by later writers as a shrew, although there is no hint in Plato to this effect. His domestic affairs seem to have taken a secondary place to friendships in the pattern of his life. His relations with youth bore the Greek peculiarity of affection for boys, but in Socrates' case this was not gross.

Despite his unconventionality, he was a patriotic citizen, counting it a great privilege to be an Athenian and zealously observing the laws of his country. But loyalty, as he conceived it, *implied*, rather than precluded, a searching criticism of his city's ways and institutions. It was the loyalty of a free, open, searching mind, intent upon improving and not merely preserving the *status quo*.

His Love of Philosophy: The Socratic Mission

It was inevitable that a man of Socrates' bent should display a penchant for philosophy. He is said to have studied under Archelaus, the first native Athenian philosopher, and he was also familiar with the teachings of the Sophists—humanistic philosophers and paid educators who traveled from city to city. But, preferring intellectual leisure to lucrative employment, he was too poor to take formal instruction from the Sophists, whose "wisdom," moreover, he regarded as somewhat hollow. He also studied science, becoming familiar with the doctrines of the Sicilian Empedocles about biological evolution, the theories of the Italian Alcmaeon about the brain as the organ of mental life, the mathematical doctrines of Pythagoras and Zeno, and the theory of Diogenes of Apollonia that everything consists of "air." But he soon became disillusioned by the flat contradictions of such rival tenets; and when one day he read in the book of Anaxagoras (the first important philosopher to live in Athens) that "mind" is the cause of the natural order, the concept struck him with the force of revelation. Reading on, he discovered that Anaxagoras introduced a cosmic mind to explain only the initial impetus given to matter and then employed mechanical principles to explain the general structure of reality. Socrates, in contrast, vowed that he would try really to understand mind and its place in the cosmos. Thenceforth his main endeavor was to search his own mind and the minds of his fellow citizens in an attempt to discover the essence of man and of goodness.

By the time he was thirty-five, Socrates had acquired a considerable reputation as a wit and wise man, and he became the center of a circle of admirers. One member of this circle, Chaerephon, asked the oracle at Delphi, shrine of the god Apollo, "Is there any one wiser than Socrates?" The priest-ess answered that there was no one. This response was treated by Socrates with characteristic humor and modesty—if he was wise, he said, it was be-cause he knew that he did not know anything, whereas those who professed wisdom were not only ignorant but too unwise to realize it. But, underneath the humor, he was intensely serious, and he took the word of the oracle as a sign that he had been set apart by the god to convince his fellow citizens of their ignorance and to search unremittingly for wisdom. He gave up every-thing for this "mission"; in consequence, he paid little attention to money matters and was plunged into considerable poverty in later life.

In pursuing his mission, Socrates was trying to explore the human mind and to reach the truth by dint of question and answer, dialogue and debate. This give-and-take method of investigation by discussion is called "dialectic" or "the Socratic method"—and it is still the essential method of the philoso-pher. It may be carried on between two or more persons or within the mind of a single inquirer, as he puts questions to himself and wrestles with his an-swers. Usually its objective is to establish a definition, to fix in mind the es-sential reality of some basic value or property. Each proposed definition is tested by a process of critical examination. Is it internally consistent? Does it fit the facts? Does it agree with what we already know? In formulating and testing the definition, the philosopher continually refers to the particu-lar data of experience; but he examines the particulars as instances of a type, and he defines the type—the "idea," "form," or "universal"—by establish-ing its significance in the particulars.

His Trial and Death

The years of Socrates' mission and the last thirty years of his life fell mainly in the period of the war with Sparta, when Athens was fighting for her existence. As we gather from the pages of the great historian Thucydides, it was a period of intense crisis and civil strife. Toward the close of this diffi-cult time, it became apparent that Athens was losing the war, and revolutions were taking place within the city. Socrates, by his independence, his critical spirit, and his refusal to adopt unjust methods, offended both the democratic and aristocratic parties.

The circumstances were as follows. In the summer of 406 B.C., the Athe-nians staved off final defeat at the hands of Sparta by a great naval victory. But the victory cost twenty-five vessels and four thousand lives, and the commanders of the Athenian fleet were charged with criminal negligence for not trying to rescue their men. The prosecution demanded that the ordinary legal processes be suspended and that the commanders be convicted *en bloc* by a single vote. Socrates, as it happened, was at this time a Senator—the only political office he ever held—and a member of the "Presidency," a kind of executive committee with power to decide whether the proposal to try the commanders *en bloc* should be put to a vote. When the presidents resisted, their lives were threatened by the prosecution, and Socrates alone stood firm at the risk of his life. His protest was overborne: the generals were tried and condemned in a body, and six of them were executed at the hands of the authorities.

This incident occurred under the democracy; but later, when the Thirty Oligarchs established their dictatorship, Socrates again proved his courage and moral integrity. The Thirty tried to implicate him in their criminality by ordering him and four others to seize Leon of Salamis, a rich man whose property the Thirty wished to confiscate. The four others obeyed and Leon was murdered; but Socrates defied the order. In consequence, he might have been killed but for a timely counter-revolution, which ended the terror.

In 404 B.C. the city was finally compelled to surrender. After a short and bloody interval of oligarchical dictatorship, the old democratic form of government was restored. But the political situation remained tense, and the ruling democrats were fearful of counter-revolution. It was Socrates' misfortune that a number of his former close associates had proved themselves traitors or vicious enemies of the democratic cause. Alcibiades, Socrates' young friend, had been a brilliant general of the Athenian army, but when he was accused of religious sacrilege and ordered to stand trial, he deserted to Sparta and became a most formidable enemy of the Athenian state. Similarly, Critias and Charmides, two associates of Socrates, had been leaders of the violent oligarchical dictatorship which was established at the conclusion of the war. Inevitably, Socrates, who had long been known as a vigorous critic of democratic follies, was suspected of subversive activities. Political motives, combined with their intense dislike of Socrates' unconventional teachings, prompted Anytus, a prominent democratic politician, and two lesser associates, Meletus and Lycon, to bring charges against Socrates in 399 B.C., about four years after the war's end. The indictment, as recorded by the later historian Diogenes Laertius, read:

> Socrates is guilty of not worshipping the gods whom the State worships, but introducing new and unfamiliar religious practices; and, further, of corrupting the young. The prosecutor demands the death penalty.

The main "offense," not specified in the indictment or at the trial, was that Socrates had fostered the anti-democratic spirit that had inspired the oligarchical revolutions. According to an amnesty that had been officially declared in the year 404–403, no one could be prosecuted for political offences committed before that date. Hence the accusations in the formal indictment were, to some extent, trumpery charges, designed to bring Socrates to trial for an offense that, perforce, remained unspecified. Yet the charges were not merely manufactured: there was widespread hostility against Socrates for his critical spirit and his unremitting search for a new rationale and norm for life. In the eyes of conservatives, he *had* blasphemed and corrupted youth. Indeed, he had questioned the very foundation of the social order, and the guardians of the *status quo,* hurt to the quick, retaliated by seeking to impose the ultimate penalty—death.

Tried before five hundred jurors selected by lot, Socrates spoke with such uncompromising independence that he angered the jury and provoked the death penalty. Some of his friends made a last-minute attempt to effect his escape, but he would brook no such disgraceful tactics. After a serene philosophical conversation with a group of intimates in his prison cell, he drank the fatal hemlock.

Such, in brief outline, is the story of Socrates. Now let us fill in some of the details by examining a number of Plato's dialogues.

The Apology*

CHARACTERS

SOCRATES

MELETUS

SCENE.—The Court of Justice.

Socrates. I cannot tell what impression my accusers have made upon you, Athenians: for my own part, I know that they nearly made me forget who I was, so plausible were they; and yet they have scarcely uttered one single word of truth. But of all their many falsehoods, the one which astonished me most, was when they said that I was a clever speaker, and that you must be careful not to let me mislead you. I thought that it was most impudent of them not to be ashamed to talk in that way; for as soon as I open my mouth the lie will be exposed, and I shall prove that I am not a clever speaker in any way at all: unless, indeed, by a clever speaker they mean a man who speaks the truth. If that is their meaning, I agree with them that I am a much greater orator than they. My accusers, then, I repeat, have said little or nothing that is true; but from me you shall hear the whole truth. Certainly you will not hear an elaborate speech, Athenians, drest up, like theirs, with words and phrases. I will say to you what I have to say, without preparation, and in the words which come first, for I believe that my cause is just; so let none of you expect anything else. Indeed, my friends, it would hardly be seemly for me, at my age, to come before you like a young man with his specious falsehoods. But there is one thing, Athenians, which I do most earnestly beg and entreat of you. Do not be surprised and do not interrupt, if in my defence I speak in the same way that I am accustomed to speak in the marketplace, at the tables of the money-changers,

* The following dialogues of Plato are from the translation of F. J. Church, first published by Macmillan and Company, London, 1880.

where many of you have heard me, and elsewhere. The truth is this. I am more than seventy years old, and this is the first time that I have ever come before a Court of Law; so your manner of speech here is quite strange to me. If I had been really a stranger, you would have forgiven me for speaking in the language and the fashion of my native country: and so now I ask you to grant me what I think I have a right to claim. Never mind the style of my speech— it may be better or it may be worse—give your whole attention to the question, Is what I say just, or is it not? That is what makes a good judge, as speaking the truth makes a good advocate.

I have to defend myself, Athenians, first against the old false charges of my old accusers, and then against the later ones of my present accusers. For many men have been accusing me to you, and for very many years, who have not uttered a word of truth: and I fear them more than I fear Anytus and his companions, formidable as they are. But, my friends, those others are still more formidable; for they got hold of most of you when you were children, and they have been more persistent in accusing me with lies, and in trying to persuade you that there is one Socrates, a wise man, who speculates about the heavens, and who examines into all things that are beneath the earth, and who can "make the worse appear the better reason." These men, Athenians, who spread abroad this report, are the accusers whom I fear; for their hearers think that persons who pursue such inquiries never believe in the gods. And then they are many, and their attacks have been going on for a long time: and they spoke to you when you were at the age most readily to believe them: for you were all young, and many of you were children: and there was no one to answer them when they attacked me. And the most unreasonable thing of all is that commonly I do not even know their names: I cannot tell you who they are, except in the case of the comic poets. But all the rest who have been trying to prejudice you against me, from motives of spite and jealousy, and sometimes, it may be, from conviction, are the enemies whom it is hardest to meet. For I cannot call any one of them forward in Court, to cross-examine him: I have, as it were, simply to fight with shadows in my defence, and to put questions which there is no one to answer. I ask you, therefore, to believe that, as I say, I have been attacked by two classes of accusers—first by Meletus and his friends, and then by those older ones of whom I have spoken. And, with your leave, I will defend myself first against my old enemies; for you heard their accusations first, and they were much more persistent than my present accusers are.

Well, I must make my defence, Athenians, and try in the short time allowed me to remove the prejudice which you have had against me for a long time. I hope that I may manage to do this, if it be good for you and for me, and that my defence may be successful; but I am quite aware of the nature of my task, and I know that it is a difficult one. Be the issue, however, as God wills, I must obey the law, and make my defence.

Let us begin again, then, and see what is the charge which has given rise to the prejudice against me, which was what Meletus relied on when he drew his indictment. What is the calumny which my enemies have been spreading about me? I must assume that they are formally accusing me, and read their indictment. It would run somewhat in this fashion: "Socrates is an evil-doer, who meddles with inquiries into things beneath the earth, and in heaven, and who 'makes the worse appear the better reason,' and who teaches others these same things." That is what they say; and in the Comedy of Aristophanes [*The Clouds*] you yourselves saw a man called Socrates swinging round in a basket, and saying that he walked the air, and talking a great deal of nonsense about matters of which I understand nothing, either more or less. I do not mean to disparage that kind of knowledge, if there is any man who possesses it. I trust Meletus may never be able to prosecute me for that. But, the truth is, Athenians, I have nothing to do with these matters, and almost all of you are yourselves my witnesses of this. I beg all of you who have ever heard me converse, and they are many, to inform your neighbors and tell them if any of you have ever heard me conversing about such matters, either more or less. That will show you that the other common stories about me are as false as this one.

But, the fact is, that not one of these stories is true; and if you have heard that I undertake to educate men, and exact money from them for so doing, that is not true either; though I think that it would be a fine thing to be able to educate men, as Gorgias of Leontini, and Prodicus of Ceos, and Hippias of Elis do. For each of them, my friends, can go into any city, and persuade the young men to leave the society of their fellow-citizens, with any of whom they might associate for nothing, and to be only too glad to be allowed to pay money for the privilege of associating with themselves. And I believe that there is another wise man from Paros residing in Athens at this moment. I happened to meet Callias, the son of Hipponicus, a man who has spent more money on the Sophists than every one else put together. So I said to him—he has two sons—Callias, if your two sons had been foals or calves, we could have hired a trainer for them who would have made them perfect in the excellence which belongs to their nature. He would have been either a groom or a farmer. But whom do

you intend to take to train them, seeing that they are men? Who understands the excellence which belongs to men and to citizens? I suppose that you must have thought of this, because of your sons. Is there such a person, said I, or not? Certainly there is, he replied. Who is he, said I, and where does he come from, and what is his fee? His name is Evenus, Socrates, he replied: he comes from Paros, and his fee is five minæ. Then I thought that Evenus was a fortunate person if he really understood this art and could teach so cleverly. If I had possessed knowledge of that kind, I should have given myself airs and prided myself on it. But, Athenians, the truth is that I do not possess it.

Perhaps some of you may reply: But, Socrates, what is this pursuit of yours? Whence come these calumnies against you? You must have been engaged in some pursuit out of the common. All these stories and reports of you would never have gone about, if you had not been in some way different from other men. So tell us what your pursuits are, that we may not give our verdict in the dark. I think that that is a fair question, and I will try to explain to you what it is that has raised these calumnies against me, and given me this name. Listen, then: some of you perhaps will think that I am jesting; but I assure you that I will tell you the whole truth. I have gained this name, Athenians, simply by reason of a certain wisdom. But by what kind of wisdom? It is by just that wisdom which is, I believe, possible to men. In that, it may be, I am really wise. But the men of whom I was speaking just now must be wise in a wisdom which is greater than human wisdom, or in some way which I cannot describe, for certainly I know nothing of it myself, and if any man says that I do, he lies and wants to slander me. Do not interrupt me, Athenians, even if you think that I am speaking arrogantly. What I am going to say is not my own: I will tell you who says it, and he is worthy of your credit. I will bring the god of Delphi to be the witness of the fact of my wisdom and of its nature. You remember Chærephon. From youth upwards he was my comrade; and he went into exile with the people,[1] and with the people he returned. And you remember, too, Chærephon's character; how vehement he was in carrying through whatever he took in hand. Once he went to Delphi and ventured to put this question to the oracle, —I entreat you again, my friends, not to cry out,—he asked if there was any man who was wiser than I: and the priestess answered that there was no man. Chærephon himself is dead, but his brother here will confirm what I say.

Now see why I tell you this. I am going to explain to you the origin of my unpopularity. When I heard of the oracle I began to reflect: What can God mean by this dark saying? I know very well that I am not wise, even in the smallest degree. Then what can he mean by saying that I am the wisest of men? It cannot be that he is speaking falsely, for he is a god and cannot lie. And for a long time I was at a loss to understand his meaning: then, very reluctantly, I turned to seek for it in this manner. I went to a man who was reputed to be wise, thinking that there, if anywhere, I should prove the answer wrong, and meaning to point out to the oracle its mistake, and to say, "You said that I was the wisest of men, but this man is wiser than I am." So I examined the man—I need not tell you his name, he was a politician—but this was the result, Athenians. When I conversed with him I came to see that, though a great many persons, and most of all he himself, thought that he was wise, yet he was not wise. And then I tried to prove to him that he was not wise, though he fancied that he was: and by

so doing I made him, and many of the bystanders, my enemies. So when I went away, I thought to myself, "I am wiser than this man: neither of us probably knows anything that is really good, but he thinks that he has knowledge, when he has not, while I, having no knowledge, do not think that I have. I seem, at any rate, to be a little wiser than he is on this point: I do not think that I know what I do not know." Next I went to another man who was reputed to be still wiser than the last, with exactly the same result. And there again I made him, and many other men, my enemies.

Then I went on to one man after another, seeing that I was making enemies every day, which caused me much unhappiness and anxiety: still I thought that I must set God's command above everything. So I had to go to every man who seemed to possess any knowledge, and search for the meaning of the oracle: and, Athenians, I must tell you the truth; verily, by the dog of Egypt, this was the result of the search which I made at God's bidding. I found that the men, whose reputation for wisdom stood highest, were nearly the most lacking in it; while others, who were looked down on as common people, were much better fitted to learn. Now, I must describe to you the wanderings which I undertook, like a series of Heraclean labors, to make full proof of the oracle. After the politicians, I went to the poets, tragic, dithyrambic, and others, thinking that there I should find myself manifestly more ignorant than they. So I took up the poems on which I thought that they had spent most pains, and asked them what they meant, hoping at the same time to learn something from them. I am ashamed to tell you the truth, my friends, but I must say it. Almost any one of the bystanders could have talked about the works of these poets better than the poets themselves. So I soon found that it is not

[1] Chærephon was forced into exile during the antidemocratic dictatorship of the Thirty in 404 B.C.

by wisdom that the poets create their works, but by a certain natural power and by inspiration, like soothsayers and prophets, who say many fine things, but who understand nothing of what they say. The poets seemed to me to be in a similar case. And at the same time I perceived that, because of their poetry, they thought that they were the wisest of men in other matters too, which they were not. So I went away again, thinking that I had the same advantage over the poets that I had over the politicians.

Finally, I went to the artizans, for I knew very well that I possessed no knowledge at all, worth speaking of, and I was sure that I should find that they knew many fine things. And in that I was not mistaken. They knew what I did not know, and so far they were wiser than I. But, Athenians, it seemed to me that the skilled artizans made the same mistake as the poets. Each of them believed himself to be extremely wise in matters of the greatest importance, because he was skilful in his own art: and this mistake of theirs threw their real wisdom into the shade. So I asked myself, on behalf of the oracle, whether I would choose to remain as I was, without either wisdom or their ignorance, or to possess both, as they did. And I made answer to myself and to the oracle that it was better for me to remain as I was.

By reason of this examination, Athenians, I have made many enemies of a very fierce and bitter kind, who have spread abroad a great number of calumnies about me, and people say that I am "a wise man." For the bystanders always think that I am wise myself in any matter wherein I convict another man of ignorance. But, my friends, I believe that only God is really wise: and that by this oracle he meant that men's wisdom is worth little or nothing. I do not think that he meant that Socrates was wise.

He only made use of my name, and took me as an example, as though he would say to men, "He among you is the wisest, who, like Socrates, knows that in very truth his wisdom is worth nothing at all." And therefore I still go about testing and examining every man whom I think wise, whether he be a citizen or a stranger, as God has commanded me; and whenever I find that he is not wise, I point out to him on the part of God that he is not wise. And I am so busy in this pursuit that I have never had leisure to take any part worth mentioning in public matters, or to look after my private affairs. I am in very great poverty by reason of my service to God.

And besides this, the young men who follow me about, who are the sons of wealthy persons and have a great deal of spare time, take a natural pleasure in hearing men cross-examined: and they often imitate me among themselves: then they try their hands at cross-examining other people. And, I imagine, they find a great abundance of men who think that they know a great deal, when in fact they know little or nothing. And then the persons who are cross-examined, get angry with me instead of with themselves, and say that Socrates is an abominable fellow who corrupts young men. And when they are asked, "Why, what does he do? what does he teach?" they do not know what to say; but, not to seem at a loss, they repeat the stock charges against all philosophers, and allege that he investigates things in the air and under the earth, and that he teaches people to disbelieve in the gods, and "to make the worse appear the better reason." For, I fancy, they would not like to confess the truth, which is that they are shown up as ignorant pretenders to knowledge that they do not possess. And so they have been filling your ears with their bitter calumnies for a long time, for they are zealous and numerous and bitter against me; and they are well disciplined and plausible in speech. On these grounds Meletus and Anytus and Lycon have attacked me. Meletus is indignant with me on the part of the poets, and Anytus on the part of the artizans and politicians, and Lycon on the part of the orators. And so, as I said at the beginning, I shall be surprised if I am able, in the short time allowed me for my defence, to remove from your minds this prejudice which has grown so strong. What I have told you, Athenians, is the truth: I neither conceal, nor do I suppress anything, small or great. And yet I know that it is just this plainness of speech which makes me enemies. But that is only a proof that my words are true, and that the prejudice against me, and the causes of it, are what I have said. And whether you look for them now or hereafter, you will find that they are so.

What I have said must suffice as my defence against the charges of my first accusers. I will try next to defend myself against that "good patriot" Meletus, as he calls himself, and my later accusers. Let us assume that they are a new set of accusers, and read their indictment, as we did in the case of the others. It runs thus. He says that Socrates is an evil-doer who corrupts the youth, and who does not believe in the gods whom the city believes in, but in other new divinities. Such is the charge. Let us examine each point in it separately. Meletus says that I do wrong by corrupting the youth: but I say, Athenians, that he is doing wrong; for he is playing off a solemn jest by bringing men lightly to trial, and pretending to have a great zeal and interest in matters to which he has never given a moment's thought. And now I will try to prove to you that it is so.

Come here, Meletus. Is it not a fact that you think it very important that the younger men should be as excellent as possible?

Meletus. It is.

Socr. Come then: tell the judges, who is it who improves them? You take so much interest in the matter that of course you know that. You are accusing me, and bringing me to trial, because, as you say, you have discovered that I am the corrupter of the youth. Come now, reveal to the judges who improves them. You see, Meletus, you have nothing to say; you are silent. But don't you think that this is a scandalous thing? Is not your silence a conclusive proof of what I say, that you have never given a moment's thought to the matter? Come, tell us, my good sir, who makes the young men better citizens?

Mel. The laws.

Socr. My excellent sir, that is not my question. What man improves the young, who starts with a knowledge of the laws?

Mel. The judges here, Socrates.

Socr. What do you mean, Meletus? Can they educate the young and improve them?

Mel. Certainly.

Socr. All of them? or only some of them?

Mel. All of them.

Socr. By Hêrê that is good news! There is a great abundance of benefactors. And do the listeners here improve them, or not?

Mel. They do.

Socr. And do the senators?

Mel. Yes.

Socr. Well then, Meletus; do the members of the Assembly corrupt the younger men? or do they again all improve them?

Mel. They too improve them.

Socr. Then all the Athenians, apparently, make the young into fine fellows except me, and I alone corrupt them. Is that your meaning?

Mel. Most certainly; that is my meaning.

Socr. You have discovered me to be a

most unfortunate man. Now tell me: do you think that the same holds good in the case of horses? Does one man do them harm and every one else improve them? On the contrary, is it not one man only, or a very few—namely, those who are skilled in horses—who can improve them; while the majority of men harm them, if they use them, and have to do with them? Is it not so, Meletus, both with horses and with every other animal? Of course it is, whether you and Anytus say yes or no. And young men would certainly be very fortunate persons if only one man corrupted them, and every one else did them good. The truth is, Meletus, you prove conclusively that you have never thought about the youth in your life. It is quite clear, on your own showing, that you take no interest at all in the matters about which you are prosecuting me.

Now, be so good as to tell us, Meletus, is it better to live among good citizens or bad ones? Answer, my friend: I am not asking you at all a difficult question. Do not bad citizens do harm to their neighbors and good citizens good.

Mel. Yes.

Socr. Is there any man who would rather be injured than benefited by his companions? Answer, my good sir: you are obliged by the law to answer. Does any one like to be injured?

Mel. Certainly not.

Socr. Well then; are you prosecuting me for corrupting the young, and making them worse men, intentionally or unintentionally?

Mel. For doing it intentionally.

Socr. What, Meletus? Do you mean to say that you, who are so much younger than I, are yet so much wiser than I, that you know that bad citizens always do evil, and that good citizens always do good, to those with whom they come in contact,

while I am so extraordinarily stupid as not to know that if I make any of my companions a rogue, he will probably injure me in some way, and as to commit this great crime, as you allege, intentionally? You will not make me believe that, nor any one else either, I should think. Either I do not corrupt the young at all; or if I do, I do so unintentionally: so that you are a liar in either case. And if I corrupt them unintentionally, the law does not call upon you to prosecute me for a fault like that, which is an involuntary one: you should take me aside and admonish and instruct me: for of course I shall cease from doing wrong involuntarily, as soon as I know that I have been doing wrong. But you declined to instruct me: you would have nothing to do with me: instead of that, you bring me up before the Court, where the law sends persons, not for instruction, but for punishment.

The truth is, Athenians, as I said, it is quite clear that Meletus has never paid the slightest attention to these matters. However, now tell us, Meletus, how do you say that I corrupt the younger men? Clearly, according to your indictment, by teaching them not to believe in the gods of the city, but in other new divinities instead. You mean that I corrupt young men by that teaching, do you not?

Mel. Yes: most certainly; I mean that.

Socr. Then in the name of these gods of whom we are speaking, explain yourself a little more clearly to me and to the judges here. I cannot understand what you mean. Do you mean that I teach young men to believe in some gods, but not in the gods of the city? Do you accuse me of teaching them to believe in strange gods? If that is your meaning, I myself believe in some gods, and my crime is not that of absolute atheism. Or do you mean that I do not believe in the gods at all myself, and that I teach other people not to believe in them either?

Mel. I mean that you do not believe in the gods in any way whatever.

Socr. Wonderful, Meletus! Why do you say that? Do you mean that I believe neither the sun nor the moon to be gods, like other men?

Mel. I swear he does not, judges: he says that the sun is a stone, and the moon earth.

Socr. My dear Meletus, do you think that you are prosecuting Anaxagoras? You must have a very poor opinion of the judges, and think them very unlettered men, if you imagine that they do not know that the works of Anaxagoras of Clazomenæ are full of these doctrines. And so young men learn these things from me, when they can often buy places in the theater [2] for a drachma at most, and laugh Socrates to scorn, were he to pretend that these doctrines, which are very peculiar doctrines too, were his. But please tell me, do you really think that I do not believe in the gods at all?

Mel. Most certainly I do. You are a complete atheist.

Socr. No one believes that, Meletus, and I think that you know it to be a lie yourself. It seems to me, Athenians, that Meletus is a very insolent and wanton man, and that he is prosecuting me simply in the insolence and wantonness of youth. He is like a man trying an experiment on me, by asking me a riddle that has no answer. "Will this wise Socrates," he says to himself, "see that I am jesting and contradicting myself? or shall I outwit him and every one else who hears me?" Meletus seems to me to contradict himself in his indictment: it is as if he were to say, "Socrates is a

wicked man who does not believe in the gods, but who believes in the gods." But that is mere trifling.

Now, my friends, let us see why I think that this is his meaning. Do you answer me, Meletus: and do you, Athenians, remember the request which I made to you at starting, and do not interrupt me if I talk in my usual way.

Is there any man, Meletus, who believes in the existence of things pertaining to men and not in the existence of men? Make him answer the question, my friends, without these absurd interruptions. Is there any man who believes in the existence of horsemanship and not in the existence of horses? or in flute-playing and not in flute-players? There is not, my excellent sir. If you will not answer, I will tell both you and the judges that. But you must answer my next question. Is there any man who believes in the existence of divine things and not in the existence of divinities?

Mel. There is not.

Socr. I am very glad that the judges have managed to extract an answer from you. Well then, you say that I believe in divine beings, whether they be old or new ones, and that I teach others to believe in them; at any rate, according to your statement, I believe in divine beings. That you have sworn in your deposition. But if I believe in divine beings, I suppose it follows necessarily that I believe in divinities. Is it not so? It is. I assume that you grant that, as you do not answer. But do we not believe that divinities are either gods themselves or the children of the gods? Do you admit that?

Mel. I do.

Socr. Then you admit that I believe in divinities: now, if these divinities are gods, then, as I say, you are jesting and asking a riddle, and asserting that I do not believe in the gods, and at the same time that I do,

[2] Socrates here alludes to the references to Anaxagoras by Aristophanes, Euripedes, and other Greek dramatists. Anaxagoras' doctrine that the sun is a stone is mentioned in the *Orestes* of Euripedes.

since I believe in divinities. But if these divinities are the illegitimate children of the gods, either by the nymphs or by other mothers, as they are said to be, then, I ask, what man could believe in the existence of the children of the gods, and not in the existence of the gods? That would be as strange as believing in the existence of the offspring of horses and asses, and not in the existence of horses and asses. You must have indicted me in this manner, Meletus, either to test my skill, or because you could not find any crime that you could accuse me of with truth. But you will never contrive to persuade any man, even of the smallest understanding, that a belief in divine things and things of the gods does not necessarily involve a belief in divinities, and in the gods, and in heroes.

But in truth, Athenians, I do not think that I need say very much to prove that I have not committed the crime for which Meletus is prosecuting me. What I have said is enough to prove that. But, I repeat, it is certainly true, as I have already told you, that I have incurred much unpopularity and made many enemies. And that is what will cause my condemnation, if I am condemned; not Meletus, nor Anytus either, but the prejudice and suspicion of the multitude. They have been the destruction of many good men before me, and I think that they will be so again. There is no fear that I shall be their last victim.

Perhaps some one will say: "Are you not ashamed, Socrates, of following pursuits which are very likely now to cause your death?" I should answer him with justice, and say: My friend, if you think that a man of any worth at all ought to reckon the chances of life and death when he acts, or that he ought to think of anything but whether he is acting rightly or wrongly, and as a good or a bad man would act, you are grievously mistaken. According

to you, the demigods who died at Troy would be men of no great worth, and among them the son of Thetis, who thought nothing of danger when the alternative was disgrace. For when his mother, a goddess, addressed him, as he was burning to slay Hector, I suppose in this fashion, "My son, if thou avengest the death of thy comrade Patroclus, and slayest Hector, thou wilt die thyself, for 'fate awaits thee straightway after Hector's death,' " he heard what she said, but he scorned danger and death; he feared much more to live a coward, and not to avenge his friend. "Let me punish the evil-doer and straightway die," he said, "that I may not remain here by the beaked ships, a scorn of men, encumbering the earth." Do you suppose that he thought of danger or of death? For this, Athenians, I believe to be the truth. Wherever a man's post is, whether he has chosen it of his own will, or whether he has been placed at it by his commander, there it is his duty to remain and face the danger, without thinking of death, or of any other thing, except dishonor.

When the generals whom you chose to command me, Athenians, placed me at my post at Potidæa, and at Amphipolis, and at Delium, I remained where they placed me, and ran the risk of death, like other men: and it would be very strange conduct on my part if I were to desert my post now from fear of death or of any other thing, when God has commanded me, as I am persuaded that he has done, to spend my life in searching for wisdom, and in examining myself and others. That would indeed be a very strange thing: and then certainly I might with justice be brought to trial for not believing in the gods: for I should be disobeying the oracle, and fearing death, and thinking myself wise, when I was not wise. For to fear death, my friends, is only to think ourselves wise, without being wise:

for it is to think that we know what we do not know. For anything that men can tell, death may be the greatest good that can happen to them: but they fear it as if they knew quite well that it was the greatest of evils. And what is this but that shameful ignorance of thinking that we know what we do not know? In this matter too, my friends, perhaps I am different from the mass of mankind: and if I were to claim to be at all wiser than others, it would be because I do not think that I have any clear knowledge about the other world, when, in fact, I have none. But I do know very well that it is evil and base to do wrong, and to disobey my superior, whether he be man or god. And I will never do what I know to be evil, and shrink in fear from what, for all that I can tell, may be a good. And so, even if you acquit me now, and do not listen to Anytus' argument that, if I am to be acquitted, I ought never to have been brought to trial at all; and that, as it is, you are bound to put me to death, because, as he said, if I escape, all your children will forthwith be utterly corrupted by practising what Socrates teaches; if you were therefore to say to me, "Socrates, this time we will not listen to Anytus: we will let you go; but on this condition, that you cease from carrying on this search of yours, and from philosophy; if you are found following those pursuits again, you shall die": I say, if you offered to let me go on these terms, I should reply:—Athenians, I hold you in the highest regard and love; but I will obey God rather than you: and as long as I have breath and strength I will not cease from philosophy, and from exhorting you, and declaring the truth to every one of you whom I meet, saying, as I am wont: "My excellent friend, you are a citizen of Athens, a city which is very great and very famous for wisdom and power of mind; are you not ashamed of caring so much for

the making of money, and for reputation, and for honor? Will you not think or care about wisdom, and truth, and the perfection of your soul?" And if he disputes my words, and says that he does care about these things, I shall not forthwith release him and go away: I shall question him and cross-examine him and test him: and if I think that he has not virtue, though he says that he has, I shall reproach him for setting the lower value on the most important things, and a higher value on those that are of less account. This I shall do to every one whom I meet, young or old, citizen or stranger: but more especially to the citizens, for they are more nearly akin to me. For, know well, God has commanded me to do so. And I think that no better piece of fortune has ever befallen you in Athens than my service to God. For I spend my whole life in going about and persuading you all to give your first and chiefest care to the perfection of your souls, and not till you have done that to think of your bodies, or your wealth; and telling you that virtue does not come from wealth, but that wealth, and every other good thing which men have, whether in public, or in private, comes from virtue. If then I corrupt the youth by this teaching, the mischief is great: but if any man says that I teach anything else, he speaks falsely. And therefore, Athenians, I say, either listen to Anytus, or do not listen to him: either acquit me, or do not acquit me: but be sure that I shall not alter my way of life; no, not if I have to die for it many times.

Do not interrupt me, Athenians. Remember the request which I made to you, and listen to my words. I think that it will profit you to hear them. I am going to say something more to you, at which you may be inclined to cry out: but do not do that. Be sure that if you put me to death, who am what I have told you that I am, you will do yourselves more harm than me. Meletus and Anytus can do me no harm: that is impossible: for I am sure that God will not allow a good man to be injured by a bad one. They may indeed kill me, or drive me into exile, or deprive me of my civil rights; and perhaps Meletus and others think those things great evils. But I do not think so: I think that it is a much greater evil to do what he is doing now, and to try to put a man to death unjustly. And now, Athenians, I am not arguing in my own defence at all, as you might expect me to do: I am trying to persuade you not to sin against God, by condemning me, and rejecting his gift to you. For if you put me to death, you will not easily find another man to fill my place. God has sent me to attack the city, as if it were a great and noble horse, to use a quaint simile, which was rather sluggish from its size, and which needed to be aroused by a gadfly: and I think that I am the gadfly that God has sent to the city to attack it; for I never cease from settling upon you, as it were, at every point, and rousing, and exhorting, and reproaching each man of you all day long. You will not easily find any one else, my friends, to fill my place: and if you take my advice, you will spare my life. You are vexed, as drowsy persons are, when they are awakened, and of course, if you listened to Anytus, you could easily kill me with a single blow, and then sleep on undisturbed for the rest of your lives, unless God were to care for you enough to send another man to arouse you. And you may easily see that it is God who has given me to your city: a mere human impulse would never have led me to neglect all my own interests, or to endure seeing my private affairs neglected now for so many years, while it made me busy myself unceasingly in your interests, and go to each man of

you by himself, like a father, or an elder brother, trying to persuade him to care for virtue. There would have been a reason for it, if I had gained any advantage by this conduct, or if I had been paid for my exhortations; but you see yourselves that my accusers, though they accuse me of everything else without blushing, have not had the effrontery to say that I ever either exacted or demanded payment. They could bring no evidence of that. And I think that I have sufficient evidence of the truth of what I say in my poverty.

Perhaps it may seem strange to you that, though I am so busy in going about in private with my counsel, yet I do not venture to come forward in the assembly, and take part in the public councils. You have often heard me speak of my reason for this, and in many places: it is that I have a certain divine sign from God, which is the divinity that Meletus has caricatured in his indictment. I have had it from childhood: it is a kind of voice, which whenever I hear it, always turns me back from something which I was going to do, but never urges me to act. It is this which forbids me to take part in politics. And I think that it does well to forbid me. For, Athenians, it is quite certain that if I had attempted to take part in politics, I should have perished at once and long ago, without doing any good either to you or to myself. And do not be vexed with me for telling the truth. There is no man who will preserve his life for long, either in Athens or elsewhere, if he firmly opposes the wishes of the people, and tries to prevent the commission of much injustice and illegality in the State. He who would really fight for justice, must do so as a private man, not in public, if he means to preserve his life, even for a short time.

I will prove to you that this is so by very strong evidence, not by mere words, but by what you value highly, actions. Listen then to what has happened to me, that you may know that there is no man who could make me consent to do wrong from the fear of death; but that I would perish at once rather than give way. What I am going to tell you may be a commonplace in the Courts of Law; nevertheless it is true. The only office that I ever held in the State, Athenians, was that of Senator. When you wished to try the ten generals, who did not rescue their men after the battle of Arginusæ, in a body, which was illegal, as you all came to think afterwards, the tribe Antiochis, to which I belong, held the presidency. On that occasion I alone of all the presidents opposed your illegal action, and gave my vote against you. The speakers were ready to suspend me and arrest me; and you were clamoring against me, and crying out to me to submit. But I thought that I ought to face the danger out in the cause of law and justice, rather than join with you in your unjust proposal, from fear of imprisonment or death. That was before the destruction of the democracy. When the oligarchy came, the Thirty sent for me, with four others, to the Council-Chamber, and ordered us to bring over Leon the Salaminian from Salamis, that they might put him to death. They were in the habit of frequently giving similar orders to many others, wishing to implicate as many men as possible in their crimes. But then I again proved, not by mere words, but by my actions, that, if I may use a vulgar expression, I do not care a straw for death; but that I do care very much indeed about not doing anything against the laws of God or man. That government with all its power did not terrify me into doing anything wrong; but when we left the Council-Chamber, the other four went over to Salamis, and brought Leon across to Athens; and I went away

home: and if the rule of the Thirty had not been destroyed soon afterwards, I should very likely have been put to death for what I did then. Many of you will be my witnesses in this matter.

Now do you think that I should have remained alive all these years, if I had taken part in public affairs, and had always maintained the cause of justice like an honest man, and had held it a paramount duty, as it is, to do so? Certainly not, Athenians, nor any other man either. But throughout my whole life, both in private, and in public, whenever I have had to take part in public affairs, you will find that I have never yielded a single point in a question of right and wrong to any man; no, not to those whom my enemies falsely assert to have been my pupils.[3] But I was never any man's teacher. I have never withheld myself from any one, young or old, who was anxious to hear me converse while I was about my mission; neither do I converse for payment, and refuse to converse without payment: I am ready to ask questions of rich and poor alike, and if any man wishes to answer me, and then listen to what I have to say, he may. And I cannot justly be charged with causing these men to turn out good or bad citizens: for I never either taught, or professed to teach any of them any knowledge whatever. And if any man asserts that he ever learnt or heard any thing from me in private, which every one else did not hear as well as he, be sure that he does not speak the truth.

Why is it, then, that people delight in spending so much time in my company? You have heard why, Athenians. I told you the whole truth when I said that they delight in hearing me examine persons who think that they are wise when they are not wise. It is certainly very amusing to listen to that. And, I say, God has commanded

[3] For example, Critias and Alcibiades.

me to examine men in oracles, and in dreams, and in every way in which the divine will was ever declared to man. This is the truth, Athenians, and if it were not the truth, it would be easily refuted. For if it were really the case that I have already corrupted some of the young men, and am now corrupting others, surely some of them, finding as they grew older that I had given them evil counsel in their youth, would have come forward today to accuse me and take their revenge. Or if they were unwilling to do so themselves, surely their kinsmen, their fathers, or brothers, or other relatives, would, if I had done them any harm, have remembered it, and taken their revenge. Certainly I see many of them in Court. Here is Crito, of my own deme and of my own age, the father of Critobulus; here is Lysanias of Sphettus, the father of Æschinus: here is also Antiphon of Cephisus, the father of Epigenes. Then here are others, whose brothers have spent their time in my company; Nicostratus, the son of Theozotides, and brother of Theodotus —and Theodotus is dead, so he at least cannot entreat his brother to be silent: here is Paralus, the son of Demodocus, and the brother of Theages: here is Adeimantus, the son of Ariston, whose brother is Plato here: and Æantodorus, whose brother is Aristodorus. And I can name many others to you, some of whom Meletus ought to have called as witnesses in the course of his own speech: but if he forgot to call them then, let him call them now—I will stand aside while he does so—and tell us if he has any such evidence. No, on the contrary, my friends, you will find all these men ready to support me, the corrupter, the injurer of their kindred, as Meletus and Anytus call me. Those of them who have been already corrupted might perhaps have some reason for supporting me: but what reason can their relatives, who are grown up, and

who are uncorrupted, have, except the reason of truth and justice, that they know very well that Meletus is a liar, and that I am speaking the truth?

Well, my friends, this, together it may be with other things of the same nature, is pretty much what I have to say in my defence. There may be some one among you who will be vexed when he remembers how, even in a less important trial than this, he prayed and entreated the judges to acquit him with many tears, and brought forward his children and many of his friends and relatives in Court, in order to appeal to your feelings; and then finds that I shall do none of these things, though I am in what he would think the supreme danger. Perhaps he will harden himself against me when he notices this: it may make him angry, and he may give his vote in anger. If it is so with any of you—I do not suppose that it is, but in case it should be so— I think that I should answer him reasonably if I said: "My friend, I have kinsmen too, for, in the words of Homer, 'I am not born of stocks and stones,' but of woman"; and so, Athenians, I have kinsmen, and I have three sons, one of them a lad, and the other two still children. Yet I will not bring any of them forward before you, and implore you to acquit me. And why will I do none of these things? It is not from arrogance, Athenians, nor because I hold you cheap: whether or no I can face death bravely is another question: but for my own credit, and for your credit, and for the credit of our city, I do not think it well, at my age, and with my name, to do anything of that kind. Rightly or wrongly, men have made up their minds that in some way Socrates is different from the mass of mankind. And it will be a shameful thing if those of you who are thought to excel in wisdom, or in bravery, or in any other virtue, are going to act in this fashion. I have often seen men with a reputation behaving in a strange way at their trial, as if they thought it a terrible fate to be killed, and as though they expected to live for ever, if you did not put them to death. Such men seem to me to bring discredit on the city: for any stranger would suppose that the best and most eminent Athenians, who are selected by their fellow-citizens to hold office, and for other honors, are no better than women. Those of you, Athenians, who have any reputation at all, ought not to do these things: and you ought not to allow us to do them: you should show that you will be much more merciless to men who make the city ridiculous by these pitiful pieces of acting, than to men who remain quiet.

But apart from the question of credit, my friends, I do not think that it is right to entreat the judge to acquit us, or to escape condemnation in that way. It is our duty to convince his mind by reason. He does not sit to give away justice to his friends, but to pronounce judgment: and he has sworn not to favor any man whom he would like to favor, but to decide questions according to law. And therefore we ought not to teach you to forswear yourselves; and you ought not to allow yourselves to be taught, for then neither you nor we would be acting righteously. Therefore, Athenians, do not require me to do these things, for I believe them to be neither good nor just nor holy; and, more especially do not ask me to do them today, when Meletus is prosecuting me for impiety. For were I to be successful, and to prevail on you by my prayers to break your oaths, I should be clearly teaching you to believe that there are no gods; and I should be simply accusing myself by my defence of not believing in them. But, Athenians, that is very far from the truth. I do believe in the gods as no one of my accusers believes in them: and to you and to God I commit my cause to be decided as is best for you and for me.

[He is found guilty by 281 votes to 220.]

I am not vexed at the verdict which you have given, Athenians, for many reasons. I expected that you would find me guilty; and I am not so much surprised at that, as at the numbers of the votes. I, certainly, never thought that the majority against me would have been so narrow. But now it seems that if only thirty votes had changed sides, I should have escaped. So I think that I have escaped Meletus, as it is: and not only have I escaped him; for it is perfectly clear that if Anytus and Lycon had not come forward to accuse me too, he would not have obtained the fifth part of the votes, and would have had to pay a fine of a thousand drachmæ.

So he proposes death as the penalty. Be it so. And what counter-penalty shall I propose to you, Athenians? What I deserve, of course, must I not? What then do I deserve to pay or to suffer for having determined not to spend my life in ease? I neglected the things which most men value, such as wealth, and family interests, and military commands, and popular oratory, and all the political appointments, and clubs, and factions, that there are in Athens; for I thought that I was really too conscientious a man to preserve my life if I engaged in these matters. So I did not go where I should have done no good either to you or to myself. I went instead to each one of you by himself, to do him, as I say, the greatest of services, and strove to persuade him not to think of his affairs, until he had thought of himself, and tried to make himself as perfect and wise as possible; nor to think of the affairs of Athens, until he had thought of Athens herself; and in all cases to bestow his thoughts on things in the same manner. Then what do I deserve for such a life? Something good, Athenians, if I am really to propose what I deserve; and something good which it would be suitable to me to receive. Then what is a suitable reward to be given to a poor benefactor, who requires leisure to exhort you? There is no reward, Athenians, so suitable for him as a public maintenance in the Prytaneum. It is a much more suitable reward for him than for any of you who has won a victory at the Olympic games with his horse or his chariots. Such a man only makes you seem happy, but I make you really happy: and he is not in want, and I am. So if I am to propose the penalty which I really deserve, I propose this, a public maintenance in the Prytaneum.

Perhaps you think me stubborn and arrogant in what I am saying now, as in what I said about the entreaties and tears. It is not so, Athenians; it is rather that I am convinced that I never wronged any man intentionally, though I cannot persuade you of that, for we have conversed together only a little time. If there were a law at Athens, as there is elsewhere, not to finish a trial of life and death in a single day, I think that I could have convinced you of it: but now it is not easy in so short a time to clear myself of the gross calumnies of my enemies. But when I am convinced that I have never wronged any man, I shall certainly not wrong myself, or admit that I deserve to suffer any evil, or propose any evil for myself as a penalty. Why should I? Lest I should suffer the penalty which Meletus proposes, when I say that I do not know whether it is a good or an evil? Shall I choose instead of it something which I know to be an evil, and propose that as a penalty? Shall I propose imprisonment? And why should I pass the rest of my days in prison, the slave of successive officials?

Or shall I propose a fine, with imprisonment until it is paid? I have told you why I will not do that. I should have to remain in prison for I have no money to pay a fine with. Shall I then propose exile? Perhaps you would agree to that. Life would indeed be very dear to me, if I were unreasonable enough to expect that strangers would cheerfully tolerate my discussions and reasonings, when you who are my fellow-citizens cannot endure them, and have found them so burdensome and odious to you, that you are seeking now to be released from them. No, indeed, Athenians, that is not likely. A fine life I should lead for an old man, if I were to withdraw from Athens, and pass the rest of my days in wandering from city to city, and continually being expelled. For I know very well that the young men will listen to me, wherever I go, as they do here; and if I drive them away, they will persuade their elders to expel me: and if I do not drive them away, their fathers and kinsmen will expel me for their sakes.

Perhaps some one will say, "Why cannot you withdraw from Athens, Socrates, and hold your peace?" It is the most difficult thing in the world to make you understand why I cannot do that. If I say that I cannot hold my peace, because that would be to disobey God, you will think that I am not in earnest and will not believe me. And if I tell you that no better thing can happen to a man than to converse every day about virtue and the other matters about which you have heard me conversing and examining myself and others, and that an unexamined life is not worth living, then you will believe me still less. But that is the truth, my friends, though it is not easy to convince you of it. And, what is more, I am not accustomed to think that I deserve any punishment. If I had been rich, I would have proposed as large a fine as I could pay: that would have done me no harm. But I am not rich enough to pay a fine, unless you are willing to fix it at a sum within my means. Perhaps I could pay you a mina: so I propose that. Plato here, Athenians, and Crito, and Critobulus, and Apollodorus bid me propose thirty minæ, and they will be sureties for me. So I propose thirty minæ. They will be sufficient sureties to you for the money.

[*He is condemned to death.*]

You have not gained very much time, Athenians, and, as the price of it, you will have an evil name from all who wish to revile the city, and they will cast in your teeth that you put Socrates, a wise man, to death. For they will certainly call me wise, whether I am wise or not, when they want to reproach you. If you would have waited for a little while, your wishes would have been fulfilled in the course of nature; for you see that I am an old man, far advanced in years, and near to death. I am speaking not to all of you, only to those who have voted for my death. And now I am speaking to them still. Perhaps, my friends, you think that I have been defeated because I was wanting in the arguments by which I could have persuaded you to acquit me, if, that is, I had thought it right to do or to say anything to escape punishment. It is not so. I have been defeated because I was wanting, not in arguments, but in overboldness and effrontery: because I would not plead before you as you would have liked to hear me plead, or appeal to you with weeping and wailing, or say and do many other things, which I maintain are unworthy of me, but which you have been accustomed to from other men. But when I was defending myself, I thought that I ought not to do anything unmanly because of the danger which I ran, and I have not changed my mind now. I would very much

rather defend myself as I did, and die, than as you would have had me do, and live. Both in a law suit, and in war, there are some things which neither I nor any other man may do in order to escape from death. In battle a man often sees that he may at least escape from death by throwing down his arms and falling on his knees before the pursuer to beg for his life. And there are many other ways of avoiding death in every danger, if a man will not scruple to say and to do anything. But, my friends, I think that it is a much harder thing to escape from wickedness than from death; for wickedness is swifter than death. And now I, who am old and slow, have been overtaken by the slower pursuer: and my accusers, who are clever and swift, have been overtaken by the swifter pursuer, which is wickedness. And now I shall go hence, sentenced by you to death; and they will go hence, sentenced by truth to receive the penalty of wickedness and evil. And I abide by this award as well as they. Perhaps it was right for these things to be so: and I think that they are fairly measured.

And now I wish to prophesy to you, Athenians who have condemned me. For I am going to die, and that is the time when men have most prophetic power. And I prophesy to you who have sentenced me to death, that a far severer punishment than you have inflicted on me, will surely overtake you as soon as I am dead. You have done this thing, thinking that you will be relieved from having to give an account of your lives. But I say that the result will be very different from that. There will be more men who will call you to account, whom I have held back, and whom you did not see. And they will be harder masters to you than I have been, for they will be younger, and you will be more angry with them. For if you think that you will restrain men from reproaching you for your evil lives by putting them to death, you are very much mistaken. That way of escape is hardly possible, and it is not a good one. It is much better, and much easier, not to silence reproaches, but to make yourselves as perfect as you can. This is my parting prophecy to you who have condemned me.

With you who have acquitted me I should like to converse touching this thing that has come to pass, while the authorities are busy, and before I go to the place where I have to die. So, I pray you, remain with me until I go hence: there is no reason why we should not converse with each other while it is possible. I wish to explain to you, as my friends, the meaning of what has befallen me. A wonderful thing has happened to me, judges—for you I am right in calling judges. The prophetic sign, which I am wont to receive from the divine voice, has been constantly with me all through my life till now, opposing me in quite small matters if I were not going to act rightly. And now you yourselves see what has happened to me; a thing which might be thought, and which is sometimes actually reckoned, the supreme evil. But the sign of God did not withstand me when I was leaving my house in the morning, nor when I was coming up hither to the Court, nor at any point in my speech, when I was going to say anything: though at other times it has often stopped me in the very act of speaking. But now, in this matter, it has never once withstood me, either in my words or my actions. I will tell you what I believe to be the reason of that. This thing that has come upon me must be a good: and those of us who think that death is an evil must needs be mistaken. I have a clear proof that that is so; for my accustomed sign would certainly have opposed me, if I had not been going to fare well.

And if we reflect in another way we shall see that we may well hope that death is a good. For the state of death is one of two things: either the dead man wholly ceases to be, and loses all sensation; or, according to the common belief, it is a change and a migration of the soul unto another place. And if death is the absence of all sensation, and like the sleep of one whose slumbers are unbroken by any dreams, it will be a wonderful gain. For if a man had to select that night in which he slept so soundly that he did not even see any dreams, and had to compare with it all the other nights and days of his life, and then had to say how many days and nights in his life he had spent better and more pleasantly than this night, I think that a private person, nay, even the great King [of Persia] himself, would find them easy to count, compared with the others. If that is the nature of death, I for one count it a gain. For then it appears that eternity is nothing more than a single night. But if death is a journey to another place, and the common belief be true, that there are all who have died, what good could be greater than this, my judges? Would a journey not be worth taking, at the end of which, in the other world, we should be released from the self-styled judges who are here, and should find the true judges, who are said to sit in judgment below, such as Minos, and Rhadamanthus, and Æacus, and Triptolemus, and the other demi-gods who were just in their lives? Or what would you not give to converse with Orpheus and Musæus and Hesiod and Homer? I am willing to die many times, if this be true. And for my own part I should have a wonderful interest in meeting there Palamedes, and Ajax the son of Telamon, and the other men of old who have died through an unjust judgment, and in comparing my experiences with theirs. That I think would be no small pleasure. And, above all, I could spend my time in examining those who are there, as I examine men here, and in finding out which of them is wise, and which of them thinks himself wise, when he is not wise. What would we not give, my judges, to be able to examine the leader of the great expedition against Troy, or Odysseus, or Sisyphus, or countless other men and women whom we could name? It would be an infinite happiness to converse with them, and to live with them, and to examine them. Assuredly there they do not put men to death for doing that. For besides the other ways in which they are happier than we are, they are immortal, at least if the common belief be true.

And you too, judges, must face death with a good courage, and believe this as a truth, that no evil can happen to a good man, either in life, or after death. His fortunes are not neglected by the gods; and what has come to me today has not come by chance. I am persuaded that it was better for me to die now, and to be released from trouble: and that was the reason why the sign never turned me back. And so I am hardly angry with my accusers, or with those who have condemned me to die. Yet it was not with this mind that they accused me and condemned me, but meaning to do me an injury. So far I may find fault with them.

Yet I have one request to make of them. When my sons grow up, visit them with punishment, my friends, and vex them in the same way that I have vexed you, if they seem to you to care for riches, or for any other thing, before virtue: and if they think that they are something, when they are nothing at all, reproach them, as I have reproached you, for not caring for what they should, and for thinking that they are great men when in fact they are worthless. And if you will do this, I myself and my sons will have received our deserts at your hands.

But now the time has come, and we must go hence; I to die, and you to live. Whether life or death is better is known to God, and to God only.

Crito

CHARACTERS OF THE DIALOGUE

SOCRATES

CRITO

SCENE.—The prison of Socrates.

Socrates. Why have you come at this hour, Crito? Is it not still early?

Crito. Yes, very early.

Socr. About what time is it?

Crito. It is just day-break.

Socr. I wonder that the jailor was willing to let you in.

Crito. He knows me now, Socrates, I come here so often; and besides, I have done him a service.

Socr. Have you been here long?

Crito. Yes; some time.

Socr. Then why did you sit down without speaking? why did you not wake me at once?

Crito. Indeed, Socrates, I wish that I myself were not so sleepless and sorrowful. But I have been wondering to see how sweetly you sleep. And I purposely did not wake you, for I was anxious not to disturb your repose. Often before, all through your life, I have thought that your temper was a happy one; and I think so more than ever now, when I see how easily and calmly you bear the calamity that has come to you.

Socr. Nay, Crito, it would be absurd if at my age I were angry at having to die.

Crito. Other men as old are overtaken by similar calamities, Socrates; but their age does not save them from being angry with their fate.

Socr. That is so: but tell me, why are you here so early?

Crito. I am the bearer of bitter news, Socrates: not bitter, it seems, to you; but to me, and to all your friends, both bitter and grievous: and to none of them, I think, is it more grievous than to me.

Socr. What is it? Has the ship come from Delos, at the arrival of which I am to die?

Crito. No, it has not actually arrived: but I think that it will be here today, from the news which certain persons have brought from Sunium, who left it there. It is clear from their news that it will be here today; and then, Socrates, tomorrow your life will have to end.

Socr. Well, Crito, may it end fortunately. Be it so, if so the gods will. But I do not think that the ship will be here today.

Crito. Why do you suppose not?

Socr. I will tell you. I am to die on the day after the ship arrives, am I not?

Crito. That is what the authorities say.

Socr. Then I do not think that it will come today, but tomorrow. I judge from a certain dream which I saw a little while ago in the night: so it seems to be fortunate that you did not wake me.

Crito. And what was this dream?

Socr. A fair and comely woman, clad in white garments, seemed to come to me, and call me and say, "O Socrates—

The third day hence shalt thou fair Phthia reach." [1]

Crito. What a strange dream, Socrates!

Socr. But its meaning is clear; at least to me, Crito.

Crito. Yes, too clear, it seems. But, O my good Socrates, I beseech you for the last time to listen to me and save yourself. For to me your death will be more than a single disaster: not only shall I lose a friend the like of whom I shall never find again, but many persons, who do not know you and me well, will think that I might have saved you if I had been willing to spend money, but that I neglected to do so. And what character could be more disgraceful than the character of caring more for money than for one's friends? The world will never believe that we were anxious to save you, but that you yourself refused to escape.

Socr. But, my excellent Crito, why should we care so much about the opinion of the world? The best men, of whose opinion it is worth our while to think, will believe that we acted as we really did.

Crito. But you see, Socrates, that it is necessary to care about the opinion of the world too. This very thing that has happened to you proves that the multitude can do a man not the least, but almost the greatest harm, if he be falsely accused to them.

Socr. I wish that the multitude were able to do a man the greatest harm, Crito, for then they would be able to do him the greatest good too. That would have been well. But, as it is, they can do neither. They cannot make a man either wise or foolish: they act wholly at random.

Crito. Well, be it so. But tell me this, Socrates. You surely are not anxious about

[1] Homer, *Iliad*, ix, 363.

me and your other friends, and afraid lest, if you escape, the informers should say that we stole you away, and get us into trouble, and involve us in a great deal of expense, or perhaps in the loss of all our property, and, it may be, bring some other punishment upon us besides? If you have any fear of that kind, dismiss it. For of course we are bound to run those risks, and still greater risks than those if necessary, in saving you. So do not, I beseech you, refuse to listen to me.

Socr. I am anxious about that, Crito, and about much besides.

Crito. Then have no fear on that score. There are men who, for no very large sum, are ready to bring you out of prison into safety. And then, you know, these informers are cheaply bought, and there would be no need to spend much upon them. My fortune is at your service, and I think that it is sufficient: and if you have any feeling about making use of my money, there are strangers in Athens, whom you know, ready to use theirs; and one of them, Simmias of Thebes, has actually brought enough for this very purpose. And Cebes and many others are ready too. And therefore, I repeat, do not shrink from saving yourself on that ground. And do not let what you said in the Court, that if you went into exile you would not know what to do with yourself, stand in your way; for there are many places for you to go to, where you will be welcomed. If you choose to go to Thessaly, I have friends there who will make much of you, and shelter you from any annoyance from the people of Thessaly.

And besides, Socrates, I think that you will be doing what is wrong, if you abandon your life when you might preserve it. You are simply playing the game of your enemies; it is exactly the game of those who wanted to destroy you. And what is more, to me you seem to be abandoning your children too: you will leave them to take their chance in life, as far as you are concerned, when you might bring them up and educate them. Most likely their fate will be the usual fate of children who are left orphans. But you ought not to beget children unless you mean to take the trouble of bringing them up and educating them. It seems to me that you are choosing the easy way, and not the way of a good and brave man, as you ought, when you have been talking all your life long of the value that you set upon virtue. For my part, I feel ashamed both for you, and for us who are your friends. Men will think that the whole of this thing which has happened to you—your appearance in court to take your trial, when you need not have appeared at all; the very way in which the trial was conducted; and then lastly this, for the crowning absurdity of the whole affair, is due to our cowardice. It will look as if we had shirked the danger out of miserable cowardice; for we did not save you, and you did not save yourself, when it was quite possible to do so, if we had been good for anything at all. Take care, Socrates, lest these things be not evil only, but also dishonorable to you and to us. Consider then; or rather the time for consideration is past; we must resolve; and there is only one plan possible. Everything must be done tonight. If we delay any longer, we are lost. O Socrates, I implore you not to refuse to listen to me.

Socr. My dear Crito, if your anxiety to save me be right, it is most valuable: but if it be not right, its greatness makes it all the more dangerous. We must consider then whether we are to do as you say, or not; for I am still what I always have been, a man who will listen to no voice but the voice of the reasoning which on consideration I find to be truest. I cannot cast aside my former arguments because this misfortune has come to me. They seem to me to be as true as ever they were, and I hold exactly the same ones in honor and esteem as I used to: and if we have no better reasoning to substitute for them, I certainly shall not agree to your proposal, not even though the power of the multitude should scare us with fresh terrors, as children are scared with hobgoblins, and inflict upon us new fines, and imprisonments, and deaths. How then shall we most fitly examine the question? Shall we go back first to what you say about the opinions of men, and ask if we used to be right in thinking that we ought to pay attention to some opinions, and not to others? Used we to be right in saying so before I was condemned to die, and has it now become apparent that we were talking at random, and arguing for the sake of argument, and that it was really nothing but play and nonsense? I am anxious, Crito, to examine our former reasoning with your help, and to see whether my present position will appear to me to have affected its truth in any way, or not; and whether we are to set it aside, or to yield assent to it. Those of us who thought at all seriously, used always to say, I think, exactly what I said just now, namely, that we ought to esteem some of the opinions which men form highly, and not others. Tell me, Crito, if you please, do you not think that they were right? For you, humanly speaking, will not have to die tomorrow, and your judgment will not be biassed by that circumstance. Consider then: do you not think it reasonable to say that we should not esteem all the opinions of men, but only some, nor the opinions of all men, but only of some men? What do you think? Is not this true?

Crito. It is.

Socr. And we should esteem the good opinions, and not the worthless ones?

Crito. Yes.

Socr. But the good opinions are those of the wise, and the worthless ones those of the foolish?

Crito. Of course.

Socr. And what used we to say about this? Does a man who is in training, and who is in earnest about it, attend to the praise and blame and opinion of all men, or of the one man only who is a doctor or a trainer?

Crito. He attends only to the opinion of the one man.

Socr. Then he ought to fear the blame and welcome the praise of this one man, not of the many?

Crito. Clearly.

Socr. Then he must act and exercise, and eat and drink in whatever way the one man who is his master, and who understands the matter, bids him; not as others bid him?

Crito. That is so.

Socr. Good. But if he disobeys this one man, and disregards his opinion and his praise, and esteems instead what the many, who understand nothing of the matter, say, will he not suffer for it?

Crito. Of course he will.

Socr. And how will he suffer? In what direction, and in what part of himself?

Crito. Of course in his body. That is disabled.

Socr. You are right. And, Crito, to be brief, is it not the same, in everything? And, therefore, in questions of right and wrong, and of the base and the honorable, and of good and evil, which we are now considering, ought we to follow the opinion of the many and fear that, or the opinion of the one man who understands these matters (if we can find him), and feel more shame and fear before him than before all other men? For if we do not follow him, we shall cripple and maim that part of us which, we used to say, is improved by right and disabled by wrong. Or is this not so?

Crito. No, Socrates, I agree with you.

Socr. Now, if, by listening to the opinions of those who do not understand, we disable that part of us which is improved by health and crippled by disease, is our life worth living, when it is crippled? It is the body, is it not?

Crito. Yes.

Socr. Is life worth living with the body crippled and in a bad state?

Crito. No, certainly not.

Socr. Then is life worth living when that part of us which is maimed by wrong and benefited by right is crippled? Or do we consider that part of us, whatever it is, which has to do with right and wrong to be of less consequence than our body?

Crito. No, certainly not.

Socr. But more valuable?

Crito. Yes, much more so.

Socr. Then, my excellent friend, we must not think so much of what the many will say of us; we must think of what the one man, who understands right and wrong, and of what Truth herself will say of us. And so you are mistaken to begin with, when you invite us to regard the opinion of the multitude concerning the right and the honorable and the good, and their opposites. But, it may be said, the multitude can put us to death?

Crito. Yes, that is evident. That may be said, Socrates.

Socr. True. But, my excellent friend, to me it appears that the conclusion which we have just reached, is the same as our conclusion of former times. Now consider whether we still hold to the belief, that we should set the highest value, not on living, but on living well?

Crito. Yes, we do.

Socr. And living well and honorably and rightly mean the same thing: do we hold to that or not?

Crito. We do.

Socr. Then, starting from these premises, we have to consider whether it is right or not right for me to try to escape from prison, without the consent of the Athenians. If we find that is right, we will try: if not, we will let it alone. I am afraid that considerations of expense, and of reputation, and of bringing up my children, of which you talk, Crito, are only the reflections of our friends, the many, who lightly put men to death, and who would, if they could, as lightly bring them to life again, without a thought. But reason, which is our guide, shows us that we can have nothing to consider but the question which I asked just now: namely, shall we be doing right if we give money and thanks to the men who are to aid me in escaping, and if we ourselves take our respective parts in my escape? Or shall we in truth be doing wrong, if we do all this? And if we find that we should be doing wrong, then we must not take any account either of death, or of any other evil that may be the consequence of remaining quietly here, but only of doing wrong.

Crito. I think that you are right, Socrates. But what are we to do?

Socr. Let us consider that together, my good sir, and if you can contradict anything that I say, do so, and I will be convinced: but if you cannot, do not go on repeating to me any longer, my dear friend, that I should escape without the consent of the Athenians. I am very anxious to act with your approval: I do not want you to think me mistaken. But now tell me if you agree with the doctrine from which I start, and try to answer my questions as you think best.

Crito. I will try.

Socr. Ought we never to do wrong intentionally at all; or may we do wrong in some ways, and not in others? Or, as we have often agreed in former times, is it never either good or honorable to do wrong? Have all our former conclusions been forgotten in these few days? Old men as we were, Crito, did we not see, in days gone by, when we were gravely conversing with each other, that we were no better than children? Or is not what we used to say most assuredly the truth, whether the world agrees with us or not? Is not wrong-doing an evil and a shame to the wrong-doer in every case, whether we incur a heavier or a lighter punishment than death as the consequence of doing right? Do we believe that?

Crito. We do.

Socr. Then we ought never to do wrong at all?

Crito. Certainly not.

Socr. Neither, if we ought never to do wrong at all, ought we to repay wrong with wrong, as the world thinks we may?

Crito. Clearly not.

Socr. Well then, Crito, ought we to do evil to any one?

Crito. Certainly I think not, Socrates.

Socr. And is it right to repay evil with evil, as the world thinks, or not right?

Crito. Certainly it is not right.

Socr. For there is no difference, is there, between doing evil to a man, and wronging him?

Crito. True.

Socr. Then we ought not to repay wrong with wrong or do harm to any man, no matter what we may have suffered from him. And in conceding this, Crito, be careful that you do not concede more than you mean. For I know that only a few men hold, or ever will hold this opinion. And so those who hold it, and those who do not, have no common ground of argument; they can of necessity only look with contempt on each other's belief. Do you therefore consider very carefully whether you agree with me and share my opinion. Are we to start in

our inquiry from the doctrine that it is never right either to do wrong, or to repay wrong with wrong, or to avenge ourselves on any man who harms us, by harming him in return? Or do you disagree with me and dissent from my principle? I myself have believed in it for a long time, and I believe in it still. But if you differ in any way, explain to me how. If you still hold to our former opinion, listen to my next point.

Crito. Yes, I hold to it, and I agree with you. Go on.

Socr. Then, my next point, or rather my next question, is this: Ought a man to perform his just agreements, or may he shuffle out of them?

Crito. He ought to perform them.

Socr. Then consider. If I escape without the state's consent, shall I be injuring those whom I ought least to injure, or not? Shall I be abiding by my just agreements or not?

Crito. I cannot answer your question, Socrates. I do not understand it.

Socr. Consider it in this way. Suppose the laws and the commonwealth were to come and appear to me as I was preparing to run away (if that is the right phrase to describe my escape) and were to ask, "Tell us, Socrates, what have you in your mind to do? What do you mean by trying to escape, but to destroy us the laws, and the whole city, so far as in you lies? Do you think that a state can exist and not be overthrown, in which the decisions of law are of no force, and are disregarded and set at nought by private individuals?" How shall we answer questions like that, Crito? Much might be said, especially by an orator, in defence of the law which makes judicial decisions supreme. Shall I reply, "But the state has injured me: it has decided my cause wrongly." Shall we say that?

Crito. Certainly we will, Socrates.

Socr. And suppose the laws were to reply, "Was that our agreement? or was it that you would submit to whatever judgments the state should pronounce?" And if we were to wonder at their words, perhaps they would say, "Socrates, wonder not at our words, but answer us; you yourself are accustomed to ask questions and to answer them. What complaint have you against us and the city, that you are trying to destroy us? Are we not, first, your parents? Through us your father took your mother and begat you. Tell us, have you any fault to find with those of us that are the laws of marriage?" "I have none," I should reply. "Or have you any fault to find with those of us that regulate the nurture and education of the child, which you, like others, received? Did not we do well in bidding your father educate you in music and gymnastic?" "You did," I should say. "Well then, since you were brought into the world and nurtured and educated by us, how, in the first place, can you deny that you are our child and our slave, as your fathers were before you? And if this be so, do you think that your rights are on a level with ours? Do you think that you have a right to retaliate upon us if we should try to do anything to you. You had not the same rights that your father had, or that your master would have had, if you had been a slave. You had no right to retaliate upon them if they ill-treated you, or to answer them if they reviled you, or to strike them back if they struck you, or to repay them evil with evil in any way. And do you think that you may retaliate on your country and its laws? If we try to destroy you, because we think it right, will you in return do all that you can to destroy us, the laws, and your country, and say that in so doing you are doing right, you, the man, who in truth thinks so much of virtue? Or are you too wise to see that your country is worthier, and more august, and more sacred, and holier, and held in higher honor both by the gods and by all men of understanding, than your father and your mother and all your other ancestors; and that it is your bounden duty to reverence it, and to submit to it, and to approach it more humbly than you would approach your father, when it is angry with you; and either to do whatever it bids you to do or to persuade it to excuse you; and to obey in silence if it orders you to endure stripes or imprisonment, or if it send you to battle to be wounded or to die? That is what is your duty. You must not give way, nor retreat, nor desert your post. In war, and in the court of justice, and everywhere, you must do whatever your city and your country bid you do, or you must convince them that their commands are unjust. But it is against the law of God to use violence to your father or to your mother; and much more so is it against the law of God to use violence to your country." What answer shall we make, Crito? Shall we say that the laws speak truly, or not?

Crito. I think that they do.

Socr. "Then consider, Socrates," perhaps they would say, "if we are right in saying that by attempting to escape you are attempting to injure us. We brought you into the world, we nurtured you, we educated you, we gave you and every other citizen a share of all the good things we could. Yet we proclaim that if any man of the Athenians is dissatisfied with us, he may take his goods and go away whithersoever he pleases: we give that permission to every man who chooses to avail himself of it, so soon as he has reached man's estate, and sees us, the laws, and the administration of our city. No one of us stands in his way or forbids him to take his goods and go wherever he likes, whether it be to an Athenian colony, or to any foreign country, if he is dissatisfied with us and with the city. But we say that every man of you who remains here, seeing how we administer justice, and how we govern the city in other matters, has agreed, by the very fact of remaining here, to do whatsoever we bid him. And, we say, he who disobeys us, does a threefold wrong: he disobeys us who are his parents, and he disobeys us who fostered him, and he disobeys us after he has agreed to obey us, without persuading us that we are wrong. Yet we did not bid him sternly to do whatever we told him. We offered him an alternative; we gave him his choice, either to obey us, or to convince us that we were wrong: but he does neither.

"These are the charges, Socrates, to which we say that you will expose yourself, if you do what you intend; and that not less, but more than other Athenians." And if I were to ask, "And why?" they might retort with justice that I have bound myself by the agreement with them more than other Athenians. They would say, "Socrates, we have very strong evidence that you were satisfied with us and with the city. You would not have been content to stay at home in it more than other Athenians, unless you had been satisfied with it more than they. You never went away from Athens to the festivals, save once to the Isthmian games, nor elsewhere except on military service; you never made other journeys like other men; you had no desire to see other cities or other laws; you were contented with us and our city. So strongly did you prefer us, and agree to be governed by us: and what is more, you begat children in this city, you found it so pleasant. And besides, if you had wished, you might at your trial have offered to go into exile. At that time you could have done with the state's consent, what you are trying now to do without it. But then you gloried in being willing to die. You said that you preferred death to exile. And now you are not ashamed of those words: you do not respect

us the laws, for you are trying to destroy us: and you are acting just as a miserable slave would act, trying to run away, and breaking the covenant and agreement which you made to submit to our government. First, therefore, answer this question. Are we right, or are we wrong, in saying that you have agreed not in mere words, but in reality, to live under our government?" What are we to say, Crito? Must we not admit that it is true?

Crito. We must, Socrates.

Socr. Then they would say, "Are you not breaking your covenants and agreements with us? And you were not led to make them by force or by fraud: you had not to make up your mind in a hurry. You had seventy years in which you might have gone away, if you had been dissatisfied with us, or if the agreement had seemed to you unjust. But you preferred neither Lacedæmon nor Crete, though you are fond of saying that they are well governed, nor any other state, either of the Hellenes, or the Barbarians. You went away from Athens less than the lame and the blind and the cripple. Clearly you, far more than other Athenians, were satisfied with the city, and also with us who are its laws: for who would be satisfied with a city which had no laws? And now will you not abide by your agreement? If you take our advice, you will, Socrates: then you will not make yourself ridiculous by going away from Athens.

"For consider: what good will you do yourself or your friends by thus transgressing, and breaking your agreement? It is tolerably certain that they, on their part, will at least run the risk of exile, and of losing their civil rights, or of forfeiting their property. For yourself, you might go to one of the neighboring cities, to Thebes or to Megara for instance—for both of them are well governed—but, Socrates, you will come as an enemy to these commonwealths; and all who care for their city will look askance at you, and think that you are a subverter of law. And you will confirm the judges in their opinion, and make it seem that their verdict was a just one. For a man who is a subverter of law, may well be supposed to be a corrupter of the young and thoughtless. Then will you avoid well-governed states and civilized men? Will life be worth having, if you do? Or will you consort with such men, and converse without shame— about what, Socrates? About the things which you talk of here? Will you tell them that virtue, and justice, and institutions, and law are the most precious things that men can have? And do you not think that that will be a shameful thing in Socrates? You ought to think so. But you will leave these places; you will go to the friends of Crito in Thessaly: for there there is most disorder and licence: and very likely they will be delighted to hear of the ludicrous way in which you escaped from prison, dressed up in peasant's clothes, or in some other disguise which people put on when they are running away, and with your appearance altered. But will no one say how you, an old man, with probably only a few more years to live, clung so greedily to life that you dared to transgress the highest laws? Perhaps not, if you do not displease them. But if you do, Socrates, you will hear much that will make you blush. You will pass your life as the flatterer and the slave of all men; and what will you be doing but feasting in Thessaly? It will be as if you had made a journey to Thessaly for an entertainment. And where will be all our old sayings about justice and virtue then? But you wish to live for the sake of your children? You want to bring them up and educate them? What? will you take them with you to Thessaly, and bring them up and

educate them there? Will you make them strangers to their own country, that you may bestow this benefit on them too? Or supposing that you leave them in Athens, will they be brought up and educated better if you are alive, though you are not with them? Yes; your friends will take care of them. Will your friends take care of them if you make a journey to Thessaly, and not if you make a journey to Hades? You ought not to think that, at least if those who call themselves your friends are good for anything at all.

"No, Socrates, be advised by us who have fostered you. Think neither of children, nor of life, nor of any other thing before justice, that when you come to the other world you may be able to make your defence before the rulers who sit in judgment there. It is clear that neither you nor any of your friends will be happier, or juster, or holier in this life, if you do this thing, nor will you be happier after you are dead. Now you will go away wronged, not by us, the laws, but by men. But if you repay evil with evil, and wrong with wrong in this shameful way, and break your agreements and covenants with us, and injure those whom you should least injure, yourself, and your friends, and your country, and us, and so escape, then we shall be angry with you while you live, and when you die our brethren, the laws in Hades, will not receive you kindly; for they will know that on earth you did all that you could to destroy us. Listen then to us, and let not Crito persuade you to do as he says."

Know well, my dear friend Crito, that this is what I seem to hear, as the worshippers of Cybele seem, in their frenzy, to hear the music of flutes: and the sound of these words rings loudly in my ears, and drowns all other words. And I feel sure that if you try to change my mind you will speak in vain; nevertheless, if you think that you will succeed, say on.

Crito. I can say no more, Socrates.

Socr. Then let it be, Crito: and let us do as I say, seeing that God so directs us.

Phaedo (Death Scene)

CHARACTERS OF THE DIALOGUE

SOCRATES

CRITO

A GROUP OF INTIMATE FRIENDS

SCENE.—The prison of Socrates at the close of a long conversation.

When Socrates had finished speaking Crito said, Be it so, Socrates. But have you any commands for your friends or for me about your children, or about other things? How shall we serve you best?

Simply by doing what I always tell you, Crito. Take care of your own selves, and you will serve me and mine and yourselves in all that you do, even though you make no promises now. But if you are careless of your own selves, and will not follow the path of life which we have pointed out in our discussions both today and at other times, all your promises now, however profuse and earnest they are, will be of no avail.

We will do our best, said Crito. But how shall we bury you?

As you please, he answered; only you must catch me first, and not let me escape you. And then he looked at us with a smile and said, My friends, I cannot convince Crito that I am the Socrates who has been conversing with you, and arranging his arguments in order. He thinks that I am the body which he will presently see a corpse, and he asks how he is to bury me. All the arguments which I have used to prove that I shall not remain with you after I have drunk the poison, but that I shall go away to the happiness of the blessed, with which I tried to comfort you and myself, have been thrown away on him. Do you therefore be my sureties to him, as he was my surety at the trial, but in a different way. He was surety for me then that I would remain; but you must be my sureties to him that I shall go away when I am dead, and not remain with you: then he will feel my death less; and when he sees my body being burnt or buried, he will not be grieved because he thinks that I am suffering dreadful things: and at my funeral he will not say that it is Socrates whom he is laying out, or bearing to the grave, or burying. For, dear Crito, he continued, you must know that to use words wrongly is not only a fault in itself; it also creates evil in the soul. You must be of good cheer, and say that you are burying my body: and you must bury it as you please, and as you think right.

With these words he rose and went into another room to bathe himself: Crito went with him and told us to wait. So we waited, talking of the argument, and discussing it, and then again dwelling on the greatness of the calamity which had fallen upon us: it seemed as if we were going to lose a father, and to be orphans for the rest of our life. When he had bathed, and his children had been brought to him,—he had two sons quite little, and one grown up,—and the women of his family were come, he spoke with them in Crito's presence, and gave them his last commands; then he sent the women and children away, and returned to us. By that time it was near the hour of sunset, for he had been a long while within. When he came back to us from the bath he sat down, but not much was said after that. Presently the servant of the Eleven came and stood before him and said, "I know that I shall not find you unreasonable like other men, Socrates. They are angry with me and curse me when I bid them drink the poison because the authorities make me do it. But I have found you all along the noblest and gentlest and best man that has ever come here; and now I am sure that you will not be angry with me, but with those who you know are to blame. And so farewell, and try to bear what must be as lightly as you can; you know why I have come." With that he turned away weeping, and went out.

Socrates looked up at him, and replied, Farewell: I will do as you say. Then he turned to us and said, How courteous the man is! And the whole time that I have been here, he has constantly come in to see me, and sometimes he has talked to me, and has been the best of men; and now, how generously he weeps for me! Come, Crito, let us obey him: let the poison be brought if it is ready; and if it is not ready, let it be prepared.

Crito replied: Nay, Socrates, I think that the sun is still upon the hills; it has not set. Besides, I know that other men take the poison quite late, and eat and drink heartily, and even enjoy the company of their chosen friends, after the announcement has been made. So do not hurry; there is still time.

Socrates replied: And those whom you speak of, Crito, naturally do so; for they think that they will be gainers by so doing. And I naturally shall not do so; for I think that I should gain nothing by drinking the poison a little later, but my own contempt for so greedily saving up a life which is already spent. So do not refuse to do as I say.

Then Crito made a sign to his slave who was standing by; and the slave went out, and after some delay returned with the man who was to give the poison, carrying it prepared in a cup. When Socrates saw him, he asked, You understand these things, my good sir, what have I to do?

You have only to drink this, he replied, and to walk about until your legs feel heavy, and then lie down; and it will act of itself. With that he handed the cup to Socrates, who took it quite cheerfully, Echecrates, without trembling, and without any change of color or of feature, and looked up at the man with that fixed glance of his, and asked, What say you to making a libation from this draught? May I, or not? We only prepare so much as we think sufficient, Socrates, he answered. I understand, said Socrates. But I suppose that I may, and must, pray to the gods that my journey hence may be prosperous: that is my prayer; be it so. With these words he put the cup to his lips and drank the poison quite calmly and cheerfully. Till then most of us had been able to control our grief fairly well; but when we saw him drinking, and then the poison finished, we could do so no longer: my tears came fast in spite of myself, and I covered my face and wept for myself: it was not for him, but at my own misfortune in losing such a friend. Even before that Crito had been unable to restrain his tears, and had gone away; and Apollodorus, who had never once ceased weeping the whole time, burst into a loud cry, and made us one and all break down by his sobbing and grief, except only Socrates himself. What are you doing, my friends? he exclaimed. I sent away the women chiefly in order that they might not offend in this way; for I have heard that a man should die in silence. So calm yourselves and bear up. When we heard that we were ashamed, and we ceased from weeping. But he walked about, until he said that his legs were getting heavy, and then he lay down on his back, as he was told. And the man who gave the poison began to examine his feet and legs, from time to time: then he pressed his foot hard, and asked if there was any feeling in it; and Socrates said, No: and then his legs, and so higher and higher, and showed us that he was cold and stiff. And Socrates felt himself, and said that when it came to his heart, he should be gone. He was already growing cold about the groin, when he uncovered his face, which had been covered, and spoke for the last time. Crito, he said, I owe a cock to Asclepius; do not forget to pay it. It shall be done, replied Crito. Is there anything else that you wish? He made no answer to this question; but after a short interval there was a movement, and the man uncovered him, and his eyes were fixed. Then Crito closed his mouth and his eyes.

Such was the end, Echecrates, of our friend, a man, I think, who was the wisest and justest, and the best man that I have ever known.

PART TWO

The Ways of Knowing

INTRODUCTORY NOTE

ONE OF THE MAIN divisions of philosophy is epistemology, or the theory of knowledge. Epistemology asks such fundamental questions as these: How much do we know? How much *can* we know? *How* do we know? How can we distinguish between appearance and reality? We shall be dealing with such questions as these in this Part. Since the problem of truth is at the heart of epistemological inquiry, we shall concentrate mainly on the question: How can we find out what is true?

This question became a matter of keen and widespread interest with the great flowering of science in the seventeenth and eighteenth centuries. The discoveries of such great scientists as Kepler, Galileo, Newton, Gilbert, and Harvey and the rapid development of mathematics and natural science forced men to reflect upon the nature of scientific knowledge and the means to its attainment.

The principal cleavage among philosophers was between the *rationalists* and the *empiricists*. The rationalists, among them Descartes, Spinoza, and Leibniz, relied chiefly upon reason as the source of genuine knowledge, taking the methods of mathematics, especially geometry, as their model. The empiricists, among them Locke, Berkeley, and Hume, depended mainly upon experience, regarding the methods of hypothesis, observation, and experiment as the principal foundations of knowledge. Actually, the differences between the two groups were not so sharp as they are often represented. Both groups recognized the necessity of a combination of experience and reason, but they veered toward opposite sides in their emphasis.

The plan of our discussion in Part Two will be as follows: First, we shall examine rationalism, using the philosophy of Descartes as our example. Then, we shall turn to empiricism, drawing on the ideas of a great American philosopher, Charles Peirce, as illustrative. We shall then consider William James and John Dewey as spokesmen for pragmatism, a movement closely related to the empiricism of Peirce. Finally, having examined the pragmatic theory of truth, we shall study two rival doctrines—the correspondence theory as formulated by Bertrand Russell, and the coherence theory as interpreted by Brand Blanshard.

3

The Way of the Rationalist

RENÉ DESCARTES (1596–1650)

Descartes' father was Councillor of the Parliament of Brittany and owner of a fair amount of landed property. His mother, apparently consumptive, died during his infancy and left him with enfeebled health. Anxious to surround the delicate boy with every care, his father entrusted Descartes' education to the Jesuits. It was at the newly established Jesuit college at La Fléche that the young Descartes fell in love with geometry.

Leaving school at seventeen, Descartes spent the next four years in Paris studying law. For the next several years, he lived as a traveler and a soldier, serving as a volunteer in three European armies, in the Netherlands, Bavaria, and Hungary. During this period, when he had a good deal of time to reflect, he came to doubt the value of everything he had learned with the single exception of mathematics.

On November 10, 1619, he had the remarkable experience to which he refers at the beginning of Part II of the *Discourse on Method*. He spent this cold November day in a stove-heated room, meditating about mathematical and scientific ideas that had been tumbling through his mind for several days. Exhausted nervously, he finally fell asleep and had three strange dreams. The first, which was full of ominous symbolism, terrified him, and he interpreted it as a rebuke for his past life. In the second dream, he seemed to hear a clap of thunder and, half awaking, he appeared to be surrounded by bright sparks of light. He interpreted the thunder as the Spirit of Truth descending to take possession of his mind. In the third dream, which was mild and reassuring, he found a volume of Latin poetry on a table and, opening it, read the words *Quid vitae sectabor iter* (What way of life shall I follow?). Then, in his dream, an unknown man approached and presented him with a piece of Latin verse beginning *Est et non* (Yes and no). He interpreted the words in the volume of poetry and the *est et non* as symbolizing human knowledge and pointing the way to a life of philosophical reflection.

51

As a result of these dreams, which he thought were inspired by God, and the intense intellectual activity that preceded them, he saw himself at the parting of the ways, and he resolved thenceforth to follow the path of philosophy and scientific research.

Although Descartes has not given us a detailed account of "the foundations of a wonderful science" which he believed he had discovered at this time, we know he had the conviction that the method of mathematics could be generalized to apply to all the sciences and that thereby certainty could be gained. Moreover, he conceived the method of applying algebraic symbolism to geometry and of using coordinates to describe geometrical figures; in other words, he founded analytical geometry. Finally, he was convinced that science and philosophy should form one whole, subject to a single method.

He vowed that no ties of marriage or society should deter him from a life of intellectual research devoted to the development of these insights. Although he continued to travel and to study "the great book of the world" for the next nine years (1619–1628), he still found time to work on various problems of mathematics and science. Growing tired of his wanderings at last, in 1628 he sold his inherited estates in France and settled in a quiet country house in Holland. With abundant leisure and a few servants to take care of his material needs, he formed the habit of staying in bed until about noon, reading, writing, or meditating. He soon acquired a wide reputation and was visited by, or corresponded with, many notable scientists and philosophers of the age. During this sojourn in Holland, he had what was apparently his only love affair. The daughter who was the issue of this alliance died at the age of five, much to her father's sorrow.

In the autumn of 1649, Descartes accepted an invitation from Queen Christina of Sweden to spend a winter at her court. An imperious though learned monarch, Christina thought that she had the right to command his services at any hour she chose. Daily at five in the morning throughout the bitterly cold winter, Descartes was ushered into the presence of the Queen, where he discoursed to her about philosophy while he stood shivering on the marble floor. Unused to the biting climate and the rigors of such early rising, he caught pneumonia and died in March 1650, a few days before his fifty-fifth birthday.

systematic doubt

Cogito ergo sum

act - intuition - reason organizing perceptions

God - Is he? Is He a Deceiver?

Meditations on the First Philosophy
dualism - 64

in Which the Existence of God
innate ideas

and the Distinction Between Mind

and Body Are Demonstrated*

MEDITATION I

Of the things which may be brought within the sphere of the doubtful.

It is now some years since I detected how many were the false beliefs that I had from my earliest youth admitted as true, and how doubtful was everything I had since constructed on this basis; and from that time I was convinced that I must once for all seriously undertake to rid myself of all the opinions which I had formerly accepted, and commence to build anew from the foundation, if I wanted to establish any firm and permanent structure in the sciences. But as this enterprise appeared to be a very great one, I waited until I had attained an age so mature that I could not hope that at any later date I should be better fitted to execute my design. This reason caused me to delay so long that I should feel that I was doing wrong were I to occupy in deliberation the time that yet remains to me for action. Today, then, since very opportunely for the plan I have in view I have delivered my mind from every care [and am happily agitated by no passions] and since I have procured for myself an assured leisure in a peaceable retirement, I shall at last seri-

ously and freely address myself to the general upheaval of all my former opinions.

Now for this object it is not necessary that I should show that all of these are false—I shall perhaps never arrive at this end. But inasmuch as reason already persuades me that I ought no less carefully to withhold my assent from matters which are not entirely certain and indubitable than from those which appear to me manifestly to be false, if I am able to find in each one some reason to doubt, this will suffice to justify my rejecting the whole. And for that end it will not be requisite that I should examine each in particular, which would be an endless undertaking; for owing to the fact that the destruction of the foundations of necessity brings with it the downfall of the rest of the edifice, I shall only in the first place attack those principles upon which all my former opinions rested.

All that up to the present time I have accepted as most true and certain I have learned either from the senses or through the senses; but it is sometimes proved to me that these senses are deceptive, and it is wiser not to trust entirely to any thing by which we have once been deceived.

But it may be that although the senses

* The following excerpts from the *Meditations* are from *The Philosophical Works of Descartes*, translated by Elizabeth S. Haldane and G. R. T. Ross, and published by Cambridge at the University Press, 1931. Reprinted by permission.

sometimes deceive us concerning things which are hardly perceptible, or very far away, there are yet many others to be met with as to which we cannot reasonably have any doubt, although we recognize them by their means. For example, there is the fact that I am here, seated by the fire, attired in a dressing gown, having this paper in my hands and other similar matters. And how could I deny that these hands and this body are mine, were it not perhaps that I compare myself to certain persons, devoid of sense, whose cerebella are so troubled and clouded by the violent vapors of black bile, that they constantly assure us that they think they are kings when they are really quite poor, or that they are clothed in purple when they are really without covering, or who imagine that they have an earthenware head or are nothing but pumpkins or are made of glass. But they are mad, and I should not be any the less insane were I to follow examples so extravagant.

At the same time I must remember that I am a man, and that consequently I am in the habit of sleeping, and in my dreams representing to myself the same things or sometimes even less probable things, than do those who are insane in their waking moments. How often has it happened to me that in the night I dreamt that I found myself in this particular place, that I was dressed and seated near the fire, whilst in reality I was lying undressed in bed! At this moment it does indeed seem to me that it is with eyes awake that I am looking at this paper; that this head which I move is not asleep, that it is deliberately and of set purpose that I extend my hand and perceive it; what happens in sleep does not appear so clear nor so distinct as does all this. But in thinking over this I remind myself that on many occasions I have in sleep been deceived by similar illusions, and in dwelling carefully on this reflection I see so manifestly that there are no certain indications by which we may clearly distinguish wakefulness from sleep that I am lost in astonishment. And my astonishment is such that it is almost capable of persuading me that I now dream.

Now let us assume that we are asleep and that all these particulars, e.g. that we open our eyes, shake our head, extend our hands, and so on, are but false delusions; and let us reflect that possibly neither our hands nor our whole body are such as they appear to us to be. At the same time we must at least confess that the things which are represented to us in sleep are like painted representations which can only have been formed as the counterparts of something real and true, and that in this way those general things at least, i.e. eyes, a head, hands, and a whole body, are not imaginary things, but things really existent. For, as a matter of fact, painters, even when they study with the greatest skill to represent sirens and satyrs by forms the most strange and extraordinary, cannot give them natures which are entirely new, but merely make a certain medley of the members of different animals; or if their imagination is extravagant enough to invent something so novel that nothing similar has ever before been seen, and that then their work represents a thing purely fictitious and absolutely false, it is certain all the same that the colors of which this is composed are necessarily real. And for the same reason, although these general things, to wit, [a body], eyes, a head, and such like, may be imaginary, we are bound at the same time to confess that there are at least some other objects yet more simple and more universal, which are real and true; and of these just in the same way as with certain real colors, all these images of things which dwell in our thoughts, whether true and real or false and fantastic, are formed.

To such a class of things pertains corporeal nature in general, and its extension, the figure of extended things, their quantity or magnitude and number, as also the place in which they are, the time which measures their duration, and so on.

That is possibly why our reasoning is not unjust when we conclude from this that Physics, Astronomy, Medicine and all other sciences which have as their end the consideration of composite things, are very dubious and uncertain; but that Arithmetic, Geometry and other sciences of that kind which only treat of things that are very simple and very general, without taking great trouble to ascertain whether they are actually existent or not, contain some measure of certainty and an element of the indubitable. For whether I am awake or asleep, two and three together always form five, and the square can never have more than four sides, and it does not seem possible that truths so clear and apparent can be suspected of any falsity [or uncertainty].

Nevertheless I have long had fixed in my mind the belief that an all-powerful God existed by whom I have been created such as I am. But how do I know that He has not brought it to pass that there is no earth, no heaven, no extended body, no magnitude, no place, and that nevertheless [I possess the perceptions of all these things and that] they seem to me to exist just exactly as I now see them? And, besides, as I sometimes imagine that others deceive themselves in the things which they think they know best, how do I know that I am not deceived every time that I add two and three, or count the sides of a square, or judge of things yet simpler, if anything simpler can be imagined? But possibly God has not desired that I should be thus deceived, for He is said to be supremely good. If, however, it is contrary to His goodness

to have made me such that I constantly deceive myself, it would also appear to be contrary to His goodness to permit me to be sometimes deceived, and nevertheless I cannot doubt that He does permit this.

There may indeed be those who would prefer to deny the existence of a God so powerful, rather than believe that all other things are uncertain. But let us not oppose them for the present, and grant that all that is said of a God is a fable; nevertheless in whatever way they suppose that I have arrived at the state of being that I have reached—whether they attribute it to fate or to accident, or make out that it is by a continual succession of antecedents, or by some other method—since to err and deceive oneself is a defect, it is clear that the greater will be the probability of my being so imperfect as to deceive myself ever, as is the Author to whom they assign my origin the less powerful. To these reasons I have certainly nothing to reply, but at the end I feel constrained to confess that there is nothing in all that I formerly believed to be true, of which I cannot in some measure doubt, and that not merely through want of thought or through levity, but for reasons which are very powerful and maturely considered; so that henceforth I ought not the less carefully to refrain from giving credence to these opinions than to that which is manifestly false, if I desire to arrive at any certainty [in the sciences].

But it is not sufficient to have made these remarks, we must also be careful to keep them in mind. For these ancient and commonly held opinions still revert frequently to my mind, long and familiar custom having given them the right to occupy my mind against my inclination and rendered them almost masters of my belief; nor will I ever lose the habit of deferring to them or of placing my confidence in them, so long as I consider them as they really are, *i.e.* opinions in some measure doubtful, as I have just shown, and at the same time highly probable, so that there is much more reason to believe than to deny them. That is why I consider that I shall not be acting amiss, if, taking of set purpose a contrary belief, I allow myself to be deceived, and for a certain time pretend that all these opinions are entirely false and imaginary, until at last, having thus balanced my former prejudices with my latter [so that they cannot divert my opinions more to one side than to the other], my judgment will no longer be dominated by bad usage or turned away from the right knowledge of the truth. For I am assured that there can be neither peril nor error in this course, and that I cannot at present yield too much to distrust, since I am not considering the question of action, but only of knowledge.

I shall then suppose, not that God who is supremely good and the fountain of truth, but some evil genius not less powerful than deceitful, has employed his whole energies in deceiving me; I shall consider that the heavens, the earth, colors, figures, sound, and all other external things are nought but the illusions and dreams of which this genius has availed himself in order to lay traps for my credulity; I shall consider myself as having no hands, no eyes, no flesh, no blood, nor any senses, yet falsely believing myself to possess all these things; I shall remain obstinately attached to this idea, and if by this means it is not in my power to arrive at the knowledge of any truth, I may at least do what is in my power [i.e. suspend my judgment], and with firm purpose avoid giving credence to any false thing, or being imposed upon by this arch deceiver, however powerful and deceptive he may be. But this task is a laborious one, and insensibly a certain lassitude leads me into the course of my ordinary life. And just as a captive who in sleep enjoys imaginary

liberty, when he begins to suspect that his liberty is but a dream, fears to awaken, and conspires with these agreeable illusions that the deception may be prolonged, so insensibly of my own accord I fall back into my former opinions, and I dread awakening from this slumber, lest the laborious wakefulness which would follow the tranquillity of this repose should have to be spent not in daylight, but in the excessive darkness of the difficulties which have just been discussed.

Meditation II

Of the Nature of the Human Mind; and that it is more easily known than the Body.

The Meditation of yesterday filled my mind with so many doubts that it is no longer in my power to forget them. And yet I do not see in what manner I can resolve them; and, just as if I had all of a sudden fallen into very deep water, I am so disconcerted that I can neither make certain of setting my feet on the bottom, nor can I swim and so support myself on the surface. I shall nevertheless make an effort and follow anew the same path as that on which I yesterday entered, *i.e.* I shall proceed by setting aside all that in which the least doubt could be supposed to exist, just as if I had discovered that it was absolutely false; and I shall ever follow in this road until I have met with something which is certain, or at least, if I can do nothing else, until I have learned for certain that there is nothing in the world that is certain. Archimedes, in order that he might draw the terrestrial globe out of its place, and transport it elsewhere, demanded only that one point should be fixed and immovable; in the same way I shall have the right to conceive high hopes if I am happy enough to discover one thing only which is certain and indubitable.

I suppose, then, that all the things that I see are false; I persuade myself that nothing has ever existed of all that my fallacious memory represents to me. I consider that I possess no senses; I imagine that body, figure, extension, movement and place are but the fictions of my mind. What, then, can be esteemed as true? Perhaps nothing at all, unless that there is nothing in the world that is certain.

But how can I know there is not something different from those things that I have just considered, of which one cannot have the slightest doubt? Is there not some God, or some other being by whatever name we call it, who puts these reflections into my mind? That is not necessary, for is it not possible that I am capable of producing them myself? I myself, am I not at least something? But I have already denied that I had senses and body. Yet I hesitate, for what follows from that? Am I so dependent on body and senses that I cannot exist without these? But I was persuaded that there was nothing in all the world, that there was no heaven, no earth, that there were no minds, nor any bodies: was I not then likewise persuaded that I did not exist? Not at all; of a surety I myself did exist since I persuaded myself of something [or merely because I thought of something]. But there is some deceiver or other, very powerful and very cunning, who ever employs his ingenuity in deceiving me. Then without doubt I exist also if he deceives me, and let him deceive me as much as he will, he can never cause me to be nothing so long as I think that I am something. So that after having reflected well and carefully examined all things, we must come to the definite conclusion that this proposition: I am, I exist, is necessarily true each time that I pronounce it, or that I mentally conceive it.

But I do not yet know clearly enough what I am, I who am certain that I am; and hence I must be careful to see that I do not imprudently take some other object in place of myself, and thus that I do not go astray in respect of this knowledge that I hold to be the most certain and most evident of all that I have formerly learned. That is why I shall now consider anew what I believed myself to be before I embarked upon these last reflections; and of my former opinions I shall withdraw all that might even in a small degree be invalidated by the reasons which I have just brought forward, in order that there may be nothing at all left beyond what is absolutely certain and indubitable.

What then did I formerly believe myself to be? Undoubtedly I believed myself to be a man. But what is a man? Shall I say a reasonable animal? Certainly not; for then I should have to inquire what an animal is, and what is reasonable; and thus from a single question I should insensibly fall into an infinitude of others more difficult; and I should not wish to waste the little time and leisure remaining to me in trying to unravel subtleties like these. But I shall rather stop here to consider the thoughts which of themselves spring up in my mind, and which were not inspired by anything beyond my own nature alone when I applied myself to the consideration of my being. In the first place, then, I considered myself as having a face, hands, arms, and all that system of members composed of bones and flesh as seen in a corpse which I designated by the name of body. In addition to this I considered that I was nourished, that I walked, that I felt, and that I thought, and I referred all these actions to the soul: but I did not stop to consider what the soul was, or if I did stop, I imagined that it was something extremely rare and subtle like a wind, a flame, or an ether, which was spread throughout my grosser parts. As to body I had no manner of doubt about its nature, but thought I had a very clear knowledge of it; and if I had desired to explain it according to the notions that I had then formed of it, I should have described it thus: By the body I understand all that which can be defined by a certain figure: something which can be confined in a certain place, and which can fill a given space in such a way that every other body will be excluded from it; which can be perceived either by touch, or by sight, or by hearing, or by taste, or by smell: which can be moved in many ways not, in truth, by itself, but by something which is foreign to it, by which it is touched [and from which it receives impressions]: for to have the power of self-movement, as also of feeling or of thinking, I did not consider to appertain to the nature of body: on the contrary, I was rather astonished to find that faculties similar to them existed in some bodies.

But what am I, now that I suppose that there is a certain genius which is extremely powerful, and, if I may say so, malicious, who employs all his powers in deceiving me? Can I affirm that I possess the least of all those things which I have just said pertain to the nature of body? I pause to consider, I resolve all these things in my mind, and find none of which I can say that it pertains to me. It would be tedious to stop to enumerate them. Let us pass to the attributes of soul and see if there is any one which is in me? What of nutrition or walking [the first mentioned]? But if it is so that I have no body it is also true that I can neither walk nor take nourishment. Another attribute is sensation. But one cannot feel without body, and besides I have thought I perceived many things during sleep that I recognized in my waking moments as not having been experienced at all. What of thinking? I find here that thought is an attribute that belongs to me; it alone cannot be separated from me. I am, I exist, that is certain. But how often? Just when I think; for it might possibly be the case if I ceased entirely to think, that I should likewise cease altogether to exist. I do not now admit anything which is not necessarily true: to speak accurately I am not more than a thing which thinks, that is to say a mind or a soul, or an understanding, or a reason, which are terms whose significance was formerly unknown to me. I am, however, a real thing and really exist; but what thing? I have answered: a thing which thinks.

And what more? I shall exercise my imagination [in order to see if I am not something more]. I am not a collection of members which we call the human body: I am not a subtle air distributed through these members, I am not a wind, a fire, a vapor, a breath, nor anything at all which I can imagine or conceive; because I have assumed that all these were nothing. Without changing that supposition I find that I only leave myself certain of the fact that I am somewhat. But perhaps it is true that these same things which I supposed were non-existent because they are unknown to me, are really not different from the self which I know. I am not sure about this, I shall not dispute about it now; I can only give judgment on things that are known to me. I know that I exist, and I inquire what I am, I whom I know to exist. But it is very certain that the knowledge of my existence taken in its precise significance does not depend on things whose existence is not yet known to me; consequently it does not depend on those which I can feign in imagination. And indeed the very term *feign* in imagination proves to me my error, for I really do this if I image myself a something, since to imagine is nothing else than to contemplate the figure or image of a corporeal thing. But I already know for certain that I am, and that it may be that all these images, and, speaking generally, all things that relate to the nature of body are nothing but dreams [and chimeras]. For this reason I see clearly that I have as little reason to say, "I shall stimulate my imagination in order to know more distinctly what I am," than if I were to say, "I am now awake, and I perceive somewhat that is real and true: but because I do not yet perceive it distinctly enough, I shall go to sleep of express purpose, so that my dreams may represent the perception with greatest truth and evidence." And, thus, I know for certain that nothing of all that I can understand by means of my imagination belongs to this knowledge which I have of myself, and that it is necessary to recall the mind from this mode of thought with the utmost diligence in order that it may be able to know its own nature with perfect distinctness.

But what then am I? A thing which thinks. What is a thing which thinks? It is a thing which doubts, understands, [conceives], affirms, denies, wills, refuses, which also imagines and feels.

Certainly it is no small matter if all these things pertain to my nature. But why should they not so pertain? Am I not that being who now doubts nearly everything, who nevertheless understands certain things, who affirms that one only is true, who denies all the others, who desires to know more, is averse from being deceived, who imagines many things, sometimes indeed despite his will, and who perceives many likewise, as by the intervention of the bodily organs? Is there nothing in all this which is as true as it is certain that I exist, even though I should always sleep and though he who has given me being employed all his ingenuity in deceiving me? Is there likewise any one of these attributes which can be distinguished from my thought, or which might be said to be separated from myself? For it is so evident of itself that it is I who doubts, who understands, and who desires, that there is no reason here to add anything to explain it. And I have certainly the power of imagining likewise; for although it may happen (as I formerly supposed) that none of the things which I imagine are true, nevertheless this power of imagining does not cease to be really in use, and it forms part of my thought. Finally, I am the same who feels, that is to say, who perceives certain things, as by the organs of sense, since in truth I see light, I hear noise, I feel heat. But it will be said that these phenomena are false and that I am dreaming. Let it be so; still it is at least quite certain that it seems to me that I see light, that I hear noise and that I feel heat. That cannot be false; properly speaking it is what is in me called feeling; and used in this precise sense that is no other thing than thinking.

From this time I begin to know what I am with a little more clearness and distinction than before; but nevertheless it still seems to me, and I cannot prevent myself from thinking, that corporeal things, whose images are framed by thought, which are tested by the senses, are much more distinctly known than that obscure part of me which does not come under the imagination. Although really it is very strange to say that I know and understand more distinctly these things whose existence seems to me dubious, which are unknown to me, and which do not belong to me, than others of the truth of which I am convinced, which are known to me and which pertain to my real nature, in a word, than myself. But I see clearly how the case stands: my mind loves to wander, and cannot yet suffer itself to be retained within the just limits of truth. Very good, let us once more give it the freest rein, so that, when afterwards we seize the proper occasion for pulling up, it may the more easily be regulated and controlled.

Let us begin by considering the commonest matters, those which we believe to be the most distinctly comprehended, to wit, the bodies which we touch and see; not indeed bodies in general, for these general ideas are usually a little more confused, but let us consider one body in particular. Let us take for example, this piece of wax: it has been taken quite freshly from the hive, and it has not yet lost the sweetness of the honey which it contains; it still retains somewhat of the odor of the flowers from which it has been culled; its color, its figure, its size are apparent; it is hard, cold, easily handled, and if you strike it with the finger, it will emit a sound. Finally all the things which are requisite to cause us distinctly to recognize a body, are met within it. But notice that while I speak and approach the fire what remained of the taste is exhaled, the smell evaporates, the color alters, the figure is destroyed, the size increases, it becomes liquid, it heats, scarcely can one handle it, and when one strikes it, no sound is emitted. Does the same wax remain after this change? We must confess that it remains; none would judge otherwise. What then did I know so distinctly in this piece of wax? It could certainly be nothing of all that the senses brought to my notice, since all these things which fall under taste, smell, sight, touch, and hearing, are found to be changed, and yet the same wax remains.

Perhaps it was what I now think, viz. that this wax was not that sweetness of honey, nor that agreeable scent of flowers, nor that particular whiteness, nor that figure, nor that sound, but simply a body which a little before appeared to me as perceptible under these forms, and which

is now perceptible under others. But what, precisely, is it that I imagine when I form such conceptions? Let us attentively consider this, and, abstracting from all that does not belong to the wax, let us see what remains. Certainly nothing remains excepting a certain extended thing which is flexible and movable. But what is the meaning of flexible and movable? Is it not that I imagine that this piece of wax being round is capable of becoming square and of passing from a square to a triangular figure? No, certainly it is not that, since I imagine it admits of an infinitude of similar changes, and I nevertheless do not know how to compass the infinitude by my imagination, and consequently this conception which I have of the wax is not brought about by the faculty of imagination. What now is this extension? Is it not also unknown? For it becomes greater when the wax is melted, greater when it is boiled, and greater still when the heat increases; and I should not conceive [clearly] according to truth what wax is, if I did not think that even this piece that we are considering is capable of receiving more variations in extension than I have ever imagined. We must then grant that I could not even understand through the imagination what this piece of wax is, and that it is my mind alone which perceives it. I say this piece of wax in particular, for as to wax in general it is yet clearer. But what is this piece of wax which cannot be understood excepting by the [understanding or] mind? It is certainly the same that I see, touch, imagine, and finally it is the same which I have always believed it to be from the beginning. But what must particularly be observed is that its perception is neither an act of vision, nor of touch, nor of imagination, and has never been such although it may have appeared formerly to be so, but only an intuition of the mind, which may be imperfect and confused as it was formerly, or clear and distinct as it is at present, according as my attention is more or less directed to the elements which are found in it, and of which it is composed.

Yet in the meantime I am greatly astonished when I consider [the great feebleness of mind] and its proneness to fall [insensibly] into error; for although without giving expression to my thoughts I consider all this in my own mind, words often impede me and I am almost deceived by the terms of ordinary language. For we say that we see the same wax, if it is present, and not that we simply judge that it is the same from its having the same color and figure. From this I should conclude that I knew the wax by means of vision and not simply by the intuition of the mind; unless by chance I remember that, when looking from a window and saying I see men who pass in the street, I really do not see them, but infer that what I see is men, just as I say that I see wax. And yet what do I see from the window but hats and coats which may cover automatic machines? Yet I judge these to be men. And similarly solely by the faculty of judgment which rests in my mind, I comprehend that which I believed I saw with my eyes. *inference*

A man who makes it his aim to raise his knowledge above the common should be ashamed to derive the occasion for doubting from the forms of speech invented by the vulgar; I prefer to pass on and consider whether I had a more evident and perfect conception of what the wax was when I first perceived it, and when I believed I knew it by means of the external senses or at least by the common sense as it is called, that is to say by the imaginative faculty, or whether my present conception is clearer now that I have most carefully examined what it is, and in what way it can be known. It would certainly be absurd

to doubt as to this. For what was there in this first perception which was distinct? What was there which might not as well have been perceived by any of the animals? But when I distinguish the wax from its external forms, and when, just as if I had taken from it its vestments, I consider it quite naked, it is certain that although some error may still be found in my judgment, I can nevertheless not perceive it thus without a human mind.

But finally what shall I say of this mind, that is, of myself, for up to this point I do not admit in myself anything but mind? What then, I who seem to perceive this piece of wax distinctly, do I not know myself, not only with much more truth and certainty, but also with much more distinctness and clearness? For if I judge that the wax is or exists from the fact that I see it, it certainly follows much more clearly that I am or that I exist myself from the fact that I see it. For it may be that what I see is not really wax, it may also be that I do not possess eyes with which to see anything; but it cannot be that when I see, or (for I no longer take account of the distinction) when I think I see, that I myself who think am nought. So if I judge that the wax exists from the fact that I touch it, the same thing will follow, to wit, that I am; and if I judge that my imagination, or some other cause, whatever it is, persuades me that the wax exists, I shall still conclude the same. And what I have here remarked of wax may be applied to all other things which are external to me [and which are met with outside of me]. And further, if the [notion or] perception of wax has seemed to me clearer and more distinct, not only after the sight or the touch, but also after many other causes have rendered it quite manifest to me, with how much more [evidence] and distinctness must it be said that I now know myself, since all the reasons which contribute to the knowledge of wax, or any other body whatever, are yet better proofs of the nature of my mind! And there are so many other things in the mind itself which may contribute to the elucidation of its nature, that those which depend on body such as these just mentioned, hardly merit being taken into account.

But finally here I am, having insensibly reverted to the point I desired, for, since it is now manifest to me that even bodies are not properly speaking known by the senses or by the faculty of imagination, but by the understanding only, and since they are not known from the fact that they are seen or touched, but only because they are understood, I see clearly that there is nothing which is easier for me to know than my mind. But because it is difficult to rid oneself so promptly of an opinion to which one was accustomed for so long, it will be well that I should halt a little at this point, so that by the length of my meditation I may more deeply imprint on my memory this new knowledge.

Meditation III

Of God: that He exists.

I shall now close my eyes, I shall stop my ears, I shall call away all my senses, I shall efface even from my thoughts all the images of corporeal things, or at least (for that is hardly possible) I shall esteem them as vain and false; and thus holding converse only with myself and considering my own nature, I shall try little by little to reach a better knowledge of and a more familiar acquaintanceship with myself. I am a thing that thinks, that is to say, that doubts, affirms, denies, that knows a few things, that is ignorant of many [that loves, that hates], that wills, that desires, that also imagines and perceives; for as I

remarked before, although the things which I perceive and imagine are perhaps nothing at all apart from me and in themselves, I am nevertheless assured that these modes of thought that I call perceptions and imaginations, inasmuch only as they are modes of thought, certainly reside [and are met with] in me.

And in the little that I have just said, I think I have summed up all that I really know, or at least all that hitherto I was aware that I knew. In order to try to extend my knowledge further, I shall now look around more carefully and see whether I cannot still discover in myself some other things which I have not hitherto perceived. I am certain that I am a thing which thinks; but do I not then likewise know what is requisite to render me certain of a truth? Certainly in this first knowledge there is nothing that assures me of its truth, excepting the clear and distinct perception of that which I state, which would not indeed suffice to assure me that what I say is true, if it could ever happen that a thing which I conceived so clearly and distinctly could be false; and accordingly it seems to me that already I can establish as a general rule that all things which I perceive very clearly and very distinctly are true.

At the same time I have before received and admitted many things to be very certain and manifest, which yet I afterwards recognized as being dubious. What then were these things? They were the earth, sky, stars and all other objects which I apprehended by means of the senses. But what did I clearly [and distinctly] perceive in them? Nothing more than that the ideas or thoughts of these things were presented to my mind. And not even now do I deny that these ideas are met with in me. But there was yet another thing which I affirmed, and which, owing to the habit which I had formed of believing it, I thought I perceived very clearly, although in truth I did not perceive it at all, to wit, that there were objects outside of me from which these ideas proceeded, and to which they were entirely similar. And it was in this that I erred, or, if perchance my judgment was correct, this was not due to any knowledge arising from my perception.

But when I took anything very simple and easy in the sphere of arithmetic or geometry into consideration, e.g. that two and three together made five, and other things of the sort, were not these present to my mind so clearly as to enable me to affirm that they were true? Certainly if I judged that since such matters could be doubted, this would not have been so for any other reason than that it came into my mind that perhaps a God might have endowed me with such a nature that I may have been deceived even concerning things which seemed to me most manifest. But every time that this preconceived opinion of the sovereign power of a God presents itself to my thought, I am constrained to confess that it is easy to Him, if He wishes it, to cause me to err, even in matters in which I believe myself to have the best evidence. And, on the other hand, always when I direct my attention to things which I believe myself to perceive very clearly, I am so persuaded of their truth that I let myself break out into words such as these: Let who will deceive me, He can never cause me to be nothing while I think that I am, or some day cause it to be true to say that I have never been, it being true now to say that I am, or that two and three make more or less than five, or any such thing in which I see a manifest contradiction. And certainly, since I have no reason to believe that there is a God who is a deceiver, and as I have not yet satisfied myself that there is a God at all, the reason for doubt which depends on this opinion

alone is very slight, and so to speak metaphysical. But in order to be able altogether to remove it, I must inquire whether there is a God as soon as the occasion presents itself; and if I find that there is a God, I must also inquire whether He may be a deceiver; for without a knowledge of these two truths I do not see that I can ever be certain of anything.

And in order that I may have an opportunity of inquiring into this in an orderly way [without interrupting the order of meditation which I have proposed to myself, and which is little by little to pass from the notions which I find first of all in my mind to those which I shall later on discover in it] it is requisite that I should consider in which of these kinds there is, properly speaking, truth or error to be found. Of my thoughts some are, so to speak, images of the things, and to these alone is the title "idea" properly applied; examples are my thought of a man or of a chimera, of heaven, of an angel, or [even] of God. But other thoughts possess other forms as well. For example in willing, fearing, approving, denying, though I always perceive something as the subject of the action of my mind, yet by this action I always add something else to the idea which I have of that thing; and of the thoughts of this kind some are called volitions or affections, and others judgments.

Now as to what concerns ideas, if we consider them only in themselves and do not relate them to anything else beyond themselves, they cannot properly speaking be false; for whether I imagine a goat or a chimera, it is not the less true that I imagine the one than the other. We must not fear likewise that falsity can enter into will and into affections, for although I may desire evil things, or even things that never existed, it is not the less true that I desire them. Thus there remains no more than the judgments which we make, in which I must take the greatest care not to deceive myself. But the principal error and the commonest which we may meet with in them, consists in my judging that the ideas which are in me are similar or conformable to the things which are outside me; for without doubt if I considered the ideas only as certain modes of my thoughts, without trying to relate them to anything beyond, they could scarcely give me material for error.

But among these ideas, some appear to me to be innate, some adventitious, and others to be formed [or invented] by myself; for, as I have the power of understanding what is called a thing, or a truth, or a thought, it appears to me that I hold this power from no other source than my own nature. But if I now hear some sound, if I see the sun, or feel the heat, I have hitherto judged that these sensations proceeded from certain things that exist outside of me; and finally it appears to me that sirens, hippogryphs, and the like, are formed out of my own mind. But again I may possibly persuade myself that all these ideas are of the nature of those which I term adventitious, or else they are all innate, or all fictitious: for I have not yet clearly discovered their true origin.

And my principal task in this place is to consider, in respect to those ideas which appear to me to proceed from certain objects that are outside me, what are the reasons which cause me to think them similar to these objects. It seems indeed in the first place that I am taught this lesson by nature; and, secondly, I experience in myself that these ideas do not depend on my will nor therefore on myself—for they often present themselves to my mind in spite of my will. Just now, for instance, whether I will or whether I do not will, I feel heat, and thus I persuade myself that this feeling, or at least this idea of heat, is produced in me by something which is different from me, i.e., by the heat of the fire near which I sit. And nothing seems to me more obvious than to judge that this object imprints its likeness rather than anything else upon me.

Now I must discover whether these proofs are sufficiently strong and convincing. When I say that I am so instructed by nature, I merely mean a certain spontaneous inclination which impels me to believe in this connection, and not a natural light which makes me recognize that it is true. But these two things are very different; for I cannot doubt that which the natural light causes me to believe to be true, as, for example, it has shown me that I am from the fact that I doubt, or other facts of the same kind. And I possess no other faculty whereby to distinguish truth from falsehood, which can teach me that what this light shows me to be true is not really true, and no other faculty that is equally trustworthy. But as far as [apparently] natural impulses are concerned, I have frequently remarked, when I had to make active choice between virtue and vice, that they often enough led me to the part that was worse; and this is why I do not see any reason for following them in what regards truth and error.

And as to the other reason, which is that these ideas must proceed from objects outside me, since they do not depend on my will, I do not find it any more convincing. For just as these impulses of which I have spoken are found in me, notwithstanding that they do not always concur with my will, so perhaps there is in me some faculty fitted to produce these ideas without the assistance of any external things, even though it is not yet known by me; just as,

1, 2, 3 - rejecteous

apparently, they have hitherto always been found in me during sleep without the aid of any external objects.

3 And finally, though they did proceed from objects different from myself, it is not a necessary consequence that they should resemble these. On the contrary, I have noticed that in many cases there was a great difference between the object and its idea. I find, for example, two completely diverse ideas of the sun in my mind; the one derives its origin from the senses, and should be placed in the category of adventitious ideas; according to this idea the sun seems to be extremely small; but the other is derived from astronomical reasonings, *i.e.*, is elicited from certain notions that are innate in me, or else it is formed by me in some other manner; in accordance with it the sun appears to be several times greater than the earth. These two ideas cannot, indeed, both resemble the same sun, and reason makes me believe that the one which seems to have originated directly from the sun itself, is the one which is most dissimilar to it.

All this causes me to believe that until the present time it has not been by a judgment that was certain [or premeditated], but only by a sort of blind impulse that I believed that things existed outside of, and different from me, which, by the organs of my senses, or by some other method whatever it might be, conveyed these ideas or images to me [and imprinted on me their similitudes].

But there is yet another method of inquiring whether any of the objects of which I have ideas within me exist outside of me. If ideas are only taken as certain modes of thought, I recognize amongst them no difference or inequality, and all appear to proceed from me in the same manner; but when we consider them as images, one representing one thing and the other another, it is clear that they are very different one from the other. There is no doubt that those which represent to me substances are something more, and contain so to speak more objective reality within them [that is to say, by representation participate in a higher degree of being or perfection] than those that simply represent modes or accidents; and that idea again by which I understand a supreme God, eternal, infinite, [immutable], omniscient, omnipotent, and Creator of all things which are outside of Himself, has certainly more objective reality in itself than those ideas by which finite substances are represented.

Now it is manifest by the natural light that there must at least be as much reality in the efficient and total cause as in its effect. For, pray, whence can the effect derive its reality, if not from its cause? And in what way can this cause communicate this reality to it, unless it possessed it in itself? And from this it follows, not only that something cannot proceed from nothing, but likewise that what is more perfect —that is to say, which has more reality within itself—cannot proceed from the less perfect. And this is not only evidently true of those effects which possess actual or formal reality, but also of the ideas in which we consider merely what is termed objective reality. To take an example, the stone which has not yet existed not only cannot now commence to be unless it has been produced by something which possesses within itself, either formally or eminently, all that enters into the composition of the stone [*i.e.*, it must possess the same things or other more excellent things than those which exist in the stone] and heat can only be produced in a subject in which it did not previously exist by a cause that is of an order [degree or kind] at least as perfect as heat, and so in all other cases. But further, the idea of heat, or of a stone, cannot exist in me unless it has been placed within me by some cause which possesses within it at least as much reality as that which I conceive to exist in the heat or the stone. For although this cause does not transmit anything of its actual or formal reality to my idea, we must not for that reason imagine that it is necessarily a less real cause; we must remember that [since every idea is a work of the mind] its nature is such that it demands of itself no other formal reality than that which it borrows from my thought, of which it is only a mode [*i.e.*, a manner or way of thinking]. But in order that an idea should contain some one certain objective reality rather than another, it must without doubt derive it from some cause in which there is at least as much formal reality as this idea contains of objective reality. For if we imagine that something is found in an idea which is not found in the cause, it must then have been derived from nought; but, however imperfect may be this mode of being by which a thing is objectively [or by representation] in the understanding by its idea, we cannot certainly say that this mode of being is nothing, nor, consequently, that the idea derives its origin from nothing.

Nor must I imagine that, since the reality that I consider in these ideas is only objective, it is not essential that this reality should be formally in the causes of my ideas, but that it is sufficient that it should be found objectively. For just as this mode of objective existence pertains to ideas by their proper nature, so does the mode of formal existence pertain to the causes of those ideas (this is at least true of the first and principal) by the nature peculiar to them. And although it may be the case that one idea gives birth to another idea, that

cannot continue to be so indefinitely; for in the end we must reach an idea whose cause shall be so to speak an archetype, in which the whole reality [or perfection] which is so to speak objectively [or by representation] in these ideas is contained formally [and really]. Thus the light of nature causes me to know clearly that the ideas in me are like [pictures or] images which can, in truth, easily fall short of the perfection of the objects from which they have been derived, but which can never contain anything greater or more perfect.

And the longer and the more carefully that I investigate these matters, the more clearly and distinctly do I recognize their truth. But what am I to conclude from it all in the end? It is this, that if the objective reality of any one of my ideas is of such a nature as clearly to make me recognize that it is not in me either formally or eminently, and that consequently I cannot myself be the cause of it, it follows of necessity that I am not alone in the world, but that there is another being which exists, or which is the cause of this idea. On the other hand, had no such an idea existed in me, I should have had no sufficient argument to convince me of the existence of any being beyond myself; for I have made very careful investigation everywhere and up to the present time have been able to find no other ground.

But of my ideas, beyond that which represents me to myself, as to which there can here be no difficulty, there is another which represents a God, and there are others representing corporeal and inanimate things, others angels, others animals, and others again which represent to me men similar to myself.

As regards the ideas which represent to me other men or animals, or angels, I can however easily conceive that they might be formed by an admixture of the other ideas which I have of myself, of corporeal things, and of God, even although there were apart from me neither men nor animals, nor angels, in all the world.

And in regard to the ideas of corporeal objects, I do not recognize in them anything so great or so excellent that they might not have possibly proceeded from myself; for if I consider them more closely, and examine them individually, as I yesterday examined the idea of wax, I find that there is very little in them which I perceive clearly and distinctly. Magnitude or extension in length, breadth, or depth, I do so perceive; also figure which results from a termination of this extension, the situation which bodies of different figure preserve in relation to one another, and movement or change of situation; to which we may also add substance, duration and number. As to other things such as light, colors, sounds, scents, tastes, heat, cold and the other tactile qualities, they are thought by me with so much obscurity and confusion that I do not even know if they are true or false, *i.e.*, whether the ideas which I form of these qualities are actually the ideas of real objects or not [or whether they only represent chimeras which cannot exist in fact]. For although I have before remarked that it is only in judgments that falsity, properly speaking, or formal falsity, can be met with, a certain material falsity may nevertheless be found in ideas, *i.e.*, when these ideas represent what is nothing as though it were something. For example, the ideas which I have of cold and heat are so far from clear and distinct that by their means I cannot tell whether cold is merely a privation of heat, or heat a privation of cold, or whether both are real qualities, or are not such. And inasmuch as [since ideas resemble images] there cannot be any ideas which do not appear to represent some things, if it is correct to say that cold is

merely a privation of heat, the idea which represents it to me as something real and positive will not be improperly termed false, and the same holds good of other similar ideas.

To these it is certainly not necessary that I should attribute any author other than myself. For if they are false, *i.e.*, if they represent things which do not exist, the light of nature shows me that they issue from nought, that is to say, that they are only in me in so far as something is lacking to the perfection of my nature. But if they are true, nevertheless because they exhibit so little reality to me that I cannot even clearly distinguish the thing represented from non-being, I do not see any reason why they should not be produced by myself.

As to the clear and distinct idea which I have of corporeal things, some of them seem as though I might have derived them from the idea which I possess of myself, as those which I have of substance, duration, number, and such like. For [even] when I think that a stone is a substance, or at least a thing capable of existing of itself, and that I am a substance also, although I conceive that I am a thing that thinks and not one that is extended, and that the stone on the other hand is an extended thing which does not think, and that thus there is a notable difference between the two conceptions—they seem, nevertheless, to agree in this, that both represent substances. In the same way, when I perceive that I now exist and further recollect that I have in former times existed, and when I remember that I have various thoughts of which I can recognize the number, I acquire ideas of duration and number which I can afterwards transfer to any object that I please. But as to all the other qualities of which the ideas of corporeal things are composed, to wit, extension, figure, situation and motion, it is true that they are not formally in me, since I am only a thing that thinks; but because they are merely certain modes of substance [and so to speak the vestments under which corporeal substance appears to us] and because I myself am also a substance, it would seem that they might be contained in me eminently.

Hence there remains alone the idea of God, concerning which we must consider whether it is not something that is capable of proceeding from me myself. By the name God I understand a substance that is infinite, [eternal, immutable], independent, all-knowing, all-powerful, and by which I myself and everything else, if anything else does exist, have been created. Now all these characteristics are such that the more diligently I attend to them, the less do they appear capable of proceeding from me alone; hence, from what has already been said, we must conclude that God necessarily exists.

For although the idea of substance is within me owing to the fact that I am substance, nevertheless I should not have the idea of an infinite substance—since I am finite—if it had not proceeded from some substance which was veritably infinite.

Nor should I imagine that I do not perceive the infinite by a true idea, but only by the negation of the finite, just as I perceive repose and darkness by the negation of movement and of light; for, on the contrary, I see that there is manifestly more reality in infinite substance than in finite, and therefore that in some way I have in me the notion of the infinite earlier than the finite—to wit, the notion of God before that of myself. For how would it be possible that I should know that I doubt and desire, that is to say, that something is lacking to me, and that I am not quite perfect, unless I had within me some idea of a Being more perfect than myself, in comparison with which I should recognize the deficiencies of my nature?

And we cannot say that this idea of God is perhaps materially false and that consequently I can derive it from nought [i.e., that possibly it exists in me because I am imperfect], as I have just said is the case with ideas of heat, cold and other such things; for, on the contrary, as this idea is very clear and distinct and contains within it more objective reality than any other, there can be none which is of itself more true, nor any in which there can be less suspicion of falsehood. The idea, I say, of this Being who is absolutely perfect and infinite, is entirely true; for although, perhaps, we can imagine that such a Being does not exist, we cannot nevertheless imagine that His idea represents nothing real to me, as I have said of the idea of cold. This idea is also very clear and distinct; since all that I conceive clearly and distinctly of the real and the true, and of what conveys some perfection, is in its entirety contained in this idea. And this does not cease to be true although I do not comprehend the infinite, or though in God there is an infinitude of things which I cannot comprehend, nor possibly even reach in any way by thought; for it is of the nature of the infinite that my nature, which is finite and limited, should not comprehend it; and it is sufficient that I should understand this, and that I should judge that all things which I clearly perceive and in which I know that there is some perfection, and possibly likewise an infinitude of properties of which I am ignorant, are in God formally or eminently, so that the idea which I have of Him may become the most true, most clear, and most distinct of all the ideas that are in my mind.

But possibly I am something more than I suppose myself to be, and perhaps all those perfections which I attribute to God are in some way potentially in me, although they do not yet disclose themselves, or issue in action. As a matter of fact I am already sensible that my knowledge increases [and perfects itself] little by little, and I see nothing which can prevent it from increasing more and more into infinitude; nor do I see, after it has thus been increased [or perfected], anything to prevent my being able to acquire by its means all the other perfections of the Divine nature; nor finally why the power I have of acquiring these perfections, if it really exists in me, shall not suffice to produce the ideas of them.

At the same time I recognize that this cannot be. For, in the first place, although it were true that every day my knowledge acquired new degrees of perfection, and that there were in my nature many things potentially which are not yet there actually, nevertheless these excellences do not pertain to [or make the smallest approach to] the idea which I have of God in whom there is nothing merely potential [but in whom all is present really and actually]; for it is an infallible token of imperfection in my knowledge that it increases little by little. And further, although my knowledge grows more and more, nevertheless I do not for that reason believe that it can ever be actually infinite, since it can never reach a point so high that it will be unable to attain to any greater increase. But I understand God to be actually infinite, so that He can add nothing to His supreme perfection. And finally I perceive that the objective being of an idea cannot be produced by a being that exists potentially only, which properly speaking is nothing, but only by a being which is formal or actual.

To speak the truth, I see nothing in all that I have just said which by the light of nature is not manifest to anyone who desires to think attentively on the subject; but when I slightly relax my attention, my mind, finding its vision somewhat obscured and so to speak blinded by the images of sensible objects, I do not easily recollect the reason why the idea that I possess of a being more perfect than I, must necessarily have been placed in me by a being which is really more perfect; and this is why I wish here to go on to inquire whether I, who have this idea, can exist if no such being exists.

And I ask, from whom do I then derive my existence? Perhaps from myself or from my parents, or from some other source less perfect than God; for we can imagine nothing more perfect than God, or even as perfect as He is.

But [were I independent of every other and] were I myself the author of my being, I should doubt nothing and I should desire nothing, and finally no perfection would be lacking to me; for I should have bestowed on myself every perfection of which I possessed any idea and should thus be God. And it must not be imagined that those things that are lacking to me are perhaps more difficult of attainment than those which I already possess; for, on the contrary, it is quite evident that it was a matter of much greater difficulty to bring to pass that I, that is to say, a thing or a substance that thinks, should emerge out of nothing, than it would be to attain to the knowledge of many things of which I am ignorant, and which are only the accidents of this thinking substance. But it is clear that if I had of myself possessed this greater perfection of which I have just spoken [that is to say, if I had been the author of my own existence], I should not at least have denied myself the things which are the more easy to acquire [to wit, many branches of knowledge of which my nature is destitute]; nor should I have deprived myself of the things contained in the idea which I form of God, because there are none of them which seem to me specially difficult to acquire: and if there were any that were more difficult to acquire, they would certainly appear to me to be such (supposing I myself were the origin of the other things which I possess) since I should discover in them that my powers were limited.

But though I assume that perhaps I have always existed just as I am at present, neither can I escape the force of this reasoning, and imagine that the conclusion to be drawn from this is, that I need not seek for any author of my existence. For all the course of my life may be divided into an infinite number of parts, none of which is in any way dependent on the other; and thus from the fact that I was in existence a short time ago it does not follow that I must be in existence now, unless some cause at this instant, so to speak, produces me anew, that is to say, conserves me. It is as a matter of fact perfectly clear and evident to all those who consider with attention the nature of time, that, in order to be conserved in each moment in which it endures, a substance has need of the same power and action as would be necessary to produce and create it anew, supposing it did not yet exist; so that the light of nature shows us clearly that the distinction between creation and conservation is solely a distinction of the reason.

All that I thus require here is that I should interrogate myself, if I wish to know whether I possess a power which is capable of bringing it to pass that I who now am shall still be in the future; for since I am nothing but a thinking thing, or at least since thus far it is only this portion of myself which is precisely in question at present, if such power did reside in me, I should certainly be conscious of it. But I am conscious of nothing of the kind, and by this I know

clearly that I depend on some being different from myself.

Possibly, however, this being on which I depend is not that which I call God, and I am created either by my parents or by some other cause less perfect than God. This cannot be, because, as I have just said, it is perfectly evident that there must be at least as much reality in the cause as in the effect; and thus since I am a thinking thing, and possess an idea of God within me, whatever in the end be the cause assigned to my existence, it must be allowed that it is likewise a thinking thing and that it possesses in itself the idea of all the perfections which I attribute to God. We may again inquire whether this cause derives its origin from itself or from some other thing. For if from itself, it follows by the reasons before brought forward, that this cause must itself be God; for since it possesses the virtue of self-existence, it must also without doubt have the power of actually possessing all the perfections of which it has the idea, that is, all those which I conceive as existing in God. But if it derives its existence from some other cause than itself, we shall again ask, for the same reason, whether this second cause exists by itself or through another, until from one step to another, we finally arrive at an ultimate cause, which will be God.

And it is perfectly manifest that in this there can be no regression into infinity, since what is in question is not so much the cause which formerly created me, as that which conserves me at the present time.

Nor can we suppose that several causes may have concurred in my production, and that from one I have received the idea of one of the perfections which I attribute to God, and from another the idea of some other, so that all these perfections indeed exist somewhere in the universe, but not as complete in one unity which is God. On the contrary, the unity, the simplicity or the inseparability of all things which are in God is one of the principal perfections which I conceive to be in Him. And certainly the idea of this unity of all Divine perfections cannot have been placed in me by any cause from which I have not likewise received the ideas of all the other perfections; for this cause could not make me able to comprehend them as joined together in an inseparable unity without having at the same time caused me in some measure to know what they are [and in some way to recognize each one of them].

Finally, so far as my parents [from whom it appears I have sprung] are concerned, although all that I have ever been able to believe of them were true, that does not make it follow that it is they who conserve me, nor are they even the authors of my being in any sense, in so far as I am a thinking being; since what they did was merely to implant certain disposition in that matter in which the self—i.e., the mind, which alone I at present identify with myself—is by me deemed to exist. And thus there can be no difficulty in their regard, but we must of necessity conclude from the fact alone that I exist, or that the idea of a Being supremely perfect—that is of God—is in me, that the proof of God's existence is grounded on the highest evidence.

It only remains to me to examine into the manner in which I have acquired this idea from God; for I have not received it through the senses, and it is never presented to me unexpectedly, as is usual with the ideas of sensible things when these things present themselves, or seem to present themselves, to the external organs of my senses; nor is it likewise a fiction of my mind, for it is not in my power to take from or to add anything to it; and consequently the only alternative is that it is innate in me, just as the idea of myself is innate in me.

And one certainly ought not to find it strange that God, in creating me, placed this idea within me to be like the mark of the workman imprinted on his work; and it is likewise not essential that the mark shall be something different from the work itself. For from the sole fact that God created me it is most probable that in some way he has placed his image and similitude upon me, and that I perceive this similitude (in which the idea of God is contained) by means of the same faculty by which I perceive myself—that is to say, when I reflect on myself I not only know that I am something [imperfect], incomplete and dependent on another, which incessantly aspires after something which is better and greater than myself, but I also know that He on whom I depend possesses in Himself all the great things towards which I aspire [and the ideas of which I find within myself], and that not indefinitely or potentially alone, but really, actually and infinitely; and that thus He is God. And the whole strength of the argument which I have here made use of to prove the existence of God consists in this, that I recognize that it is not possible that my nature should be what it is, and indeed that I should have in myself the idea of a God, if God did not veritably exist—a God, I say, whose idea is in me, i.e., who possesses all those supreme perfections of which our mind may indeed have some idea but without understanding them all, who is liable to no errors or defect [and who has none of all those marks which denote imperfection]. From this it is manifest that He cannot be a deceiver, since the light of nature teaches us that fraud and deception necessarily proceed from some defect.

But before I examine this matter with more care, and pass on to the consideration of other truths which may be derived from it, it seems to me right to pause for a while in order to contemplate God Himself, to ponder at leisure his marvelous attributes, to consider, and admire, and adore, the beauty of his light so resplendent, at least so far as the strength of my mind, which is in some measure dazzled by the sight, will allow me to do so. For just as faith teaches us that supreme felicity of the other life consists only in this contemplation of the Divine Majesty, so we continue to learn by experience that a similar meditation, though incomparably less perfect, causes us to enjoy the greatest satisfaction of which we are capable in this life. . . .

MEDITATION VI

Of the existence of Material Things, and of the real distinction between the Soul and Body of Man.

. . . First of all I shall recall to my memory those matters which I hitherto held to be true, as having perceived them through the senses, and the foundations on which my belief has rested; in the next place I shall examine the reasons which have since obliged me to place them in doubt; in the last place I shall consider which of them I must now believe.

First of all, then, I perceived that I had a head, hands, feet, and all other members of which this body—which I considered as a part, or possibly even as the whole, of myself—is composed. Further I was sensible that this body was placed amidst many others, from which it was capable of being affected in many different ways, beneficial and hurtful, and I remarked that a certain feeling of pleasure accompanied those that were beneficial, and pain those which were harmful. And in addition to this pleasure and pain, I also experienced hunger, thirst, and other similar appetites, as also certain

corporeal inclinations towards joy, sadness, anger, and other similar passions. And outside myself, in addition to extension, figure, and motions of bodies, I remarked in them hardness, heat, and all other tactile qualities, and, further, light and color, and scents and sounds, the variety of which gave me the means of distinguishing the sky, the earth, the sea, and generally all the other bodies, one from the other. And certainly, considering the ideas of all these qualities which presented themselves to my mind, and which alone I perceived properly or immediately, it was not without reason that I believed myself to perceive objects quite different from my thought, to wit, bodies from which those ideas proceeded; for I found by experience that these ideas presented themselves to me without my consent being requisite, so that I could not perceive any object, however desirous I might be, unless it were present to the organs of sense; and it was not in my power not to perceive it, when it was present. And because the ideas which I perceived through the senses were much more lively, more clear, and even, in their own way, more distinct than any of those which I could of myself frame in meditation, or than those I found impressed on my memory, it appeared as though they could not have proceeded from my mind, so that they must necessarily have been produced in me by some other things. And having no knowledge of those objects excepting the knowledge which the ideas themselves gave me, nothing was more likely to occur to my mind than that the objects were similar to the ideas which were caused. And because I likewise remembered that I had formerly made use of my senses rather than my reason, and recognized that the ideas which I formed of myself were not so distinct as those which I perceived through the senses, and that they were most frequently even composed of portions of these last, I persuaded myself easily that I had no idea in my mind which had not formerly come to me through the senses. Nor was it without some reason that I believed that this body (which by a certain special right I call my own) belonged to me more properly and more strictly than any other; for in fact I could never be separated from it as from other bodies; I experienced in it and on account of it all my appetites and affections, and finally I was touched by the feeling of pain and the titillation of pleasure in its parts, and not in the parts of other bodies which were separated from it. But when I inquired, why, from some, I know not what, painful sensation, there follows sadness of mind, and from the pleasurable sensation there arises joy, or why this mysterious emotion of the stomach which I call hunger causes me to desire to eat, and dryness of throat causes a desire to drink, and so on, I could give no reason excepting that nature taught me so; for there is certainly no affinity (that I at least can understand) between the craving of the stomach and the desire to eat, any more than between the perception of whatever causes pain and the thought of sadness which arises from this perception. And in the same way it appeared to me that I had learned from nature all the other judgments which I formed regarding the objects of my senses, since I remarked that these judgments were formed in me before I had the leisure to weigh and consider any reasons which might oblige me to make them.

But afterwards many experiences little by little destroyed all the faith which I had rested in my senses; for I from time to time observed that those towers which from afar appeared to me to be round, more closely observed seemed square, and that colossal statues raised on the summit of these towers, appeared as quite tiny statues when viewed from the bottom; and so in an infinitude of other cases I found error in judgments founded on the external senses. And not only in those founded on the external senses, but even in those founded on the internal as well; for is there anything more intimate or more internal than pain? And yet I have learned from some persons whose arms or legs have been cut off, that they sometimes seemed to feel pain in the part which had been amputated, which made me think that I could not be quite certain that it was a certain member which pained me, even although I felt pain in it. And to those grounds of doubt I have lately added two others, which are very general; the first is that I never have believed myself to feel anything in waking moments which I cannot also sometimes believe myself to feel when I sleep, and as I do not think that these things which I seem to find in sleep, proceed from objects outside of me, I do not see any reason why I should have this belief regarding objects which I seem to perceive while awake. The other was that being still ignorant, or rather supposing myself to be ignorant, of the author of my being, I saw nothing to prevent me from having been so constituted by nature that I might be deceived even in matters which seemed to me to be most certain. And as to the grounds on which I was formerly persuaded of the truth of sensible objects, I had not much trouble in replying to them. For since nature seemed to cause me to lean towards many things from which reason repelled me, I did not believe that I should trust much to the teachings of nature. And although the ideas which I receive by the senses do not depend on my will, I did not think that one should for that reason conclude that they proceeded from things different from myself, since possibly some faculty might be discovered in me— though hitherto unknown to me—which produced them.

But now that I begin to know myself better, and to discover more clearly the author of my being, I do not in truth think that I should rashly admit all the matters which the senses seem to teach us, but, on the other hand, I do not think that I should doubt them all universally.

And first of all, because I know that all things which I apprehend clearly and distinctly can be created by God as I apprehend them, it suffices that I am able to apprehend one thing apart from another clearly and distinctly in order to be certain that the one is different from the other, since they may be made to exist in separation at least by the omnipotence of God; and it does not signify by what power this separation is made in order to compel me to judge them to be different: and, therefore, just because I know certainly that I exist, and that meanwhile I do not remark that any other thing necessarily pertains to my nature or essence, excepting that I am a thinking thing, I rightly conclude that my essence consists solely in the fact that I am a thinking thing [or a substance whose whole essence or nature is to think]. And although possibly (or rather certainly, as I shall say in a moment) I possess a body with which I am very intimately conjoined, yet because, on the one side, I have a clear and distinct idea of myself inasmuch as I am only a thinking and unextended thing, and as, on the other, I possess a distinct idea of body, inasmuch as it is only an extended and unthinking thing, it is certain that this I [that is to say, my soul by which I am what I am], is entirely and absolutely distinct from my body, and can exist without it. . . .

. . . There is a great difference between mind and body, inasmuch as body is by nature always divisible, and the mind is entirely indivisible. For, as a matter of fact, when I consider the mind, that is to say, myself inasmuch as I am only a thinking thing, I cannot distinguish in myself any parts, but apprehend myself to be clearly one and entire; and although the whole mind seems to be united to the whole body, yet if a foot, or an arm, or some other part, is separated from my body, I am aware that nothing has been taken away from my mind. And the faculties of willing, feeling, conceiving, etc., cannot be properly speaking said to be its parts, for it is one and the same mind which employs itself in willing and in feeling and understanding. But it is quite otherwise with corporeal or extended objects, for there is not one of these imaginable by me which my mind cannot easily divide into parts, and which consequently I do not recognize as being divisible; this would be sufficient to teach me that the mind or soul of man is entirely different from the body, if I have not already learned it from other sources. . . .

From this it is quite clear that, notwithstanding the supreme goodness of God, the nature of man, inasmuch as it is composed of mind and body, cannot be otherwise than sometimes a source of deception. For if there is any cause which excites, not in the foot but in some parts of the nerves which are extended between the foot and the brain, or even the brain itself, the same movement which usually is produced when the foot is detrimentally affected, pain will be experienced as though it were in the foot, and the sense will thus naturally be deceived; for since the same movement in the brain is capable of causing but one sensation in the mind, and this sensation is much more frequently excited by a cause which hurts the foot than by another existing in some other quarter, it is reasonable that it should convey to the mind pain in the foot rather than in any other part of the body. And although the parchedness of the throat does not always proceed, as it usually does, from the fact that drinking is essential for the health of the body, but sometimes comes from quite a different cause, as is the case with dropsical patients, it is yet much better that it should mislead on this occasion than if, on the other hand, it were always to deceive us when the body is in good health; and so on in similar cases.

And certainly this consideration is of great service to me, not only in enabling me to recognize all the errors to which my nature is subject, but also in enabling me to avoid them or to correct them more easily. For knowing that all my senses more frequently indicate to me truth than falsehood respecting the things which concern that which is beneficial to the body, and being able almost always to avail myself of many of them in order to examine one particular thing, and, besides that, being able to make use of my memory in order to connect the present with the past, and of my understanding which already has discovered all the causes of my errors, I ought no longer to fear that falsity may be found in matters every day presented to me by my senses. And I ought to set aside all the doubts of these past days as hyperbolical and ridiculous, particularly that very common uncertainty respecting sleep, which I could not distinguish from the waking state; for at present I find a very notable difference between the two, inasmuch as our memory can never connect our dreams one with the other, or with the whole course of our lives, as it unites events which happen to us while we are awake. And, as a matter of fact, if someone, while I was awake, quite suddenly appeared to me and disappeared as fast as do the images which I see in sleep, so that I could not know from whence the form came nor whither it went, it would not be without reason that I should deem it a specter or a phantom formed by my brain [and similar to those which I form in sleep], rather than a real man. But when I perceive things as to which I know distinctly both the place from which they proceed, and that in which they are, and the time at which they appeared to me; and when, without any interruption, I can connect the perceptions which I have of them with the whole course of my life, I am perfectly assured that these perceptions occur while I am waking and not during sleep. And I ought in no wise to doubt the truth of such matters, if, after having called up all my senses, my memory, and my understanding, to examine them, nothing is brought to evidence by any one of them which is repugnant to what is set forth by the others. For because God is in no wise a deceiver, it follows that I am not deceived in this. But because the exigencies of action often oblige us to make up our minds before having leisure to examine matters carefully, we must confess that the life of man is very frequently subject to error in respect to individual objects, and we must in the end acknowledge the infirmity of our nature.

COMMENT

In considering Descartes' philosophy as an example of rationalism, we shall concentrate upon an exposition of his method.

Of primary significance is Descartes' intense desire for certainty: "I always had an excessive desire to learn to distinguish the true from the false, in order to see clearly in my actions and to walk with confidence in this life." [1]

[1] *Discourse on Method,* Part I, in *The Philosophical Works of Descartes,* trans. by Elizabeth S. Haldane and G. R. T. Ross (Cambridge University Press, 1931) I, p. 87.

He believed that the key to certainty, the way in which to dispel his innumerable doubts, lay in a sound and logical method of reasoning. The proper employment of reason, he believed, would make vast provinces accessible to human knowledge.

Descartes asserted that all certain knowledge is based upon two mental operations: *intuition*—which he also called "the natural light of reason"—and *deduction*. His definitions of these terms are contained in his *Rules for the Direction of the Mind:*

> By *intuition* I understand, not the fluctuating testimony of the senses, nor the misleading judgment that proceeds from the blundering constructions of imagination, but the conception which an unclouded and attentive mind gives us so readily and distinctly that we are wholly freed from doubt about that which we understand. Or, what comes to the same thing, *intuition* is the undoubting conception of an unclouded and attentive mind, and springs from the light of reason alone. . . .
>
> By *deduction* . . . we understand all necessary inference from other facts that are known with certainty. . . . Many things are known with certainty, though not by themselves evident, but only deduced from true and known principles by the continuous and uninterrupted action of a mind that has a clear vision of each step in the process. It is in a similar way that we know that the last link in a long chain is connected with the first, even though we do not take in by means of one and the same act of vision all the intermediate links on which that connection depends, but only remember that we have taken them successively under review and that each single one is united to its neighbor, from the first even to the last. . . . But the first principles themselves are given by intuition alone, while, on the contrary, the remote conclusions are furnished only by deduction.[2]

In formulating these definitions, Descartes was thinking specifically of the method of mathematics, particularly geometry. The certainty of rigorous mathematical reasoning, he believed, consists in starting with meanings and insights so clear and distinct that they cannot be doubted, and then accepting nothing as true unless it follows no less evidently from these foundations. An intuited truth is such that reason has only to understand its meaning fully to see that it *must* be true. Examples of intuitions are the insights that five is more than four, that a triangle is bounded by only three lines, and that things equal to the same thing are equal to each other. Given such manifest and self-evident premises, our conclusion will be certain provided that it is *necessarily* implied by what precedes and that nothing is admitted in the steps of reasoning that does not thus necessarily follow. Thus, in a chain of reasoning symbolized by letters, if p implies q, and q implies r, and r implies s, then s is certain provided that p is certain and that each subsequent step

[2] *Rules for the Direction of the Mind*, in *ibid.*, pp. 7–8.

leading to *s* is also certain. Descartes believed that thinkers have succeeded in the past and will succeed in the future to the extent that they have rigorously employed, or will employ, intuition and deduction.

With this conception of reasoning in mind, he summed up his method in four rules, which are stated in Part II of the *Discourse:*

1. *The rule of certainty.* This rule is (*a*) to accept nothing as true that we do not unquestionably recognize to be such, and (*b*) carefully to avoid all precipitation and prejudice so as to reach judgments so clear and distinct that they cannot be doubted. Only what we *know* to be true is to be admitted into the sphere of belief: thus Descartes aimed not at mere probability, but at absolute certainty. This rule compelled him to reject all beliefs that are at all dubious.

He recognized two causes as chiefly responsible for error: precipitate judgment, due to insufficient care, and prejudiced judgment, due to habit or emotional bias. Many beliefs are tenaciously held not because they are seen with clearness and distinctness to be true but because, in our haste or bias, we feel a very strong inclination to believe them. "I term that clear," he declared, "which is present and apparent to an attentive mind. . . . But the distinct is that which is so precise and different from all other objects that it contains within itself nothing but what is clear." [3] A judgment is worthy of belief only if all the ideas in it and the judgment as a whole are thus clear and distinct.

2. *The rule of division.* We should analyze each of the difficulties involved in our problem into its smallest and simplest parts. If we then attack each of the subordinate parts separately, we shall find it easier to understand and deal with the simple than the complex. When we have thus discovered elements so simple, so clear, and so distinct that the mind cannot break them down into still more simple parts, we can know these elements by a direct awareness exempt from illusion and error; and after this analysis, reason can more surely reconstruct the complex objects of thought.

3. *The rule of order.* We should carry on our reflections in due order, starting with the simplest ideas and proceeding, step by step, to the more and more complex. Descartes had in mind a deductive chain of reasoning in which each stage follows necessarily from the preceding stage, reason always being careful to follow the one and only right order. Every step in this process must command certainty, since it is guaranteed by *intuition,* that "undoubting conception of an unclouded and attentive mind."

4. *The rule of enumeration and review.* In a long chain of reasoning, we are apt to make a slip—to think that we grasp something clearly and distinctly when in fact we do not, or to remember incorrectly some earlier stage in the reasoning. Whenever the smallest link is thus impaired, the chain of reasoning is broken, and all certainty is lost. Hence, it is necessary to re-

[3] *The Principles of Philosophy,* in *ibid.,* I, p. 237.

count and review the steps again and again so as to be absolutely sure that there has been no trick of memory or mistake in reasoning. Certainty is attained only when every link is so firmly grasped, and every connection has been so often reviewed, that the mind finally gathers together the links into an indissoluble, self-evident whole, which it views, as it were, all at the same time. Intuition then can grasp this whole as certain, just as it has grasped the initial premises and each successive step as certain.

Systematic Doubt

The success of the Cartesian method depends upon having a sure foundation upon which to build and thereafter upon successfully applying the first rule—to admit nothing that is uncertain. Therefore Descartes resolved to doubt everything that he could possibly doubt, provisionally retaining only those ordinary maxims of conduct that are necessary in order to live decently. To doubt in this methodical way is not to consider something false or improbable but to recognize that it is not *absolutely* certain. The function of systematic doubt is to find a solid foundation for science and philosophy and thus to dispel scepticism.

The kind of indubitable foundation for which Descartes was searching is not any formal principle of logic or mathematics, such as the principle that one and the same proposition cannot be both true and false. Such a principle, although a necessary foundation of reasoning, tells us nothing about *what exists* and hence cannot provide the necessary basis for a philosophy or science of *reality*. The kind of premise that he sought, therefore, must be such that its truth cannot be doubted; it must be self-evident and not deduced from something else; and it must refer to something actually existing.

In resolutely admitting nothing except what is certain, Descartes was forced to doubt almost everything that he had ever believed:

1. *Sensory experience.* He began by doubting the evidence of his senses. "Can I doubt," he asked, "that I am sitting here by the fire in my dressing gown?" Yes, he replied. Sane men are often subject to illusions and madmen to hallucinations, and I may be in like plight. Moreover, in dreams I seem to see objects and have experiences which do not exist. What I take to be a waking experience may be an unusually stubborn dream. It is possible that I am dreaming at this very instant.

2. *Memory.* My memory at times has tricked me and may be tricking me now. The past that I *think* I remember may be only an illusion.

3. *Expectation.* Just as I may be mistaken about my past, so I may be mistaken about my future.

4. *Other people.* I have no indubitable knowledge of other people, since I am aware of them only through my fallible senses of hearing, touch, and

sight. All the people who apparently surround me may be only figures in a prolonged dream.

5. *My body*. I know my body only through sensory experience, and this can be deceiving. It is possible that I have no body and that my mind is only entertaining the false impression that I do have one.

6. *The external world*. Not only can I doubt any *particular* object of sense-experience; I can also doubt that there is any external world at all. It is true that the very clear ideas of physical science—such as the ideas of measurable extension and motion—are much more difficult to doubt than are the comparatively vague and inexact impressions of color, sound, touch, and taste. But it is conceivable that some kind of god or demon is deceiving me even with respect to these most clear ideas. It may be that there exists in reality neither earth nor heavens, nor any extended object, but that a supernatural being has put all these false notions into my mind.

7. *Mathematical truths*. It would seem that I can be quite certain about simple mathematical truths—whether I am awake or dreaming, it is surely true that two and three make five. But I, being finite, am fallible, and I may be deceived even in my most profound convictions. If there be an evil demon, no less cunning and deceitful than powerful, he may be using all his ingenuity to deceive me. Perhaps he may be deceiving me even when I am doing a simple mathematical operation.

It would seem that nothing at all is left to believe; but something remains even when doubt has done its worst. "I suppose myself to be deceived," Descartes exclaimed; "doubtless, then, I exist, since I am deceived." My very act of doubting proves something that I cannot doubt. "I think, therefore I am."

Here is the first principle—the absolute and indubitable certainty—for which Descartes was searching, and here also is the main point of departure of modern epistemology. The certainty of self-consciousness had been proclaimed earlier by St. Augustine (354–430) and St. Thomas Aquinas (1225?–1274). But Descartes gave the idea wide currency, backing it up with systematic doubt, and without admitting the element of faith essential to Augustine and Aquinas. No one before him had so deliberately adopted doubt as a method of procedure or employed it so boldly and sweepingly. Most later philosophers have agreed that the existence of mind is more certain than the existence of matter, and that the existence of *my* mind—for *me* —is more certain than the existence of other minds. Modern philosophy has largely radiated out from this focal point.

When I say "I think, therefore I am," what do I mean by "I"? Clearly I mean a *thinking being*—hence thought enters into the very essence of the self. Thought is to be understood in a broad sense; perception, memory, imagination, desire, will, reason—all are forms of thought, and, through introspection, we are immediately aware of all these mental operations. Descartes was not, at this point, prepared to describe the exact nature of the *being* that thinks. "A thing that thinks," the materialist Hobbes objected, "may be something corporeal; and the opposite of this has been assumed; not proved." To this objection Descartes replied: "But really I did not assume the opposite, neither did I use it as the basis of my argument; I left it wholly undetermined until Meditation VI, in which its proof is given." [4] At this stage, then, Descartes was prepared to say only that there is thought, which consists of conscious mental operations, and that there is a thinker. By a "thinker," however, he meant a "substance"—that is to say, an enduring *thing* that has changing states or characteristics (which he calls "accidents.") "It is certain," he declared, "that no thought can exist apart from a thing that thinks; no activity, no accident can be without a substance in which to exist." [5] What is certain, then, is that there is an "I"—a thinking thing—with its various forms of thought.

Application of the Method to Metaphysics

Descartes thus had a starting point—the certainty of his own existence. He noted that the truth of this first premise—"I think, therefore I am"—was *clearly* and *distinctly* perceived. Since it is this clear and distinct perception that guarantees the truth of the premise, it seemed to him that he could take as a general rule that all that is thus very clearly and distinctly perceived is true.

But what else can he know? It is doubtful whether anything else can be certain so long as there is the possibility of a deceiving demon. This difficulty must somehow be removed. (The "deceiving demon" must not be understood too literally. It is a kind of literary device to indicate the possibility that thinking may be utterly treacherous and that whatever exists may be entirely irrational.) Descartes must show that reality is not irrational and that very careful reasoning can be trusted. He can do this by proving that a rational and beneficent God, rather than a malicious and deceitful demon, is the foundation of whatever is real, for if God is indeed the basis of reality, surely our most careful reasoning is trustworthy—God would not be a deceiver.

Descartes' first argument for the existence of God may appear complex, but it is actually quite simple, consisting of four steps: (1) I have an idea of God. (2) Everything, including my idea, has a cause. (3) Since the greater cannot proceed from the less, nothing less than God is adequate to explain my idea of God. (4) Therefore God exists.

---

[4] *Reply to Third Objections,* in *ibid.,* II, p. 63.
[5] *Ibid.,* p. 64.

Descartes advanced a second argument for God, once again starting with "I think, therefore I am." He argued (still using the first person pronoun) that God is the cause, not only of my idea of God, but of *me*. This is an argument by elimination: (1) I am not the cause of myself, for if I were, I would not be the highly imperfect and fallible being that I know myself to be. (2) No other finite being could be the sufficient cause of my existence, for if such a being existed, it in turn would have to be explained, as would any prior finite cause as well. I would thus have to trace the causal process back from stage to stage to the *ultimate* cause, an eternal and necessary being who requires no explanation beyond himself. Only such an infinite cause could be conceived as existing, not merely through my life, but through all the lives involved in the total succession of finite beings—and only such a cause would be adequate to *maintain* as well as to originate the entire succession. (3) The ultimate cause could not be multiple, because I conceive of God as absolutely one, and the cause of this idea must be no less perfect than its effect, not falling short of the idea in its unity or in any other respect. (4) The only possibility that remains is that an infinite and monotheistic God is the cause. Therefore God exists.

In Meditation V, which has been omitted in the present book, Descartes presented a third argument for God's existence—a restatement of the so-called Ontological Argument of Saint Anselm, an early medieval philosopher. Since this argument is dealt with at some length in Part Four, we shall not consider it here.

The importance of God in Descartes' system, as we have pointed out, is that He is used to guarantee not a system of dogma but science and philosophy. Science and philosophy are based upon reason and memory, and God is needed to guarantee their reliability. God, being perfect, would not deceive me—he would not, like a malignant demon, so mislead me as to invalidate my most vivid memory and careful reasoning. Descartes' constructive argument started with "I think, therefore I am." But, almost surreptitiously, he came to admit three other "self-evident truths":

1. Whatever is clearly and distinctly perceived is true.
2. Nothing can be without a cause.
3. The cause must be at least as great as the effect.

From these premises he has deduced two additional "truths":

4. God exists.
5. God, being perfect, cannot deceive me.

The remainder of his argument follows rather quickly. He argued for the existence of other minds and material objects alike on the grounds of God's veracity. This means not that all my ideas are true but simply that the faculties God has given me are reliable when used correctly—without prejudice, hastiness, or naïveté. I can trust only "firm conceptions born in a sound and attentive mind from the light of reason alone" and rigorous deductions from these conceptions.

God has given me such a strong and unavoidable inclination to believe in a physical world that He would be deceitful if no such world existed. But I can be sure only of my very clear and distinct ideas of external reality. Impressions of color, odor, sound, touch, and taste, not being susceptible of precise mathematical formulation, are too unclear to be regarded as trustworthy reports of the real properties of material bodies. But *extension* can be measured; and we cannot even conceive of a material body apart from extension, since an unextended body is a contradiction in terms. Therefore the very essence of body is to be extended.

A further argument, using *permanence* as the criterion of what is real, is introduced in Meditation II. Descartes pointed out that a piece of wax, if heated, will change its color, odor, taste, and tactile qualities. Nothing remains constant except extension, flexibility, and mobility. But flexibility is not a property of all bodies, and mobility is relational (*i.e.*, a thing can be said to move only by reference to another thing). Hence extension is the only *intrinsic* quality of matter.

Just as I have a very strong inclination to believe in a physical world, so I have an equally strong inclination to believe that other people are not mere dream phantoms or physical automata but real persons like myself. In this regard also, God would not deceive me.

Descartes recognized two distinct realms of being. One is the world described by physics, a world which does not depend upon our thoughts. It would continue to exist and operate if there were no human beings at all. Its essence is to be extended. The other is the world whose essence is thought— perception, willing, feeling, reasoning, imagining, and the corresponding ideas or mental representations.

A human being, as a compound of mind and body, belongs to both realms. How a person can thus be both two and one poses a difficult problem. Despite the apparent paradox, Descartes believed that mind and body, although radically different, are harmoniously combined in the human organism, and that the unextended mind somehow interacts with the extended body.

Application of the Method to Natural Science

Even when Descartes turned to natural science, his ideal of attaining certainty remained the same. All of natural science appears to be subject to rational deduction from self-evident premises. "As for physics," he declared, "I should believe myself to know nothing of it if I were able to say only how things may be without demonstrating that they cannot be otherwise; for having reduced physics to the laws of mathematics, it is possible to do this, and I believe that I can do it in all that little I believe myself to know." [6]

In practice, however, he was forced to qualify or abandon such extreme claims. The deduction of physics from mathematics and metaphysics, it appears, applies only to *general* principles. In more specialized research, he discovered that brute fact eludes determination by pure deductive reasoning. He was guided to this conclusion by his own experience as a keen observer of nature, dissecting the bodies of various animals and investigating experimentally the weight of air, the laws of light and sound, the characteristics of various oils, waters, spirits, and salts, and other natural phenomena. Not only did he discover that he must himself fall back upon empirical methods, but he strongly recommended to others that such observations and experiments be conducted.

Although, as we have said, Descartes thought that the quite general principles of natural science could be demonstrated *a priori*, he believed that experience serves a valuable function as an additional check and confirmation. Such empirical checking-up should be carried out to make doubly certain of the principles. In Book VI of the *Discourse*, he confessed that it is necessary to combine experience with *a priori* principles in order to derive the special hypotheses of science and to devise crucial experiments to decide between the alternative hypotheses that are thus derived.

Thus his conception of method was not so extreme and one-sided as is often supposed. He recognized that there are two ways of reaching knowledge—by pure reason and by experience—and that in natural science both are indispensable.

Criticism

Descartes was the first thinker to construct a rationalistic theory of knowledge using mathematics as a model of correct reasoning. In this sense, he was a highly original philosopher who brought about a veritable revolution in human thought. The demand for intellectual order, rigor, and discipline stated in his four rules and his method of systematic doubt have exercised a very useful function in making science and philosophy more stringent and pure. In the application of his rules to metaphysics and physical science, he often displayed great perspicacity.

Nevertheless, he did not sufficiently realize the importance of experience in the pursuit of truth. Although he recognized the necessity for observation and experiment in science, he wrongly supposed that the main principles of physics could be deduced from a rationalistic metaphysics. He was also mistaken in supposing that the methods of mathematics could be extended to metaphysical reasoning. *A priori* reason is applicable to mathematics because

[6] Letter to Mersenne, March 11, 1649. Quoted by Ralph M. Blake, "The Role of Experience in Descartes' Theory of Knowledge," *Philosophical Review*, XXXVIII, 1929, p. 126.

it *is* mathematics—a nonempirical science. Pure deduction, by itself, cannot give us truth about matters of fact—it can give us only logical consistency. For example, a number of alternative systems of geometry have been worked out by such modern mathematicians, as Lobatchewsky, Minkowsky, and Riemann—each system of geometry equally consistent, and each conceivably applicable to the real world. But which one in fact does apply can be discovered only by the empirical method of hypothesis and observation. It used to be taken for granted that the physical world conforms to Euclid's geometry, but Einstein advanced the hypothesis that the universe conforms instead to Riemann's geometry, in which all space is curved and there are no straight lines. The decisive test, which confirmed Einstein's theory, was the observation by astronomers that light rays bend as they travel through space. No *a priori* reasoning could suffice to decide the question—or any other question about matters of fact. In failing adequately to grasp this crucial difference between a formal, nonempirical science, such as geometry, and an inquiry into the factual nature of existence, Descartes veered too far in the direction of a pure rationalism.

The quest for certainty, which is the basic motive of Descartes' theory of knowledge, is mainly a will-of-the-wisp. Certainty is attainable only within a very narrow range. Even his "indubitable" first premise—"I think, therefore I am"—does not provide the kind of certainty that he supposed. Doubt implies *thought*—this is certain. But does it imply an enduring thinker—a *thing*, or *substance*, that thinks? Is there a thinking self that somehow remains selfsame amid all the changing thoughts? Buddha, Hume, James, Russell, and others have doubted it, and Descartes nowhere proves it. Even if we should grant that thought implies a thinker, the most that Descartes would seem to be justified in concluding is the momentary existence of the thinker and his thought. For it must not be forgotten that he had rejected as uncertain all memory of the past and all expectation of the future. The only consistent position that remains is what philosophers call "a solipsism of the moment"—namely, a belief only in one's immediate, *present* existence and experience.

The criterion of truth that Descartes introduced at this stage of his argument is "clear and distinct perception." Unfortunately, this criterion is itself not too clear. Did he mean that a *concept* that is clear and distinct must be true? Or did he mean that a *judgment* that is clear and distinct must be true? Strictly speaking, *concepts* cannot be true or false—the *concept* of a unicorn may be very "clear and distinct," but it is only a judgment or proposition, such as "Unicorns exist," that can be true or false. The clarity and distinctness of the concept in no way guarantees the truth of an assertion about it. What Descartes may have meant, however, is that the criterion of truth is clear and distinct insight into self-evidence or implication—insight that a judgment must be true or that it follows necessarily from some other judgment. But if, as Descartes insisted, the human mind is quite fallible, a person may *think* that he has a clear and distinct insight when in fact he does not. It is notorious that our psychological *feeling* that we know something clearly and distinctly may be mistaken. Our mental hospitals are full of people who have unreliable feelings of this sort, and normal people also have such feelings.

After stating his criterion of truth, Descartes tried to prove the existence of God, introducing two new premises: (1) nothing can be without a cause, and (2) the cause must be at least as great as the effect. He regarded these premises as self-evident. But are they? Some philosophers have admitted the possibility of uncaused events. In the modern theory of "emergent evolution," moreover, it is maintained that *new* things or qualities come into existence, and that the effect, being novel, *is* greater than its cause. The world is in the making, and much in the present is greater than its causes in the past.

In trying to prove the existence of God, Descartes became involved in a circular argument. He had doubted the reliability of memory—not just some memories, but *all* memory—and he had to demonstrate God's existence in order to eliminate the possibility of the deceiving demon and to establish the general veracity of memory. But, since one must remember each past stage in the argument, it is necessary to *use* memory in the very process of "proving" God's existence. He thus took for granted what he set out to prove—the reliability of memory. He also made use of the basic principles of logic, which are the foundation of all reasoning. If even such a simple arithmetical proposition as "$2 + 3 = 5$" is doubtful, the basic principles of logic must also be doubtful. But if memory and the principles of logic are doubtful *until* I prove the existence of God, I can never prove the existence of God. On the other hand, if memory and the principles of logic are *not* doubtful, then it is unnecessary to prove God's existence in order to guarantee them. Thus, Descartes' arguments for the existence of God are either epistemologically superfluous or circular.

His first argument for God—that nothing less than God is adequate to explain his idea of God—is unconvincing. It is based upon the premise, which we have already questioned, that everything must have a cause equal or superior to itself; and it involves the very dubious contention that the *idea* of an Infinite and Perfect Being is itself, in a sense, infinite and perfect, and so requires an infinite and perfect Cause. Why should we suppose that the idea of God is itself godlike? On the contrary, it would seem that human beings have a very imperfect conception of an Infinite and Perfect Being, and that this imperfect grasp is quite within the human compass.

Descartes' second and third arguments for God will be criticized in Chapter 11. At present, it will suffice to say that many, if not most, philosophers regard them as fallacious.

The shakiness of his three "proofs" of God's existence is a critical weakness, since he bases his argument both for other minds and for matter on the ground of God's veracity.

We shall not criticize his theory of mind and body here, except to note that so sharp a dualism presents considerable difficulties. Likewise, we shall pass over his scientific doctrines, many of which have been superseded or remain unverifiable speculations.

What is the upshot of our criticism? It is this: Descartes was an intellectual giant who did a great deal to make philosophical and scientific method more rigorous; but he overemphasized the rationalistic elements in knowledge and was unable to attain his own ideal of demonstrative certainty. Like most great men, he was great in his errors as well as in his achievements.

4

The Way of the Empiricist

CHARLES SANDERS PEIRCE (1839–1914)

Peirce was born in Cambridge, Massachusetts, the second son of Benjamin Peirce, a professor at Harvard and one of America's foremost mathematicians. At the time of Peirce's birth, Cambridge was one of the main centers of American culture, and the Peirce home was a principal gathering place of celebrities. Such famous scientists as Louis Agassiz and Asa Gray and such great literary figures as Longfellow, Emerson, and Oliver Wendell Holmes were frequent guests. Peirce's father, himself remarkable, gave his son Charles an impressive education in logic, mathematics, philosophy, and experimental science. At the age of twelve, Charles set up a chemical laboratory in which he undertook some rather advanced experiments. At Harvard, which he attended from the age of sixteen until he was twenty, he did not buckle down to a strict routine of study but roamed over a vast philosophical and scientific literature. After being graduated, he continued his studies at Harvard, receiving a Master's degree in mathematics and an additional degree in chemistry.

This wide reading and scientific training was supplemented by a great deal of practical experience in scientific research. He was an assistant for three years in the Harvard astronomical observatory, where he carried out the investigations published in *Photometric Researches* (1878), the only one of his books to appear during his lifetime. He also conducted extensive scientific research for the United States Coastal and Geodetic Survey, with which he was associated from 1861 to 1891. His researches led to important original contributions in chemistry, astronomy, optics, the theory of gravity and pendulum movement, and the determination of weights and measures.

During the 1860's he found time to give a number of lecture courses at Harvard on logic and the history of science, and from 1879 to 1884, he was a lecturer in logic at the Johns Hopkins University. But he never received a permanent university appointment, largely because his ideas were too bold and original and his personality was too eccentric. Publishers showed themselves indifferent to an author who had no official university backing; and consequently a great deal of his writing was never presented to the public during his own lifetime. His reputation at Harvard also suffered as a result of his divorce from his first wife, who belonged to a very respectable family and was popular in Cambridge. Although he contracted a happy second marriage to a French woman, he never quite regained his status in the eyes of the community.

In his younger days, Peirce was a member, along with William James and Oliver Wendell Holmes, Jr., of an intimate circle of brilliant thinkers in Cambridge; but as he grew older he became more isolated. In 1881, at the age of forty-eight, he retired to Milford, Pennsylvania, where he lived in seclusion with his French wife. Here he waged a gradually losing battle against poverty, eking out a small income by writing articles for popular scientific magazines. Dogged by his creditors and seeking intellectual refuge, he would retire to his attic, pulling up a rope ladder after him so that no one could follow. To make matters worse, in the last years of his life, he suffered from slow cancer. When he finally became too ill to do any sustained work, he was supported mainly by the charity of William James and a few other friends.

During these final years of illness and poverty, he heroically persevered in his philosophical labors, often writing the whole night through. Nothing daunted him—not physical pain, the lack of a publisher, the isolation from friends, the failure to achieve public recognition. He continued to write even when he trembled so much that he was compelled to steady one hand against the other. Only death, at the age of seventy-five, could quell his spirit.

The Fixation of Belief*

I

Few persons care to study logic, because everybody conceives himself to be proficient enough in the art of reasoning already. But I observe that this satisfaction is limited to one's own ratiocination, and does not extend to that of other men.

We come to the full possession of our power of drawing inferences the last of all our faculties, for it is not so much a natural gift as a long and difficult art. The history of its practice would make a grand subject for a book. The medieval schoolman, following the Romans, made logic the earliest of a boy's studies after grammar, as being very easy. So it was as they understood it. Its fundamental principle, according to them, was, that all knowledge rests on either authority or reason; but that

* Reprinted from *Popular Science Monthly*, 1877, with a few slight omissions.

whatever is deduced by reason depends ultimately on a premise derived from authority. Accordingly, as soon as a boy was perfect in the syllogistic procedure, his intellectual kit of tools was held to be complete.

To Roger Bacon, that remarkable mind who in the middle of the thirteenth century was almost a scientific man, the schoolmen's conception of reasoning appeared only an obstacle to truth. He saw that experience alone teaches anything—a proposition which to us seems easy to understand, because a distinct conception of experience has been handed down to us from former generations; which to him also seemed perfectly clear, because its difficulties had not yet unfolded themselves. Of all kinds of experience, the best, he thought, was interior illumination, which teaches many things about Nature which the external senses could never discover, such as the transubstantiation of bread.

Four centuries later, the more celebrated Bacon, in the first book of his "Novum Organum," gave his clear account of experience as something which must be opened to verification and reëxamination. But, superior as Lord Bacon's conception is to earlier notions, a modern reader who is not in awe of his grandiloquence is chiefly struck by the inadequacy of his view of scientific procedure. That we have only to make some crude experiments, to draw up briefs of the results in certain blank forms, to go through these by rule, checking off everything disproved and setting down the alternatives, and that thus in a few years physical science would be finished up— what an idea! "He wrote on science like a Lord Chancellor," indeed.

The early scientists, Copernicus, Tycho, Brahe, Kepler, Galileo and Gilbert, had methods more like those of their modern brethren. Kepler undertook to draw a curve through the places of Mars; and his greatest service to science was in impressing on men's minds that this was the thing to be done if they wished to improve astronomy; that they were not to content themselves with inquiring whether one system of epicycles was better than another but that they were to sit down by the figures and find out what the curve, in truth, was. He accomplished this by his incomparable energy and courage, blundering along in the most inconceivable way (to us), from one irrational hypothesis to another, until, after trying twenty-two of these, he fell, by the mere exhaustion of his invention, upon the orbit which a mind well furnished with the weapons of modern logic would have tried almost at the outset.[1]

In the same way, every work of science great enough to be remembered for a few generations affords some exemplification of the defective state of the art of reasoning of the time when it was written; and each chief step in science has been a lesson in logic. It was so when Lavoisier and his contemporaries took up the study of Chemistry. The old chemist's maxim had been, "Lege, lege, lege, labora, ora, et relege." [2] Lavoisier's method was not to read and pray, not to dream that some long and complicated chemical process would have a certain effect, to put it into practice with dull patience, after its inevitable failure, to dream that with some modification it would have another result, and to end by publishing the last dream as a fact: his way was to carry his mind into his laboratory, and to make of his alembics and cucurbits instruments of thought, giving a new conception of reasoning as something which was

[1] Twenty-one years later (in 1893), Peirce retracted this criticism of Kepler, saying that it was a "foolish remark" made because he had not as yet read the original work of Kepler, which was "a marvellous piece of inductive reasoning." [Editor]

[2] "Read, read, read, work, pray, and read again."

to be done with one's eyes open, by manipulating real things instead of words and fancies . . .

II

The object of reasoning is to find out, from the consideration of what we already know, something else which we do not know. Consequently, reasoning is good if it be such as to give a true conclusion from true premises, and not otherwise. Thus, the question of validity is purely one of fact and not of thinking. A being the premises and B being the conclusion, the question is, whether these facts are really so related that if A is B is. If so, the inference is valid; if not, not. It is not in the least the question whether, when the premises are accepted by the mind, we feel an impulse to accept the conclusion also. It is true that we do generally reason correctly by nature. But that is an accident; the true conclusion would remain true if we had no impulse to accept it; and the false one would remain false, though we could not resist the tendency to believe in it.

We are, doubtless, in the main logical animals, but we are not perfectly so. Most of us, for example, are naturally more sanguine and hopeful than logic would justify. We seem to be so constituted that in the absence of any facts to go upon we are happy and self-satisfied; so that the effect of experience is continually to counteract our hopes and aspirations. Yet a lifetime of the application of this corrective does not usually eradicate our sanguine disposition. Where hope is unchecked by any experience, it is likely that our optimism is extravagant. Logicality in regard to practical matters is the most useful quality an animal can possess, and might, therefore, result from the action of natural selection; but outside of these it is probably of more advantage to the animal to have his mind filled with pleasing and encouraging visions, independently of their truth; and thus, upon unpractical subjects, natural selection might occasion a fallacious tendency of thought.

That which determines us, from given premises, to draw one inference rather than another, is some habit of mind, whether it be constitutional or acquired. The habit is good or otherwise, according as it produces true conclusions from true premises or not; and an inference is regarded as valid or not, without reference to the truth or falsity of its conclusion specially, but according as the habit which determines it is such as to produce true conclusions in general or not. The particular habit of mind which governs this or that inference may be formulated in a proposition whose truth depends on the validity of the inferences which the habit determines; and such a formula is called a *guiding principle* of inference. Suppose, for example, that we observe that a rotating disk of copper quickly comes to rest when placed between the poles of a magnet, and we infer that this will happen with every disk of copper. The guiding principle is, that what is true of one piece of copper is true of another. Such a guiding principle with regard to copper would be much safer than with regard to many other substances —brass, for example.

A book might be written to signalize all the most important of these guiding principles of reasoning. It would probably be, we must confess, of no service to a person whose thought is directed wholly to practical subjects, and whose activity moves along thoroughly beaten paths. The problems which present themselves to such a mind are matters of routine which he has learned once for all to handle in learning his business. But let a man venture into an unfamiliar field, or where his results are not continually checked by experience, and all history shows that the most masculine intellect will ofttimes lose his orientation and waste his efforts in directions which bring him no nearer to his goal, or even carry him entirely astray. He is like a ship on the open sea, with no one on board who understands the rules of navigation. And in such a case some general study of the guiding principles of reasoning would be sure to be found useful.

The subject could hardly be treated, however, without being first limited; since almost any fact may serve as a guiding principle. But it so happens that there exists a division among facts, such that in one class are all those which are absolutely essential as guiding principles, while in the other are all those which have any other interest as objects of research. This division is between those which are necessarily taken for granted in asking whether a certain conclusion follows from certain premises, and those which are not implied in that question. A moment's thought will show that a variety of facts are already assumed when the logical question is first asked. It is implied, for instance, that there are such states of mind as doubt and belief—that a passage from one to the other is possible, the object of thought remaining the same, and that this transition is subject to some rules which all minds are alike bound by. As these are facts which we must already know before we can have any clear conception of reasoning at all, it cannot be supposed to be any longer of much interest to inquire into their truth or falsity. On the other hand, it is easy to believe that those rules of reasoning which are deduced from the very idea of the process are the ones which are the most essential; and, indeed, that so long as it conforms to these it will, at least, not lead to false conclusions from true premises. In point of fact, the importance of what may be deduced from the assumptions involved in the logi-

cal question turns out to be greater than might be supposed, and this for reasons which it is difficult to exhibit at the outset. The only one which I shall here mention is, that conceptions which are really products of logical reflections, without being readily seen to be so, mingle with our ordinary thoughts, and are frequently the causes of great confusion. This is the case, for example, with the conception of quality. A quality as such is never an object of observation. We can see that a thing is blue or green, but the quality of being blue and the quality of being green are not things which we see; they are products of logical reflections. The truth is, that commonsense, or thought as it first emerges above the level of the narrowly practical, is deeply imbued with that bad logical quality to which the epithet *metaphysical* is commonly applied; and nothing can clear it up but a severe course of logic.

III

We generally know when we wish to ask a question and when we wish to pronounce a judgment, for there is a dissimilarity between the sensation of doubting and that of believing.

But this is not all which distinguishes doubt from belief. There is a practical difference. Our beliefs guide our desires and shape our actions. The Assassins, or followers of the Old Man of the Mountain, used to rush into death at his least command, because they believed that obedience to him would insure everlasting felicity. Had they doubted this, they would not have acted as they did. So it is with every belief, according to its degree. The feeling of believing is a more or less sure indication of there being established in our nature some habit which will determine our actions. Doubt never has such an effect.

Nor must we overlook a third point of

difference. Doubt is an uneasy and dissatisfied state from which we struggle to free ourselves and pass into the state of belief; while the latter is a calm and satisfactory state which we do not wish to avoid, or to change to a belief in anything else. On the contrary, we cling tenaciously, not merely to believing, but to believing just what we do believe.

Thus, both doubt and belief have positive effects upon us, though very different ones. Belief does not make us act at once, but puts us into such a condition that we shall behave in a certain way, when the occasion arises. Doubt has not the least effect of this sort, but stimulates us to action until it is destroyed. This reminds us of the irritation of a nerve and the reflex action produced thereby; while for the analogue of belief, in the nervous system, we must look to what are called nervous associations—for example, to that habit of the nerves in consequence of which the smell of a peach will make the mouth water.

IV

The irritation of doubt causes a struggle to attain a state of belief. I shall term this struggle *inquiry*, though it must be admitted that this is sometimes not a very apt designation.

The irritation of doubt is the only immediate motive for the struggle to attain belief. It is certainly best for us that our beliefs should be such as may truly guide our actions so as to satisfy our desires; and this reflection will make us reject any belief which does not seem to have been so formed as to insure this result. But it will only do so by creating a doubt in the place of that belief. With the doubt, therefore, the struggle begins, and with the cessation of doubt it ends. Hence, the sole object of inquiry is the settlement of opinion. We

may fancy that this is not enough for us, and that we seek not merely an opinion, but a true opinion. But put this fancy to the test, and it proves groundless; for as soon as a firm belief is reached we are entirely satisfied, whether the belief be false or true. And it is clear that nothing out of the sphere of our knowledge can be our object, for nothing which does not affect the mind can be a motive for a mental effort. The most that can be maintained is, that we seek for a belief that we shall *think* to be true. But we think each one of our beliefs to be true, and, indeed, it is mere tautology to say so.

That the settlement of opinion is the sole end of inquiry is a very important proposition. It sweeps away, at once, various vague and erroneous conceptions of proof. A few of these may be noticed here.

1. Some philosophers have imagined that to start an inquiry it was only necessary to utter a question or set it down on paper, and have even recommended us to begin our studies with questioning everything! But the mere putting of a proposition into the interrogative form does not stimulate the mind to any struggle after belief. There must be a real and living doubt, and without this all discussion is idle.

2. It is a very common idea that a demonstration must rest on some ultimate and absolutely indubitable propositions. These, according to one school, are first principles of a general nature; according to another, are first sensations. But, in point of fact, an inquiry, to have that completely satisfactory result called demonstration, has only to start with propositions perfectly free from all actual doubt. If the premises are not in fact doubted at all, they cannot be more satisfactory than they are.

3. Some people seem to love to argue a point after all the world is fully convinced of it. But no further advance can be made.

When doubt ceases, mental action on the subject comes to an end; and, if it did go on, it would be without a purpose.

v

If the settlement of opinion is the sole object of inquiry, and if belief is of the nature of a habit, why should we not attain the desired end, by taking any answer to a question, which we may fancy, and constantly reiterating it to ourselves, dwelling on all which may conduce to that belief, and learning to turn with contempt and hatred from anything which might disturb it? This simple and direct method is really pursued by many men. I remember once being entreated not to read a certain newspaper lest it might change my opinion upon free-trade. "Lest I might be entrapped by its fallacies and misstatements," was the form of expression. "You are not," my friend said, "a special student of political economy. You might, therefore, easily be deceived by fallacious arguments upon the subject. You might, then, if you read this paper, be led to believe in protection. But you admit that free-trade is the true doctrine; and you do not wish to believe what is not true." I have often known this system to be deliberately adopted. Still oftener, the instinctive dislike of an undecided state of mind, exaggerated into a vague dread of doubt, makes men cling spasmodically to the views they already take. The man feels that, if he only holds to his belief without wavering, it will be entirely satisfactory. Nor can it be denied that a steady and immovable faith yields great peace of mind. It may, indeed, give rise to inconveniences, as if a man should resolutely continue to believe that fire would not burn him, or that he would be eternally damned if he received his *ingesta* otherwise than through a stomach-pump. But then the man who adopts this method will not allow that its inconveniences are greater than its advantages. He will say, "I hold steadfastly to the truth and the truth is always wholesome." And in many cases it may very well be that the pleasure he derives from his calm faith overbalances any inconveniences resulting from its deceptive character. Thus, if it be true that death is annihilation, then the man who believes that he will certainly go straight to heaven when he dies, provided he has fulfilled certain simple observances in this life, has a cheap pleasure which will not be followed by the least disappointment. A similar consideration seems to have weight with many persons in religious topics, for we frequently hear it said, "Oh, I could not believe so-and-so, because I should be wretched if I did." When an ostrich buries its head in the sand as danger approaches, it very likely takes the happiest course. It hides the danger, and then calmly says there is no danger; and, if it feels perfectly sure there is none, why should it raise its head to see? A man may go through life, systematically keeping out of view all that might cause a change in his opinions, and if he only succeeds—basing his method, as he does, on two fundamental psychological laws—I do not see what can be said against his doing so. It would be an egotistical impertinence to object that his procedure is irrational, for that only amounts to saying that his method of settling belief is not ours. He does not propose to himself to be rational, and indeed, will often talk with scorn of man's weak and illusive reason. So let him think as he pleases.

But this method of fixing belief, which may be called the method of tenacity, will be unable to hold its ground in practice. The social impulse is against it. The man who adopts it will find that other men think differently from him, and it will be apt to occur to him in some saner moment that their opinions are quite as good as his own, and this will shake his confidence in his belief. This conception, that another man's thought or sentiment may be equivalent to one's own, is a distinctly new step, and a highly important one. It arises from an impulse too strong in man to be suppressed, without danger of destroying the human species. Unless we make ourselves hermits, we shall necessarily influence each other's opinions; so that the problem becomes how to fix belief, not in the individual merely, but in the community.

Let the will of the state act, then, instead of that of the individual. Let an institution be created which shall have for its object to keep correct doctrines before the attention of the people, to reiterate them perpetually, and to teach them to the young; having at the same time power to prevent contrary doctrines from being taught, advocated, or expressed. Let all possible causes of a change of mind be removed from men's apprehensions. Let them be kept ignorant, lest they should learn of some reason to think otherwise than they do. Let their passions be enlisted, so that they may regard private and unusual opinions with hatred and horror. Then, let all men who reject the established belief be terrified into silence. Let the people turn out and tar-and-feather such men, or let inquisitions be made into the manner of thinking of suspected persons, and, when they are found guilty of forbidden beliefs, let them be subjected to some signal punishment. When complete agreement could not otherwise be reached, a general massacre of all who have not thought in a certain way has proved a very effective means of settling opinion in a country. If the power to do this be wanting, let a list of opinions be drawn up, to which no man of the least independence of thought can assent, and let the faithful be required to accept all these propositions, in order to segregate them as radically as possible from the influence of the rest of the world.

This method has, from the earliest times, been one of the chief means of upholding correct theological and political doctrines, and of preserving their universal or catholic character. In Rome, especially, it has been practiced from the days of Numa Pompilius to those of Pius Nonus. This is the most perfect example in history; but wherever there is a priesthood—and no religion has been without one—this method has been more or less made use of. Wherever there is an aristocracy, or a guild, or any association of a class of men whose interests depend, or are supposed to depend, on certain propositions, there will be inevitably found some traces of this natural product of social feeling. Cruelties always accompany this system; and when it is consistently carried out, they become atrocities of the most horrible kind in the eyes of any rational man. Nor should this occasion surprise, for the officer of a society does not feel justified in surrendering the interests of that society for the sake of mercy, as he might his own private interests. It is natural, therefore, that sympathy and fellowship should thus produce a most ruthless power.

In judging this method of fixing belief, which may be called the method of authority, we must, in the first place, allow its immeasurable mental and moral superiority to the method of tenacity. Its success is proportionately greater; and, in fact, it has over and over again worked the most majestic results. The mere structures of stone which it has caused to be put together—in Siam, for example, in Egypt, and in Europe—have many of them a sublimity hardly more than rivaled by the greatest works of Nature. And, except the geological epochs, there are no periods of time so vast as those which are measured by some of these organized faiths. If we scrutinize the matter closely, we shall find that there has not been one of their creeds which has remained always the same; yet the change is so slow as to be imperceptible during one person's life, so that individual belief remains sensibly fixed. For the mass of mankind, then, there is perhaps no better method than this. If it is their highest impulse to be intellectual slaves, then slaves they ought to remain.

But no institution can undertake to regulate opinions upon every subject. Only the most important ones can be attended to, and on the rest men's minds must be left to the action of natural causes. This imperfection will be no source of weakness so long as men are in such a state of culture that one opinion does not influence another—that is, so long as they cannot put two and two together. But in the most priest-ridden states some individuals will be found who are raised above that condition. These men possess a wider sort of social feeling; they see that men in other countries and in other ages have held to very different doctrines from those which they themselves have been brought up to believe; and they cannot help seeing that it is the mere accident of their having been taught as they have, and of their having been surrounded with the manners and associations they have, that has caused them to believe as they do and not far differently. Nor can their candor resist the reflection that there is no reason to rate their own views at a higher value than those of other nations and other centuries; thus giving rise to doubts in their minds.

They will further perceive that such doubts as these must exist in their minds with reference to every belief which seems to be determined by the caprice either of themselves or of those who originated the popular opinions. The willful adherence to a belief, and the arbitrary forcing of it upon others, must, therefore, both be given up. A different new method of settling opinions must be adopted, that shall not only produce an impulse to believe, but shall also decide what proposition it is which is to be believed. Let the action of natural preferences be unimpeded, then, and under their influence let men, conversing together and regarding matters in different lights, gradually develop beliefs in harmony with natural causes. This method resembles that by which conceptions of art have been brought to maturity. The most perfect example of it is to be found in the history of metaphysical philosophy. Systems of this sort have not usually rested upon any observed facts, at least not in any great degree. They have been chiefly adopted because their fundamental propositions seemed "agreeable to reason." This is an apt expression; it does not mean that which agrees with experience, but that which we find ourselves inclined to believe. Plato, for example, finds it agreeable to reason that the distances of the celestial spheres from one another should be proportional to the different lengths of strings which produce harmonious chords. Many philosophers have been led to their main conclusions by considerations like this; but this is the lowest and least developed form which the method takes, for it is clear that another man might find Kepler's theory, that the celestial spheres are proportional to the inscribed and circumscribed spheres of the different regular solids, more agreeable to *his* reason. But the shock of opinions will soon lead men to rest on preferences of a far more universal nature. Take, for example, the doctrine that man only acts selfishly—that is, from the consideration that acting in one way will afford him more pleasure than acting in another. This rests on no fact in the world, but it has had a wide acceptance as being the only reasonable theory.

This method is far more intellectual and respectable from the point of view of reason than either of the others which we have noticed. But its failure has been the most manifest. It makes of inquiry something similar to the development of taste; but taste, unfortunately, is always more or less a matter of fashion, and accordingly metaphysicians have never come to any fixed agreement, but the pendulum has swung backward and forward between a more material and a more spiritual philosophy, from the earliest times to the latest. And so from this, which has been called the *a priori* method, we are driven, in Lord Bacon's phrase, to a true induction. We have examined into this *a priori* method as something which promised to deliver our opinions from their accidental and capricious element. But development, while it is a process which eliminates the effect of some casual circumstances, only magnifies that of others. This method, therefore, does not differ in a very essential way from that of authority. The government may not have lifted its finger to influence my convictions; I may have been left outwardly quite free to choose, we will say, between monogamy and polygamy, and, appealing to my conscience only, I may have concluded that the latter practice is in itself licentious. But when I come to see that the chief obstacle to the spread of Christianity among a people of as high culture as the Hindoos has been a conviction of the immorality of our way of treating women, I cannot help seeing that, though governments do not interfere, sentiments in their development will be very greatly determined by accidental causes. Now, there are some people, among whom I must suppose that my reader is to be found, who, when they see that any belief of theirs is determined by any circumstance extraneous to the facts, will from that moment not merely admit in words that that belief is doubtful, but will experience a real doubt of it, so that it ceases in some degree to be a belief.

To satisfy our doubts, therefore, it is necessary that a method should be found by which our beliefs may be caused by nothing human, but by some external permanency—by something upon which our thinking has no effect. Some mystics imagine that they have such a method in a private inspiration from on high. But that is only a form of the method of tenacity, in which the conception of truth as something public is not yet developed. Our external permanency would not be external, in our sense, if it was restricted in its influence to one individual. It must be something which affects, or might affect, every man. And, though these affections are necessarily as various as are individual conditions, yet the method must be such that the ultimate conclusion of every man shall be the same. Such is the method of science. Its fundamental hypothesis, restated in more familiar language, is this: There are Real things, whose characters are entirely independent of our opinions about them; those realities affect our senses according to regular laws, and, though our sensations are as different as are our relations to the objects, yet, by taking advantage of the laws of perception, we can ascertain by reasoning how things really are; and any man, if he have sufficient experience and he reason enough about it, will be led to the one True conclusion. The new conception here involved is that of Reality. It may be asked how I know that there are any realities. If this hypothesis is the sole support of my method of inquiry, my method of inquiry must not be used to support my hypothesis. The reply is this: 1. If investigation cannot be regarded as proving that there are Real things, it at least does not lead to a contrary conclusion; but the method and the conception on which it is based remain ever in harmony. No doubts of the method, therefore, necessarily arise from its practice, as is the case with all the others. 2. The feeling which gives rise to any method of fixing belief is a dissatisfaction at two repugnant propositions. But here already is a vague concession that there is some *one* thing to which a proposition should conform. Nobody, therefore, can really doubt that there are realities, for, if he did, doubt would not be a source of dissatisfaction. The hypothesis, therefore, is one which every mind admits. So that the social impulse does not cause men to doubt it. 3. Everybody uses the scientific method about a great many things, and only ceases to use it when he does not know how to apply it. 4. Experience of the method has not led us to doubt it, but, on the contrary, scientific investigation has had the most wonderful triumphs in the way of settling opinion. These afford the explanation of my not doubting the method or the hypothesis which it supposes; and not having any doubt, nor believing that anybody else whom I could influence has, it would be the merest babble for me to say more about it. If there be anybody with a living doubt upon the subject, let him consider it. . . .

This is the only one of the four methods which presents any distinction of a right and a wrong way. If I adopt the method of tenacity, and shut myself out from all influences, whatever I think necessary to doing this, is necessary according to that method. So with the method of authority: the state may try to put down heresy by means which, from a scientific point of view, seem very ill-calculated to accomplish its purposes; but the only test *on that*

method is what the state thinks; so that it cannot pursue the method wrongly. So with the a priori method. The very essence of it is to think as one is inclined to think. All metaphysicians will be sure to do that, however they may be inclined to judge each other to be perversely wrong. The Hegelian system recognizes every natural tendency of thought as logical, although it is certain to be abolished by countertendencies. Hegel thinks there is a regular system in the succession of these tendencies, in consequence of which, after drifting one way and the other for a long time, opinion will at last go right. And it is true that metaphysicians get the right ideas at last; Hegel's system of Nature represents tolerably the science of that day; and one may be sure that whatever scientific investigation has put out of doubt will presently receive *a priori* demonstration on the part of the metaphysicians. But with the scientific method the case is different. I may start with known and observed facts to proceed to the unknown; and yet the rules which I follow in doing so may not be such as investigation would approve. The test of whether I am truly following the method is not an immediate appeal to my feelings and purposes, but, on the contrary, itself involves the application of the method. Hence it is that bad reasoning as well as good reasoning is possible; and this fact is the foundation of the practical side of logic.

It is not to be supposed that the first three methods of settling opinion present no advantage whatever over the scientific method. On the contrary, each has some peculiar convenience of its own. The *a priori* method is distinguished for its comfortable conclusions. It is the nature of the process to adopt whatever belief we are inclined to, and there are certain flatteries to the vanity of man which we all believe by nature, until we are awakened from our pleasing dream by rough facts. The method of authority will always govern the mass of mankind; and those who wield the various forms of organized force in the state will never be convinced that dangerous reasoning ought not to be suppressed in some way. If liberty of speech is to be untrammeled from the grosser forms of constraint, then uniformity of opinion will be secured by a moral terrorism to which the respectability of society will give its thorough approval. Following the method of authority is the path of peace. Certain non-conformities are permitted; certain others (considered unsafe) are forbidden. These are different in different countries and in different ages; but, wherever you are, let it be known that you seriously hold a tabooed belief, and you may be perfectly sure of being treated with a cruelty less brutal but more refined than hunting you like a wolf. Thus, the greatest intellectual benefactors of mankind have never dared, and dare not now, to utter the whole of their thought; and thus a shade of *prima facie* doubt is cast upon every proposition which is considered essential to the security of society. Singularly enough, the persecution does not all come from without; but a man torments himself and is oftentimes most distressed at finding himself believing propositions which he has been brought up to regard with aversion. The peaceful and sympathetic man will, therefore, find it hard to resist the temptation to submit his opinions to authority. But most of all I admire the method of tenacity for its strength, simplicity, and directness. Men who pursue it are distinguished for their decision of character, which becomes very easy with such a mental rule. They do not waste time in trying to make up their minds what they want, but, fastening like lightning upon whatever alternative comes

first, they hold it to the end, whatever happens, without an instant's irresolution. This is one of the splendid qualities which generally accompany brilliant, unlasting success. It is impossible not to envy the man who can dismiss reason, although we know how it must turn out at last.

Such are the advantages which the other methods of settling opinion have over scientific investigation. A man should consider well of them; and then he should consider that, after all, he wishes his opinions to coincide with the fact, and that there is no reason why the results of those three methods should do so. To bring about this effect is the prerogative of the method of science. Upon such considerations he has to make his choice—a choice which is far more than the adoption of any intellectual opinion, which is one of the ruling decisions of his life, to which, when once made, he is bound to adhere. The force of habit will sometimes cause a man to hold on to old beliefs, after he is in a condition to see that they have no sound basis. But reflection upon the state of the case will overcome these habits, and he ought to allow reflection its full weight. People sometimes shrink from doing this, having an idea that beliefs are wholesome which they cannot help feeling rest on nothing. But let such persons suppose an analogous though different case from their own. Let them ask themselves what they would say to a reformed Mussulman who should hesitate to give up his old notions in regard to the relations of the sexes; or to a reformed Catholic who should still shrink from reading the Bible. Would they not say that these persons ought to consider the matter fully, and clearly understand the new doctrine, and then ought to embrace it, in its entirety? But, above all, let it be considered that what is more wholesome than any particular belief is integrity of belief, and that to avoid looking into the support of any belief from a fear that it may turn out rotten is quite as immoral as it is disadvantageous. The person who confesses that there is such a thing as truth, which is distinguished from falsehood simply by this, that if acted on it will carry us to the point we aim at and not astray, and then, though convinced of this, dares not know the truth and seeks to avoid it, is in a sorry state of mind indeed.

Yes, the other methods do have their merits: a clear logical conscience does cost something—just as any virtue, just as all that we cherish, costs us dear. But we should not desire it to be otherwise. The genius of a man's logical method should be loved and reverenced as his bride, whom he has chosen from all the world. He need not contemn the others; on the contrary, he may honor them deeply, and in doing so he only honors her the more. But she is the one that he has chosen, and he knows that he was right in making that choice. And having made it, he will work and fight for her, and will not complain that there are blows to take, hoping that there may be as many and as hard to give, and will strive to be the worthy knight and champion of her from the blaze of whose splendors he draws his inspiration and his courage.

How to Make Our Ideas Clear *

I

Whoever has looked into a modern treatise on logic of the common sort, will doubtless remember the two distinctions between *clear* and *obscure* conceptions, and between *distinct* and *confused* conceptions. They have lain in the books now for nigh two centuries, unimproved and unmodified, and are generally reckoned by logicians as among the gems of their doctrine.

A clear idea is defined as one which is so apprehended that it will be recognized wherever it is met with, and so that no other will be mistaken for it. If it fails of this clearness, it is said to be obscure.

This is rather a neat bit of philosophical terminology; yet, since it is clearness that they were defining, I wish the logicians had made their definition a little more plain. Never to fail to recognize an idea, and under no circumstances to mistake another for it, let it come in how recondite a form it may, would indeed imply such prodigious force and clearness of intellect as is seldom met with in this world. On the other hand, merely to have such an acquaintance with the idea as to have become familiar with it, and to have lost all hesitancy in recognizing it in ordinary cases, hardly seems to deserve the name of clearness of apprehension, since after all it only amounts to a subjective feeling of mastery which may be entirely mistaken. I take it, however, that when the logicians speak of "clearness," they mean nothing more than such a familiarity with an idea, since they regard the quality as but a small merit, which needs

* This essay is a sequel to "The Fixation of Belief." Reprinted from *Popular Science Monthly*, 1878, with some omissions.

to be supplemented by another, which they call *distinctness*.

A distinct idea is defined as one which contains nothing which is not clear. This is technical language; by the *contents* of an idea logicians understand whatever is contained in its definition. So that an idea is *distinctly* apprehended, according to them, when we can give a precise definition of it, in abstract terms. Here the professional logicians leave the subject; and I would not have troubled the reader with what they have to say, if it were not such a striking example of how they have been slumbering through ages of intellectual activity, listlessly disregarding the enginery of modern thought, and never dreaming of applying its lessons to the improvement of logic. It is easy to show that the doctrine that familiar use and abstract distinctness make the perfection of apprehension has its only true place in philosophies which have long been extinct; and it is now time to formulate the method of attaining to a more perfect clearness of thought, such as we see and admire in the thinkers of our own time.

When Descartes set about the reconstruction of philosophy, his first step was to (theoretically) permit scepticism and to discard the practice of the schoolmen of looking to authority as the ultimate source of truth. That done, he sought a more natural fountain of true principles, and professed to find it in the human mind; thus passing, in the directest way, from the method of authority to that of a priority, as described in my first paper. Self-consciousness was to furnish us with our fundamental truths, and to decide what was agreeable to reason. But since, evidently, not all ideas are true, he was led to note, as the first condition of infallibility, that they must be clear. The distinction between an idea *seeming* clear and really being so, never occurred to him. Trusting to introspection, as he did, even for a knowledge of external things, why should he question its testimony in respect to the contents of our own minds? But then, I suppose, seeing men, who seemed to be quite clear and positive, holding opposite opinions upon fundamental principles, he was further led to say that clearness of ideas is not sufficient, but that they need also to be distinct, *i.e.*, to have nothing unclear about them. What he probably meant by this (for he did not explain himself with precision) was, that they must sustain the test of dialectical examination; that they must not only seem clear at the outset, but that discussion must never be able to bring to light points of obscurity connected with them.

Such was the distinction of Descartes, and one sees that it was precisely on the level of his philosophy. It was somewhat developed by Leibnitz. This great and singular genius was as remarkable for what he failed to see as for what he saw. That a piece of mechanism could not do work perpetually without being fed with power in some form, was a thing perfectly apparent to him; yet he did not understand that the machinery of the mind can only transform knowledge, but never originate it, unless it be fed with facts of observation. He thus missed the most essential point of the Cartesian philosophy, which is, that to accept propositions which seem perfectly evident to us is a thing which, whether it be logical or illogical, we cannot help doing. Instead of regarding the matter in this way, he sought to reduce the first principles of science to formulas which cannot be denied without self-contradiction, and was apparently unaware of the great difference between his position and that of Descartes. So he reverted to the old formalities of logic, and, above all, abstract definitions played a great part in his philosophy. It was quite natural, therefore, that on observing that the method of Descartes labored under the difficulty that we may seem to ourselves to have clear apprehensions of ideas which in truth are very hazy, no better remedy occurred to him than to require an abstract definition of every important term. Accordingly, in adopting the distinction of *clear* and *distinct* notions, he described the latter quality as the clear apprehension of everything contained in the definition; and the books have ever since copied his words. There is no danger that his chimerical scheme will ever again be overvalued. Nothing new can ever be learned by analyzing definitions. Nevertheless, our existing beliefs can be set in order by this process, and order is an essential element of intellectual economy, as of every other. It may be acknowledged, therefore, that the books are right in making familiarity with a notion the first step toward clearness of apprehension, and the defining of it the second. But in omitting all mention of any higher perspicuity of thought, they simply mirror a philosophy which was exploded a hundred years ago. That much-admired "ornament of logic"—the doctrine of clearness and distinctness—may be pretty enough, but it is high time to relegate to our cabinet of curiosities the antique *bijou,* and to wear about us something better adapted to modern uses.

The very first lesson that we have a right to demand that logic shall teach us is, how to make our ideas clear; and a most important one it is, depreciated only by minds who stand in need of it. To know what we think, to be masters of our own meaning, will make a solid foundation for great and weighty thought. It is most easily learned by those whose ideas are meager and restricted; and far happier they than such as wallow helplessly in a rich mud of conceptions. A nation, it is true, may, in the

course of generations, overcome the disadvantage of an excessive wealth of language and its natural concomitant, a vast, unfathomable deep of ideas. We may see it in history, slowly perfecting its literary forms, sloughing at length its metaphysics, and, by virtue of the untirable patience which is often a compensation, attaining great excellence in every branch of mental acquirement. The page of history is not yet unrolled which is to tell us whether such a people will or will not in the long run prevail over one whose ideas (like the words of their language) are few, but which possesses a wonderful mastery over those which it has. For an individual, however, there can be no question that a few clear ideas are worth more than many confused ones. A young man would hardly be persuaded to sacrifice the greater part of his thoughts to save the rest; and the muddled head is the least apt to see the necessity of such a sacrifice. Him we can usually only commiserate, as a person with a congenital defect. Time will help him, but intellectual maturity with regard to clearness comes rather late, an unfortunate arrangement of Nature, inasmuch as clearness is of less use to a man settled in life, whose errors have in great measure had their effect, than it would be to one whose path lies before him. It is terrible to see how a single unclear idea, a single formula without meaning, lurking in a young man's head, will sometimes act like an obstruction of inert matter in an artery, hindering the nutrition of the brain, and condemning its victim to pine away in the fullness of his intellectual vigor and in the midst of intellectual plenty. Many a man has cherished for years as his hobby some vague shadow of an idea, too meaningless to be positively false; he has, nevertheless, passionately loved it, has made it his companion by day and by night, and has given to it his strength and his life, leaving all other occupations for its sake, and in short has lived with it and for it, until it has become, as it were, flesh of his flesh and bone of his bone; and then he has waked up some bright morning to find it gone, clean vanished away like the beautiful Melusina of the fable, and the essence of his life gone with it. I have myself known such a man; and who can tell how many histories of circle-squarers, metaphysicians, astrologers, and what not, may not be told in the old German story?

II

The principles set forth in the first of these papers lead, at once, to a method of reaching a clearness of thought of a far higher grade than the "distinctness" of the logicians. We have there found that the action of thought is excited by the irritation of doubt, and ceases when belief is attained; so that the production of belief is the sole function of thought. All these words, however, are too strong for my purpose. It is as if I had described the phenomena as they appear under a mental microscope. Doubt and Belief, as the words are commonly employed, relate to religious or other grave discussions. But here I use them to designate the starting of any question, no matter how small or how great, and the resolution of it. If, for instance, in a horse-car, I pull out my purse and find a five-cent nickel and five coppers, I decide, while my hand is going to the purse, in which way I will pay my fare. To call such a question Doubt, and my decision Belief, is certainly to use words very disproportionate to the occasion. To speak of such a doubt as causing an irritation which needs to be appeased, suggests a temper which is uncomfortable to the verge of insanity. Yet, looking at the matter minutely, it must be admitted that, if there is the least hesitation as to whether I shall pay the five cop-

pers or the nickel (as there will be sure to be, unless I act from some previously contracted habit in the matter), though irritation is too strong a word, yet I am excited to such small mental activity as may be necessary to deciding how I shall act. Most frequently doubts arise from some indecision, however momentary, in our action. Sometimes it is not so. I have, for example, to wait in a railway-station, and to pass the time I read the advertisements on the walls, I compare the advantages of different trains and different routes which I never expect to take, merely fancying myself to be in a state of hesitancy, because I am bored with having nothing to trouble me. Feigned hesitancy, whether feigned for mere amusement or with a lofty purpose, plays a great part in the production of scientific inquiry. However the doubt may originate, it stimulates the mind to an activity which may be slight or energetic, calm or turbulent. Images pass rapidly through consciousness, one incessantly melting into another, until at last, when all is over—it may be in a fraction of a second, in an hour, or after long years—we find ourselves decided as to how we should act under such circumstances as those which occasioned our hesitation. In other words, we have attained belief.

In this process we observe two sorts of elements of consciousness, the distinction between which may best be made clear by means of an illustration. In a piece of music there are the separate notes, and there is the air. A single tone may be prolonged for an hour or a day, and it exists as perfectly in each second of that time as in the whole taken together; so that, as long as it is sounding, it might be present to a sense from which everything in the past was as completely absent as the future itself. But it is different with the air, the performance of which occupies a certain time, during the portions of which only portions of it are played. It consists in an orderliness in the succession of sounds which strike the ear at different times; and to perceive it there must be some continuity of consciousness which makes the events of a lapse of time present to us. We certainly only perceive the air by hearing the separate notes; yet we cannot be said to directly hear it, for we hear only what is present at the instant, and an orderliness of succession cannot exist in an instant. These two sorts of objects, what we are *immediately* conscious of and what we are *mediately* conscious of, are found in all consciousness. Some elements (the sensations) are completely present at every instant so long as they last, while others (like thought) are actions having beginning, middle, and end, and consist in a congruence in the succession of sensations which flow through the mind. They cannot be immediately present to us, but must cover some portion of the past or future. Thought is a thread of melody running through the succession of our sensations.

We may add that just as a piece of music may be written in parts, each part having its own air, so various systems of relationship of succession subsist together between the same sensations. These different systems are distinguished by having different motives, ideas, or functions. Thought is only one such system, for its sole motive, idea, and function, is to produce belief, and whatever does not concern that purpose belongs to some other system of relations. The action of thinking may incidentally have other results; it may serve to amuse us, for example, and among *dilletanti* it is not rare to find those who have so perverted thought to the purposes of pleasure that it seems to vex them to think that the questions upon which they delight to exercise it may ever get finally settled;

and a positive discovery which takes a favorite subject out of the arena of literary debate is met with ill-concealed dislike. This disposition is the very debauchery of thought. But the soul and meaning of thought, abstracted from the other elements which accompany it, though it may be voluntarily thwarted, can never be made to direct itself toward anything but the production of belief. Thought in action has for its only possible motive the attainment of thought at rest; and whatever does not refer to belief is no part of the thought itself.

And what, then, is belief? It is the demi-cadence which closes a musical phrase in the symphony of our intellectual life. We have seen that it has just three properties: First, it is something that we are aware of; second, it appeases the irritation of doubt; and, third it involves the establishment in our nature of a rule of action, or, say, for short, a *habit.* As it appeases the irritation of doubt, which is the motive for thinking, thought relaxes, and comes to rest for a moment when belief is reached. But, since belief is a rule for action, the application of which involves further doubt and further thought, at the same time that it is a stopping-place, it is also a new starting-place for thought. That is why I have permitted myself to call it thought at rest, although thought is essentially an action. The *final* upshot of thinking is the exercise of volition, and of this thought no longer forms a part; but belief is only a stadium of mental action, an effect upon our nature due to thought, which will influence future thinking.

The essence of belief is the establishment of a habit, and different beliefs are distinguished by the different modes of action to which they give rise. If beliefs do not differ in this respect, if they appease the same doubt by producing the same rule of action, then no mere differences in the manner of consciousness of them can make them different beliefs, any more than playing a tune in different keys is playing different tunes. Imaginary distinctions are often drawn between beliefs which differ only in their mode of expression;—the wrangling which ensues is real enough, however. To believe that any objects are arranged as in Fig. I, and to believe that they are arranged [as] in Fig. 2, are one

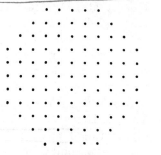

FIG. 1

and the same belief; yet it is conceivable that a man should assert one proposition and deny the other. Such false distinctions do as much harm as the confusion of beliefs really different, and are among the pitfalls of which we ought constantly to beware, especially when we are upon metaphysical ground. One singular deception of this sort, which often occurs, is to mistake the sensation produced by our own unclearness of thought for a character of the object we are thinking. Instead of perceiving that the obscurity is purely subjective, we fancy that we contemplate a quality of the object which is essentially mysterious; and if our conception be afterward presented to us in a clear form we do not recognize it as the same, owing to the absence of the feeling of unintelligibility. So long as this deception lasts, it obviously puts an impassable barrier in the way of perspicuous thinking; so that it equally interests the opponents of rational thought to perpetuate it, and its adherents to guard against it.

Another such deception is to mistake a mere difference in the grammatical construction of two words for a distinction between the ideas they express. In this pedantic age, when the general mob of writers attend so much more to words than to things, this error is common enough. When I just said that thought is an *action*, and that it consists in a *relation*, although a

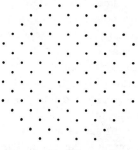

FIG. 2

person performs an action but not a relation, which can only be the result of an action, yet there was no inconsistency in what I said, but only a grammatical vagueness.

From all these sophisms we shall be perfectly safe so long as we reflect that the whole function of thought is to produce habits of action; and that whatever there is connected with a thought, but irrelevant to its purpose, is an accretion to it, but no part of it. If there be a unity among our sensations which has no reference to how we shall act on a given occasion, as when we listen to a piece of music, why, we do not call that thinking. To develop its meaning, we have, therefore, simply to determine what habits it produces, for what a thing means is simply what habits it involves. Now, the identity of a habit depends on how it might lead us to act, not merely under such circumstances as are likely to arise, but under such as might possibly occur, no matter how improbable they may be. What the habit is depends on *when* and *how* it causes us to act. As for the *when*, every stimulus to action is derived from perception; as for the *how*, every purpose of action is to produce some sensible result. Thus, we come down to what is tangible and conceivably practical, as the root of every real distinction of thought, no matter how subtle it may be; and there is no distinction of meaning so fine as to consist in anything but a possible difference of practice.

To see what this principle leads to, consider in the light of it such a doctrine as that of transubstantiation. The Protestant churches generally hold that the elements of the sacrament are flesh and blood only in a tropical sense; they nourish our souls as meat and the juice of it would our bodies. But the Catholics maintain that they are literally just that; although they possess all the sensible qualities of wafer-cakes and diluted wine. But we can have no conception of wine except what may enter into a belief, either—

1. That this, that, or the other, is wine; or,

2. That wine possesses certain properties.

Such beliefs are nothing but self-notifications that we should, upon occasion, act in regard to such things as we believe to be wine according to the qualities which we believe wine to possess. The occasion of such an action would be some sensible perception, the motive of it to produce some sensible result. Thus our action has exclusive reference to what affects the senses, our habit has the same bearing as our action, our belief the same as our habit, our conception the same as our belief; and we can consequently mean nothing by wine but what has certain effects, direct or indirect, upon our senses; and to talk of

something as having all the sensible characters of wine, yet being in reality blood, is senseless jargon. Now, it is not my object to pursue the theological question; and having used it as a logical example I drop it, without caring to anticipate the theologian's reply. I only desire to point out how impossible it is that we should have an idea in our minds which relates to anything but conceived sensible effects of things. Our idea of anything *is* our idea of its sensible effects; and if we fancy that we have any other we deceive ourselves, and mistake a mere sensation accompanying the thought for a part of the thought itself. It is absurd to say that thought has any meaning unrelated to its only function. It is foolish for Catholics and Protestants to fancy themselves in disagreement about the elements of the sacrament, if they agree in regard to all their sensible effects, here or hereafter.

It appears, then, that the rule for attaining the third grade of clearness of apprehension is as follows: Consider what effects, which might conceivably have practical bearings, we conceive the object of our conception to have. Then, our conception of these effects is the whole of our conception of the object.

III

Let us illustrate this rule by some examples; and, to begin with the simplest one possible, let us ask what we mean by calling a thing *hard*. Evidently that it will not be scratched by many other substances. The whole conception of this quality, as of every other, lies in its conceived effects. There is absolutely no difference between a hard thing and a soft thing so long as they are not brought to the test. Suppose, then, that a diamond could be crystallized in the midst of a cushion of soft cotton, and should remain there until it was finally burned up. Would it be false to say that that diamond was soft? This seems a foolish question, and would be so, in fact, except in the realm of logic. There such questions are often of the greatest utility as serving to bring logical principles into sharper relief than real discussions ever could. In studying logic we must not put them aside with hasty answers, but must consider them with attentive care, in order to make out the principles involved. We may, in the present case, modify our question, and ask what prevents us from saying that all hard bodies remain perfectly soft until they are touched, when their hardness increases with the pressure until they are scratched. Reflection will show that the reply is this: there would be no *falsity* in such modes of speech. They would involve a modification of our present usage of speech with regard to the words hard and soft, but not of their meanings. For they represent no fact to be different from what it is; only they involve arrangements of facts which would be exceedingly maladroit. This leads us to remark that the question of what would occur under circumstances which do not actually arise is not a question of fact, but only of the most perspicuous arrangement of them. For example, the question of free-will and fate in its simplest form, stripped of verbiage, is something like this: I have done something of which I am ashamed; could I, by an effort of the will, have resisted the temptation, and done otherwise? The philosophical reply is, that this is not a question of fact, but only of the arrangement of facts. Arranging them so as to exhibit what is particularly pertinent to my question—namely, that I ought to blame myself for having done wrong—it is perfectly true to say that, if I had willed to do otherwise than I did, I should have done otherwise. On the other hand, arranging the facts so as to exhibit another impor-

tant consideration, it is equally true that, when a temptation has once been allowed to work, it will, if it has a certain force, produce its effect, let me struggle how I may. There is no objection to a contradiction in what would result from a false supposition. The *reductio ad absurdum* consists in showing that contradictory results would follow from a hypothesis which is consequently judged to be false. Many questions are involved in the free-will discussion, and I am far from desiring to say that both sides are equally right. On the contrary, I am of opinion that one side denies important facts, and that the other does not. But what I do say is, that the above single question was the origin of the whole doubt; that, had it not been for this question, the controversy would never have arisen; and that this question is perfectly solved in the manner which I have indicated.

Let us next seek a clear idea of weight. This is another very easy case. To say that a body is heavy means simply that, in the absence of opposing force, it will fall. This (neglecting certain specifications of how it will fall, etc., which exist in the mind of the physicist who uses the word) is evidently the whole conception of weight. It is a fair question whether some particular facts may not *account* for gravity; but what we mean by the force itself is completely involved in its effects. . . .

IV

Let us now approach the subject of logic, and consider a conception which particularly concerns it, that of *reality*. Taking clearness in the sense of familiarity, no idea could be clearer than this. Every child uses it with perfect confidence, never dreaming that he does not understand it. As for clearness in its second grade, however, it would probably puzzle most men, even among those of a reflective turn of mind, to give an abstract definition of the real. Yet such a definition may perhaps be reached by considering the points of difference between reality and its opposite, fiction. A figment is a product of somebody's imagination; it has such characters as his thought impresses upon it. That whose characters are independent of how you or I think is an external reality. There are, however, phenomena within our own minds, dependent upon our thought, which are at the same time real in the sense that we really think them. But though their characters depend on how we think, they do not depend on what we think those characters to be. Thus, a dream has a real existence as a mental phenomenon, if somebody has really dreamt it; that he dreamt so and so, does not depend on what anybody thinks was dreamt, but is completely independent of all opinion on the subject. On the other hand, considering, not the fact of dreaming, but the thing dreamt, it retains its peculiarities by virtue of no other fact than that it was dreamt to possess them. Thus we may define the real as that whose characters are independent of what anybody may think them to be.

But, however satisfactory such a definition may be found, it would be a great mistake to suppose that it makes the idea of reality perfectly clear. Here, then, let us apply our rules. According to them, reality, like every other quality, consists in the peculiar sensible effects which things partaking of it produce. The only effect which real things have is to cause belief, for all the sensations which they excite emerge into consciousness in the form of beliefs. The question therefore is, how is true belief (or belief in the real) distinguished from false belief (or belief in fiction). Now, as we have seen in the former paper, the ideas of truth and falsehood, in their full development, apper-

tain exclusively to the scientific method of settling opinion. A person who arbitrarily chooses the propositions which he will adopt can use the word truth only to emphasize the expression of his determination to hold on to his choice. Of course, the method of tenacity never prevailed exclusively; reason is too natural to men for that. But in the literature of the dark ages we find some fine examples of it. When Scotus Erigena is commenting upon a poetical passage in which hellebore is spoken of as having caused the death of Socrates, he does not hesitate to inform the inquiring reader that Helleborus and Socrates were two eminent Greek philosophers, and that the latter having been overcome in argument by the former took the matter to heart and died of it! What sort of an idea of truth could a man have who could adopt and teach, without the qualification of a perhaps, an opinion taken so entirely at random? The real spirit of Socrates, who I hope would have been delighted to have been "overcome in argument," because he would have learned something by it, is in curious contrast with the naïve idea of the glossist, for whom discussion would seem to have been simply a struggle. When philosophy began to awake from its long slumber, and before theology completely dominated it, the practice seems to have been for each professor to seize upon any philosophical position he found unoccupied and which seemed a strong one, to intrench himself in it, and to sally forth from time to time to give battle to the others. Thus, even the scanty records we possess of those disputes enable us to make out a dozen or more opinions held by different teachers at one time concerning the question of nominalism and realism. Read the opening part of the "Historia Calamitatum" of Abelard, who was certainly as philosophical as any of his contemporaries, and see the spirit of combat which it breathes.

For him, the truth is simply his particular stronghold. When the method of authority prevailed, the truth meant little more than the Catholic faith. All the efforts of the scholastic doctors are directed toward harmonizing their faith in Aristotle and their faith in the Church, and one may search their ponderous folios through without finding an argument which goes any further. It is noticeable that where different faiths flourish side by side, renegades are looked upon with contempt even by the party whose belief they adopt; so completely has the idea of loyalty replaced that of truth-seeking. Since the time of Descartes, the defect in the conception of truth has been less apparent. Still, it will sometimes strike a scientific man that the philosophers have been less intent on finding out what the facts are, than on inquiring what belief is most in harmony with their system. It is hard to convince a follower of the *a priori* method by adducing facts; but show him that an opinion he is defending is inconsistent with what he has laid down elsewhere, and he will be very apt to retract it. These minds do not seem to believe that disputation is ever to cease; they seem to think that the opinion which is natural for one man is not so for another, and that belief will, consequently, never be settled. In contenting themselves with fixing their own opinions by a method which would lead another man to a different result, they betray their feeble hold of the conception of what truth is.

On the other hand, all the followers of science are fully persuaded that the processes of investigation, if only pushed far enough, will give one certain solution to every question to which they can be applied. One man may investigate the velocity of light by studying the transits of Venus and the aberration of the stars; another by the oppositions of Mars and the eclipses of Jupiter's satellites; a third by the method of Fizeau; a fourth by that of Foucault; a fifth by the motions of the curves of Lissajous; a sixth, a seventh, an eighth, and a ninth, may follow the different methods of comparing the measures of statical and dynamical electricity. They may at first obtain different results, but, as each perfects his method and his processes, the results will move steadily together toward a destined center. So with all scientific research. Different minds may set out with the most antagonistic views, but the progress of investigation carries them by a force outside of themselves to one and the same conclusion. This activity of thought by which we are carried, not where we wish, but to a foreordained goal, is like the operation of destiny. No modification of the point of view taken, no selection of other facts for study, no natural bent of mind even, can enable a man to escape the predestinate opinion. This great law is embodied in the conception of truth and reality. The opinion which is fated [1] to be ultimately agreed to by all who investigate, is what we mean by the truth, and the object represented in this opinion is the real. That is the way I would explain reality.

But it may be said that this view is directly opposed to the abstract definition which we have given of reality, inasmuch as it makes the characters of the real to depend on what is ultimately thought about them. But the answer to this is that, on the one hand, reality is independent, not necessarily of thought in general, but only of what you

[1] Fate means merely that which is sure to come true, and can nohow be avoided. It is a superstition to suppose that a certain sort of events are ever fated, and it is another to suppose that the word fate can never be freed from its superstitious taint. We are all fated to die. [Footnote added in later reprinting.]

or I or any finite number of men may think about it; and that, on the other hand, though the object of the final opinion depends on what that opinion is, yet what that opinion is does not depend on what you or I or any man thinks. Our perversity and that of others may indefinitely postpone the settlement of opinion; it might even conceivably cause an arbitrary proposition to be universally accepted as long as the human race should last. Yet even that would not change the nature of the belief, which alone could be the result of investigation carried sufficiently far; and if, after the extinction of our race, another should arise with faculties and disposition for investigation, that true opinion must be the one which they would ultimately come to. "Truth crushed to earth shall rise again," and the opinion which would finally result from investigation does not depend on how anybody may actually think. But the reality of that which is real does depend on the real fact that investigation is destined to lead, at last, if continued long enough, to a belief in it.

But I may be asked what I have to say to all the minute facts of history, forgotten never to be recovered, to the lost books of the ancients, to the buried secrets.

Full many a gem of purest ray serene
    The dark, unfathomed caves of ocean bear;
Full many a flower is born to blush unseen,
    And waste its sweetness on the desert air.

Do these things not really exist because they are hopelessly beyond the reach of our knowledge? And then, after the universe is dead (according to the prediction of some scientists), and all life has ceased forever, will not the shock of atoms continue though there will be no mind to know it? To this I reply that, though in no possible state of knowledge can any number

be great enough to express the relation between the amount of what rests unknown and the amount of the known, yet it is unphilosophical to suppose that, with regard to any given question (which has any clear meaning), investigation would not bring forth a solution of it, if it were carried far enough. Who would have said, a few years ago, that we could ever know of what substances stars are made whose light may have been longer in reaching us than the human race has existed? Who can be sure of what we shall not know in a few hundred years? Who can guess what would be the result of continuing the pursuit of science for ten thousand years, with the activity of the last hundred? And if it were to go on for a million, or a billion, or any number of years you please, how is it possible to say that there is any question which might not ultimately be solved?

But it may be objected, "Why make so much of these remote considerations, especially when it is your principle that only practical distinctions have a meaning?" Well, I must confess that it makes very little difference whether we say that a stone on the bottom of the ocean, in complete darkness, is brilliant or not—that is to say, that it *probably* makes no difference, remembering always that that stone *may* be fished up tomorrow. But that there are gems at the bottom of the sea, flowers in the untraveled desert, etc., are propositions which, like that about a diamond being hard when it is not pressed, concern much more the arrangement of our language than they do the meaning of our ideas.

We have, hitherto, not crossed the threshold of scientific logic. It is certainly important to know how to make our ideas clear, but they may be ever so clear without being true. . . . How to give birth to those vital and procreative ideas which multiply

into a thousand forms and diffuse themselves everywhere, advancing civilization
and making the dignity of man, is an art

not yet reduced to rules, but of the secret
of which the history of science affords some
hints.

COMMENT

The Empirical Tradition

Even before Descartes outlined his rationalistic theory of knowledge,
Francis Bacon (1561–1626), a prominent figure in the Court of Queen Elizabeth and James I of England, had set forth the basic tenets of empiricism in
his two great books *The Advancement of Learning* and *Novum Organum*.
With the intensity and earnestness of a prophet, Bacon proclaimed that induction is the true road to knowledge and that none before him had tried
this method. The statement is itself, however, a faulty induction, since even a
superficial survey of the history of science reveals that a number of Bacon's
predecessors—Roger Bacon, Leonardo da Vinci, Telesio, and Campanella,
to name but a few—were also heralds of empirical science. Even Aristotle,
whom Bacon denounced, knew very well how to handle the inductive method.
After the time of Bacon, there was a great succession of English philosophers
—Locke, Berkeley, Hume, and Mill—whose emphasis was empirical. On
the Continent, the method of empiricism has been notably represented by
the "positivists" Mach, Comte, and Poincaré.

It is customary to cite Francis Bacon as the principal representative of
empiricism, and there is much to justify the choice: He was an important
figure in the history of thought and gave eloquent expression to the faith in
science. But Bacon has not been selected here as the spokesman of empiricism
because, for our purposes, he had certain shortcomings. In particular, he
had an inadequate sense of the value of scientific imagination—the ability,
characteristic of all great scientists, to devise novel ways of explaining the
observed facts. Science can advance only by asking questions of nature—
that is, by framing and then testing hypotheses—rather than by simply accumulating and classifying data. Bacon emphasized mainly long and patient
observation, not the imaginative construction of hypotheses, which is equally
important. He was unable to tell others how "to put questions to nature," or
to do so himself. Moreover, he neglected the value of deduction in elaborating
hypotheses and working out inferences that could then be experimentally
tested. Also, he thought of science as mainly the description of nature's
qualities rather than as a measurement of nature's quantities; and this interpretation led him to minimize the importance of mathematics, the most
powerful of all methods of economizing thought and obtaining exactitude.
All in all, Bacon was a great but rather naïve prophet of the scientific method.

No one is better suited to represent the tenets of empiricism than Charles

Sanders Peirce (pronounced "purse"), the most versatile and original of American philosophers, and one of the greatest figures in the history of modern thought. Peirce is often considered a pragmatist, but his thought far transcends the limits of the pragmatic approach. As Morris R. Cohen has remarked, "Peirce's analysis of the method of science . . . is one of the best introductions to a theory of liberal or Hellenic civilization, as opposed to those of despotic societies." [1] His philosophy, in addition, constitutes an antithesis to Descartes' thesis, since it was in part conceived as an answer to Cartesianism. No one else, we contend, has criticized the rationalistic method of Descartes so profoundly, and no one has more suggestively outlined the alternative method of empiricism. Hence a consideration of Peirce will serve admirably as a contrast to the preceding section, devoted to Descartes.

The Revolt Against Cartesianism

Since "contrast is the soul of clearness," we shall begin with Peirce's very penetrating criticism of Cartesianism. It may be summarized as follows:

1. *Against the method of doubt.* Peirce sharply rejected Descartes' method of universal doubt:

> We cannot begin with complete doubt. We must begin with all the prejudices which we actually have when we enter into the study of philosophy. These prejudices are not to be dispelled by a maxim, for they are things which it does not occur to us *can* be questioned. . . . A person may, it is true, in the course of his studies, find reason to doubt what he began by believing; but in that case he doubts because he has a positive reason for it, and not on account of the Cartesian maxim. Let us not pretend to doubt in philosophy what we do not doubt in our hearts. [2]

Peirce's criticism is partly *psychological* and partly *logical.* The crux of the psychological criticism is that *real* doubt arises from the conflict of beliefs and hence involves non-doubt. It is an error to suppose that one can doubt at will. "For belief, while it lasts, is a strong habit, and as such, forces the man to believe until surprise breaks up the habit." [3] The surprise occurs when a belief comes into conflict with either some other belief or some novel experience, and a mind empty of belief cannot be surprised. If you try to doubt without such positive occasion for doubting, you are merely feigning doubt. "Do you call it *doubting* to write it down on a piece of paper that you

---

[1] *Chance, Love and Logic* (Harcourt, Brace, and Company, 1932), p. xxix.
[2] *Collected Papers of Charles Sanders Peirce,* ed. by Charles Hartshorne and Paul Weiss (Harvard University Press, 1931), V, para. 265. Following the practice of Peirce's editors, we shall hereafter give first the number of the volume, then a decimal point, then the number of the paragraph. Thus the notation of this first quotation would be 5.265. Since "The Fixation of Belief" and "How to Make Our Ideas Clear" are reprinted in the present volume, quotations from these essays have not been footnoted.
[3] 5.524.

doubt? If so, doubt has nothing to do with any serious business." [4] Underneath all the "paper doubts" will remain a solid core of beliefs, many of which will be implicit and more or less subconscious. The Cartesian method is naïve in assuming, first, that a man can be *thoroughly* aware of his beliefs and presuppositions and, second, that he can shed his beliefs at will.

Logically as well as psychologically, inquiry does not begin with an empty mind but involves beliefs as the presuppositions of inquiry. Just what these presuppositions are must be discovered *through* inquiry; but an investigator who doubted his memory, the principles of logic, the reliability of reason, and all the evidence of his senses would be completely hamstrung. The moment one advances beyond the first "self-evident" premise ("I think, therefore I am"), one must employ some of the very beliefs that one has pretended to doubt. "Descartes and others have endeavored to bolster up the light of reason by make-believe arguments from the 'veracity of God' and the like. They had better not have pretended to call that in question which they intended to prove, since the proofs, themselves, call for the same light to make them evident." [5]

2. *Against an individualistic criterion of truth.* Peirce rejected individual intuition, or "clear and distinct perception," as the test of truth, substituting a *social* criterion. The Cartesian view, it will be remembered, emphasizes intuition, defined as the individual mind's immediate insight into self-evident truth, as the ultimate source of knowledge. It thus involves a simple two-term relation between the knowing mind and the known truth—a relation that takes no account of *other* minds or *other* truths. For if the grasp of truth were dependent upon the agreement of other minds, or upon connections with other truths, it would lose its immediate and intuitive character. What guarantees the reliability of intuition is not only its immediacy but its clarity and distinctness.

According to Peirce, this Cartesian interpretation of inquiry is radically false. Descartes failed to distinguish between an idea that *seemed* clear and one that really was so, or a proposition that *seemed* self-evident and one that really was so. Philosophers have notoriously disagreed about what really is clear or self-evident. Hence the appeal to intuition simply results in assertion and counter-assertion. Peirce wittily remarked that metaphysicians who adopt the Cartesian method "will all agree that metaphysics has reached a pitch of certainty far beyond that of the physical sciences;—only they can agree on nothing else." [6] To assert, as Descartes did, that whatever is clearly and distinctly perceived is true is to abandon all tests of truth beyond in-

[4] 5.416.
[5] 2.28.
[6] 5.265.

dividual opinion. "Ideas," moreover, "may be ever so clear without being true" [7]—a fact that Descartes apparently did not grasp.

Peirce proposed a quite different approach to truth and clarity. First, he maintained that the way in which to clarify the meaning of an idea or proposition is to envisage its practical consequences. We establish clear meaning by *testing* an idea in *use*—by tracing out its concrete applications and consequences rather than by intuitive inspection or abstract definition. Secondly, Peirce contended that truth is established by public agreement rather than private insight—and not just the agreement of ignorant minds but the agreement of qualified investigators converging toward an ideal limit of accuracy and objectivity. The ultimate test of truth is that it is verified by facts open to inspection and admitted to be such by all qualified observers. So long as an "intuition" remains the object of a single individual's perspective and is not submitted to the test of *social* verification, there is nothing to guarantee its reliability. "Truth is public." [8] Thirdly, Peirce denied that we ever grasp ideas or statements in isolation and immediately discern their truth or clarity. Thinking is fundamentally contextualistic—we understand things when we relate them to other things; we connect the immediately given with the non-given. Even a very simple perception, such as your awareness of "this moment," involves such contextualistic interpretation. You are aware that it is *a* moment, a particular instance of a universal—and you are aware that it is *this* moment only because it stands in contrast to a moment ago, which you now remember, and the next moment, which you anticipate. Peirce never tired of pointing out such connections. In his theory of inquiry, he argued that we can establish the truth of statements only by fitting them into the context of our beliefs and of socially verified perceptions and judgments. It would be difficult to find a sharper contrast than that between Peirce's experimental, social, and contextualistic approach to truth and Descartes' intuitive, individual, and isolationist approach.

3. *Against the primacy of self-consciousness.* Descartes maintained that the awareness each one of us has of himself and his own mental states is the most immediate and indubitable form of knowledge. In the main, modern epistemology has accepted this point of view. Now, Peirce did not deny that in some way and to some degree each person is aware of himself and his own mental states; but he did strenuously deny that this self-knowledge is wholly immediate and private. [9] He believed that a child becomes self-conscious by comparing and contrasting himself with others, and that this process of interpreting oneself

---

[7] 5.410.
[8] Letter to William James quoted in Ralph Barton Perry, *The Thought and Character of William James* (Harvard University Press, 1935), II, p. 437.
[9] For a fuller statement of this criticism, see "Concerning Certain Faculties Claimed for Man," in *Collected Papers*, V.

through relations with others continues throughout adulthood. Consequently, self-knowledge is inseparably connected with knowledge of other people. We cannot know ourselves and our own mental states, moreover, unless our thoughts are expressed in words or other signs. Whereas Descartes had maintained that self-knowledge involves a direct two-term relation between a knowing mind and a known object ("myself"), Peirce maintained that all knowledge, including knowledge about oneself, involves at least *three* terms —sign, object signified, and interpreter. A person does not know what he is thinking, even when he is thinking about himself, unless he can put his thoughts into words or other symbols. "One's thoughts," declared Peirce, "are what he is 'saying to himself'; that is, is saying to that other self that is just coming into life in the flow of time. When one reasons, it is that critical self that one is trying to persuade; and all thought whatsoever is a sign, and is mostly in the nature of language." [10] Now, language is a means to social communication, and all words and other symbols are normally expressed in some overt, physical way, such as speaking, writing, or gesturing. Hence self-knowledge, since it is mediated through signs, involves outward, physical facts, and is social. It is therefore not prior to other forms of knowledge and has no unique, privileged status.

4. *Against the method of linear inference.* For Descartes, the attainment of knowledge involves a step-by-step process of reasoning from the simplest and clearest intuitions to the more and more complex deductions, following the one and only right order. He found the model of such reasoning in mathematics, especially Euclidean geometry. Peirce denied that it is necessary or desirable to follow such a single thread of reasoning. Even in mathematics, he pointed out, there are usually several ways of proving a theorem, and in empirical science a conclusion may be reached by many routes. "There may . . . be," he declared, "a hundred ways of thinking in passing from a premise to a conclusion." [11] And, again: "Philosophy ought to imitate the successful sciences in its method, . . . and to trust rather to the multitude and variety of its arguments than to the conclusiveness of any one. Its reasoning should not form a chain which is no stronger than its weakest link, but a cable whose fibres may be ever so slender, provided they are sufficiently numerous and intimately connected." [12]

5. *Against the quest for certainty.* Peirce believed that it is a mistake to seek, as Descartes did, for indubitable first premises and necessary deductions to certain conclusions. The notion that there are such premises and conclusions smacks of dogmatism and "blocks the road of inquiry." In oppo-

[10] 5.421.
[11] 2.54.
[12] 5.265.

sition to Descartes, Peirce urged a doctrine that he called "critical common-sensism." This doctrine may be said to consist of three main contentions:

First, the starting point of philosophy is common sense rather than indubitable intuitions. By common sense Peirce meant those fundamental beliefs that we share with almost all human beings and that our human situation forces upon us. Examples of common-sense beliefs are our conviction that fire burns, that some things are red and others blue, that we can usually trust our memories, and that there is a certain amount of order in the universe. Peirce maintained that the human mind has been conditioned by a long course of evolution to have such fundamental beliefs, and that they must be useful and generally sound to have arisen in this natural way.

Second, all opinions about matters of fact, including our common-sense beliefs, are fallible and hence subject to criticism. Peirce did not deny "that people can usually *count* with accuracy"; he did not question formal reasoning in which the sole objective is logical consistency; and he did not doubt the common-sense position that we should trust our reasoning faculties. What he said is "that people cannot obtain absolute certainty concerning matters of fact." [13] Both the factual premises and the conclusions of philosophy are never more than probable—though perhaps very highly probable.

Third, the correct method of inquiry, in philosophy as well as in science, is not Descartes' rationalistic method of intuition and deduction but an observational and experimental method. By this method we can uncover and criticize our common-sense beliefs and advance to new *probable* conclusions.

"The Fixation of Belief"

Peirce's conception of the method of inquiry is explained in his famous essays "The Fixation of Belief" and "How to Make Our Ideas Clear," reprinted in the present volume. Let us first analyze briefly "The Fixation of Belief."

After some introductory comments about the history of scientific method, Peirce discusses the object and the presuppositions of inquiry. "The object of reasoning," he declares, "is to find out, from the consideration of what we already know, something else which we do not know." This implies that we do not begin with an empty head—that some things are already known. To begin with, there are states of belief and doubt. Next, there are rules and guiding principles of reasoning, including basic rules of logic and such other more special principles of reasoning as may be involved in a particular inquiry. Finally, there are certain concepts and judgments involved even in our simplest perceptions. For example, "we can see that a thing is blue or green, but

[13] 1.149.

the quality of being blue and the quality of being green are not things which we see; they are products of logical reflection." In other words, the quality of blueness is not a particular that we perceive but a universal that we conceive, and when we "see" that a particular thing is blue, we are judging that it belongs to a *class* of things. Such judgment is immediate, unconscious, and taken for granted, but it is also fallible. We judge that something is blue when it *seems* blue to us, but it may not be blue. Once in a while a perceptual judgment turns out to be mistaken.

So far Peirce has been mainly pointing out the presuppositions of inquiry. He next considers in detail the purpose or object of inquiry. Inquiry begins as a result of the "irritation" of "real and living doubt," which arises from conflict with other beliefs or with novel environment. The doubt un-fixes belief, and the object of the inquiry is to re-fix belief by removing the irritation of doubt. "Thought in action has for its only possible motive the attainment of Thought at rest." The goal of inquiry, therefore, is "a state of satisfaction" that ends the irritation of doubt.

To understand this doctrine it is necessary to grasp what Peirce means by "belief" and "doubt." He recognizes that there is a difference between the sensations of doubting and of believing, but it is not this psychological difference that he emphasizes. There is "a practical difference" exhibited in different ways of behaving. Belief is a rule of action, and so long as it lasts, it is a strong habit. The test of belief is that we are ready to *act* on what we believe; if we have no such readiness to act, we do not believe. "Belief does not make us act at once, but puts us into such a condition that we shall behave in some certain way, when the occasion arises. Doubt has not the least such active effect, but stimulates us to inquiry until it is destroyed." When the doubt is resolved, there is once again a smoothly working habit of action. In characterizing belief and doubt in terms of action, Peirce interprets inquiry as involving overt behavior, not just inward mental processes.

But there is an inconsistency in his interpretation. If the goal of inquiry is the re-fixing of belief, it would seem that inquiry has nothing necessarily to do with truth. Indeed, Peirce says just this: "The sole object of inquiry is the settlement of opinion. We may fancy that this is not enough for us, and that we seek, not merely an opinion, but a true opinion. But put this fancy to the test, and it proves groundless; for as soon as a firm belief is reached we are entirely satisfied, whether the belief be true or false." This statement is in conflict with what he says elsewhere in the same essay: "The object of reasoning is to find out, from a consideration of what we already know, something else which we do not know. Consequently, reasoning is good if it be such as to give a true conclusion from true premises, and not otherwise. . . . The true conclusion would remain true if we had no impulse to accept it; and the false one would remain false, though we could not resist the tendency to believe in it." And, again, he declares: "A man . . . should consider that, after all, he wishes his opinions to coincide with the fact."

In later years, Peirce realized the inconsistency in these statements and renounced the view that the aim of inquiry is simply a state of satisfaction, or that the true is simply the satisfactory. He explained that the object of inquiry is a certain kind of satisfaction—the satisfaction that the truth alone can bring. Moreover, he defined truth as the conformity of our beliefs to reality, to things that exist quite independently of our feelings of satisfaction and our practical interests. According to this later statement, the object of inquiry is not merely to escape from doubt but to escape from *error*.[14]

In the original essay, Peirce goes on to distinguish four methods of fixing belief:

1. *The method of tenacity*. Many people cling tenaciously to the beliefs that they find agreeable, sealing their minds against doubt, argument, or new evidence.

2. *The method of authority*. This is the method of social indoctrination, censorship, repression, and intellectual slavery. Since the death of Peirce, it has been carried to the peak of ruthless efficiency by totalitarianism, but it is far older than the Inquisition and it is present, to some degree, in even the most liberal societies. In many respects, its success has been striking. Peirce declares: "For the mass of mankind, then, there is perhaps no better method than this. If it is their highest impulse to be intellectual slaves, then slaves they ought to remain." This remark, unless it is ironical, does less than justice to Peirce's own point of view. Actually, he was a staunch democrat and liberal who hated every form of tyranny.

3. *The method of* a priori *reason*. This is the method of those philosophers who pay very little attention to experience but seek to formulate doctrines "agreeable to reason." As an example, Peirce cites Plato's attempt to correlate astronomy with music; and in a very long footnote added in 1893 (which is here omitted) he also cites the *a priori* arguments of Descartes, Kant, and Hegel. As an example of a somewhat different type, he mentions the widespread idea that men are selfish and pleasure-seeking in all their actions—a view not supported by evidence.

4. *The method of science*. The great difference between this method and all the others is that it is based upon a realistic foundation. It assumes that: "There are Real things, whose characters are entirely independent of our opinions about them; those Reals affect our senses according to regular laws, and . . . by taking advantage of the laws of perception, we can ascertain by reasoning how things really are. . . ." The scientific criterion for judging

---

14 See Daniel J. Bronstein, "Inquiry and Meaning," in Philip P. Wiener and Frederic H. Young (eds.), *Studies in the Philosophy of Charles Sanders Peirce* (Harvard University Press, 1952), pp. 37–47, for an account of the way in which Peirce revised his opinions.

the nature of these "independent Reals" is not private inspiration but public verifiability by a community of interpreters. The mark of scientific method is that it leads competent and reasonable investigators, when confronted by adequate evidence, to reach an agreement.

If we compare the scientific method with the other three, its superiority becomes clear. It is the only method that is genuinely critical and self-corrective. None of the others can purge the mind of the dross of subjectivity and capriciousness. The method of tenacity is inherently irrational; the method of authority permits no criticism of the wisdom of the censors; the *a priori* method prompts the metaphysician to think as he is inclined to think—all three methods lack the discipline of a systematic and critical survey of the facts. On the other hand, if an investigator applies the scientific method wrongly, the rough facts will jolt him out of his mistake. Hence this is the only method that is capable of eliminating its own errors. It alone can bring about that conformity between our ideas and real things that is the sole dependable guarantee of stable beliefs.

"How to Make Our Ideas Clear"

Peirce's second essay, "How to Make Our Ideas Clear," is a sequel to "The Fixation of Belief," written for the same publication, the *Popular Science Monthly*. Unlike the first essay, it is not concerned primarily with the settlement of belief or the meaning of truth, but rather with the criterion of meaningfulness. Peirce's main purpose is to formulate a maxim for attaining clarity in our ideas and concepts.

This purpose must be understood in the light of Peirce's intellectual development. He had long been familiar with the methods of the experimental scientist. When the experimentalist does not understand the meaning of a scientific concept, hypothesis, or theory, he usually tries to clarify its meaning by some operation or experimental process. If he is confronted by two rival hypotheses, he asks himself, "What observable difference would result if I should accept one of these hypotheses rather than the other?" If no such difference is observable, he concludes that the two hypotheses have the same meaning. If an hypothesis has no observable consequences, so that it is incapable of being verified, he regards it as scientifically meaningless. Peirce hoped that this experimentalist approach to meaning might be extended to philosophical fields of inquiry. Noting the tendency of philosophers to dispute the meaning of terms, he proposed in this essay a principle of clarification akin to the method of the experimental scientist. Although he realized the impossibility of resolving philosophical disputes by laboratory experiments, he hoped to adapt the experimentalist approach to the clarification of philosophical concepts.

Writing years later (in 1905) about his "pragmatic" principle of clarification, first enunciated in "How to Make Our Ideas Clear," he said:

> . . . What is its purpose? What is it expected to accomplish? It is expected to bring to an end those prolonged disputes of philosophers which no observations of facts could settle, and yet in which each side claims to prove that the other side is in the wrong. Pragmatism maintains that in those cases the disputants must be at cross-purposes. They either attach different meanings to words, or else one side or the other (or both) uses a word without any definite meaning. What is wanted, therefore, is a method for ascertaining the real meaning of any concept, doctrine, proposition, word, or other sign.[15]

This statement formulates Peirce's principal motive in writing "How to Make Our Ideas Clear."

He takes his point of departure from Descartes' doctrine that philosophical ideas must be "clear and distinct." In the traditional books of logic, "a clear idea is defined as one which is so apprehended that it will be recognized wherever it is met with, and so that no other will be mistaken for it," and "a distinct idea is defined as one which contains nothing which is not clear." The logic books speak of two grades of clearness with respect to any idea: first, familiarity, and second, abstract definition. Peirce regards both grades as quite inadequate. We may be very familiar with an unclear idea that we never stop to analyze; and an abstract definition may be unclear because of its very abstractness—indeed, abstract terms are most in need of clarification. Hence the aim of this essay is to formulate a rule for attaining a "third grade of clearness" which will avoid the traditional appeal to mere familiarity or mere abstract definition. This third grade is to be sought in what is *more concrete* rather than more abstract.

He states his rule for attaining the third grade of clearness in two rather awkward sentences: "Consider what effects, which might conceivably have practical bearings, we conceive the object of our conception to have. Then, our conception of these effects is the whole of our conception of the object." The awkwardness results from the repetition—"conceivably," "conceive," "conception," "conception," "conception." This repetition is deliberate and was intended to prevent a possible misunderstanding. Peirce, as we have said, is proposing to clarify the more abstract by the more concrete, rather than vice versa. Hence he proposes to define meanings in terms of concrete actions and sensible effects. In discussing the meaning of the term "wine," for example, he declares that "our idea of anything *is* our idea of its sensible effects." Such statements might suggest that he finds meaning only in sensations or other concrete particulars, but this interpretation would be false. Hence, as he explains in a note written in 1906, he deliberately repeated the word "concep-

[15] 5.6.

tion" in order to emphasize that he is talking about "intellectual purport" and that he is not trying "to explain a concept . . . by anything but concepts." [16] Meaning is to be found, not in sensations or acts themselves, but in our *conceptions* of observable actions and sensible effects. Peirce was not an anti-intellectualist eschewing general ideas. He agreed with Socrates and Plato that we must try to define the meanings of *universals*, but he sought to fix these meanings by the way in which universals are exemplified by, or embodied in, *particulars*.

Another possible misunderstanding of Peirce's rule arises from his use of the word "practical." The meaning of an idea, he declares, is the conception of its practical consequences; and if, in conception, two ideas have the same practical consequences, they have the same meaning. The pragmatists, especially William James and John Dewey, have greatly emphasized this aspect of Peirce's thought. As a result, it is sometimes supposed that he denies the disinterested character of scientific inquiry. But this is a gross misinterpretation. He denounces the view that "Doing is the Be-all and the End-all of life" and insists that science is "diligent research into truth for truth's sake, without any sort of axe to grind." [17] The word "practical," as Peirce employs it, is not intended to suggest that the scientist or philosopher must have some ulterior purpose, such as to make money, or to amend his life, or to benefit his fellows. The word is employed as an *experimental,* not a moral or utilitarian, term. The meaning of an idea is best understood if we consider the *practices* involved in its use. This is the way in which an idea is clarified by an experimentalist, and this is the way that Peirce is proposing. It has nothing to do with "practicality" in the sense of being instrumental to our moral or utilitarian purposes unless by such purposes we understand the cultivation of reason. Peirce maintains that the attainment of "concrete reasonableness" is man's proper aim—and inquiry can be called a "practical" means to this goal. But such practicality *requires,* rather than precludes, objective and disinterested inquiry.

A third possible misunderstanding of Peirce's rule arises from his use of the word "consequences." The consequences of a present idea lie in the *future;* hence, if the meaning of the idea is to be found in its consequences, it might seem that all ideas necessarily refer to the future. Indeed, Peirce goes so far as to say, in an article written in 1905, that "the rational meaning of every proposition lies in the future," and that even "a belief that Christopher Columbus discovered America really refers to the future." [18] If this statement is intended to deny that we refer to the past, it is absurd, since we often have meaningful thoughts about such past events as the discovery of America. But Peirce himself often refers to our thought and knowledge of the past, and is

[16] 5.402, footnote 3.
[17] 5.429 and 1.44.
[18] 5.427 and 5.462.

quite conscious of doing so. What he means, rather, is that even an idea about the past has future consequences; if it did not, there could be no way of verifying or of discrediting it. For example, one likely consequence of the statement that "Columbus discovered America in 1492" is that we are led to expect *records* of this discovery—records which, in the future, could be consulted. It is this sort of consequence that has "practical bearing" because it offers an opportunity for scientific verification.

The real point of Peirce's emphasis on "consequences" is that, according to his view, meaningful ideas or statements are verifiable or disverifiable. Moreover, Peirce does not wish to imply that meaning is to be found solely in *actual* consequences. The consequences may be merely "conceived" or envisaged; but unless there are *some* "conceivable" consequences of a meaning, it is, according to Peirce, so unclear as to be practically worthless.

There is one other peculiarity of Peirce's language in this essay that should be noted. Although the essay is entitled "How to Make Our Ideas Clear," he more often speaks of *beliefs* than of *ideas*. This is partly because the essay is a sequel to "The Fixation of Belief" and, to a certain extent, develops the same theme expressed in the earlier essay. Another reason is that Peirce is concerned not merely with ideas in abstraction, but with ideas as they function in our beliefs about what is true or what is real. Toward the end of the essay, in a very illuminating discussion of truth and reality, he returns to a point formulated in "The Fixation of Belief"—that the mark of scientific method is that it leads competent investigators to reach an agreement. He now adds the significant contention that the very meaning of "truth" and "reality" is to be found in possible agreement among a community of investigators. Citing the way in which various scientific methods of investigating the velocity of light will finally yield the same objective conclusion, he declares:

> So with all scientific research. Different minds may set out with the most antagonistic views, but the progress of investigation carries them by a force outside themselves to one and the same conclusion. . . . The opinion which is fated to be ultimately agreed to by all who investigate is what we mean by truth, and the object represented in this opinion is the real.

This passage provides a key to the essay. The very meaning of a true statement or a real object is that it can meet the test of *social* verification. For example, saying that the moon is real or that a statement such as "the moon exists" is true can be justifiable only if all qualified observers can *see* or in some way detect the "same" body. Conversely, only one person can "see" the unreal snake which appears during delirium tremens. This interpretation of truth and reality implies that there are real things "whose characters are independent of what anybody may think them to be," and that such characters can be determined only by a community of qualified investigators converging toward an ideal limit of agreement. Now, if meaning is to have relevance to the real world it must also be determined by what is socially observable. Therefore, it must depend upon operations and objects that are *public*. Overt actions and sensible objects are public, whereas thoughts and feelings are relatively private—hence Peirce proposes that meaning be clarified by reference to such actions and objects. Only if abstractions can thus give an account of themselves in terms of concrete experience do they have any clear meaning. For example, "Let us ask what we mean by calling a thing *hard*. Evidently that it will not be scratched by many other substances. The whole conception of this quality, as of every other, lies in its conceived effects." These effects we know through public and repeatable operations, such as the act of scratching a piece of metal with a diamond point.

In Peirce's later writings, he added one very important tenet to his theory of meaning. He contended that only hypotheses that are *clear* should be admitted in scientific and philosophical inquiry. Thus his doctrine of clearness becomes a test for the admissibility of hypotheses. So long as hypotheses have "practical effects" that can be observed, they have distinctive meaning and can be verified or disverified. To understand an hypothesis means to know how to obtain evidence for or against it. If no such evidence can be obtained, the hypothesis is so vague as to be almost meaningless and hence not admissible in serious inquiry. Peirce believes that if this test were applied to metaphysical hypotheses a great and salutary house-cleaning would take place.

A Few Critical Remarks

Although Peirce's criticism of Descartes is both profound and illuminating, Peirce himself exaggerated the difference between his view of method and the Cartesian view. His attack upon the method of doubt, for example, is based partly upon misunderstanding. Descartes did not mean that he *actually* doubted the existence of an external world, the reality of other human beings, the general validity of memory, etc. Rather, he maintained that these things are not absolutely certain and therefore *can* be doubted. Peirce himself, in his doctrine of "fallibilism," carried doubt about as far as Descartes. The principal difference is that Descartes believed he had a rationalistic method whereby he could *ultimately* attain certainty in metaphysics, whereas Peirce, rejecting this rationalistic approach, maintained that the quest for certainty is a will-of-the-wisp. In this sense, Peirce was more of a doubter than Descartes.

He decried "feigned" doubts as having "nothing to do with any serious business"; but in "How to Make Our Ideas Clear" he remarks: "Feigned hesitancy, whether feigned for mere amusement or with a lofty purpose, plays a great part in the production of scientific inquiry. However the doubt may

originate, it stimulates the mind to an activity which may be slight or energetic, calm or turbulent." Here, it seems, he is really conceding the possible
value of such "feigned" doubts as Descartes entertained. For purposes of
inquiry, we may fruitfully entertain a nominal doubt so as to explore what
can be said for or against a belief. Inquiry is not necessarily prompted by "real
and living doubt": it has its own motive—curiosity or wonder. This motive
has a positive impetus which need not be called into play by the negative
stimulus of doubt.[19]

The object of inquiry, as we have seen, is not to replace the irritation of
doubt by the satisfaction of belief. Irritation might be more easily allayed and
satisfaction more quickly achieved by a stiff drink of whiskey—but inquiry
would not thereby reach its goal. The goal of inquiry is *truth,* and truth consists not in satisfaction or the re-fixing of belief but, as Peirce sometimes acknowledged, in the correspondence of our ideas with what is independently
real. In these early essays, he somewhat inconsistently clung to the plausible
but mistaken view that the goal of inquiry is the satisfaction of restored belief.

Peirce overreacted against the traditional view that meaning and truth are
to be defined in terms of mental processes, such as Descartes' intuition and *a
priori* reason. For example, he certainly exaggerated when he declared that
"the whole function" or "purpose of thought is to produce habits of action."
Thought exists no more exclusively for the sake of action than action for the
sake of thought. We often *act* so that we shall be able to think; and we often
think because we *like* to think rather than because we *need* to think. In his
later, more considered statements, Peirce did not deny this. But in the early
essays, he was reacting so strongly against the intuitional and rationalistic
method that he exaggerated the role of overt actions and sensible effects in the
business of inquiry.

An example of such exaggeration is provided by his discussion of Catholic
and Protestant interpretations of the wine used in the communion service. He
declared that "we can . . . mean nothing by wine but what has certain effects, direct or indirect, upon our senses; and to talk of something as having
all the sensible characters of wine, yet being in reality blood, is senseless
jargon." In attributing to Catholics the "senseless" belief that the wine is
"literally" blood, he was being, if not inaccurate, at least overly simple. The
official Catholic view was stated by the Council of Trent in 1547:

> If any one shall say that in the Holy Sacrament of the Eucharist there
> remains, together with the Body and Blood of Our Lord Jesus Christ, the
> substance of the Bread and Wine, and shall deny that wonderful and singular
> conversion is of the whole substance of the Bread into (His) Body and of

---

[19] For a penetrating criticism of Peirce on this score, see Arthur F. Smullyan, "Some Implications
of Critical Common-sensism," in Wiener and Young, *op. cit.,* pp. 113–115.

the Wine into (His) Blood, the species only of the Bread and Wine remaining—which conversion the Catholic Church most fittingly calls Transubstantiation—let him be anathema.

To understand this statement, it is necessary to realize that the word "substance" was used for the *inward reality* as distinguished from outward appearance, and that the word "species" meant *outward appearance* rather than inward reality. The doctrine, therefore, is that the appearance—the color, odor, taste, etc.—of the bread and wine remains the same throughout the communion service, but that the hidden and underlying substance is changed by a "miracle of transubstantiation" to a kind of identity with the Body and Blood of Jesus. Moreover, the bread or wine, when employed in the service, is a *symbol* of communion which *spiritually* unites the congregation. The words of Jesus, "Where two or three are gathered together" in Christian communion ("in my name"), move forward to the conclusion, "there am I in their midst." Both Catholics and orthodox Protestants, however much they may differ about the precise meaning of the sacramental bread and wine, accept this conclusion, which cannot be fully understood in a literalistic sense. Now, such a spiritual meaning, even though it does have outward consequences, is certainly not reducible to the conception of "sensible" effects or characteristics. The distinction between "substance" as inward reality and "species" as outward appearance is also not reducible to any merely sensible phenomena, yet it is not utterly devoid of meaning.

There are many meanings, in philosophical as well as in religious discourse, that cannot be explicated or clarified simply in terms of overt actions, sensible effects, or experimental operations. Whether we are searching for meaning or for truth, we should not neglect what happens within the human mind, even though these happenings are not open to direct public inspection. The illustrations that best serve to elucidate Peirce's theory of clarification and inquiry are taken from experimental science, but the question of how far the logical techniques of experimental science are adaptable to philosophical inquiry is debatable.

We are asked to distinguish meanings in terms of their "experimental" or "public" effects; but this method of clarification does not tell us what the meanings *are* as present in consciousness—it tells us only what the *effects* of these meanings are. Peirce's assumption is that we can infer diversity of meanings from diversity of effects and identity of meaning from identity of effects. But as Arthur O. Lovejoy, in criticizing Peirce's theory, has pointed out, such inferences are not always sound—there may be identity in effect but difference in cause.[20] The slamming of a door, for example, may be caused by either a gust of wind or a movement of an arm. Hence one cannot safely infer the nature of the cause from the character of the effect—and this is true even

[20] *Cf.* Lovejoy, "What Is the Pragmaticist Theory of Meaning? The First Phase," in *ibid.*, p. 11.

when the cause is a meaning and the effect is some overt action or sensible event. The fact is that such effects may be far too gross to permit subtle discriminations in meaning. Reference to physical actions and sensible effects may be very useful in the clarification of meanings, but it is no substitute for the direct inspection of meanings as present to a conscious and critical mind.

Nevertheless, Peirce's interpretation of inquiry, especially his account of the realistic and social basis of truth and meaning, is very rich in insights. To fully appreciate him, we should consider the much wider compass of his philosophy—a task far beyond the scope of this book. But perhaps we have said enough to indicate that he is one of the towering figures in the history of modern thought.

5

The Way of the Pragmatist

WILLIAM JAMES (1842–1910)

Born in New York City in 1842, William James grew up in a family remarkable for its high spirits, intelligence, and congeniality. His father, Henry James, Senior, a man of intense religious and philosophical disposition, used his considerable inherited fortune to surround his five children with an atmosphere of culture. The family traveled a great deal, and William, like his sister and three brothers, was educated in various schools in the United States, England, France, Germany, and Switzerland. Thus he acquired the cosmopolitanism and *savoir faire* which distinguished him throughout his life. Uncertain of the choice of a career, he dabbled in painting, then studied chemistry, physiology, and medicine at Harvard. Still unable to reach a decision, he accompanied Louis Agassiz, the great naturalist, on a field trip up the Amazon, and spent the next two years studying in Europe, mainly Germany. During this period and the subsequent three years, which he spent in America, he suffered from a profound mental depression, at times even considering suicide.

Although he completed the work for his Doctor's degree at the Harvard Medical School in 1869, it was not until 1872, when he was appointed to the post of Instructor in Physiology at Harvard, that he found regular employment. This appointment, which he called "a perfect God-send to me," contributed to a happier outlook. The last traces of his morbid mental state had apparently disappeared by 1878, when he married Miss Alice Gibbens.

By this time, aged 36, he was an established teacher of physiology and psychology at Harvard. In 1880, he became Assistant Professor of Philosophy and before long Professor. During his tenure, the Department of Philosophy attained a high point of distinction, including among its faculty Josiah Royce, Hugo Münsterberg, and George Santayana. James' own importance as an original thinker was established with the publication, in 1890, of his master work, *Principles of Psychology*, the product of eleven years of labor. Although he finally won great acclaim as a philosopher, he never succeeded in writing a philosophical work as substantial and comprehensive as this great treatise in psychology.

Among his favorite recreations was mountain climbing. In June 1899, while climbing alone in the Adirondacks, he lost his way and overstrained his heart in a desperate thirteen-hour scramble. The result was an irreparable lesion, which forced him to curtail his intellectual activities. Finally, in 1910, his heart trouble became very serious, and he died in his New Hampshire home in August of that year.

Witty, kindly, urbane, but restless and neurasthenic, James was a remarkably complex and attractive character—"a being," to quote his sister, "who would bring life and charm to a treadmill." This charm he communicated in his writing, which often lends a rollicking sprightliness to the most abstruse subjects. Despite his artistic flair, he had the scientist's keen sense of fact and the moralist's high seriousness. But his seriousness was never stuffy—he was always opposed to the snobs, the dogmatists, the dry-as-dusts, and the goody-goodies that would fence in the human spirit.

What Pragmatism Means[*]

Some years ago, being with a camping party in the mountains, I returned from a solitary ramble to find every one engaged in a ferocious metaphysical dispute. The *corpus* of the dispute was a squirrel—a live squirrel supposed to be clinging to one side of a tree-trunk; while over against the tree's opposite side a human being was imagined to stand. This human witness tries to get sight of the squirrel by moving rapidly round the tree, but no matter how fast he goes, the squirrel moves as fast in the opposite direction, and always keeps the tree between himself and the man, so that never a glimpse of him is caught. The resultant metaphysical problem now is this: *Does the man go round the squirrel or not?* He goes round the tree, sure enough, and the squir-

rel is on the tree; but does he go round the squirrel? In the unlimited leisure of the wilderness, discussion had been worn threadbare. Every one had taken sides, and was obstinate; and the numbers on both sides were even. Each side, when I appeared, therefore appealed to me to make it a majority. Mindful of the scholastic adage that whenever you meet a contradiction you must make a distinction, I immediately sought and found one, as follows: "Which party is right," I said, "depends on what you *practically mean* by 'going round' the squirrel. If you mean passing from the north of him to the east, then to the south, then to the west, and then to the north of him again, obviously the man does go round him, for he occupies these successive posi-

* From *Pragmatism: A New Name for Some Old Ways of Thinking*, Lectures II and VI. New York: Longmans, Green and Company, 1907. Reprinted by permission.

tions. But if on the contrary you mean being first in front of him, then on the right of him, then behind him, then on his left, and finally in front again, it is quite as obvious that the man fails to go round him, for by the compensating movements the squirrel makes, he keeps his belly turned towards the man all the time, and his back turned away. Make the distinction, and there is no occasion for any further dispute. You are both right and both wrong according as you conceive the verb 'to go round' in one practical fashion or the other."

Although one or two of the hotter disputants called my speech a shuffling evasion, saying they wanted no quibbling or scholastic hair-splitting, but meant just plain honest English "round," the majority seemed to think that the distinction had assuaged the dispute.

I tell this trivial anecdote because it is a peculiarly simple example of what I wish now to speak of as *the pragmatic method*. The pragmatic method is primarily a method of settling metaphysical disputes that otherwise might be interminable. Is the world one or many?—fated or free?—material or spiritual?—here are notions either of which may or may not hold good of the world; and disputes over such notions are unending. The pragmatic method in such cases is to try to interpret each notion by tracing its respective practical consequences. What difference would it practically make to any one if this notion rather than that notion were true? If no practical difference whatever can be traced, then the alternatives mean practically the same thing, and all dispute is idle. Whenever a dispute is serious, we ought to be able to show some practical difference that must follow from one side or the other's being right.

A glance at the history of the idea will show you still better what pragmatism means. The term is derived from the same Greek word πράγμα, meaning action, from which our words "practice" and "practical" come. It was first introduced into philosophy by Mr. Charles Peirce in 1878. In an article entitled "How to Make Our Ideas Clear," in the *Popular Science Monthly* for January of that year Mr. Peirce, after pointing out that our beliefs are really rules for action, said that, to develop a thought's meaning, we need only determine what conduct it is fitted to produce: that conduct is for us its sole significance. And the tangible fact at the root of all our thought-distinctions, however subtle, is that there is no one of them so fine as to consist in anything but a possible difference of practice. To attain perfect clearness in our thoughts of an object, then, we need only consider what conceivable effects of a practical kind the object may involve—what sensations we are to expect from it, and what reactions we must prepare. Our conception of these effects, whether immediate or remote, is then for us the whole of our conception of the object, so far as that conception has positive significance at all.

This is the principle of Peirce, the principle of pragmatism. It lay entirely unnoticed by any one for twenty years, until I, in an address before Professor Howison's Philosophical Union at the University of California, brought it forward again and made a special application of it to religion. By that date (1898) the times seemed ripe for its reception. The word "pragmatism" spread, and at present it fairly spots the pages of the philosophic journals. On all hands we find the "pragmatic movement" spoken of, sometimes with respect, sometimes with contumely, seldom with clear understanding. It is evident that the term applies itself conveniently to a number of tendencies that hitherto have lacked a collective name, and that it has "come to stay."

To take in the importance of Peirce's principle, one must get accustomed to applying it to concrete cases. I found a few years ago that Ostwald, the illustrious Leipzig chemist, had been making perfectly distinct use of the principle of pragmatism in his lectures on the philosophy of science, though he had not called it by that name.

"All realities influence our practice," he wrote me, "and that influence is their meaning for us. I am accustomed to put questions to my classes in this way: In what respects would the world be different if this alternative or that were true? If I can find nothing that would become different, then the alternative has no sense."

That is, the rival views mean practically the same thing, and meaning, other than practical, there is for us none. Ostwald in a published lecture gives this example of what he means. Chemists have long wrangled over the inner constitution of certain bodies called "tautomerous." Their properties seemed equally consistent with the notion that an instable hydrogen atom oscillates inside of them, or that they are instable mixtures of two bodies. Controversy raged, but never was decided. "It would never have begun," says Ostwald, "if the combatants had asked themselves what particular experimental fact could have been made different by one or the other view being correct. For it would then have appeared that no difference of fact could possibly ensue; and the quarrel was as unreal as if, theorizing in primitive times about the raising of dough by yeast, one party should have invoked a 'brownie,' while another insisted on an 'elf' as the true cause of the phenomenon." [1]

It is astonishing to see how many philosophical disputes collapse into insignificance the moment you subject them to this simple test of tracing a concrete consequence. There can *be* no difference anywhere that doesn't *make* a difference elsewhere—no difference in abstract truth that doesn't express itself in a difference in concrete fact and in conduct consequent upon that fact, imposed on somebody, somehow, somewhere, and somewhen. The whole function of philosophy ought to find out what definite difference it will make to you and me, at definite instants of our life, if this world-formula or that world-formula be the true one.

There is absolutely nothing new in the pragmatic method. Socrates was an adept at it. Aristotle used it methodically. Locke, Berkeley, and Hume made momentous contributions to truth by its means. Shadworth Hodgson keeps insisting that realities are only what they are "known as." But these forerunners of pragmatism used it in fragments: they were preluders only. Not until in our time has it generalized itself, become conscious of a universal mission, pretended to a conquering destiny. I believe in that destiny, and I hope I may end by inspiring you with my belief.

Pragmatism represents a perfectly familiar attitude in philosophy, the empiricist attitude, but it represents it, as it seems to me, both in a more radical and in a less objectionable form than it has ever yet assumed. A pragmatist turns his back resolutely and once for all upon a lot of inveterate habits dear to professional philoso-

---

[1] "Theorie und Praxis," *Zeitschrift des Oesterreich-ischen Ingenieur-u. Architecten-Vereines*, 1905, Nr.

4 u. 6. I find a still more radical pragmatism than Ostwald's in an address by Professor W. S. Franklin: "I think that the sickliest notion of physics, even if a student gets it, is that it is 'the science of masses, molecules, and the ether.' And I think that the healthiest notion, even if a student does not wholly get it, is that physics is the science of the ways of taking hold of bodies and pushing them!" (*Science*, January 2, 1903.)

phers. He turns away from abstraction and insufficiency, from verbal solutions, from bad *a priori* reasons, from fixed principles, closed systems, and pretended absolutes and origins. He turns towards concreteness and adequacy, towards facts, towards action and towards power. That means the empiricist temper regnant and the rationalist temper sincerely given up. It means the open air and possibilities of nature, as against dogma, artificiality, and the pretence of finality in truth.

At the same time it does not stand for any special results. It is a method only. But the general triumph of that method would mean an enormous change in . . . the "temperament" of philosophy. Teachers of the ultra-rationalistic type would be frozen out, much as the courtier type is frozen out in republics, as the ultramontane type of priest is frozen out in protestant lands. Science and metaphysics would come much nearer together, would in fact work absolutely hand in hand.

Metaphysics has usually followed a very primitive kind of quest. You know how men have always hankered after unlawful magic, and you know what a great part in magic *words* have always played. If you have his name, or the formula of incantation that binds him, you can control the spirit, genie, afrite, or whatever the power may be. Solomon knew the names of all the spirits, and having their names, he held them subject to his will. So the universe has always appeared to the natural mind as a kind of enigma, of which the key must be sought in the shape of some illuminating or power-bringing word or name. That word names the universe's *principle,* and to possess it is after a fashion to possess the universe itself. "God," "Matter," "Reason," "the Absolute," "Energy," are so many solving names. You can rest when you have

them. You are at the end of your metaphysical quest.

But if you follow the pragmatic method, you cannot look on any such word as closing your quest. You must bring out of each word its practical cash-value, set it at work within the stream of your experience. It appears less as a solution, then, than as a program for more work, and more particularly as an indication of the ways in which existing realities may be *changed.*

Theories thus become instruments, not answers to enigmas, in which we can rest. We don't lie back upon them, we move forward, and, on occasion, make nature over again by their aid. Pragmatism unstiffens all our theories, limbers them up and sets each one at work. Being nothing essentially new, it harmonizes with many ancient philosophic tendencies. It agrees with nominalism, for instance, in always appealing to particulars; with utilitarianism in emphasizing practical aspects; with positivism in its disdain for verbal solutions, useless questions and metaphysical abstractions.

All these, you see, are *anti-intellectualist* tendencies. Against rationalism as a pretension and a method pragmatism is fully armed and militant. But, at the outset, at least, it stands for no particular results. It has no dogmas, and no doctrines save its method. As the young Italian pragmatist Papini has well said, it lies in the midst of our theories, like a corridor in a hotel. Innumerable chambers open out of it. In one you may find a man writing an atheistic volume; in the next some one on his knees praying for faith and strength; in a third a chemist investigating a body's properties. In a fourth a system of idealistic metaphysics is being excogitated; in a fifth the impossibility of metaphysics is being shown. But they all own the corridor, and all must pass through it if they want a practicable way of getting into or out of their respective rooms.

No particular results then, so far, but only an attitude of orientation, is what the pragmatic method means. *The attitude of looking away from first things, principles, "categories," supposed necessities; and of looking towards last things, fruits, consequences, facts.*

So much for the pragmatic method! . . . Meanwhile the word pragmatism has come to be used in a still wider sense, as meaning also a certain *theory of truth.* . . .

Truth, as any dictionary will tell you, is a property of certain of our ideas. It means their "agreement," as falsity means their "disagreement," with "reality." Pragmatists and intellectualists both accept this definition as a matter of course. They begin to quarrel only after the question is raised as to what may precisely be meant by the term "agreement," and what by the term "reality," when reality is taken as something for our ideas to agree with.

In answering these questions the pragmatists are more analytic and painstaking, the intellectualists more offhand and irreflective. The popular notion is that a true idea must copy its reality. Like other popular views, this one follows the analogy of the most usual experience. Our true ideas of sensible things do indeed copy them. Shut your eyes and think of yonder clock on the wall, and you get just such a true picture or copy of its dial. But your idea of its "works" (unless you are a clockmaker) is much less of a copy, yet it passes muster, for it in no way clashes with the reality. Even though it should shrink to the mere word "works," that word still serves you truly; and when you speak of the "time-keeping function" of the clock, or of its spring's "elasticity," it is hard to see exactly what your ideas can copy.

You perceive that there is a problem here. Where our ideas cannot copy definitely their object, what does agreement with that object mean? Some idealists seem to say that they are true whenever they are what God means that we ought to think about that subject. Others hold the copy-view all through, and speak as if our ideas possessed truth just in proportion as they approach to being copies of the Absolute's eternal way of thinking.

These views, you see, invite pragmatistic discussion. But the great assumption of the intellectualists is that truth means essentially an inert static relation. When you've got your true idea of anything, there's an end of the matter. You're in possession; you *know;* you have fulfilled your thinking destiny. You are where you ought to be mentally; you have obeyed your categorical imperative; and nothing more need follow on that climax of your rational destiny. Epistemologically you are in stable equilibrium.

Pragmatism, on the other hand, asks its usual question. "Grant an idea or belief to be true," it says, "what concrete difference will its being true make in any one's actual life? How will the truth be realized? What experiences will be different from those which would obtain if the belief were false? What, in short, is the truth's cash-value in experiential terms?"

The moment pragmatism asks this question, it sees the answer: *True ideas are those that we can assimilate, validate, corroborate and verify. False ideas are those that we cannot.* That is the practical difference it makes to us to have true ideas; that, therefore, is the meaning of truth, for it is all that truth is known-as.

This thesis is what I have to defend. The truth of an idea is not a stagnant property inherent in it. Truth *happens* to an idea. It *becomes* true, is *made* true by events. Its verity *is* in fact an event, a process: the process namely of its verifying itself, its veri-*fication*. Its validity is the process of its valid-*ation*.

But what do the words verification and validation themselves pragmatically mean? They again signify certain practical consequences of the verified and validated idea. It is hard to find any one phrase that characterizes these consequences better than the ordinary agreement-formula—just such consequences being what we have in mind whenever we say that our ideas "agree" with reality. They lead us, namely, through the acts and other ideas which they instigate, into or up to, or towards, other parts of experience with which we feel all the while—such feeling being among our potentialities—that the original ideas remain in agreement. The connections and transitions come to us from point to point as being progressive, harmonious, satisfactory. This function of agreeable leading is what we mean by an idea's verification. . . .

To "agree" in the widest sense with a reality *can only mean to be guided either straight up to it or into its surroundings, or to be put into such working touch with it as to handle either it or something connected with it better than if we disagreed.* Better either intellectually or practically! And often agreement will only mean the negative fact that nothing contradictory from the quarter of that reality comes to interfere with the way in which our ideas guide us elsewhere. To copy a reality is, indeed, one very important way of agreeing with it, but it is far from being essential. The essential thing is the process of being guided. Any idea that helps us to *deal*, whether practically or intellectually, with either the reality or its belongings, that doesn't entangle our progress in frustrations, that *fits*, in fact, and adapts our life to the reality's whole setting, will agree sufficiently to meet the requirement. It will hold true of that reality.

Thus, *names* are just as "true" or "false" as definite mental pictures are. They set up similar verification-processes, and lead to fully equivalent practical results. . . .

The overwhelming majority of our true ideas admit of no direct or face-to-face verification—those of past history, for example, as of Cain and Abel. The stream of time can be remounted only verbally, or verified indirectly by the present prolongations or effects of what the past harbored. Yet if they agree with these verbalities and effects, we can know that our ideas of the past are true. *As true as past time itself was,* so true was Julius Caesar, so true were antediluvian monsters, all in their proper dates and settings. That past time itself was, is guaranteed by its coherence with everything that's present. True as the present *is*, the past *was* also.

Agreement thus turns out to be essentially an affair of leading—leading that is useful because it is into quarters that contain objects that are important. True ideas lead us into useful verbal and conceptual quarters as well as directly up to useful sensible termini. They lead to consistency, stability and flowing human intercourse. They lead away from eccentricity and isolation, from foiled and barren thinking. The untrammeled flowing of the leading-process, its general freedom from clash and contradiction, passes for its indirect verification; but all roads lead to Rome, and in the end and eventually, all true processes must lead to the face of directly verifying sensible experiences *somewhere*, which somebody's ideas have copied.

Such is the large loose way in which the pragmatist interprets the word agreement. He treats it altogether practically. He lets it cover any process of conduction from a present idea to a future terminus, provided only it run prosperously. It is only thus that "scientific" ideas, flying as they do beyond common sense, can be said to agree with their realities. It is, as I have already said, *as if* reality were made of ether, atoms or electrons, but we mustn't think so literally. The term "energy" doesn't even pretend to stand for anything "objective." It is only a way of measuring the surface of phenomena so as to string their changes on a simple formula.

Yet in the choice of these man-made formulas we cannot be capricious with impunity any more than we can be capricious on the common-sense practical level. We must find a theory that will *work;* and that means something extremely difficult; for our theory must mediate between all previous truths and certain new experiences. It must derange common sense and previous belief as little as possible, and it must lead to some sensible terminus or other that can be verified exactly. To "work" means both these things; and the squeeze is so tight that there is little loose play for any hypothesis. Our theories are wedged and controlled as nothing else is. Yet sometimes alternative theoretic formulas are equally compatible with all the truths we know, and then we choose between them for subjective reasons. We choose the kind of theory to which we are already partial; we follow "elegance" or "economy." Clerk-Maxwell somewhere says it would be "poor scientific taste" to choose the more complicated of two equally well-evidenced conceptions; and you will all agree with him. Truth in science is what gives us the maximum possible sum of satisfactions, taste included, but consistency both with previous truth and with novel fact is always the most imperious claimant. . . .

Our account of truth is an account of truths in the plural, of processes of leading, realized *in rebus* [in things], and having only this quality in common, that they *pay*. They pay by guiding us into or towards some part of a system that dips at numerous points into sense-percepts, which we may copy mentally or not, but with which at any rate we are now in the kind of commerce vaguely designated as verification. Truth for us is simply a collective name for verification-processes, just as health, wealth, strength, etc., are names for other processes connected with life, and also pursued because it pays to pursue them. Truth is *made,* just as health, wealth and strength are made, in the course of experience. . . .

"The true," to put it very briefly, *is only the expedient in the way of our thinking, just as "the right" is only the expedient in the way of our behaving.* Expedient in almost any fashion; and expedient in the long run and on the whole of course; for what meets expediently all the experience in sight won't necessarily meet all further experiences equally satisfactorily. Experience, as we know, has ways of *boiling over,* and making us correct our present formulas.

The "absolutely" true, meaning what no further experience will ever alter, is that ideal vanishing-point towards which we imagine that all our temporary truths will some day converge. It runs on all fours with the perfectly wise man, and with the absolutely complete experience; and, if these ideals are ever realized, they will all be realized together. Meanwhile we have to live today by what truth we can get today, and be ready tomorrow to call it falsehood. Ptolemaic astronomy, Euclidean space, Aristotelian logic, Scholastic metaphysics, were expedient for centuries, but human experience has boiled over those limits, and we now call these things only relatively true, or true within those borders of experience. "Absolutely" they are false; for we know that those limits were casual, and might have been transcended by past theorists just as they are by present thinkers. . . .

The trail of the human serpent is thus over everything. Truth independent; truth that we *find* merely; truth no longer malleable to human need; truth incorrigible, in a word; such truth exists indeed superabundantly—or is supposed to exist by rationalistically minded thinkers; but then it means only the dead heart of the living tree, and its being there means only that truth also has its paleontology, and its "prescription," and may grow stiff with years of veteran service and petrified in men's regard by sheer antiquity. But how plastic even the oldest truths nevertheless really are has been vividly shown in our day by the transformation of logical and mathematical ideas, a transformation which seems even to be invading physics. The ancient formulas are reinterpreted as special expressions of much wider principles, principles that our ancestors never got a glimpse of in their present shape and formulation. . . .

Such then would be the scope of pragmatism—first, a method; and second, a genetic theory of what is meant by truth.

JOHN DEWEY (1859–1952)

John Dewey was born in the beautiful New England town of Burlington, Vermont. "All my forefathers," he has said, "earned an honest living as farmers, wheelwrights, coopers. I was absolutely the first one in seven generations to fall from grace." [1] But his father, a grocer, loved to recite from Shakespeare and Milton, and his parents gave their four sons the advantages of a college education and of a liberal moral and religious outlook. John took his undergraduate degree at the University of Vermont and his Doctor's degree in Philosophy at Johns Hopkins in 1884.

He taught at the University of Michigan from 1884 until 1894 (except for one year at the University of Minnesota), and then, for an additional ten-year period, at the University of Chicago. During these years, he gradually shifted from Hegelian idealism to his own version of pragmatism, or, as he preferred to call it, "instrumentalism." His ideas had begun to cause some controversy even before he went to Chicago, but this was mild compared with the storm that broke out when he began to apply his pragmatic ideals as director of the "Laboratory School" for children at the University of Chicago. Aided by his wife, for seven and a half years Dewey conducted a bold educational experiment based on the concepts of "learning by doing" and "education for democracy." Whereas traditional education had sought to instill obedience and receptivity, he sought to cultivate activity, initiative, diversity, and voluntary cooperation; and in so doing, he wrought a veritable revolution in educational theory and practice. The volume in which he explained what he was trying to do, *School and Society,* was first published in 1899 and has since been trans-

---

[1] Edwin E. Slosson, *Six Major Prophets* (Boston: Little, Brown, 1917), p. 268. (From a letter of Dewey to Slosson.)

lated into a dozen European and Oriental languages and reprinted many times.

Having achieved fame both as an educator and as a philosopher, Dewey in 1904 was called to Columbia University, where he remained until his retirement in 1929. With prodigious energy, he poured forth an immense volume of publications and engaged in many educational, political, and civic activities. In 1919 he lectured at the Imperial University of Japan in Tokyo, and during the next two years at the National Universities at Peking and at Nanking, where he made a profound impression upon Chinese students and intellectuals. For briefer periods he visited Turkey in 1924, Mexico in 1926, and Soviet Russia in 1928. Later he served as a member of the international Commission of Inquiry into the charges made against Leon Trotsky at the famous Moscow trial of Trotsky's alleged confederates. This Commission, which met in Mexico City, finally issued a report, *Not Guilty* (1937), which became the object of heated political controversy.

During the later years of his life, Dewey's interests continued to broaden, as indicated by the wide range of his writings—on education, religion, art, politics, ethics, logic, epistemology, and metaphysics. His many social and intellectual activities, however, did not prevent him from rearing a large family and forming many warm personal friendships. When he died at the age of ninety-two, he had had a more comprehensive and profound impact on the modern world than any other American philosopher.

His personality was not as vivid as James', and his literary style is not as readable. Modest, unobtrusive, somewhat halting in speech, and ultra-democratic in manner, Dewey the human being has sometimes seemed to be quite different from Dewey the bold and independent thinker. This contrast has led many people to misinterpret and vulgarize his ideas and to underestimate his native radicalism. But if, as has been claimed, Dewey is more representative of democratic America than any other thinker, it is an intellectually adventurous and daring America that he represents.

The Influence of Darwinism on Philosophy *

I

That the publication of *The Origin of Species* marked an epoch in the development of the natural sciences is well known to the layman. That the combination of the very words origin and species embodied an intellectual revolt and introduced

* From *The Influence of Darwin on Philosophy and Other Essays in Contemporary Thought*. New York: Henry Holt and Company, 1910. Reprinted by permission.

a new intellectual temper is easily overlooked by the expert. The conceptions that had reigned in the philosophy of nature and knowledge for two thosuand years, the conceptions that had become the familiar furniture of the mind, rested on the assumption of the superiority of the fixed and final; they rested upon treating change and origin as signs of defect and unreality. In laying hands upon the sacred ark of absolute permanency, in treating the forms that had been regarded as types of fixity and perfection as originating and passing away, *The Origin of Species* introduced a mode of thinking that in the end was bound to transform the logic of knowledge, and hence the treatment of morals, politics, and religion.

No wonder, then, that the publication of Darwin's book, a half century ago, precipitated a crisis. The true nature of the controversy is easily concealed from us, however, by the theological clamor that attended it. The vivid and popular features of the anti-Darwinian row tended to leave the impression that the issue was between science on one side and theology on the other. Such was not the case—the issue lay primarily within science itself, as Darwin himself early recognized. The theological outcry he discounted from the start, hardly noticing it save as it bore upon the "feelings of his female relatives." But for two decades before final publication he contemplated the possibility of being put down by his scientific peers as a fool or as crazy; and he set, as the measure of his success, the degree in which he should affect three men of science: Lyell in geology, Hooker in botany, and Huxley in zoölogy.

Religious considerations lent fervor to the controversy, but they did not provoke it. Intellectually, religious emotions are not creative but conservative. They attach themselves readily to the current view of the world and consecrate it. They steep and dye intellectual fabrics in the seething vat of emotions; they do not form their warp and woof. There is not, I think, an instance of any large idea about the world being independently generated by religion. Although the ideas that rose up like armed men against Darwinism owed their intensity to religious associations, their origin and meaning are to be sought in science and philosophy, not in religion.

II

Few words in our language foreshorten intellectual history as much as does the word species. The Greeks, in initiating the intellectual life of Europe, were impressed by characteristic traits of the life of plants and animals; so impressed indeed that they made these traits the key to defining nature and to explaining mind and society. And truly, life is so wonderful that a seemingly successful reading of its mystery might well lead men to believe that the key to the secrets of heaven and earth was in their hands. The Greek rendering of this mystery, the Greek formulation of the aim and standard of knowledge, was in the course of time embodied in the word species, and it controlled philosophy for two thousand years. To understand the intellectual face-about expressed in the phrase "Origin of Species," we must, then, understand the long dominant idea against which it is a protest.

Consider how men were impressed by the facts of life. Their eyes fell upon certain things slight in bulk, and frail in structure. To every appearance, these perceived things were inert and passive. Suddenly, under certain circumstances, these things—henceforth known as seeds or eggs or germs—begin to change, to change rapidly in size, form, and qualities. Rapid and extensive changes occur, however, in many things—as when wood is touched by fire. But the changes in the living thing are orderly; they are cumulative; they tend constantly in one direction; they do not, like other changes, destroy or consume, or pass fruitless into wandering flux, they realize and fulfil. Each successive stage, no matter how unlike its predecessor, preserves its net effect and also prepares the way for a fuller activity on the part of its successor. In living beings, changes do not happen as they seem to happen elsewhere, any which way; the earlier changes are regulated in view of later results. This progressive organization does not cease till there is achieved a true final term, a *telos,* a completed, perfected end. This final form exercises in turn a plenitude of functions, not the least noteworthy of which is production of germs like those from which it took its own origin, germs capable of the same cycle of self-fulfilling activity.

But the whole miraculous tale is not yet told. The same drama is enacted to the same destiny in countless myriads of individuals so sundered in time, so severed in space, that they have no opportunity for mutual consultation and no means of interaction. As an old writer quaintly said, "things of the same kind go through the same formalities"—celebrate, as it were, the same ceremonial rites.

This formal activity which operates throughout a series of changes and holds them to a single course; which subordinates their aimless flux to its own perfect manifestation; which, leaping the boundaries of space and time, keeps individuals distant in space and remote in time to a uniform type of structure and function: this principle seemed to give insight into the very nature of reality itself. To it Aristotle gave the name, *eidos.* This term the scholastics translated as *species.*

The force of this term was deepened by its application to everything in the universe that observes order in flux and manifests constancy through change. From the casual drift of daily weather, through the uneven recurrence of seasons and unequal return of seed time and harvest, up to the majestic sweep of the heavens—the image of eternity in time—and from this to the unchanging pure and contemplative intelligence beyond nature lies one unbroken fulfilment of ends. Nature as a whole is a progressive realization of purpose strictly comparable to the realization of purpose in any single plant or animal.

The conception of *eidos,* species, a fixed form and final cause, was the central principle of knowledge as well as of nature. Upon it rested the logic of science. Change as change is mere flux and lapse; it insults intelligence. Genuinely to know is to grasp a permanent end that realizes itself through changes, holding them thereby within the metes and bounds of fixed truth. Completely to know is to relate all special forms to their one single end and good: pure contemplative intelligence. Since, however, the scene of nature which directly confronts us is in change, nature as directly and practically experienced does not satisfy the conditions of knowledge. Human experience is in flux, and hence the instrumentalities of sense-perception and of inference based upon observation are condemned in advance. Science is compelled to aim at realities lying behind and beyond the processes of nature, and to carry on its search for these realities by means of rational forms transcending ordinary modes of perception and inference.

There are, indeed, but two alternative courses. We must either find the appropriate objects and organs of knowledge in the mutual interactions of changing things; or else, to escape the infection of change, we *must* seek them in some transcendent and supernal region. The human mind, deliberately as it were, exhausted the logic of the changeless, the final, and the transcendent, before it essayed adventure on the pathless wastes of generation and transformation. We dispose all too easily of the efforts of the schoolmen to interpret nature and mind in terms of real essences, hidden forms, and occult faculties, forgetful of the seriousness and dignity of the ideas that lay behind. We dispose of them by laughing at the famous gentleman who accounted for the fact that opium put people to sleep on the ground it had a dormitive faculty. But the doctrine, held in our own day, that knowledge of the plant that yields the poppy consists in referring the peculiarities of an individual to a type, to a universal form, a doctrine so firmly established that any other method of knowing was conceived to be unphilosophical and unscientific, is a survival of precisely the same logic. This identity of conception in the scholastic and anti-Darwinian theory may well suggest greater sympathy for what has become unfamiliar as well as greater humility regarding the further unfamiliarities that history has in store.

Darwin was not, of course, the first to question the classic philosophy of nature and of knowledge. The beginnings of the revolution are in the physical science of the sixteenth and seventeenth centuries. When Galileo said: "It is my opinion that the earth is very noble and admirable by reason of so many and so different alterations and generations which are incessantly made therein," he expressed the changed temper that was coming over the world; the transfer of interest from the permanent to the changing. When Descartes said: "The nature of physical things is much more easily conceived when they are beheld coming gradually into existence, than when they are only considered as produced at once in a finished and perfect state," the modern world became self-conscious of the logic that was henceforth to control it, the logic of which Darwin's *Origin of Species* is the latest scientific achievement. Without the methods of Copernicus, Kepler, Galileo, and their successors in astronomy, physics, and chemistry, Darwin would have been helpless in the organic sciences. But prior to Darwin the impact of the new scientific method upon life, mind, and politics, had been arrested, because between these ideal or moral interests and the inorganic world intervened the kingdom of plants and animals. The gates of the garden of life were barred to the new ideas; and only through this garden was there access to mind and politics. The influence of Darwin upon philosophy resides in his having conquered the phenomena of life for the principle of transition, and thereby freed the new logic for application to mind and morals and life. When he said of species what Galileo had said of the earth, *eppur si muove* [and yet it does move], he emancipated, once for all, genetic and experimental ideas as an organon of asking questions and looking for explanations.

III

The exact bearings upon philosophy of the new logical outlook are, of course, as yet, uncertain and inchoate. We live in the twilight of intellectual transition. One must add the rashness of the prophet to the stubbornness of the partizan to venture a systematic exposition of the influence upon philosophy of the Darwinian method. At best, we can but inquire as to its general bearing—the effect upon mental temper and complexion, upon that body of half-conscious, half-instinctive intellectual aversions and preferences which determine, after all, our more deliberate intellectual enterprises.

In this vague inquiry there happens to exist as a kind of touchstone a problem of long historic currency that has also been much discussed in Darwinian literature. I refer to the old problem of design *versus* chance, mind *versus* matter, as the causal explanation, first or final, of things.

As we have already seen, the classic notion of species carried with it the idea of purpose. In all living forms, a specific type is present directing the earlier stages of growth to the realization of its own perfection. Since this purposive regulative principle is not visible to the senses, it follows that it must be an ideal or rational force. Since, however, the perfect form is gradually approximated through the sensible changes, it also follows that in and through a sensible realm a rational ideal force is working out its own ultimate manifestation. These inferences were extended to nature: (*a*) She does nothing in vain; but all for ulterior purpose. (*b*) Within natural sensible events there is therefore contained a spiritual causal force, which as spiritual escapes perception, but is apprehended by an enlightened reason. (*c*) The manifestation of this principle brings about a subordination of matter and sense to its own realization, and this ultimate fulfilment is the goal of nature and man. The design argument thus operated in two directions. Purposefulness accounted for the intelligibility of nature and the possibility of science, while the absolute or cosmic character of this purposefulness gave sanction and worth to the moral and religious endeavors of man. Science was underpinned and morals authorized by one and the same principle, and their mutual agreement was eternally guaranteed.

This philosophy remained, in spite of sceptical and polemic outbursts, the official and the regnant philosophy of Europe for over two thousand years. The expulsion of fixed first and final causes from astronomy, physics, and chemistry had indeed given the doctrine something of a shock. But, on the other hand, increased acquaintance with the details of plant and animal life operated as a counterbalance and perhaps even strengthened the argument from design. The marvelous adaptations of organisms to their environment, of organs to the organism, of unlike parts of a complex organism— like the eye—to the organ itself; the foreshadowing by lower forms of the higher; the preparation in earlier stages of growth for organs that only later had their functioning—these things were increasingly recognized with the progress of botany, zoölogy, paleontology, and embryology. Together, they added such prestige to the design argument that by the late eighteenth century it was, as approved by the sciences of organic life, the central point of theistic and idealistic philosophy.

The Darwinian principle of natural selection cut straight under this philosophy. If all organic adaptations are due simply to constant variation and the elimination of those variations which are harmful in the struggle for existence that is brought about by excessive reproduction, there is no call for a prior intelligent causal force to plan and preordain them. Hostile critics charged Darwin with materialism and with making chance the cause of the universe.

Some naturalists, like Asa Gray, favored the Darwinian principle and attempted to reconcile it with design. Gray held to what may be called design on the installment plan. If we conceive the "stream of variations" to be itself intended, we may suppose that each successive variation was designed from the first to be selected. In that case, variation, struggle and selection simply define the mechanism of "secondary causes" through which the "first cause" acts; and the doctrine of design is none the worse off because we know more of its *modus operandi*.

Darwin could not accept this mediating proposal. He admits or rather he asserts that it is "impossible to conceive this immense and wonderful universe including man with his capacity of looking far backwards and far into futurity as the result of blind chance or necessity."[1] But nevertheless he holds that since variations are in useless as well as useful directions, and since the latter are sifted out simply by the stress of the conditions of struggle for existence, the design argument as applied to living beings is unjustifiable; and its lack of support there deprives it of scientific value as applied to nature in general. If the variations of the pigeon, which under artificial selection give the pouter pigeon, are not preordained for the sake of the breeder, by what logic do we argue that variations resulting in natural species are predesigned?[2]

IV

So much for some of the more obvious facts of the discussion of design *versus* chance, as causal principles of nature and of life as a whole. We brought up this discussion, you recall, as a crucial instance. What does our touchstone indicate as to the bearing of Darwinian ideas upon philosophy? In the first place, the new logic outlaws, flanks, dismisses—what you will—one type of problems and substitutes for it another type. Philosophy forswears inquiry after absolute origins and absolute finalities in order to explore specific values and the specific conditions that generate them.

Darwin concluded that the impossibility of assigning the world to chance as a whole and to design in its parts indicated the in-

solubility of the question. Two radically different reasons, however, may be given as to why a problem is insoluble. One reason is that the problem is too high for intelligence; the other is that the question in its very asking makes assumptions that render the question meaningless. The latter alternative is unerringly pointed to in the celebrated case of design *versus* chance. Once admit that the sole verifiable or fruitful object of knowledge is the particular set of changes that generate the object of study together with the consequences that then flow from it, and no intelligible question can be asked about what, by assumption, lies outside. To assert—as is often asserted —that specific values of particular truth, social bonds and forms of beauty, if they can be shown to be generated by concretely knowable conditions, are meaningless and in vain; to assert that they are justified only when they and their particular causes and effects have all at once been gathered up into some inclusive first cause and some exhaustive final goal, is intellectual atavism. Such argumentation is reversion to the logic that explained the extinction of fire by water through the formal essence of aqueousness and the quenching of thirst by water through the final cause of aqueousness. Whether used in the case of the special event or that of life as a whole, such logic only abstracts some aspect of the existing course of events in order to reduplicate it as a petrified eternal principle by which to explain the very changes of which it is the formalization.

When Henry Sidgwick casually remarked in a letter that as he grew older his interest in what or who made the world was altering into interest in what kind of a world it is anyway, his voicing of a common experience of our own day illustrates also the nature of that intellectual transformation effected by the Darwinian logic. Interest

[1] *Life and Letters,* Vol. I, p. 282; *cf.* 285.
[2] *Life and Letters,* Vol. II, pp. 146, 170, 245; Vol. I, pp. 283–84. See also the closing portion of his *Variations of Animals and Plants under Domestication.*

shifts from the wholesale essence back of special changes to the question of how special changes serve and defeat concrete purposes; shifts from an intelligence that shaped things once for all to the particular intelligences which things are even now shaping; shifts from an ultimate goal of good to the direct increments of justice and happiness that intelligent administration of existent conditions may beget and that present carelessness or stupidity will destroy or forego.

In the second place, the classic type of logic inevitably set philosophy upon proving that life *must* have certain qualities and values—no matter how experience presents the matter—because of some remote cause and eventual goal. The duty of wholesale justification inevitably accompanies all thinking that makes the meaning of special occurrences depend upon something that once and for all lies behind them. The habit of derogating from present meanings and uses prevents our looking the facts of experience in the face; it prevents serious acknowledgment of the evils they present and serious concern with the goods they promise but do not as yet fulfill. It turns thought to the business of finding a wholesale transcendent remedy for the one and guarantee for the other. One is reminded of the way many moralists and theologians greeted Herbert Spencer's recognition of an unknowable energy from which welled up the phenomenal physical processes without and the conscious operations within. Merely because Spencer labeled his unknowable energy "God," this faded piece of metaphysical goods was greeted as an important and grateful concession to the reality of the spiritual realm. Were it not for the deep hold of the habit of seeking justification for ideal values in the remote and transcendent, surely this reference of them to an unknowable absolute would be despised in comparison with the demonstrations of experience that knowable energies are daily generating about us precious values.

The displacing of this wholesale type of philosophy will doubtless not arrive by sheer logical disproof, but rather by growing recognition of its futility. Were it a thousand times true that opium produces sleep because of its dormitive energy, yet the inducing of sleep in the tired, and the recovery to waking life of the poisoned, would not be thereby one least step forwarded. And were it a thousand times dialectically demonstrated that life as a whole is regulated by a transcendent principle to a final inclusive goal, none the less truth and error, health and disease, good and evil, hope and fear in the concrete, would remain just what and where they now are. To improve our education, to ameliorate our manners, to advance our politics, we must have recourse to specific conditions of generation.

Finally, the new logic introduces responsibility into the intellectual life. To idealize and rationalize the universe at large is after all a confession of inability to master the courses of things that specifically concern us. As long as mankind suffered from this impotency, it naturally shifted a burden of responsibility that it could not carry over to the more competent shoulders of the transcendent cause. But if insight into specific conditions of value and into specific consequences of ideas is possible, philosophy must in time become a method of locating and interpreting the more serious of the conflicts that occur in life, and a method of projecting ways for dealing with them: a method of moral and political diagnosis and prognosis.

The claim to formulate *a priori* the legislative constitution of the universe is by its nature a claim that may lead to elaborate dialectic developments. But it is also one that removes these very conclusions from subjection to experimental test, for, by definition, these results make no differences in the detailed course of events. But a philosophy that humbles its pretentions to the work of projecting hypotheses for the education and conduct of mind, individual and social, is thereby subjected to test by the way in which the ideas it propounds work out in practice. In having modesty forced upon it, philosophy also acquires responsibility.

Doubtless I seem to have violated the implied promise of my earlier remarks and to have turned both prophet and partizan. But in anticipating the direction of the transformations in philosophy to be wrought by the Darwinian genetic and experimental logic, I do not profess to speak for any save those who yield themselves consciously or unconsciously to this logic. No one can fairly deny that at present there are two effects of the Darwinian mode of thinking. On the one hand there are many making sincere and vital efforts to revise our traditional philosophic conceptions in accordance with its demands. On the other hand, there is as definitely a recrudescence of absolutistic philosophies; an assertion of a type of philosophic knowing distinct from that of the sciences, one which opens to us another kind of reality from that to which the sciences give access; an appeal through experience to something that essentially goes beyond experience. This reaction affects popular creeds and religious movements as well as technical philosophies. The very conquest of the biological sciences by the new ideas has led many to proclaim an explicit and rigid separation of philosophy from science.

Old ideas give way slowly; for they are more than abstract logical forms and categories. They are habits, predispositions, deeply engrained attitudes of aversion and preference. Moreover, the conviction persists—though history shows it to be a hallucination—that all the questions that the human mind has asked are questions that can be answered in terms of the alternatives that the questions themselves present. But in fact intellectual progress usually occurs through sheer abandonment of questions together with both of the alternatives they assume—an abandonment that results from their decreasing vitality and a change of urgent interest. We do not solve them: we get over them. Old questions are solved by disappearing, evaporating, while new questions corresponding to the changed attitude of endeavor and preference take their place. Doubtless the greatest dissolvent in contemporary thought of old questions, the greatest precipitant of new methods, new intentions, new problems, is the one effected by the scientific revolution that found its climax in *The Origin of Species.*

COMMENT

The Origins of Pragmatism

The word "pragmatism" was introduced into modern philosophy by Charles Peirce to designate the "method of ascertaining the meaning of hard words and abstract conceptions" [1] which he had advocated in "How to Make Our Ideas Clear" (1878). Even before he wrote this essay, Peirce had expressed the basic principle of his pragmatism in a review (1871) of Fraser's edition of

[1] *Collected Papers of Charles Sanders Peirce* (Harvard University Press, 1931–1935), V, para. 464.

Berkeley's *Works,* in which he offered the following "rule for avoiding the deceits of language": "Do things fulfill the same function practically? Then let them be signified by the same word. Do they not? Then let them be distinguished." [2] In neither of these early statements did Peirce use the word "pragmatism." But in 1898, at the University of California, William James delivered a lecture entitled "Philosophical Conceptions and Practical Results," in which he hailed Peirce not only as the founder of pragmatism but as the originator of the term. It appears that Peirce used the word orally for some time before he first committed it to print in 1902, when he contributed an article on the subject to Baldwin's *Philosophical Dictionary.*

The terms "pragmatic" and "pragmatism" were suggested to Peirce by his study of Kant. In *The Metaphysic of Morals,* Kant distinguished between "pragmatic" and "practical." The former term, deriving from the Greek *pragma* (things done), applies to the rules of art or technique based upon experience; the latter term applies to moral rules which Kant regarded as *a priori.* Hence Peirce, wishing to emphasize an experimental and non-*a priori* type of reasoning, chose the word "pragmatic" to designate his way of clarifying meanings.

The pragmatic movement first sprang to life in the early eighteen-seventies in the "Metaphysical Club," a philosophical discussion group founded by Peirce, which included among its members William James and Oliver Wendell Holmes, Jr. Two of the brilliant young members of the club, Chauncey Wright and Nicholas St. John Green, emphasized the practical bearing and function of ideas. They thus suggested to Peirce the criterion of clarity which he expressed in "How to Make Our Ideas Clear." But this essay lay unnoticed for twenty years until James, in his address of 1898, pointed to Peirce as the founder of an important new philosophical movement.

As Peirce initially used the term, pragmatism referred to a maxim for the clarification of ideas and hypotheses, not for their verification; it was a theory of meaning, not of truth. Later he also used the term to designate the rule that only hypotheses that are *clear* should be admitted in scientific or philosophical inquiry. As interpreted and amplified by James, "pragmatism" became a theory of truth and so changed into something alien to Peirce's way of thinking. "The modern movement known as pragmatism," Ralph Barton Perry has remarked, "is largely the result of James' misunderstanding of Peirce." [3]

While James was developing his own version of pragmatism, John Dewey was working along similar lines at the University of Michigan and later at the University of Chicago. As early as 1886, he and James began to exchange

2 *North American Review,* CXIII (1871), p. 469.
3 *The Thought and Character of William James,* Briefer Version (Harvard University Press, 1935), p. 281.

letters, and in 1903, in the Preface to *Studies in Logical Theory,* Dewey acknowledged "a preëminent obligation" to James. In certain ways, however, Dewey shows a closer affinity to Peirce—for example, in his close study of the experimental methods of natural science, in his rejection of James' criterion of emotional satisfaction as a test of truth, in his emphasis on the *social* bearing of ideas, and in his opposition to all "intuitionist" theories of knowledge.

There were other important contributors to pragmatism, such as George Herbert Mead (1863–1931) in America and Frederick Canning Scott Schiller (1864–1937) in England; but Peirce, James, and Dewey are the towering figures.

The Pragmatism of James

Underlying James' pragmatism is an interpretation of human nature which he elaborated in his famous *Principles of Psychology.* All animals, including man, select and respond to those stimuli that fulfill their interests and practical needs:

> The dog singles out of any situation its smells, and the horse its sounds, because they may reveal facts of practical moment, and are instinctively exciting to these several creatures. The infant notices the candle-flame or the window, and ignores the rest of the room, because those objects give him a vivid pleasure. So, the country boy dissociates the blackberry, the chestnut, and the wintergreen from the vague mass of other shrubs and trees, for their practical uses.[4]

The higher mental activities are likewise motivated and discriminatory. Reason, for example, operates under the pressure of interests, extracting and linking together ideas that are germane to its purposes—as when a sailor, at the moment of shipwreck, "sees at a glance" just what needs to be done. Reasoning is a way of problem-solving, and the ideas reasoned about are "ideo-motor" dispositions, which tend to discharge themselves in action. So regarded, the human mind is not a substance or independent "stuff" but an activity by means of which the organism copes with its environment. This conception of the mind is very closely related to James' pragmatism.

Another characteristic doctrine is his contention that knowledge is essentially direct and concrete. If knowing is to be consummated, concepts must lead to percepts, abstract ideas must point the way to concrete experiences. Mediating knowledge through abstract ideas is simply a means of extending the scope of experience by the method of temporary substitution. The act of knowing is not completed until immediate acquaintance—direct confrontation of the object—takes the place of reference. In one of his first articles,

---

[4] William James, *Psychology* (Henry Holt, 1893), p. 363.

"The Function of Consciousness," James insisted that "sensible things, these mere matters of acquaintance," are both the initiating stimuli and the ultimate objects of knowledge:

> Condemned though they be by some thinkers, these sensations are the mother-earth, the anchorage, the stable rock, the first and last limits, the *terminus a quo* [the first limit or starting point] and the *terminus ad quem* [the last limit or goal] of the mind. To find such sensational termini should be our aim with all our higher thought. They end discussion; they destroy the false conceit of knowledge; and without them we are all at sea with each other's meanings. . . . We can never be sure we understand each other till we are able to bring the matter to this test.[5]

It is but a step from these initial doctrines—that the mind is essentially practical and that knowledge is presentational—to the basic tenets of James' pragmatism. He began his account of pragmatism by enunciating a theory of meaning, which he modestly attributed to Peirce. He maintained that we find out what an idea really means by defining the practical difference that it will conceivably make in sensible experience:

> . . . The tangible fact at the root of all our thought-distinctions, however subtle, is that there is no one of them so fine as to consist in anything but a possible difference of practice. To attain perfect clearness in our thoughts of an object, then, we need only consider what conceivable effects of a practical kind the object may involve—what sensations we are to expect from it, and what reactions we must prepare.[6]

There is no doubt that we often think of clearness in this practical way. Clear directions, for example, are those that we can follow with the least trouble and that will bring us most quickly to our destination. "Go five blocks to the right, four blocks to the left, and look for the house number 728 three doors from the corner on the east side of the street." If the directions are sufficiently clear, we will be able to find our way without fumbling or groping. Different directions will make some practical difference in concrete, sensible experiences. If no such practical difference is discoverable, the various meanings, however variously expressed, are the same. This is the general tenor of James' theory of meaning.

James' theory is not the same as the theory of Peirce, even though it seems at first glance to be very similar. James defined meaning in terms of the *sensations* the idea leads us to expect, whereas Peirce defined it in terms of habit, a *general* attitude of response. James thought of meaning in terms of its practical uses, whereas Peirce, although he also employed the word "practical," had in mind a disinterested experimental clarification of meaning

[5] *Mind*, X (1885); reprinted in *The Meaning of Truth* (Longmans, Green, 1910), pp. 39–40.
[6] *Pragmatism: A New Name for Some Old Ways of Thinking* (Longmans, Green, 1907), pp. 46–47.

rather than a utilitarian criterion. To James, a meaning is clear if it is useful; to Peirce, it is clear if it is testable in terms of some conceivable operations. James went on to elaborate a pragmatic theory of truth, whereas Peirce's "pragmatism" stopped with a theory of meaning—except that he added the significant corollary that only clear hypotheses are admissible in inquiry.

James' conception of truth follows from his psychological doctrine that the mind is essentially interested, selective, goal-seeking. An idea or belief owes its existence to some interest. If there are no interested minds, there can be no ideas or opinions. The opinion, or idea, is true when the inciting interest is satisfied. A statement that cannot be tested by action is empty verbiage; and the testing involves the effort to satisfy an interest. A belief, therefore, is true if it *works*—that is, if it is successful in satisfying an interest. Truth is satisfaction.

The word "satisfaction," however, is ambiguous. If an interest is cognitive —a desire to *know*—the satisfaction of the interest is the fulfillment of the cognitive impulse. In this case, according to James, truth means logical verification—an idea is true if it leads to the sensible experiences that it promises. If I think that there is a panda bear in the zoo, and if I actually find a panda bear when I get there, then my cognitive interest is satisfied and the idea is true. At times, James seems to be saying that *all* truth, in the last analysis, consists in such verification. For example, he declared:

> True ideas lead us into useful verbal and conceptual quarters as well as directly up to useful sensible termini. . . . The untrammelled flowing of the leading-process, its general freedom from clash and contradiction, passes for its indirect verification; but all roads lead to Rome, and in the end and eventually, all true processes must lead to the face of directly verifying sensible experiences *somewhere,* which somebody's ideas have copied.[7]

In another passage, he added that "verifiability . . . is as good as verification," and that often "we are so sure that verification is possible that we omit it." [8]

Side by side with this doctrine that truth consists of logical verification or verifiability, there appears another, more radical doctrine, that truth consists not only in cognitive but in noncognitive satisfaction. An idea, or opinion, is said to be true if it "works" in yielding maximal satisfaction. This view led James to make such sweeping statements as the following:

> The true is the name for whatever proves itself to be good in the way of belief. . . .[9]

[7] *Ibid.,* p. 215.
[8] *Ibid.,* p. 207.
[9] *Ibid.,* p. 76.

The true . . . is only the expedient in the way of our thinking. . . . Expedient in almost any fashion, . . . in the long run and on the whole of course.[10]

. . . We cannot reject any hypothesis if consequences useful to life flow from it. . . .[11]

. . . If the hypothesis of God works satisfactorily in the widest sense of the word, it is true. . . .[12]

In these statements, truth is conceived in terms of the *value* of results.

At this point, James' terminology is rather confusing. He sometimes used the word "verification" to include the testing of an idea or belief in terms of the satisfaction that it yields, whereas elsewhere he meant by "verification" the testing of an hypothesis by such evidence as inductive science customarily employs. These are two quite different ways of testing, and it is confusing to use "verification" to cover both meanings. We shall therefore reserve the term for the second method. We can then say that James had two distinguishable theories of truth: one that defines "truth" as the power of a belief to bring personal or social satisfaction, and one that conceives of hypotheses as predictions or plans of action to be tested by factual experiment or observation, and that defines "truth" in terms of such testing.

There is no way of reconciling these two theories completely, and hence there is a real inconsistency in James' interpretation of truth. The best one can do is to suggest that he intended to distinguish between different kinds of truth corresponding to different sorts of satisfactions. At least, his emphasis shifted as he moved from the scientific to the moral and religious field. In the case of scientific hypotheses, the interest to be satisfied is mainly cognitive, and further observations and experiments must confirm, not conflict with, the hypotheses. Here, truth can be interpreted as verification or verifiability. A true *moral* belief, on the other hand, is one that proves to be good in its consequences. And in religion, where precise scientific information is unavailable, we should consider true such beliefs as would appear most fruitful and satisfactory in our lives.

In James' more cautious statements, satisfaction, apart from verification, is offered not as evidence of truth, but as justifying belief when truth is doubtful. Truth requires something more than satisfaction—it must lead to what is verifiably real. For example, in *The Meaning of Truth,* a sequel to *Pragmatism,* James declared:

> The pragmatist calls satisfactions indispensable for truth-building, but I have everywhere called them insufficient unless reality be also incidentally led to. If the reality assumed were cancelled from the pragmatist's universe of dis-

[10] *Ibid.,* p. 222.
[11] *Ibid.,* p. 273.
[12] *Ibid.,* p. 299.

course, he would straightway give the name of falsehoods to the beliefs remaining, in spite of all their satisfactoriness.[13]

A great many of the criticisms that have been directed against James would have been avoided if he had consistently adhered to this more cautious and logical position.

Some of the implications of James' interpretation of truth become clearer if we contrast it with rival views. There are two other main interpretations: the correspondence theory and the coherence theory.

1. *Correspondence.* According to this ancient and venerable theory, a proposition is true if it faithfully represents or portrays some matter of fact. As often stated, the theory involves the notion that ideas somehow copy external objects. But James contended that ideas are not to be regarded as copies or replicas of things. An idea need not resemble its object; we can shut our eyes and picture a clock on a wall, but if instead we try to think of the "time-keeping function" of the clock, or of the elasticity of its spring, it is difficult to see how our idea can be a copy. A great deal of our thinking, as a matter of fact, is non-imagistic and cannot be said to portray or resemble an external object in any literal sense.

If the proponent of the correspondence theory means that something "inside" the mind—an opinion or belief—corresponds to something "outside" the mind, we must ask just what is meant by "outside." Does it mean outside of all possible experience? How then can we ever compare the belief or opinion with this extra-experiential object to tell whether the one really corresponds to the other? Since it is impossible to know a thing in itself independently of all knowers, the correspondence test so interpreted is unworkable. James therefore proposed to substitute for the test of correspondence the test of actual confrontation. That there are tigers in India is true if we can go to India and actually confront tigers. Thus truth is not a connection between something *in* experience and something outside it: it is the efficiency of an idea in leading to some future verifying experience.

2. *Coherence.* The coherence theory maintains that truth is a property of an extensive body of consistent propositions—a property that is applicable to any one proposition in such a system by virtue of its consistency with the other propositions in the system. True propositions hang together to make a harmonious and consistent whole; false propositions do not. A dream, for example, is inconsistent with our waking experiences, and hence cannot be regarded as true.

James was quite as much opposed to this theory as to the correspondence theory, for it emphasizes the coherence of a hypothesis with other parts of knowledge accumulated to date, whereas James puts primary stress upon

[13] *Op. cit.*, p. 195.

future consequences. What beliefs *do* and how well they succeed are more significant than the fact that they are consistent with a pre-existing body of knowledge. Ideas are not, like the pieces of a jig-saw puzzle, static things to fit into a ready-made pattern—they are flexible tools to control the future.

The rejection of the correspondence and coherence theories, James believed, means the abandonment of fixed, absolute, eternal "truths." Since the truth represents a successful adjustment between human purposes and the environment, it is man-made and subject to human limitations. If the adjustment varies, the truth also will vary. The same statement can be true for one person and false for another; or it can be true for a person at one time and false for him at another time; or it can be more or less true, or more or less false, as its satisfactoriness fluctuates. In so far as James emphasized subjective satisfaction rather than scientific verification, the implications of his theory of truth are relativistic.

The Instrumentalism of Dewey

In reviewing *Pragmatism,* Dewey pointed out that James inconsistently defined truth in terms of both verification and ethical satisfaction. "Good consequences," Dewey declared, are relevant to truth only if they serve to verify an idea or hypothesis, and "this is, at times, unequivocally recognized by James":

> But at other times any good which flows from acceptance of a belief is treated as if it were an evidence, *in so far,* of the truth of the idea. This holds particularly when theological notions are under consideration. . . . Since Mr. James has referred to me as saying "truth is what gives satisfaction," I may remark (apart from the fact that I do not think I ever said that truth is what *gives* satisfaction) that I have never identified any satisfaction with the truth of an idea, save *that* satisfaction which arises when the idea as working hypothesis or tentative method is applied to prior existences in such a way as to fulfill what it intends.[14]

By such fulfillment of intention Dewey meant "the advent of the object intended," its confrontation in experience—or some other process of verification. Confrontation will resolve a very specific question about some observable matter of fact, but more is involved in the verification of a complex hypothesis, such as Einstein's theory of relativity. In this case, no simple observation will suffice, and it is necessary to consider the capacity of the theory to render systematically intelligible a large body of facts and to be fruitful in leading to new discoveries.

Like James, Dewey is prepared to say that the truth of an hypothesis is its successful working. The "success" to which he refers, however, is not any

[14] "What Pragmatism Means by Practical," *Journal of Philosophy,* V (1908), pp. 93–94.

incidental ethical satisfaction but success in resolving the *specific* problem that has evoked the inquiry. An hypothesis is true if it "works" to transform a perplexed, confused, and discordant situation, which has incited the inquiry, into a clear, orderly, and satisfactory situation, which brings the inquiry to a close. "Satisfactory" means satisfactory for the immediate purpose at hand. Hence it is necessary to distinguish an inquiry that is predominantly practical, such as one whose aim is to discover how to build a bridge, from an inquiry that is predominantly scientific, such as one that seeks to know the structure of the benzine molecule.

> In the former the practical commitment involved in overt action is much more serious than in the latter. An astronomer or chemist performs overt actions, but they are for the sake of knowledge; they serve to test and develop his conceptions and theories. In practical matters, the main result desired lies outside of knowledge.[15]

In such statements, Dewey avoids the more extravagant claims of pragmatism, recognizing that scientific inquiry has methods and goals of its own which distinguish it from narrowly practical pursuits. He is thoroughly aware that factual verification is crucial to scientific inquiry, and he wishes greatly to extend, rather than to restrict, the application of science to human affairs.

However much he differed in some respects from James, Dewey fully agreed with the forward-looking and empirical temper of James' pragmatism—"the attitude of looking away from first things, principles, 'categories,' supposed necessities; and of looking toward last things, fruits, consequences, facts." He also agreed that thinking is essentially instrumental to the attainment of human purposes, although the purposes of the scientist are to be distinguished from the purposes of the practical man of affairs. Like James, moreover, he vehemently rejected a dualism of experience and nature: the stuff of the world is natural events such as we directly experience. His interpretation of inquiry, however, was more akin to Peirce's experimentalism than to James' ethical pragmatism. The result is a constellation of ideas that can be described as "experimental naturalism." Perhaps the best brief expression of this naturalistic philosophy is to be found in Dewey's essay "The Influence of Darwinism upon Philosophy," reprinted in the present volume.

In this essay, Dewey argues that the Darwinian revolution in science necessitates a comparable revolution in philosophy. The philosopher, using a method like that of the biologist, should forswear "inquiry after absolute origins and absolute finalities in order to explore specific values and the specific conditions that generate them." First and final causes, as allegedly lying behind and beyond nature, are beyond the reach of science, and the philosopher should turn away from such illusory objects. For him as for the sci-

[15] *How We Think* (D. C. Heath, 1933), p. 115.

entist, things should be understood in terms of their origins and functions, and inquiry should be empirical in method and practical in motivation.

Conceiving philosophical and scientific method in this way, Dewey regards fruitful inquiry as essentially active and prospective rather than passive and retrospective:

> Intelligence develops within the sphere of action for the sake of possibilities not yet given. . . . Intelligence *as* intelligence is inherently forward-looking. . . . A pragmatic intelligence is a creative intelligence, not a routine mechanic. . . . Intelligence is . . . instrumental *through* action to the determination of the qualities of future experience.[16]

Accordingly, Dewey proposes to determine meanings and test beliefs by examining the *consequences* that flow from them. What can the idea or belief promise for the future? How can it help us in resolving our perplexities? What predictions are implied by the hypothesis and how can they be verified?

Such questions apply even to propositions about the past, and even these propositions must be verified in terms of future consequences: "The past event has left effects, consequences, that are present and that will continue in the future. Our belief about it, if genuine, must also modify action in *some* way and so have objective effects. If these two sets of effects interlock harmoniously, then the judgment is true." [17] For example, the assassination of Lincoln *had* consequences, such as records of the event. My belief about it *has* consequences, such as expectations that the records will be so-and-so. If the two sets of consequences harmoniously coincide so that my expectations are fulfilled, the statement is true.

Dewey regarded this emphasis on consequences as the essential characteristic of pragmatism. "The term 'pragmatic,' " he declared, "means only the rule of referring all thinking, all reflective considerations, to *consequences* for final meaning and test." [18] This insistence upon consequent rather than antecedent phenomena is, as we have noted, like the pragmatism of James except that it does not define truth in terms of emotional satisfactions and the play of desires.

Even though Dewey differed from James in this respect, he agreed that inquiry springs from felt need and results in practical gain. Reflective thought characteristically arises when there is some difficulty, conflict, or crisis that disrupts the ordinary routine of living. The difficulty is then diagnosed, alternative solutions or explanations are formulated and tested, and, if some one of these alternatives is finally corroborated by overt acts or experiments, the problem is solved. The point of inquiry so conceived is not merely to understand existence but to *change* it. Truth is not thought of as a static cor-

---

[16] *Creative Intelligence* (Henry Holt, 1917), p. 65.
[17] *The Influence of Darwin on Philosophy and Other Essays* (Henry Holt, 1910), p. 160.
[18] *Essays in Experimental Logic* (University of Chicago Press, 1916), p. 330.

respondence between an idea and what was *antecedently* real—it is not merely
the disclosure of a reality that existed prior to and independent of knowing.
The inquiry is a creative process directed by purpose and bringing about a
control over, and thus a change in, the experienced objects; and truth and
knowledge are attained when the inciting problems are resolved by the reconstruction of experience.

In denying that knowledge reveals "antecedent" objects, and in asserting
that the act of knowing partly determines its object, Dewey seems to reject
the possibility of genuinely objective knowledge: "Knowing is one kind of
interaction which goes on within the world. . . . What is known is seen to be
a product in which the act of observation plays a necessary role. Knowing is
seen to be a participant in what is finally known." [19] Each person, according to Dewey, is limited to his own particular perspective, and every thing
known is an object-from-a-perspective. Moreover, "there are an indefinite
number of heres, nows, and perspectives. As many as there are existences." [20]
The implications of such passages are highly relativistic. If each person can
know a thing only in relation to himself as a knower, if his perspective is
unique, and if this perspective makes an essential difference in the object
known, he cannot know the thing as it *really is* apart from himself.

In developing his theory of inquiry, Dewey distinguished between the
purposes of philosophical inquiry and those of scientific inquiry. The purpose
of philosophy, as he saw it, is criticism—a "criticism of beliefs, institutions,
customs, policies with respect to their bearing upon good." This view of
philosophy, he declared, is "a version of the old saying that philosophy is
love of wisdom, of wisdom that is not knowledge and which nevertheless cannot be without knowledge." [21] Philosophy seeks wisdom; science seeks knowledge. Hence the former is mainly concerned with criticism, the latter with
description. Both wisdom and knowledge are instrumental to human need,
but the need is specific to the type of inquiry.

Criticism

Although there is much that is stimulating and valuable in the pragmatism
of James and Dewey, there are also some grave difficulties and objections.
Some of these apply only to the more extreme theory of James, but others
apply to the theory of Dewey as well. Let us begin with the more extreme
doctrines.

James was mistaken in believing that "the true is only the expedient in
the way of our thinking." In the first place, this is not what we mean by "true."
As Josiah Royce remarked, James would apparently require a witness on
the stand to swear "to tell the expedient, the whole expedient, and nothing

[19] *The Quest for Certainty* (New York: Minton, Balch, 1929), p. 204.
[20] *Journal of Philosophy*, XXIV (1927), p. 63.
[21] *Experience and Nature* (W. W. Norton, 1929), pp. 408–9.

but the expedient, so help him future experience." [22] Such an oath is certainly not the same as swearing to tell the truth! When we say that a belief is expedient, what do we mean? Do we mean that it is *expedient* that the belief is expedient? Surely not. We mean that it is *true* that the belief is expedient. That a belief actually has good consequences is a truth to be verified, not just an expediency. Clearly, we cannot substitute the concept of expediency for the concept of truth. James has tried to attach a new meaning to an old word, but the meaning does not fit.

James might have admitted that truth does not *mean* mere expediency in belief and still have contended that in practice the two coincide. It is not the case, however, that all true beliefs are expedient and that all expedient beliefs are true. There are truths so trivial that it would be a waste of time to discover or entertain them. It may be possible, for example, to discover exactly how many hairs you have on your head, but it would scarcely pay for anyone to count them or for you to have them counted. Of course, we often waste our time finding out useless truths, but this only emphasizes the fact that truth and utility do not always coincide. The true and the useful are not merely distinct but sometimes opposed. It may be disadvantageous for a patient to hold a true opinion about the nature of his illness, for the truth may add greatly to his misery or jeopardize his chance to recover. Similarly, the truths of nuclear physics which were instrumental in making the hydrogen bomb may, in the long run and on the whole, have terrible consequences; but these consequences will not make the truths any the less true. We have cited examples of truths that are harmful, but it is just as easy to cite falsehoods that are useful. A lie to save a life or to deceive an enemy in wartime may have very desirable consequences, and a mistaken religious belief may be very consoling. Hence a judgment can be true but not useful or useful but not true.

Even the more logical and moderate view that truth is verification or verifiability poses difficulties. If to "verify" is to find evidence that really does prove an idea to be true, then it would certainly follow that all verified or verifiable ideas *are* true. But it does not follow that all true ideas can be verified. Suppose that you are playing cards and someone asks whether, in a previous hand, you held the six of hearts. You maintain that you did, but your opponent maintains that you did not, and no one feels sure of his memory. In the meantime the cards have been reshuffled and all traces have been lost. Either your opinion or the opinion of your opponent is true, but neither is verifiable.[23] There are, of course, many such unverifiable questions about one's past, about remote events in history, or about things spatially beyond

[22] *The Philosophy of Loyalty* (Macmillan, 1908), p. 332.
[23] I borrow this illustration from G. E. Moore, *Philosophical Studies* (Harcourt, Brace, 1922), p. 101.

the reach of observation—questions to which no verifiable answer can be given because no sufficient evidence can be found. Yet logic and common sense require that the answers be either true or false.

It might still be maintained that verification is the only *test* of truth. A statement is verified if we find out what follows from it and if we then look to the facts and discover that these implications are confirmed. But this is not the *only* way of establishing truth. First, we know some truths by acquaintance. If I am staring at a red patch, I know by direct acquaintance that the patch, as an immediate datum, is red. Second, we know some truths, such as mathematical propositions, by intuition or deductive reasoning. I intuitively grasp that two plus two equals four, and I know that a conclusion logically follows from its premises by a process of deduction rather than factual verification. In practice, the test of logical consistency is of great importance, not only in *a priori* sciences such as geometry but in natural sciences such as physics. One of the main criteria for judging the truth of an hypothesis is that it is consistent both internally and as regards previously established theories and laws. The empiricists have emphasized the test of factual verification and the rationalists have emphasized the test of logical consistency; but, as Whitehead has said, it is as foolish for the rationalists and empiricists to attack each other as for the two ends of a worm to quarrel.[24]

If the pragmatists should abandon the exaggerated claim that truth *is* verification or verifiability and the equally exaggerated claim that verification is the *only* test of truth, they could still maintain that verification is an extremely important test. But this is an assertion that no informed person would deny. Verification is an ordinary and indispensable procedure of scientific method, and it is admitted as an essential test of truth by all reasonable scientists and philosophers, whether or not they are pragmatists. It is difficult to see what distinguishes the pragmatic doctrine of verification from ordinary empiricism unless it includes such exaggerated claims as we have found to be untenable.

Aside from the theory of truth, pragmatism is more a temper than a distinctive creed. It is a way of approaching philosophical problems—of getting down to the concrete particulars and judging issues in terms of the practical and human differences that they make. This approach is a very effective broom to sweep away the cobwebs of vague and unprofitable speculation. But there are still some doubts that can trouble a conscientious thinker. These can be summarized under three headings: practicalism, futurism, and relativism.

1. *Practicalism*. It is important that the emphasis upon being practical should not act as a blinker to limit vision. We can admit that thinking originates in practical needs, and yet recognize that the advent of the thinking

24 Cited by L. S. Stebbing, *A Modern Introduction to Logic* (London: Methuen, 1930), p. 344.

habit opens vast new possibilities that are not, in any limited sense, practical. The person who never thinks because he *likes* to think, but only because he *needs* to think, is a very servile and limited being. Although it is well to insist, as Dewey does, upon the social uses of science and philosophy, it is wrong to reduce philosophy or science to a mere instrument of something else— even of social betterment. As a profound humanitarian, Dewey strove to free human beings from bondage to material necessity, but the mark of such freedom is the enjoyment of feeling, imagination, and thought for their own sakes. Thinking for the joy of thinking is not only self-justifying but the highest mode of living. Sometimes the pragmatists lose sight of this fact.

2. *Futurism.* The emphasis of both James and Dewey upon the future— "that strange pragmatic reduction of yesterday to tomorrow" [25]—can be overdone. There is some truth but much falsity in Dewey's statement that "anticipation is . . . more primary than recollection; projection than summoning of the past; the prospective than the retrospective. . . . Imaginative recovery of the bygone is indispensable to successful invasion of the future, but its status is that of an instrument." [26] On the contrary, disinterested knowledge of the past—the vision of eons of cosmic evolution and the vivid procession of human history—brings immense enrichment and liberation to the human mind. How poor and stunted life would be without the heritage of the past! If you cut away the past the present collapses, quite as much as if you cut away the future. Most of the spiritual depth and inwardness of life depends upon mental rehearsal and interpretation of our acts, which otherwise would be merely outward and mechanical; and until we look back on the acts we have no adequate basis for interpreting them. We seldom, if ever, can forejudge the future without some memory of the past. Hence it is rather silly to disparage the past for the sake of the future, since the future has no meaning without reference to the past. Even verification, which the pragmatists insist upon so strongly, is meaningless unless there is a backward reference. At the end of the process, we confront the verifying facts with the same proposition that we entertained at the beginning and realize that the facts confirm the proposition. Unless we can recall our hypothesis and say, "This is what I meant," there is no verification.

3. *Relativism.* There is a questionable strain of epistemological relativism in the pragmatism of both James and Dewey. James' more extreme theory of truth is patently relativistic, since it denies that the true has any objective content apart from the interests and satisfactions of individuals. But even Dewey, with his doctrine of the relativity of the known to the unique and changing perspectives of the knower, lends support to relativism.

[25] George Santayana, "Dewey's Naturalistic Metaphysics," *Journal of Philosophy*, XXII (1925), p. 686.
[26] *Creative Intelligence*, op. cit., pp. 12, 14.

It may be said in rebuttal, that statements are true when they conform to objective facts. If a person says there are polar bears in Alaska, and there *really are* polar bears in Alaska, then the statement is true. And it is not just true for me and false for you, or true on Monday and false on Tuesday. Of course, the meanings of *words* change, and in that sense, the "truth" of a statement changes. For example, the words "Roosevelt is *now* President" were true in 1940 but are false today, because the word "now" denoted a different time in 1940 than it denotes at present. But if Roosevelt *was* President in 1940, it will remain forever true that he was President then. Similarly, words may vary in meaning from one person to another. As James points out, the phrase "The man goes round the squirrel" has one meaning when interpreted by one disputant and a quite different meaning when interpreted by his antagonist. But this insight—that the same words have different meanings, and that disputes can often be terminated by pointing out these diverse meanings—is at least as old as Socrates. We must distinguish this truism, which no one will dispute, from the relativistic doctrine that a statement *having one and the same meaning* can be both true and false. Once all ambiguity has been eliminated, the statement "The man goes round the squirrel" is true if it conforms to the facts and false if it does not. *Belief* is relative, since it depends upon the character and situation of the knower, but *truth* is not.

We would be making a great mistake to conclude that pragmatism is but a false and outmoded way of thinking. It continues to exert a profound influence upon contemporary thought, and it contains many insights that are both important and salutary. Perhaps its value can be suggested by the following description by John Jay Chapman of a social gathering at the home of a friend, Mrs. Henry Whitman, in Boston:

> I remember a curious Bostonian cockfight at her studio, where Professor Royce and Judge Oliver Wendell Holmes were pitted against each other to talk about the Infinite. Royce won, of course, . . . by involving the subject in such adamantine cobwebs of voluminous rolling speculation that no one could regain his senses thereafter. He not only cut the ground from under everyone's feet; but he pulled down the sun and moon, and raised up the ocean, and everyone was shipwrecked and took to small planks and cups of tea.[27]

Holmes, the friend of James and Peirce, was a pragmatist, whereas Royce was of the old-fashioned school of metaphysics. Holmes lost the argument, but he had a greater humility, a keener sense of reality, and a firmer hold on the perennially human point of view than Royce. If homely realism and practical concern for man's lot have tended to supersede the daring flights of metaphysicians, the pragmatists, such as James, Dewey, and Holmes, are in large measure responsible. This change one may count as either a loss or a gain.

[27] *Memories and Milestones* (New York: Moffatt, Yard, 1915), p. 106. Cited by Max H. Fisch, *Classic American Philosophers* (New York: Appleton-Century-Crofts, 1951), p. 7.

6

The Meaning of Truth

BERTRAND RUSSELL (1872–)

The second son of Viscount Amberly and grandson of Lord John Russell, a famous liberal Prime Minister, Bertrand Russell was born on May 18, 1872, in the lovely valley of the Wye (described in Wordsworth's *Tintern Abbey*). His mother died when he was two years old and his father when he was three, so the boy was brought up in the home of his grandfather. Until he went to Cambridge University, at the age of eighteen, he lived a solitary life, supervised by German and Swiss governesses and English tutors and seeing little of other children. But Cambridge opened to him "a new world of infinite delight." Here he found mathematics and philosophy extremely exciting and formed warm friendships with a number of brilliant young men, including the philosophers McTaggart, Moore, and Whitehead.

After leaving Cambridge in 1894, Russell spent some time abroad, at first as attaché at the British Embassy in Paris. He married at the end of a year's service in the Embassy—he was then 22—and went to Germany to study economics and politics. His wife, the sister of Logan Pearsall Smith, well-known essayist, and a Philadelphia Quaker, persuaded him to spend three months in America in 1896. After these travels, the young couple settled down in a workman's cottage in Sussex, where Russell, with enough income to support his family without other remuneration, devoted himself intensively to philosophy and mathematics.

The next two decades were the most intellectually productive in his long career. During this period he wrote a series of important books, including *A Critical Exposition of the Philosophy of Leibniz* (1900), *The Principles of Mathematics* (1903), *Principia Mathematica* (with Whitehead, 1910–1913), and *Our Knowledge of the External World* (1914). These books, especially *Principia Mathematica*, which was the result of twelve years of intense labor, firmly established Russell's reputation as one of the great figures in modern thought.

157

Always interested in politics, Russell was profoundly disturbed by the outbreak of World War I and was quite unsatisfied with the melodramatic explanations of the belligerent governments. His bold defense of conscientious objectors and his anti-war publications brought him fines and imprisonment, as well as loss of his position as Fellow at Trinity College, Cambridge. He emerged from the war a changed man, aware of great social perils and pathological depths in human nature that he had never suspected. Ever since, he has devoted a large part of his time and energy to writing about human affairs, especially politics, education, and morals.

In 1921, after seventeen years of married life, his first marriage was dissolved, and he then wed Dora Winifred Black, who bore him a daughter and son. In 1927, he and his wife established a "modern" experimental school for about twenty girls and boys, with Bertrand Russell as headmaster and Dora Russell as headmistress. His participation in the school ended in 1934, when he was divorced from Dora. Upon the death of his elder brother in 1931, he succeeded to the family earldom; and in 1934 he remarried, thus making Helen Patricia Spence, a young and beautiful woman, the Countess Russell.

During his elder years, he has continued to live a busy and adventurous life, traveling widely, lecturing frequently, and writing prolifically. In 1950 he received the Nobel prize for literature—an award well merited.

Truth and Falsehood[*]

Our knowledge of truths, unlike our knowledge of things, has an opposite, namely error. So far as things are concerned, we may know them or not know them, but there is no positive state of mind which can be described as erroneous knowledge of things, so long, at any rate, as we confine ourselves to knowledge by acquaintance. Whatever we are acquainted with must be something; we may draw wrong inferences from our acquaintance, but the acquaintance itself cannot be deceptive. Thus there is no dualism as regards acquaintance. But as regards knowledge of truths, there is a dualism. We may believe what is false as well as what is true. We know that on very many subjects different people hold different and incompatible opinions: hence some beliefs must be erroneous. Since erroneous beliefs are often held just as strongly as true beliefs, it becomes a difficult question how they are to be distinguished from true beliefs. How are we to know, in a given case, that our belief is not erroneous? This

* From The Problems of Philosophy. London, New York, and Toronto: Oxford University Press, 1912. Reprinted by permission.

is a question of the very greatest difficulty, to which no completely satisfactory answer is possible. There is, however, a preliminary question which is rather less difficult, and that is: What do we *mean* by truth and falsehood? It is this preliminary question which is to be considered in this chapter.

In this chapter we are not asking how we can know whether a belief is true or false: we are asking what is meant by the question whether a belief is true or false. It is to be hoped that a clear answer to this question may help us to obtain an answer to the question what beliefs are true, but for the present we ask only "What is truth?" and "What is falsehood?" not "What beliefs are true?" and "What beliefs are false?" It is very important to keep these different questions entirely separate, since any confusion between them is sure to produce an answer which is not really applicable to either.

There are three points to observe in the attempt to discover the nature of truth, three requisites which any theory must fulfill.

(1) Our theory of truth must be such as to admit of its opposite, falsehood. A good many philosophers have failed adequately to satisfy this condition: they have constructed theories according to which all our thinking ought to have been true, and have then had the greatest difficulty in finding a place for falsehood. In this respect our theory of belief must differ from our theory of acquaintance, since in the case of acquaintance it was not necessary to take account of any opposite.

(2) It seems fairly evident that if there were no beliefs there could be no falsehood, and no truth either, in the sense in which truth is correlative to falsehood. If we imagine a world of mere matter, there would be no room for falsehood in such a world, and although it would contain what may be called "facts," it would not contain any truths, in the sense in which truths are things of the same kind as falsehoods. In fact, truth and falsehood are properties of beliefs and statements: hence a world of mere matter, since it would contain no beliefs or statements, would also contain no truth or falsehood.

(3) But, as against what we have just said, it is to be observed that the truth or falsehood of a belief always depends upon something which lies outside the belief itself. If I believe that Charles I died on the scaffold, I believe truly, not because of any intrinsic quality of my belief, which could be discovered by merely examining the belief, but because of an historical event which happened two and a half centuries ago. If I believe that Charles I died in his bed, I believe falsely: no degree of vividness in my belief, or of care in arriving at it, prevents it from being false, again because of what happened long ago, and not because of any intrinsic property of my belief. Hence, although truth and falsehood are properties of beliefs, they are properties dependent upon the relations of the beliefs to other things, not upon any internal quality of the beliefs.

The third of the above requisites leads us to adopt the view—which has on the whole been commonest among philosophers—that truth consists in some form of correspondence between belief and fact. It is, however, by no means an easy matter to discover a form of correspondence to which there are no irrefutable objections. By this partly—and partly by the feeling that, if truth consists in a correspondence of thought with something outside thought, thought can never know when truth has been attained—many philosophers have been led to try to find some definition of truth which shall not consist in relation to something wholly outside belief. The most important attempt at a definition of this sort is the theory that truth consists in *coherence*. It is said that the mark of falsehood is failure to cohere in the body of our beliefs, and that it is the essence of a truth to form part of the completely rounded system which is The Truth.

There is, however, a great difficulty in this view, or rather two great difficulties. The first is that there is no reason to suppose that only *one* coherent body of beliefs is possible. It may be that, with sufficient imagination, a novelist might invent a past for the world that would perfectly fit on to what we know, and yet be quite different from the real past. In more scientific matters, it is certain that there are often two or more hypotheses which account for all the known facts on some subject, and although, in such cases, men of science endeavor to find facts which will rule out all the hypotheses except one, there is no reason why they should always succeed.

In philosophy, again, it seems not uncommon for two rival hypotheses to be both able to account for all the facts. Thus, for example, it is possible that life is one long dream, and that the outer world has only that degree of reality that the objects of dreams have; but although such a view does not seem inconsistent with known facts, there is no reason to prefer it to the common-sense view, according to which other people and things do really exist. Thus coherence as the definition of truth fails because there is no proof that there can be only one coherent system.

The other objection to this definition of truth is that it assumes the meaning of "coherence" known, whereas, in fact, "coherence" presupposes the truth of the laws of logic. Two propositions are coherent when both may be true, and are incoherent when one at least must be false. Now in order to know whether two propositions can both be true, we must know such truths as the law of contradiction. For example, the two propositions, "this tree is a beech" and "this tree is not a beech," are not coherent, because of the law of contradiction. But if the law of contradiction itself were subjected to the test of coherence, we should find that, if we choose to suppose it false, nothing will any longer be incoherent with anything else. Thus the laws of logic supply the skeleton or framework within which the test of coherence applies, and they themselves cannot be established by this test.

For the above two reasons, coherence cannot be accepted as giving the *meaning* of truth, though it is often a most important *test* of truth after a certain amount of truth has become known.

Hence we are driven back to *correspondence with fact* as constituting the nature of truth. It remains to define precisely what we mean by "fact," and what is the nature of the correspondence which must subsist between belief and fact, in order that belief may be true.

In accordance with our three requisites, we have to seek a theory of truth which (1) allows truth to have an opposite, namely falsehood, (2) makes truth a property of beliefs, but (3) makes it a property wholly dependent upon the relation of the beliefs to outside things.

The necessity of allowing for falsehood makes it impossible to regard belief as a relation of the mind to a single object, which could be said to be what is believed. If belief were so regarded, we should find that, like acquaintance, it would not admit of the opposition of truth and falsehood, but would have to be always true. This may be made clear by examples. Othello believes falsely that Desdemona loves Cassio. We cannot say that this belief consists in a relation to a single object, "Desdemona's love for Cassio," for if there were such an object, the belief would be true. There is in fact no such object, and therefore Othello cannot have any relation to such an object. Hence his belief cannot possibly consist in a relation to this object.

It might be said that his belief is a relation to a different object, namely "that Desdemona loves Cassio"; but it is almost as difficult to suppose that there is such an object as this, when Desdemona does not love Cassio, as it was to suppose that there is "Desdemona's love for Cassio." Hence it will be better to seek for a theory of belief which does not make it consist in a relation of the mind to a single object.

It is common to think of relations as though they always held between *two* terms, but in fact this is not always the case. Some relations demand three terms, some four, and so on. Take, for instance, the relation "between." So long as only two terms come in, the relation "between" is impossible: three terms are the smallest number that render it possible. York is between London and Edinburgh; but if London and Edinburgh were the only places in the world, there could be nothing which was between one place and another. Similarly *jealousy* requires three people: there can be no such relation that does not involve three at least. Such a proposition as "A wishes B to promote C's marriage with D" involves a relation of four terms; that is to say, A and B and C and D all come in, and the relation involved cannot be expressed otherwise than in a form involving all four. Instances might be multiplied indefinitely, but enough has been said to show that there are relations which require more than two terms before they can occur.

The relation involved in *judging* or *believing* must, if falsehood is to be duly allowed for, be taken to be a relation between several terms, not between two. When Othello believes that Desdemona loves Cassio, he must not have before his mind a single object, "Desdemona's love for Cassio," or "that Desdemona loves Cassio," for that would require that there should be objective falsehoods, which subsist independently of any minds; and this, though not logically refutable, is a theory to be avoided if possible. Thus it is easier to account for falsehood if we take judgment to be a relation in which the mind and the various objects concerned all occur severally; that is to say, Desdemona and loving and Cassio must all be terms in the relation which subsists when Othello believes that Desdemona loves Cassio. This relation, therefore, is a relation of four terms, since Othello also is one of the terms of the relation. When we say that it is a relation of four terms, we do not mean that Othello has a certain relation to Desdemona, and has the same relation to loving and also to Cassio. This may be true of some other relation than believing; but believing, plainly, is not a relation which Othello has to *each* of the three terms concerned, but to *all* of them together: there is only one example of the relation of believing involved, but this one example knits together four terms. Thus the actual occurrence, at the moment when Othello is entertaining his belief, is that the relation called "believing" is knitting together into one complex whole the four terms Othello, Desdemona, loving, and Cassio. What is called belief or judgment is nothing but this relation of believing or judging, which relates a mind to several things other than itself. An *act* of belief or of judgment is the occurrence between certain terms at some particular time, of the relation of believing or judging.

We are now in a position to understand what it is that distinguishes a true judgment from a false one. For this purpose we will adopt certain definitions. In every act of judgment there is a mind which judges, and there are terms concerning which it judges. We will call the mind the *subject* in the judgment, and the remaining terms the *objects*. Thus, when Othello judges that Desdemona loves Cassio, Othello is the subject, while the objects are Desdemona and loving and Cassio. The subject and the objects together are called the *constituents* of the judgment. It will be observed that the relation of judging has what is called a "sense" or "direction." We may say, metaphorically, that it puts its objects in a certain *order*, which we may indicate by means of the order of the words in the sentence. (In an inflected language, the same thing will be indicated by inflections, *e.g.*, by the difference between nominative and accusative.) Othello's judgment that Cassio loves Desdemona differs from his judgment that Desdemona loves Cassio, in spite of the fact that it consists of the same constituents, because the relation of judging places the constituents in a different order in the two cases. Similarly, if Cassio judges that Desdemona loves Othello, the constituents of the judgment are still the same, but their order is different. This property of having a "sense" or "direction" is one which the relation of judging shares with all other relations. The "sense" of relations is the ultimate source of order and series and a host of mathematical concepts; but we need not concern ourselves further with this aspect.

We spoke of the relation called "judging" or "believing" as knitting together into one complex whole the subject and the objects. In this respect, judging is exactly like every other relation. Whenever a relation holds between two or more terms, it unites the terms into a complex whole. If Othello loves Desdemona, there is such

a complex whole as "Othello's love for Desdemona." The terms united by the relation may be themselves complex, or may be simple, but the whole which results from their being united must be complex. Wherever there is a relation which relates certain terms, there is a complex object formed of the union of those terms; and conversely, wherever there is a complex object, there is a relation which relates its constituents. When an act of believing occurs, there is a complex, in which "believing" is the uniting relation, and subject and objects are arranged in a certain order by the "sense" of the relation of believing. Among the objects, as we saw in considering "Othello believes that Desdemona loves Cassio," one must be a relation—in this instance, the relation "loving." But this relation, as it occurs in the act of believing, is not the relation which creates the unity of the complex whole consisting of the subject and the objects. The relation "loving," as it occurs in the act of believing, is one of the objects—it is a brick in the structure, not the cement. The cement is the relation "believing." When the belief is *true,* there is another complex unity, in which the relation which was one of the objects of the belief relates the other objects. Thus, *e.g.*, if Othello believes *truly* that Desdemona loves Cassio, then there is a complex unity, "Desdemona's love for Cassio," which is composed exclusively of the *objects* of the belief, in the same order as they had in the belief, with the relation which was one of the objects occurring now as the cement that binds together the other objects of the belief. On the other hand, when a belief is *false,* there is no such complex unity composed only of the objects of the belief. If Othello believes *falsely* that Desdemona loves Cassio, then there is no such complex unity as "Desdemona's love for Cassio."

Thus a belief is *true* when it *corresponds*

to a certain associated complex, and *false* when it does not. Assuming, for the sake of definiteness, that the objects of the belief are two terms and a relation, the terms being put in a certain order by the "sense" of the believing, then if the two terms in that order are united by the relation into a complex, the belief is true; if not, it is false. This constitutes the definition of truth and falsehood that we were in search of. Judging or believing is a certain complex unity of which a mind is a constituent; if the remaining constituents, taken in the order which they have in the belief, form a complex unity, then the belief is true; if not, it is false.

Thus although truth and falsehood are properties of beliefs, yet they are in a sense extrinsic properties, for the condition of the truth of a belief is something not involving beliefs, or (in general) any mind at all, but only the *objects* of the belief. A mind, which believes, believes truly when there is a *corresponding* complex not involving the mind, but only its objects. This correspondence ensures truth, and its absence entails falsehood. Hence we account simultaneously for the two facts that be-

liefs (*a*) depend on minds for their *existence*, (*b*) do not depend on minds for their *truth*.

We may restate our theory as follows: If we take such a belief as "Othello believes that Desdemona loves Cassio," we will call Desdemona and Cassio the *object-terms*, and loving the *object-relation*. If there is a complex unity "Desdemona's love for Cassio," consisting of the object-terms related by the object-relation in the same order as they have in the belief, then this complex unity is called the *fact corresponding to the belief*. Thus a belief is true when there is a corresponding fact, and is false when there is no corresponding fact.

It will be seen that minds do not *create* truth or falsehood. They create beliefs, but when once the beliefs are created, the mind cannot make them true or false, except in the special case where they concern future things which are within the power of the person believing, such as catching trains. What makes a belief true is a *fact*, and this fact does not (except in exceptional cases) in any way involve the mind of the person who has the belief. . . .

BRAND BLANSHARD (1892–   )

One of the most erudite of living philosophers, Blanshard was educated at the Universities of Michigan, Columbia, Oxford, and Harvard. He has taught at Michigan, Columbia, Swarthmore, Harvard, and, since 1945, at Yale. In 1952–1953, he delivered the Gifford Lectures in Scotland. His principal work is *The Nature of Thought*, published in two volumes in 1939. This is a searching analysis of the knowing process, including its relation to epistemology, psychology, logic, and metaphysics. Blanshard writes in the main tradition of idealism, but his work is replete with original insights.

Coherence as the Nature of Truth*

To think is to seek understanding. And to seek understanding is an activity of mind that is marked off from all other activities by a highly distinctive aim. This aim . . . is to achieve systematic vision, so to apprehend what is now unknown to us as to relate it, and relate it necessarily, to what we know already. We think to solve problems; and our method of solving problems is to build a bridge of intelligible relation from the continent of our knowledge to the island we wish to include in it. Sometimes this bridge is causal, as when we try to explain a disease; sometimes teleological, as when we try to fathom the move of an opponent over the chess board; sometimes geometrical, as in Euclid. But it is always systematic; thought in its very nature is the attempt to bring something unknown or imperfectly known into a sub-system of knowledge, and thus also into that larger system that forms the world of accepted beliefs. That is what explanation is. *Why* is it that thought desires this ordered vision? Why should such a vision give satisfaction when it comes? To these questions there is no answer, and if there were, it would be an answer only because it had succeeded in supplying the characteristic satisfaction to this unique desire.

But may it not be that what satisfies thought fails to conform to the real world? Where is the guarantee that when I have brought my ideas into the form my ideal requires, they should be *true?* . . . In our long struggle with the relation of thought to reality we saw that if thought and things are conceived as related only externally, then knowledge is luck; there is no necessity whatever that what satisfies intelligence should coincide with what really is. It may do so, or it may not; on the principle that there are many misses to one bull's-eye, it more probably does not. But if we get rid of the misleading analogies through which this relation has been conceived, of copy and original, stimulus and organism, lantern and screen, and go to thought itself with the question what reference to an object means, we get a different and more hopeful answer. To think of a thing is to get that thing itself in some degree within the mind. To think of a color or an emotion is to have that within us which if it *were developed and completed,* would identify itself with the object. In short, if we accept its own report, thought is related to reality as the partial to the perfect fulfilment of a purpose. The more adequate its grasp the more nearly does it approximate, the more fully does it realize in itself, the nature and relations of its objects.

Thought thus appears to have two ends, one immanent, one transcendent. On the one hand it seeks fulfilment in a special kind of satisfaction, the satisfaction of systematic vision. On the other hand it seeks fulfilment in its object. Now it was the chief contention of our second book that these ends are one. Indeed unless they are accepted as one, we could see no alter-

* From *The Nature of Thought,* Vol. II. New York: The Macmillan Company; London: G. Allen & Unwin, 1940. Reprinted by permission.

native to scepticism. If the pursuit of thought's own ideal were merely an elaborate self-indulgence that brought us no nearer to reality, or if the apprehension of reality did not lie in the line of thought's interest, or still more if both of these held at once, the hope of knowledge would be vain. Of course it may really be vain. If anyone cares to doubt whether the framework of human logic has any bearing on the nature of things, he may be silenced perhaps, but he cannot be conclusively answered. One may point out to him that the doubt itself is framed in accordance with that logic, but he can reply that thus we are taking advantage of his logico-centric predicament; further, that any argument we can offer accords equally well with his hypothesis and with ours, with the view that we are merely flies caught in a logical net and the view that knowledge reveals reality. And what accords equally well with both hypotheses does not support either to the exclusion of the other. But while such doubt is beyond reach by argument, neither is there anything in its favor. It is a mere suspicion which is, and by its nature must remain, without any positive ground; and as such it can hardly be discussed. Such suspicions aside, we can throw into the scale of our theory the impressive fact of the advance of knowledge. It has been the steadfast assumption of science whenever it came to an unsolved problem that there was a key to it to be found, that if things happened thus rather than otherwise they did so for a cause or reason, and that if this were not forthcoming it was never because it was lacking, but always because of a passing blindness in ourselves. Reflection has assumed that pursuit of its own immanent end is not only satisfying but revealing, that so far as the immanent end is achieved we are making progress toward the transcendent end as well. Indeed, that

these ends coincide is the assumption of every act of thinking whatever. To think is to raise a question; to raise a question is to seek an explanation; to seek an explanation is to assume that one may be had; so to assume is to take for granted that nature in that region is intelligible. Certainly the story of advancing knowledge unwinds as if self-realization in thought meant also a coming nearer to reality.

That these processes are really one is the metaphysical base on which our belief in coherence is founded. If one admits that the pursuit of a coherent system has actually carried us to what everyone would agree to call knowledge, why not take this ideal as a guide that will conduct us farther? What better key can one ask to the structure of the real? Our own conviction is that we should take this immanent end of thought in all seriousness as the clue to the nature of things. We admit that it may prove deceptive, that somewhere thought may end its pilgrimage in frustration and futility before some blank wall of the unintelligible. There are even those who evince their superior insight by taking this as a foregone conclusion and regarding the faith that the real is rational as the wishful thinking of the "tender-minded." Their attitude appears to us a compound made up of one part timidity, in the form of a refusal to hope lest they be disillusioned; one part muddled persuasion that to be sceptical is to be sophisticated; one part honest dullness in failing to estimate rightly the weight of the combined postulate and success of knowledge; one part genuine insight into the possibility of surds in nature. But whatever its motives, it is a view that goes less well with the evidence than the opposite and brighter view. That view is that reality is a system, completely ordered and fully intelligible, with which thought in its advance is more and more identifying itself. We may look at the growth of knowledge, individual or social, either as an attempt by our own minds to return to union with things as they are in their ordered wholeness, or the affirmation through our minds of the ordered whole itself. And if we take this view, our notion of truth is marked out for us. Truth is the approximation of thought to reality. It is thought on its way home. Its measure is the distance thought has traveled, under guidance of its inner compass, toward that intelligible system which unites its ultimate object with its ultimate end. Hence at any given time the degree of truth in our experience as a whole is the degree of system it has achieved. The degree of truth of a particular proposition is to be judged in the first instance by its coherence with experience as a whole, ultimately by its coherence with that further whole, all-comprehensive and fully articulated, in which thought can come to rest.

But it is time we defined more explicitly what coherence means. To be sure, no fully satisfactory definition can be given; and as Dr. Ewing says, "It is wrong to tie down the advocates of the coherence theory to a precise definition. What they are doing is to describe an ideal that has never yet been completely clarified but is none the less immanent in all our thinking." [1] Certainly this ideal goes far beyond mere consistency. Fully coherent knowledge would be knowledge in which every judgment entailed, and was entailed by, the rest of the system. Probably we never find in fact a system where there is so much of interdependence. What it means may be clearer if we take a number of familiar systems and arrange them in a series tending to such coherence as a limit. At the bottom would be a junk-

[1] *Idealism* (London: Methuen, 1934), p. 231.

heap, where we could know every item but one and still be without any clue as to what that remaining item was. Above this would come a stone-pile, for here you could at least infer that what you would find next would be a stone. A machine would be higher again, since from the remaining parts one could deduce not only the general character of a missing part, but also its special form and function. This is a high degree of coherence, but it is very far short of the highest. You could remove the engine from a motor-car while leaving the other parts intact, and replace it with any one of thousands of other engines, but the thought of such an interchange among human heads or hearts shows at once that the interdependence in a machine is far below that of the body. Do we find then in organic bodies the highest conceivable coherence? Clearly not. Though a human hand, as Aristotle said, would hardly be a hand when detached from the body, still it would be something definite enough; and we can conceive systems in which even this something would be gone. Abstract a number from the number series and it would be a mere unrecognizable x; similarly, the very thought of a straight line involves the thought of the Euclidean space in which it falls. It is perhaps in such systems as Euclidean geometry that we get the most perfect examples of coherence that have been constructed. If any proposition were lacking, it could be supplied from the rest; if any were altered, the repercussions would be felt through the length and breadth of the system. Yet even such a system as this falls short of ideal system. Its postulates are unproved; they are independent of each other, in the sense that none of them could be derived from any other or even from all the others together; its clear necessity is bought by an abstractness so extreme as to have left out nearly everything that belongs to the character of actual things. A completely satisfactory system would have none of these defects. No proposition would be arbitrary, every proposition would be entailed by the others jointly and even singly,[2] no proposition would stand outside the system. The integration would be so complete that no part could be seen for what it was without seeing its relation to the whole, and the whole itself could be understood only through the contribution of every part.

It may be granted at once that in common life we are satisfied with far less than this. We accept the demonstrations of the geometer as complete, and do not think of reproaching him because he begins with postulates and leaves us at the end with a system that is a skeleton at the best. In physics, in biology, above all in the social sciences, we are satisfied with less still. We test judgments by the amount of coherence which in that particular subject-matter it seems reasonable to expect. We apply, perhaps unconsciously, the advice of Aristotle, and refrain from asking demonstration in the physical sciences, while in mathematics we refuse to accept less. And such facts may be thought to show that we make no actual use of the ideal standard just described. But however much this standard may be relaxed within the limits of a particular science, its influence is evident in the grading of the sciences generally. It is

precisely in those sciences that approach most nearly to system as here defined that we achieve the greatest certainty, and precisely in those that are most remote from such system that our doubt is greatest whether we have achieved scientific truth at all. Our immediate exactions shift with the subject-matter; our ultimate standard is unvarying.

Now if we accept coherence as the test of truth, does that commit us to any conclusions about the *nature* of truth or reality? I think it does, though more clearly about reality than about truth. It is past belief that the fidelity of our thought to reality should be rightly measured by coherence if reality itself were not coherent. To say that the nature of things may be *in*coherent, but we shall approach the truth about it precisely so far as our thoughts become coherent, sounds very much like nonsense. And providing we retained coherence as the test, it would still be nonsense even if truth were conceived as correspondence. On this supposition we should have truth when, our thought having achieved coherence, the correspondence was complete between that thought and its object. But complete correspondence between a coherent thought and an incoherent object seems meaningless. It is hard to see, then, how anyone could consistently take coherence as the test of truth unless he took it also as a character of reality.

Does acceptance of coherence as a test commit us not only to a view about the structure of reality but also to a view about the nature of truth? This is a more difficult question. As we saw at the beginning of the chapter, there have been some highly reputable philosophers who have held that the answer to "What is the test of truth?" is "Coherence," while the answer to "What is the nature or meaning of truth?" is "Cor-

[2] Coherence can be defined without this point, which, as Dr. Ewing remarks (*Idealism*, p. 231), makes the case harder to establish. In no mathematical system, for example, would anyone dream of trying to deduce all the other propositions from any proposition taken singly. But when we are describing an ideal, such a fact is not decisive, and I follow Joachim in holding that in a perfectly coherent system every proposition would entail all others, if only for the reason that its meaning could never be fully understood without apprehension of the system in its entirety.

respondence." These questions are plainly distinct. Nor does there seem to be any direct path from the acceptance of coherence as the test of truth to its acceptance as the nature of truth. Nevertheless there is an indirect path. If we accept coherence as our test, we must use it everywhere. We must therefore use it to test the suggestion that truth *is* other than coherence. But if we do, we shall find that we must reject the suggestion as leading to *in*coherence. Coherence is a pertinacious concept and, like the well-known camel, if one lets it get its nose under the edge of the tent, it will shortly walk off with the whole.

Suppose that, accepting coherence as the test, one rejects it as the nature of truth in favor of some alternative; and let us assume, for example, that this alternative is correspondence. This, we have said, is incoherent; why? Because if one holds that truth is correspondence, one cannot intelligibly hold either that it is tested by coherence or that there is any dependable test at all. Consider the first point. Suppose that we construe experience into the most coherent picture possible, remembering that among the elements included will be such secondary qualities as colors, odors, and sounds. Would the mere fact that such elements as these are coherently arranged prove that anything precisely corresponding to them exists "out there"? I cannot see that it would, even if we knew that the two arrangements had closely corresponding patterns. If on one side you have a series of elements a, b, c . . . , and on the other a series of elements a, β, γ . . . , arranged in patterns that correspond, you have no proof as yet that the *natures* of these elements correspond. It is therefore impossible to argue from a high degree of coherence within experience to its correspondence in the same degree with any-

thing outside. And this difficulty is typical. If you place the nature of truth in one sort of character and its test in something quite different, you are pretty certain, sooner or later, to find the two falling apart. In the end, the only test of truth that is not misleading is the special nature or character that is itself constitutive of truth.

Feeling that this is so, the adherents of correspondence sometimes insist that correspondence shall be its own test. But then the second difficulty arises. If truth does consist in correspondence, no test can be sufficient. For in order to know that experience corresponds to fact, we must be able to get at that fact, unadulterated with idea, and compare the two sides with each other. And we have seen in the last chapter that such fact is not accessible. When we try to lay hold of it, what we find in our hands is a judgment which is obviously not itself the indubitable fact we are seeking, and which must be checked by some fact beyond it. To this process there is no end. And even if we did get at the fact directly, rather than through the veil of our ideas, that would be no less fatal to correspondence. This direct seizure of fact presumably gives us truth, but since that truth no longer consists in correspondence of idea with fact, the main theory has been abandoned. In short, if we can know fact only through the medium of our own ideas, the original forever eludes us; if we can get at the facts directly, we have knowledge whose truth is not correspondence. The theory is forced to choose between scepticism and self-contradiction.

Thus the attempt to combine coherence as the test of truth with correspondence as the nature of truth will not pass muster by its own test. The result is *in*coherence. We believe that an application of the test to other theories of truth would lead to a like result. The argument is: assume co-herence as the test, and you will be driven by the incoherence of your alternatives to the conclusion that it is also the nature of truth.

COMMENT

The Three Main Theories of Truth

In Chapter 5, we reviewed the pragmatist theory of truth. If we shear away James' more exaggerated view (which defines truth in terms of satisfaction or expediency), the remaining doctrine is that truth is verification or verifiability. Let us call this the verification theory of truth. It is accepted not only by moderate pragmatism but also by the flourishing contemporary philosophical movement called "logical empiricism," to which such important thinkers as Moritz Schlick (1882–1936), Rudolf Carnap (1891–   ), and Ludwig Wittgenstein (1889–1951) have contributed.

The core of logical empiricism is its reliance on verifiability as the criterion of meaning. In this respect, it is closely affiliated with the method of clarification advocated by Charles Peirce in "How to Make Our Ideas Clear." When the logical empiricists turn to the subject of truth, they sharply distinguish between *logical* and *factual* truth. Logical truth, as in pure mathematics and formal logic, is interpreted as consistency. "Two plus two equals four" is consistent and therefore true, whereas "two plus two equals five" is inconsistent and therefore false. When it comes to factual truth, the logical empiricists employ the criterion of empirical verification. They try to discover the ultimate observational basis of factual propositions and to test the propositions by the relevant observations. The observations which they regard as scientifically reliable are public, repeatable, and objective rather than private, unrepeatable, and subjective. This theory is so close to the position of Peirce and moderate pragmatism that no selection from any of the epistemological writings of the logical empiricists is included in the present volume.

There are, however, two other principal theories of truth—the correspondence theory and the coherence theory, which were touched upon briefly in our exposition of James' thought. The preceding selection from Bertrand Russell represents the correspondence theory, and the selection from Brand Blanshard represents the coherence theory. Let us consider each in turn.

Realism and the Correspondence Theory

During the long period in which Russell has been writing—almost sixty years—he has continued to develop, modify, and change his ideas. The views which we shall now briefly consider are those expressed in *The Problems of*

Philosophy (1912)—a relatively early work. In this book Russell rejected the idealistic doctrine that whatever exists must be in some sense mental and maintained the "realistic" theory that knowledge of physical things involves four factors: (1) a knowing self, (2) an act of awareness, (3) the "sense data" of which we are immediately aware, and (4) the physical objects known through the mediation of the sense data.

Each of us, according to this view, is a self aware of objects. What is the nature of this awareness? Russell distinguishes between two ways of knowing—knowing by *acquaintance* and knowing by *description*. We have acquaintance with anything of which we are directly aware. When I am actually seeing and touching a table, for example, I am acquainted, not with the physical table itself, but with the sensible qualities that make up the appearance of the table—its color, shape, smoothness, hardness, etc. We thus have acquaintance in sensation with the data of the outer senses, and we also have acquaintance in introspection with the data of mental processes—thoughts, feelings, desires, etc.—and of course we have memories of both types of data. Russell believes that we are also acquainted with *universals* of various kinds, such as *triangularity*. Like Plato, he argues that we have a kind of direct awareness of these universals.

But no one is acquainted with physical objects or other people's minds; these we know by *description, i.e.,* indirectly, through the mediation of signs or symbols. Since I am not a mind reader, I know the minds of my friends in this way, through written and spoken words, facial expressions, gestures, etc. Similarly, I know physical objects through their sensible appearances. I am not directly acquainted with the physical sun—that huge and distant physical mass, with its vastly complex atomic structure. I am acquainted only with a sense datum—a bright yellow shape—which I regard as an appearance of the sun, resulting from my sensory reaction to light rays which have traveled millions of miles through space. There is a causal relation between the physical sun and "seeing the sun," and also some degree of resemblance between the sense datum and the physical object (*e.g.,* the sense datum is round and the sun is supposedly a round lump of very hot matter). The existence of physical objects, which are causally related to our sense data and are believed to bear some resemblance to these sense data, is known only by inference. Russell admits that we can never prove the existence of physical objects; yet he accepts their existence as the simplest and most plausible hypothesis to account for the facts of ordinary sense perception and the findings of physical science.

Thus far, in our summary of Russell's epistemology, we have been considering the knowledge of *things* as known either by acquaintance or description. In addition, Russell discusses the knowledge of *truths.* This sort of knowledge occurs when we believe a statement that corresponds with facts.

A statement is expressed in words which form a sentence, but the same statement can be expressed in different words or different sentences. Thus a sentence can be translated from English into French without changing in meaning, or the same statement can be expressed in different ways in the same language. For example, the sentences "Booth shot Lincoln" and "Lincoln was shot by Booth" differ in structure but express the same proposition. Truth depends upon *what* is said, not upon *how* it is said. But it also depends upon something other than the statement; namely, upon the facts. In the absence of corresponding facts, the statement is false.

Thus truth has an opposite—falsehood. In this sense, it differs from acquaintance, which does not admit of deception. For example, when I am acquainted with a red patch there is no deception. I can be deceived only if I make some inference—for example, that the red patch represents the cover of a book. But as soon as I make an inference, my belief may be either true or false. The "book" that I think I see may be an illusion. Hence a satisfactory theory of truth must admit of falsehood.

When one believes a true statement, such as "Robert Browning loved Elizabeth Barrett," one is referring to real facts or events which serve to make the statement true. But when Othello believes a false statement, that "Desdemona loves Cassio," there seems to be no corresponding fact or event and hence no *object* to which the belief is directed. Yet it seems quite clear that *something* is being believed by Othello. One might suppose that there are peculiar entities called "objective falsehoods," and that one of these has been, as it were, lying in wait for Othello to believe it.

To avoid so implausible an explanation, Russell points out that the difficulty arises from supposing that, when one believes a falsehood, there is simply a *dual* relation between the mind and an object. If, instead, we think of belief as a *multiple* relation between the mind and several objects, we can explain falsehood without assuming the objective existence of falsehoods. When we make a mistake we make a wrong mental connection—as when we mistakenly connect a red sense datum with a physical object. Othello's error consists in connecting the terms—Desdemona, loving, and Cassio—in the wrong way; that is, in a way to which no actual fact or event corresponds. When, on the other hand, a person makes the right mental connections, so that the object-terms are related in the belief as the objects are related in fact, the belief is true. This would be the case when we correctly judge that Robert Browning loved Elizabeth Barrett. Hence, a mind believes truly "when there is a *corresponding* complex not involving the mind, but only its objects. This correspondence ensures truth, and its absence entails falsehood."

As Russell points out, this theory "(1) allows truth to have an opposite, namely falsehood, (2) makes truth a property of beliefs, but (3) makes it a property wholly dependent upon the relation of the beliefs to outside things."

The correspondence theory, as thus set forth, is clearly distinguishable from the verification theory. It maintains that there are objective matters of fact and beliefs related to these matters of fact in ways which make the beliefs true or false quite independently of whether either alternative can be verified. Indeed, according to Russell, there is no reason to suppose that all true propositions are verifiable. He also rejects *coherence* as a definition of truth, although he retains it as an important *test* of truth. Since his criticism of the coherence theory is clearly stated in the preceding selection, we shall not recapitulate his arguments.

We have been discussing *factual* truth, not *logical* truth. In more recent works, Russell agrees with the logical empiricists in distinguishing between these two kinds of truth, and in interpreting logical truth as consistency and logical falsehood as contradiction. With respect to factual truth, he has continued to hold to a correspondence theory—phrased somewhat differently in his later works.

Idealism and the Coherence Theory

The coherence theory is the view that truth is to be found in the most consistent and comprehensive system of propositions. The truth of any single proposition is to be judged by its coherence with this system. This doctrine has been most closely associated with the tradition of idealism, especially "absolute idealism."

The fundamental emphasis of absolute idealism, as we find in the philosophy of, for example, G. W. F. Hegel (1770–1831), is upon total integration. According to this point of view, the whole of reality is a system in which each part is relational. Hence the part cannot be understood in isolation—any more than a single line in a well-integrated painting can be understood and appreciated in isolation from the rest of the painting, or a single theorem in geometry understood in isolation from the geometrical system of which it is a part. Hence, to see things together, in their interconnection and unity, is to see them truly; to see things apart, as isolated, fragmentary, and contradictory, is to see them falsely. No proposition taken in isolation is wholly true because no thing taken in isolation is wholly real. Complete or absolute truth is attained only when all fragmentariness disappears and all contradictions vanish within a final, all-inclusive organization of meanings.

With this emphasis upon comprehensive unity, the absolute idealists reject any dualistic system of metaphysics, such as that of Descartes, which would sharply divide reality into mind and matter. Although they agree with Descartes' view that we directly know our own minds and our own mental experiences, they disagree with his contention that our ideas represent external *physical* things. The whole of reality is a unity because it is one both in kind and in structure—a unified system of spirit or mind. But it is worth noting that Spinoza (1632–1677), without embracing idealism, maintained that all reality is a systematic unity and that truth is a kind of coherence. For him, both mind and matter are real, but they are aspects of a single comprehensive being, called Substance or God. One does not have to be an idealist to hold the coherence theory of truth, but most of its spokesmen have been idealists.

Absolute idealism found its classic expression in the philosophy of Hegel, but it received a very impressive formulation in more recent philosophies, such as the systems of Francis Herbert Bradley (1846–1924) in England and Josiah Royce (1855–1916) in the United States. Since the beginning of the century, idealism has suffered a decline in competition with more naturalistic philosophical movements, such as materialism, pragmatism, and logical empiricism, but it still remains one of the great philosophical movements.

Among its contemporary spokesmen, one of the most impressive is Brand Blanshard. There are three steps in Blanshard's argument: he undertakes to prove (1) that coherence is the test of truth, (2) that it is the mark of reality, and (3) that it is the nature of truth.

1. *The test of truth.* Blanshard points out that the activity of knowing has two ends, one "immanent" and the other "transcendent." The immanent end is to attain a state of insight that will satisfy an inner demand—the craving to know. The transcendent end is to reveal things as they really are.

What is the *test* that thought, in its double purposiveness, has reached its goal? Blanshard examines various "tests" of truth—the voice of authority, the warrant of mystical experience, "working" as defined by the pragmatist, self-evidence, and correspondence with fact. He contends that each one of these, in so far as it is valid, turns out to be coherence in disguise. His argument is too long even to summarize, but we shall at least consider his criticism of the correspondence theory.

Let us examine three types of judgment: a judgment about an event in the past, a judgment about a present object of reference, and a judgment about an object of "acquaintance." Consider first the historical judgment: "Burr killed Hamilton in a duel." Correspondence as a test of truth is here unworkable because there is no way of comparing the judgment with the original event. One of the terms that allegedly corresponds has irrevocably disappeared with the flight of time. Consequently, we must fall back upon some other test, and this test turns out to be coherence:

If this belief about Hamilton is true, then a thousand references in newspapers, magazines, and books, and almost endless facts about the fortunes of Hamilton's family, about the later life of Burr, and about American constitutional history fall into place in a consistent picture. If it is false, then the most credible journalists, historians and statesmen, generation after generation, may be so deluded about events that happen before the eyes of a nation that no single historical fact is any longer above suspicion. If evidence of this weight is to be rejected, then in consistency we must go on to reject almost every hint that takes us beyond immediate perception. And intellectually speaking, that would pull our house about our heads. What really tests the judgment is the extent of our accepted world that is implicated with it and would be carried down with it if it fell. And that is the test of coherence.[1]

Let us next take a judgment about a present object of reference: "That is a cardinal on the branch yonder." It would seem that the test of correspondence is easy to apply in this case: to assure yourself that there is a correspondence between the judgment and the fact, you simply look at the branch and see the cardinal. But the test is by no means so simple. In the first place, you recognize the cardinal because you have a *concept* of what a cardinal is, and this involves innumerable connections with a larger system of meanings:

> The idea of living organisms, the thought of the bird kingdom and its outstanding characteristics, the notions of flight and a peculiar song and a determinate color—these and many other notions are so bound up with the identification that our thought would lose its character with the removal of any one of them.[2]

The concept of a cardinal thus has meaning only when it is implicated in a coherent system of ideas. And secondly, as Russell would point out, what we directly perceive is not the cardinal but certain sense data—colored shapes and noises. These we take to be the *appearance* of a cardinal. But if we try to verify this appearance by the test of correspondence, we again run into trouble. The theory supposes that there are two entities: (*A*) the appearance, and (*B*) the external object. We directly know *A*, the appearance, but not *B*, the object. But if we do not know *B*—if it can never be confronted—we can never know that *B* corresponds to *A*, or to any judgment we make about *A*. Hence we must again fall back upon the test of coherence. If the appearance fits coherently into the larger pattern of our knowledge and experience, we judge the object to be real. If not, we judge it to be false.

Finally, let us consider a judgment about an object of acquaintance: "I have a toothache." Here it would seem absolutely certain that the proposition corresponds with the fact. At the moment that I feel the aching tooth, I surely am directly aware of the correspondence between the judgment and the ache.

[1] *The Nature of Thought* (London: Allen and Unwin, and New York: Macmillan, 1940), II, p. 227.
[2] *Ibid.*, pp. 228–229.

But again, grasp of the truth is not so simple as it appears; the judgment turns out to be quite complicated:

> "I," that is, a self; "have," that is, a relation of ownership; "a," that is, one member of a class; "toothache," that is, a special kind of pain connected with a particular point in the body; every one of these elements is included and asserted as real; every one of them goes beyond sense data; yet every one of them must be given in fact if the verification is to be completed.[3]

Thus, what appears to be a matter of simple acquaintance really involves interpretation and reference.

Blanshard argues that in the case of even simpler judgments—as simple as we can make them—there is always an element of interpretation that goes beyond mere acquaintance with data. Suppose I respond to the toothache with a mere "Ouch!" If this is nothing more than an exclamation—a thoughtless wincing of my nervous system—there is no judgment and hence nothing to be called true or false. But if the "Ouch" really signifies the mental recognition of a pain (even though the "I," the "have," the "a," and "tooth" are left out), there is implicit reference beyond the immediate datum. The pain, for example, is recognized as *now*. "But 'now' means membership in a series; 'the present,' as Landor says, 'like a note in music, is nothing but as it appertains to what is past and what is to come'; and past and future are not data."[4] Moreover, if the pain is grasped as of a certain kind and degree (for example, sharp and intense), it is recognized as falling at a certain point within a scale of degrees and a range of qualities. By such examples, Blanshard seeks to show that the data of sensation are suffused with thought and judgment.

He thus questions Russell's distinction between knowledge by acquaintance and knowledge by description. The "sense data" that Russell and other contemporary realists talk about are neither so sensory nor so given as their name implies. The factor of thought is no less necessary than the factor of sense if there is to be any knowledge or any grasp of truth. What is sensorily given, if it could ever be isolated, would be too meager to constitute knowledge or to establish the truth of any judgment. Hence, there is no knowledge of acquaintance without the sort of concepts and judgments that enter into description. Moreover, as soon as we begin to describe, we relate our impressions to a system of meanings, and we are then compelled, as before, to fall back upon coherence as the test of truth. In the final analysis, Blanshard maintains, no other test will work.

2. *The mark of reality.* If coherence is the only effective *test* of truth, this surely implies that reality is coherent. As Blanshard points out in the preced-

---

[3] *Ibid.*, p. 230.
[4] *Ibid.*, p. 231.

ing selection, "To say that the nature of things may be *in*coherent, but [that] we shall approach the truth about it precisely so far as our thoughts become coherent, sounds very much like nonsense." Hence he concludes that coherence is not only the test of truth but the mark of reality.

But just how coherent is reality? The more we know about reality, the more we find system, interconnection, consistent and comprehensive order. The progress of science has been a steady movement in this direction. Hence Blanshard feels that we are justified in concluding that "reality is a system, completely ordered and fully intelligible, with which thought in its advance is more and more identifying itself." He admits that proof of such a system, all-inclusive and perfectly integrated, is not possible. To *know* so perfect a system would be completely to fulfill the theoretic impulse, and this of course no man has done. But at least, the more we know, the more reality appears in this guise. Hence there is nothing to forbid the conclusion that as thought approximates its immanent end, the achievement of systematic vision, it also approximates its transcendent end, the apprehension of reality.

3. *The nature of truth.* To say that the *test* of truth is coherence but that the *nature* of truth is correspondence leads to intellectual *in*coherence. Hence, according to the test, this will not pass muster. If coherence is one thing and correspondence is something quite different, then no amount of coherence will be proof of correspondence. The truth-seeker will always be plagued by the possibility that coherence is merely subjective. The test of truth and the nature of truth, being quite different, will fall apart. But if we apprehend truth in the very act of testing it—if coherence is not only the test but the very nature of truth—then we are not condemned to seek a truth that we can never verify. "In the end, the only test of truth that is not misleading is the special nature or character that is itself constitutive of truth." We must therefore conclude that truth *is* coherence.

If these contentions are sound, truth is a matter of degree. Absolute truth applies only to the most complete and integrated system of thought; but the system of present knowledge always falls short of this absolute limit. The measure of truth is the extent to which our thought approximates this upper limit of coherence. For example, the astronomical system of Ptolemy is not so true as that of Copernicus, the system of Copernicus is not so true as that of Newton, and the system of Newton is not so true as that of Einstein. Each later system of scientific explanation is more inclusive and unified, and hence exhibits a higher degree of truth.

Conclusion

We shall not undertake a comprehensive criticism of the foregoing conceptions of truth. In discussing pragmatism in the preceding chapter, we have already advanced some criticisms of the view that truth is verification or verifiability. In addition, the foregoing selection from Russell contains a brief criticism of the coherence theory, and we have indicated something of the tenor of Blanshard's criticism of the correspondence theory.

The correspondence theory has the merit of insisting that there are independent facts to which our beliefs, if they are to be true, must conform. This interpretation accords with both common sense and the objective methods of science. Indeed, it seems obviously correct to say that the truth of a belief consists in its agreement with, or correspondence to, an existing state of affairs. But the main question is how we are to grasp these independent facts to which our beliefs must conform. And here, the answer of the realist has sometimes been rather naïve. He has spoken as if we could seize the "given" or the "datum" as bare, brute fact, quite apart from interpretation or judgment; or he has taken it for granted that the "datum" reveals the independent physical object. "Facts," particularly "facts" independent of experience, are not simply apprehended; they have to be established by acts of judgment. Moreover, it is impossible directly to compare a present proposition with a past, future, or unexperienced object. Such comparison would require the past, the future, or the unexperienced object to be now present for comparison, and this is impossible. Hence the alleged correspondence between the proposition and the object cannot be directly confirmed. Evidently, there must be a process of inference and judgment which the correspondence theory, in itself, does not delineate.

In emphasizing the judgmental element in knowledge, the coherence theory has made a necessary contribution. In general, we test the truth of statements by seeing if they will fit in with all the other statements that we are prepared to believe. Although the coherence theory has the merit of thus insisting upon the systematic character of our knowledge, it seems to go too far when it *identifies* truth with the coherence of our judgments. If a new race of poets should arise who could imagine a set of propositions that would be more consistent and coherent than the whole body of our science, that would not make the propositions true. Knowledge must be not only coherent but anchored to what is independently real.

We have now completed our survey of epistemology. Beginning with Descartes, we have examined the two principal methods of arriving at truth, rationalism and empiricism, and we have surveyed various conceptions of meaning and truth as formulated by pragmatists, realists, and idealists. These epistemological theories are intimately related to the metaphysical doctrines in Part Three. The separation of epistemology and metaphysics is rather artificial, and the metaphysicians that we shall next examine have much to say about truth and knowledge.

PART THREE

The Nature of Reality

INTRODUCTORY NOTE

IN PART TWO we have been concerned mainly with epistemology, or the theory of knowledge—especially with the meaning of truth and the methods of its attainment. In Part Three we shall be concerned primarily with metaphysics, or the theory of reality. It is impossible, however, to sharply separate epistemology and metaphysics. For example, in Part Two, we studied the philosophy of Descartes, which is as important for metaphysics as for epistemology; and in Part Three we shall examine the philosophies of Berkeley, Hume, and Kant, which have contributed as greatly to epistemology as to metaphysics. The difference between Part Two and Part Three, therefore, is not an absolute difference in subject matter but a relative difference in emphasis.

We shall consider the question "What is the fundamental nature of man and the surrounding universe?" This question directs attention to "the metaphysics of the microcosm"—of the "I" or self as a small part of the whole scheme of things—and to "the metaphysics of the macrocosm"—of the great, all-enveloping system of reality. We shall not attempt to separate these two inquiries, and, indeed, any sharp separation would be artificial. But each of the theories that we shall consider will throw light upon the nature of the human person and the nature of his total environment. We shall discuss five answers—not all mutually exclusive:

1. *The answer of the teleologist.* This interpretation finds the principal explanation of the nature of existence in "teleology" (from the Greek word *telos,* meaning end or goal). Teleology is the doctrine that reality is ordered by goals, ends, purposes, values. It seeks to explain the past and the present in terms of the future; it asserts, that is, that things occur to realize future ends.

2. *The answer of the materialist.* As opposed to the teleologist, the materialist tries to explain the present and the future in terms of past or antecedent

causes, and these causes are conceived to be material, such as the movement of physical atoms.

3. *The answer of the idealist.* Like the materialist, the idealist denies ultimate dualism, but unlike the materialist, he regards mind rather than matter as the basic stuff.

4. *The answer of the sceptic.* In contrast with all positive theorists, the sceptic contends that it is impossible to know the real nature of the external world and the deeper underlying nature of the human being.

5. *The answer of the theist.* The view of the theist may be combined with teleology, dualism, idealism, or vitalism, but it is incompatible with a complete materialism or an absolute scepticism. It conceives of human beings and animals as the creatures of God and of nature as God's handiwork.

In addition to these five answers, there is the answer of the dualist, as illustrated by the philosophy of Descartes, which we examined in Chapter 3. The dualist recognizes two distinct and irreducible kinds of being—mind and matter—and regards man as a combination of the two. Although Descartes defined the essence of the mind as thought and the essence of body as extension, he maintained that the two substances, the physical and the mental, interact within the pineal gland of the human brain. Although no one would now assign so crucial a role to the pineal gland and few philosophers would now distinguish mind and matter so sharply, Descartes' basic concept of dualism remains one of the principal answers to the central question of metaphysics. The reader should bear this answer in mind while considering the alternative theories presented in Part Three.

7

Teleology

ARISTOTLE (384 B.C.–322 B.C.)

The greatest proponent of a teleological interpretation of existence is Aristotle. He was born in Stagira, a town in Macedonia colonized by Greeks. At the time of his birth, Socrates had been dead for fifteen years and Plato was thirty-three. Aristotle's father Nichomachus, having achieved some renown, became court physician to King Amyntas II of Macedonia. Refusing to follow his father's profession, Aristotle at the age of eighteen migrated to Athens, where he lived for twenty years as a member of Plato's school, the Academy. When the master died, Aristotle left Athens to spend four years on the coast of Asia Minor, engaged mainly in biological research. During this period he married, and his wife eventually bore him a daughter. Subsequently he married a second time and had two sons, one adopted and one natural.

Meanwhile Philip, the son of Amyntas, having become King of Macedonia, invited Aristotle to take charge of the education of his son Alexander, then thirteen years old. In consequence of accepting this invitation, Aristotle must have acquired intimate knowledge of court affairs, but he makes no mention of the great Macedonian empire built up by Philip and Alexander the Great. Perhaps he was too close to kings to be greatly impressed by courtly glitter.

He stayed with Philip for seven years, until the monarch's death, and lingered at the court for about a year after Alexander's accession to the throne. Then he returned to Athens to resume his philosophical career. At this time the Academy was being reorganized, and Xenocrates, a second-rate philosopher, was made head. Evidently disappointed at the choice, Aristotle withdrew and founded a school of his own, the Lyceum. He directed the school for twelve years, his greatest period of productivity.

Aristotle's reputation and the prosperity of his school suffered from the anti-Macedonian reaction which took place after Alexander's death in 323 B.C. Accused of impiety, Aristotle, unlike Socrates, fled to the island of Euboea, vowing that he would not "give the Athenians a second chance of sinning against philosophy." A year later, in 322 B.C., he died of a stomach disease, at the age of sixty-three.

His writings, as they have come down to us, lack the beauty of Plato's dialogues and are without wit, personal charm, or poetry. He also wrote popular works, including dialogues, which were praised by Cicero for "the incredible flow and sweetness of their diction"; but by an unhappy chance only his more technical writings have been preserved. The works that remain touch upon almost every phase of human knowledge, and they establish Aristotle's reputation not only as an extremely versatile philosopher but as an accomplished biologist.

From *The Physics* *

1. [*Explanation of Change*]

Our first step must be to recognize that one thing does not act upon nor become affected by nor turn into any other thing at random, except "in an incidental sense." We could not describe a man's "pallid whiteness" as arising from his "being cultured" unless this had been incidentally connected with a quality opposed to whiteness—*i.e.*, "swarthy blackness." White can arise only from "not-white"; and by not-white I do not mean just any quality at random that happens to be other than white, but black or some intermediate color. "Being cultured," in turn, does not arise from anything at random, but from the "*un*cultured"—unless, of course, we postulate some quality intermediate between the two.

Qualities are restricted similarly in their disappearance. White does not pass into the quality of being cultured, except in an incidental sense; strictly speaking, it can pass only into the opposite of white—*i.e.*, not into anything at all that happens to be other than white, but into black or some intermediate color. So too, "being cultured" will not pass into anything at random, but only into the state of being uncultured, or else into some state intermediate between the two.

It is the same with everything else. Even composite structures, as distinguished from simple qualities, follow the same law; we overlook this aspect, however, because the corresponding lack of structure has received no name. Nevertheless, a particular harmony or arrangement of parts can only have arisen from a state in which that particular arrangement was lacking; and when it is destroyed it will pass not into anything at random, but into that state which is its specific opposite. Whether such an arrange-

---

* Parts 1, 3, 4, and 5 are from *Aristotle: Containing Selections from Seven of the Most Important Books of Aristotle,* translated by Philip Wheelwright, copyright by the Odyssey Press, 1935, 1951. Part 2 is a translation by Henry M. Magid in *Landmarks for Beginners in Philosophy,* copyright by the editors, Irwin Edman and Herbert W. Schneider: Reynal and Hitchcock; Henry Holt and Company, 1941. Reprinted by permission.

ment of parts is called a harmony or an order or a combination is immaterial: the rule holds good in any case. In fact, it holds good even of a house or a statue or any other such product. A house comes into existence out of materials previously unjoined; a statue, or anything else that has been molded into shape, out of a material previously unwrought; all such constructions involving either a combination or an ordering of parts.

This being so, we may conclude that whenever anything is created or destroyed it necessarily passes out of or into either its opposite or some intermediate state. And since each group of intermediates is derived from some pair of opposites (colors, for instance, from white and black), it follows that whatever comes into existence by a natural process is either itself one of a pair of opposites or a product of such a pair. . . .

"Coming into existence" takes place in several ways: (1) by change of shape, as a bronze statue; (2) by accretion, as things that grow; (3) by subduction, as a Hermes chiseled from a block of marble; (4) by combination, as a house; and (5) by "qualitative alteration," where the material itself assumes different properties. In all of these cases it is evident that the process of coming into existence presupposes a substratum which is already existing.

Hence it appears that whatever "becomes" is always composite: there is something [a new element of form] that comes into existence, and something else that becomes it. This "something else" may be conceived in a double sense: as the enduring substratum, or as the original qualification which in the process is replaced by its opposite. In the example previously employed, "uncultured" is the original qualification, "man" is the subject; in the making of a statue the lack of form, shape, and

order is the original qualification, while the bronze or stone or gold is the subject. If we grant, then, that all things are determined by causes and basic principles, of which they are the essential, not the accidental, result, it plainly follows that everything comes into existence at one and the same time from the subject and from a certain form. For "cultured man" consists, so to speak, of both "man" and "cultured"; and the meaning of the composite term can be analyzed into these two component meanings. Elements like these, then, are the conditions of any becoming.

The subject of any change is numerically one, but with a duality of form. A man, or gold, or any other "material susceptible of form," can be regarded as a unit, and is the essential basis of the process that transpires; but the "lack of form" and its opposite are related to the process only incidentally. At the same time it is also possible to regard the acquired form—the order, or the state of culture attained—as something unitary. Thus we must recognize a sense in which the principles are two, and another sense in which they are three. From one point of view it seems enough to take as principles some pair of opposites such as cultured vs. uncultured, hot vs. cold, or joined vs. unjoined; but there is another point of view from which this interpretation is inadequate, inasmuch as opposites cannot be acted on by each other. We therefore solve the difficulty by postulating a substratum distinct from either of the opposites which successively inhere in it, and not itself the opposite of anything. . . .

What the underlying substratum is, can be understood by analogy. As bronze is to a completed statue, wood to a bed, and still unformed materials to the objects fashioned from them, so the underlying substratum is to anything substantial, particular, and existent. . . .

2. [The Four Causes]

In the first place, one calls cause that which composes a thing, and that from which it arises. Thus one can say in this sense that bronze is the cause of the statue, and silver is the cause of the phial; and one applies this way of speaking to all things of the same kind. (Material cause.) In a second sense, the cause is the form and the model of things; it is the essential character of the thing and its kind. Thus in music, the cause of the octave is the ratio 2:1, and, in a more general way, it is number; and with number, it is the part which enters into its definition. (Formal cause.) In a third sense, the cause is the source from which movement or rest comes. Thus he who, in a certain case, has given advice to act is the cause of the acts which are accomplished; the father is the cause of the child; and generally speaking that which acts is the cause of that which is done; that which produces a change is the cause of the change produced. (Efficient cause.) Fourthly, cause signifies the end and the goal of a thing. Thus health is the cause of walking. If we ask, "Why is he walking?" the answer is, "In order to be well," and when we say this, we believe that we have the cause of the walking. This meaning applies to all the intermediaries who contribute to the attainment of the final end, after the first mover has started the movement. For example, dieting and purgation, or drugs and the instruments of the surgeon can be regarded as means to health; and the only difference is that some are acts and others are instruments. (Final cause.)

These are briefly the meanings of the word cause. In accordance with this diversity of senses, a single thing can have several causes at the same time, and not simply. Thus, for the statue, one can assign to it as causes both the art of the sculptor who has made it and the bronze of which it is made and not in any other sense than as a statue. The two causes are not to be understood in the same sense; they differ in that one is the material and the other is the source of the movement. It is also because of this that there can be said to be things that are reciprocally the causes of each other. Thus exercise is the cause of health, and health is the cause of exercise; but not in the same sense, for, in the first case, health is the end, while in the second health is the source of the movement. Moreover, a single thing is at times the cause of opposite results; for, the same thing which is the cause of a given effect when it is present, can be the cause of an opposite effect when it is absent. For example, the absence of the pilot can be considered the cause of the loss of the ship, because the presence of the same pilot could have guaranteed its safety.

All the causes mentioned can be reduced to these four very obvious kinds. The letters of the alphabet are the cause of the syllables; the material is the cause of the things which art produces; fire and the other elements are the causes of the bodies which they compose; the parts are the cause of the whole, and the propositions are the causes of the conclusions which are drawn from them. Each of these is a cause since it is that out of which the other thing comes. Of these, the causes are either the subject of the thing, as parts relative to the whole; or the essential character of the thing, as the whole and the synthesis and the form; or the source of change or rest, as the germ, the physician, the giver of advice, and in general that which has effects; and finally, in the fourth place, the end and the good of other things; the attainment of the best is that for the sake of which the thing exists, and it would make no difference whether one said the real or the apparent good.

3. [Luck and Chance]

"Luck" and "pure spontaneous chance" are sometimes included in the list of explanatory factors, and many things are said to come about "as luck would have it" or "by chance." In what sense may luck and chance be included among the types of determining factor just enumerated? Further, is luck the same thing as pure chance or something different? And exactly what is each of them?

Some people question even their existence. Nothing, they declare, happens fortuitously; whatever we ascribe to luck or pure chance has been somehow determined. Take, for instance, the case of a man who goes to market and "as luck would have it" meets someone whom he wanted but did not expect to meet: his going to market, they say, was responsible for this. So they argue that of any other occurrence ascribed to luck there is always some more positive explanation to be found. Luck [they say] cannot have been the reason, for it would be paradoxical to regard luck as something real. Further, they consider it noteworthy that none of the ancient philosophers mentioned luck when discussing the reasons of becoming and perishing—an indication, apparently, that they disbelieved in the possibility of fortuitous occurrences.

Yet it is odd that while people theoretically accept the venerable argument which assumes that every chance happening and stroke of luck can be attributed to some reason or other, they nevertheless continue to speak of some things as matters of luck, others not. The earlier philosophers ought to have taken some account of this popular distinction, but among their various principles—love and strife, mind, fire, etc.—luck finds no place. The omission is equally surprising whether we suppose them to have disbelieved in luck or to have believed in but disregarded it; for at any rate they were not above employing the idea in their explanations. Empedocles, for example, remarks that air is sifted up into the sky not uniformly but "as it may chance"; or, in the words of his *Cosmogony*, "Now it 'happened' to run this way, now that." And the parts of animals, he declares, came to be what they are purely by chance.

Some go so far as to attribute the heavens and all the worlds to "chance happenings," declaring that the vortex—*i.e.*, the motion which separated and arranged the entire universe in its present order—arose "of itself." We may well be surprised at this assertion that while the existence and generation of animals and plants must be attributed not to chance but to nature or mind or something of the sort (what issues from a particular sperm or seed is obviously not a matter of chance, since from one kind of seed there comes forth an olive, from another a man), yet the heavens and the divinest of visible things have come into existence spontaneously and have no determining factors such as animals and plants have. Even if this were true, it would be something to give us pause, and ought to have elicited some comment. For apart from the generally paradoxical nature of such a theory it is rather odd that people should accept it when they can find no evidence of spontaneous occurrences among celestial phenomena but plenty of such evidence among the things in which they deny the presence of chance. The evidence is just the opposite of what should have been expected if their theory were true.

There are other people who, while accepting luck as a determining factor of things, regard it as something divinely mysterious, inscrutable to human intelligence.

Accordingly we must investigate the nature of luck and chance, and see whether they are the same as each other or different, and how they fit into our classification of determining factors.

To begin with, when we see certain things occurring in a certain way either uniformly or "as a general rule," we obviously would not ascribe them to mere luck. A stroke of luck is not something that comes to pass either by uniform necessity or as a general rule. But as there is also a third sort of event which is found to occur, which everyone speaks of as being a matter of luck, and which we all know is meant when the word "lucky" is used, it is plain that such a thing as luck and "pure spontaneous chance" must exist.

Some events "serve a purpose," others do not. Of the former class, some are in accordance with the intention of the purposer, others not; but both are in the class of things that serve a purpose. Evidently, then, even among occurrences that are not the predictable (*i.e.,* neither the constant nor normal) results of anyone's actual intention, there are some which may be spoken of as serving a purpose. What serves a purpose may have originated either in thought or in nature: in either case when its occurrence is accidental [1] we call it a matter of luck. Just as everything has both an essential nature and a number of incidental attributes, so when anything is considered as a determining factor it may have similarly a twofold aspect. When a man builds a house, for instance, his faculty of housebuilding is the essential determinant of the house, while the fact that he is blond or cultured is only incidental to that result. The essential determinant can be calculated, but the incidentally related factors are incalculable, for any number of them may inhere in one subject.

[1] *I.e.,* when in the case of deliberate actions the result is unforeseen, and when in the case of natural occurrences the result is neither certain nor usual.

As already explained, then, we attribute to chance or luck whatever happens [accidentally] in such a way as to serve a purpose. (The specific difference between chance and luck will be explained later; for the present it is enough to emphasize that both of them refer to actions that happen to serve a purpose.) As an illustration, suppose that we wish to solicit a man for a contribution of money. Had we known where he was we should have gone there and accosted him. But if with some other end in view we go to a place which it is not our invariable nor even our usual practice to visit, then, since the end effected (getting the money) is not a spontaneous process of nature, but is the type of thing that results from conscious choice and reflection, we describe the meeting as a stroke of luck. It would not be a matter of luck, however, if we were to visit the place for the express purpose of seeking our man, or if we regularly went there when taking up subscriptions. Luck, then, is evidently an incidental aspect of the real reason of something in the sphere of actions that involve purposive choice and reflection. Hence, since choice implies "intelligent reflection," we may conclude that luck and intelligent reflection both refer to the same sphere of things and activities. . . .

According as the result of a fortuitous action is good or bad we speak of good and bad luck. In more serious matters we use the terms "good fortune" and "misfortune"; and when we escape by a hair's breadth some great evil or just miss some great good we consider ourselves fortunate or unfortunate accordingly—the margin having been so slight that we can reflect upon the good or ill in question as if it were actually present. Moreover, as all luck is unstable (for nothing invariable or normal could be attributed to luck), we are right in regarding good fortune as also unstable.

Both luck and spontaneous chance, then, as has been said, are determining factors in a purely incidental sense and are attributed to the type of occurrence which is neither constant nor normal and which might have been aimed at for its own sake.

The difference between luck and chance is that "chance" is the more inclusive term. Every case of luck is a case of chance, but not all cases of chance are cases of luck.

Luck, together with lucky or unlucky occurrences, is spoken of only in connection with agents that are capable of enjoying good [or ill] fortune and of performing moral actions. It follows, then, that luck always has some reference to conduct—a conclusion which is further enforced by the popular belief that "good fortune" is the same, or practically the same, as "happiness"; and that happiness, as it involves "well-doing," is a kind of "moral action." Hence only what is capable of moral conduct can perform actions that are lucky or the reverse. Luck does not pertain to the activities of a lifeless thing, a beast, or a child, for these exercise no "deliberate choice." If we call them lucky or unlucky we are speaking figuratively—as when Protarchus speaks of altar stones as fortunate because they are treated with reverence while their fellows are trampled underfoot. All such objects are affected by luck only in so far as a moral agent may deal with them in a manner that is lucky or unlucky [to himself].

"Pure spontaneous chance," on the other hand, is found both among the lower animals and in many lifeless things. We say of a horse, for example, that it went "by chance" to a place of safety, meaning that it was not for the sake of safety that it went there. Again, we say of a tripod that it fell onto its feet "by chance," because although it could then be used to sit on, it did not fall for the sake of that.

[The distinction, then, may be summarized as follows.] We attribute to "pure chance" all those events which are such as ordinarily admit of a telic explanation, but which happen on this occasion to have been produced without any reference to the actual result. The word "luck," on the other hand, is restricted to that special type of chance events which (1) are possible objects of choice, and (2) affect persons capable of exercising choice. . . . The difference between chance and luck becomes clearest when applied to the productions of nature: when she produces a monster we attribute it to chance but we do not call nature unlucky. Even this, however, is not quite the same type of situation as that of the horse who chances to escape; for the horse's escape was due to factors independent of the horse, while the reasons for nature's miscarriages are private to herself.

Thus we have explained the meaning of, and distinction between, chance and luck. Both, it may be added, belong to the order of "propelling factors" or "sources of movement"; for the determining factors to which they are incidental are either natural forces or intelligent agents—the particular kinds of which are too numerous to mention.

Inasmuch as the results of chance and luck, while of a sort that nature or a conscious intelligence might well have intended, have in fact emerged as a purely incidental result of some determinative process, and as there can be nothing incidental without something prior for it to be incidental to, it is clear that an incidental connection presupposes a determinative relation that is authentic and direct. Chance and luck, then, presuppose intelligence and nature as determinative agents. Hence, however true it may be that the heavens are due to spontaneous chance, intelligence and nature must be the prior reasons, not only of many other things, but of this universe itself.

4. [*The Meaning of Nature*]

Some things exist by nature, some from other causes. Animals and their bodily organs, plants, and the physical elements—earth, fire, air, and water—such things as these we say exist "by nature." There is one particular in which all the objects just named are observed to differ from things that are not constituted by nature: each of them has within itself a principle of movement and rest—whether this movement be locomotion, or growth and decrease, or qualitative change. In such objects as beds and coats, on the other hand —provided we are speaking [not of their materials but] of the beds and coats themselves as products of craftwork—there is no inherent tendency to change. Of course, in respect of the stone or earth or composite matter of which such things are made, they do to that extent have such a tendency.[2] This, however, is a purely incidental aspect; [although it offers, to be sure, additional evidence that] what causes a thing to change or be at rest is its "nature"—*i.e.*, the nature that belongs to it primarily, not as an incidental attribute. As an illustration of what is meant by this last qualification, consider the case of a physician who cures himself. It would not be *quâ* patient that he possessed the art of healing; it would merely happen that in this exceptional case the same man was doctor and patient. So it is with all artificial products: none of them has within itself the principle of its own production. But while in some cases (*e.g.,* a house or any other such product of manual labor) the moving principle resides in some external agent, there are also cases where the principle is found as an inci-

[2] It is *quâ* wood or other heavy material that a bed tends to fall, not *quâ* bed.

dental attribute within the thing produced.

Since this is what is meant by "nature," anything may be said to "have a nature" so far as it possesses within itself a principle of the sort just described. Whatever possesses such a principle is "something substantial, a concrete thing"; for it is *subject* [to change], and subjects are what have inherent natures. We may note also the phrase "according to nature," which is applied not only to the things themselves but also to their essential attributes. When, for example, fire is borne upwards, that phenomenon *is* not nature, nor does it *have* a nature, but it takes place *in accordance with nature*. This, then, is the distinction between nature, [existing] by nature, and [being or occurring] in accordance with nature.

5. [*Teleology and Necessity in Nature*]

We must now explain in what sense nature belongs to the class of telic determinants. Then we shall consider what is meant by necessity when spoken of with reference to natural phenomena; for people are constantly appealing to necessity as the cause of things, arguing that since the hot and the cold and all the other qualities are each of a certain definitive nature, the objects which they characterize must exist and be created by necessity. Even those who admit some further determining principle of things, such as Love and Strife, or Mind, do not consistently adhere to their explanations [but fall back upon the idea of necessity].

[With reference to our first question] it may be objected that nature does not act with reference to a goal nor by reason of the fact that one thing is better than another, but for the same reason that it rains —not to make the corn grow, but of necessity. When rain falls, so the argument runs, it is simply because the rising vapor has be-

come cooled, and being cooled turns to water, which descends, causing the corn to
grow; on the same basis as, when rain
spoils the crops on the threshing-floor, we
do not suppose that it fell for the sake of
spoiling them but that it merely happened
to do so. Why, then, should it not be the
same with the organic parts of nature?
Take the case of our teeth, for example—
the front teeth sharp and suitable for tearing the food, the back ones broad and flat,
suitable for grinding it—may they not have
grown up thus by simple necessity,[3] and
their adaptation to their respective functions be purely a coincidence? The same
argument can be offered about any organic
structure to which purpose is commonly
ascribed; and it is further explained that
where the organic structures happen to have
been formed *as if* they had been arranged
on purpose, the creatures which thus happen to be suitably organized have survived,
while the others have perished—as Empedocles relates of his "man-faced ox-
creatures."

While these and similar arguments may
cause difficulties, they certainly do not represent the truth. For in the first place,
(1) teeth and all other natural phenomena
come about in a certain way if not invariably at least normally, and this is inconsistent with the meaning of luck or chance.
We do not appeal to luck or coincidence in
explaining the frequency of rain in winter
nor of heat in mid-summer; we would, however, if the situation were to be reversed.
As every occurrence must be ascribed either
to coincidence or to purpose, if such cases
as the foregoing cannot be ascribed to coincidence or chance, they must be ascribed
to purpose. But since even our opponents
will admit that all such occurrences are

[3] *I.e.*, by virtue of material and efficient determinants [causes] only, and without reference to any
telic determinant [final cause].

natural events, it follows that there is such
a thing as purpose in nature and its processes.

(2) Furthermore, [in any human art or
technique] where there is an end to be
achieved, the first and each succeeding step
of the operation are performed for the sake
of that end. As in human operations, so in
the processes of nature; and as in nature,
so in each human undertaking—unless
there is something to interfere. Human operations, however, are for the sake of an
end; hence natural processes must be so
too. If a house, for example, had been a
natural product it would have been made
by the same successive stages as it passed
through when made by human technique;
and if natural objects could be duplicated
artificially it would be by the same series
of steps as now produce them in nature. In
art and in nature alike each stage is for
the sake of the one that follows; for generally speaking, human technique either
gives the finishing touches to what nature
has had to leave incomplete, or else imitates
her. Hence, if the operations that constitute
a human technique are for the sake of an
end, it is clear that this must be no less true
of natural processes. The relation of earlier
to later terms of the series is the same for
both.

(3) This is most clearly true in the case
of the lower animals, whose behavior is admittedly independent of any conscious technique or experimentation or deliberation—
so much so, in fact, that it is debated
whether the work of spiders, ants, and the
like is due to intelligence or to some other
faculty. Passing gradually down the scale
we find that plants too produce organs subservient to their "natural end": leaves, for
instance, are put forth to provide shade for
the fruit. Hence, if it is both "by nature"
and also "for a purpose" that the swallow
builds its nest and the spider its web, and

that plants put forth leaves for the sake of the fruit and push down rather than up with their roots for the sake of nourishment, it is evident that the type of determining factor which we have called telic is operative in the objects and processes of nature.

[What, then, is a telic determinant?] Consider first that nature exists under a twofold aspect—as "composed of materials" and "as consisting in the ways in which things are shaping up"; that by the second of these aspects is meant "the perfected results at which processes tend to arrive," and that all the earlier stages in any process are for the sake of such perfected results [*i.e.*, are telically determined by them]: it follows that the telic determinant of a thing is nothing other than the "way in which it tends to shape up" [*i.e.*, its "form"].

No human technique is free from error: the man of letters makes mistakes in grammar, and the physician may administer a wrong dose. Hence it is not surprising that there should be errors in the processes of nature too. Just as in the arts and other human techniques there are certain procedures which correctly serve their specific ends, while to aim at such ends and miss them is to fail; so it presumably is with nature, and what we call freaks are simply failures or errors in respect of nature's proper ends. . . .

[A consequence of Empedocles' theory [4]] is that it would be entirely a matter of chance what might spring up from a given seed. But such an assertion would be a denial of nature and of the whole natural order. For we call anything "natural" when by virtue of an "initiating principle" inherent in itself it progresses continuously toward some goal. Such principles do not

all make for the same goal, nor, on the other hand, is the goal picked at random; but each inner principle makes always for the same goal of its own, if nothing interferes. There are other cases, to be sure, where a certain end, as well as the means of attaining it, may come about entirely by luck. Thus we call it a stroke of luck that a stranger should come and before departing pay the ransom; for the ransom is paid just as if payment of it had been the stranger's purpose in coming, although actually it was not. In this case the result achieved is incidental [to the stranger's real purpose in coming]; since luck, as we have already explained, is incidental causation. But when a certain result is achieved either invariably or normally, it is no incidental or merely lucky occurrence; and in the processes of nature each result is achieved if not invariably at least normally, provided nothing hinders.

There are some who deny the existence of purpose in nature on the ground that they can never detect the physical force in the act of deliberating. Such an argument is illogical, for human techniques also may be carried on without deliberation. Yet if the shipbuilding art were inherent in the timber the construction of the ship would then proceed naturally in the same way as it now proceeds by human skill—showing that if purpose is inherent in human techniques it must inhere in nature too.

The processes of nature are best illustrated by the case of a doctor who doctors himself. Nature similarly is agent and patient at once.

In conclusion, it is clear that nature is a "determining principle," whose manner of determination is telic.

As for necessity, does it exist conditionally or unconditionally? People tend to think of necessity as something inherent in

---

[4] That "man headed ox-creatures" and countless other such combinations originally arose at random, but being ill-adapted did not survive.

the process of production; which is pretty much as if they should suppose that a wall might be built by [an accidental conjunction of] necessary forces—*i.e.,* that as heavy things are naturally borne downward and light things toward the top, so the stones and foundations would necessarily fall to the lowest place, the earth more lightly rising above, and the wood, because it was lightest of all, forming the roof. But while it is true that the wall cannot be built unless these materials [with their respective properties] are present; still, being only its material conditions, they will not suffice to account for the completed wall, which is brought into existence for the sake of sheltering us and protecting our goods. And so with all other cases of working toward an end: although the end cannot be attained without certain materials possessing definitive properties, these are only the material precondition of its attainment; properly speaking, what brings it into existence is a certain purpose. Suppose, for example, we were to ask why a saw is what it is. In order that it may perform a certain work and thereby serve a certain end, we should reply. But [let us suppose] this work cannot be performed unless the saw is made of iron. We may then declare that if it is to be truly a saw and perform its function it "must necessarily" be made of iron. Necessity, then, is conditional. It is not of the same order as the end; for while necessity resides only in the "material pre-

conditions," the "end or purpose" is found in the definition. . . .

From the foregoing analogy it is plain that when we speak of necessity we are referring to the "material aspect" of nature and the changes proper to that aspect. While the natural scientist must deal with the material aspect too, his primary concern is with the "purposive aspect"; for the goal may determine the material changes, but these do not determine the goal. The principle that determines the goal, or inherent purpose, of a thing is to be found in its meaning and definition. In the case of human techniques, when we have determined what kind of a house we want, certain materials must then "of necessity" be either had or got in order to build it; and when we have determined what we mean by health, certain things become necessary in order to secure it. [So it is with nature]: if man has a certain meaning, certain antecedent conditions are requisite to his existence, and these conditions will in turn presuppose others.

From another point of view we may refer necessity to the definition of a thing. For if we define sawing as a particular kind of scission, it will follow that this cannot be accomplished unless the saw possesses teeth of a particular character, and to have such a character the teeth must be made of iron. The definition, no less than the physical object, contains parts which are, so to speak, its matter.

COMMENT

Aristotle's Basic Concepts

Aristotle employs certain key concepts that must be understood if we are to grasp his argument. Perhaps the most important of these concepts are *substance* and *attributes, matter* and *form, potentiality* and *actuality,* the *four causes,* and *motion.* His interpretation of these concepts in itself constitutes a very penetrating analysis of the nature of reality.

1. *Substance* and *attributes.* Aristotle distinguishes a "primary" and a "secondary" meaning of substance. In the primary sense, a substance is an absolutely individual thing: *this* man, *this* dog, *this* apple, *this* rock. In the secondary sense, a substance is a *class* of things, such as "man," "dog," "apple," "rock"—one of the kinds of things that we find in nature and that we note in describing and classifying objects. In both senses, a substance is distinguished from the changeable qualities that attach to things.

For example, the following poem distinguishes between the thing and its qualities and illustrates both the primary and secondary meanings of substance:

> Hurray! said the bear,
> I'm a bear!
> I'm a bear when I eat,
> I'm a bear when I sleep,
> I'm a series of events,
> Of causal predicaments,
> A verbal symbolization,
> And a temporal relation.
> But in every provisionality
> Or circumstantiality
> I never abrogate
> My single blessed state
> Of a bear.[1]

The bear that sings the song, this particular bear, is a substance in the primary sense. But its song indicates that it is also *a* bear, a member of a class (genus or species); and this *class* is a substance in the secondary sense.

Aristotle notes two basic characteristics of a primary substance. First, it is always grammatically a subject and never a predicate. It *has* various predicates, but it is not predicable of something else. In the example cited, the bear is a subject to which we can attribute various qualities, and it is not a mere quality or characteristic of something else. Second, a substance, while remaining numerically one, admits of innumerable alterations. The bear, for example, is the same bear whether it is lying down, sitting up, running, or standing still, and it is successively young and old. Thus a primary substance is a relatively fixed and permanent factor in a world of change.

Similarly, as the bear's song indicates, a *secondary* substance is a class which remains invariant "in every provisionality or circumstantiality," for the bear always remains *a* bear. Moreover, the secondary substance is a class

[1] Edward Godfrey Cox, *Naming Day in the Garden of Eden* (University of Washington Book Store, 1930), p. 30.

of *subjects*—that is to say, a class of primary substances exhibiting various changing characteristics.

The changing characteristics of the substance are called its attributes. They are *universals* in the sense that they can apply to an indefinite number of particular things. For example, the attribute of being musical can apply to many human beings. Aristotle did not suppose, as Plato apparently did, that universals have an existence or being apart from particular things. The universal is simply the characteristic common to all members of the group— as, for example, redness is to be found in all red things. The theory that universals are *in* things gives an empirical tone to Aristotle's thought. Science, he believed, has no need for pure disembodied forms, unrealized in the actual world. It should be observational in method, finding those attributes or universals that are actually in things.

2. *Matter* and *form*. Primary substances can be analyzed into two constituent factors, matter and form. Matter is the stuff of which the thing consists, and this stuff may be the same in kind as the stuff of which quite different things consist. Thus gold is the stuff out of which rings, bracelets, watch casings, and many other things are made. This conception of matter is extended beyond any merely physical stuff. For example, psychological dispositions are the matter out of which a man's character is formed, and various propositions are the matter out of which an argument is made.

The form is the determination or organization given to the matter. Wherever there is matter there is form, and wherever there is form there is matter. The concepts of matter and form are relative—what is form from one standpoint is matter from another standpoint. A piece of lumber, for example, has a certain form—namely, a shape or structure. But the lumber, in turn, is the matter used, for example, in making a table, and the table, with its form, is matter used by an interior decorator in furnishing a home. One can even think of homes as matter out of which a city is made, and of cities as matter that enters into the larger form of a nation.

In a primary substance, the matter and form are thought of as combined to make an individual thing. The substance is *this* matter combined with *this* form to make this particular entity. But matter and form can also be conceived generically. For example, flesh and bones, in general, are the matter out of which human bodies, in general, are made.

3. *Potentiality and actuality*. Thus far we have been looking at substances statically. If we now look at them dynamically—as moving, changing things —we also have a twofold division: *potentiality*, what *may* be, and *actuality*, what *is*. Of a given acorn we can say, this is not *actually* an oak, but it is *potentially* an oak. When once the development is complete, we can say that the oak tree is an actuality.

Potentiality is related to matter and actuality is related to form. Matter has the potentiality of being shaped into a certain form. Lumber, for example, has the potentiality of becoming a table, a door, a fence, etc. But when the lumber takes on the form of the completed thing, we can say that a certain potentiality has been actualized. This conception of development from the potential to the actual imparts a certain characteristic flavor to Aristotle's metaphysics. Whereas Plato was primarily interested in *being,* the static and enduring, Aristotle was more interested in *becoming,* the change and development everywhere going on in nature.

Since potentiality involves what *may* be, and since matter usually has many potentialities, matter is more indeterminate than form; but it is not utterly amorphous and indeterminate. A male baby, for example, is potentially a man but not an elephant, umbrella, volcano, or a woman. The potentiality of a thing is limited by its real characteristics and tendencies.

4. *The four causes.* The conception of reality involved in these antitheses of matter and form and actuality and potentiality finds more detailed expression in the doctrine of the four causes. Aristotle used the word "cause" in a broad sense to include any "why or wherefore"—any factor that makes a thing what it is. A complete explanation requires a statement of all four causes: (*a*) the *material* cause, or the elements out of which the thing is made; (*b*) the *formal* cause, or the mold into which the material is put; (*c*) the *efficient* cause, or the means by which the change is wrought; and (*d*) the *final* cause, or the end for which the process occurs. Let us examine briefly each of these causes.

a. The material cause. Matter acts as a cause because it sets limits to the form and character of a thing and remains in the final product. Each kind of matter has characteristic properties: water is flowing, bronze is hard, lead is heavy, etc. We say, "You can't make a silk purse out of a sow's ear," implying that the final product is influenced by the stuff that goes into it.

b. The formal cause. The form of a thing is the pattern or formula that expresses its nature. In addition to "essential" properties, which the thing *must* have, there are "accidental" properties which the thing may or may not have. Thus a human being, to exist at all, must possess human nature, but he can vary in accidental properties, such as his weight or the color of his complexion. To explain something in terms of a formal cause is to point to its formal properties, essential or accidental, in answering the question "why." For example, if we explain a man's behavior by declaring, "It is human nature to act in this way," we are referring to what we take to be an essential property. If we say, "He did this because he is tall," we are pointing to a more accidental property. But in either case we would be referring to the way in which the man "shapes up"—the form of his body or mind.

c. The efficient cause. The efficient cause is the force or agent that brings about the change. For example, the activity of the sculptor is the efficient cause of a statue, and a bolt of lightning is the efficient cause of a certain forest fire. Thus the efficient cause is a power that acts upon matter to bring it into a determinate form.

d. The final cause. The final cause is the end, aim, or completed result of the process. We may ask why the process took place, meaning for what end or purpose. The final cause of, for example, taking quinine might be to cure malaria and thus to regain health. The emphasis upon final causality gives Aristotle's philosophy a thoroughly teleological character.

There is a tendency for the formal, efficient, and final causes to coalesce. In the building of a house, the *plan* of the house is the formal cause, this plan as it exists in the mind of the architect or builder is part of the efficient cause, and the plan as the end to be achieved in the completed house is the final cause. Similarly, in the growth of a tree, the form of the fully developed tree is the final and formal cause, and the parent tree, which exhibits the form, is the efficient cause. The material cause, on the other hand, is the relatively independent and passive factor, having a potentiality without power to actualize itself until it is acted upon by the final-formal-efficient cause.

5. *Motion.* The effect of the propelling causes upon the matter is to set up a "motion" which forces the matter to assume a specific form. Motion is thus the actualization of potentiality. This is a broader meaning than we give to the term "motion" at the present time: it includes not only change of place (motion in our modern sense) but change in quality and quantity.

Since motion is matter taking on form, the form must be lacking in the matter before the motion takes place. This lack is called *privation.* For example, if a person *becomes* wise, he is unwise in the beginning, and thus lack of wisdom is the privation presupposed by the motion. Whenever a potentiality is actualized, it can be taken for granted that the actuality was lacking at the start.

Motion may be either artificial or natural. The motion is artificial if the form is imposed upon the matter by some external force or agency. A piece of gold, for example, will not spontaneously form itself into a bracelet but must be wrought into this shape by a craftsman. On the other hand, a motion is natural if it results from an inherent tendency in the matter. An acorn, for example, naturally tends to grow into a tree, and a gaseous body naturally tends to expand into a larger and more diffuse shape.

The Teleological Interpretation of Reality

Having defined the key concepts in Aristotle's philosophy, we are in a position to formulate his theory of teleology. A teleological interpretation of reality emphasizes the role of final causes. It thus differs from mechanism—the doctrine that all phenomena are totally explicable in terms of physically efficient causes. In the next chapter, we shall consider the theory that the world can be explained in terms of moving atoms and the void. Aristotle was thoroughly opposed to this type of mechanistic theory, maintaining that motions can be fully explained only in terms of ends or purposes.

He begins by distinguishing between "nature" and "art," a distinction corresponding to natural and artificial motions. *Nature,* in one sense of the term, is an *inherent* tendency to bring about change. Thus the tendency of a seed to germinate and grow is part of its nature, and the tendency of smoke to rise and spread is part of *its* nature. *Art,* on the other hand, is the activity of an *external* agent in imposing form upon matter. When a doctor, by the use of medicines, makes his patients well, he is practicing the art of medicine, and when a tailor, by cutting and sewing cloth, makes a suit of clothes, he is practicing the art of tailoring. Aristotle remarks that we also give the name of nature to the products of nature, and the name of art to the products of art.

It is fairly obvious that human art must be explained, in part, teleologically. The doctor treats his patients for the sake of health, and the painter creates his pictures for the sake of beauty. Most human activities are goal-seeking and hence can be fully explained only in terms of final causes. But Aristotle believes that even the "art" of animals—such as that of the bee in making its honeycomb or the beaver in building its dam—is instinctively goal-directed; and that nature—the inherent tendency of a thing to actualize its potentialities—is likewise teleological. This does not mean that *every* characteristic of an animal can be explained teleologically. Whereas an eye, as a functional organ, must be explained by reference to its end or function, the particular color of the eye is the result of non-teleological causes (since blue and brown eyes can see equally well).

Although Aristotle believed that we should not always look for a final cause, his approach to the problems of organic life was primarily teleological. He maintained that final causes, for the biologist, are generally more important than merely material or efficient causes. The earlier phases of a natural process must be explained by the later, by the climax or culmination; the organ must be explained by its function, the body by the life that it sustains, and the life of each species must be understood by reference to the highest level it ever attains. Thus the end, or final cause, of each species is to realize the fully developed characteristics of that form, that kind of being. The basic structure of an animal is not due to the purpose of the *individual* animal but to a kind of vital force that impels it to realize the development characteristic of its *type*. Although described as acting for a purpose, nature is not a conscious agent but a kind of unconscious inner drive or propulsion.

The principal mistake of earlier Greek scientists and philosophers, Aristotle declared, is that they sought material and efficient causes to the neglect of formal and final causes. In one sphere, however, Aristotle himself recognized that final causes are inoperative. This is the realm of coincidence. For example, when a flower seed that has begun to germinate is swept away by a flooding stream, we should not try to explain this event teleologically but should rather attribute it to coincidence. By "coincidence" Aristotle meant the accidental meeting of two or more chains of causation. In the example cited, one set of causes led to the germination of the seed by the brink of the stream; another set of causes brought the spring rains and the consequent flooding; and the two chains fortuitously merged in the sweeping away of the seed, thus frustrating a normal natural result, namely, the growth of a flower.

When a coincidence serves or defeats a purpose, it is called by Aristotle a case of *luck* or *chance*. The word "chance" is the more inclusive term: "Every case of luck is a case of chance, but not all cases of chance are cases of luck." If a person, while shopping, accidentally meets a long-sought friend, this is good luck—because the meeting happens to serve a purpose. But if he accidentally meets someone he wishes to avoid, this is bad luck, since it frustrates a purpose. Without *conscious* motives, which are accidentally served or impeded, there can be no good or bad luck. But "chance," a wider term, applies not only to cases of luck but also to coincidences that abet or hinder *unconscious* teleological tendencies. When an animal, incapable of conscious purposiveness, accidentally moves out of the way of an advancing avalanche, we should call this a fortunate chance rather than "good luck." Both chance and luck are not *actually* teleological but *seemingly* so: they do not happen as a result of teleological tendencies but aid or hinder these tendencies.

The climax of Aristotle's teleological theory of reality is to be found in his conception of God as "the Unmoved Mover." As the highest and best of beings, God is the unchanging source of all changes—"an eternal Thinker eternally thinking the selfsame eternal thoughts." Hence He does not act as a providential God, answering prayers and intervening in particular circumstances. Instead, He acts as a final cause—"the object of the world's desire." His function is to impart motion to the whole order by serving as a kind of supreme goal. Nature has a tendency to move toward God, who acts, so to speak, as a kind of magnet. In addition to the Unmoved Mover, there are subordinate intelligences (like the angels of Christian theology) which aspire toward God and move the heavenly spheres.

A Brief Appraisal

No one today would defend all the details of Aristotle's teleological interpretation of reality. Nevertheless, most psychologists, social scientists, and philosophers maintain that we must refer to goals and purposes in explaining much of human behavior. Purposiveness is so characteristic of human beings that the person who seems to lack a goal is denounced as a "drifter" or "ne'er do well." To deny that purposes ever operate in human life verges on the absurd or contradictory. Whitehead somewhere remarks that scientists animated by the *purpose* of proving that they are purposeless constitute an interesting subject for study.

Moreover, there certainly *appears* to be teleological activity at the subhuman level; for example:

> . . . when a dog hides an unfinished bone in a very unusual place; . . . when rooks take fresh-water mussels to a great height and let them fall on the single shingle beneath so that they are broken; when a mother weasel, accompanied by one of her offspring, about to be overtaken on the links, seizes the youngster in her mouth, dashes on ahead, and lays it in a sandy hole; when beavers cut a canal right through a large island in a river; when mares, some past foaling, unite to lift up between them a number of foals on the occasion of a great flood.[2]

Such illustrations can be multiplied indefinitely, and they certainly suggest that human purposes have their instinctive counterparts in animals.

On the other hand, Aristotle's conception of *unconscious* teleology, especially at the level of plants and lower animals, is paradoxical. One can certainly question the notion of purpose that is not the purpose of any mind. Of course, in a purely temporal sense, there is an end to every process. In this sense, the full development of the oak is the end toward which the acorn moves. But it is hazardous to interpret this temporal finis as a goal or end in a *teleological* sense. Whereas a conscious purpose acts as a cause and helps to realize itself, there appears to be no reason to suppose that a *temporal* end, such as the culminating phase of a tree's growth, is actually operating as a cause to bring about its own realization.

The functional adaptation of organisms to their environments is not necessarily a sign of the operation of final causes. Darwin advanced an alternative explanation. All plants and animals, he maintained, multiply more rapidly than the means of subsistence, and therefore many perish. Most of those that survive are in some way better fitted to cope with their environments than the perishing. Their greater life span is the result of fortunate chance variations which are transmitted, through heredity, to their offspring. The accumulation of such variations, generation after generation, gradually produces a change in type, perhaps the evolution of a new species. Consequently, there is adaptation without design, an appearance of purposiveness without purpose, a seeming teleology in which there is no more ultimate explanation than the sifting out of the functional from the unfunctional by a mechanical process of selection. Whether natural selection without teleology is *sufficient* to account for evolution is one of the great questions of science.

Finally, Aristotle's belief that God is "the object of the world's desire" seems to require elucidation. How literally are we to understand his lan-

---

[2] J. Arthur Thomson, *The System of Animate Nature* (Henry Holt, 1920), I, pp. 335–336.

guage? Does fire as it darts upward aspire toward divinity? Do the stars in their courses yearn toward God, and is this the reason for their motion? Obviously there are difficulties in any such interpretation. One of the classic arguments for God—that nature exhibits a design which implies God as a designer—is somewhat akin to Aristotle's view of the Unmoved Mover; but it leads to the conception of God as an artificer and not merely as a final cause. In Chapter 11, "The Answer of the Theist," we shall review this question of the relation of God to design and purpose in nature.

There can be no doubt that much of Aristotle's philosophy is extremely valuable. Such concepts as *substance, matter* and *form, actuality* and *potentiality,* and the *four causes* have played a great role in the history of thought and are potent instruments of analysis. Some of these concepts have been sharply criticized by later thinkers—for example, the concept of substance by Hume, and the concept of final cause by Hobbes. Yet Aristotle remains one of the giants of human thought; and the idea of teleology which is at the heart and core of his interpretation of reality remains one of the root concepts of metaphysics.

8

Materialism

TITUS LUCRETIUS CARUS (95?–52? B.C.)

We know nothing certain about the life of Lucretius. St. Jerome, a hostile critic, declared that he had fits of madness, composed his poem during intervals of sanity, and killed himself in his forty-fourth year. This report, as George Santayana has remarked, must be taken with a large grain of salt. From his book we discover that he revered Epicurus, detested religious superstition, and delighted in the bounty of nature.

From *On the Nature of Things*[*]

1. [*Prayer to the creative force of nature (personified as Venus) to inspire the poet, to bless his patron Memmius, and to bring peace.*]

Mother of Aeneas's sons, joy of men and gods, Venus the life-giver, who beneath the gliding stars of heaven fillest with life the sea that carries the ships and the land that bears the crops; for thanks to thee every tribe of living things is conceived, and comes forth to look upon the light of the sun. Thou, goddess, thou dost turn to flight the winds and the clouds of heaven, thou at thy coming; for thee earth, the quaint artificer, puts forth her sweet-scented flowers; for thee the levels of ocean smile, and the sky, its anger past, gleams with spreading light. For when once the face of the spring day is revealed and the teeming breeze of the west wind is loosed from prison and blows strong, first the birds in high heaven herald thee, goddess, and thine approach, their hearts thrilled with thy might. Then the tame beasts grow wild and bound over the fat pastures, and swim the racing rivers; so surely enchained by thy charm each follows thee in hot desire

* Translated by Cyril Bailey. Oxford University Press, London, 1910, 1921. Reprinted by permission.

whither thou goest before to lead him on. Yea, through seas and mountains and tearing rivers and the leafy haunts of birds and verdant plains thou dost strike fond love into the hearts of all, and makest them in hot desire to renew the stock of their races, each after his own kind. And since thou alone art pilot to the nature of things, and nothing without thine aid comes forth into the bright coasts of light, nor waxes glad nor lovely, I long that thou shouldest be my helper in writing these verses, which I essay to trace on the nature of things for the son of the Memmii, my friend, whom thou, goddess, through all his life hast willed to be bright with every grace beyond his fellows. Therefore the more, goddess, grant a lasting loveliness to my words. Bring it to pass that meantime the wild works of warfare may be lulled to sleep over all seas and lands. For thou only canst bless mortal men with quiet peace, since 'tis Mavors [Mars], the lord of hosts, who guides the wild works of war, and he upon thy lap oft flings himself back, conquered by the eternal wound of love; and then pillowing his shapely neck upon thee and looking up he feeds with love his greedy eyes, gazing wistfully towards thee, while, as he lies back, his breath hangs upon thy lips. Do thou, goddess, as he leans resting on thy sacred limbs, bend to embrace him and pour forth sweet petition from thy lips, seeking, great lady, gentle peace for the Romans.

2. [*The universe is composed of atoms and the void.*]

. . . All nature then, as it is of itself, is built of these two things: for there are bodies and the void, in which they are placed and where they move hither and thither. For that body exists is declared by the feeling which all share alike; and unless faith in this feeling be firmly grounded at once and prevail, there will be naught to which we can make appeal about things hidden, so as to prove aught by the reasoning of the mind. And next, were there not room and empty space, which we call void, nowhere could bodies be placed, nor could they wander at all hither and thither in any direction; and this I have above shown to you but a little while before. Besides these there is nothing which you could say is parted from all body and sundered from void, which could be discovered, as it were a third nature in the list. For whatever shall exist, must needs be something in itself; and if it suffer touch, however small and light, it will increase the count of body by a bulk great or maybe small, if it exists at all, and be added to its sum. But if it is not to be touched, inasmuch as it cannot on any side check anything from wandering through it and passing on its way, in truth it will be that which we call empty void. Or again, whatsoever exists by itself, will either do something or suffer itself while other things act upon it, or it will be such that things may exist and go on in it. But nothing can do or suffer without body, nor afford room again, unless it be void and empty space. And so besides void and bodies no third nature by itself can be left in the list of things, which might either at any time fall within the purview of our senses, or be grasped by any one through reasoning of the mind.

3. [*The atoms are solid and indestructible.*]

Bodies, moreover, are in part the first-beginnings of things, in part those which are created by the union of first-beginnings. Now the true first-beginnings of things, no force can quench; for they by their solid body prevail in the end. Albeit it seems hard to believe that there can be found among things anything of solid body. For the thunderbolt of heaven passes through walled houses, as do shouts and cries; iron grows white hot in the flame, and stones seethe in fierce fire and leap asunder; then too the hardness of gold is relaxed and softened by heat, and the ice of brass yields beneath the flame and melts; warmth and piercing cold ooze through silver, since when we have held cups duly in our hands we have felt both alike, when the dewy moisture of water was poured in from above. So true is it that in things there is seen to be nothing solid. But yet because true reasoning and the nature of things constrains us, give heed, until in a few verses we set forth that there are things which exist with solid and everlasting body, which we show to be the seeds of things and their first-beginnings, out of which the whole sum of things now stands created.

First, since we have found existing a twofold nature of things far differing, the nature of body and of space, in which all things take place, it must needs be that each exists alone by itself and unmixed. For wherever space lies empty, which we call the void, body is not there; moreover, wherever body has its station, there is by no means empty void. Therefore the first bodies are solid and free from void. Moreover, since there is void in things created, solid matter must needs stand all round, nor can anything by true reasoning be shown to hide void in its body and hold it within, except you grant that what keeps it in is solid. Now it can be nothing but a union of matter, which could keep in the void in things. Matter then, which exists with solid body, can be everlasting, when all else is dissolved. Next, if there were nothing which was empty and void, the whole would be solid; unless on the other hand there were bodies determined, to fill all the places that they held, the whole universe would be but empty void space.

Body, then, we may be sure, is marked off from void turn and turn about, since there is neither a world utterly full nor yet quite empty. There are therefore bodies determined, such as can mark off void space from what is full. These cannot be broken up when hit by blows from without, nor again can they be pierced to the heart and undone, nor by any other way can they be assailed and made to totter; all of which I have above shown to you but a little while before. For it is clear that nothing could be crushed in without void, or broken or cleft in twain by cutting, nor admit moisture nor likewise spreading cold or piercing flame, whereby all things are brought to their end. And the more each thing keeps void within it, the more is it assailed to the heart by these things and begins to totter. Therefore, if the first bodies are solid and free from void, as I have shown, they must be everlasting. Moreover, if matter had not been everlasting, ere this all things had wholly passed away to nothing, and all that we see had been born again from nothing. But since I have shown above that nothing can be created from nothing, nor can what has been begotten be summoned back to nothing, the first-beginnings must needs be of immortal body, into which at their last day all things can be dissolved, that there may be matter enough for renewing things. Therefore the first-beginnings are of solid singleness, nor in any other way can they be preserved through the ages from infinite time now gone and renew things.

4. [*The undetermined swerve of the atoms makes free will possible.*]

Herein I would fain that you should learn this too, that when first-bodies are being carried downwards straight through the void by their own weight, at times quite undetermined and at undetermined spots they push a little from their path: yet only just so much as you could call a change of trend. But if they were not used to swerve, all things would fall downwards through the deep void like drops of rain, nor could collision come to be, nor a blow brought to pass for the first-beginnings: so nature would never have brought aught to being. . . .

Once again, if every motion is always linked on, and the new always arises from the old in order determined, nor by swerving do the first-beginnings make a certain start of movement to break through the decrees of fate, so that cause may not follow cause from infinite time; whence comes this free will for living things all over the earth, whence, I ask, is it wrested from fate, this will whereby we move forward, where pleasure leads each one of us, and swerve likewise in our motions neither at determined times nor in a determined direction of place, but just where our mind has carried us? For without doubt it is his own will which gives to each one a start for this movement, and from the will the motions pass flooding through the limbs. Do you not see too how, when the barriers are flung open, yet for an instant of time the eager might of the horses cannot burst out so suddenly as their mind itself desires? For the whole store of matter throughout the whole body must be roused to movement, that then aroused through every limb it may strain and follow the eager longing of the mind; so that you see a start of movement is brought to pass from the heart, and comes forth first of all from the will of the mind, and then afterwards is spread through all the body and limbs. Nor is it the same as when we move forward impelled by a blow from the strong might and strong constraint of another. For then it is clear to see that all the matter of the body moves and is hurried on against our will,

until the will has reined it back throughout the limbs. Do you not then now see that, albeit a force outside pushes many men and constrains them often to go forward against their will and to be hurried away headlong, yet there is something in our breast, which can fight against it and withstand it? And at its bidding too the store of matter is constrained now and then to turn throughout the limbs and members, and, when pushed forward, is reined back and comes to rest again. Wherefore in the seeds too you must needs allow likewise that there is another cause of motion besides blows and weights, whence comes this power born in us, since we see that nothing can come to pass from nothing. For weight prevents all things coming to pass by blows, as by some force without. But that the very mind feels not some necessity within in doing all things, and is not constrained like a conquered thing to bear and suffer, this is brought about by the tiny swerve of the first-beginnings in no determined direction of place and at no determined time.

5. [*The atoms themselves are without color, heat, sound, taste, smell, and sentience.*]

Come now, listen to discourse gathered by my joyful labor, lest by chance you should think that these white things, which you perceive shining bright before your eyes are made of white first-beginnings, or that things which are black are born of black seeds; or should believe that things which are steeped in any other color you will, bear this color because the bodies of matter are dyed with a color like it. For the bodies of matter have no color at all, neither like things nor again unlike them. And if by chance it seems to you that the mind cannot project itself into these bodies, you wander far astray. For since those born blind, who have never descried the light of the sun, yet know bodies by touch, never linked with color for them from the outset of their life, you may know that for our mind too, bodies painted with no tint may become a clear concept. Again, we ourselves feel that whatever we touch in blind darkness is not dyed with any color. And since I convince you that this may be, I will now teach you that the first-beginnings are deprived of all color. . . .

But lest by chance you think that the first-bodies abide bereft only of color, they are also sundered altogether from warmth and cold, and fiery heat, and are carried along barren of sound and devoid of taste, nor do they give off any scent of their own from their body. Even as when you set about to make the delicious liquid of marjoram or myrrh, or scent of nard, which breathes nectar to the nostrils, first of all it is right to seek, in so far as you may and can find it, the nature of scentless oil, which may send off no breath of perfume to the nostrils, so that it may as little as possible taint and ruin with its own strong smell the scents mingled in its body and boiled along with it. Therefore after all the first-beginnings of things are bound not to bring to the begetting of things their own scent or sound, since they cannot give anything off from themselves, nor in the same way acquire any taste at all, nor cold, nor once more warm and fiery heat . . . and the rest: yet since they are such as to be created mortal, the pliant of soft body, the brittle of crumbling body, the hollow of rare, they must needs all be kept apart from the first-beginnings, if we wish to place immortal foundations beneath things, on which the sum of life may rest; lest you see all things pass away utterly into nothing.

It must needs be that you should admit that all things which we see have sense are yet made of insensible first-beginnings. The clear facts, which are known for all to see, neither refute this nor fight against it, but rather themselves lead us by the hand and constrain us to believe that, as I say, living things are begotten of insensible things. Why we may see worms come forth alive from noisome dung, when the soaked earth has gotten muddiness from immeasurable rains; moreover, we may see all things in like manner change themselves. Streams, leaves, and glad pastures change themselves into cattle, cattle change their nature into our bodies, and from our bodies the strength of wild beasts often gains increase, and the bodies of birds strong of wing. And so nature changes all foods into living bodies, and out of food brings to birth all the senses of living things, in no far different way than she unfolds dry logs into flames and turns all things into fires. Do you not then see now that it is of great matter in what order all the first-beginnings of things are placed, and with what others mingled they give and receive motions?

6. [*Feeling and thought result from the combinations of the atoms.*]

Moreover, since there is pain when the bodies of matter, disturbed by some force throughout the living flesh and limbs, tremble each in their abode within, and when they settle back into their place, comforting pleasure comes to pass, you may know that the first-beginnings cannot be assailed by any pain, and can find no pleasure in themselves: inasmuch as they are not made of any bodies of first-beginnings, through whose newness of movement they may be in pain or find any enjoyment of life-giving delight. They are bound then not to be endowed with any sensation.

Again, if, in order that all living things may be able to feel, we must after all assign sensation to their first-beginnings, what of those whereof the race of men has its peculiar increment? You must think that they are shaken with quivering mirth and laugh aloud and sprinkle face and cheeks with the dew of their tears. And they have the wit to say much about the mingling of things, and they go on to ask what are their first-beginnings; inasmuch as, being made like to whole mortal men, they too must needs be built of other particles in their turn, and those again of others, so that you may never dare to make a stop: nay, I will press hard on you, so that, whatsoever you say speaks and laughs and thinks, shall be composed of other particles which do these same things. But if we perceive this to be but raving madness, and a man can laugh, though he has not the increment of laughing atoms, and can think and give reasons with learned lore, though he be not made of seeds thoughtful and eloquent, why should those things, which, as we see, have feeling, any the less be able to exist, mingled of seeds which lack sense in every way?

And so, we are all sprung from heavenly seed; there is the one father of us all, from whom when life-giving earth, the mother, has taken within her the watery drops of moisture, teeming she brings forth the goodly crops and the glad trees and the race of men; she brings forth too all the tribes of the wild beasts, when she furnishes the food, on which all feed their bodies and pass a pleasant life and propagate their offspring; wherefore rightly has she won the name of mother. Even so, when once sprung from earth, sinks back into the earth, and what was sent down from the coasts of the sky, returns again, and the regions of heaven receive it. Nor does death so destroy things as to put an end to the bodies of matter, but only scatters their union. Then she joins anew one with others, and brings it to pass that all things thus alter their forms, and change their

colors, and receive sensations, and in an instant of time yield them up again, so that you may know that it matters with what others the first-beginnings of things are bound up and in what position and what motions they mutually give and receive, and may not think that what we see floating on the surface of things or at times coming to birth, and on a sudden passing away, can abide in the possession of eternal first-bodies. Nay, indeed, even in my verses it is of moment with what others and in what order each letter is placed. For the same letters signify sky, sea, earth, rivers, sun, the same too crops, trees, living creatures; if not all, yet by far the greater part, are alike, but it is by position that things sound different. So in things themselves likewise when meetings, motions, order, position, shapes are changed, things too are bound to be changed.

7. [*The mind will perish but it is foolish to fear death.*]

And since the mind is one part of man, which abides rooted in a place determined, just as are ears and eyes and all the other organs of sense which guide the helm of life; and, just as hand and eye or nostrils, sundered apart from us, cannot feel nor be, but in fact are in a short time melted in corruption, so the mind cannot exist by itself without the body. . . .

Death, then, is naught to us, nor does it concern us a whit, inasmuch as the nature of the mind is but a mortal possession. And even as in the time gone by we felt no ill, when the Poeni came from all sides to the shock of battle, when all the world, shaken by the hurrying turmoil of war, shuddered and reeled beneath the high coasts of heaven, in doubt to which people's sway must fall all human power by land and sea; so, when we shall be no more, when there shall have come the parting of body and soul, by whose union we are made one, you may know that nothing at all will be able to happen to us, who then will be no more, or stir our feeling; no, not if earth shall be mingled with sea, and sea with sky. And even if the nature of mind and the power of soul has feeling, after it has been rent asunder from our body, yet it is naught to us, who are made one by the mating and marriage of body and soul. Nor, if time should gather together our substance after our decease and bring it back again as it is now placed, if once more the light of life should be vouchsafed to us, yet, even were that done, it would not concern us at all, when once the remembrance of our former selves were snapped in twain. And even now we care not at all for the selves that we once were, not at all are we touched by any torturing pain for them. For when you look back over all the lapse of immeasurable time that now is gone, and think how manifold are the motions of matter, you could easily believe this too, that these same seeds, whereof we now are made, have often been placed in the same order as they are now; and yet we cannot recall that in our mind's memory; for in between lies a break in life, and all the motions have wandered everywhere far astray from sense. For, if by chance there is to be grief and pain for a man, he must needs himself too exist at that time, that ill may befall him. Since death forestalls this, and prevents the being of him, on whom these misfortunes might crowd, we may know that we have naught to fear in death, and that he who is no more cannot be wretched, and that it were no whit different if he had never at any time been born, when once immortal death hath stolen away mortal life.

GEORGE SANTAYANA (1863–1952)

Santayana was born in Madrid of Spanish parents but spent most of his life outside of Spain. His mother, through an earlier marriage, had American connections, and brought her young son to Boston when he was nine. He stayed to graduate from Boston Latin School and Harvard College, and, after further study in Germany and England, he returned to teach philosophy at Harvard alongside his old masters, Josiah Royce and William James. In 1912, upon receipt of a legacy from his mother's estate, he resigned his professorship to live abroad. He spent the period of World War I in England and the postwar period in Rome. During World War II he took up residence in a Catholic hospital in Rome and remained there, in serene detachment, until his death in 1952.

Throughout a literary career of more than sixty years, he wrote a remarkable variety of books, including poetry, fiction, autobiography, literary essays, and systematic philosophy. These works, exquisite in style and urbane in thought, are among the classics of literature.

Although Catholic by tradition, Santayana was materialist by conviction and drew his inspiration from diverse sources. "I recited my Lucretius with as much gusto as my Saint Augustine," he declared; "and gradually Lucretius sank deeper and became more satisfying." The result is a material-ism strangely blended with Catholic and Platonic ideas, and expressed with gentle irony.

Lucretius. From *Three Philosophical Poets*[*]

There is perhaps no important poem the antecedents of which can be traced so exhaustively as can those of the work of Lucretius, *De Rerum Natura*. These antecedents, however, do not lie in the poet himself. If they did, we should not be able to trace them, since we know nothing, or next to nothing, about Lucretius the man. In a chronicon, compiled by St. Jerome largely out of Suetonius, in which miscellaneous events are noted which occurred in each successive year, we read for the year 94 B.C.: "Titus Lucretius, poet, is born. After a love-philter had turned him mad, and he had written, in the intervals of his insanity, several books which Cicero revised, he killed himself by his own hand in the forty-fourth year of his age."

The love-philter in this report sounds apocryphal; and the story of the madness and suicide attributes too edifying an end to an atheist and Epicurean not to be suspected. If anything lends color to the story it is a certain consonance which we may feel between its tragic incidents and the genius of the poet as revealed in his work, where we find a strange scorn of love, a strange vehemence, and a high melancholy. It is by no means incredible that the author of such a poem should have been at some time the slave of a pathological passion, that his vehemence and inspiration

should have passed into mania, and that he should have taken his own life. But the untrustworthy authority of St. Jerome cannot assure us whether what he repeats is a tradition founded on fact or an ingenious fiction.

Our ignorance of the life of Lucretius is not, I think, much to be regretted. His work preserves that part of him which he himself would have wished to preserve. Perfect conviction ignores itself, proclaiming the public truth. To reach this no doubt requires a peculiar genius which is called intelligence; for intelligence is quickness in seeing things as they are. But where intelligence is attained, the rest of a man, like the scaffolding to a finished building, becomes irrelevant. We do not wish it to intercept our view of the solid structure, which alone was intended by the artist—if he was building for others, and was not a coxcomb. It is his intellectual vision that the naturalist in particular wishes to hand down to posterity, not the shabby incidents that preceded that vision in his own person. These incidents, even if they were by chance interesting, could not be repeated in us; but the vision into which the thinker poured his faculties, and to which he devoted his vigils, is communicable to us also, and may become a part of ourselves.

Since Lucretius is thus identical for us

* Harvard University Press, 1927. Reprinted by permission. Footnotes omitted.

with his poem, and is lost in his philosophy, the antecedents of Lucretius are simply the stages by which his conception of nature first shaped itself in the human mind. To retrace these stages is easy; some of them are only too familiar; yet the very triteness of the subject may blind us to the grandeur and audacity of the intellectual feat involved. A naturalistic conception of things is a great work of imagination,— greater, I think, than any dramatic or moral mythology: it is a conception fit to inspire great poetry, and in the end, perhaps, it will prove the only conception able to inspire it.

We are told of the old Xenophanes that he looked up into the round heaven and cried, "The All is One." What is logically a truism may often be, imaginatively, a great discovery, because no one before may have thought of the obvious analogy which the truism registers. So, in this case, the unity of all things is logically an evident, if barren, truth; for the most disparate and unrelated worlds would still be a multitude, and so an aggregate, and so, in some sense, a unity. Yet it was a great imaginative feat to cast the eye deliberately round the entire horizon, and to draw mentally the sum of all reality, discovering that reality makes such a sum, and may be called one; as any stone or animal, though composed of many parts, is yet called one in common parlance. It was doubtless some prehistoric man of genius, long before Xenophanes, who first applied in this way to all things together that notion of unity and wholeness which everybody had gained by observation of things singly, and who first ventured to speak of "the world." To do so is to set the problem for all natural philosophy, and in a certain measure to anticipate the solution of that problem; for it is to ask how things hang together, and to assume that they do hang together in one way or another.

To cry "The All is One," and to perceive that all things are in one landscape and form a system by their juxtaposition, is the rude beginning of wisdom in natural philosophy. But it is easy to go farther, and to see that things form a unity in a far deeper and more mysterious way. One of the first things, for instance, that impresses the poet, the man of feeling and reflection, is that these objects that people the world all pass away, and that the place thereof knows them no more. Yet, when they vanish, nothingness does not succeed; other things arise in their stead. Nature remains always young and whole in spite of death at work everywhere; and what takes the place of what continually disappears is often remarkably like it in character. Universal instability is not incompatible with a great monotony in things; so that while Heraclitus lamented that everything was in flux, Ecclesiastes, who was also entirely convinced of that truth, could lament that there was nothing new under the sun.

This double experience of mutation and recurrence, an experience at once sentimental and scientific, soon brought with it a very great thought, perhaps the greatest thought that mankind has ever hit upon, and which was the chief inspiration of Lucretius. It is that all we observe about us, and ourselves also, may be so many passing forms of a permanent substance. This substance, while remaining the same in quantity and in inward quality, is constantly redistributed; in its redistribution it forms those aggregates which we call things, and which we find constantly disappearing and reappearing. All things are dust, and to dust they return; a dust, however, eternally fertile, and destined to fall perpetually into new, and doubtless beautiful, forms. This notion of substance lends a much greater unity to the outspread world; it persuades us that all things pass into one another, and have a common ground from which they spring successively, and to which they return.

The spectacle of inexorable change, the triumph of time, or whatever we may call it, has always been a favorite theme for lyric and tragic poetry, and for religious meditation. To perceive universal mutation, to feel the vanity of life, has always been the beginning of seriousness. It is the condition for any beautiful, measured, or tender philosophy. Prior to that, everything is barbarous, both in morals and in poetry; for until then mankind has not learned to renounce anything, has not outgrown the instinctive egotism and optimism of the young animal, and has not removed the center of its being, or of its faith, from the will to the imagination.

To discover substance, then, is a great step in the life of reason, even if substance be conceived quite negatively as a term that serves merely to mark, by contrast, the unsubstantiality, the vanity, of all particular moments and things. That is the way in which Indian poetry and philosophy conceived substance. But the step taken by Greek physics, and by the poetry of Lucretius, passes beyond. Lucretius and the Greeks, in observing universal mutation and the vanity of life, conceived behind appearance a great intelligible process, an evolution in nature. The reality became interesting, as well as the illusion. Physics became scientific, which had previously been merely spectacular.

Here was a much richer theme for the poet and philosopher, who was launched upon the discovery of the ground and secret causes of this gay or melancholy flux. The understanding that enabled him to discover

these causes did for the European what no Indian mystic, what no despiser of understanding anywhere, suffers himself to do; namely, to dominate, foretell, and transform this changing show with a virile, practical intelligence. The man who discovers the secret springs of appearances opens to contemplation a second positive world, the workshop and busy depths of nature, where a prodigious mechanism is continually supporting our life, and making ready for it from afar by the most exquisite adjustments. The march of this mechanism, while it produces life and often fosters it, yet as often makes it difficult and condemns it to extinction. This truth, which the conception of natural substance first makes intelligible, justifies the elegies which the poets of illusion and disillusion have always written upon human things. It is a truth with a melancholy side; but being a truth, it satisfies and exalts the rational mind, that craves truth as truth, whether it be sad or comforting, and wishes to pursue a possible, not an impossible, happiness.

So far, Greek science had made out that the world was one, that there was a substance, that this was a physical substance, distributed and moving in space. It was matter. The question remained, What is the precise nature of matter, and how does it produce the appearances we observe? The only answer that concerns us here is that given by Lucretius; an answer he accepted from Epicurus, his master in everything, who in turn had accepted it from Democritus. Now Democritus had made a notable advance over the systems that selected one obvious substance, like water, or collected all the obvious substances, as Anaxagoras had done, and tried to make the world out of them. Democritus thought that the substance of everything ought not to have any of the qualities present in some things and absent in others; it ought to have only the qualities present in all things. It should be *merely* matter. Materiality, according to him, consisted of extension, figure, and solidity; in the thinnest ether, if we looked sharp enough, we should find nothing but particles possessing these properties. All other qualities of things were apparent only, and imputed to them by a convention of the mind. The mind was a born mythologist, and projected its feelings into their causes. Light, color, taste, warmth, beauty, excellence, were such imputed and conventional qualities; only space and matter were real. But empty space was no less real than matter. Consequently, although the atoms of matter never changed their form, real changes could take place in nature, because their position might change in a real space.

Unlike the useless substance of the Indians, the substance of Democritus could offer a calculable ground for the flux of appearances; for this substance was distributed unequally in the void, and was constantly moving. Every appearance, however fleeting, corresponded to a precise configuration of substance; it arose with that configuration and perished with it. This substance, accordingly, was physical, not metaphysical. It was no dialectical term, but a scientific anticipation, a prophecy as to what an observer who should be properly equipped would discover in the interior of bodies. Materialism is not a system of metaphysics; it is a speculation in chemistry and physiology, to the effect that, if analysis could go deep enough, it would find that all substance was homogeneous, and that all motion was regular.

Though matter was homogeneous, the forms of the ultimate particles, according to Democritus, were various; and sundry combinations of them constituted the sundry objects in nature. Motion was not, as the vulgar (and Aristotle) supposed, unnatural, and produced magically by some moral cause; it had been eternal and was native to the atoms. On striking, they rebounded; and the mechanical currents or vortices which these contacts occasioned formed a multitude of stellar systems, called worlds, with which infinite space was studded.

Mechanism as to motion, atomism as to structure, materialism as to substance, that is the whole system of Democritus. It is as wonderful in its insight, in its sense for the ideal demands of method and understanding, as it is strange and audacious in its simplicity. Only the most convinced rationalist, the boldest prophet, could embrace it dogmatically; yet time has largely given it the proof. If Democritus could look down upon the present state of science, he would laugh, as he was in the habit of doing, partly at the confirmation we can furnish to portions of his philosophy, and partly at our stupidity that cannot guess the rest.

There are two maxims in Lucretius that suffice, even to this day, to distinguish a thinker who is a naturalist from one who is not. "Nothing," he says, "arises in the body in order that we may use it, but what arises brings forth its use." This is that discarding of final causes on which all progress in science depends. The other maxim runs: "One thing will grow plain when compared with another: and blind night shall not obliterate the path for thee, before thou hast thoroughly scanned the ultimate things of nature; so much will things throw light on things." Nature is her own standard; and if she seems to us unnatural, there is no hope for our minds.

The ethics of Democritus, in so far as we may judge from scanty evidence, were merely descriptive or satirical. He was an aristocratic observer, a scorner of fools.

Nature was laughing at us all; the wise man considered his fate and, by knowing it, raised himself in a measure above it. All living things pursued the greatest happiness they could see their way to; but they were marvelously short-sighted; and the business of the philosopher was to foresee and pursue the greatest happiness that was really possible. This, in so rough a world, was to be found chiefly in abstention and retrenchment. If you asked for little, it was more probable that the event would not disappoint you. It was important not to be a fool, but it was very hard.

The system of Democritus was adopted by Epicurus, but not because Epicurus had any keenness of scientific vision. On the contrary, Epicurus, the Herbert Spencer of antiquity, was in his natural philosophy an encyclopedia of second-hand knowledge. Prolix and minute, vague and inconsistent, he gathered his scientific miscellany with an eye fixed not on nature, but on the exigencies of an inward faith,—a faith accepted on moral grounds, deemed necessary to salvation, and defended at all costs, with any available weapon. It is instructive that materialism should have been adopted at that juncture on the same irrelevant moral grounds on which it has usually been rejected.

Epicurus, strange as it may sound to those who have heard, with horror or envy, of wallowing in his sty, Epicurus was a saint. The ways of the world filled him with dismay. The Athens of his time, which some of us would give our eyes to see, retained all its splendor amid its political decay; but nothing there interested or pleased Epicurus. Theaters, porches, gymnasiums, and above all the agora, reeked, to his sense, with vanity and folly. Retired in his private garden, with a few friends and disciples, he sought the ways of peace; he lived abstemiously; he spoke gently; he

gave alms to the poor; he preached against wealth, against ambition, against passion. He defended free-will because he wished to exercise it in withdrawing from the world, and in not swimming with the current. He denied the supernatural, since belief in it would have a disquieting influence on the mind, and render too many things compulsory and momentous. There was no future life: the art of living wisely must not be distorted by such wild imaginings.

All things happened in due course of nature; the gods were too remote and too happy, secluded like good Epicureans, to meddle with earthly things. Nothing ruffled what Wordsworth calls their "voluptuous unconcern." Nevertheless, it was pleasant to frequent their temples. There, as in the spaces where they dwelt between the worlds, the gods were silent and beautiful, and wore the human form. Their statues, when an unhappy man gazed at them, reminded him of happiness; he was refreshed and weaned for a moment from the senseless tumult of human affairs. From those groves and hallowed sanctuaries the philosopher returned to his garden strengthened in his wisdom, happier in his isolation, more friendly and more indifferent to all the world. Thus the life of Epicurus, as St. Jerome bears witness, was "full of herbs, fruits, and abstinences." There was a hush in it, as of bereavement. His was a philosophy of the decadence, a philosophy of negation, and of flight from the world.

Although science for its own sake could not interest so monkish a nature, yet science might be useful in buttressing the faith, or in removing objections to it. Epicurus therefore departed from the reserve of Socrates, and looked for a natural philosophy that might support his ethics. Of all the systems extant—and they were legion—he found that of Democritus the most helpful and edifying. Better than any other it would persuade men to renounce the madness that must be renounced and to enjoy the pleasures that may be enjoyed. But, since it was adopted on these external and pragmatic grounds, the system of Democritus did not need to be adopted entire. In fact, one change at least was imperative. The motion of the atoms must not be wholly regular and mechanical. Chance must be admitted, that Fate might be removed. Fate was a terrifying notion. It was spoken of by the people with superstitious unction. Chance was something humbler, more congenial to the man in the street. If only the atoms were allowed to deflect a little now and then from their courses, the future might remain unpredictable, and free-will might be saved. Therefore, Epicurus decreed that the atoms deflected, and fantastic arguments were added to show that this intrusion of chance would aid in the organization of nature; for the declension of the atoms, as it is called, would explain how the original parallel downpour of them might have yielded to vortices, and so to organized bodies. Let us pass on.

Materialism, like any system of natural philosophy, carries with it no commandments and no advice. It merely describes the world, including the aspirations and consciences of mortals, and refers all to a material ground. The materialist, being a man, will not fail to have preferences, and even a conscience, of his own; but his precepts and policy will express, not the logical implications of his science, but his human instincts, as inheritance and experience may have shaped them. Any system of ethics might accordingly coexist with materialism; for if materialism declares certain things (like immortality) to be impossible, it cannot declare them to be undesirable. Nevertheless, it is not likely that

a man so constituted as to embrace materialism will be so constituted as to pursue things which he considers unattainable. There is therefore a psychological, though no logical, bond between materialism and a homely morality.

The materialist is primarily an observer; and he will probably be such in ethics also; that is, he will have no ethics, except the emotion produced upon him by the march of the world. If he is an *esprit fort* [strong spirit] and really disinterested, he will love life; as we all love perfect vitality, or what strikes us as such, in gulls and porpoises. This, I think, is the ethical sentiment psychologically consonant with a vigorous materialism: sympathy with the movement of things, interest in the rising wave, delight at the foam it bursts into, before it sinks again. Nature does not distinguish the better from the worse, but the lover of nature does. He calls better what, being analogous to his own life, enhances his vitality and probably possesses some vitality of its own. This is the ethical feeling of Spinoza, the greatest of modern naturalists in philosophy; and we shall see how Lucretius, in spite of his fidelity to the ascetic Epicurus, is carried by his poetic ecstasy in the same direction.

But mark the crux of this union: the materialist will love the life of nature when he loves his own life; but if he should hate his own life, how should the life of nature please him? Now Epicurus, for the most part, hated life. His moral system, called hedonism, recommends that sort of pleasure which has no excitement and no risk about it. This ideal is modest, and even chaste, but it is not vital. Epicurus was remarkable for his mercy, his friendliness, his utter horror of war, of sacrifice, of suffering. These are not sentiments that a genuine naturalist would be apt to share. Pity and repentance, Spinoza said, were vain and evil; what increased a man's power and his joy increased his goodness also. The naturalist will believe in a certain hardness, as Nietzsche did; he will incline to a certain scorn, as the laughter of Democritus was scornful. He will not count too scrupulously the cost of what he achieves; he will be an imperialist, rapt in the joy of achieving something. In a word, the moral hue of materialism in a formative age, or in an aggressive mind, would be aristocratic and imaginative; but in a decadent age, or in a soul that is renouncing everything, it would be, as in Epicurus, humanitarian and timidly sensual.

We have now before us the antecedents and components of Lucretius' poem on nature. There remains the genius of the poet himself. The greatest thing about this genius is its power of losing itself in its object, its impersonality. We seem to be reading not the poetry of a poet about things, but the poetry of things themselves. That things have their poetry, not because of what we make them symbols of, but because of their own movement and life, is what Lucretius proves once for all to mankind. . . .

Poetic dominion over things as they are is seen best in Shakespeare for the ways of men, and in Lucretius for the ways of nature. Unapproachably vivid, relentless, direct in detail, he is unflinchingly grand and serious in his grouping of the facts. It is the truth that absorbs him and carries him along. He wishes us to be convinced and sobered by the fact, by the overwhelming evidence of thing after thing, raining down upon us, all bearing witness with one voice to the nature of the world.

Suppose, however,—and it is a tenable supposition,—that Lucretius is quite wrong in his science, and that there is no space, no substance, and no nature. His poem would then lose its pertinence to our lives and personal convictions; it would not lose its imaginative grandeur. We could still conceive a world composed as he describes. Fancy what emotions those who lived in such a world would have felt on the day when a Democritus or a Lucretius revealed to them their actual situation. How great the blindness or the madness dissipated, and how wonderful the vision gained! How clear the future, how intelligible the past, how marvelous the swarming atoms, in their unintentional, perpetual fertility! What the sky is to our eyes on a starry night, that every nook and cranny of nature would resemble, with here and there the tentative smile of life playing about those constellations. Surely that universe, for those who lived in it, would have had its poetry. It would have been the poetry of naturalism. Lucretius, thinking he lived in such a world, heard the music of it, and wrote it down.

And yet, when he set himself to make his poem out of the system of Epicurus, the greatness of that task seems to have overwhelmed him. He was to unfold for the first time, in sonorous but unwieldy Latin, the birth and nature of all things, as Greek subtlety had discerned them. He was to dispel superstition, to refute antagonists, to lay the sure foundations of science and of wisdom, to summon mankind compellingly from its cruel passions and follies to a life of simplicity and peace. He was himself combative and distracted enough—as it is often our troubles, more than our attainments, that determine our ideals. Yet in heralding the advent of human happiness, and in painting that of the gods, he was to attain his own, soaring upon the strong wings of his hexameters into an ecstasy of contemplation and enthusiasm. When it is so great an emotion to read these verses, what must it have been to compose them? Yet could he succeed? Could such great things fall to his lot? Yes, they might, if only the creative forces of nature, always infinite and always at hand, could pass into his brain and into his spirit; if only the seeds of corruption and madness, which were always coursing through the air, could be blown back for a moment; and if the din of civil conflicts could be suspended while he thought and wrote. To a fortunate conjunction of atoms, a child owes his first being. To a propitious season and atmosphere, a poet owes his inspiration and his success. Conscious that his undertaking hangs upon these chance conjunctions, Lucretius begins by invoking the powers he is about to describe, that they may give him breath and genius enough to describe them. And at once these powers send him a happy inspiration, perhaps a happy reminiscence of Empedocles. There are two great perspectives which the moralist may distinguish in the universal drift of atoms,—a creative movement, producing what the moralist values, and a destructive movement, abolishing the same. Lucretius knows very well that this distinction is moral only, or as people now say, subjective. No one else has pointed out so often and so clearly as he that nothing arises in this world not helped to life by the death of some other thing; so that the destructive movement creates and the creative movement destroys. Yet from the point of view of any particular life or interest, the distinction between a creative force and a destructive force is real and all-important. To make it is not to deny the mechanical structure of nature, but only to show how this mechanical structure is fruitful morally, how the outlying parts of it are friendly or hostile to me or to you, its local and living products.

This double coloring of things is supremely interesting to the philosopher; so much so that before his physical science has reached the mechanical stage, he will doubtless regard the double aspect which things present to him as a dual principle in these things themselves. So Empedocles had spoken of Love and Strife as two forces which respectively gathered and disrupted the elements, so as to carry on between them the Penelope's labor of the world, the one perpetually weaving fresh forms of life, and the other perpetually undoing them.

It needed but a slight concession to traditional rhetoric in order to exchange these names, Love and Strife, which designated divine powers in Empedocles, into the names of Venus and Mars, which designated the same influences in Roman mythology. The Mars and Venus of Lucretius are not moral forces, incompatible with the mechanism of atoms; they are this mechanism itself, in so far as it now produces and now destroys life, or any precious enterprise, like this of Lucretius in composing his saving poem. Mars and Venus, linked in each other's arms, rule the universe together; nothing arises save by the death of some other thing. Yet when what arises is happier in itself, or more congenial to us, than what is destroyed, the poet says that Venus prevails, that she woos her captive lover to suspend his unprofitable raging. At such times it is spring on earth; the storms recede (I paraphrase the opening passage), the fields are covered with flowers, the sunshine floods the serene sky, and all the tribes of animals feel the mighty impulse of Venus in their hearts. The corn ripens in the plains, and even the sea bears in safety the fleets that traverse it.

Not least, however, of these works of Venus is the Roman people. Never was the formative power of nature better illustrated than in the vitality of this race, which conquered so many other races, or than in its assimilative power, which civilized and pacified them. Legend had made

Venus the mother of Aeneas, and Aeneas the progenitor of the Romans. Lucretius seizes on this happy accident and identifies the Venus of fable with the true Venus, the propitious power in all nature, of which Rome was indeed a crowning work. But the poet's work, also, if it is to be accomplished worthily, must look to the same propitious movement for its happy issue and for its power to persuade. Venus must be the patron of his art and philosophy. She must keep Memmius from the wars, that he may read, and be weaned from frivolous ambitions; and she must stop the tumult of constant sedition, that Lucretius may lend his undivided mind to the precepts of Epicurus, and his whole heart to a sublime friendship, which prompts him to devote to intense study all the watches of the starry night, plotting the course of each invisible atom, and mounting almost to the seat of the gods.

This impersonation in the figure of Venus of whatever makes for life would not be legitimate—it would really contradict a mechanical view of nature—if it were not balanced by a figure representing the opposite tendency, the no less universal tendency towards death.

The Mars of the opening passage, subdued for a moment by the blandishments of love, is raging in all the rest of the poem in his irrepressible fury. These are the two sides of every transmutation, that in creating, one thing destroys another; and this transmutation being perpetual,—nothing being durable except the void, the atoms, and their motion,—it follows that the tendency towards death is, for any particular thing, the final and victorious tendency. The names of Venus and Mars, not being essential to the poet's thought, are allowed to drop out, and the actual processes they stand for are described nakedly; yet, if the poem had ever been finished, and Lucretius

had wished to make the end chime with the beginning, and represent, as it were, one great cycle of the world, it is conceivable that he might have placed at the close a mythical passage to match that at the beginning; and we might have seen Mars aroused from his luxurious lethargy, reasserting his immortal nature, and rushing, firebrand in hand, from the palace of love to spread destruction throughout the universe, till all things should burn fiercely, and be consumed together. Yet not quite all; for the goddess herself would remain, more divine and desirable than ever in her averted beauty. Instinctively into her bosom the God of War would sink again, when weary and drunk with slaughter; and a new world would arise from the scattered atoms of the old.

These endless revolutions, taken in themselves, exactly balance; and I am not sure that, impartially considered, it is any sadder that new worlds should arise than that this world should always continue. Besides, nature cannot take from us more than she has given, and it would be captious and thankless in us to think of her as destructive only, or destructive essentially, after the unspeculative fashion of modern pessimists. She destroys to create, and creates to destroy, her interest (if we may express it so) being not in particular things, nor in their continuance, but solely in the movement that underlies them, in the flux of substance beneath. Life, however, belongs to form, and not to matter; or in the language of Lucretius, life is an *eventum*, a redundant ideal product or incidental aspect, involved in the equilibration of matter; as the throw of sixes is an *eventum*, a redundant ideal product or incidental aspect, occasionally involved in shaking a dice-box. Yet, as this throw makes the acme and best possible issue of a game of dice, so life is the acme and best possible issue of the dance of atoms; and it is from the point of view of this *eventum* that the whole process is viewed by us, and is judged. Not until that happy chance has taken place, do we exist morally, or can we reflect or judge at all. The philosopher is at the top of the wave, he is the foam in the rolling tempest; and as the wave must have risen before he bursts into being, all that he lives to witness is the fall of the wave. The decadence of all he lives by is the only prospect before him; his whole philosophy must be a prophecy of death. Of the life that may come after, when the atoms come together again, he can imagine nothing; the life he knows and shares, all that is life to him, is waning and almost spent.

Therefore Lucretius, who is nothing if not honest, is possessed by a profound melancholy. Vigorous and throbbing as are his pictures of spring, of love, of ambition, of budding culture, of intellectual victory, they pale before the vivid strokes with which he paints the approach of death—fatigue of the will, lassitude in pleasure, corruption and disintegration in society, the soil exhausted, the wild animals tamed or exterminated, poverty, pestilence, and famine at hand; and for the individual, almost at once, the final dissipation of the atoms of his soul, escaping from a relaxed body, to mingle and lose themselves in the universal flow. Nothing comes out of nothing, nothing falls back into nothing, if we consider substance; but everything comes from nothing and falls back into nothing if we consider things—the objects of love and of experience. Time can make no impression on the void or on the atoms; nay, time is itself an *eventum* created by the motion of atoms in the void; but the triumph of time is absolute over persons, and nations, and worlds.

In treating of the soul and of immortality Lucretius is an imperfect psychologist and an arbitrary moralist. His zeal to prove that the soul is mortal is inspired by the wish to dispel all fear of future punishments, and so to liberate the mind for the calm and tepid enjoyment of this world. There is something to be gained in this direction, undoubtedly, especially if tales about divine vengeance to come are used to sanction irrational practices, and to prevent poor people from improving their lot. At the same time, it is hardly fair to assume that hell is the only prospect which immortality could possibly open to any of us; and it is also unfair not to observe that the punishments which religious fables threaten the dead with are, for the most part, symbols for the actual degradation which evil-doing brings upon the living; so that the fear of hell is not more deterrent or repressive than experience of life would be if it were clearly brought before the mind.

There is another element in this polemic against immortality which, while highly interesting and characteristic of a decadent age, betrays a very one-sided and, at bottom, untenable ideal. This element is the fear of life. Epicurus had been a pure and tender moralist, but pusillanimous. He was so afraid of hurting and of being hurt, so afraid of running risks or tempting fortune, that he wished to prove that human life was a brief business, not subject to any great transformations, nor capable of any great achievements. He taught accordingly that the atoms had produced already all the animals they could produce, for though infinite in number the atoms were of few kinds. Consequently the possible sorts of being were finite and soon exhausted; this world, though on the eve of destruction, was of recent date. The worlds around it, or to be produced in future, could not afford anything essentially different. All the suns were much alike, and there was nothing new under them. We need not, then, fear the world; it is an explored and domestic scene,—a home, a little garden, six feet of earth for a man to stretch in. If people rage and make a great noise, it is not because there is much to win, or much to fear, but because people are mad. Let me not be mad, thought Epicurus; let me be reasonable, cultivating sentiments appropriate to a mortal who inhabits a world morally comfortable and small, and physically poor in its infinite monotony. The well-known lines of Fitzgerald echo this sentiment perfectly:

A Book of Verses underneath the Bough,
A Jug of Wine, a Loaf of Bread—and Thou
   Beside me singing in the Wilderness—
Oh, Wilderness were Paradise enow!

But what if the shadow of incalculable possibilities should fall across this sunny retreat? What if after death we should awake in a world to which the atomic philosophy might not in the least apply? Observe that this suggestion is not in the least opposed to any of the arguments by which science might prove the atomic theory to be correct. All that Epicurus taught about the universe now before us might be perfectly true of it; but what if tomorrow a new universe should have taken its place? The suggestion is doubtless gratuitous, and no busy man will be much troubled by it; yet when the heart is empty it fills itself with such attenuated dreams. The muffled pleasures of the wise man, as Epicurus conceived him, were really a provocation to supernaturalism. They left a great void; and before long supernaturalism—we shall see it in Dante—actually rushed in to quicken the pulses of life with fresh hopes and illusions, or at least (what may seem better than nothing) with terrors and fanatical zeal. With such tendencies already afoot as the myths and dogmas of Plato had betrayed, it was imperative for Epi-

curus to banish anxiously all thought of what might follow death. To this end are all his arguments about the material nature of the soul and her incapacity to survive the body.

To say that the soul is material has a strange and barbarous sound to modern ears. We live after Descartes, who taught the world that the essence of the soul was consciousness; and to call consciousness material would be to talk of the blackness of white. But ancient usage gave the word soul a rather different meaning. The essence of the soul was not so much to be conscious as to govern the formation of the *Aristotle* body, to warm, move, and guide it. And if we think of the soul exclusively in this light, it will not seem a paradox, it may even seem a truism, to say that the soul must be material. For how are we to conceive that preëxisting consciousness should govern the formation of the body, move, warm, or guide it? A spirit capable of such a miracle would in any case not be human, but altogether divine. The soul that Lucretius calls material should not, then, be identified with consciousness, but with the ground of consciousness, which is at the same time the cause of life in the body. This he conceives to be a swarm of very small and volatile atoms, a sort of ether, resident in all living seeds, breathed in abundantly during life and breathed out at death.

Even if this theory were accepted, however, it would not prove the point which Lucretius has chiefly at heart, namely, that an after-life is impossible. The atoms of the soul are indestructible, like all atoms; and if consciousness were attached to the fortunes of a small group of them, or of one only (as Leibniz afterwards taught), consciousness would continue to exist after these atoms had escaped from the body and were shooting through new fields of space.

Indeed, they might be the more aroused by that adventure, as a bee might find the sky or the garden more exciting than the hive. All that Lucretius urges about the divisibility of the soul, its diffused bodily seat, and the perils it would meet outside fails to remove the ominous possibility that troubles him.

To convince us that we perish at death he has to rely on vulgar experience and inherent probability: what changes is not indestructible; what begins, ends; mental growth, health, sanity, accompany the fortunes of the body as a whole (not demonstrably those of the soul-atoms); the passions are relevant to bodily life and to an earthly situation; we should not be ourselves under a different mask or in a new setting; we remember no previous existence if we had one, and so, in a future existence, we should not remember this. These reflections are impressive, and they are enforced by Lucretius with his usual vividness and smack of reality. Nothing is proved scientifically by such a deliverance, yet it is good philosophy and good poetry; it brings much experience together and passes a lofty judgment upon it. The artist has his eye on the model; he is painting death to the life.

If these considerations succeed in banishing the dread of an after-life, there remains the distress which many feel at the idea of extinction; and if we have ceased to fear death, like Hamlet, for the dreams that may come after it, we may still fear death instinctively, like a stuck pig. Against this instinctive horror of dying Lucretius has many brave arguments. Fools, he says to us, why do you fear what never can touch you? While you still live, death is absent; and when you are dead, you are so dead that you cannot know you are dead, nor regret it. You will be as much at ease as before you were born. Or is what

troubles you the childish fear of being cold in the earth, or feeling its weight stifling you? But you will not be there; the atoms of your soul—themselves unconscious—will be dancing in some sunbeam far away, and you yourself will be nowhere; you will absolutely not exist. Death is by definition a state that excludes experience. If you fear it, you fear a word.

To all this, perhaps, Memmius, or some other recalcitrant reader, might retort that what he shrank from was not the metaphysical state of being dead, but the very real agony of dying. Dying is something ghastly, as being born is something ridiculous; and, even if no pain were involved in quitting or entering this world, we might still say what Dante's Francesca says of it: *Il modo ancor m' offende,*—"I shudder at the way of it." Lucretius, for his part, makes no attempt to show that everything is as it should be; and if our way of coming into this life is ignoble, and our way of leaving it pitiful, that is no fault of his nor of his philosophy. If the fear of death were merely the fear of dying, it would be better dealt with by medicine than by argument. There is, or there might be, an art of dying well, of dying painlessly, willingly, and in season,—as in those noble partings which Attic gravestones depict,—especially if we were allowed, as Lucretius would allow us, to choose our own time.

But the radical fear of death, I venture to think, is something quite different. It is the love of life. Epicurus, who feared life, seems to have missed here the primordial and colossal force he was fighting against. Had he perceived that force, he would have been obliged to meet it in a more radical way, by an enveloping movement, as it were, and an attack from the rear. The love of life is not something rational, or founded on experience of life. It is something antecedent and spontaneous. It is that Venus Genetrix which covers the earth with its flora and fauna. It teaches every animal to seek its food and its mate, and to protect its offspring; as also to resist or fly from all injury to the body, and most of all from threatened death. It is the original impulse by which good is discriminated from evil, and hope from fear.

Nothing could be more futile, therefore, than to marshal arguments against that fear of death which is merely another name for the energy of life, or the tendency to self-preservation. Arguments involve premises, and these premises, in the given case, express some particular form of the love of life; whence it is impossible to conclude that death is in no degree evil and not at all to be feared. For what is most dreaded is not the agony of dying, nor yet the strange impossibility that when we do not exist we should suffer for not existing. What is dreaded is the defeat of a present will directed upon life and its various undertakings. Such a present will cannot be argued away, but it may be weakened by contradictions arising within it, by the irony of experience, or by ascetic discipline. To introduce ascetic discipline, to bring out the irony of experience, to expose the self-contradictions of the will, would be the true means of mitigating the love of life; and if the love of life were extinguished, the fear of death, like smoke rising from that fire, would have vanished also.

Indeed, the force of the great passage against the fear of death, at the end of the third book of Lucretius, comes chiefly from the picture it draws of the madness of life. His philosophy deprecates covetousness, ambition, love, and religion; it takes a long step towards the surrender of life, by surrendering all in life that is ardent, on the ground that it is painful in the end and ignominious. To escape from it all is a great deliverance. And since genius must be ar-

dent about something, Lucretius pours out his enthusiasm on Epicurus, who brought this deliverance and was the saviour of mankind. Yet this was only a beginning of salvation, and the same principles carried further would have delivered us from the Epicurean life and what it retained that was Greek and naturalistic: science, friendship, and the healthy pleasures of the body. Had it renounced these things also, Epicureanism would have become altogether ascetic, a thorough system of mortification, or the pursuit of death. To those who sincerely pursue death, death is no evil, but the highest good. No need in that case of elaborate arguments to prove that death should not be feared, because it is nothing; for in spite of being nothing—or rather because it is nothing—death can be loved by a fatigued and disillusioned spirit, just as in spite of being nothing—or rather because it is nothing—it must be hated and feared by every vigorous animal.

One more point, and I have done with this subject. Ancient culture was rhetorical. It abounded in ideas that are verbally plausible, and pass muster in a public speech, but that, if we stop to criticize them, prove at once to be inexcusably false. One of these rhetorical fallacies is the maxim that men cannot live for what they cannot witness. What does it matter to you, we may say in debate, what happened before you were born, or what may go on after you are buried? And the orator who puts such a challenge may carry the audience with him, and raise a laugh at the expense of human sincerity. Yet the very men who applaud are proud of their ancestors, care for the future of their children, and are very much interested in securing legally the execution of their last will and testament. What may go on after their death concerns them deeply, not because they expect to watch the event from hell or heaven, but because they are interested ideally in what that event shall be, although they are never to witness it. Lucretius himself, in his sympathy with nature, in his zeal for human enlightenment, in his tears for Iphigenia, long since dead, is not moved by the hope of observing, or the memory of having observed, what excites his emotion. He forgets himself. He sees the whole universe spread out in its true movement and proportions; he sees mankind freed from the incubus of superstition, and from the havoc of passion. The vision kindles his enthusiasm, exalts his imagination, and swells his verse into unmistakable earnestness.

If we follow Lucretius, therefore, in narrowing the sum of our personal fortunes to one brief and partial glimpse of earth, we must not suppose that we need narrow at all the sphere of our moral interests. On the contrary, just in proportion as we despise superstitious terrors and sentimental hopes, and as our imagination becomes self-forgetful, we shall strengthen the direct and primitive concern which we feel in the world and in what may go on there, before us, after us, or beyond our ken. If, like Lucretius and every philosophical poet, we range over all time and all existence, we shall forget our own persons, as he did, and even wish them to be forgotten, if only the

things we care for may subsist or arise. He who truly loves God, says Spinoza, cannot wish that God should love him in return. One who lives the life of the universe cannot be much concerned for his own. After all, the life of the universe is but the locus and extension of ours. The atoms that have once served to produce life remain fit to reproduce it; and although the body they might animate later would be a new one, and would have a somewhat different career, it would not, according to Lucretius, be of a totally new species; perhaps not more unlike ourselves than we are unlike one another, or than each of us is unlike himself at the various stages of his life.

The soul of nature, in the elements of it, is then, according to Lucretius, actually immortal; only the human individuality, the chance composition of those elements, is transitory; so that, if a man could care for what happens to other men, for what befell him when young or what may overtake him when old, he might perfectly well care, on the same imaginative principle, for what may go on in the world for ever. The finitude and injustice of his personal life would be broken down; the illusion of selfishness would be dissipated; and he might say to himself, I have imagination, and nothing that is real is alien to me.

COMMENT

Ancient and Modern Materialism

The task of commenting upon the readings in this chapter has been greatly simplified by the inclusion of the essay by George Santayana. Little need be added to his interpretation of the Roman poet, and his own reflections upon human destiny and the nature of the universe are too lucid to require analysis. One feels that his genius is akin to that of Lucretius, and that the implications of materialism remain as fresh and pertinent for him as for his ancient predecessor.

This may seem strange to a reader familiar with the history of ideas. Have not science and the naturalistic philosophy based upon it undergone an immense revolution since the time of Lucretius? Even the more modern materialism of Hobbes and La Mettrie appears quaint and archaic in the light of recent science and philosophy. We can no longer conceive of matter in the form of tiny indivisible particles, like the motes of dust that we see dancing about in a shaft of sunlight. The atomic theory has been transplanted from metaphysical speculation to experimental research, and the resulting discoveries have radically transformed it.

Few people would now question the existence of atoms, but the atoms are no longer conceived as inert, eternal, and indivisible particles moving in a featureless void. Instead of being inert, they are made up of electrical charges which behave like waves. Instead of being eternal, they emit radiations and are subject to splittings and fusions. Instead of being indivisible, they can be analyzed into electrons, protons, neutrons, mesons, positrons, and so on. Instead of moving in a void, they are enmeshed in "electromagnetic fields" within "curved" space-time. These modern concepts of radiation, fission, quanta, waves, fields, and relativity are a far cry from Lucretius.

Yet the naturalistic temper of his philosophy as distinguished from the archaic details of his science remains as up-to-date as ever. Nothing in modern physics contradicts his vision of all things arising from and returning to a material base. W. H. Mallock, in a free poetic translation of a passage from Lucretius, has expressed the essence of this naturalism:

> No single thing abides; but all things flow
> Fragment to fragment clings—the things thus grow
> Until we know and name them. By degrees
> They melt, and are no more the things we know.
>
> Globed from the atoms falling slow or swift
> I see the suns, I see the systems lift
> Their forms; and even the systems and the suns
> Shall go back slowly to the eternal drift.
>
> Thou too, oh earth—thine empires, lands, and seas—
> Least, with thy stars, of all the galaxies,
> Globed from the drift like these, like these thou too
> Shalt go. Thou art going, hour by hour, like these.[1]

Lucretius, the ancient poet, and Santayana, the modern philosopher, share this naturalistic vision.

[1] William Hurrell Mallock, *Lucretius on Life and Death, in the Metre of Omar Khayyam* (London: A. C. Black, 1900).

Can Materialism Explain Secondary Qualities?

Extreme materialism tries to explain every process in terms of matter and motion quantitatively described. "Primary qualities," which are abstract and measurable, are conceived to be more ultimate or objective, whereas "secondary qualities," which are concrete and unmeasureable, are regarded as more derivative or subjective. This distinction was first clearly stated by Democritus:

> There are two kinds of knowledge: real knowledge and obscure knowledge. To obscure knowledge belong all things of sight, sound, odor, taste, and touch; real knowledge is distinct from this . . . Sweet and bitter, heat and cold, and color, are only opinions; there is nothing true but atoms and the void.[2]

For Democritus, the only objective properties of things are size, shape, weight, and motion. All other qualities, such as sound, color, odor, taste, and touch, are sensations in us caused by the motions and arrangements of the atoms.

This theory was revived by Galileo and was reformulated by Hobbes, Locke, Newton, and other influential modern thinkers. It has figured very prominently in modern theories of perception. Warmth, for example, is explained as the reaction of our sense organs and nervous systems to molecular motions; sound, as our reaction to air waves; color, as our reaction to electromagnetic vibrations. Thus the "secondary qualities"—colors, sounds, odors, and so on—exist, as such, only for our minds. In the absence of our mental reactions, the universe is a pretty dull and abstract affair—a collection of soundless, colorless, and odorless particles, in various arrangements, drifting through space and time.

Lucretius, departing from the views of Democritus, had a different theory. He agreed that the atoms individually are without any of the secondary qualities, but maintained that these qualities spring into existence when the atoms are combined in certain ways. "The first-bodies," he tells us, are not only "bereft . . . of color, they are also sundered altogether from warmth and cold, and fiery heat, and are carried along barren of sound and devoid of taste, nor do they give off any scent of their own from their body." But these qualities *are* properties of compounds, formed by combinations of atoms. The compounds, being new and different entities, have color, sound, odor, taste, and heat, none of which can belong to the atoms as individual particles. When we perceive these secondary qualities we are grasping real objective properties, for the complex body perceived by our senses is as real as the atoms.

There are difficulties in both the Lucretian and the Democritean theory.

[2] Translated by Philip Wheelwright, *The Way of Philosophy* (Odyssey Press, 1954), p. 162

Some critics have objected that if the atoms of Lucretius are devoid of secondary qualities, it is difficult to understand how by mere juxtaposition or arrangement they can produce things which possess these qualities. This difficulty is increased by the contention that the atoms are utterly unchangeable, possessing the secondary qualities neither before nor after they combine. It would seem that elementary particles that are themselves unmodifiable could not by their combination give rise to entities having radically new qualities. Perhaps more serious is the fact that Lucretius rests his theory upon a rather naïve trust in perception. He insists that we see objects as they really are, that our senses do not deceive us. Perhaps! We naturally attribute the sounds, colors, odors, tastes, and tactile qualities which we perceive to supposedly real external objects. But there is evidence to show that these qualities depend upon physiological and psychological reactions in the perceiving organisms. To suppose that our senses perfectly reveal the nature of the external world is, therefore, a very big assumption.

The theory of Democritus, with its modern counterparts, can also be challenged. The primary qualities may be no less subjective than the secondary. If the sounds and colors that I perceive do not exist in the external world but come into being when my mind is acted upon in certain ways, why may not the same be true of the shapes and motions which I seem to perceive in things? As we shall see when we study Berkeley, it can be argued that the considerations that drive us to conclude that the secondary qualities are subjective apply also to the primary qualities.

On the other hand, some philosophers maintain that *both* primary and secondary qualities are objective. They would agree with Lucretius that compounds, if not more elementary bodies, possess secondary qualities. The real world, they believe, has the vivid colors, odors, sounds, tastes, and tactile qualities that it appears to have. The problem, to which we shall return in the next chapter, is difficult, and no solution is obviously the right one. But it seems unlikely that an adequate solution can be worked out in terms of a simple materialism.

Can Materialism Explain Life?

Can a materialist account for the difference between animate and inanimate things?

An extreme materialist will not admit any such fundamental cleavage. Plant and animal activity, he will maintain, is reducible simply to physical and chemical forces exactly like those found in inorganic bodies. Living things are composed exclusively of substances that may also be found in non-living things, and there are no teleological or vitalistic forces that explain life. In opposition to this point of view, "vitalists" such as Henri Bergson (1859–1941) maintain that life is distinct and fundamentally different from non-life.

There certainly *appears* to be a gap between living organisms and mere physical mechanisms. No machine grows by what it feeds on. No machine has the capacity to produce a germ which will develop into another thing like itself—Ford cars do not produce little Ford cars. No machine can grow new tissue and thus repair its own injuries. No machine has memories. No machine has purposes or expectations. No machine, not even an "electronic brain," sets problems for itself to solve—it can solve only those problems "fed" into it. A man can invent a machine or, like Luther Burbank, breed a new species of organism, but a machine cannot invent another machine or breed even the lowliest organism. No machine is conscious of itself or of other things. "Electronic brains" can perform computations far beyond the power of a human mind and machines can simulate the behavior of animate creatures, but there still remains a great chasm between the most adroit machines and real organisms. To say that machines can reason, remember, criticize, plan, love, or imagine is to speak in a purely metaphorical sense.

Unlike extreme reductive materialists, Lucretius did not deny that living beings have distinctive characteristics. He was a believer in what is now called the doctrine of "emergence"—the theory that new qualities, including mental functions, spring into existence as a result of the complex combinations of material elements. He pointed out that men can speak and laugh and think whereas it would be absurd to attribute these capacities to atoms. A human organism, made up of innumerable atoms, has vital characteristics which the atoms taken singly do not possess. Just as the meaning of a sentence results from the combinations of meaningless letters, so life results from the meetings and configurations of lifeless atoms. Applied to evolution, this theory means the recognition of diverse levels of complexity and organization, each with its emergent qualities, and the interpretation of these levels as successive stages in an evolutionary process. We associate this type of theory with such modern philosophers as Samuel Alexander (1859–1938), but it was maintained by Lucretius two thousand years ago.

Its implications are, in the wide sense of the word, "materialistic." Life, it declares, arises out of matter and is a function of complex material bodies. "Out of dust man arises and to dust will he return." Vital processes cannot survive the dissolution of the body any more than a football game can continue after the disbanding of the opposing teams.

The adequacy of this type of theory to explain life is a subject of much dispute. Some philosophers maintain that the phenomena of life are so essentially disparate from and discontinuous with merely material happenings that they cannot possibly "emerge" from a previous state of lifeless matter. To maintain the doctrine of emergence, it is said, is to assert the miracle of creation out of nothing. "Wherever mind is taken to begin" in this way, declares

G. F. Stout, "it bursts into being like a shot out of a pistol that is not previously in the pistol." [3]

A considerable number of philosophers and biologists, moreover, have argued that no purely materialistic theory can explain the facts of organic evolution. The usual explanation is in terms of Darwin's theory of random variations, struggle for existence, and survival of the fittest—and there are interesting anticipations of Darwinism in Lucretius' poem. But if mere survival is the sole requirement, it is difficult to account for the upward drive of life to high and unstable evolutionary levels. Some of the very simplest species are today what they were at the remotest times of the paleozoic era, a half billion years ago. They are as perfectly adapted as any organisms, judged by their capacity to survive. Why did not life stop at this very stable level? Why has it gone on, complicating itself more and more dangerously? "The truth is that adaptation explains the sinuosities of the movement of evolution," declared the famous French philosopher Henri Bergson, "but not its general directions, still less the movement itself." [4] Throughout organic nature, he argued, there is a persistent vital impetus which explains the vast ascending movement of evolution. Life is in no sense a product of matter. It is an opposite current that builds up organisms out of matter. Matter is governed by the Law of Entropy—the tendency of purely material systems to run down through the loss of radiant energy. But life moves in the opposite direction from matter and stores up and concentrates energy and evolves ever higher and more complex beings. This philosophy of "creative evolution," as Bergson dubbed it, makes a clean break with materialism.

If scientists should eventually succeed in producing life—not something that merely simulates life but something indubitably alive—by synthesis of certain chemicals, this feat would refute Bergson's contention that life is underivable from "matter." But even so, materialism would not be proved—what we take to be inorganic matter might be organic. This is the view that has been elaborately formulated by Alfred North Whitehead (1861–1947), who interprets evolution as the development of complex organisms from antecedent states of simpler organisms. Just as disease viruses are very elementary organisms, so are atoms—though they are organisms of a different type. Hence evolution does not involve a leap from the inorganic to the organic, as in the theory of Lucretius, but merely a greater and greater complication of organisms. The philosophy of Whitehead, like that of Bergson, thus represents an alternative to materialism.

[3] *Mind and Matter* (Cambridge at the University Press, 1931), p. 110.
[4] *Creative Evolution* (Henry Holt, 1911), p. 102.

Can Materialism Explain the Relation Between Mind and Body?

Ever since the time of Descartes, one of the main concerns of philosophy and psychology has been "the mind-body problem." Body and mind appear to be very different and yet intimately connected. To what extent *are* they different, and how are they connected? Let us glance at the answers that materialism might give to this question.

The most extreme position is the virtual denial that we have minds at all. Extreme reductive materialism interprets human beings as very complex mechanisms, like the electronic computing machines which have often been compared to human brains. Some forms of "Behaviorism" (a type of mechanistic psychology) virtually deny that there are any genuinely mental processes, such as reasoning, willing, feeling, perceiving, remembering, or imagining. "Thinking" is defined as the movement of the larynx, or other purely physical motions. "Joy" means nothing but certain detectable changes in eyes, lungs, muscles, glands, etc. A view so obviously inadequate scarcely needs refutation. It is like the play that purports to be *Hamlet* but omits the Prince of Denmark from the cast!

A second and more tenable type of materialism—called "epiphenomenalism"—admits that there *are* mental processes but regards them as mere ineffectual by-products of physical processes. The only causal relations are between physical events and *other* physical events, or between physical antecedents and mental consequents. Our thoughts and feelings are caused by molecular changes in the brain or other physical processes and have no causal efficacy of their own. The mind has as little to do with the movement of the body as the shadow cast by a locomotive has to do with the racing of the locomotive. The rather shocking implications of this type of materialism are stated by William James in his inimitable style:

> If we knew thoroughly the nervous system of Shakespeare, and as thoroughly all his environing conditions, we should be able, according to the theory of automatism, to show why at a given period of his life his hand came to trace on certain sheets of paper those crabbed little black marks which we for shortness' sake call the manuscript of *Hamlet*. We should understand the rationale of every erasure and alteration therein, and we should understand all this without in the slightest degree acknowledging the existence of the thoughts in Shakespeare's mind. The words and sentences would be taken, not as signs of anything beyond themselves, but as little outward facts, pure and simple. In like manner, the automaton theory affirms, we might exhaustively write the biography of those two hundred pounds, more or less, of warmish albuminoid matter called Martin Luther, without ever implying that it felt.
>
> But, on the other hand, nothing in all this could prevent us from giving an equally complete account of either Luther's or Shakespeare's spiritual history,

an account in which every gleam of thought and emotion should find its place. The mind-history would run alongside of the body-history of each man, and each point in the one would correspond to, but not react upon, a point in the other. So the melody floats from the harp-string, but neither checks nor quickens its vibrations; so the shadow runs alongside the pedestrian, but in no way influences his steps.

As a mere *conception,* and so long as we confine our view to the nervous centers themselves, few things are more seductive than this radically mechanical theory of their action. And yet our consciousness *is there,* and has in all probability been evolved, like all other functions, for a use—it is to the highest degree improbable *a priori* that it should have no use. Its use *seems* to be that of *selection;* but to select, it must be efficacious. States of consciousness which feel right are held fast to; those which feel wrong are checked. If the "holding" and the "checking" of the conscious states severally mean also the efficacious reinforcing or inhibiting of the correlated neural processes, then it would seem as if the presence of the states of mind might help to steer the nervous system and keep it in the path which to the consciousness seemed best. Now on the average what seems best to consciousness is really best for the creature. It is a well-known fact that pleasures are generally associated with beneficial, pains with detrimental, experiences. All the fundamental vital processes illustrate this law. Starvation; suffocation; privation of food, drink, and sleep; work when exhausted; burns, wounds, inflammation; the effects of poison, are as disagreeable as filling the hungry stomach, enjoying rest and sleep after fatigue, exercise after rest, and a sound skin and unbroken bones at all times, are pleasant. . . .

Probability and circumstantial evidence thus run dead against the theory that our actions are *purely* mechanical in their causation. From the point of view of descriptive Psychology (even though we be bound to assume . . . that all our feelings have brain-processes for their condition of existence, and can be remotely traced in every instance to currents coming from the outer world) we have no clear reason to doubt that the feelings may react so as to further or to dampen the processes to which they are due. I shall therefore not hesitate . . . to use the language of common-sense. I shall talk as if consciousness kept actively pressing the nerve-centers in the direction of its own ends, and was no mere impotent and paralytic spectator of life's game.[5]

The theory that James is here criticizing is not a doctrine which Lucretius entertained. As we have already observed, Lucretius formulated a theory of emergence which permitted him to recognize the reality and causal efficacy of mental characteristics. Also, his theory of "swerving" atoms, with the concomitant belief in free will, represents a distinct departure from a strict mechanistic determinism.

This theory, although unsubstantiated and somewhat naïvely stated, is similar to the famous "principle of indeterminacy" formulated in 1927 by Werner Heisenberg, a German physicist. Heisenberg found that it is impos-

[5] *Psychology* (Henry Holt, 1893), pp. 102–104.

sible to determine the position and the velocity of an electron simultaneously —*i.e.*, to state that the electron is at a precise spot while moving at a specific speed. This uncertainty, he maintained, is caused not by the inadequacy of scientific measurement and observation but by the capriciousness of the external physical order. Nature itself is "throwing dice" in a somewhat unpredictable way.

A number of distinguished scientists, such as Arthur Eddington and James Jeans, have interpreted Heisenberg's principle of indeterminacy as supporting the doctrine of free will. If physical events, they reason, are somewhat indeterminate and unpredictable, the human mind may be exempt from rigid determinism. Eddington suggests that the indeterminacy may exist in living matter and more particularly in the human brain, and that free choice may influence the movements of the brain-atoms in one direction rather than another. There has been much dispute as to whether this application of Heisenberg's principle is justifiable; but it is a modern analogue of Lucretius' theory of swerving atoms and free will.

It would take too much space to discuss the complicated puzzle of the relation between body and mind. One suspects that no extreme doctrine, such as reductive materialism or Descartes' exaggerated dualism ("the dogma of the ghost in the machine"), will suffice, and that a person is a psychophysical organism in which body and mind are so intimately connected as to constitute a single system. Such unity is already recognized in psychiatry and psychosomatic medicine.

There is another possibility, however, that we should very carefully consider. This is idealism—to which we shall turn in the next chapter.

9

Idealism

GEORGE BERKELEY (1685–1753)

Berkeley was born in Kilkenny County, Ireland. His parents, having a comfortable income, gave him a good education at Kilkenny School and Trinity College, Dublin. While scarcely more than a boy, he began to fill notebooks with original philosophical reflections. His first major publication, *An Essay Toward a New Theory of Vision,* appeared when he was twenty-four, and *Principles of Human Knowledge,* which set forth his whole idealistic philosophy, was published only a year later. Finding that his ideas were ridiculed if not neglected, he reformulated his argument in *Three Dialogues Between Hylas and Philonous,* which appeared in 1713. Thus, by the time he was twenty-eight, he had published his three major works, remarkable both for the felicity of their style and for the daring and profundity of their thought.

During this period of his greatest literary activity, Berkeley was a fellow and tutor at Trinity College, but he spent the next years after publishing his *Dialogues* in London, France, and Italy. In London, he became the friend of Pope, Steele, Addison, and Swift. Subsequently he traveled in Europe as secretary and chaplain to an earl and tutor to a bishop's son. While in Sicily, he lost the manuscript of the second part of *The Principles of Human Knowledge* and never had the heart to rewrite it.

Returning to Ireland, he was appointed Lecturer in Greek and Theology at Trinity College and eventually an ecclesiastical Dean (1724). Shortly thereafter, to his immense surprise, he inherited three thousand pounds from Hester Van Homrigh (Swift's former friend "Vanessa"), a lady whom he had met once and then only casually.

At about the same time, he conceived the project of founding a college in the Bermudas for training missionaries to the Indians and clergymen for the American colonists. By his eloquence and personal charm, he was able to obtain a considerable sum to finance his project from private donors and the promise of twenty thousand pounds from the House of Commons. With a new wife, he set sail for America in 1728. But Walpole, the Prime Minister, refused to fulfill the promise of Parliament, and Berkeley remained for three years at Newport, Rhode Island, his hopes gradually diminishing. Finally, in 1731, despairing of further aid and saddened by the death of an infant daughter, he sailed with his wife and tiny son back to England.

His later life was spent as Bishop of Cloyne and head of a growing family. He divided his time between ecclesiastical duties, philosophical studies, agitation for social reform, and family affairs. His main publication in these years was *Siris* (1744), a rather odd work in which he extolled the medicinal virtues of tar-water and expounded an idealistic interpretation of the Universe. In the final year of his life, Berkeley and his family moved to Oxford, where, "suddenly and without the least previous notice or pain," he died in 1753.

Three Dialogues*

THE FIRST DIALOGUE

Philonous. Good morning, *Hylas:* I did not expect to find you abroad so early.

Hyl. It is indeed something unusual; but my thoughts were so taken up with a subject I was discoursing of last night, that finding I could not sleep, I resolved to rise and take a turn in the garden.

Phil. It happened well, to let you see what innocent and agreeable pleasures you lose every morning. Can there be a pleasanter time of the day, or a more delightful season of the year? That purple sky, those wild but sweet notes of birds, the fragrant bloom upon the trees and flowers, the gentle influence of the rising sun, these and a thousand nameless beauties of nature in-

spire the soul with secret transports; its faculties too being at this time fresh and lively, are fit for these meditations, which the solitude of a garden and tranquillity of the morning naturally dispose us to. But I am afraid I interrupt your thoughts: for you seemed very intent on something.

Hyl. It is true, I was, and shall be obliged to you if you will permit me to go on in the same vein; not that I would by any means deprive myself of your company, for my thoughts always flow more easily in conversation with a friend, than when I am alone: but my request is, that you would suffer me to impart my reflections to you.

Phil. With all my heart, it is what I should have requested myself if you had not prevented me.

Hyl. I was considering the odd fate of

---

*London, 1713. Second unchanged edition, 1725. Third edition, 1734. The present text is that of A. Campbell Fraser, *The Works of George Berkeley*. Oxford: Clarendon Press, 1871. (With omissions.)

those men who have in all ages, through an affectation of being distinguished from the vulgar, or some unaccountable turn of thought, pretended either to believe nothing at all, or to believe the most extravagant things in the world. This however might be borne, if their paradoxes and scepticism did not draw after them some consequences of general disadvantage to mankind. But the mischief lieth here; that when men of less leisure see them who are supposed to have spent their whole time in the pursuits of knowledge professing an entire ignorance of all things, or advancing such notions as are repugnant to plain and commonly received principles, they will be tempted to entertain suspicions concerning the most important truths, which they had hitherto held sacred and unquestionable.

Phil. I entirely agree with you, as to the ill tendency of the affected doubts of some philosophers, and fantastical conceits of others. I am even so far gone of late in this way of thinking, that I have quitted several of the sublime notions I had got in their schools for vulgar opinions. And I give it you on my word, since this revolt from metaphysical notions, to the plain dictates of nature and common sense, I find my understanding strangely enlightened, so that I can now easily comprehend a great many things which before were all mystery and riddle.

Hyl. I am glad to find there was nothing in the accounts I heard of you.

Phil. Pray, what were those?

Hyl. You were represented in last night's conversation, as one who maintained the most extravagant opinion that ever entered into the mind of man, to wit, that there is no such thing as *material substance* in the world.

Phil. That there is no such thing as what Philosophers call *material substance,* I am seriously persuaded: but, if I were made to

see anything absurd or sceptical in this, I should then have the same reason to renounce this that I imagine I have now to reject the contrary opinion.

Hyl. What! can anything be more fantastical, more repugnant to common sense, or a more manifest piece of Scepticism, than to believe there is no such thing as *matter?*

Phil. Softly, good *Hylas.* What if it should prove, that you, who hold there is, are, by virtue of that opinion, a greater sceptic, and maintain more paradoxes and repugnances to common sense, than I who believe no such thing?

Hyl. You may as soon persuade me, the part is greater than the whole, as that, in order to avoid absurdity and Scepticism, I should ever be obliged to give up my opinion in this point.

Phil. Well then, are you content to admit that opinion for true, which, upon examination, shall appear most agreeable to common sense, and remote from Scepticism?

Hyl. With all my heart. Since you are for raising disputes about the plainest things in nature, I am content for once to hear what you have to say.

Phil. Pray, *Hylas,* what do you mean by a *sceptic?*

Hyl. I mean what all men mean, one that doubts of everything.

Phil. He then who entertains no doubt concerning some particular point, with regard to that point cannot be thought a sceptic.

Hyl. I agree with you.

Phil. Whether doth doubting consist in embracing the affirmative or negative side of a question?

Hyl. In neither; for whoever understands English cannot but know that *doubting* signifies a suspense between both.

Phil. He then that denieth any point, can no more be said to doubt of it, than he who affirmeth it with the same degree of assurance.

Hyl. True.

Phil. And, consequently, for such his denial is no more to be esteemed a sceptic than the other.

Hyl. I acknowledge it.

Phil. How cometh it to pass then, *Hylas,* that you pronounce me a *sceptic,* because I deny what you affirm, to wit, the existence of Matter? Since, for aught you can tell, I am as peremptory in my denial, as you in your affirmation.

Hyl. Hold, *Philonous,* I have been a little out in my definition; but every false step a man makes in discourse is not to be insisted on. I said indeed that a *sceptic* was one who doubted of everything; but I should have added, or who denies the reality and truth of things.

Phil. What things? Do you mean the principles and theorems of sciences? But these you know are universal intellectual notions, and consequently independent of Matter; the denial therefore of this doth not imply the denying them.

Hyl. I grant it. But are there no other things? What think you of distrusting the senses, of denying the real existence of sensible things, or pretending to know nothing of them. Is not this sufficient to denominate a man a *sceptic?*

Phil. Shall we therefore examine which of us it is that denies the reality of sensible things, or professes the greatest ignorance of them; since, if I take you rightly, he is to be esteemed the greatest *sceptic?*

Hyl. That is what I desire.

Phil. What mean you by Sensible Things?

Hyl. Those things which are perceived by the senses. Can you imagine that I mean anything else?

Phil. Pardon me, *Hylas,* if I am desirous clearly to apprehend your notions, since this may much shorten our inquiry. Suffer me then to ask you this further question. Are those things only perceived by the senses which are perceived immediately? Or, may those things properly be said to be *sensible* which are perceived mediately, or not without the intervention of others?

Hyl. I do not sufficiently understand you.

Phil. In reading a book, what I immediately perceive are the letters, but mediately, or by means of these, are suggested to my mind the notions of God, virtue, truth, &c. Now, that the letters are truly sensible things, or perceived by sense, there is no doubt: but I would know whether you take the things suggested by them to be so too.

Hyl. No, certainly; it were absurd to think *God* or *virtue* sensible things, though they may be signified and suggested to the mind by sensible marks, with which they have an arbitrary connection.

Phil. It seems then, that by *sensible things* you mean those only which can be perceived *immediately* by sense?

Hyl. Right.

Phil. Doth it not follow from this, that though I see one part of the sky red, and another blue, and that my reason doth thence evidently conclude there must be some cause of that diversity of colors, yet that cause cannot be said to be a sensible thing, or perceived by the sense of seeing?

Hyl. It doth.

Phil. In like manner, though I hear variety of sounds, yet I cannot be said to hear the causes of those sounds?

Hyl. You cannot.

Phil. And when by my touch I perceive a thing to be hot and heavy, I cannot say, with any truth or propriety, that I feel the cause of its heat or weight?

Hyl. To prevent any more questions of this kind, I tell you once for all, that by *sensible things* I mean those only which are perceived by sense, and that in truth the senses perceive nothing which they do not perceive immediately: for they make no inferences. The deducing therefore of causes or occasions from effects and appearances, which alone are perceived by sense, entirely relates to reason.

Phil. This point then is agreed between us—that *sensible things are those only which are immediately perceived by sense.* You will further inform me, whether we immediately perceive by sight anything beside light, and colors, and figures; or by hearing, anything but sounds; by the palate, anything beside tastes; by the smell, beside odors; or by the touch, more than tangible qualities.

Hyl. We do not.

Phil. It seems, therefore, that if you take away all sensible qualities, there remains nothing sensible?

Hyl. I grant it.

Phil. Sensible things therefore are nothing else but so many sensible qualities, or combinations of sensible qualities?

Hyl. Nothing else.

Phil. Heat is then a sensible thing?

Hyl. Certainly.

Phil. Doth the reality of sensible things consist in being perceived? or, is it something distinct from their being perceived, and that bears no relation to the mind?

Hyl. To *exist* is one thing, and to be *perceived* is another.

Phil. I speak with regard to sensible things only: and of these I ask, whether by their real existence you mean a subsistence exterior to the mind, and distinct from their being perceived?

Hyl. I mean a real absolute being, distinct from, and without any relation to their being perceived.

Phil. Heat therefore, if it be allowed a real being, must exist without the mind?

Hyl. It must.

Phil. Tell me, *Hylas,* is this real existence equally compatible to all degrees of heat, which we perceive; or is there any reason why we should attribute it to some, and deny it to others? and if there be, pray let me know that reason.

Hyl. Whatever degree of heat we perceive by sense, we may be sure the same exists in the object that occasions it.

Phil. What! the greatest as well as the least?

Hyl. I tell you, the reason is plainly the same in respect of both: they are both perceived by sense; nay, the greater degree of heat is more sensibly perceived; and consequently, if there is any difference, we are more certain of its real existence than we can be of the reality of a lesser degree.

Phil. But is not the most vehement and intense degree of heat a very great pain?

Hyl. No one can deny it.

Phil. And is any unperceiving thing capable of pain or pleasure?

Hyl. No certainly.

Phil. Is your material substance a senseless being, or a being endowed with sense and perception?

Hyl. It is senseless without doubt.

Phil. It cannot therefore be the subject of pain?

Hyl. By no means.

Phil. Nor consequently of the greatest heat perceived by sense, since you acknowledge this to be no small pain?

Hyl. I grant it.

Phil. What shall we say then of your external object; is it a material Substance, or no?

Hyl. It is a material substance with the sensible qualities inhering in it.

Phil. How then can a great heat exist in it, since you own it cannot in a material substance? I desire you would clear this point.

Hyl. Hold, *Philonous,* I fear I was out in yielding intense heat to be a pain. It should seem rather, that pain is something distinct from heat, and the consequence or effect of it.

Phil. Upon putting your hand near the fire, do you perceive one simple uniform sensation, or two distinct sensations?

Hyl. But one simple sensation.

Phil. Is not the heat immediately perceived?

Hyl. It is.

Phil. And the pain?

Hyl. True.

Phil. Seeing therefore they are both immediately perceived at the same time, and the fire affects you only with one simple, or uncompounded idea, it follows that this same simple idea is both the intense heat immediately perceived, and the pain; and, consequently, that the intense heat immediately perceived, is nothing distinct from a particular sort of pain.

Hyl. It seems so.

Phil. Again, try in your thoughts, *Hylas,* if you can conceive a vehement sensation to be without pain or pleasure.

Hyl. I cannot.

Phil. Or can you frame to yourself an idea of sensible pain or pleasure, in general, abstracted from every particular idea of heat, cold, tastes, smells? &c.

Hyl. I do not find that I can.

Phil. Doth it not therefore follow, that sensible pain is nothing distinct from those sensations or ideas,—in an intense degree?

Hyl. It is undeniable; and, to speak the truth, I begin to suspect a very great heat cannot exist but in a mind perceiving it.

Phil. What! are you then in that *sceptical* state of suspense, between affirming and denying?

Hyl. I think I may be positive in the point. A very violent and painful heat cannot exist without the mind.

Phil. It hath not therefore, according to you, any real being?

Hyl. I own it.

Phil. Is it therefore certain, that there is no body in nature really hot?

Hyl. I have not denied there is any real heat in bodies. I only say, there is no such thing as an intense real heat.

Phil. But, did you not say before that all degrees of heat were equally real; or, if there was any difference, that the greater were more undoubtedly real than the lesser?

Hyl. True: but it was because I did not then consider the ground there is for distinguishing between them, which I now plainly see. And it is this:—because intense heat is nothing else but a particular kind of painful sensation; and pain cannot exist but in a perceiving being; it follows that no intense heat can really exist in an unperceiving corporeal substance. But this is no reason why we should deny heat in an inferior degree to exist in such a substance.

Phil. But how shall we be able to discern those degrees of heat which exist only in the mind from those which exist without it?

Hyl. That is no difficult matter. You know the least pain cannot exist unperceived; whatever, therefore, degree of heat is a pain exists only in the mind. But, as for all other degrees of heat, nothing obliges us to think the same of them.

Phil. I think you granted before that no unperceiving being was capable of pleasure, any more than of pain.

Hyl. I did.

Phil. And is not warmth, or a more gentle degree of heat than what causes uneasiness, a pleasure?

Hyl. What then?

Phil. Consequently, it cannot exist without the mind in an unperceiving substance, or body.

Hyl. So it seems.

Phil. Since, therefore, as well those degrees of heat that are not painful, as those that are, can exist only in a thinking substance; may we not conclude that external bodies are absolutely incapable of any degree of heat whatsoever?

Hyl. On second thoughts, I do not think it is so evident that warmth is a pleasure, as that a great degree of heat is a pain.

Phil. I do not pretend that warmth is as great a pleasure as heat is a pain. But, if you grant it to be even a small pleasure, it serves to make good my conclusion.

Hyl. I could rather call it an *indolence.* It seems to be nothing more than a privation of both pain and pleasure. And that such a quality or state as this may agree to an unthinking substance, I hope you will not deny.

Phil. If you are resolved to maintain that warmth, or a gentle degree of heat, is no pleasure, I know not how to convince you otherwise, than by appealing to your own sense. But what think you of cold?

Hyl. The same that I do of heat. An intense degree of cold is a pain; for to feel a very great cold, is to perceive a great uneasiness: it cannot therefore exist without the mind; but a lesser degree of cold may, as well as a lesser degree of heat.

Phil. Those bodies, therefore, upon whose application to our own, we perceive a moderate degree of heat, must be concluded to have a moderate degree of heat or warmth in them; and those, upon whose application we feel a like degree of cold, must be thought to have cold in them.

Hyl. They must.

Phil. Can any doctrine be true that necessarily leads a man into an absurdity?

Hyl. Without doubt it cannot.

Phil. Is it not an absurdity to think that the same thing should be at the same time both cold and warm?

Hyl. It is.

Phil. Suppose now one of your hands hot, and the other cold, and that they are both at once put into the same vessel of water, in an intermediate state; will not the water seem cold to one hand, and warm to the other?

Hyl. It will.

Phil. Ought we not therefore, by our principles, to conclude it is really both cold and warm at the same time, that is, according to your own concession, to believe an absurdity?

Hyl. I confess it seems so.

Phil. Consequently, the principles themselves are false, since you have granted that no true principle leads to an absurdity.

Hyl. But, after all, can anything be more absurd than to say, *there is no heat in the fire?*

Phil. To make the point still clearer; tell me whether, in two cases exactly alike, we ought not to make the same judgment?

Hyl. We ought.

Phil. When a pin pricks your finger, doth it not rend and divide the fibers of your flesh?

Hyl. It doth.

Phil. And when a coal burns your finger, doth it any more?

Hyl. It doth not.

Phil. Since, therefore, you neither judge the sensation itself occasioned by the pin, nor anything like it to be in the pin; you should not, conformably to what you have now granted, judge the sensation occasioned by the fire, or anything like it, to be in the fire.

Hyl. Well, since it must be so, I am content to yield this point, and acknowledge that heat and cold are only sensations existing in our minds. But there still remain qualities enough to secure the reality of external things.

Phil. But what will you say, *Hylas,* if it shall appear that the case is the same with regard to all other sensible qualities, and that they can no more be supposed to exist without the mind, than heat and cold?

Hyl. Then indeed you will have done something to the purpose; but that is what I despair of seeing proved.

Phil. Let us examine them in order. What think you of *tastes*—do they exist without the mind, or no?

Hyl. Can any man in his senses doubt whether sugar is sweet, or wormwood bitter?

Phil. Inform me, *Hylas.* Is a sweet taste a particular kind of pleasure or pleasant sensation, or is it not?

Hyl. It is.

Phil. And is not bitterness some kind of uneasiness or pain?

Hyl. I grant it.

Phil. If therefore sugar and wormwood are unthinking corporeal substances existing without the mind, how can sweetness and bitterness, that is, pleasure and pain, agree to them?

Hyl. Hold, *Philonous,* I now see what it was deluded me all this time. You asked whether heat and cold, sweetness and bitterness, were not particular sorts of pleasure and pain; to which I answered simply, that they were. Whereas I should have thus distinguished:—those qualities, as perceived by us, are pleasures or pains; but not as existing in the external objects. We must not therefore conclude absolutely, that there is no heat in the fire, or sweetness in the sugar, but only that heat or sweetness, as perceived by us, are not in the fire or sugar. What say you to this?

Phil. I say it is nothing to the purpose

Our discourse proceeded altogether concerning sensible things, which you defined to be, *the things we immediately perceive by our senses.* Whatever other qualities, therefore, you speak of, as distinct from these, I know nothing of them, neither do they at all belong to the point in dispute. You may, indeed, pretend to have discovered certain qualities which you do not perceive, and assert those insensible qualities exist in fire and sugar. But what use can be made of this to your present purpose, I am at a loss to conceive. Tell me then once more, do you acknowledge that heat and cold, sweetness and bitterness (meaning those qualities which are perceived by the senses), do not exist without the mind?

Hyl. I see it is to no purpose to hold out, so I give up the cause as to those mentioned qualities. Though I profess it sounds oddly, to say that sugar is not sweet.

Phil. But, for your further satisfaction, take this along with you: that which at other times seems sweet, shall, to a distempered palate, appear bitter. And, nothing can be plainer than that divers persons perceive different tastes in the same food; since that which one man delights in, another abhors. And how could this be, if the taste was something really inherent in the food?

Hyl. I acknowledge I know not how.

Phil. In the next place, *odors* are to be considered. And, with regard to these, I would fain know whether what has been said of tastes doth not exactly agree to them? Are they not so many pleasing or displeasing sensations?

Hyl. They are.

Phil. Can you then conceive it possible that they should exist in an unperceiving thing?

Hyl. I cannot.

Phil. Or, can you imagine that filth and

ordure affect those brute animals that feed on them out of choice, with the same smells which we perceive in them?

Hyl. By no means.

Phil. May we not therefore conclude of smells, as of the other forementioned qualities, that they cannot exist in any but a perceiving substance or mind.

Hyl. I think so.

Phil. Then as to *sounds,* what must we think of them: are they accidents really inherent in external bodies, or not?

Hyl. That they inhere not in the sonorous bodies is plain from hence; because a bell struck in the exhausted receiver of an air-pump sends forth no sound. The air, therefore, must be thought the subject of sound.

Phil. What reason is there for that, *Hylas?*

Hyl. Because, when any motion is raised in the air, we perceive a sound greater or lesser, according to the air's motion; but without some motion in the air, we never hear any sound at all.

Phil. And granting that we never hear a sound but when some motion is produced in the air, yet I do not see how you can infer from thence, that the sound itself is in the air.

Hyl. It is this very motion in the external air that produces in the mind the sensation of *sound.* For, striking on the drum of the ear, it causeth a vibration, which by the auditory nerves being communicated to the brain, the soul is thereupon affected with the sensation called *sound.*

Phil. What! is sound then a sensation?

Hyl. I tell you, as perceived by us, it is a particular sensation in the mind.

Phil. And can any sensation exist without the mind?

Hyl. No, certainly.

Phil. How then can sound, being a sensation, exist in the air, if by the *air* you mean a senseless substance existing without the mind?

Hyl. You must distinguish, *Philonous,* between sound as it is perceived by us, and as it is in itself; or (which is the same thing) between the sound we immediately perceive, and that which exists without us. The former, indeed, is a particular kind of sensation, but the latter is merely a vibrative or undulatory motion in the air.

Phil. I thought I had already obviated that distinction, by the answer I gave when you were applying it in a like case before. But, to say no more of that, are you sure then that sound is really nothing but motion?

Hyl. I am.

Phil. Whatever therefore agrees to real sound, may with truth be attributed to motion?

Hyl. It may.

Phil. It is then good sense to speak of *motion* as of a thing that is *loud, sweet, acute, or grave.*

Hyl. I see you are resolved not to understand me. Is it not evident those accidents or modes belong only to sensible sound, or *sound* in the common acceptation of the word, but not to *sound* in the real and philosophic sense; which, as I just now told you, is nothing but a certain motion of the air?

Phil. It seems then there are two sorts of sound—the one vulgar, or that which is heard, the other philosophical and real?

Hyl. Even so.

Phil. And the latter consists in motion?

Hyl. I told you so before.

Phil. Tell me, *Hylas,* to which of the senses, think you, the idea of motion belongs? to the hearing?

Hyl. No, certainly; but to the sight and touch.

Phil. It should follow then, that, according to you, real sounds may possibly be *seen* or *felt*, but never *heard*.

Hyl. Look you, *Philonous*, you may, if you please, make a jest of my opinion, but that will not alter the truth of things. I own, indeed, the inferences you draw me into, sound something oddly; but common language, you know, is framed by, and for the use of the vulgar: we must not therefore wonder, if expressions adapted to exact philosophic notions seem uncouth and out of the way.

Phil. Is it come to that? I assure you, I imagine myself to have gained no small point, since you make so light of departing from common phrases and opinions; it being a main part of our inquiry, to examine whose notions are widest of the common road, and most repugnant to the general sense of the world. But, can you think it no more than a philosophical paradox, to say that *real sounds are never heard,* and that the idea of them is obtained by some other sense? And is there nothing in this contrary to nature and the truth of things?

Hyl. To deal ingenuously, I do not like it. And, after the concessions already made, I had as well grant that sounds too have no real being without the mind.

Phil. And I hope you will make no difficulty to acknowledge the same of *colors.*

Hyl. Pardon me: the case of colors is very different. Can anything be plainer than that we see them on the objects?

Phil. The objects you speak of are, I suppose, corporeal Substances existing without the mind?

Hyl. They are.

Phil. And have true and real colors inhering in them?

Hyl. Each visible object hath that color which we see in it.

Phil. How! is there anything visible but what we perceive by sight?

Hyl. There is not.

Phil. And, do we perceive anything by sense which we do not perceive immediately?

Hyl. How often must I be obliged to repeat the same thing? I tell you, we do not.

Phil. Have patience, good *Hylas;* and tell me once more, whether there is anything immediately perceived by the senses, except sensible qualities. I know you asserted there was not; but I would now be informed, whether you still persist in the same opinion.

Hyl. I do.

Phil. Pray, is your corporeal substance either a sensible quality, or made up of sensible qualities?

Hyl. What a question that is! who ever thought it was?

Phil. My reason for asking was, because in saying, *each visible object hath that color which we see in it,* you make visible objects to be corporeal substances; which implies either that corporeal substances are sensible qualities, or else that there is something beside sensible qualities perceived by sight: but, as this point was formerly agreed between us, and is still maintained by you, it is a clear consequence, that your corporeal substance is nothing distinct from sensible qualities.

Hyl. You may draw as many absurd consequences as you please, and endeavor to perplex the plainest things; but you shall never persuade me out of my senses. I clearly understand my own meaning.

Phil. I wish you would make me understand it too. But, since you are unwilling to have your notion of corporeal substance examined, I shall urge that point no further. Only be pleased to let me know, whether the same colors which we see exist in external bodies, or some other.

Hyl. The very same.

Phil. What! are then the beautiful red and purple we see on yonder clouds really in them? Or do you imagine they have in themselves any other form than that of a dark mist or vapor?

Hyl. I must own, *Philonous,* those colors are not really in the clouds as they seem to be at this distance. They are only apparent colors.

Phil. Apparent call you them? how shall we distinguish these apparent colors from real?

Hyl. Very easily. Those are to be thought apparent which, appearing only at a distance, vanish upon a nearer approach.

Phil. And those, I suppose, are to be thought real which are discovered by the most near and exact survey.

Hyl. Right.

Phil. Is the nearest and exactest survey made by the help of a microscope, or by the naked eye?

Hyl. By a microscope, doubtless.

Phil. But a microscope often discovers colors in an object different from those perceived by the unassisted sight. And, in case we had microscopes magnifying to any assigned degree, it is certain that no object whatsoever, viewed through them, would appear in the same color which it exhibits to the naked eye.

Hyl. And what will you conclude from all this? You cannot argue that there are really and naturally no colors on objects: because by artificial managements they may be altered, or made to vanish.

Phil. I think it may evidently be concluded from your own concessions, that all the colors we see with our naked eyes are only apparent as those on the clouds, since they vanish upon a more close and accurate inspection which is afforded us by a microscope. Then, as to what you say by way of prevention: I ask you whether the real and natural state of an object is better discovered by a very sharp and piercing sight, or by one which is less sharp?

Hyl. By the former without doubt.

Phil. Is it not plain from *Dioptrics* that microscopes make the sight more penetrating, and represent objects as they would appear to the eye in case it were naturally endowed with a most exquisite sharpness?

Hyl. It is.

Phil. Consequently the microscopical representation is to be thought that which best sets forth the real nature of the thing, or what it is in itself. The colors, therefore, by it perceived are more genuine and real than those perceived otherwise.

Hyl. I confess there is something in what you say.

Phil. Besides, it is not only possible but manifest, that there actually are animals whose eyes are by nature framed to perceive those things which by reason of their minuteness escape our sight. What think you of those inconceivably small animals perceived by glasses? must we suppose they are all stark blind? Or, in case they see, can it be imagined their sight hath not the same use in preserving their bodies from injuries, which appears in that of all other animals? And if it hath, is it not evident they must see particles less than their own bodies, which will present them with a far different view in each object from that which strikes our senses? Even our own eyes do not always represent objects to us after the same manner. In the *jaundice* every one knows that all things seem yellow. Is it not therefore highly probable those animals in whose eyes we discern a very different texture from that of ours, and whose bodies abound with different humors, do not see the same colors in every object that we do? From all which, should it not seem to follow that all colors are equally apparent, and that none of those which we perceive are really inherent in any outward object?

Hyl. It should.

Phil. The point will be past all doubt, if you consider that, in case colors were real properties or affections inherent in external bodies, they could admit of no alteration without some change wrought in the very bodies themselves: but, is it not evident from what hath been said that, upon the use of microscopes, upon a change happening in the humors of the eye, or a variation of distance, without any manner of real alteration in the thing itself, the colors of any object are either changed, or totally disappear? Nay, all other circumstances remaining the same, change but the situation of some objects, and they shall present different colors to the eye. The same thing happens upon viewing an object in various degrees of light. And what is more known than that the same bodies appear differently colored by candlelight from what they do in the open day? Add to these the experiment of a prism which, separating the heterogeneous rays of light, alters the color of any object, and will cause the whitest to appear of a deep blue or red to the naked eye. And now tell me whether you are still of opinion that every body hath its true real color inhering in it; and, if you think it hath, I would fain know farther from you, what certain distance and position of the object, what peculiar texture and formation of the eye, what degree or kind of light is necessary for ascertaining that true color, and distinguishing it from apparent ones.

Hyl. I own myself entirely satisfied, that they are all equally apparent, and that there is no such thing as color really inhering in external bodies, but that it is altogether in the light. And what confirms me in this opinion is that in proportion to the light colors are still more or less vivid; and if there be no light, then are there no colors perceived. Besides, allowing there are colors on external objects, yet, how is it possible for us to perceive them? For no external body affects the mind, unless it acts first on our organs of sense. But the only action of bodies is motion; and motion cannot be communicated otherwise than by impulse. A distant object therefore cannot act on the eye, nor consequently make itself or its properties perceivable to the soul. Whence it plainly follows that it is immediately some contiguous substance, which, operating on the eye, occasions a perception of colors: and such is light.

Phil. How! is light then a substance?

Hyl. I tell you, *Philonous,* external light is nothing but a thin fluid substance, whose minute particles being agitated with a brisk motion, and in various manners reflected from the different surfaces of outward objects to the eyes, communicate different motions to the optic nerves; which, being propagated to the brain, cause therein various impressions; and these are attended with the sensations of red, blue, yellow, &c.

Phil. It seems then the light doth no more than shake the optic nerves.

Hyl. Nothing else.

Phil. And, consequent to each particular motion of the nerves, the mind is affected with a sensation, which is some particular color.

Hyl. Right.

Phil. And these sensations have no existence without the mind.

Hyl. They have not.

Phil. How then do you affirm that colors are in the light; since by *light* you understand a corporeal substance external to the mind?

Hyl. Light and colors, as immediately perceived by us, I grant cannot exist without the mind. But, in themselves they are only the motions and configurations of certain insensible particles of matter.

Phil. Colors, then, in the vulgar sense, or taken for the immediate objects of sight, cannot agree to any but a perceiving substance.

Hyl. That is what I say.

Phil. Well then, since you give up the point as to those sensible qualities which are alone thought colors by all mankind beside, you may hold what you please with regard to those invisible ones of the philosophers. It is not my business to dispute about them; only I would advise you to bethink yourself, whether, considering the inquiry we are upon, it be prudent for you to affirm—*the red and blue which we see are not real colors, but certain unknown motions and figures, which no man ever did or can see, are truly so.* Are not these shocking notions, and are not they subject to as many ridiculous inferences, as those you were obliged to renounce before in the case of sounds?

Hyl. I frankly own, *Philonous,* that it is in vain to stand out any longer. Colors, sounds, tastes, in a word all those termed *secondary qualities,* have certainly no existence without the mind. But, by this acknowledgment I must not be supposed to derogate anything from the reality of Matter or external objects; seeing it is no more than several philosophers maintain, who nevertheless are the farthest imaginable from denying Matter. For the clearer understanding of this, you must know sensible qualities are by philosophers divided into *primary* and *secondary.* The former are Extension, Figure, Solidity, Gravity, Motion, and Rest. And these they hold exist really in bodies. The latter are those above enumerated; or, briefly, all sensible qualities beside the Primary, which they assert are only so many sensations or ideas existing nowhere but in the mind. But all this, I doubt not, you are apprised of. For my part, I have been a long time sensible there was such an opinion current among philosophers, but was never thoroughly convinced of its truth until now.

Phil. You are still then of opinion that *extension* and *figures* are inherent in external unthinking substances?

Hyl. I am.

Phil. But what if the same arguments which are brought against Secondary Qualities will hold good against these also?

Hyl. Why then I shall be obliged to think, they too exist only in the mind.

Phil. Is it your opinion the very figure and extension which you perceive by sense exist in the outward object or material substance?

Hyl. It is.

Phil. Have all other animals as good grounds to think the same of the figure and extension which they see and feel?

Hyl. Without doubt, if they have any thought at all.

Phil. Answer me, *Hylas.* Think you the senses were bestowed upon all animals for their preservation and well-being in life? or were they given to men alone for this end?

Hyl. I make no question but they have the same use in all other animals.

Phil. If so, is it not necessary they should be enabled by them to perceive their own limbs, and those bodies which are capable of harming them?

Hyl. Certainly.

Phil. A mite therefore must be supposed to see his own foot, and things equal or even less than it, as bodies of some considerable dimension; though at the same time they appear to you scarce discernible, or at best as so many visible points?

Hyl. I cannot deny it.

Phil. And to creatures less than the mite they will seem yet larger?

Hyl. They will.

Phil. Insomuch that what you can hardly discern will to another extremely minute animal appear as some huge mountain?

Hyl. All this I grant.

Phil. Can one and the same thing be at the same time in itself of different dimensions?

Hyl. That were absurd to imagine.

Phil. But, from what you have laid down it follows that both the extension by you perceived, and that perceived by the mite itself, as likewise all those perceived by lesser animals, are each of them the true extension of the mite's foot; that is to say, by your own principles you are led into an absurdity.

Hyl. There seems to be some difficulty in the point.

Phil. Again, have you not acknowledged that no real inherent property of any object can be changed without some change in the thing itself?

Hyl. I have.

Phil. But, as we approach to or recede from an object, the visible extension varies, being at one distance ten or a hundred times greater than at another. Doth it not therefore follow from hence likewise that it is not really inherent in the object?

Hyl. I own I am at a loss what to think.

Phil. Your judgment will soon be determined, if you will venture to think as freely concerning this quality as you have done concerning the rest. Was it not admitted as a good argument, that neither heat nor cold was in the water, because it seemed warm to one hand and cold to the other?

Hyl. It was.

Phil. Is it not the very same reasoning to conclude there is no extension or figure in an object, because to one eye it shall seem little, smooth, and round, when at the same time it appears to the other, great, uneven, and angular?

Hyl. The very same. But does this latter fact ever happen?

Phil. You may at any time make the experiment, by looking with one eye bare, and with the other through a microscope.

Hyl. I know not how to maintain it, and yet I am loath to give up *extension*, I see so many odd consequences following upon such a concession.

Phil. Odd, say you? After the concessions already made, I hope you will stick at nothing for its oddness.[1] But, on the other hand, should it not seem very odd, if the general reasoning which includes all other sensible qualities did not also include extension? If it be allowed that no idea nor anything like an idea can exist in an unperceiving substance, then surely it follows that no figure or mode of extension, which we can either perceive or imagine, or have any idea of, can be really inherent in Matter; not to mention the peculiar difficulty there must be in conceiving a material substance, prior to and distinct from extension, to be the *substratum* of extension. Be the sensible quality what it will—figure, or sound, or color; it seems alike impossible it should subsist in that which doth not perceive it.

Hyl. I give up the point for the present, reserving still a right to retract my opinion, in case I shall hereafter discover any false step in my progress to it.

Phil. That is a right you cannot be denied. Figures and extensions being dispatched, we proceed next to *motion*. Can a real motion in any external body be at the same time both very swift and very slow?

Hyl. It cannot.

Phil. Is not the motion of a body swift in a reciprocal proportion to the time it takes up in describing any given space? Thus a body that describes a mile in an hour moves

---

[1] The remainder of the present paragraph was not contained in the first and second editions.

three times faster than it would in case it described only a mile in three hours.

Hyl. I agree with you.

Phil. And is not time measured by the succession of ideas in our minds?

Hyl. It is.

Phil. And is it not possible ideas should succeed one another twice as fast in your mind as they do in mine, or in that of some spirit of another kind?

Hyl. I own it.

Phil. Consequently, the same body may to another seem to perform its motion over any space in half the time that it doth to you. And the same reasoning will hold as to any other proportion: that is to say, according to your principles (since the motions perceived are both really in the object) it is possible one and the same body shall be really moved the same way at once, both very swift and very slow. How is this consistent either with common sense, or with what you just now granted?

Hyl. I have nothing to say to it.

Phil. Then as for *solidity;* either you do not mean any sensible quality by that word, and so it is beside our inquiry: or if you do, it must be either hardness or resistance. But both the one and the other are plainly relative to our senses: it being evident that what seems hard to one animal may appear soft to another, who hath greater force and firmness of limbs. Nor is it less plain that the resistance I feel is not in the body.

Hyl. I own the very sensation of resistance, which is all you immediately perceive, is not in the *body,* but the cause of that sensation is.

Phil. But the causes of our sensations are not things immediately perceived, and therefore not sensible. This point I thought had been already determined.

Hyl. I own it was; but you will pardon me if I seem a little embarrassed: I know not how to quit my old notions.

Phil. To help you out, do but consider that if *extension* be once acknowledged to have no existence without the mind, the same must necessarily be granted of motion, solidity, and gravity—since they all evidently suppose extension. It is therefore superfluous to inquire particularly concerning each of them. In denying extension, you have denied them all to have any real existence.

Hyl. I wonder, *Philonous,* if what you say be true, why those philosophers who deny the Secondary Qualities any real existence, should yet attribute it to the Primary. If there is no difference between them, how can this be accounted for?

Phil. It is not my business to account for every opinion of the philosophers. But, among other reasons which may be assigned for this, it seems probable that pleasure and pain being rather annexed to the former than the latter may be one. Heat and cold, tastes and smells, have something more vividly pleasing or disagreeable than the ideas of extension, figure, and motion affect us with. And, it being too visibly absurd to hold that pain or pleasure can be in an unperceiving Substance, men are more easily weaned from believing the external existence of the Secondary than the Primary Qualities. You will be satisfied there is something in this, if you recollect the difference you made between an intense and more moderate degree of heat; allowing the one a real existence, while you denied it to the other. But, after all, there is no rational ground for that distinction; for, surely an indifferent sensation is as truly *a sensation* as one more pleasing or painful; and consequently should not any more than they be supposed to exist in an unthinking subject.

Hyl. It is just come into my head, *Philonous,* that I have somewhere heard of a distinction between absolute and sensible extension. Now, though it be acknowledged that *great* and *small,* consisting merely in the relation which other extended beings have to the parts of our own bodies, do not really inhere in the Substances themselves; yet nothing obliges us to hold the same with regard to *absolute extension,* which is something abstracted from *great* and *small,* from this or that particular magnitude or figure. So likewise as to motion; *swift* and *slow* are altogether relative to the succession of ideas in our own minds. But, it doth not follow, because those modifications of motion exist not without the mind, that therefore absolute motion abstracted from them doth not.

Phil. Pray what is it that distinguishes one motion, or one part of extension, from another? Is it not something sensible, as some degree of swiftness or slowness, some certain magnitude or figure peculiar to each?

Hyl. I think so.

Phil. These qualities, therefore, stripped of all sensible properties, are without all specific and numerical differences, as the schools call them.

Hyl. They are.

Phil. That is to say, they are extension in general, and motion in general.

Hyl. Let it be so.

Phil. But it is a universally received maxim that *Everything which exists is particular.* How then can motion in general, or extension in general, exist in any corporeal Substance?

Hyl. I will take time to solve your difficulty.

Phil. But I think the point may be speedily decided. Without doubt you can tell whether you are able to frame this or that idea. Now I am content to put our dispute on this issue. If you can frame in your thoughts a distinct abstract idea of motion or extension; divested of all those

sensible modes, as swift and slow, great and small, round and square, and the like, which are acknowledged to exist only in the mind, I will then yield the point you contend for. But, if you cannot, it will be unreasonable on your side to insist any longer upon what you have no notion of.

Hyl. To confess ingenuously, I cannot.

Phil. Can you even separate the ideas of extension and motion from the ideas of all those qualities which they who make the distinction term *secondary?*

Hyl. What! is it not an easy matter to consider extension and motion by themselves, abstracted from all other sensible qualities? Pray how do the mathematicians treat of them?

Phil. I acknowledge, *Hylas,* it is not difficult to form general propositions and reasonings about those qualities, without mentioning any other; and, in this sense, to consider or treat of them abstractedly. But, how doth it follow that, because I can pronounce the word *motion* by itself, I can form the idea of it in my mind exclusive of body? Or, because theorems may be made of extension and figures, without any mention of *great* or *small,* or any other sensible mode or quality, that therefore it is possible such an abstract idea of extension, without any particular size or figure, or sensible quality, should be distinctly formed, and apprehended by the mind? Mathematicians treat of quantity, without regarding what other sensible qualities it is attended with, as being altogether indifferent to their demonstrations. But, when laying aside the words, they contemplate the bare ideas, I believe you will find, they are not the pure abstracted ideas of extension.

Hyl. But what say you to *pure intellect?* May not abstracted ideas be framed by that faculty?

Phil. Since I cannot frame abstract ideas at all, it is plain I cannot frame them by the help of *pure intellect;* whatsoever faculty you understand by those words. Besides, not to inquire into the nature of pure intellect and its spiritual objects, as *virtue, reason, God,* or the like, thus much seems manifest, that sensible things are only to be perceived by sense, or represented by the imagination. Figures, therefore, and extension, being originally perceived by sense, do not belong to pure intellect: but, for your further satisfaction, try if you can frame the idea of any figure, abstracted from all particularities of size, or even from other sensible qualities.

Hyl. Let me think a little. . . . I do not find that I can.

Phil. And can you think it possible that should really exist in nature which implies a repugnancy in its conception?

Hyl. By no means.

Phil. Since therefore it is impossible even for the mind to disunite the ideas of extension and motion from all other sensible qualities, doth it not follow, that where the one exist there necessarily the other exist likewise?

Hyl. It should seem so.

Phil. Consequently, the very same arguments which you admitted as conclusive against the Secondary Qualities are, without any further application of force, against the Primary too. Besides, if you will trust your senses, is it not plain all sensible qualities coexist, or to them appear as being in the same place? Do they ever represent a motion, or figure, as being divested of all other visible and tangible qualities?

Hyl. You need say no more on this head. I am free to own, if there be no secret error or oversight in our proceedings hitherto, that all sensible qualities are alike to be denied existence without the mind. But, my fear is that I have been too liberal in my former concessions, or overlooked some fallacy or other. In short, I did not take time to think.

Phil. For that matter, *Hylas,* you may take what time you please in reviewing the progress of our inquiry. You are at liberty to recover any slips you might have made, or offer whatever you have omitted which makes for your first opinion.

Hyl. One great oversight I take to be this—that I did not sufficiently distinguish the *object* from the *sensation.* Now, though this latter may not exist without the mind, yet it will not thence follow that the former cannot.

Phil. What object do you mean? The object of the senses?

Hyl. The same.

Phil. It is then immediately perceived?

Hyl. Right.

Phil. Make me to understand the difference between what is immediately perceived, and a sensation.

Hyl. The sensation I take to be an act of the mind perceiving; besides which, there is something perceived; and this I call the *object.* For example, there is red and yellow on that tulip. But then the act of perceiving those colors is in me only, and not in the tulip.

Phil. What tulip do you speak of? Is it that which you see?

Hyl. The same.

Phil. And what do you see beside color, figure, and extension?

Hyl. Nothing.

Phil. What you would say then is that the red and yellow are coexistent with the extension; is it not?

Hyl. That is not all; I would say they have a real existence without the mind, in some unthinking substance.

Phil. That the colors are really in the tulip which I see is manifest. Neither can it be denied that this tulip may exist independent of your mind or mine; but, that any immediate object of the senses—that is, any idea, or combination of ideas—should exist in an unthinking substance, or exterior to all minds, is in itself an evident contradiction. Nor can I imagine how this follows from what you said just now, to wit, that the red and yellow were on the tulip *you saw,* since you do not pretend to *see* that unthinking substance.

Hyl. You have an artful way, *Philonous,* of diverting our inquiry from the subject.

Phil. I see you have no mind to be pressed that way. To return then to your distinction between *sensation* and *object;* if I take you right, you distinguish in every perception two things, the one an action of the mind, the other not.

Hyl. True.

Phil. And this action cannot exist in, or belong to, any unthinking thing; but, whatever beside is implied in a perception may?

Hyl. That is my meaning.

Phil. So that if there was a perception without any act of the mind, it were possible such a perception should exist in an unthinking substance?

Hyl. I grant it. But it is impossible there should be such a perception.

Phil. When is the mind said to be active?

Hyl. When it produces, puts an end to, or changes, anything.

Phil. Can the mind produce, discontinue, or change anything, but by an act of the will?

Hyl. It cannot.

Phil. The mind therefore is to be accounted *active* in its perceptions so far forth as *volition* is included in them?

Hyl. It is.

Phil. In plucking this flower I am active; because I do it by the motion of my hand, which was consequent upon my volition; so likewise in applying it to my nose. But is either of these smelling?

Hyl. No.

Phil. I act too in drawing the air through my nose; because my breathing so rather than otherwise is the effect of my volition. But neither can this be called *smelling:* for, if it were, I should smell every time I breathed in that manner?

Hyl. True.

Phil. Smelling then is somewhat consequent to all this?

Hyl. It is.

Phil. But I do not find my will concerned any further. Whatever more there is—as that I perceive such a particular smell, or any smell at all—this is independent of my will, and therein I am altogether passive. Do you find it otherwise with you, *Hylas?*

Hyl. No, the very same.

Phil. Then, as to seeing, is it not in your power to open your eyes, or keep them shut; to turn them this or that way?

Hyl. Without doubt.

Phil. But, doth it in like manner depend on your will that in looking on this flower you perceive *white* rather than any other color? Or, directing your open eyes towards yonder part of the heaven, can you avoid seeing the sun? Or is light or darkness the effect of your volition?

Hyl. No certainly.

Phil. You are then in these respects altogether passive?

Hyl. I am.

Phil. Tell me now, whether *seeing* consists in perceiving light and colors, or in opening and turning the eyes?

Hyl. Without doubt, in the former.

Phil. Since therefore you are in the very perception of light and colors altogether passive, what is become of that action you were speaking of as an ingredient in every sensation? And, doth it not follow from your own concessions, that the perception of light and colors, including no action in it, may exist in an unperceiving substance? And is not this a plain contradiction?

Hyl. I know not what to think of it.

Phil. Besides, since you distinguish the *active* and *passive* in every perception, you must do it in that of pain. But how is it possible that pain, be it as little active as you please, should exist in an unperceiving substance? In short, do but consider the point, and then confess ingenuously, whether light and colors, tastes, sounds, &c., are not all equally passions or sensations in the soul. You may indeed call them *external objects,* and give them in words what subsistence you please. But, examine your own thoughts, and then tell me whether it be not as I say?

Hyl. I acknowledge, *Philonous,* that, upon a fair observation of what passes in my mind, I can discover nothing else but that I am a thinking being, affected with variety of sensations; neither is it possible to conceive how a sensation should exist in an unperceiving substance. But then, on the other hand, when I look on sensible things in a different view, considering them as so many modes and qualities, I find it necessary to suppose a material *substratum,* without which they cannot be conceived to exist.

Phil. Material substratum call you it? Pray, by which of your senses came you acquainted with that being?

Hyl. It is not itself sensible; its modes and qualities only being perceived by the senses.

Phil. I presume then it was by reflection and reason you obtained the idea of it?

Hyl. I do not pretend to any proper positive idea of it. However, I conclude it exists, because qualities cannot be conceived to exist without a support.

Phil. It seems then you have only a relative notion of it, or that you conceive it not otherwise than by conceiving the relation it bears to sensible qualities?

Hyl. Right.

Phil. Be pleased therefore to let me know wherein that relation consists.

Hyl. Is it not sufficiently expressed in the term *substratum* or *substance?*

Phil. If so, the word *substratum* should import that it is spread under the sensible qualities or accidents?

Hyl. True.

Phil. And consequently under extension?

Hyl. I own it.

Phil. It is therefore somewhat in its own nature entirely distinct from extension?

Hyl. I tell you, extension is only a mode, and Matter is something that supports modes. And is it not evident the thing supported is different from the thing supporting?

Phil. So that something distinct from, and exclusive of, extension is supposed to be the *substratum* of extension?

Hyl. Just so.

Phil. Answer me, *Hylas.* Can a thing be spread without extension? or is not the idea of extension necessarily included in *spreading?*

Hyl. It is.

Phil. Whatsoever therefore you suppose spread under anything must have in itself an extension distinct from the extension of that thing under which it is spread?

Hyl. It must.

Phil. Consequently, every corporeal substance being the *substratum* of extension must have in itself another extension, by which it is qualified to be a *substratum* and so on to infinity? And I ask whether this be not absurd in itself, and repugnant to what you granted just now, to wit, that the *substratum* was something distinct from and exclusive of extension?

Hyl. Aye, but, *Philonous,* you take me wrong. I do not mean that Matter is *spread* in a gross literal sense under extension. The word *substratum* is used only to express in general the same thing with *substance.*

Phil. Well then, let us examine the relation implied in the term *substance.* Is it not that it stands under accidents?

Hyl. The very same.

Phil. But, that one thing may stand under or support another, must it not be extended?

Hyl. It must.

Phil. Is not therefore this supposition liable to the same absurdity with the former?

Hyl. You still take things in a strict literal sense; that is not fair, *Philonous.*

Phil. I am not for imposing any sense on your words: you are at liberty to explain them as you please. Only, I beseech you, make me understand something by them. You tell me Matter supports or stands under accidents. How! is it as your legs support your body?

Hyl. No; that is the literal sense.

Phil. Pray let me know any sense, literal or not literal, that you understand it in. . . . How long must I wait for an answer, *Hylas?*

Hyl. I declare I know not what to say. I once thought I understood well enough what was meant by Matter's supporting accidents. But now, the more I think on it the less can I comprehend it; in short I find that I know nothing of it.

Phil. It seems then you have no idea at all, neither relative nor positive, of Matter; you know neither what it is in itself, nor what relation it bears to accidents?

Hyl. I acknowledge it.

Phil. And yet you asserted that you could not conceive how qualities or accidents should really exist, without conceiving at the same time a material support of them?

Hyl. I did.

Phil. That is to say, when you conceive the real existence of qualities, you do withal conceive something which you cannot conceive?

Hyl. It was wrong I own. But still I fear there is some fallacy or other. Pray what think you of this? It is just come into my head that the ground of all our mistake lies in your treating of each quality by itself. Now, I grant that each quality cannot singly subsist without the mind. Color cannot without extension, neither can figure without some other sensible quality. But, as the several qualities united or blended together form entire sensible things, nothing hinders why such things may not be supposed to exist without the mind.

Phil. Either, *Hylas,* you are jesting, or have a very bad memory. Though indeed we went through all the qualities by name one after another, yet my arguments, or rather your concessions, nowhere tended to prove that the Secondary Qualities did not subsist each alone by itself; but, that they were not *at all* without the mind. Indeed, in treating of figure and motion we concluded they could not exist without the mind, because it was impossible even in thought to separate them from all secondary qualities, so as to conceive them existing by themselves. But then this was not the only argument made use of upon that occasion. But (to pass by all that hath been hitherto said, and reckon it for nothing, if you will have it so) I am content to put the whole upon this issue. If you can conceive it possible for any mixture or combination of qualities, or any sensible object whatever, to exist without the mind, then I will grant it actually to be so.

Hyl. If it comes to that the point will soon be decided. What more easy than to conceive a tree or house existing by itself, independent of, and unperceived by, any mind whatsoever? I do at this present time conceive them existing after that manner.

Phil. How say you, *Hylas,* can you see a thing which is at the same time unseen?

Hyl. No, that were a contradiction.

Phil. Is it not as great a contradiction to

talk of *conceiving* a thing which is *unconceived?*

Hyl. It is.

Phil. The tree or house therefore which you think of is conceived by you?

Hyl. How should it be otherwise?

Phil. And what is conceived is surely in the mind?

Hyl. Without question, that which is conceived is in the mind.

Phil. How then came you to say, you conceived a house or tree existing independent and out of all minds whatsoever?

Hyl. That was I own an oversight; but stay, let me consider what led me into it.— It is a pleasant mistake enough. As I was thinking of a tree in a solitary place where no one was present to see it, methought that was to conceive a tree as existing unperceived or unthought of—not considering that I myself conceived it all the while. But now I plainly see that all I can do is to frame ideas in my own mind. I may indeed conceive in my own thoughts the idea of a tree, or a house, or a mountain, but that is all. And this is far from proving that I can conceive them *existing out of the minds of all Spirits.*

Phil. You acknowledge then that you cannot possibly conceive how any one corporeal sensible thing should exist otherwise than in a mind?

Hyl. I do.

Phil. And yet you will earnestly contend for the truth of that which you cannot so much as conceive?

Hyl. I profess I know not what to think; but still there are some scruples remain with me. Is it not certain I *see* things at a distance? Do we not perceive the stars and moon, for example, to be a great way off? Is not this, I say, manifest to the senses?

Phil. Do you not in a dream too perceive those or the like objects?

Hyl. I do.

Phil. And have they not then the same appearance of being distant?

Hyl. They have.

Phil. But you do not thence conclude the apparitions in a dream to be without the mind?

Hyl. By no means.

Phil. You ought not therefore to conclude that sensible objects are without the mind, from their appearance or manner wherein they are perceived.

Hyl. I acknowledge it. But doth not my sense deceive me in those cases?

Phil. By no means. The idea or thing which you immediately perceive, neither sense nor reason informs you that it actually exists without the mind. By sense you only know that you are affected with such certain sensations of light and colors, &c. And these you will not say are without the mind.

Hyl. True: but, beside all that, do you not think the sight suggests something of *outness* or *distance?*

Phil. Upon approaching a distant object, do the visible size and figure change perpetually, or do they appear the same at all distances?

Hyl. They are in a continual change.

Phil. Sight therefore doth not suggest or any way inform you that the visible object you immediately perceive exists at a distance,[2] or will be perceived when you advance farther onward; there being a continued series of visible objects succeeding each other during the whole time of your approach.

Hyl. It doth not; but still I know, upon seeing an object, what object I shall perceive after having passed over a certain distance: no matter whether it be exactly the same or no: there is still something of distance suggested in the case.

[2] See the "Essay towards a New Theory of Vision," and its "Vindication."—AUTHOR, 1734.

Phil. Good *Hylas,* do but reflect a little on the point, and then tell me whether there be any more in it than this:—From the ideas you actually perceive by sight, you have by experience learned to collect what other ideas you will (according to the standing order of nature) be affected with, after such a certain succession of time and motion.

Hyl. Upon the whole, I take it to be nothing else.

Phil. Now, is it not plain that if we suppose a man born blind was on a sudden made to see, he could at first have no experience of what may be suggested by sight?

Hyl. It is.

Phil. He would not then, according to you, have any notion of distance annexed to the things he saw; but would take them for a new set of sensations existing only in his mind?

Hyl. It is undeniable.

Phil. But, to make it still more plain: is not *distance* a line turned endwise to the eye?

Hyl. It is.

Phil. And can a line so situated be perceived by sight?

Hyl. It cannot.

Phil. Doth it not therefore follow that distance is not properly and immediately perceived by sight?

Hyl. It should seem so.

Phil. Again, is it your opinion that colors are at a distance?

Hyl. It must be acknowledged they are only in the mind.

Phil. But do not colors appear to the eye as coexisting in the same place with extension and figures?

Hyl. They do.

Phil. How can you then conclude from sight that figures exist without, when you acknowledge colors do not; the sensible appearance being the very same with regard to both?

Hyl. I know not what to answer.

Phil. But, allowing that distance was truly and immediately perceived by the mind, yet it would not thence follow it existed out of the mind. For, whatever is immediately perceived is an idea: and can any *idea* exist out of the mind?

Hyl. To suppose that were absurd: but, inform me, *Philonous,* can we perceive or know nothing beside our ideas?

Phil. As for the rational deducing of causes from effects, that is beside our inquiry. And, by the senses you can best tell whether you perceive anything which is not immediately perceived. And I ask you, whether the things immediately perceived are other than your own sensations or ideas? You have indeed more than once, in the course of this conversation, declared yourself on those points; but you seem, by this last question, to have departed from what you then thought.

Hyl. To speak the truth, *Philonous,* I think there are two kinds of objects:—the one perceived immediately, which are likewise called *ideas;* the other are real things or external objects, perceived by the mediation of ideas, which are their images and representations. Now, I own ideas do not exist without the mind; but the latter sort of objects do. I am sorry I did not think of this distinction sooner; it would probably have cut short your discourse.

Phil. Are those external objects perceived by sense, or by some other faculty?

Hyl. They are perceived by sense.

Phil. How! is there anything perceived by sense which is not immediately perceived?

Hyl. Yes, *Philonous,* in some sort there is. For example, when I look on a picture or statue of Julius Cæsar, I may be said after a manner to perceive him (though not immediately) by my senses.

Phil. It seems then you will have our ideas, which alone are immediately perceived, to be pictures of external things: and that these also are perceived by sense, inasmuch as they have a conformity or resemblance to our ideas?

Hyl. That is my meaning.

Phil. And, in the same way that Julius Cæsar, in himself invisible, is nevertheless perceived by sight; real things, in themselves imperceptible, are perceived by sense.

Hyl. In the very same.

Phil. Tell me, *Hylas,* when you behold the picture of Julius Cæsar, do you see with your eyes any more than some colors and figures, with a certain symmetry and composition of the whole?

Hyl. Nothing else.

Phil. And would not a man who had never known anything of Julius Cæsar see as much?

Hyl. He would.

Phil. Consequently he hath his sight, and the use of it, in as perfect a degree as you?

Hyl. I agree with you.

Phil. Whence comes it then that your thoughts are directed to the Roman emperor, and his are not? This cannot proceed from the sensations or ideas of sense by you then perceived; since you acknowledge you have no advantage over him in that respect. It should seem therefore to proceed from reason and memory: should it not?

Hyl. It should.

Phil. Consequently, it will not follow from that instance that anything is perceived by sense which is not immediately perceived. Though I grant we may, in one acceptation, be said to perceive sensible things mediately by sense—that is, when,

from a frequently perceived connection, the immediate perception of ideas by one sense suggest to the mind others, perhaps belonging to another sense, which are wont to be connected with them. For instance, when I hear a coach drive along the streets, immediately I perceive only the sound; but, from the experience I have had that such a sound is connected with a coach, I am said to hear the coach. It is nevertheless evident that, in truth and strictness, nothing can be *heard* but *sound;* and the coach is not then properly perceived by sense, but suggested from experience. So likewise when we are said to see a red-hot bar of iron; the solidity and heat of the iron are not the objects of sight, but suggested to the imagination by the color and figure which are properly perceived by that sense. In short, those things alone are actually and strictly perceived by any sense, which would have been perceived in case that same sense had then been first conferred on us. As for other things, it is plain they are only suggested to the mind by experience, grounded on former perceptions. But, to return to your comparison of Cæsar's picture, it is plain, if you keep to that, you must hold the real things or archetypes of our ideas are not perceived by sense, but by some internal faculty of the soul, as reason or memory. I would therefore fain know what arguments you can draw from reason for the existence of what you call *real things* or *material objects.* Or, whether you remember to have seen them formerly as they are in themselves; or, if you have heard or read of any one that did.

Hyl. I see, *Philonous,* you are disposed to raillery; but that will never convince me.

Phil. My aim is only to learn from you the way to come at the knowledge of *material beings.* Whatever we perceive is perceived immediately or mediately: by sense;

or by reason and reflection. But, as you have excluded sense, pray show me what reason you have to believe their existence; or what *medium* you can possibly make use of to prove it, either to mine or your own understanding.

Hyl. To deal ingenuously, *Philonous,* now I consider the point, I do not find I can give you any good reason for it. But, thus much seems pretty plain, that it is at least possible such things may really exist. And, as long as there is no absurdity in supposing them, I am resolved to believe as I did, till you bring good reasons to the contrary.

Phil. What! is it come to this, that you only believe the existence of material objects, and that your belief is founded barely on the possibility of its being true? Then you will have me bring reasons against it: though another would think it reasonable the proof should lie on him who holds the affirmative. And, after all, this very point which you are now resolved to maintain, without any reason, is in effect what you have more than once during this discourse seen good reason to give up. But, to pass over all this; if I understand you rightly, you say our ideas do not exist without the mind; but that they are copies, images, or representations, of certain originals that do?

Hyl. You take me right.

Phil. They are then like external things?

Hyl. They are.

Phil. Have those things a stable and permanent nature, independent of our senses; or are they in a perpetual change, upon our producing any motions in our bodies, suspending, exerting, or altering, our faculties or organs of sense?

Hyl. Real things, it is plain, have a fixed and real nature, which remains the same notwithstanding any change in our senses, or in the posture and motion of our bodies; which indeed may affect the ideas in our minds, but it were absurd to think they had the same effect on things existing without the mind.

Phil. How then is it possible that things perpetually fleeting and variable as our ideas should be copies or images of anything fixed and constant? Or, in other words, since all sensible qualities, as size, figure, color, &c., that is, our ideas, are continually changing upon every alteration in the distance, medium, or instruments of sensation; how can any determinate material objects be properly represented or painted forth by several distinct things, each of which is so different from and unlike the rest? Or, if you say it resembles some one only of our ideas, how shall we be able to distinguish the true copy from all the false ones?

Hyl. I profess, *Philonous,* I am at a loss. I know not what to say to this.

Phil. But neither is this all. Which are material objects in themselves—perceptible or imperceptible?

Hyl. Properly and immediately nothing can be perceived but ideas. All material things, therefore, are in themselves insensible, and to be perceived only by our ideas.

Phil. Ideas then are sensible, and their archetypes or originals insensible?

Hyl. Right.

Phil. But how can that which is sensible be like that which is insensible? Can a real thing, in itself *invisible,* be like a *color;* or a real thing, which is not *audible,* be like a *sound?* In a word, can anything be like a sensation or idea, but another sensation or idea?

Hyl. I must own, I think not.

Phil. Is it possible there should be any doubt on the point? Do you not perfectly know your own ideas?

Hyl. I know them perfectly; since what I do not perceive or know can be no part of my idea.

Phil. Consider, therefore, and examine

them, and then tell me if there be anything in them which can exist without the mind? or if you can conceive anything like them existing without the mind?

Hyl. Upon inquiry, I find it is impossible for me to conceive or understand how anything but an idea can be like an idea. And it is most evident that *no idea can exist without the mind.*

Phil. You are therefore, by our principles, forced to deny the reality of sensible things; since you made it to consist in an absolute existence exterior to the mind. That is to say, you are a downright sceptic. So I have gained my point, which was to show your principles led to Scepticism.

Hyl. For the present I am, if not entirely convinced, at least silenced.

Phil. I would fain know what more you would require in order to a perfect conviction. Have you not had the liberty of explaining yourself all manner of ways? Were any little slips in discourse laid hold and insisted on? Or were you not allowed to retract or reinforce anything you had offered, as best served your purpose? Hath not everything you could say been heard and examined with all the fairness imaginable? In a word, have you not in every point been convinced out of your own mouth? and, if you can at present discover any flaw in any of your former concessions, or think of any remaining subterfuge, any new distinction, color, or comment whatsoever, why do you not produce it?

Hyl. A little patience, *Philonous.* I am at present so amazed to see myself ensnared, and as it were imprisoned in the labyrinths you have drawn me into, that on the sudden it cannot be expected I should find my way out. You must give me time to look about me and recollect myself?

Phil. Hark; is not this the college bell?

Hyl. It rings for prayers.

Phil. We will go in then, if you please, and meet here again tomorrow morning. In the meantime, you may employ your thoughts on this morning's discourse, and try if you can find any fallacy in it, or invent any new means to extricate yourself.

Hyl. Agreed.

THE SECOND DIALOGUE

Hylas. I beg your pardon, *Philonous,* for not meeting you sooner. All this morning my head was so filled with our late conversation that I had not leisure to think of the time of the day, or indeed of anything else.

Philonous. I am glad you were so intent upon it, in hopes if there were any mistakes in your concessions, or fallacies in my reasonings from them, you will now discover them to me.

Hyl. I assure you I have done nothing ever since I saw you but search after mistakes and fallacies, and, with that view, have minutely examined the whole series of yesterday's discourse: but all in vain, for the notions it led me into, upon review, appear still more clear and evident; and, the more I consider them, the more irresistibly do they force my assent.

Phil. And is not this, think you, a sign that they are genuine, that they proceed from nature, and are conformable to right reason? Truth and beauty are in this alike, that the strictest survey sets them both off to advantage; while the false luster of error and disguise cannot endure being reviewed, or too nearly inspected.

Hyl. I own there is a great deal in what you say. Nor can any one be more entirely satisfied of the truth of those odd consequences, so long as I have in view the reasonings that lead to them. But, when these are out of my thoughts, there seems, on the other hand, something so satisfactory, so natural and intelligible, in the modern way of explaining things that, I profess, I know not how to reject it.

Phil. I know not what way you mean.

Hyl. I mean the way of accounting for our sensations or ideas.

Phil. How is that?

Hyl. It is supposed the soul makes her residence in some part of the brain, from which the nerves take their rise, and are thence extended to all parts of the body; and that outward objects, by the different impressions they make on the organs of sense, communicate certain vibrative motions to the nerves; and these being filled with spirits propagate them to the brain or seat of the soul, which, according to the various impressions or traces thereby made in the brain, is variously affected with ideas.

Phil. And call you this an explication of the manner whereby we are affected with ideas?

Hyl. Why not, *Philonous;* have you anything to object against it?

Phil. I would first know whether I rightly understand your hypothesis. You make certain traces in the brain to be the causes or occasions of our ideas. Pray tell me whether by the *brain* you mean any sensible thing.

Hyl. What else think you I could mean?

Phil. Sensible things are all immediately perceivable; and those things which are immediately perceivable are ideas; and these exist only in the mind. Thus much you have, if I mistake not, long since agreed to.

Hyl. I do not deny it.

Phil. The brain therefore you speak of, being a sensible thing, exists only in the mind. Now, I would fain know whether you think it reasonable to suppose that one idea or thing existing in the mind occasions all other ideas. And, if you think so, pray how do you account for the origin of that primary idea or brain itself?

Hyl. I do not explain the origin of our ideas by that brain which is perceivable to sense, this being itself only a combination of sensible ideas, but by another which I imagine.

Phil. But are not things imagined as truly *in the mind* as things perceived?

Hyl. I must confess they are.

Phil. It comes, therefore, to the same thing; and you have been all this while accounting for ideas by certain motions or impressions of the brain, that is, by some alterations in an idea, whether sensible or imaginable it matters not.

Hyl. I begin to suspect my hypothesis.

Phil. Besides spirits, all that we know or conceive are our own ideas. When, therefore, you say all ideas are occasioned by impressions in the brain, do you conceive this brain or no? If you do, then you talk of ideas imprinted in an idea causing that same idea, which is absurd. If you do not conceive it, you talk unintelligibly, instead of forming a reasonable hypothesis.

Hyl. I now clearly see it was a mere dream. There is nothing in it.

Phil. You need not be much concerned at it; for after all, this way of explaining things, as you called it, could never have satisfied any reasonable man. What connection is there between a motion in the nerves, and the sensations of sound or color in the mind? Or how is it possible these should be the effect of that?

Hyl. But I could never think it had so little in it as now it seems to have.

Phil. Well then, are you at length satisfied that no sensible things have a real existence; and that you are in truth an arrant *sceptic?*

Hyl. It is too plain to be denied.

Phil. Look! are not the fields covered with a delightful verdure? Is there not something in the woods and groves, in the rivers and clear springs, that soothes, that delights, that transports the soul? At the prospect of the wide and deep ocean, or some huge mountain whose top is lost in the clouds, or of an old gloomy forest, are not our minds filled with a pleasing horror? Even in rocks and deserts is there not an agreeable wildness? How sincere a pleasure is it to behold the natural beauties of the earth! To preserve and renew our relish for them, is not the veil of night alternately drawn over her face, and doth she not change her dress with the seasons? How aptly are the elements disposed! What variety and use in the meanest productions of nature! What delicacy, what beauty, what contrivance, in animal and vegetable bodies! How exquisitely are all things suited, as well to their particular ends, as to constitute opposite parts of the whole! And, while they mutually aid and support, do they not also set off and illustrate each other? Raise now your thoughts from this ball of earth to all those glorious luminaries that adorn the high arch of heaven. The motion and situation of the planets, are they not admirable for use and order? Were those (miscalled *erratic*) globes ever known to stray, in their repeated journeys through the pathless void? Do they not measure areas round the sun ever proportioned to the times? So fixed, so immutable are the laws by which the unseen Author of nature actuates the universe. How vivid and radiant is the luster of the fixed stars! How magnificent and rich that negligent profusion with which they appear to be scattered throughout the whole azure vault! Yet, if you take the telescope, it brings into your sight a new host of stars that escape the naked eye. Here they seem contiguous and minute, but to a nearer view immense orbs of light at various distances, far sunk in the abyss of space. Now you must call imagination to your aid. The feeble narrow sense cannot descry innumerable worlds revolving round the central fires; and in those

worlds the energy of an all-perfect Mind displayed in endless forms. But, neither sense nor imagination are big enough to comprehend the boundless extent, with all its glittering furniture. Though the laboring mind exert and strain each power to its utmost reach, there still stands out ungrasped a surplusage immeasurable. Yet all the vast bodies that compose this mighty frame, how distant and remote soever, are by some secret mechanism, some divine art and force, linked in a mutual dependence and intercourse with each other, even with this earth, which was almost slipped from my thoughts and lost in the crowd of worlds. Is not the whole system immense, beautiful, glorious beyond expression and beyond thought! What treatment, then, do those philosophers deserve, who would deprive these noble and delightful scenes of all reality? How should those Principles be entertained that lead us to think all the visible beauty of the creation a false imaginary glare? To be plain, can you expect this Scepticism of yours will not be thought extravagantly absurd by all men of sense?

Hyl. Other men may think as they please; but for your part you have nothing to reproach me with. My comfort is, you are as much a sceptic as I am.

Phil. There, *Hylas,* I must beg leave to differ from you.

Hyl. What! have you all along agreed to the premises, and do you now deny the conclusion, and leave me to maintain those paradoxes by myself which you led me into? This surely is not fair.

Phil. I deny that I agreed with you in those notions that led to Scepticism. You indeed said the *reality* of sensible things consisted in an *absolute existence* out of the minds of spirits, or distinct from their being perceived. And, pursuant to this notion of reality, you are obliged to deny sensible things any real existence: that is, according to your own definition, you profess yourself a sceptic. But I neither said nor thought the reality of sensible things was to be defined after that manner. To me it is evident, for the reasons you allow of, that sensible things cannot exist otherwise than in a mind or spirit. Whence I conclude, not that they have no real existence, but that, seeing they depend not on my thought, and have an existence distinct from being perceived by me, *there must be some other mind wherein they exist.* As sure, therefore, as the sensible world really exists, so sure is there an infinite omnipresent Spirit, who contains and supports it.

Hyl. What! this is no more than I and all Christians hold; nay, and all others too who believe there is a God, and that He knows and comprehends all things.

Phil. Aye, but here lies the difference. Men commonly believe that all things are known or perceived by God, because they believe the being of a God; whereas I, on the other side, immediately and necessarily conclude the being of a God, because all sensible things must be perceived by him. . . . It is evident that the things I perceive are my own ideas, and that no idea can exist unless it be in a mind. Nor is it less plain that these ideas or things by me perceived, either themselves or their archetypes, exist independently of my mind; since I know myself not to be their author, it being out of my power to determine at pleasure what particular ideas I shall be affected with upon opening my eyes or ears. They must therefore exist in some other mind, whose will it is they should be exhibited to me. The things, I say, immediately perceived are ideas or sensations, call them which you will. But how can any idea or sensation exist in, or be produced by, anything but a mind or spirit? This indeed is inconceivable; and to assert that which is inconceivable is to talk nonsense: is it not?

Hyl. Without doubt.

Phil. But, on the other hand, it is very conceivable that they should exist in and be produced by a Spirit; since this is no more than I daily experience in myself, inasmuch as I perceive numberless ideas; and, by an act of my will, can form a great variety of them, and raise them up in my imagination: though, it must be confessed, these creatures of the fancy are not altogether so distinct, so strong, vivid, and permanent, as those perceived by my senses, which latter are called *real things.* From all which I conclude, *there is a Mind which affects me every moment with all the sensible impressions I perceive.* And, from the variety, order, and manner of these, I conclude the Author of them to be *wise, powerful, and good, and beyond comprehension.* . . .

THE THIRD DIALOGUE

Philonous. Tell me, *Hylas,* what are the fruits of yesterday's meditation? Hath it confirmed you in the same mind you were in at parting? or have you since seen cause to change your opinion?

Hyl. Truly my opinion is that all our opinions are alike vain and uncertain. What we approve today, we condemn tomorrow. We keep a stir about knowledge, and spend our lives in the pursuit of it, when, alas! we know nothing all the while: nor do I think it possible for us ever to know anything in this life. Our faculties are too narrow and too few. Nature certainly never intended us for speculation.

Phil. What! say you we can know nothing, *Hylas?*

Hyl. There is not that single thing in the world whereof we can know the real nature, or what it is in itself.

Phil. Will you tell me I do not really know what fire or water is?

Hyl. You may indeed know that fire appears hot, and water fluid; but this is no more than knowing what sensations are produced in your own mind, upon the application of fire and water to your organs of sense. Their internal constitution, their true and real nature, you are utterly in the dark as to *that*.

Phil. Do I not know this to be a real stone that I stand on, and that which I see before my eyes to be a real tree?

Hyl. Know? No, it is impossible you or any man alive should know it. All you know is, that you have such a certain idea or appearance in your own mind. But what is this to the real tree or stone? I tell you that color, figure, and hardness, which you perceive, are not the real natures of those things, or in the least like them. The same may be said of all other real things or corporeal substances which compose the world. They have none of them anything of themselves, like those sensible qualities by us perceived. We should not therefore pretend to affirm or know anything of them, as they are in their own nature.

Phil. But surely, *Hylas*, I can distinguish gold, for example, from iron: and how could this be, if I knew not what either truly was?

Hyl. Believe me, *Philonous*, you can only distinguish between your own ideas. That yellowness, that weight, and other sensible qualities, think you they are really in the gold? They are only relative to the senses and have no absolute existence in nature. And in pretending to distinguish the species of real things, by the appearances in your mind, you may perhaps act as wisely as he that should conclude two men were of a different species, because their clothes were not of the same color.

Phil. It seems, then, we are altogether put off with the appearances of things, and those false ones too. The very meat I eat, and the cloth I wear, have nothing in them like what I see and feel.

Hyl. Even so.

Phil. But is it not strange the whole world should be thus imposed on, and so foolish as to believe their senses? And yet I know not how it is, but men eat, and drink, and sleep, and perform all the offices of life, as comfortably and conveniently as if they really knew the things they are conversant about.

Hyl. They do so: but you know ordinary practice does not require a nicety of speculative knowledge. Hence the vulgar retain their mistakes, and for all that make a shift to bustle through the affairs of life. But philosophers know better things.

Phil. You mean, they know that they *know nothing*.

Hyl. That is the very top and perfection of human knowledge.

Phil. But are you all this while in earnest, *Hylas;* and are you seriously persuaded that you know nothing real in the world? Suppose you are going to write, would you not call for pen, ink, and paper, like another man; and do you not know what it is you call for?

Hyl. How often must I tell you, that I know not the real nature of any one thing in the universe? I may indeed upon occasion make use of pen, ink, and paper. But, what any one of them is in its own true nature, I declare positively I know not. And the same is true with regard to every other corporeal thing. And, what is more, we are not only ignorant of the true and real nature of things, but even of their existence. It cannot be denied that we perceive such certain appearances or ideas; but it cannot be concluded from thence that bodies really exist. Nay, now I think on it, I must, agreeably to my former concessions, further declare that it is impossible any real corporeal thing should exist in nature.

Phil. You amaze me. Was ever anything more wild and extravagant than the notions you now maintain: and is it not evident you are led into all these extravagances by the belief of *material substance?* This makes you dream of those unknown natures in everything. It is this occasions your distinguishing between the reality and sensible appearances of things. It is to this you are indebted for being ignorant of what everybody else knows perfectly well. Nor is this all: you are not only ignorant of the true nature of everything, but you know not whether any thing really exists, or whether there are any true natures at all; forasmuch as you attribute to your material beings an absolute or external existence, wherein you suppose their reality consists. And, as you are forced in the end to acknowledge such an existence means either a direct repugnancy, or nothing at all, it follows that you are obliged to pull down your own hypothesis of material Substance, and positively to deny the real existence of any part of the universe. And so you are plunged into the deepest and most deplorable *Scepticism* that ever man was. Tell me, *Hylas,* is it not as I say?

Hyl. I agree with you. *Material substance* was no more than an hypothesis, and a false and groundless one too. I will no longer spend my breath in defense of it. But, whatever hypothesis you advance, or whatsoever scheme of things you introduce in its stead, I doubt not it will appear every whit as false: let me but be allowed to question you upon it. That is, suffer me to serve you in your own kind, and I warrant it shall conduct you through as many perplexities and contradictions, to the very same state of Scepticism that I myself am in at present.

Phil. I assure you, *Hylas,* I do not pretend to frame any hypothesis at all. I am of a vulgar cast, simple enough to believe my senses, and leave things as I find them. To be plain, it is my opinion that the real things are those very things I see and feel, and perceive by my senses. These I know, and, finding they answer all the necessities and purposes of life, have no reason to be solicitous about any other unknown beings. A piece of sensible bread, for instance, would stay my stomach better than ten thousand times as much of that insensible, unintelligible, real bread you speak of. It is likewise my opinion that colors and other sensible qualities are on the objects. I cannot for my life help thinking that snow is white, and fire hot. You indeed, who by *snow* and *fire* mean certain external, unperceived, unperceiving substances, are in the right to deny whiteness or heat to be affections inherent in them. But I, who understand by those words the things I see and feel, am obliged to think like other folks. And, as I am no sceptic with regard to the nature of things, so neither am I as to their existence. That a thing should be really perceived by my senses, and at the same time not really exist, is to me a plain contradiction; since I cannot prescind or abstract, even in thought, the existence of a sensible thing from its being perceived. Wood, stones, fire, water, flesh, iron, and the like things, which I name and discourse of, are things that I know. And I should not have known them but that I perceived them by my senses; and things perceived by the senses are immediately perceived; and things immediately perceived are ideas; and ideas cannot exist without the mind; their existence therefore consists in being perceived; when, therefore, they are actually perceived there can be no doubt of their existence. Away then with all that Scepticism, all those ridiculous philosophical doubts. What a jest is it for a philosopher to question the existence of sensible things, till he hath it proved to him from the veracity of

God; or to pretend our knowledge in this point falls short of intuition or demonstration! I might as well doubt of my own being, as of the being of those things I actually see and feel.

Hyl. Not so fast, *Philonous:* you say you cannot conceive how sensible things should exist without the mind. Do you not?

Phil. I do

Hyl. Supposing you were annihilated, cannot you conceive it possible that things perceivable by sense may still exist?

Phil. I can; but then it must be in another mind. When I deny sensible things an existence out of the mind, I do not mean my mind in particular, but all minds. Now, it is plain they have an existence exterior to my mind; since I find them by experience to be independent of it. There is therefore some other mind wherein they exist, during the intervals between the times of my perceiving them: as likewise they did before my birth, and would do after my supposed annihilation. And, as the same is true with regard to all other finite created spirits, it necessarily follows there is an *omnipresent eternal Mind,* which knows and comprehends all things, and exhibits them to our view in such a manner, and according to such rules, as He Himself hath ordained, and are by us termed the *laws of nature.*

Hyl. Answer me, *Philonous.* Are all our ideas perfectly inert beings? Or have they any agency included in them?

Phil. They are altogether passive and inert.

Hyl. And is not God an agent, a being purely active?

Phil. I acknowledge it.

Hyl. No idea therefore can be like unto, or represent the nature of God?

Phil. It cannot.

Hyl. Since therefore you have no idea of the mind of God, how can you conceive it possible that things should exist in His mind? Or, if you can conceive the mind of God, without having an idea of it, why may not I be allowed to conceive the existence of Matter, notwithstanding I have no idea of it?

Phil. As to your first question: I own I have properly no *idea,* either of God or any other spirit; for these being active, cannot be represented by things perfectly inert, as our ideas are. I do nevertheless know that I, who am a spirit or thinking substance, exist as certainly as I know my ideas exist. Farther, I know what I mean by the terms *I* and *myself;* and I know this immediately or intuitively, though I do not perceive it as I perceive a triangle, a color, or a sound. The Mind, Spirit, or Soul is that indivisible unextended thing which thinks, acts, and perceives. I say *indivisible,* because unextended; and *unextended,* because extended, figured, movable things are ideas; and that which perceives ideas, which thinks and wills, is plainly itself no idea, nor like an idea. Ideas are things inactive, and perceived. And Spirits a sort of beings altogether different from them. I do not therefore say my soul is an idea, or like an idea. However, taking the word *idea* in a large sense, my soul may be said to furnish me with an idea, that is, an image or likeness of God, though indeed extremely inadequate. For, all the notion I have of God is obtained by reflecting on my own soul, heightening its powers, and removing its imperfections. I have, therefore, though not an inactive idea, yet in *myself* some sort of an active thinking image of the Deity. And, though I perceive Him not by sense, yet I have a notion of Him, or know Him by reflection and reasoning. My own mind and my own ideas I have an immediate knowledge of; and, by the help of these, do mediately apprehend the possibility of the existence of other spirits and ideas. Further, from my own being, and from the dependency I find in myself and my ideas, I do, by an act of reason, necessarily infer the existence of a God, and of all created things in the mind of God. So much for your first question. For the second: I suppose by this time you can answer it yourself. For you neither perceive Matter objectively, as you do an inactive being or idea; nor know it, as you do yourself, by a reflex act; neither do you mediately apprehend it by similitude of the one or the other; nor yet collect it by reasoning from that which you know immediately. All which makes the case of *Matter* widely different from that of the *Deity.*

Hyl. You say your own soul supplies you with some sort of an idea or image of God. But, at the same time, you acknowledge you have, properly speaking, no *idea* of your own soul. You even affirm that spirits are a sort of beings altogether different from ideas. Consequently that no idea can be like a spirit. We have therefore no idea of any spirit. You admit nevertheless that there is spiritual Substance, although you have no idea of it; while you deny there can be such a thing as material Substance, because you have no notion or idea of it. Is this fair dealing? To act consistently, you must either admit Matter or reject Spirit. What say you to this?

Phil. I say, in the first place, that I do not deny the existence of material substance, merely because I have no notion of it, but because the notion of it is inconsistent; or, in other words, because it is repugnant that there should be a notion of it. Many things, for aught I know, may exist, whereof neither I nor any other man hath or can have any idea or notion whatsoever. But then those things must be possible, that is, nothing inconsistent must be included in their definition. I say, secondly, that, although we believe things to exist which we do not perceive, yet we may not believe that any particular thing exists, without some reason for such belief: but I have no reason for believing the existence of Matter. I have no immediate intuition thereof: neither can I immediately from my sensations, ideas, notions, actions, or passions, infer an unthinking, unperceiving, inactive Substance, either by probable deduction, or necessary consequence. Whereas the being of my Self, that is, my own soul, mind, or thinking principle, I evidently know by reflection. You will forgive me if I repeat the same things in answer to the same objections. In the very notion or definition of *material Substance,* there is included a manifest repugnance and inconsistency. But this cannot be said of the notion of Spirit. That ideas should exist in what doth not perceive, or be produced by what doth not act, is repugnant. But, it is no repugnancy to say that a perceiving thing should be the subject of ideas, or an active thing the cause of them. It is granted we have neither an immediate evidence nor a demonstrative knowledge of the existence of other finite spirits; but it will not thence follow that such spirits are on a foot with material substances: if to suppose the one be inconsistent, and it be not inconsistent to suppose the other; if the one can be inferred by no argument, and there is a probability for the other; if we see signs and effects indicating distinct finite agents like ourselves, and see no sign or symptom whatever that leads to a rational belief of Matter. I say, lastly, that I have a notion of Spirit, though I have not, strictly speaking, an idea of it. I do not perceive it as an idea, or by means of an idea, but know it by reflection.

Hyl. Notwithstanding all you have said, to me it seems that, according to your own way of thinking, and in consequence of your own principles, it should follow that *you* are only a system of floating ideas, without any substance to support them. Words are not to be used without a meaning. And, as there is no more meaning in *spiritual Substance* than in *material Substance,* the one is to be exploded as well as the other.

Phil. How often must I repeat, that I know or am conscious of my own being; and that *I myself* am not my ideas, but somewhat else, a thinking, active principle that perceives, knows, wills, and operates about ideas. I know that I, one and the same self, perceive both colors and sounds: that a color cannot perceive a sound, nor a sound a color: that I am therefore one individual principle, distinct from color and sound; and, for the same reason, from all other sensible things and inert ideas. But, I am not in like manner conscious either of the existence or essence of Matter. On the contrary, I know that nothing inconsistent can exist, and that the existence of Matter implies an inconsistency. Further, I know what I mean when I affirm that there is a spiritual substance or support of ideas, that is, that a spirit knows and perceives ideas. But, I do not know what is meant when it is said that an unperceiving substance hath inherent in it and supports either ideas or the archetypes of ideas. There is therefore upon the whole no parity of case between Spirit and Matter.

Hyl. I own myself satisfied in this point. But, do you in earnest think the real existence of sensible things consists in their being actually perceived? If so; how comes it that all mankind distinguish between them? Ask the first man you meet, and he shall tell you, *to be perceived* is one thing, and *to exist* is another.

Phil. I am content, *Hylas,* to appeal to the common sense of the world for the truth of my notion. Ask the gardener why he thinks yonder cherry-tree exists in the gar-

den, and he shall tell you, because he sees and feels it; in a word, because he perceives it by his senses. Ask him why he thinks an orange-tree not to be there, and he shall tell you, because he does not perceive it. What he perceives by sense, that he terms a real being, and saith it *is* or *exists;* but, that which is not perceivable, the same, he saith, hath no being.

Hyl. Yes, *Philonous,* I grant the existence of a sensible thing consists in being perceivable, but not in being actually perceived.

Phil. And what is perceivable but an idea? And can an idea exist without being actually perceived? These are points long since agreed between us.

Hyl. But, be your opinion never so true, yet surely you will not deny it is shocking, and contrary to the common sense of men. Ask the fellow whether yonder tree hath an existence out of his mind: what answer think you he would make?

Phil. The same that I should myself, to wit, that it doth exist out of his mind. But then to a Christian it cannot surely be shocking to say, the real tree, existing without his mind, is truly known and comprehended by (that is, *exists in*) the infinite mind of God. Probably he may not at first glance be aware of the direct and immediate proof there is of this; inasmuch as the very being of a tree, or any other sensible thing, implies a mind wherein it is. But the point itself he cannot deny. The question between the Materialists and me is not, whether things have a *real* existence out of the mind of this or that person, but, whether they have an *absolute* existence, distinct from being perceived by God, and exterior to all minds. This indeed some heathens and philosophers have affirmed, but whoever entertains notions of the Deity suitable to the Holy Scriptures will be of another opinion.

Hyl. But, according to your notions, what difference is there between real things, and chimeras formed by the imagination, or the visions of a dream, since they are all equally in the mind?

Phil. The ideas formed by the imagination are faint and indistinct; they have, besides, an entire dependence on the will. But the ideas perceived by sense, that is, real things, are more vivid and clear; and, being imprinted on the mind by a spirit distinct from us, have not the like dependence on our will. There is therefore no danger of confounding these with the foregoing: and there is as little of confounding them with the visions of a dream, which are dim, irregular, and confused. And, though they should happen to be never so lively and natural, yet, by their not being connected, and of a piece with the preceding and subsequent transactions of our lives, they might easily be distinguished from realities. In short, by whatever method you distinguish *things* from *chimeras* on your scheme, the same, it is evident, will hold also upon mine. For, it must be, I presume, by some perceived difference; and I am not for depriving you of any one thing that you perceive.

Hyl. But still, *Philonous,* you hold, there is nothing in the world but spirits and ideas. And this, you must needs acknowledge, sounds very oddly.

Phil. I own the word *idea,* not being commonly used for *thing,* sounds something out of the way. My reason for using it was, because a necessary relation to the mind is understood to be implied by that term; and it is now commonly used by philosophers to denote the immediate objects of the understanding. But, however oddly the proposition may sound in words, yet it includes nothing so very strange or shocking in its sense; which in effect amounts to no more than this, to wit, that

there are only things perceiving, and things perceived; or that every unthinking being is necessarily, and from the very nature of its existence, perceived by some mind; if not by a finite created mind, yet certainly by the infinite mind of God, in whom "we live, and move, and have our being." Is this as strange as to say, the sensible qualities are not on the objects: or that we cannot be sure of the existence of things, or know anything of their real natures, though we both see and feel them, and perceive them by all our senses? . . .

Hyl. But the denying Matter, *Philonous,* or corporeal Substance; there is the point. You can never persuade me that this is not repugnant to the universal sense of mankind. Were our dispute to be determined by most voices, I am confident you would give up the point, without gathering the votes.

Phil. I wish both our opinions were fairly stated and submitted to the judgment of men who had plain common sense, without the prejudices of a learned education. Let me be represented as one who trusts his senses, who thinks he knows the things he sees and feels, and entertains no doubts of their existence; and you fairly set forth with all your doubts, your paradoxes, and your scepticism about you, and I shall willingly acquiesce in the determination of any indifferent person. That there is no substance wherein ideas can exist beside spirit is to me evident. And that the objects immediately perceived are ideas, is on all hands agreed. And that sensible qualities are objects immediately perceived no one can deny. It is therefore evident there can be no *substratum* of those qualities but spirit; in which they exist, not by way of mode or property, but as a thing perceived in that which perceives it. I deny therefore that there is any unthinking *substratum* of the objects of sense, and in that acceptation that there is any material substance.

But if by *material substance* is meant only sensible body, that which is seen and felt (and the unphilosophical part of the world, I dare say, mean no more), then I am more certain of matter's existence than you or any other philosopher pretend to be. If there be anything which makes the generality of mankind averse from the notions I espouse, it is a misapprehension that I deny the reality of sensible things: but, as it is you who are guilty of that and not I, it follows that in truth their aversion is against your notions and not mine. I do therefore assert that I am as certain as of my own being, that there are bodies or corporeal substances (meaning the things I perceive by my senses); and that, granting this, the bulk of mankind will take no thought about, nor think themselves at all concerned in the fate of those unknown natures and philosophical quiddities which some men are so fond of.

Hyl. What say you to this? Since, according to you, men judge of the reality of things by their senses, how can a man be mistaken in thinking the moon a plain lucid surface, about a foot in diameter; or a square tower, seen at a distance, round; or an oar, with one end in the water, crooked?

Phil. He is not mistaken with regard to the ideas he actually perceives, but in the inferences he makes from his present perceptions. Thus, in the case of the oar, what he immediately perceives by sight is certainly crooked; and so far he is in the right. But, if he thence conclude that upon taking the oar out of the water he shall perceive the same crookedness; or that it would affect his touch as crooked things are wont to do: in that he is mistaken. In like manner, if he shall conclude from what he perceives in one station, that, in case he advances towards the moon or tower, he should still be affected with the like ideas, he is mistaken. But his mistake lies not in what he perceives immediately and at present (it being a manifest contradiction to suppose he should err in respect of that), but in the wrong judgment he makes concerning the ideas he apprehends to be connected with those immediately perceived: or, concerning the ideas that, from what he perceives at present, he imagines would be perceived in other circumstances. The case is the same with regard to the Copernican system. We do not here perceive any motion of the earth: but it were erroneous thence to conclude, that, in case we were placed at as great a distance from that as we are now from the other planets, we should not then perceive its motion.

Hyl. I understand you; and must needs own you say things plausible enough: but, give me leave to put you in mind of one thing. Pray, *Philonous,* were you not formerly as positive that Matter existed, as you are now that it does not?

Phil. I was. But here lies the difference. Before my positiveness was founded, without examination, upon prejudice; but now, after inquiry, upon evidence.

Hyl. After all, it seems our dispute is rather about words than things. We agree in the thing, but differ in the name. That we are affected with ideas from without is evident; and it is no less evident that there must be (I will not say archetypes, but) powers without the mind, corresponding to those ideas. And, as these powers cannot subsist by themselves, there is some subject of them necessarily to be admitted, which I call *Matter,* and you call *Spirit.* This is all the difference.

Phil. Pray, *Hylas,* is that powerful being, or subject of powers, extended?

Hyl. It hath not extension; but it hath the power to raise in you the idea of extension.

Phil. It is therefore itself unextended?

Hyl. I grant it.

Phil. Is it not also active?

Hyl. Without doubt: otherwise, how could we attribute powers to it?

Phil. Now let me ask you two questions: *First,* whether it be agreeable to the usage either of philosophers or others to give the name *Matter* to an unextended active being? And, *Secondly,* whether it be not ridiculously absurd to misapply names contrary to the common use of language?

Hyl. Well then, let it not be called Matter, since you will have it so, but some *third nature* distinct from Matter and Spirit. For what reason is there why you should call it Spirit? Does not the notion of spirit imply that it is thinking, as well as active and unextended?

Phil. My reason is this: because I have a mind to have some notion of meaning in what I say: but I have no notion of any action distinct from volition, neither can I conceive volition to be anywhere but in a spirit; therefore, when I speak of an active being, I am obliged to mean a spirit. Beside, what can be plainer than that a thing which hath no ideas in itself cannot impart them to me; and, if it hath ideas, surely it must be a spirit. To make you comprehend the point still more clearly if it be possible: I assert as well as you that, since we are affected from without, we must allow powers to be without, in a being distinct from ourselves. So far we are agreed. But then we differ as to the kind of this powerful being. I will have it to be spirit, you Matter, or I know not what (I may add too, you know not what) third nature. Thus, I prove it to be spirit. From the effects I see produced I conclude there are actions; and, because actions, volitions; and, because there are volitions, there must be a will. Again, the things I perceive must have an existence, they or their archetypes, out of my mind: but, being ideas, neither they nor their archetypes can exist otherwise than in an understanding; there is therefore an understanding. But will and understanding constitute in the strictest sense a mind or spirit. The powerful cause, therefore, of my ideas is in strict propriety of speech a *spirit.* . . .

COMMENT

Do We Perceive Material Objects?

The speakers in the preceding *Dialogues* are Hylas, a "materialist," and Philonous, who represents Berkeley himself. Physical objects, according to Philonous, have no existence independent of thought. The whole universe is made up of minds and the immaterial objects of minds—nothing more. This doctrine, which is called "idealism," may strike beginning students as exceedingly odd; but it is quite possible that the Universe *is* very odd, and the arguments for idealism are strong. Since Berkeley is not only the founder but also the clearest expositor of modern idealism, we shall consider his work in some detail.

Berkeley begins his argument, in *Essay Towards a New Theory of Vision,* by attacking the common-sense assumption that we directly perceive spatial relation. Distance, he maintains, is not seen but inferred. Assuming that objects are constant in size, we judge them to be near if they appear large and far away if they look small. The effect of perspective, as when the two sides of a railroad track seem to converge in the distance, or when one object appears higher in the field of vision than another, is to indicate relative distance. Certain colors, such as the purplish haze of mountains, suggest remoteness, and certain other colors, such as clear, distinct hues, suggest nearness. Eye strain in seeing very near or very distant things, the felt accommodation of the eyes and eye muscles when objects move backward or forward in the field of vision, and the confusion in outline and double imagery when objects are seen at very close range are additional clues to spatial location. The tactile signs of distance are quite different from the visual signs; and we learn to correlate the two sets of signs as a result of long experience. Hence a man born blind and suddenly made to see would have to learn gradually to interpret the visual signs and to correlate visual and tactile data. Berkeley shows by means of this analysis that our impressions of distance originate largely in the mind. But he does not, in this book, disclose the full sweep of his idealism.

In his later books, Berkeley argues that we perceive not material objects but concrete sense data, which he calls "ideas." (He uses the word *idea* to denote the immediate object of perception—the sense datum—reserving the word *notion* to denote the object of introspection—the introspective datum.) A cherry, for example, is soft, red, sweet, round, and odorous. The softness, that is, is felt, the red color is seen, the sweetness is tasted, the roundness is perceived by sight or touch, and the odor is smelled. The very being of these qualities consists in their being perceived. What we call a cherry is simply the complex, or sum total, of all these sensible qualities. If we try to think of a cherry as something distinct and separate from its qualities, we reduce it to an utter abstraction that can have no reality or meaning. It is an object perceived by a mind and can exist in no other way.

Someone might reply that we can still *conceive* of a cherry as existing apart from a mind. To this objection Berkeley replies that it is impossible ever to think of *anything* that is not related to a mind:

> But, say you, surely there is nothing easier than for me to imagine trees, for instance, in a park, or books existing in a closet, and nobody by to perceive them. I answer, you may so, there is no difficulty in it. But what is all this, I beseech you, more than framing in your mind certain ideas which you call *books* and *trees*, and at the same time omitting to frame the idea of any one that may perceive them? But do not you yourself perceive or think of them all the while? . . . When we do our utmost to conceive the existence of external bodies, we are all the while only contemplating our own ideas.[1]

Thus everyone is in the predicament of knowing immediately the ideas of his own mind. All else can only be inferred.

[1] *Principles of Human Knowledge*, #23.

Can We Infer Material Objects?

Berkeley examines four attempted inferences to non-mental entities: (1) the inference to concrete physical objects, (2) the inference to objects having only primary qualities, (3) the inference to substance, and (4) the inference to matter as unknown cause.

1. *The inference to concrete physical objects.* The inference to concrete objects is the view that our "mental pictures," with all their concrete sensuous content, are copies of external physical objects—that things actually possess the colors, shapes, textures, odors, tastes, and sounds revealed in immediate experience. Our ideas literally picture material things as they are.

In attacking this view, Berkeley argues that our impressions ("ideas") are too variable and relative to be faithful copies of independently existing objects. Colored objects change their hue as we approach them; the "same" food will taste different to different people or to the same person at different times; the temperature of a room will seem more or less warm depending upon the condition of the perceiver. By such examples, which we need not multiply, Berkeley shows that things appear to have extremely variable and even incompatible qualities. But a physical thing cannot at one and the same time have opposite qualities, such as heat and cold, or be so changeable. Hence, we must conclude that our ideas are not exact copies of external things.

Material, he also points out, means "other-than-mental." Hence, by definition, no material thing can be like an idea. Nothing can be like a sensation or idea but another sensation or idea. "How can that which is sensible," he asks, "be like that which is insensible? Can a real thing in itself *invisible* be like a *color;* or a real thing which is not *audible* be like a *sound?*" [2] The hypothesis of exact resemblance between an idea of sense and an unsensed material thing is illogical.

The very attempt to separate the sensation from the thing, which is implied in regarding the one as the duplicate of the other, seems to Berkeley an attempt to separate the inseparable. For him, the objects *are* the ideas and nothing more:

> Light and colors, heat and cold, extension and figures—in a word the things we see and feel—what are they but so many sensations, notions, ideas, or impressions on the sense? And is it possible to separate, even in thought, any of these from perception? For my part, I might as easily divide a thing from itself. . . . In truth, the object and the sensation are the same thing, and cannot therefore be abstracted from each other.[3]

[2] *Dialogues,* I.
[3] *Principles of Human Knowledge,* #5.

It is a manifest contradiction to suppose that concrete ideas of sense can exist unsensed, or that exact duplicates of ideas can exist in an unexperienced physical world.

2. *The inference to objects having only primary qualities.* Descartes, Locke, and their followers were prepared to concede that "secondary qualities"—colors, odors, sounds, tastes, and tactile qualities—are not actually inherent in physical objects. Were I in the dark, for example, a peach would have no color; if I did not bite into it, the taste would not exist; if I did not feel it, it would not be soft, etc. All such qualities are like the tickle of a feather, which is not *in* the feather but in one's reaction to it. So, likewise, colors, odors, sounds, tastes, and touch impressions are not in the external things but in our mental reactions to these things. Physical objects emit "particles" which, by impact upon the nervous system, *cause* the ideas of secondary qualities to arise in the mind. But, according to the same philosophers, there also are "primary qualities"—extension, figure, motion, rest, solidity, and number—which physical science requires to describe the external world. These qualities exist in the physical things, whether we perceive them or not.

This distinction between primary and secondary qualities was made for two main reasons. First, the secondary qualities are so variable and fluctuating that they cannot be considered objective, whereas the primary qualities are relatively stable and fixed. Secondly, the laws of the physical science of the day were framed in terms of primary but not secondary qualities and therefore seemed to imply the objectivity of the former but not of the latter. This impression was reinforced by scientific explanations of perception, which described color, sound, odor, etc., as psychological reactions to external motions.

Berkeley offers a three-pronged rebuttal to this separation of primary and secondary qualities. First, he contends that primary qualities are quite as relative and mind-dependent as secondary qualities. A tower looks tiny when seen from a distance but large at close quarters; the shape of a table top appears to change as perspectives change; a nut that seems solid to a child seems relatively fragile to a blacksmith; a tree that appears to be in motion as we sail by in a boat seems stationary when we drop anchor. Thus primary qualities, as directly perceived, are also relative to the perceiver.

Secondly, the supposition that our *ideas* of the primary qualities resemble the physical things can never be put to the test. According to Locke's own theory, nothing is available in experience except our ideas; matter is never experienced. Hence there is no way of comparing our ideas with material objects in order to judge whether the latter in any way correspond to the former. If all we ever perceive are the effects produced in our minds, then the supposed cause is imperceptible and unknowable. To assume that it has a certain sort of nature—that it possesses primary qualities, for example, but not secondary—is mere guesswork.

Thirdly, the primary qualities cannot exist all by themselves. There can be no motion without something to be moved, no extension without something to be extended, no shape without something to be shaped, no number without something to be numbered, no solidity without something to be solid. Actually, the primary qualities are known only in inextricable relation to secondary qualities. The sensation of extension, for example, comes to us only by way of our sight and touch. When it comes by sight, it is invariably conjoined with sense data of color; when it comes by touch, it is invariably conjoined with tactile sense data. Bare extension, disengaged from all secondary qualities, is never experienced, and we cannot even imagine what it would be like to experience it. We cannot make a physical world out of such mere abstractions.

3. *The inference to substance.* Locke distinguished between the qualities of an object and the underlying substance in which the qualities supposedly inhere. After we have taken note of all the colors, shapes, motions, textures, odors, or other qualities, whether primary or secondary, that might conceivably characterize an object, there remains something more—an unexperienced substratum which "supports" whatever qualities are finally deemed to be objective. This substance is an indefinite, indefinable something of which we can form no positive idea. Unlike Aristotle's "substance," which is conceived to be the more permanent core of *experienceable* qualities, Locke's substance turns out to be no more than an unknown x, a deeper and hidden nature, which underlies all assignable properties of the object. Nevertheless, Locke believed that this mysterious substratum must exist to hold the qualities together and give them necessary support.

Berkeley emphatically rejects this conception. Since Locke's substance is indefinable and inexperienceable, there is no way of verifying its existence. Obviously there can be no evidence for something that, by its very definition, is absolutely unknown and unknowable.

Berkeley also finds that the notion of *support*, which the substance supposedly gives to the qualities, is very unclear: "It is evident *support* cannot be taken in its usual or literal sense, as when we say that pillars support a building. In what sense therefore must it be taken? For my part, I am not able to discover any sense at all that can be applicable to it." [4] Such ill-defined concepts can win no credence from a critical thinker.

Berkeley also objects to the concept of "substance" because of its abstractness. In the Introduction to *Principles of Human Knowledge,* he launches a determined attack against abstract ideas, charging that they are mere dust clouds raised by philosophers who then foolishly complain that they cannot

[4] *Ibid.,* #16.

see. Universals, such as "triangle," do not exist; there are only particular triangles of a definite character. Everyone who responds fully to the word *triangle* thinks of a concrete triangular shape. The image thus formed in the mind may become a representative sign of other triangles, but any actually existing thing or quality is always concrete and particular. Berkeley, holding this nominalistic view of universals, rejects the notion of "substance" as too abstract to have genuine meaning.

As we have already indicated, a "thing" for Berkeley is not a mysterious "something" possessing certain qualities. It is nothing but a collection of ideas of sense. A beefsteak, for example, is just a complex of sense data—the brown color, the irregular shape, the appetizing aroma, the meaty taste, the texture that we feel with our tongue. There is no need to speak of a physical substance somehow distinct from these concrete qualities. Certain "ideas" are observed repeatedly to go together and are accounted one distinct thing, signified by the word "beefsteak." But the *thing* is just the collection of ideas —nothing more. Unlike Hume, whom we shall discuss in the next chapter, Berkeley retained the concept of spiritual substance, in the sense of an enduring self. He agreed with Descartes that thought requires a thinker. But sense qualities, he was convinced, do not require a physical substance in which to inhere.

4. *The inference to matter as unknown cause.* An opponent, such as Hylas is represented to be, may try to meet Berkeley's arguments by a rather large dose of scepticism. He may finally be driven to admit that we cannot attribute either primary or secondary qualities to matter and that the conception of substance is untenable. But he may still insist that *something* exists in the external world and helps to cause our ideas. This something has no assignable qualities except that it is non-mental.

Berkeley's answer is brief. If outer reality is absolutely unknown, we have no reason to suppose that it is non-mental. That which has no assignable qualities is nothing and does not even exist. Like Locke's substance, it is a meaningless abstraction.

The Inference to an Ideal Objective Order

Thus far we have been considering the negative aspects of Berkeley's argument, his attacks on the hypothesis of the "materialist" rather than his own hypothesis. Let us now examine the constructive portion of his argument.

Like everyone else, Berkeley distinguished between dreams and waking perceptions, between illusions and realities. Real objects are usually more vivid and distinct than illusory objects; they are not, like the figments of imagination, of our own making; they exhibit a superior order and coherence; they change or recur in predictable ways, permitting us to formulate "laws of nature"; they seem to continue to exist in the intervals between our experiences. For example, a candle burns down even when we are not present; a dog gets hungry when we are absent and do not feed it; a hill gradually erodes, whether we observe it or not. Such things, we have ample reason to suppose, exist and go on changing even when we do not perceive them.

The materialist concludes from these marks of objectivity that there must be physical objects independent of perceptions. But opposed to this hypothesis are all of the foregoing arguments against materialism. Is there any other alternative?

Berkeley believes that there is. He points out that all the marks of objectivity are features of experience, not of any thing or substance *beyond* experience. They simply mean that experience has a certain regularity and dependable character—that we can make verifiable predictions as to what we shall experience. We can predict, for example, that when we again perceive a candle after an hour's interval it will be of diminished size.

In accounting for such facts, it is sound empirical method to stick close to actual experience. What sorts of things do I actually know? I know ideas because I actually experience them. I know myself, my own mind and mental operations, because I have an immediate introspective awareness of myself and my own mental states. Suppose I try to interpret reality in terms of immediate experience, recognizing that others have similar minds and experiences.

First, there is my mind and other finite minds. Second, there are my ideas and the ideas of other finite minds. Third, there is a far greater Mind, or God, which I can conceive as analogous to my own mind although immeasurably greater. Fourth, there are His ideas, which, in their regular order, constitute nature. Being omnipotent, God can communicate ideas to us by a kind of divine mental telepathy. The "real objects" which we perceive, not being of our own imagining, have their cause, but that cause is not matter; it is God. He coordinates my experiences and the experiences of all other finite spirits so that we live in a dependable and common "world."

The natural universe has a kind of double existence. On the one hand, it is a steady, interconnected, and comprehensive set of ideas in the Divine Mind; and, on the other hand, it is a regular and somewhat repetitious set of ideas in finite minds, communicated to them by God. Berkeley's account does not indicate whether we somehow share in God's ideas, or whether He gives us a corresponding but independent set of ideas. Of course, God has an infinitely larger stock of ideas than all finite minds put together. He conserves objects in the intervals when no finite mind is perceiving them. The burning candle which continues to exist when no finite mind sees it depends upon perception (its *esse est percipi*), but the perception involved in this instance is God's, not man's.

This idealistic hypothesis is supported by Berkeley's interpretation of causation. Like David Hume (whom we shall study in the next chapter), he maintained that no inspection of our sense data discloses any causal force or power. We say, for example, that cold makes water freeze. But the closest inspection fails to disclose any *power* in cold that *makes* water become solid. All we actually observe is that cold is followed by the solidification of water; we discover a sequence, nothing more. Unlike Hume, however, Berkeley maintained that we do have insight into causal connection through knowledge of our mental operations. We have introspective awareness of ourselves as active, volitional, creative beings, with the power to produce imaginary ideas. It is a natural inference that the power to produce perceived ideas is similarly mental, the difference being that imaginary ideas are created by finite minds whereas perceived ideas are created and communicated to us by an Infinite Mind.

To a religious person such as Berkeley, this idealistic interpretation has an immense appeal. He sees the Universe as through and through spiritual— a system of spirits with God the supreme author and creator. But his idealism also has great logical advantages, since it bears so close a relation to the immediate facts of experience and relieves us of such unempirical abstractions as Locke's substances and primary qualities. It adheres to the logical principle of parsimony—the principle that we should suppose no more entities than necessary to explain the given facts. Materialists believe in substances and material entities; but they never find them in experience—they find only ideas. The world would look the same and behave in the same way if these unexperienced things were omitted. Berkeley proposes to omit them. Thus he achieves an immense housecleaning, getting rid of a tremendous amount of metaphysical rubbish.

At the same time, he preserves science intact. Science does not need substances or invisible matter: it needs only laws. If the external causes of our minds and their experiences have a constant nature, the ideas of sense which are their effects will exhibit lawful regularities and permit scientific predictions. God, as a non-material cause, can have a nature as constant as that of any material cause. When God is substituted for matter in Berkeley's metaphysics, all the laws of science still hold good, but their metaphysical basis has been reinterpreted. Atheism and other heresies creep in when scientists forget the empirical foundations of their science and engage in metaphysical speculation about imperceivable entities. They thus turn legitimate science into illegitimate metaphysics. Genuine science rests upon *perceptions* and will not err so long as it remains true to its concrete, empirical basis. Berkeley believes that he is recalling science to its true foundations.

Finally, he argues that his philosophy rarely contradicts common sense. Most men believe in God, and almost everyone supposes that objects have the concrete qualities that they appear to have. Berkeley's idealism retains the belief in God and interprets objects as the sets of qualities immediately perceived. The color and the odor of a tulip are not illusory—they are as real as any qualities. The philosopher who dissolves the tulip into invisible and intangible particles is the one who is really at odds with common sense. The ordinary man, according to Berkeley, is right: we see things as they are.

The Idealism of Hegel and Kant

Berkeley was the founder of modern idealism, but Kant and Hegel were more influential proponents of this philosophy. Because the metaphysical works of these famous German philosophers are extremely difficult and do not serve as the best introduction to philosophy, this book includes no selection from Hegel and none from the non-ethical writings of Kant. The omission of their writings is compensated by the inclusion of the selection by Brand Blanshard in Chapter 6. The very essence of Absolute Idealism, which stems from Kant and Hegel, is to combine the doctrine that reality is mental with the doctrine, so well expressed by Blanshard, that coherence is the key to truth and the fundamental mark of reality.

Kant, it should be pointed out, was less an idealist than Hegel. In *The Critique of Pure Reason,* he undertook to prove that all genuine scientific knowledge, whether in mathematics or in the natural sciences, is universally valid, but that speculative metaphysics, which seeks to go beyond experience to determine the ultimate and absolute nature of things, cannot be established upon any sound and dependable basis. Science is reliable because it deals with *phenomena*—things as they *appear* in human experiences; but metaphysics is unreliable because it tries to interpret *noumena*—things as they are in themselves apart from experience. The world of ultimate reality, in contrast to the world of appearance, can never be known to reason. The noumenal realities must be interpreted, if at all, by moral conviction and religious faith —not by science or pure theoretical philosophy.

The phenomena, Kant insisted, exhibit spatial and temporal forms and rational connections, such as cause and effect. In grasping these forms and connections, consciousness is an awareness of meanings—not passive contemplation but active judgment, not mere perception but synthetic interpretation. We can never know things as they are apart from these synthetic modes of apprehension and judgment, which are the necessary conditions of all human experience. To interpret *ultimate* reality as either finite or infinite, one or many, mechanistic or teleological, mental or material, is to attempt to probe the ultimate nature of existence—and this human reason can never do.

To call Kant an "idealist" tends to be misleading in view of his denial that an idealistic metaphysics can ever be theoretically justified. He emphasized the role of mind in experience, his moral and religious faith inclined him in the direction of idealism, and he greatly influenced the idealistic tradition—

but otherwise he is not an idealist. In his critical agnosticism, he is allied to sceptics such as David Hume, "positivists" such as Auguste Comte, and "logical empiricists" such as Moritz Schlick and Rudolph Carnap, rather than to speculative metaphysics. He argued for belief in God, freedom of the will, and immortality—but as a necessary article of moral faith rather than as a doctrine that can be established by theoretical reason.

Hegel, on the other hand, had no such sceptical view. He believed that the processes of nature are within the world-mind, that they are the very reasonings, or objectifications, of that mind. The laws of science and the concepts of philosophy are the tracing of world-thought. The changes within nature and human affairs are the working out of cosmic reasons or purposes. Every human spirit and every thing is a part of the Absolute—the total unity. Hence we are inextricably in touch with reality, and Kant's distinction between things as they appear to us and things as they are in themselves is invalid. Hegel was a full-fledged idealist, offering to disclose the ultimate meaning of things. Thus Kant prepared the ground for Absolute Idealism by emphasizing the coherence of knowledge and the mind's contribution to experience, but Hegel erected the structure.

Some Critical Questions

Idealism seems to the present writer, if not true, at least irrefutable. But certain critical questions will occur to a reflective reader:

1. *Is the essence of an object to be perceived?* Over and over again, Berkeley insisted that "things" are mere collections of "ideas" and that ideas cannot exist unless they are perceived. The plausibility of his contention depends upon his constant use of the word *idea*. We think of "idea" as something in the mind and therefore as incapable of existing apart from the mind. Hence, if we are told that an apple consists entirely of "ideas," it is natural for us to suppose that the apple can exist only in some mind. But "idea," as Berkeley used it, really means "immediate object of thought or experience" (including both imaginative and perceptual experience). If we understand idea in this sense, there is a possibility, not lightly to be dismissed, that an object known as a set of ideas may continue to exist when the thought of it ceases.

The point can be illustrated by an amusing passage from Lewis Carroll's *Through the Looking Glass*. Alice is warned by Tweedledum and Tweedledee not to awaken the Red King:

> "He's dreaming now," said Tweedledee: "and what do you think he's dreaming about?"
> Alice said, "Nobody can guess that."
> "Why about *you!*" Tweedledee exclaimed, clapping his hands triumphantly. "And if he left off dreaming about you, where do you suppose you'd be?"
> "Where I am now, of course," said Alice.

"Not you!" Tweedledee retorted contemptuously. "You'd be nowhere. Why, you're only a sort of thing in his dream!"

"If that there King was to wake," added Tweedledum, "you'd go out—bang! —just like a candle!"

The delicious absurdity of this passage depends upon the supposition of Tweedledum and Tweedledee that to *exist* is to be *borne in mind,* and that when Alice is not borne in mind by the Red King she cannot exist. But no real person is merely a thought or idea in anybody's mind.

This point would be admitted by Berkeley. His formula for summing up the nature of reality is *"esse est percipi aut percipere,"* not just *"esse est percipi."* Being is to perceive *or* to be perceived—only *perceivers* can exist unperceived. But if a person can exist independently of someone's idea of him, why cannot a *thing* exist independently? To argue that an apple must be in our minds because we are thinking of it is like arguing that a person must be in our minds because we are thinking of him. If we distinguish clearly between the act of thinking and the object of thought, the act of perceiving and the object perceived, there is no absurdity in supposing that things may exist even when they are unperceived or unthought.

2. *Is the "egocentric predicament" a reason for believing in idealism?* Berkeley pointed out that everyone's knowledge is incurably egocentric. Even when I think of the unobserved interior of the earth, I am *thinking* about it, and, in that sense, it is an object before my mind. Every object we ever perceive or think about in any way stands *ipso facto* in relation to our minds. Does this "egocentric predicament" [5] provide a valid argument for idealism?

Ralph Barton Perry answers in the negative. The fact that no one can eliminate himself as the subject of his own experiences proves nothing at all about the nature of the external world. We may have good reason to suppose that there are unknown stars, unexperienced atoms, unsighted grains of sand in the Sahara Desert, and unobserved physical processes beneath the earth's crust. Our reasons for believing in them should be judged on the basis of logic and evidence and should not be rejected merely because no one can think about these matters without using his mind.

3. *Does the relativity of perception prove idealism?* The fact that sense data are relative to the perceiver can scarcely be denied; but does it prove idealism? So long as we can explain *why* things appear differently to different observers, we can still maintain that there are real objective qualities.

Let us consider one of Berkeley's own examples. He pointed out that if one hand has been chilled and the other warmed, and both hands are put simultaneously into the same pan of water, the water will seem warm to one hand and cool to the other. But this is just what we should expect if the water

[5] *Cf.* Ralph Barton Perry, *Present Philosophical Tendencies* (Longmans, Green, 1929), pp. 129–132.

is *really* tepid. What the person who puts his hands in the water feels is not the temperature of the water but the temperature in his hands—and the pre-heated hand naturally has a different temperature than the prechilled hand. If the two hands remain in the water long enough, the temperature of the water will finally pervade them, and then the water will feel tepid to *both* hands. Similarly, if light and color are truly objective, an object will naturally appear to have a different color in a different light. Or if a microscope enables us to see features of an object that were before invisible, it is not surprising that we see colors and shapes that we did not see before. However variously things may *appear,* we can often distinguish between "appearances" and "realities." Whether we can do this in a sufficient number of cases to invalidate Berkeley's argument is a question worth debating.

4. *Does the inseparability of primary and secondary qualities commit us to idealism?* Suppose we grant Berkeley's contention that primary and secondary qualities are inseparable. We might therefore conclude that both are objective (*not* mind-dependent) rather than that both are subjective (mind-dependent). Some critics maintain that Berkeley's arguments fail to show that even secondary qualities are "in the mind." They believe that colors, sounds, odors, and textures (though perhaps not tastes) are no less objective than the primary qualities.

Another alternative would be the agnostic position that things-in-themselves are unknowable, and that consequently we can no more assert idealism than we can assert materialism. This is the position favored by Kant, Hume, and the positivists—all of whom admit the inseparability of primary and secondary qualities.

But it is also possible to reject Berkeley's thesis that primary and secondary qualities are inseparable. Actually, there is a very significant difference between the two sets of qualities. The secondary qualities are *sensory* properties, whereas the primary qualities are *formal* characteristics—the structures, relations, and quantities of things. This difference may justify the supposition that the primary qualities have a different epistemological status than the secondary qualities.

According to modern scientific theories of perception, the secondary qualities seem to depend upon physiological and mental factors and thus appear to be qualitative events in the perceiving organisms. Sounds seem to depend upon organic reactions to air-waves; colors upon organic reactions to electro-magnetic vibrations; etc. Our *impressions* of primary qualities are similarly dependent upon our minds, but there is a significant difference: the laws of physics are framed in terms of abstract orders and quantitative relations—primary qualities—rather than in terms of concrete secondary qualities. We therefore have scientific warrant for believing that our impressions of pri-

mary but not of secondary qualities have objective counterparts—*if* science
is dealing with a real objective world.   . . . .

Relational properties cannot exist all by themselves; they must attach to
the things related. On this point Berkeley is perfectly right. Yet it is conceivable that physical science reveals the relational structure of the real
world without revealing its content. Atoms may exist and conform to Einstein's equations even though their ultimate qualitative nature remains a
mystery.

5. *Can we test the correspondence between ideas and things?* Once we distinguish between objects as we apprehend them and objects as they really
are, how can we ever know that the former agree with the latter? Not only
Berkeley but Kant and Hegel as well maintained that the correspondence
test of truth is unworkable. We have already considered this question in
Chapter 6, but a few additional remarks may be helpful.

The impossibility of directly comparing ideas (or sense data) with things
outside experience must be admitted. But we can *infer* things that we do not
experience. No one, for example, *directly* observes another person's toothache, but he can be reasonably certain that the other person *is* suffering
toothache. Such indirect knowledge involves the interpretation of signs, and
we can often infer from signs what we cannot observe.

It is a striking fact that the signs of minds differ very markedly from the
signs of external things. When we hear a person talk, see him gesture, or read
what he has written, we are interpreting signs of a very different sort than
when we are looking at a rock. The first set of signs are clearly indicative of
a thinking person and his thoughts, whereas the second set of signs, to all
appearances, indicates something non-conscious and non-intelligent. It seems
a bit fantastic and gratuitous to attribute a *mind* to the rock, or even to the
system of nature of which the rock is a minute part. The sensible aspects of
human behavior from which we infer a human mind have little resemblance
to the sensible characteristics of nature from which Berkeley would have us
infer God. Perhaps Kant and the positivists are right—perhaps we can never
know the rock as a thing-in-itself—but such clues as we have for judging the
nature of inorganic things are quite different from the clues whereby we infer
the minds of our friends and acquaintances. Reality *appears* to be dualistic,
made up of both mental and physical qualities, and it involves a sharp break
with common sense to suppose that this appearance is quite illusory.

There are other critical questions that we might ponder. For example,
Berkeley's attack upon abstract ideas, his rejection of such abstract notions
as "substance," "matter," and "primary qualities," involves the whole question of the meaning of universals and the validity of abstract thought. The
contrast between Berkeley's pluralistic idealism and Hegel's monistic idealism suggests the great issue of monism *versus* pluralism—the question

whether reality, in its basic structure, is one or many. This issue, in turn, gives rise to the question whether relations are "internal" or "external"— whether the things being related cannot exist apart from their relations, or whether they can enter or leave these relations without prejudice to their existence and basic characteristics. The contrast between Berkeley's emphasis upon perception and Kant's emphasis upon synthetic judgment poses the complex problem of the nature of mental activity and its relation to knowledge. Berkeley, Kant, and Hegel have raised issues of profound and lasting importance. Perhaps their greatest service is to stimulate us to think rather than to give us final answers.

10

Scepticism

DAVID HUME (1711–1776)

Born in Edinburgh, Hume was the youngest son of a gentleman landowner. His father died when he was an infant, and he was reared by his mother, who, somewhat critical of his bookish tendencies, is said to have remarked that "oor Davie's a fine good-natured crater but uncommon wake-minded." Hume's studies at the University of Edinburgh instilled in him a love of literature and philosophy which kept him from settling down to a legal or business career. He decided to devote his life to scholarly pursuits, and at the age of twenty-three crossed the Channel to live in France, studying at La Fleche, where Descartes had gone to school.

There he completed, before he reached the age of twenty-five, his greatest philosophical work, the *Treatise of Human Nature.* In his brief autobiography he remarked that the book "fell dead-born from the press." Although this remark is an exaggeration, it suggests Hume's great disappointment that his ideas did not find a wider public. His *An Enquiry Concerning Human Understanding* (1748) and *An Enquiry Concerning the Principles of Morals* (1751), which restated principal parts of the *Treatise,* were somewhat more popular, but his literary reputation was based mainly upon his *Political Discourses* (1752) and his *History of England,* published in 1755 and following years. He also wrote *Dialogues Concerning Natural Religion,* which he regarded as a bit too shocking to publish during his own lifetime.

Although the income from his books gradually increased and he remained a frugal bachelor, he had to find other means of livelihood. Early in his career, he applied first to the University of Edinburgh and then to the University of Glasgow for a teaching position, but both universities rejected him because of the heterodoxy of his views. For a short time he was tutor to a lunatic, the Marquis of Annandale, and then secretary to a general, St. Clair. Thereafter he secured a six-year post as Keeper of Advocates' Library in Edinburgh, and from 1763 to 1765 served as secretary to the British Embassy in Paris. His French acquaintances included the most famous intellectuals of the period—D'Alembert, Diderot, Holbach, and Rousseau. After his sojourn in France, he spent two years in London (1767–1769) as Under Secretary of State for Scotland. In Great Britain as in France, he was a friend of distinguished wits, such as Burke, Gibbon, and Adam Smith. Having received a moderate pension, he finally retired to Edinburgh, where he lived quietly with his sister until his death in 1776.

In a self-obituary, he describes himself as follows:

> I was a man of mild disposition, of command of temper, of an open, social and cheerful humor, capable of attachment but little susceptible of enmity, and of great moderation in all my passions. Even my love of literary fame, my ruling passion, never soured my temper, notwithstanding my frequent disappointments.

This characterization appears to be entirely accurate. Hume was a canny Scot, with a kindly, humorous, equable disposition.

From *A Treatise of Human Nature* and *An Enquiry Concerning Human Understanding* *

1. [*Impressions and Ideas*]

Everyone will readily allow, that there is a considerable difference between the perceptions of the mind, when a man feels the pain of excessive heat, or the pleasure of moderate warmth, and when he afterwards recalls to his memory this sensation, or anticipates it by his imagination. These faculties may mimic or copy the perceptions of the senses; but they never can entirely reach the force and vivacity of the original sentiment. The utmost we say of them, even when they operate with greatest vigor, is, that they represent their object in so lively a manner, that we could *almost* say we feel or see it: But, except the mind be disordered by disease or madness, they never can arrive at such a pitch of vivacity, as to render these perceptions altogether undistinguishable. All the colors of poetry, however splendid, can never paint natural objects in such a manner as to make the description be taken for a real landskip. The most lively thought is still inferior to the dullest sensation.

We may observe a like distinction to run through all the other perceptions of the

* Section 1 combines excerpts from the *Treatise* and the *Enquiry;* sections 2, 4, 5, and 7 are from the *Enquiry;* sections 3 and 6 are from the *Treatise.* The *Treatise* was published in 1739; the *Enquiry* in 1748

mind. A man in a fit of anger, is actuated in a very different manner from one who only thinks of that emotion. If you tell me, that any person is in love, I easily understand your meaning, and form a just conception of his situation; but never can mistake that conception for the real disorders and agitations of the passion. When we reflect on our past sentiments and affections, our thought is a faithful mirror, and copies its objects truly; but the colors which it employs are faint and dull, in comparison of those in which our original perceptions were clothed. It requires no nice discernment or metaphysical head to mark the distinction between them.

Here therefore we may divide all the perceptions of the mind into two classes or species, which are distinguished by their different degrees of force and vivacity. The less forcible and lively are commonly denominated *Thoughts* or *Ideas.* The other species want a name in our language, and in most others; I suppose, because it was not requisite for any, but philosophical purposes, to rank them under a general term or appellation. Let us, therefore, use a little freedom, and call them *Impressions;* employing that word in a sense somewhat different from the usual. By the term *impression,* then, I mean all our more lively perceptions, when we hear, or see, or feel, or love, or hate, or desire, or will. And impressions are distinguished from ideas, which are the less lively perceptions, of which we are conscious, when we reflect on any of those sensations or movements above mentioned. . . .

Impressions may be divided into two kinds, those of *sensation,* and those of *reflection.* The first kind arises in the soul originally, from unknown causes. The second is derived, in a great measure, from our ideas, and that in the following order. An impression first strikes upon the senses, and makes us perceive heat or cold, thirst or hunger, pleasure or pain, of some kind or other. Of this impression there is a copy taken by the mind, which remains after the impression ceases; and this we call an idea. This idea of pleasure or pain, when it returns upon the soul, produces the new impressions of desire and aversion, hope and fear, which may properly be called impressions of reflection, because derived from it. These again are copied by the memory and imagination, and become ideas: which, perhaps, in their turn, give rise to other impressions and ideas; so that the impressions of reflection, are not only antecedent to their correspondent ideas, but posterior to those of sensation, and derived from them. . . .

We find, by experience, that when any impression has been present with the mind, it again makes its appearance there as an idea; and this it may do after two different ways: either when, in its new appearance, it retains a considerable degree of its first vivacity, and is somewhat intermediate betwixt an impression and an idea; or when it entirely loses that vivacity, and is a perfect idea. The faculty by which we repeat our impressions in the first manner, is called the *memory,* and the other the *imagination.* It is evident, at first sight, that the ideas of the memory are much more lively and strong than those of the imagination, and that the former faculty paints its objects in more distinct colors than any which are employed by the latter. When we remember any past event, the idea of it flows in upon the mind in a forcible manner; whereas, in the imagination, the perception is faint and languid, and cannot, without difficulty, be preserved by the mind steady and uniform for any considerable time. Here, then, is a sensible difference betwixt one species of ideas and another.

There is another difference betwixt these

two kinds of ideas, which is no less evident, namely, that though neither the ideas of the memory nor imagination, neither the lively nor faint ideas, can make their appearance in the mind, unless their correspondent impressions have gone before to prepare the way for them, yet the imagination is not restrained to the same order and form with the original impressions; while the memory is in a manner tied down in that respect, without any power of variation.

Nothing, at first view, may seem more unbounded than the thought of man, which not only escapes all human power and authority, but is not even restrained within the limits of nature and reality. To form monsters, and join incongruous shapes and appearances, costs the imagination no more trouble than to conceive the most natural and familiar objects. And while the body is confined to one planet, along which it creeps with pain and difficulty; the thought can in an instant transport us into the most distant regions of the universe; or even beyond the universe, into the unbounded chaos, where nature is supposed to lie in total confusion. What never was seen, or heard of, may yet be conceived; nor is anything beyond the power of thought, except what implies an absolute contradiction.

But though our thought seems to possess this unbounded liberty, we shall find, upon a nearer examination, that it is really confined within very narrow limits, and that all this creative power of the mind amounts to no more than the faculty of compounding, transposing, augmenting, or diminishing the materials afforded us by the senses and experience. When we think of a golden mountain, we only join two consistent ideas, *gold*, and *mountain*, with which we were formerly acquainted. A virtuous horse we can conceive; because, from our own feeling, we can conceive virtue; and this we

may unite to the figure and shape of a horse, which is an animal familiar to us. In short, all the materials of thinking are derived either from our outward or inward sentiment: the mixture and composition of these belongs alone to the mind and will. Or, to express myself in philosophical language, all our ideas or more feeble perceptions are copies of our impressions or more lively ones. . . .

Here, therefore, is a proposition, which not only seems, in itself, simple and intelligible; but, if a proper use were made of it, might render every dispute equally intelligible, and banish all that jargon, which has so long taken possession of metaphysical reasonings, and drawn disgrace upon them. All ideas, especially abstract ones, are naturally faint and obscure: the mind has but a slender hold of them: they are apt to be confounded with other resembling ideas; and when we have often employed any term, though without a distinct meaning, we are apt to imagine it has a determinate idea annexed to it. On the contrary, all impressions, that is, all sensations, either outward or inward, are strong and vivid: the limits between them are more exactly determined: nor is it easy to fall into any error or mistake with regard to them. When we entertain, therefore, any suspicion that a philosophical term is employed without any meaning or idea (as is but too frequent), we need but enquire, *from what impression is that supposed idea derived?* And if it be impossible to assign any, this will serve to confirm our suspicion. By bringing ideas into so clear a light we may reasonably hope to remove all dispute, which may arise, concerning their nature and reality.

2. [*The Forms of Reasoning*]

All the objects of human reason or enquiry may naturally be divided into two kinds, to wit, *Relations of Ideas,* and *Matters of Fact*. Of the first kind are the sciences of Geometry, Algebra, and Arithmetic; and in short, every affirmation which is either intuitively or demonstratively certain. *That the square of the hypothenuse is equal to the square of the two sides,* is a proposition which expresses a relation between these figures. *That three times five is equal to the half of thirty,* expresses a relation between these numbers. Propositions of this kind are discoverable by the mere operation of thought, without dependence on what is anywhere existent in the universe. Though there never were a circle or triangle in nature, the truths demonstrated by Euclid would for ever retain their certainty and evidence.

Matters of fact, which are the second objects of human reason, are not ascertained in the same manner; nor is our evidence of their truth, however great, of a like nature with the foregoing. The contrary of every matter of fact is still possible; because it can never imply a contradiction, and is conceived by the mind with the same facility and distinctness, as if ever so comformable to reality. *That the sun will not rise tomorrow* is no less intelligible a proposition, and implies no more contradiction than the affirmation, *that it will rise*. We should in vain, therefore, attempt to demonstrate its falsehood. Were it demonstratively false, it would imply a contradiction, and could never be distinctly conceived by the mind.

It may, therefore, be a subject worthy of curiosity, to enquire what is the nature of that evidence which assures us of any real existence and matter of fact, beyond the present testimony of our senses, or the records of our memory. This part of philosophy, it is observable, has been little cultivated; either by the ancients or moderns; and therefore our doubts and errors, in the prosecution of so important an enquiry, may be the more excusable; while we march through such difficult paths without any guide or direction. They may even prove useful, by exciting curiosity, and destroying that implicit faith and security, which is the bane of all reasoning and free enquiry. The discovery of defects in the common philosophy, if any such there be, will not, I presume, be a discouragement, but rather an incitement, as is usual, to attempt something more full and satisfactory than has yet been proposed to the public.

All reasonings concerning matter of fact seem to be founded on the relation of *Cause and Effect*. By means of that relation alone we can go beyond the evidence of our memory and senses. If you were to ask a man, why he believes any matter of fact, which is absent; for instance, that his friend is in the country, or in France; he would give you a reason; and this reason would be some other fact; as a letter received from him, or the knowledge of his former resolutions and promises. A man finding a watch or any other machine in a desert island, would conclude that there had once been men in that island. All our reasonings concerning fact are of the same nature. And here it is constantly supposed that there is a connection between the present fact and that which is inferred from it. Were there nothing to bind them together, the inference would be entirely precarious. The hearing of an articulate voice and rational discourse in the dark assures us of the presence of some person: Why? because these are the effects of the human make and fabric, and closely connected with it. If we anatomize all the other reasonings of this nature, we shall find that they are founded on the relation of cause and effect, and that this relation is either near or remote, direct or collateral. Heat and light are collateral effects of fire, and the one effect may justly be inferred from the other.

If we would satisfy ourselves, therefore, concerning the nature of that evidence, which assures us of matters of fact, we must enquire how we arrive at the knowledge of cause and effect.

I shall venture to affirm, as a general proposition, which admits of no exception, that the knowledge of this relation is not, in any instance, attained by reasonings *a priori;* but arises entirely from experience, when we find that any particular objects are constantly conjoined with each other. Let an object be presented to a man of ever so strong natural reason and abilities; if that object be entirely new to him, he will not be able, by the most accurate examination of its sensible qualities, to discover any of its causes or effects. Adam, though his rational faculties be supposed, at the very first, entirely perfect, could not have inferred from the fluidity and transparency of water that it would suffocate him, or from the light and warmth of fire that it would consume him. No object ever discovers, by the qualities which appear to the senses, either the causes which produced it, or the effects which will arise from it; nor can our reason, unassisted by experience, ever draw any inference concerning real existence and matter of fact.

This proposition, *that causes and effects are discoverable, not by reason but by experience,* will readily be admitted with regard to such objects, as we remember to have once been altogether unknown to us; since we must be conscious of the utter inability, which we then lay under, of foretelling what would arise from them. Present two smooth pieces of marble to a man who has no tincture of natural philosophy; he will never discover that they will adhere together in such a manner as to require great force to separate them in a direct line, while they make so small a resistance to a lateral pressure. Such events, as bear little analogy to the common course of nature, are also readily confessed to be known only by experience; nor does any man imagine that the explosion of gunpowder, or the attraction of a loadstone, could ever be discovered by arguments *a priori.* In like manner, when an effect is supposed to depend upon an intricate machinery or secret structure of parts, we make no difficulty in attributing all our knowledge of it to experience. Who will assert that he can give the ultimate reason, why milk or bread is proper nourishment for a man, not for a lion or a tiger? . . .

3. [*The Idea of Causation*]

We must consider the idea of *causation,* and see from what origin it is derived. It is impossible to reason justly, without understanding perfectly the idea concerning which we reason; and it is impossible perfectly to understand any idea, without tracing it up to its origin, and examining that primary impression, from which it arises. The examination of the impression bestows a clearness on the idea; and the examination of the idea bestows a like clearness on all our reasoning.

Let us therefore cast our eye on any two objects, which we call cause and effect, and turn them on all sides, in order to find that impression, which produces an idea of such prodigious consequence. At first sight I perceive, that I must not search for it in any of the particular *qualities* of the objects; since, whichever of these qualities I pitch on, I find some object that is not possessed of it, and yet falls under the denomination of cause or effect. And indeed there is nothing existent, either externally or internally, which is not to be considered either as a cause or an effect; though it is plain there is no one quality which universally belongs to all beings, and gives them a title to that denomination.

The idea then of causation must be derived from some *relation* among objects; and that relation we must now endeavor to discover. I find in the first place, that whatever objects are considered as causes or effects, are *contiguous;* and that nothing can operate in a time or place, which is ever so little removed from those of its existence. Though distant objects may sometimes seem productive of each other, they are commonly found upon examination to be linked by a chain of causes, which are contiguous among themselves, and to the distant objects; and when in any particular instance we cannot discover this connection, we still presume it to exist. We may therefore consider the relation of *contiguity* as essential to that of causation. . . .

The second relation I shall observe as essential to causes and effects, is . . . that of *priority* of time in the cause before the effect. . . .

[A third] relation betwixt cause and effect . . . is their *constant conjunction.* Contiguity and succession are not sufficient to make us pronounce any two objects to be cause and effect, unless we perceive that these two relations are preserved in several instances. . . . Thus we remember to have seen that species of object we call *flame,* and to have felt that species of sensation we call *heat.* We likewise call to mind their constant conjunction in all past instances. Without any farther ceremony, we call the one *cause* and the other *effect,* and infer the existence of the one from that of the other. . . .

There is [also] a *necessary connection* to be taken into consideration; and that relation is of much greater importance. . . .

What is our idea of necessity, when we say that two objects are necessarily connected together? Upon this head I repeat, what I have often had occasion to observe, that as we have no idea that is not derived from an impression, we must find some impression that gives rise to this idea of necessity, if we assert we have really such an idea. In order to this, I consider in what objects necessity is commonly supposed to lie; and, finding that it is always ascribed to causes and effects, I turn my eye to two objects supposed to be placed in that relation, and examine them in all the situations of which they are susceptible. I immediately perceive that they are *contiguous* in time and place, and that the object we call cause *precedes* the other we call effect. In no one instance can I go any further, nor is it possible for me to discover any third relation betwixt these objects. I therefore enlarge my view to comprehend several instances, where I find like objects always existing in like relations of contiguity and succession. At first sight this seems to serve but little to my purpose. The reflection on several instances only repeats the same objects; and therefore can never give rise to a new idea. But upon further enquiry I find, that the repetition is not in every particular the same, but produces a new impression, and by that means the idea which I at present examine. For after a frequent repetition I find, that upon the appearance of one of the objects, the mind is *determined* by custom to consider its usual attendant, and to consider it in a stronger light upon account of its relation to the first object. It is this impression, then, or *determination,* which affords me the idea of necessity. . . .

Suppose two objects to be presented to us, of which the one is the cause and the other the effect; it is plain that, from the simple consideration of one, or both these objects, we never shall perceive the tie by which they are united, or be able certainly to pronounce, that there is a connection betwixt them. It is not, therefore, from any one instance, that we arrive at the idea of cause and effect, of a necessary connection of power, of force, of energy, and of efficacy. Did we never see any but particular conjunctions of objects, entirely different from each other, we should never be able to form any such ideas [as cause and effect].

But, again, suppose we observe several instances in which the same objects are always conjoined together, we immediately conceive a connection betwixt them, and begin to draw an inference from one to another. This multiplicity of resembling instances, therefore, constitutes the very essence of power or connection, and is the source from which the idea of it arises. . . .

Though the several resembling instances, which give rise to the idea of power, have no influence on each other, and can never produce any new quality *in the object,* which can be the model of that idea, yet the *observation* of this resemblance produces a new impression *in the mind,* which is its real model. For after we have observed the resemblance in a sufficient number of instances, we immediately feel a determination of the mind to pass from one object to its usual attendant, and to conceive it in a stronger light upon account of that relation. This determination is the only effect of the resemblance; and, therefore, must be the same with power or efficacy, whose idea is derived from the resemblance. The several instances of resembling conjunctions lead us into the notion of power and necessity. These instances are in themselves totally distinct from each other, and have no union but in the mind, which observes them, and collects their ideas. Necessity, then, is the effect of this observation, and

is nothing but an internal impression of the mind, or a determination to carry our thoughts from one object to another. Without considering it in this view, we can never arrive at the most distant notion of it, or be able to attribute it either to external or internal objects, to spirit or body, to causes or effects. . . .

The idea of necessity arises from some impression. There is no impression conveyed by our senses, which can give rise to that idea. It must, therefore, be derived from some internal impression, or impression of reflection. There is no internal impression which has any relation to the present business, but that propensity, which custom produces, to pass from an object to the idea of its usual attendant. This, therefore, is the essence of necessity. Upon the whole, necessity is something that exists in the mind, not in objects; nor is it possible for us ever to form the most distant idea of it, considered as a quality in bodies. Either we have no idea of necessity, or necessity is nothing but that determination of the thought to pass from causes to effects, and from effects to causes, according to their experienced union.

Thus, as the necessity, which makes two times two equal to four, or three angles of a triangle equal to two right ones, lies only in the act of the understanding, by which we consider and compare these ideas; in like manner, the necessity of power, which unites causes and effects, lies in the determination of the mind to pass from the one to the other. The efficacy or energy of causes is neither placed in the causes themselves, nor in the Deity, nor in the concurrence of these two principles; but belongs entirely to the soul, which considers the union of two or more objects in all past instances. It is here that the real power of causes is placed, along with their connection and necessity. . . .

4. [*Will the Future Resemble the Past?*]

It must certainly be allowed, that nature has kept us at a great distance from all her secrets, and has afforded us only the knowledge of a few superficial qualities of objects; while she conceals from us those powers and principles on which the influence of those objects entirely depends. Our senses inform us of the color, weight, and consistence of bread; but neither sense nor reason can ever inform us of those qualities which fit it for the nourishment and support of a human body. Sight or feeling conveys an idea of the actual motion of bodies; but as to that wonderful force or power, which would carry on a moving body for ever in a continued change of place, and which bodies never lose but by communicating it to others; of this we cannot form the most distant conception. But notwithstanding this ignorance of natural powers and principles, we always presume, when we see like sensible qualities, that they have like secret powers, and expect that effects, similar to those which we have experienced, will follow from them. If a body of like color and consistence with that bread, which we have formerly eat, be presented to us, we make no scruple of repeating the experiment, and foresee, with certainty, like nourishment and support. Now this is a process of the mind or thought, of which I would willingly know the foundation. It is allowed on all hands that there is no known connection between the sensible qualities and the secret powers; and consequently, that the mind is not led to form such a conclusion concerning their constant and regular conjunction, by anything which it knows of their nature. As to past *Experience,* it can be allowed to give *direct* and *certain* information of those precise objects only, and that precise period of time, which fell under its cognizance: but why this experience should be extended to future times, and to other objects, which for aught we know, may be only in appearance similar; this is the main question on which I would insist. The bread, which I formerly eat, nourished me; that is, a body of such sensible qualities was, at that time, endued with such secret powers: but does it follow, that other bread must also nourish me at another time, and that like sensible qualities must always be attended with like secret powers? The consequence seems nowise necessary. At least, it must be acknowledged that there is here a consequence drawn by the mind; that there is a certain step taken; a process of thought, and an inference, which wants to be explained. These two propositions are far from being the same, *I have found that such an object has always been attended with such an effect,* and *I foresee, that other objects, which are, in appearance, similar, will be attended with similar effects.* I shall allow, if you please, that the one proposition may justly be inferred from the other: I know, in fact, that it always is inferred. But if you insist that the inference is made by a chain of reasoning, I desire you to produce that reasoning. . . .

All reasonings may be divided into two kinds, namely, demonstrative reasoning, or that concerning relations of ideas, and moral reasoning, or that concerning matter of fact and existence. That there are no demonstrative arguments in the case seems evident; since it implies no contradiction that the cause of nature may change, and that an object, seemingly like those which we have experienced, may be attended with different or contrary effects. May I not clearly and distinctly conceive that a body, falling from the clouds, and which, in all other respects, resembles snow, has yet the taste of salt or feeling of fire? Is there any more intelligible proposition than to affirm, that all the trees will flourish in December and January, and decay in May and June? Now whatever is intelligible, and can be distinctly conceived, implies no contradiction, and can never be proved false by any demonstrative argument or abstract reasoning *a priori*.

If we be, therefore, engaged by arguments to put trust in past experience, and make it the standard of our future judgment, these arguments must be probable only, or such as regard matter of fact and real existence, according to the division above mentioned. But that there is no argument of this kind, must appear, if our explication of that species of reasoning be admitted as solid and satisfactory. We have said that all arguments concerning existence are founded on the relation of cause and effect; that our knowledge of that relation is derived entirely from experience; and that all our experimental conclusions proceed upon the supposition that the future will be conformable to the past. To endeavor, therefore, the proof of this last supposition by probable arguments, or arguments regarding existence, must be evidently going in a circle, and taking that for granted, which is the very point in question. . . .

Should it be said that, from a number of uniform experiments, we *infer* a connection between the sensible qualities and the secret powers; this, I must confess, seems the same difficulty, couched in different terms. The question still recurs, on what process of argument this *inference* is founded? Where is the medium, the interposing ideas, which join propositions so very wide of each other? It is confessed that the color, consistence, and other sensible qualities of bread appear not, of themselves, to have any connection with the secret powers of nourishment and support. For otherwise we could infer these secret

powers from the first appearance of these sensible qualities, without the aid of experience; contrary to the sentiment of all philosophers, and contrary to plain matter of fact. Here, then, is our natural state of ignorance with regard to the powers and influence of all objects. How is this remedied by experience? It only shows us a number of uniform effects, resulting from certain objects, and teaches us that those particular objects, at that particular time, were endowed with such powers and forces. When a new object, endowed with similar sensible qualities, is produced, we expect similar powers and forces, and look for a like effect. From a body of like color and consistence with bread we expect like nourishment and support. But this surely is a step or progress of the mind, which wants to be explained. When a man says, *I have found, in all past instances, such sensible qualities conjoined with such secret powers:* And when he says, *Similar sensible qualities will always be conjoined with similar secret powers,* he is not guilty of a tautology, nor are these propositions in any respect the same. You say that the one proposition is an inference from the other. But you must confess that the inference is not intuitive; neither is it demonstrative: Of what nature is it, then? To say it is experimental, is begging the question. For all inferences from experience suppose, as their foundation, that the future will resemble the past, and that similar powers will be conjoined with similar sensible qualities. If there be any suspicion that the course of nature may change, and that the past may be no rule for the future, all experience becomes useless, and can give rise to no inference or conclusion. It is impossible, therefore, that any arguments from experience can prove this resemblance of the past to the future; since all these arguments are founded on the supposition of that resemblance. Let the course of things be allowed hitherto ever so regular; that alone, without some new argument or inference, proves not that, for the future, it will continue so. In vain do you pretend to have learned the nature of bodies from your past experience. Their secret nature, and consequently all their effects and influence, may change, without any change in their sensible qualities. This happens sometimes, and with regard to some objects: Why may it not happen always, and with regard to all objects? What logic, what process of argument secures you against this supposition? My practice, you say, refutes my doubts. But you mistake the purport of my question. As an agent, I am quite satisfied in the point; but as a philosopher, who has some share of curiosity, I will not say scepticism, I want to learn the foundation of this inference. No reading, no enquiry has yet been able to remove my difficulty, or give me satisfaction in a matter of such importance. Can I do better than propose the difficulty to the public, even though, perhaps, I have small hopes of obtaining a solution? We shall at least, by this means, be sensible of our ignorance, if we do not augment our knowledge.

5. [Can We Know External Objects?]

It seems evident, that men are carried, by a natural instinct or prepossession, to repose faith in their senses; and that, without any reasoning, or even almost before the use of reason, we always suppose an external universe, which depends not on our perception, but would exist, though we and every sensible creature were absent or annihilated. Even the animal creation are governed by a like opinion, and preserve this belief of external objects, in all their thoughts, designs, and actions.

It seems also evident, that, when men follow this blind and powerful instinct of nature, they always suppose the very images, presented by the senses, to be the external objects, and never entertain any suspicion, that the one are nothing but representations of the other. This very table, which we see white, and which we feel hard, is believed to exist, independent of our perception, and to be something external to our mind, which perceives it. Our presence bestows not being on it: our absence does not annihilate it. It preserves its existence uniform and entire, independent of the situation of intelligent beings, who perceive or contemplate it.

But this universal and primary opinion of all men is soon destroyed by the slightest philosophy, which teaches us, that nothing can ever be present to the mind but an image or perception, and that the senses are only the inlets, through which these images are conveyed, without being able to produce any immediate intercourse between the mind and the object. The table, which we see, seems to diminish, as we remove farther from it: but the real table, which exists independent of us, suffers no alteration: it was, therefore, nothing but its image, which was present to the mind. These are the obvious dictates of reason; and no man, who reflects, ever doubted, that the existences, which we consider, when we say, *this house* and *that tree,* are nothing but perceptions in the mind, and fleeting copies or representations of other existences, which remain uniform and independent.

So far, then, are we necessitated by reasoning to contradict or depart from the primary instincts of nature, and to embrace a new system with regard to the evidence of our senses. But here philosophy finds herself extremely embarrassed, when she would justify this new system, and obviate the cavils and objections of the sceptics. She can no longer plead the infallible and irresistible instinct of nature: for that led us to a quite different system, which is acknowledged fallible and even erroneous. And to justify this pretended philosophical system, by a chain of clear and convincing argument, or even any appearance of argument, exceeds the power of all human capacity.

By what argument can it be proved, that the perceptions of the mind must be caused by external objects, entirely different from them, though resembling them (if that be possible) and could not arise either from the energy of the mind itself, or from the suggestion of some invisible and unknown spirit, or from some other cause still more unknown to us? It is acknowledged, that, in fact, many of these perceptions arise not from anything external, as in dreams, madness, and other diseases. And nothing can be more inexplicable than the manner, in which body should so operate upon mind as ever to convey an image of itself to a substance, supposed of so different, and even contrary a nature.

It is a question of fact, whether the perceptions of the senses be produced by external objects, resembling them: how shall this question be determined? By experience surely; as all other questions of a like nature. But here experience is, and must be entirely silent. The mind has never anything present to it but the perceptions, and cannot possibly reach any experience of their connection with objects. The supposition of such a connection is, therefore, without any foundation in reasoning.

To have recourse to the veracity of the Supreme Being, in order to prove the veracity of our senses, is surely making a very unexpected circuit. If his veracity were at all concerned in this matter, our senses would be entirely infallible; because it is not possible that he can ever deceive. Not to mention, that, if the external world be once called in question, we shall be at a loss to find arguments, by which we may prove the existence of that Being or any of his attributes.

This is a topic, therefore, in which the profounder and more philosophical sceptics will always triumph, when they endeavor to introduce an universal doubt into all subjects of human knowledge and enquiry. Do you follow the instincts and propensities of nature, may they say, in assenting to the veracity of sense? But these lead you to believe that the very perception or sensible image is the external object. Do you disclaim this principle, in order to embrace a more rational opinion, that the perceptions are only representations of something external? You here depart from your natural propensities and more obvious sentiments; and yet are not able to satisfy your reason, which can never find any convincing argument from experience to prove, that the perceptions are connected with any external objects. . . .

It is universally allowed by modern enquirers, that all the sensible qualities of objects, such as hard, soft, hot, cold, white, black, &c. are merely secondary, and exist not in the objects themselves, but are perceptions of the mind, without any external archetype or model, which they represent. If this be allowed, with regard to secondary qualities, it must also follow, with regard to the supposed primary qualities of extension and solidity; nor can the latter be any more entitled to that denomination than the former. The idea of extension is entirely acquired from the senses of sight and feeling; and if all the qualities, perceived by the senses, be in the mind, not in the object, the same conclusion must reach the idea of extension, which is wholly dependent on the sensible ideas or the ideas of secondary qualities. . . .

Thus the first philosophical objection to

the evidence of sense or to the opinion of external existence consists in this, that such an opinion, if rested on natural instinct, is contrary to reason, and if referred to reason, is contrary to natural instinct, and at the same time carries no rational evidence with it, to convince an impartial enquirer. The second objection goes farther, and represents this opinion as contrary to reason: at least, if it be a principle of reason, that all sensible qualities are in the mind, not in the object. Bereave matter of all its intelligible qualities, both primary and secondary, you in a manner annihilate it, and leave only a certain unknown, inexplicable *something*, as the cause of our perceptions; a notion so imperfect, that no sceptic will think it worth while to contend against it.

6. [*The Idea of Self*]

There are some philosophers, who imagine we are every moment intimately conscious of what we call our *self;* that we feel its existence and its continuance in existence; and are certain, beyond the evidence of a demonstration, both of its perfect identity and simplicity. The strongest sensation, the most violent passion, say they, instead of distracting us from this view, only fix it the more intensely, and make us consider their influence on *self* either by their pain or pleasure. To attempt a further proof of this were to weaken its evidence; since no proof can be derived from any fact of which we are so intimately conscious; nor is there any thing, of which we can be certain, if we doubt of this.

Unluckily all these positive assertions are contrary to that very experience which is pleaded for them; nor have we any idea of *self*, after the manner it is here explained. For, from what impression could this idea be derived? This question it is impossible to answer without a manifest contradiction and absurdity; and yet it is a question which must necessarily be answered, if we would have the idea of self pass for clear and intelligible. It must be some one impression that gives rise to every real idea. But self or person is not any one impression, but that to which our several impressions and ideas are supposed to have a reference. If any impression gives rise to the idea of self, that impression must continue invariably the same, through the whole course of our lives; since self is supposed to exist after that manner. But there is no impression constant and invariable. Pain and pleasure, grief and joy, passions and sensations succeed each other, and never all exist at the same time. It cannot therefore be from any of these impressions, or from any other, that the idea of self is derived; and consequently there is no such idea.

But further, what must become of all our particular perceptions upon this hypothesis? All these are different, and distinguishable, and separable from each other, and may be separately considered, and may exist separately, and have no need of any thing to support their existence. After what manner therefore do they belong to self, and how are they connected with it? For my part, when I enter most intimately into what I call *myself*, I always stumble on some particular perception or other, of heat or cold, light or shade, love or hatred, pain or pleasure. I never can catch *myself* at any time without a perception, and never can observe any thing but the perception. When my perceptions are removed for any time, as by sound sleep, so long am I insensible of *myself*, and may truly be said not to exist. And were all my perceptions removed by death, and could I neither think, nor feel, nor see, nor love, nor hate, after the dissolution of my body, I should be entirely annihilated, nor do I conceive what is further requisite to make me a perfect nonentity. If any one, upon serious and unprejudiced reflection, thinks he has a different notion of *himself*, I must confess I can reason no longer with him. All I can allow him is, that he may be in the right as well as I, and that we are essentially different in this particular. He may, perhaps, perceive something simple and continued, which he calls *himself;* though I am certain there is no such principle in me.

But setting aside some metaphysicians of this kind, I may venture to affirm of the rest of mankind, that they are nothing but a bundle or collection of different perceptions, which succeed each other with an inconceivable rapidity, and are in a perpetual flux and movement. Our eyes cannot turn in their sockets without varying our perceptions. Our thought is still more variable than our sight; and all our other senses and faculties contribute to this change; nor is there any single power of the soul, which remains unalterably the same, perhaps for one moment. The mind is a kind of theater, where several perceptions successively make their appearance; pass, repass, glide away, and mingle in an infinite variety of postures and situations. There is properly no *simplicity* in it at one time, nor identity in different, whatever natural propension we may have to imagine that simplicity and identity. The comparison of the theater must not mislead us. They are the successive perceptions only, that constitute the mind; nor have we the most distant notion of the place where these scenes are represented, or of the materials of which it is composed.

7. [On the Proper Limits of Enquiry]

The *imagination* of man is naturally sublime, delighted with whatever is remote and extraordinary, and running, without control, into the most distant parts of space and time in order to avoid the objects, which custom has rendered too familiar to it. A correct *Judgment* observes a contrary method, and avoiding all distant and high enquiries, confines itself to common life and to such subjects as fall under daily practice and experience; leaving the more sublime topics to the embellishment of poets and orators, or to the arts of priests and politicians. . . . Those who have a propensity to philosophy, will still continue their researches; because they reflect, that, besides the immediate pleasure, attending such an occupation, philosophical decisions are nothing but the reflections of common life, methodized and corrected. But they will never be tempted to go beyond common life, so long as they consider the imperfection of those faculties which they employ, their narrow reach, and their inaccurate operations. While we cannot give a satisfactory reason, why we believe, after a thousand experiments, that a stone will fall, or fire burn; can we ever satisfy ourselves concerning any determination, which we may form, with regard to the origin of worlds, and the situation of nature, from, and to eternity?

This narrow limitation, indeed, of our enquiries, is, in every respect, so reasonable that it suffices to make the slightest examination into the natural powers of the human mind and to compare them with their objects, in order to recommend it to us. We shall then find what are the proper subjects of science and enquiry.

It seems to me, that the only objects of the abstract science or of demonstration are quantity and number, and that all attempts to extend this more perfect species of knowledge beyond these bounds are mere sophistry and illusion. As the component parts of quantity and number are entirely similar, their relations become intricate and involved; and nothing can be more curious, as well as useful, than to trace, by a variety of mediums, their equality or inequality, through their different appearances. But as all other ideas are clearly distinct and different from each other, we can never advance farther, by our utmost scrutiny, than to observe this diversity, and, by an obvious reflection, pronounce one thing not to be another. Or if there be any difficulty in these decisions, it proceeds entirely from the undeterminate meaning of words, which is corrected by juster definitions. That *the square of the hypothenuse is equal to the squares of the other two sides,* cannot be known, let the terms be ever so exactly defined, without a train of reasoning and enquiry. But to convince us of this proposition, *that where there is no property, there can be no injustice,* it is only necessary to define the terms, and explain injustice, to be a violation of property. This proposition is, indeed, nothing but a more imperfect definition. It is the same case with all those pretended syllogistical reasonings, which may be found in every other branch of learning, except the sciences of quantity and number; and these may safely, I think, be pronounced the only proper objects of knowledge and demonstration.

All other enquiries of men regard only matter of fact and existence; and these are evidently incapable of demonstration. Whatever *is* may *not be.* No negation of a fact can involve a contradiction. The non-existence of any being, without exception, is as clear and distinct an idea as its exist-

ence. The proposition, which affirms it not to be, however false, is no less conceivable and intelligible, than that which affirms it to be. The case is different with the sciences, properly so called. Every proposition, which is not true, is there confused and unintelligible. That the cube root of 64 is equal to the half of 10, is a false proposition, and can never be distinctly conceived. But that Cæsar, or the angel Gabriel, or any being never existed, may be a false proposition, but still is perfectly conceivable, and implies no contradiction.

The existence, therefore, of any being can only be proved by arguments from its cause or its effect; and these arguments are founded entirely on experience. If we reason *a priori,* anything may appear able to produce anything. The falling of a pebble may, for aught we know, extinguish the sun; or the wish of a man control the planets in their orbits. It is only experience, which teaches us the nature and bounds of cause and effect, and enables us to infer the existence of one object from that of another. . . .

When we run over libraries, persuaded of these principles, what havoc must we make? If we take in our hand any volume; of divinity or school metaphysics, for instance; let us ask, *Does it contain any abstract reasoning concerning quantity or number?* No. *Does it contain any experimental reasoning concerning matter of fact and existence?* No. Commit it then to the flames: for it can contain nothing but sophistry and illusion.

COMMENT

Impressions and Ideas

The supreme advocate of the sceptical spirit is David Hume. He is a member of the sequence of classic British empiricists, which includes such great figures as Bacon, Locke, Berkeley, and Mill. More consistent in his empiricism than his predecessors, Hume pushed the sceptical implications of this approach to its logical extreme. Many philosophers have tried to refute his arguments, but his influence continues to be immense.

A thorough empiricist, Hume traced all knowledge back to some original basis in experience. The stream of experience, he pointed out, is made up of *perceptions,* a term he employed to designate any mental content whatever. He divided perceptions into *impressions,* the original sensations or feelings, and *ideas,* the images, copies, or representations of these originals. It is important to note that Hume, unlike Locke and Berkeley, reserved the word "idea" for mental copies or representations of original data.

Impressions are (1) more forcible or vivid than ideas, and (2) prior in occurrence to ideas, being their necessary cause or source. There are two types of impressions—those of *sensation* and those of *reflection.* Impressions of sensation are the data that come from the external senses—sight, hearing, touch, taste, and smell. Impressions of reflection, such as emotions and desires, are internal to the mind and are frequently occasioned by ideas. The *idea* of death, for example, may arouse the impression of fear. The impressions of reflection are, in this sense, less original than impressions of sensation. But both types of impression may be copied by the memory and imagination; and simple ideas, which are exact copies of impressions, may be combined in many different ways to form complex ideas. Unlike simple ideas, our complex ideas need not exactly resemble impressions. We can imagine a mermaid without ever having seen one, but the *constituents* of the complex idea—in this instance, the idea of a fish and the idea of a woman—must ultimately go back to original impressions.

Hume's practice of tracing ideas back to their original impressions becomes a *logical test* of the soundness of concepts. If a concept, such as that of substance, cannot be traced back to some reliable basis in impressions, it immediately becomes suspect. A fertile source of confusion in our thinking is the tendency to impute to outer things the qualities that belong to internal impressions. Thus an internal feeling of necessity may be falsely imputed to some outer chain of events. The human mind, if it does not carefully analyze the sources of its ideas, is prone to fall into such errors. Hume's philosophy consists largely in exposing these pitfalls in our thinking.

Criticism of the Idea of Causation

The most famous example of this critical method is Hume's analysis of the idea of causation. He began by pointing out that this idea is extremely crucial in our thinking. "The only connection or relation of objects," he declared, "which can lead us beyond the immediate impressions of our memory and senses, is that of cause and effect; and that because it is the only one on which we can found a just inference from one object to another." [1] We infer external objects only because we suppose them to be the causes of the immediate data of experience. The idea of causation is thus the basis of empirical science and the ultimate ground for belief in an external world. For Hume, scientific knowledge as a whole stands or falls according to whether causation can be validated as a principle of reasoning.

Upon analysis, the idea of causation breaks up into four notions: (1) *succession,* (2) *contiguity,* (3) *constant conjunction,* and (4) *necessary connection.* Hume maintained that the first three notions can be defended—we can verify them by recalling the original sensory impressions from which they are derived. But *necessity* cannot thus be verified—try as we may, we cannot trace it back to any sensory impression. It turns out, therefore, to be a confused and illegitimate notion. Let us now consider the details of Hume's analysis:

1. *Succession.* The existence of a cause-and-effect relation, by definition, presupposes the existence of a temporal order of succession, since the cause must be immediately prior to the effect. If vigorous exercise, for example, is the cause of a good appetite, the exercise is temporally prior. But since cause and effect are in contact, the time interval between the two may be very slight.

2. *Contiguity.* The cause is contiguous in time and space with the effect. To cite a modern illustration, the blowing of a noontime whistle in Los Angeles is not a cause of workers' leaving a factory in New York, more than three thousand miles away; if a whistle blew a year ago, it is not the cause of workers' laying down their tools today. But the blowing of a whistle in the New York factory, in which the workers knock off for lunch a moment later, may truly be called a causal factor in the work-stoppage. What may appear to be causal action at a distance in time or space is really a chain of causes connecting the distant with the near object, each cause and each effect in the chain being in direct contact.

3. *Constant Conjunction.* If a certain event is the sufficient cause of a given effect, repetition of the cause will be followed by repetition of the effect. A rock thrown against a window will break the pane of glass, and other window panes will break under exactly similar impact.

Hume maintained that we actually observe succession, contiguity, and constant conjunction in cause-and-effect relations. To this extent, there is no serious difficulty in verifying the conception of cause and effect.

4. *Necessary connection.* We habitually suppose, however, that there is another factor involved in causation—namely, necessary connection. We suppose that *B,* an effect, not only follows *A,* the cause, but that it *must*

---

[1] *A Treatise of Human Nature,* ed. by L. A. Selby-Bigge (Oxford: Clarendon Press, 1896), p. 89.

follow—that there is a power, a force, an efficacy in the cause that *dictates* the effect.

Necessity can be conceived as either *logical* or *physical*. There is logical necessity when we can infer a conclusion from premises, as in mathematical computation. In arithmetic, for example, two plus one equals three. We know this to be true because any other conclusion is contradictory. We might suppose that it is similarly necessary logically that heat should make water boil. But there is an enormous difference between these two instances. We cannot imagine that two and one will not add up to three (since contradiction would be involved), but we can easily imagine that fire will not make water boil— it might conceivably make it freeze. There is nothing contradictory in such an assumption. Every event, Hume remarked, is utterly distinct and therefore separable from every other event, and evidently there is no necessary *logical* connection between events thus inherently separable.

But is there an actual *physical* connection? Do we observe a power or force in the cause that necessitates the effect? Hume answered with an emphatic *no*. Causal action cannot be observed. We observe *sequence* but not *con*sequence. The sun rises and the air becomes warm; we note the conjunction of events but we do not observe the sun's rays *causing* the warmth. So it is in general: we discover that one event mysteriously follows another event —we observe the *how* but never the *why*.

We may *think* that we have direct consciousness of necessary connection in the process of willing. For example, a person may *will* to move a huge stone and then proceed to do so. But his awareness, according to Hume, reveals nothing of the force producing the physical action. He has merely the consciousness of his intention followed by a perception of the ensuing event—he perceives a mere conjunction, not a necessary connection. Admittedly, he has a certain sense of willing and a certain sense of strain, but he observes no necessary connection between these and the events that follow. The whole *modus operandi* of mind influencing body remains profoundly mysterious.

If all that we ever observe is mere sequence, whence arises the idea of necessity? Hume's explanation is that the original basis for the idea is not an impression of sensation but an impression of reflection. We have an inward feeling, the sense of transition from one perception to another, which we wrongly impute to outer events. When we observe often and without exception that event *B* follows event *A*, a firm association of ideas becomes established in our minds: the thought of *A* irresistibly carries the mind to the thought of *B*. Hence arises a strong sense of expectation, that every *A* will be followed by a *B*, and this sense is the original impression from which is derived the idea of necessary connection. Repeated confirmation of such expectations in a great variety of instances induces the generalized belief that for every event a cause can be found. The *force* of the conviction of necessity, however, lies in the strength of expectation. We have observed so many instances of *A-then-B* that we habitually think in terms of *A-therefore-B*. But the "therefore" is merely subjective, a customary mental connection rather than a real external rod of necessity.

Sceptical Implications

Hume was quick to draw the consequences from his theory of causation. One implication is that our common-sense idea that the future will resemble the past is merely an assumption, an expectation begotten by habit, not a rational conviction. Since we never discover an objective necessity binding effect to cause, we have no reason to assume that this cause-and-effect relation must continue to hold. The sun has risen many times, but this does not mean that it will rise tomorrow. There is no "law" that the sun must rise: there is only inexplicable repetition.

Indeed, we cannot even say that it is *probable* that the sun will rise tomorrow. Probability is based upon regularity, and this is just what we have no right to assume. Every event is, so far as we can see, "loose and separate" from every other; and hence every moment we start from scratch with no logical basis for prediction. The previous regularity of nature may be just a run of luck; for all we know to the contrary, something may happen in the very next moment to upset nature's apple cart.

It may be said in reply that we *count* on the ordinary course of events. But we do not *rationally* count on it: we *bet* on it, so to speak, and we are so used to the betting that we overlook the irrational nature of the bet. Practically speaking, we have to bet on the future if we are to survive, but we must not mistake this practical necessity for a logical insight. Nature repeats the same tales again and again, but *why* she repeats them, and whether she will continue to repeat them, we cannot tell. The scientist, in this regard, has no better insight than the rest of us.

Since we have no reason to say that nature *must* be regular, we have no logical ground for excluding the possibility of miracles. Nevertheless, Hume was strongly disinclined to believe in them because of insufficient evidence. When a so-called miracle is reported, we should ask ourselves whether it is more credible to believe that the miracle actually occurred or to suppose that the report is false. The latter alternative seemed to Hume the more credible, because we can explain the *report* upon the basis of rumor, ignorance, superstition, deceit, or fallacious inference—factors of which we have common knowledge—whereas if we suppose the miracle to be true, we are flying in the face of the uniformity of all our past experience. It has often been said in criticism of Hume that he has here overstated his case. Elsewhere, at any rate, he took the view that we have no rational presumption in favor of the uniformity of nature.

We have yet to consider one of the most significant applications of Hume's analysis of causation—namely, his attack upon the arguments for an external world. Both Locke and Berkeley, whose arguments he had primarily in mind, inferred the existence of an external world on the basis of a theory of causation. They reasoned that the regular character of experience, which is largely determined for us independently of our wills, must have some external cause. Locke found the cause in material substances and primary qualities; Berkeley in God and the ideas which He imprints upon our minds. Now Hume, in attack, went to the nerve of the argument and maintained that we are not justified in employing the idea of cause in this way.

Up to a point, he agreed with Locke and Berkeley. He fully accepted their destructive arguments: the argument of Locke that secondary qualities are subjective, and the argument of Berkeley that primary qualities and material substances are not extramentally real. He agrees that external physical objects cannot be known directly—that the objects with which we are directly acquainted are merely sense-data:

> It is universally allowed by modern enquirers that all the sensible qualities of objects, such as hard, soft, hot, cold, white, black, etc., are merely secondary, and exist not in the objects themselves, but are perceptions of the mind, without any external archetype or model which they represent. If this be allowed with regard to secondary qualities, it must also follow with regard to the supposed primary qualities of extension and solidity. . . . Nothing can ever be present to the mind but an image or perception . . . ; and no man who reflects ever doubted that the existences which we consider when we say *this house* and *that tree* are nothing but perceptions in the mind. . . .[2]

We know directly only perceptions; all else is inference. But at this point Hume parted company with Locke and Berkeley. Locke and Berkeley supposed that the regular character of experience implies an external world as its cause, but Hume maintained that cause is only a kind of associational connection between items *within* experience. We often observe a relation of cause and effect between *perceptions,* but we can never observe it between perceptions and *external objects:*

> The only conclusion we can draw from the existence of one thing to that of another is by means of the relation of cause and effect, which shows that there is a connection betwixt them, and that the existence of one is dependent on that of the other. . . . But as no beings are ever present to the mind but perceptions, it follows that we may observe a conjunction or a relation of cause and

2 *An Enquiry Concerning Human Understanding,* 2nd ed., ed. by L. A. Selby-Bigge (Oxford: Clarendon Press, 1902), pp. 154, 152.

effect between different perceptions, but can never observe it between perceptions and objects. 'Tis impossible, therefore, that from the existence or any of
the qualities of the former, we can ever form any conclusion concerning the
existence of the latter. . . .[3]

What emerges from this devastating criticism? If we are resolved thus to
stay within the closed circle of experience, we can either accept our perceptions as the ultimate character of existence or say that there may be something more—*some* kind of external world—but that we cannot know what
that something more is. There is little basis here for positive belief.

A final twist to Hume's scepticism is his denial of a substantial self. Just
as Berkeley rejected Locke's doctrine of material substance, so Hume for
similar reasons rejected Berkeley's doctrine of a mental substance. He denied
that we ever have an *impression* of a self, and in the absence of any such impression, he saw no way of proving that a self exists. All the content of experience is fleeting, evanescent, whereas the self is supposed to be identical
through succeeding states. Impressions, being variable and evanescent, are
incapable of revealing a permanent self; and to *infer* an unexperienced self
as the necessary cause of our mental states is to project illegitimately the
relation of cause and effect, which is through and through experiential, beyond the circle of experience.

Moreover, why should *thoughts* imply a *thinker?* An impression or idea,
being distinct, requires nothing in which to inhere: "Since all our perceptions
are different from each other, and from everything else in the universe, they
are also distinct and separable, and may be considered as separately existent,
and may exist separately, and have no need of anything else to support their
existence." [4] Therefore, a "thinker" may simply be a certain series of
thoughts, connected with one another by causal relations. Such thoughts may
form parts of one biography, just as successive notes may be parts of one
tune. We need not suppose that a category of grammar, the first person singular, is also a category of reality. The "I," in the sense of an enduring ego, may
be only a convenient grammatical fiction.

Hume thus reduced reality, so far as it can be verified, to a stream of "perceptions" neither caused nor sustained by any mental or material substance.
Existence is made up of mental facts, perceptions, with no selves to which the
perceptions belong and no material world in which they reside.

Whence comes, then, our idea of an identical self—a spiritual substance—
or an identical thing—a material substance? Why do we suppose that there
are enduring entities behind the flux of experience? The answer, Hume believed, is that we notice relatively permanent or recurrent qualities in experience, and we try to account for them by supposing self-identical objects that

[3] *Treatise, op. cit.,* p. 212.
[4] *Ibid.,* p. 233.

persist underneath all changes and between the gaps of experience. Hence we speak of the "same" table and the "same" person, although actually there is constant change, if we would but notice it.

The preceding discussion has emphasized the sceptical aspects of Hume's philosophy. This scepticism, if accepted as a basis for living, would have an extremely paralyzing effect. Hume avoided this paralysis by falling back upon what he termed "natural instinct." We instinctively tend to believe many doctrines that we cannot *logically* justify; and, indeed, we must do so for the purposes of living. Hence common sense and science are justified in assuming that the future *will* resemble the past, and every man is justified in adopting the working faith that is necessary to live a sensible life. "Be a philosopher," Hume admonished, "but amidst all your philosophy, be still a man." [5] We must act and reason and believe, even though we cannot, by the most diligent intellectual inquiry, satisfy ourselves concerning the intellectual foundations of belief.

Despite the ultrasceptical nature of some of Hume's theoretical conclusions, he was far from being a complete sceptic. He acknowledged the reliability of mathematical knowledge, and, in practice, he accepted the natural sciences. Moreover, in his social and ethical philosophy, which we do not have space to examine here, his sceptical proclivities were held in check. Theoretically, he was a sceptic in epistemology, metaphysics, and theology, but not in mathematics, the natural sciences, the social sciences, and ethics.

Taking Stock

The debt of later philosophers to David Hume can scarcely be overestimated. Kant claimed that Hume awoke him from his "dogmatic slumbers," but Hume also had an immense effect on many other thinkers down to the present time. Positivists and logical empiricists in particular have been dancing to his tune. In general, he encouraged philosophers to make a fresh start, to critically interrogate experience instead of taking insufficiently analyzed assumptions for granted.

Yet Hume, like every other philosopher, had his limitations. Perhaps his greatest limitation was his tendency to think of every perception or event as discrete and separate. In this respect, he did not anticipate the movement of science since his day. Whether in the "field" theories of physical science, the "organismic" theories of biology, the "Gestalt" theories of psychology, or the "culture-pattern" theories of the social sciences, the tendency has been to recognize essential relations and real connections. In view of the verdict of science and the relations found in direct experience, there seems to be no supportable reason to accept Hume's vision of "a world of this and that," in which selves are no more than bundles of perceptions, things are no more than

[5] *Enquiry, op. cit.,* p. 9.

collections of qualities, and every quality and perception is "loose and separate" from every other. In this respect, the empiricism of James and Dewey, which acknowledges the connectedness of things, is keener and more perceptive than the empiricism of Hume.

If there *are* essential relations binding things together, Hume's contention that there is only a loose, associational connection between cause and effect must be regarded as inadequate. Hume, in a sense, contradicted himself, for when he maintained that the strength of our mental expectation *causes* us to believe in necessary connection, he was employing the very category of causality which he had called into question. On the basis of his view, it is very difficult to explain why nature so frequently repeats herself. Such constant conjunctions seem utterly inexplicable if there is no more than a chance connection between cause and effect, but they cease to be strange if effects are genuinely connected with or determined by their causes. Some philosophers, such as Alfred North Whitehead, have maintained that we *do* sometimes perceive real causal connections, but even if we do not, we have much reason to suppose that they exist.

We also have reason to think that the self *is* substantial. Hume considered only two alternatives: an *invariable* self and *no* self. But there is another possibility—the most plausible one—that there is a continually developing self. Hume maintained, however, that there is no introspective awareness of a self, whether changing or unchanging. This contention can be questioned, for, in a certain sense, a person *is* self-conscious, as, for example, when he has stage-fright, and it is difficult to explain *self*-consciousness if there is no self. But consider even ordinary experiences: do "perceptions" perceive and "feelings" feel without a self to feel or perceive? It would seem more plausible to admit that there is a real self, and that each person is aware, perhaps indirectly, of himself and his own attitudes.

Suppose one were to grant Hume's point that no one is really aware of himself. This lack of self-awareness might be due not to the absence of a self but to the inherent nature of the self. A camera cannot photograph itself, because its nature or function is to photograph other things. So, similarly, a self may not be able to "photograph" itself, because, by its very nature, its function is to grasp *objects*. There might still be good reasons to believe that there is a self.

No one, at any rate, is willing to *act* as if he had no substantial existence—as if he were an affair of the moment, just a passing perception or a mere loose "bundle" of passing perceptions. Every person *feels* and *acts* as if he really had a self to be selfish about. Memory involves one's own past recognized as such, and the process of remembering is often too intense, personal, and selective to explain in terms of the mere association of ideas. It would be a wise idea that would know its own impression. There are many other mental functions besides memory—*e.g.,* purpose, attention, self-criticism, friendship— that seem to involve an active self really cognizant of itself and other selves. Hume himself remarks in the Appendix to his *Treatise* that his denial of a substantial self appears unsatisfactory.

We shall not review here one of the most crucial issues involved in Hume's scepticism—whether the mind is limited in its knowledge to its own subjective states or whether it can reach out and know real external things. This issue has already been discussed in Chapter 9, "Idealism."

We have now completed our survey of scepticism, using the philosophy of Hume as the outstanding example. As the reader peruses Hume's arguments, he must be deeply impressed by their incisiveness and penetration. Whatever criticism of thoroughgoing scepticism may be made, there can be no doubt that a sceptic of genius, such as Hume, can intensely stimulate philosophical reflection and can help greatly to make us less dogmatic and more critical.

11

Theism

SAINT ANSELM (1033?–1109)

Although Italian by birth, Saint Anselm ended his career as Archbishop of Canterbury. He is famous not only for his philosophical works but also for his interpretation of Christian theology. As Abbot of a monastery in Normandy and as Archbishop in England, he was a zealous defender of the Church against the expansion of secular power.

From the *Proslogium**

. . . I do not seek to understand that I may believe, but I believe in order to understand. For this also I believe,—that unless I believed, I should not understand. And so, Lord, do thou, who dost give understanding to faith, give me, so far as thou knowest it to be profitable, to understand that thou art as we believe; and that thou art that which we believe. And, indeed, we believe that thou art a being than which nothing greater can be conceived. Or is there no such nature, since the fool hath said in his heart, there is no God? (Psalms xiv. 1). But, at any rate, this very fool, when he hears of this being of which I speak—a being than which nothing greater can be conceived—understands what he hears, and what he understands is in his understanding; although he does not understand it to exist.

For, it is one thing for an object to be in the understanding, and another to understand that the object exists. When a painter first conceives of what he will afterwards perform, he has it in his understanding, but he does not yet understand it to be, because he has not yet performed it. But after he has made the painting, he both has it in his understanding, and he understands that it exists, because he has made it.

* Trans. by Sidney Norton Deane, Open Court Publishing Co., 1903. Reprinted by permission.

Hence, even the fool is convinced that something exists in the understanding, at least, than which nothing greater can be conceived. For, when he hears of this, he understands it. And whatever is understood, exists in the understanding. And assuredly that, than which nothing greater can be conceived, cannot exist in the understanding alone. For, <u>suppose it exists in the understanding alone: then it can be conceived to exist in reality; which is greater.</u>

<u>Therefore, if that, than which nothing greater can be conceived, exists in the understanding alone, the very being, than which nothing greater can be conceived, is one, than which a greater can be conceived.</u> But obviously this is impossible. Hence, there is no doubt that there exists a being, than which nothing greater can be conceived, and it exists both in the understanding and in reality.

And it assuredly exists so truly, that it cannot be conceived not to exist. For, it is possible to conceive of a being which cannot be conceived not to exist; and this is greater than one which can be conceived not to exist. Hence, if that, than which nothing greater can be conceived, can be conceived not to exist, it is not that, than which nothing greater can be conceived. But this is an irreconcilable contradiction. There is, then, so truly a being than which nothing greater can be conceived to exist, that it cannot even be conceived not to exist; and this being thou art, O Lord, our God.

So truly, therefore, dost thou exist, O Lord, my God, that thou canst not be conceived not to exist; and rightly. For, if a mind could conceive of a being better than thee, the creature would rise above the Creator; and this is most absurd. And, indeed, whatever else there is, except thee alone, can be conceived not to exist. To thee alone, therefore, it belongs to exist more truly than all other beings, and hence in a higher degree than all others. For, whatever else exists does not exist so truly, and hence in a less degree it belongs to it to exist. Why, then, has the fool said in his heart, there is no God, since it is so evident, to a rational mind, that thou dost exist in the highest degree of all? Why, except that he is dull and a fool?

SAINT THOMAS AQUINAS (1225?–1274)

Thomas, the son of Count Landolfo, of Aquino, was born at the ancestral castle near Naples. At the age of five, he was sent to the Benedictine monastery of Monte Cassino to be educated. When ten years old, he entered the University of Naples, where he remained for six years. He then joined the Dominican Order, very much against the will of his parents and so much to the disgust of his brothers that they kidnaped and imprisoned him in the family stronghold for two years. At last he escaped and continued his education at Paris and Cologne. In 1256, he became a Master of Theology, and thereafter taught at the University of Paris and elsewhere. During his career, he succeeded in constructing the greatest of all systems of Catholic philosophy. He died at the age of forty-nine. Three years after his death he was censured by the Bishop of Paris for his alleged heterodoxy, but in 1323 he was canonized by Pope John XXII.

From *Summa Theologica* and *Summa Contra Gentiles**

1. [*The Argument for a Necessary Being*]

[*Aquinas argues from the fact of change to an Unmoved Mover; from the fact of causation to an Uncaused Cause; and from the fact of dependence to a Necessary Being. In each case the reasoning is an inference from something dependent (change, causation, or contingent being) to something independent and self-sufficient— namely, God. The wording of his argument is elusive and difficult, especially for beginning students; but the following paragraphs state the argument from contingency with comparative lucidity.—M.R.*]

We observe in our environment how things are born and die away; they may or may not exist; to be or not to be—they are open to either alternative. All things cannot be so contingent, for what is able not to be may be reckoned as once a non-being, and were everything like that once there would have been nothing at all. Now were this true, nothing would ever have begun, for what is does not begin to be except because of something which is, and so there would be nothing even now. This is clearly hollow. Therefore all things cannot be might-not-have-beens; among them must be being whose existence is necessary.

Summa Theologica, Ia. ii. 3

Everything that is a possible-to-be has a cause, since its essence as such is equally uncommitted to the alternatives of existing and not existing. If it be credited with existence, then this must be from some cause. Causality, however, is not an infinite process. Therefore a necessary being is the conclusion. The principle of its necessity is either from outside or not. If not, then the being is inwardly necessary. If necessity comes from without, we must still propose a first being necessary of itself, since we cannot have an endless series of derivatively necessary beings.

Summa Contra Gentiles, I, 15

2. [*The Argument from Purpose or Design*]

Contrary and discordant elements . . . cannot always, or nearly always, work harmoniously together unless they be directed by something providing each and all with their tendencies to a definite end. Now in the universe we see things of diverse natures conspiring together in one scheme, not rarely or haphazardly, but approximately always or for the most part. There must be something, therefore, whose providence directs the universe.

Summa Contra Gentiles, I, 13

We observe that things without consciousness, such as physical bodies, operate with a purpose, as appears from their co-operating invariably, or almost so, in the same way in order to obtain the best result. Clearly then they reach this end by intention and not by chance. Things lacking

* From St. Thomas Aquinas, *Philosophical Texts*, trans. by Thomas Gilby, Oxford University Press, London, New York, Toronto, 1951. Reprinted by permission.

knowledge move towards an end only when directed by someone who knows and understands, as an arrow by an archer. There is consequently an intelligent being who directs all natural things to their ends; and this being we call God.

Summa Theologica, Ia. ii. 3

When diverse things are co-ordinated the scheme depends on their directed unification, as the order of battle of a whole army hangs on the plan of the commander-in-chief. The arrangement of diverse things cannot be dictated by their own private and divergent natures; of themselves they are diverse and exhibit no tendency to make a pattern. It follows that the order of many among themselves is either a matter of chance or it must be resolved into one first planner who has a purpose in mind. What comes about always, or in the great majority of cases, is not the result of accident. Therefore the whole of this world has but one planner or governor.

Summa Contra Gentiles, I, 42

DAVID HUME
(For biographical note see pages 278–279.)

From *Dialogues Concerning Natural Religion*

1. [*The Argument for a First Cause*]

The argument, replied Demea, which I would insist on is the common one. Whatever exists must have a cause or reason of its existence, it being absolutely impossible for anything to produce itself or be the cause of its own existence. In mounting up, therefore, from effects to causes, we must either go on in tracing an infinite succession, without any ultimate cause at all, or must at last have recourse to some ultimate cause that is *necessarily* existent. Now that the first supposition is absurd may be thus proved. In the infinite chain or succession of causes and effects, each single effect is determined to exist by the power and efficacy of that cause which immediately preceded; but the whole eternal chain or succession, taken together, is not determined or caused by anything, and yet it is evident that it requires a cause or reason, as much as any particular object which begins to exist in time. The question is still reasonable why this particular succession of causes existed from eternity, and not any other succession or no succession at all. If there be no necessarily existent being, any supposition which can be formed is equally possible; nor is there any more absurdity in *nothing's* having existed from eternity than there is in that succession of causes which constitutes the universe. What was it, then, which determined *something* to exist rather than *nothing,* and bestowed being on a particular possibility, exclusive of the rest? *External causes,* there are supposed to be none. *Chance* is a word without a meaning. Was it *nothing?* But that can never produce anything. We must, therefore, have recourse to a necessarily existent Being who carries the *reason* of his existence in himself, and who cannot be supposed not to exist, without an express contradiction. There is, consequently, such a Being—that is, there is a Deity.

I shall not leave it to Philo, said Cleanthes, though I know that the starting objections is his chief delight, to point out the weakness of this metaphysical reasoning. It seems to me so obviously ill-grounded, and at the same time of so little consequence to the cause of true piety and religion, that I shall myself venture to show the fallacy of it.

I shall begin with observing that there is an evident absurdity in pretending to demonstrate a matter of fact, or to prove it by any arguments *a priori*. Nothing is demonstrable unless the contrary implies a contradiction. Nothing that is distinctly conceivable implies a contradiction. Whatever we conceive as existent, we can also conceive as non-existent. There is no being, therefore, whose non-existence implies a contradiction. Consequently there is no being whose existence is demonstrable. I propose this argument as entirely decisive, and am willing to rest the whole controversy upon it.

It is pretended that the Deity is a necessarily existent being; and this necessity of his existence is attempted to be explained by asserting that, if we knew his whole essence or nature, we should perceive it to be as impossible for him not to exist, as for twice two not to be four. But it is evident that this can never happen, while our faculties remain the same as at present. It will still be possible for us, at any time, to conceive the non-existence of what we formerly conceived to exist; nor can the mind ever lie under a necessity of supposing any object to remain always in being; in the same manner as we lie under a necessity of always conceiving twice two to be four. The words, therefore, *necessary existence* have no meaning or, which is the same thing, none that is consistent.

But further, why may not the material universe be the necessarily existent Being, according to this pretended explication of necessity? We dare not affirm that we know all the qualities of matter; and, for aught we can determine, it may contain some qualities which, were they known, would make its non-existence appear as great a contradiction as that twice two is five. I find only one argument employed to prove that the material world is not the necessarily existent Being; and this argument is derived from the contingency both of the matter and the form of the world. "Any particle of matter," it is said, "may be *conceived* to be annihilated, and any form may be *conceived* to be altered. Such an annihilation or alteration, therefore, is not impossible." [1] But it seems a great partiality not to perceive that the same argument extends equally to the Deity, so far as we have any conception of him, and that the mind can at least imagine him to be non-existent or his attributes to be altered. It must be some unknown, inconceivable qualities which can make his non-existence appear impossible or his attributes unalterable; and no reason can be assigned why these qualities may not belong to matter. As they are altogether unknown and inconceivable, they can never be proved incompatible with it.

Add to this that in tracing an eternal succession of objects it seems absurd to inquire for a general cause or first author. How can anything that exists from eternity have a cause, since that relation implies a priority in time and a beginning of existence?

In such a chain, too, or succession of ob-

[1] Dr. Clarke.

jects, each part is caused by that which preceded it, and causes that which succeeds it. Where then is the difficulty? But the *whole,* you say, wants a cause. I answer that the uniting of these parts into a whole, like the uniting of several distinct countries into one kingdom, or several distinct members into one body, is performed merely by an arbitrary act of the mind, and has no influence on the nature of things. Did I show you the particular causes of each individual in a collection of twenty particles of matter, I should think it very unreasonable should you afterwards ask me what was the cause of the whole twenty. This is sufficiently explained in explaining the cause of the parts.

Though the reasonings which you have urged, Cleanthes, may well excuse me, said Philo, from starting any further difficulties, yet I cannot forbear insisting still upon another topic. It is observed by arithmeticians that the products of 9 compose always either 9 or some lesser product of 9 if you add together all the characters of which any of the former products is composed. Thus, of 18, 27, 36, which are products of 9, you make 9 by adding 1 to 8, 2 to 7, 3 to 6. Thus 369 is a product also of 9; and if you add 3, 6, and 9, you make 18, a lesser product of 9. To a superficial observer so wonderful a regularity may be admired as the effect either of chance or design; but a skilful algebraist immediately concludes it to be the work of necessity, and demonstrates that it must for ever result from the nature of these numbers. Is it not probable, I ask, that the whole economy of the universe is conducted by a like necessity, though no human algebra can furnish a key which solves the difficulty? And instead of admiring the order of natural beings, may it not happen that, could we penetrate into the intimate nature of bodies, we should clearly see why it was

absolutely impossible they could ever admit of any other disposition? So dangerous is it to introduce this idea of necessity into the present question! and so naturally does it afford an inference directly opposite to the religious hypothesis!

2. [*The Argument from Design*]

Not to lose any time in circumlocutions, said Cleanthes, . . . I shall briefly explain how I conceive this matter. Look round the world, contemplate the whole and every part of it: you will find it to be nothing but one great machine, subdivided into an infinite number of lesser machines, which again admit of subdivisions to a degree beyond what human senses and faculties can trace and explain. All these various machines, and even their most minute parts, are adjusted to each other with an accuracy which ravishes into admiration all men who have ever contemplated them. The curious adapting of means to ends, throughout all nature, resembles exactly, though it much exceeds, the productions of human contrivance—of human design, thought, wisdom, and intelligence. Since therefore the effects resemble each other, we are led to infer, by all the rules of analogy, that the causes also resemble, and that the Author of nature is somewhat similar to the mind of man, though possessed of much larger faculties, proportioned to the grandeur of the work which he has executed. By this argument *a posteriori,* and by this argument alone, do we prove at once the existence of a Deity and his similarity to human mind and intelligence.

I shall be so free, Cleanthes, said Demea, as to tell you that from the beginning I could not approve of your conclusion concerning the similarity of the Deity to men, still less can I approve of the mediums by which you endeavor to establish it. What! No demonstration of the Being of God! No abstract arguments! No proofs *a priori!* Are these which have hitherto been so much insisted on by philosophers all fallacy, all sophism? Can we reach no farther in this subject than experience and probability? I will not say that this is betraying the cause of a Deity; but surely, by this affected candor, you give advantages to atheists which they never could obtain by the mere dint of argument and reasoning.

What I chiefly scruple in this subject, said Philo, is not so much that all religious arguments are by Cleanthes reduced to experience, as that they appear not to be even the most certain and irrefragable of that inferior kind. That a stone will fall, that fire will burn, that the earth has solidity, we have observed a thousand and a thousand times; and when any new instance of this nature is presented, we draw without hesitation the accustomed inference. The exact similarity of the cases gives us a perfect assurance of a similar event, and a stronger evidence is never desired nor sought after. But wherever you depart, in the least, from the similarity of the cases, you diminish proportionably the evidence, and may at last bring it to a very weak *analogy,* which is confessedly liable to error and uncertainty. After having experienced the circulation of the blood in human creatures, we make no doubt that it takes place in Titius and Maevius; but from its circulation in frogs and fishes it is only a presumption, though a strong one, from analogy that it takes place in men and other animals. The analogical reasoning is much weaker when we infer the circulation of the sap in vegetables from our experience that the blood circulates in animals; and those who hastily followed that imperfect analogy are found, by more accurate experiments, to have been mistaken.

If we see a house, Cleanthes, we conclude, with the greatest certainty, that it had an architect or builder because this is precisely that species of effect which we have experienced to proceed from that species of cause. But surely you will not affirm that the universe bears such a resemblance to a house that we can with the same certainty infer a similar cause, or that the analogy is here entire and perfect. The dissimilitude is so striking that the utmost you can here pretend to is a guess, a conjecture, a presumption concerning a similar cause; and how that pretension will be received in the world, I leave you to consider. . . .

That all inferences, Cleanthes, concerning fact are founded on experience, and that all experimental reasonings are founded on the supposition that similar causes prove similar effects, and similar effects similar causes, I shall not at present much dispute with you. But observe, I entreat you, with what extreme caution all just reasoners proceed in the transferring of experiments to similar cases. Unless the cases be exactly similar, they repose no perfect confidence in applying their past observation to any particular phenomenon. Every alteration of circumstances occasions a doubt concerning the event; and it requires new experiments to prove certainly that the new circumstances are of no moment or importance. A change in bulk, situation, arrangement, age, disposition of the air, or surrounding bodies—any of these particulars may be attended with the most unexpected consequences. And unless the objects be quite familiar to us, it is the highest temerity to expect with assurance, after any of these changes, an event similar to that which before fell under our observation. The slow and deliberate steps of philosophers here, if anywhere, are distinguished from the precipitate march of the vulgar, who, hurried on by the smallest similitude, are incapable of all discernment or consideration.

But can you think, Cleanthes, that your usual phlegm and philosophy have been preserved in so wide a step as you have taken when you compared to the universe houses, ships, furniture, machines, and, from their similarity in some circumstances, inferred a similarity in their causes? Thought, design, intelligence, such as we discover in men and other animals, is no more than one of the springs and principles of the universe, as well as heat or cold, attraction or repulsion, and a hundred others which fall under daily observation. It is an active cause by which some particular parts of nature, we find, produce alterations on other parts. But can a conclusion, with any propriety, be transferred from parts to the whole? Does not the great disproportion bar all comparison and inference? From observing the growth of a hair, can we learn anything concerning the generation of a man? Would the manner of a leaf's blowing, even though perfectly known, afford us any instruction concerning the vegetation of a tree?

But allowing that we were to take the *operations* of one part of nature upon another for the foundation of our judgment concerning the *origin* of the whole (which never can be admitted), yet why select so minute, so weak, so bounded a principle as the reason and design of animals is found to be upon this planet? What peculiar privilege has this little agitation of the brain which we call *thought,* that we must thus make it the model of the whole universe? Our partiality in our own favor does indeed present it on all occasions, but sound philosophy ought carefully to guard against so natural an illusion.

So far from admitting, continued Philo, that the operations of a part can afford us any just conclusion concerning the origin of the whole, I will not allow any one part to form a rule for another part if the latter be very remote from the former. Is there any reasonable ground to conclude that the inhabitants of other planets possess thought, intelligence, reason, or anything similar to these faculties in men? When nature has so extremely diversified her manner of operation in this small globe, can we imagine that she incessantly copies herself throughout so immense a universe? And if thought, as we may well suppose, be confined merely to this narrow corner and has even there so limited a sphere of action, with what propriety can we assign it for the original cause of all things? The narrow views of a peasant who makes his domestic economy the rule for the government of kingdoms is in comparison a pardonable sophism.

But were we ever so much assured that a thought and reason resembling the human were to be found throughout the whole universe, and were its activity elsewhere vastly greater and more commanding than it appears in this globe, yet I cannot see why the operations of a world constituted, arranged, adjusted, can with any propriety be extended to a world which is in its embryo state, and is advancing towards that constitution and arrangement. By observation we know somewhat of the economy, action, and nourishment of a finished animal, but we must transfer with great caution that observation to the growth of a fœtus in the womb, and still more to the formation of an animalcule in the loins of its male parent. Nature, we find, even from our limited experience, possesses an infinite number of springs and principles which incessantly discover themselves on every change of her position and situation. And what new and unknown principles would actuate her in so new and unknown a situation as that of the formation of a universe, we cannot, without the utmost temerity, pretend to determine.

A very small part of this great system, during a very short time, is very imperfectly discovered to us; and do we thence pronounce decisively concerning the origin of the whole?

Admirable conclusion! Stone, wood, brick, iron, brass, have not, at this time, in this minute globe of earth, an order or arrangement without human art and contrivance; therefore, the universe could not originally attain its order and arrangement without something similar to human art. But is a part of nature a rule for another part very wide of the former? Is it a rule for the whole? Is a very small part a rule for the universe? Is nature in one situation a certain rule for nature in another situation vastly different from the former?

And can you blame me, Cleanthes, if I here imitate the prudent reserve of Simonides, who, according to the noted story, being asked by Hiero, *What God was?* desired a day to think of it, and then two days more; and after that manner continually prolonged the term, without ever bringing in his definition or description? Could you even blame me if I had answered, at first, *that I did not know,* and was sensible that this subject lay vastly beyond the reach of my faculties? You might cry out sceptic and rallier, as much as you pleased; but, having found in so many other subjects much more familiar the imperfections and even contradictions of human reason, I never should expect any success from its feeble conjectures in a subject so sublime and so remote from the sphere of our observation. When two *species* of objects have always been observed to be conjoined together, I can *infer,* by custom, the existence of one wherever I *see* the existence of the other; and this I call an argument from experience. But how this argument can have place where the objects, as in the present case, are single, individual, without parallel or specific resemblance, may be difficult to explain. And will any man tell me with a serious countenance that an orderly universe must arise from some thought and art like the human because we have experience of it? To ascertain this reasoning it were requisite that we had experience of the origin of worlds; and it is not sufficient, surely, that we have seen ships and cities arise from human art and contrivance. . . .

. . . I shall endeavor to show you, a little more distinctly, the inconveniences of that anthropomorphism which you have embraced, and shall prove that there is no ground to suppose a plan of the world to be formed in the Divine mind, consisting of distinct ideas, differently arranged, in the same manner as an architect forms in his head the plan of a house which he intends to execute.

It is not easy, I own, to see what is gained by this supposition, whether we judge of the matter by *reason* or by *experience.* We are still obliged to mount higher in order to find the cause of this cause which you had assigned as satisfactory and conclusive.

If *reason* (I mean abstract reason derived from inquiries *a priori*) be not alike mute with regard to all questions concerning cause and effect, this sentence at least it will venture to pronounce: that a mental world or universe of ideas requires a cause as much as does a material world or universe of objects, and, if similar in its arrangement, must require a similar cause. For what is there in this subject which should occasion a different conclusion or inference? In an abstract view, they are entirely alike; and no difficulty attends the one supposition which is not common to both of them.

Again, when we will needs force *experience* to pronounce some sentence, even on these subjects which lie beyond her sphere, neither can she perceive any material difference in this particular between these two kinds of worlds, but finds them to be governed by similar principles, and to depend upon an equal variety of causes in their operations. We have specimens in miniature of both of them. Our own mind resembles the one; a vegetable or animal body the other. Let experience, therefore, judge from these samples. Nothing seems more delicate, with regard to its causes, than thought; and as these causes never operate in two persons after the same manner, so we never find two persons who think exactly alike. Nor indeed does the same person think exactly alike at any two different periods of time. A difference of age, of the disposition of his body, of weather, of food, of company, of books, of passions —any of these particulars, or others more minute, are sufficient to alter the curious machinery of thought and communicate to it very different movements and operations. As far as we can judge, vegetables and animal bodies are not more delicate in their motions, nor depend upon a greater variety or more curious adjustment of springs and principles.

How, therefore, shall we satisfy ourselves concerning the cause of that Being whom you suppose the Author of nature, or, according to your system of anthropomorphism, the ideal world into which you trace the material? Have we not the same reason to trace that ideal world into another ideal world or new intelligent principle? But if we stop and go no farther, why go so far? why not stop at the material world? How can we satisfy ourselves without going on *in infinitum?* And, after all, what satisfaction is there in that infinite progression? Let us remember the story of the Indian philosopher and his elephant. It was never more applicable than to the present subject. If the material world rests upon a similar ideal world, this ideal world must rest upon some other, and so on without end. It were better, therefore, never to look beyond the present material world. By supposing it to contain the principle of its order within itself, we really assert it to be God; and the sooner we arrive at that Divine Being, so much the better. When you go one step beyond the mundane system, you only excite an inquisitive humor which it is impossible ever to satisfy.

To say that the different ideas which compose the reason of the Supreme Being fall into order of themselves and by their own nature is really to talk without any precise meaning. If it has a meaning, I would fain know why it is not as good sense to say that the parts of the material world fall into order of themselves and by their own nature. Can the one opinion be intelligible, while the other is not so?

We have, indeed, experience of ideas which fall into order of themselves and without any *known* cause. But, I am sure, we have a much larger experience of matter which does the same, as in all instances of generation and vegetation where the accurate analysis of the cause exceeds all human comprehension. We have also experience of particular systems of thought and of matter which have no order; of the first in madness, of the second in corruption. Why, then, should we think that order is more essential to one than the other? And if it requires a cause in both, what do we gain by your system, in tracing the universe of objects into a similar universe of ideas? The first step which we make leads us on for ever. It were, therefore, wise in us to limit all our inquiries to the present world, without looking farther. No satisfaction can ever be attained by these speculations which so far exceed the narrow bounds of human understanding. . . .

But to show you still more inconveniences, continued Philo, in your anthropomorphism, please to take a new survey of your principles. *Like effects prove like causes.* This is the experimental argument; and this, you say too, is the sole theological argument. . . .

Now, Cleanthes, said Philo, with an air of alacrity and triumph, mark the consequences. *First,* by this method of reasoning you renounce all claim to infinity in any of the attributes of the Deity. For, as the cause ought only to be proportioned to the effect, and the effect, so far as it falls under our cognizance, is not infinite, what pretensions have we, upon your suppositions, to ascribe that attribute to the Divine Being? You will still insist that, by removing him so much from all similarity to human creatures, we give in to the most arbitrary hypothesis, and at the same time weaken all proofs of his existence.

Secondly, you have no reason, on your theory, for ascribing perfection to the Deity, even in his finite capacity, or for supposing him free from every error, mistake, or incoherence, in his undertakings. There are many inexplicable difficulties in the works of nature which, if we allow a perfect author to be proved *a priori,* are easily solved, and become only seeming difficulties from the narrow capacity of man, who cannot trace infinite relations. But according to your method of reasoning, these difficulties become all real, and, perhaps, will be insisted on as new instances of likeness to human art and contrivance. At least, you must acknowledge that it is impossible for us to tell, from our limited views, whether this system contains any great faults or deserves any considerable praise if compared to other possible and even real systems. Could a peasant, if the *Æneid* were read to him, pronounce that poem to be absolutely faultless, or even assign to it its proper rank among the productions of human wit, he who had never seen any other production?

But were this world ever so perfect a production, it must still remain uncertain whether all the excellences of the work can justly be ascribed to the workman. If we survey a ship, what an exalted idea must we form of the ingenuity of the carpenter who framed so complicated, useful, and beautiful a machine? And what surprise must we feel when we find him a stupid mechanic who imitated others, and copied an art which, through a long succession of ages, after multiplied trials, mistakes, corrections, deliberations, and controversies, had been gradually improving? Many worlds might have been botched and bungled, throughout an eternity, ere this system was struck out; much labor lost, many fruitless trials made, and a slow but continued improvement carried on during infinite ages in the art of world-making. In such subjects, who can determine where the truth, nay, who can conjecture where the probability lies, amidst a great number of hypotheses which may be proposed, and a still greater which may be imagined?

And what shadow of an argument, continued Philo, can you produce from your hypothesis to prove the unity of the Deity? A great number of men join in building a house or ship, in rearing a city, in framing a commonwealth; why may not several deities combine in contriving and framing a world? This is only so much greater similarity to human affairs. By sharing the work among several, we may so much further limit the attributes of each, and get rid of that extensive power and knowledge which must be supposed in one deity, and which, according to you, can only serve to weaken the proof of his existence. And if such foolish, such vicious creatures as man can yet often unite in framing and executing one plan, how much more those deities or demons, whom we may suppose several degrees more perfect! . . . .

It must be a slight fabric, indeed, said Demea, which can be erected on so tottering a foundation. While we are uncertain whether there is one deity or many, whether the deity or deities, to whom we owe our existence, be perfect or imperfect, subordinate or supreme, dead or alive, what trust or confidence can we repose in them? What devotion or worship address to them? What veneration or obedience pay them? To all the purposes of life the theory of religion becomes altogether useless; and even with regard to speculative consequences its uncertainty, according to you, must render it totally precarious and unsatisfactory.

To render it still more unsatisfactory, said Philo, there occurs to me another hypothesis which must acquire an air of probability from the method of reasoning so much insisted on by Cleanthes. That like effects arise from like causes—this principle he supposes the foundation of all religion. But there is another principle of the same kind, no less certain and derived from the same source of experience, that, where several known circumstances are observed to be similar, the unknown will also be found similar. Thus, if we see the limbs of a human body, we conclude that it is also attended with a human head, though hid from us. Thus, if we see, through a chink in a wall, a small part of the sun, we conclude that were the wall removed we should see the whole body. In short, this method of reasoning is so obvious and familiar that no scruple can ever be made with regard to its solidity.

Now, if we survey the universe, so far as it falls under our knowledge, it bears a great resemblance to an animal or organized body, and seems actuated with a like principle of life and motion. A continual circulation of matter in it produces no disorder; a continual waste in every part is incessantly repaired; the closest sympathy is perceived throughout the entire system; and each part or member, in performing its proper offices, operates both to its own preservation and to that of the whole. The world, therefore, I infer, is an animal; and the Deity is the *soul* of the world, actuating it, and actuated by it.

You have too much learning, Cleanthes, to be at all surprised at this opinion which, you know, was maintained by almost all the theists of antiquity, and chiefly prevails in their discourses and reasonings. For though, sometimes, the ancient philosophers reason from final causes, as if they thought the world the workmanship of God, yet it appears rather their favorite notion to consider it as his body whose organization renders it subservient to him. And it must be confessed that, as the universe resembles more a human body than it does the works of human art and contrivance, if our limited analogy could ever, with any propriety, be extended to the whole of nature, the inference seems juster in favor of the ancient than the modern theory.

There are many other advantages, too, in the former theory which recommended it to the ancient theologians. Nothing more repugnant to all their notions because nothing more repugnant to common experience than mind without body, a mere spiritual substance which fell not under their senses nor comprehension, and of which they had not observed one single instance throughout all nature. Mind and body they knew because they felt both; an order, arrangement, organization, or internal machinery, in both they likewise knew, after the same manner; and it could not but seem reasonable to transfer this experience to the universe, and to suppose the divine mind and body to be also coeval and to have, both of them, order and arrangement naturally inherent in them and inseparable from them.

Here, therefore, is a new species of anthropomorphism, Cleanthes, on which you may deliberate, and a theory which seems not liable to any considerable difficulties. You are too much superior, surely, to systematical prejudices to find any more difficulty in supposing an animal body to be, originally, of itself or from unknown causes, possessed of order and organization, than in supposing a similar order to belong to mind. But the vulgar prejudice that body and mind ought always to accompany each other ought not, one should think, to be entirely neglected; since it is founded on vulgar experience, the only guide which you profess to follow in all these theological inquiries. And if you assert that our limited experience is an unequal standard by which to judge of the unlimited extent of nature, you entirely abandon your own hypothesis, and must thenceforward adopt our mysticism, as you call it, and admit of the absolute incomprehensibility of the Divine Nature.

This theory, I own, replied Cleanthes, has never before occurred to me, though a pretty natural one; and I cannot readily, upon so short an examination and reflection, deliver any opinion with regard to it. You are very scrupulous, indeed, said Philo, were I to examine any system of yours, I should not have acted with half that caution and reserve, in stating objections and difficulties to it. However, if anything occur to you, you will oblige us by proposing it.

Why then, replied Cleanthes, it seems to me that, though the world does, in many circumstances, resemble an animal body, yet is the analogy also defective in many circumstances the most material: no organs of sense; no seat of thought or reason; no one precise origin of motion and action. In short, it seems to bear a stronger resemblance to a vegetable than to an animal, and your inference would be so far inconclusive in favor of the soul of the world. . . .

But here, continued Philo, in examining the ancient system of the soul of the world there strikes me, all on a sudden, a new idea which, if just, must go near to subvert all your reasoning, and destroy even your first inferences on which you repose such confidence. If the universe bears a greater likeness to animal bodies and to vegetables than to the works of human art, it is more probable that its cause resembles the cause of the former than that of the latter, and its origin ought rather to be ascribed to generation or vegetation than to reason or design. Your conclusion, even according to your own principles, is therefore lame and defective.

Pray open up this argument a little further, said Demea, for I do not rightly apprehend it in that concise manner in which you have expressed it.

Our friend Cleanthes, replied Philo, as you have heard, asserts that, since no question of fact can be proved otherwise than by experience, the existence of a Deity admits not of proof from any other medium. The world, says he, resembles the works of human contrivance; therefore its cause must also resemble that of the other. Here we may remark that the operation of one very small part of nature, to wit, man, upon another very small part, to wit, that inanimate matter lying within his reach, is the rule by which Cleanthes judges of the origin of the whole; and he measures objects, so widely disproportioned, by the same individual standard. But to waive all objections drawn from this topic, I affirm that there are other parts of the universe (besides the machines of human invention) which bear still a greater resemblance to the fabric of the world, and which, therefore, afford a better conjecture concerning the universal origin of this system. These parts are animals and vegetables. The world plainly resembles more an animal or a vegetable than it does a watch or a knitting-loom. Its cause, therefore, it is more probable, resembles the cause of the former. The cause of the former is generation or vegetation. The cause, therefore, of the world we may infer to be something similar or analogous to generation or vegetation.

. . . In this little corner of the world alone, there are four principles, *reason, instinct, generation, vegetation,* which are similar to each other, and are the causes of similar effects. What a number of other principles may we naturally suppose in the immense extent and variety of the universe could we travel from planet to planet, and from system to system, in order to examine each part of this mighty fabric? Any one of these four principles above mentioned (and a hundred others which lie open to our conjecture) may afford us a theory by which to judge of the origin of the world; and it is a palpable and egregious partiality to confine our view entirely to that principle by which our own minds operate. Were this principle more intelligible on that account, such a partiality might be somewhat excusable; but reason, in its internal fabric and structure, is really as little known to us as instinct or vegetation; and perhaps, even that vague, undeterminate word *nature* to which the vulgar refer everything is not at the bottom more inexplicable. The effects of these principles are all known to us from experience; but the principles themselves and their manner of operation are totally unknown; nor is it less intelligible or less conformable to experience to say that the world arose by vegetation, from a seed shed by another world, than to say that it arose from a divine reason or contrivance, according to the sense in which Cleanthes understands it.

But methinks, said Demea, if the world had a vegetative quality and could sow the seeds of new worlds into the infinite chaos, this power would be still an additional argument for design in its author. For whence could arise so wonderful a faculty but from design? Or how can order spring from anything which perceives not that order which it bestows?

You need only look around you, replied Philo, to satisfy yourself with regard to this question. A tree bestows order and organization on that tree which springs from it, without knowing the order; an animal in the same manner on its offspring; a bird on its nest; and instances of this kind are even more frequent in the world than those of order which arise from reason and contrivance. To say that all this order in animals and vegetables proceeds ultimately from design is begging the question; nor can that great point be ascertained otherwise than by proving, *a priori,* both that order is, from its nature, inseparably attached to thought and that it can never of itself or from original unknown principles belong to matter. . . .

I must confess, Philo, replied Cleanthes, that, of all men living, the task which you have undertaken, of raising doubts and objections, suits you best and seems, in a manner, natural and unavoidable to you So great is your fertility of invention that I am not ashamed to acknowledge myself unable, on a sudden, to solve regularly such out-of-the-way difficulties as you incessantly start upon me, though I clearly see, in general, their fallacy and error. And I question not, but you are yourself, at present, in the same case, and have not the solution so ready as the objection, while you must be sensible that common sense and reason are entirely against you, and that such whimsies as you have delivered may puzzle but never can convince us.

What you ascribe to the fertility of my invention, replied Philo, is entirely owing to the nature of the subject. In subjects adapted to the narrow compass of human reason there is commonly but one determination which carries probability or conviction with it; and to a man of sound judgment all other suppositions but that one appear entirely absurd and chimerical. But in such questions as the present, a hundred contradictory views may preserve a kind of imperfect analogy, and invention has here full scope to exert itself. Without any great effort of thought, I believe that I could, in an instant, propose other systems of cosmogony which would have some faint appearance of truth, though it is a thousand, a million to one if either yours or any one of mine be the true system.

For instance, what if I should revive the old Epicurean hypothesis? This is commonly, and I believe justly, esteemed the most absurd system that has yet been proposed; yet I know not whether, with a few alterations, it might not be brought to bear a faint appearance of probability. Instead of supposing matter infinite, as Epicurus did, let us suppose it finite. A finite number of particles is only susceptible of finite transpositions; and it must happen, in an eternal duration, that every possible order or position must be tried an infinite number of times. This world, therefore, with all its events, even the most minute, has before been produced and destroyed, and will again be produced and destroyed, without any bounds and limitations. No one who

has a conception of the powers of infinite, in comparison of finite, will ever scruple this determination.

But this supposes, said Demea, that matter can acquire motion without any voluntary agent or first mover.

And where is the difficulty, replied Philo, of that supposition? Every event, before experience, is equally difficult and incomprehensible; and every event, after experience, is equally easy and intelligible. Motion, in many instances, from gravity, from elasticity, from electricity, begins in matter, without any known voluntary agent; and to suppose always, in these cases, an unknown voluntary agent is mere hypothesis and hypothesis attended with no advantages. The beginning of motion in matter itself is as conceivable *a priori* as its communication from mind and intelligence.

Besides, why may not motion have been propagated by impulse through all eternity, and the same stock of it, or nearly the same, be still upheld in the universe? As much is lost by the composition of motion, as much is gained by its resolution. And whatever the causes are, the fact is certain that matter is and always has been in continual agitation, as far as human experience or tradition reaches. There is not probably, at present, in the whole universe, one particle of matter at absolute rest.

And this very consideration, too, continued Philo, which we have stumbled on in the course of the argument suggests a new hypothesis of cosmogony that is not absolutely absurd and improbable. Is there a system, an order, an economy of things, by which matter can preserve that perpetual agitation which seems essential to it, and yet maintain a constancy in the forms which it produces? There certainly is such an economy, for this is actually the case with the present world. The continual motion of matter, therefore, in less than infinite transpositions, must produce this economy or order, and, by its very nature, that order, when once established, supports itself for many ages if not to eternity. But wherever matter is so poised, arranged, and adjusted, as to continue in perpetual motion, and yet preserve a constancy in the forms, its situation must, of necessity, have all the same appearance of art and contrivance which we observe at present. All the parts of each form must have a relation to each other and to the whole; and the whole itself must have a relation to the other parts of the universe, to the element in which the form subsists, to the materials with which it repairs its waste and decay, and to every other form which is hostile or friendly. A defect in any of these particulars destroys the form, and the matter of which it is composed is again set loose, and is thrown into irregular motions and fermentations till it unite itself to some other regular form. If no such form be prepared to receive it, and if there be a great quantity of this corrupted matter in the universe, the universe itself is entirely disordered, whether it be the feeble embryo of a world in its first beginnings that is thus destroyed or the rotten carcase of one languishing in old age and infirmity. In either case, a chaos ensues till finite though innumerable revolutions produce, at last, some forms whose parts and organs are so adjusted as to support the forms amidst a continued succession of matter.

Suppose (for we shall endeavor to vary the expression) that matter were thrown into any position by a blind, unguided force; it is evident that this first position must, in all probability, be the most confused and most disorderly imaginable, without any resemblance to those works of human contrivance which, along with a symmetry of parts, discover an adjustment of means to ends and a tendency to self-preservation. If the actuating force cease after this operation, matter must remain for ever in disorder and continue an immense chaos, without any proportion or activity. But suppose that the actuating force, whatever it be, still continues in matter, this first position will immediately give place to a second which will likewise, in all probability, be as disorderly as the first, and so on through many successions of changes and revolutions. No particular order or position ever continues a moment unaltered. The original force, still remaining in activity, gives a perpetual restlessness to matter. Every possible situation is produced, and instantly destroyed. If a glimpse or dawn of order appears for a moment, it is instantly hurried away and confounded by that never-ceasing force which actuates every part of matter.

Thus the universe goes on for many ages in a continued succession of chaos and disorder. But is it not possible that it may settle at last, so as not to lose its motion and active force (for that we have supposed inherent in it), yet so as to preserve an uniformity of appearance, amidst the continual motion and fluctuation of its parts? This we find to be the case with the universe at present. Every individual is perpetually changing, and every part of every individual; and yet the whole remains, in appearance, the same. May we not hope for such a position or rather be assured of it from the eternal revolutions of unguided matter; and may not this account for all the appearing wisdom and contrivance which is in the universe? Let us contemplate the subject a little, and we shall find that this adjustment if attained by matter of a seeming stability in the forms, with a real and perpetual revolution or motion of parts, affords a plausible, if not a true, solution of the difficulty.

It is in vain, therefore, to insist upon the

uses of the parts in animals or vegetables, and their curious adjustment to each other. I would fain know how an animal could subsist unless its parts were so adjusted? Do we not find that it immediately perishes whenever this adjustment ceases, and that its matter, corrupting, tries some new form? It happens indeed that the parts of the world are so well adjusted that some regular form immediately lays claim to this corrupted matter; and if it were not so, could the world subsist? Must it not dissolve, as well as the animal, and pass through new positions and situations till in great but finite succession it fall, at last, into the present or some such order?

It is well, replied Cleanthes, you told us that this hypothesis was suggested on a sudden, in the course of the argument. Had you had leisure to examine it, you would soon have perceived the insuperable objections to which it is exposed. No form, you say, can subsist unless it possess those powers and organs requisite for its subsistence; some new order or economy must be tried, and so on, without intermission, till at last some order which can support and maintain itself is fallen upon. But according to this hypothesis, whence arise the many conveniences and advantages which men and all animals possess? Two eyes, two ears are not absolutely necessary for the subsistence of the species. Human race might have been propagated and preserved without horses, dogs, cows, sheep, and those innumerable fruits and products which serve to our satisfaction and enjoyment. If no camels had been created for the use of man in the sandy deserts of Africa and Arabia, would the world have been dissolved? If no loadstone had been framed to give that wonderful and useful direction to the needle, would human society and the human kind have been immediately extinguished? Though the maxims of nature be in general very frugal, yet instances of this kind are far from being rare; and any one of them is a sufficient proof of design—and of a benevolent design—which gave rise to the order and arrangement of the universe.

At least, you may safely infer, said Philo, that the foregoing hypothesis is so far incomplete and imperfect, which I shall not scruple to allow. But can we ever reasonably expect greater success in any attempts of this nature? Or can we ever hope to erect a system of cosmogony that will be liable to no exceptions, and will contain no circumstance repugnant to our limited and imperfect experience of the analogy of nature? Your theory itself cannot surely pretend to any such advantage, even though you have run into *anthropomorphism*, the better to preserve a conformity to common experience. Let us once more put it to trial. In all instances which we have ever seen, ideas are copied from real objects, and are ectypal, not archetypal, to express myself in learned terms. You reverse this order and give thought the precedence. In all instances which we have ever seen, thought has no influence upon matter except where that matter is so conjoined with it as to have an equal reciprocal influence upon it. No animal can move immediately anything but the members of its own body; and, indeed, the equality of action and reaction seems to be an universal law of nature; but your theory implies a contradiction to this experience. These instances, with many more which it were easy to collect (particularly the supposition of a mind or system of thought that is eternal or, in other words, an animal ingenerable and immortal)—these instances, I say, may teach all of us sobriety in condemning each other, and let us see that as no system of this kind ought ever to be received from a slight analogy, so neither ought any to be rejected on account of a small incongruity. For that is an inconvenience from which we can justly pronounce no one to be exempted.

All religious systems, it is confessed, are subject to great and insuperable difficulties. Each disputant triumphs in his turn, while he carries on an offensive war, and exposes the absurdities, barbarities, and pernicious tenets of his antagonist. But all of them, on the whole, prepare a complete triumph for the *sceptic,* who tells them that no system ought ever to be embraced with regard to such subjects: for this plain reason that no absurdity ought ever to be assented to with regard to any subject. A total suspense of judgment is here our only reasonable resource. And if every attack, as is commonly observed, and no defense among theologians is successful, how complete must be *his* victory who remains always, with all mankind, on the offensive, and has himself no fixed station or abiding city which he is ever, on any occasion, obliged to defend?

WILLIAM JAMES
(For biographical note see pages 126–127.)

The Will to Believe*

In the recently published Life by Leslie Stephen of his brother, Fitz-James, there is an account of a school to which the latter went when he was a boy. The teacher, a certain Mr. Guest, used to converse with his pupils in this wise: "Gurney, what is the difference between justification and sanctification?—Stephen, prove the omnipotence of God!" etc. In the midst of our Harvard freethinking and indifference we are prone to imagine that here at your good old orthodox College conversation continues to be somewhat upon this order; and to show you that we at Harvard have not lost all interest in these vital subjects, I have brought with me tonight something like a sermon on justification by faith to read to you—I mean an essay in justification *of* faith, a defense of our right to adopt a believing attitude in religious matters, in spite of the fact that our merely logical intellect may not have been coerced. "The Will to Believe," accordingly, is the title of my paper.

I have long defended to my own students the lawfulness of voluntarily adopted faith; but as soon as they have got well imbued with the logical spirit, they have as a rule refused to admit my contention to be lawful philosophically, even though in point of fact they were personally all the time chock-full of some faith or other themselves. I am all the while, however, so profoundly convinced that my own position is correct, that your invitation has seemed to me a good occasion to make my statements more clear. Perhaps your minds will be more open than those with which I have hitherto had to deal. I will be as little technical as I can, though I must begin by

* An Address to the Philosophical Clubs of Yale and Brown Universities. Published in the *New World,* June 1896.

setting up some technical distinctions that will help us in the end.

I

Let us give the name of *hypothesis* to anything that may be proposed to our belief; and just as the electricians speak of live and dead wires, let us speak of any hypothesis as either *live* or *dead*. A live hypothesis is one which appeals as a real possibility to him to whom it is proposed. If I ask you to believe in the Mahdi, the notion makes no electric connection with your nature—it refuses to scintillate with any credibility at all. As an hypothesis it is completely dead. To an Arab, however (even if he be not one of the Mahdi's followers), the hypothesis is among the mind's possibilities: it is alive. This shows that deadness and liveness in an hypothesis are not intrinsic properties, but relations to the individual thinker. They are measured by his willingness to act. The maximum of liveness in an hypothesis means willingness to act irrevocably. Practically, that means belief; but there is some believing tendency wherever there is willingness to act at all.

Next, let us call the decision between two hypotheses an *option.* Options may be of several kinds. They may be—first, *living* or *dead;* secondly, *forced* or *avoidable;* thirdly, *momentous* or *trivial;* and for our purposes we may call an option a *genuine* option when it is of the forced, living, and momentous kind.

1. A living option is one in which both hypotheses are live ones. If I say to you: "Be a theosophist or be a Mohammedan," it is probably a dead option, because for you neither hypothesis is likely to be alive. But if I say: "Be an agnostic or be a Christian," it is otherwise: trained as you are, each hypothesis makes some appeal, however small, to your belief.

2. Next, if I say to you: "Choose between going out with your umbrella or without it," I do not offer you a genuine option, for it is not forced. You can easily avoid it by not going out at all. Similarly, if I say, "Either love me or hate me," "Either call my theory true or call it false," your option is avoidable. You may remain indifferent to me, neither loving nor hating, and you may decline to offer any judgment as to my theory. But if I say, "Either accept this truth or go without it," I put on you a forced option, for there is no standing place outside of the alternative. Every dilemma based on a complete logical disjunction, with no possibility of not choosing, is an option of this forced kind.

3. Finally, if I were Dr. Nansen and proposed to you to join my North Pole expedition, your option would be momentous; for this would probably be your only similar opportunity, and your choice now would either exclude you from the North Pole sort of immortality altogether or put at least the chance of it into your hands. He who refuses to embrace a unique opportunity loses the prize as surely as if he tried and failed. *Per contra,* the option is trivial when the opportunity is not unique, when the stake is insignificant, or when the decision is reversible if it later prove unwise. Such trivial options abound in the scientific life. A chemist finds an hypothesis live enough to spend a year in its verification: he believes in it to that extent. But if his experiments prove inconclusive either way, he is quit for his loss of time, no vital harm being done.

It will facilitate our discussion if we keep all these distinctions well in mind.

II

The next matter to consider is the actual psychology of human opinion. When we look at certain facts, it seems as if our passional and volitional nature lay at the root of all our convictions. When we look at others, it seems as if they could do nothing when the intellect had once said its say. Let us take the latter facts up first.

Does it not seem preposterous on the very face of it to talk of our opinions being modifiable at will? Can our will either help or hinder our intellect in its perceptions of truth? Can we, by just willing it, believe that Abraham Lincoln's existence is a myth, and that the portraits of him in *McClure's Magazine* are all of some one else? Can we, by any effort of our will, or by any strength of wish that it were true, believe ourselves well and about when we are roaring with rheumatism in bed, or feel certain that the sum of the two one-dollar bills in our pocket must be a hundred dollars? We can *say* any of these things, but we are absolutely impotent to believe them; and of just such things is the whole fabric of the truths that we do believe in made up— matters of fact, immediate or remote, as Hume said, and relations between ideas, which are either there or not there for us if we see them so, and which if not there cannot be put there by any action of our own.

In Pascal's *Thoughts* there is a celebrated passage known in literature as Pascal's wager. In it he tries to force us into Christianity by reasoning as if our concern with truth resembled our concern with the stakes in a game of chance. Translated freely his words are these: You must either believe or not believe that God is—which will you do? Your human reason cannot say. A game is going on between you and the nature of things which at the day of judgment will bring out either heads or tails. Weigh what your gains and your losses would be if you should stake all you have on heads, or God's existence: if you win in such case, you gain eternal beatitude; if you lose, you lose nothing at all. If there were an infinity of chances, and only

one for God in this wager, still you ought to stake your all on God; for though you surely risk a finite loss by this procedure, any finite loss is reasonable, even a certain one is reasonable, if there is but the possibility of infinite gain. Go, then, and take holy water, and have masses said; belief will come and stupefy your scruples—*Cela vous fera croire et vous abêtira* [This will make you believe and stupefy you]. Why should you not? At bottom, what have you to lose?

You probably feel that when religious faith expresses itself thus, in the language of the gaming-table, it is put to its last trumps. Surely Pascal's own personal belief in masses and holy water had far other springs; and this celebrated page of his is but an argument for others, a last desperate snatch at a weapon against the hardness of the unbelieving heart. We feel that a faith in masses and holy water adopted wilfully after such a mechanical calculation would lack the inner soul of faith's reality; and if we were ourselves in the place of the Deity, we should probably take particular pleasure in cutting off believers of this pattern from their infinite reward. It is evident that unless there be some pre-existing tendency to believe in masses and holy water, the option offered to the will by Pascal is not a living option. Certainly no Turk ever took to masses and holy water on its account; and even to us Protestants these means of salvation seem such foregone impossibilities that Pascal's logic, invoked for them specifically, leaves us unmoved. As well might the Mahdi write to us, saying, "I am the Expected One whom God has created in his effulgence. You shall be infinitely happy if you confess me; otherwise you shall be cut off from the light of the sun. Weigh, then, your infinite gain if I am genuine against your finite sacrifice if I am not!" His logic would be that of Pascal;

but he would vainly use it on us, for the hypothesis he offers us is dead. No tendency to act on it exists in us to any degree.

The talk of believing by our volition seems, then, from one point of view, simply silly. From another point of view it is worse than silly, it is vile. When one turns to the magnificent edifice of the physical sciences, and sees how it was reared; what thousands of disinterested moral lives of men lie buried in its mere foundations; what patience and postponement, what choking down of preference, what submission to the icy laws of outer fact are wrought into its very stones and mortar; how absolutely impersonal it stands in its vast augustness— then how besotted and contemptible seems every little sentimentalist who comes blowing his voluntary smoke-wreaths, and pretending to decide things from out of his private dream! Can we wonder if those bred in the rugged and manly school of science should feel like spewing such subjectivism out of their mouths? The whole system of loyalties which grow up in the schools of science go dead against its toleration; so that it is only natural that those who have caught the scientific fever should pass over to the opposite extreme, and write sometimes as if the incorruptibly truthful intellect ought positively to prefer bitterness and unacceptableness to the heart in its cup.

It fortifies my soul to know
That though I perish, Truth is so—

sings Clough, while Huxley exclaims: "My only consolation lies in the reflection that, however bad our posterity may become, so far as they hold by the plain rule of not pretending to believe what they have no reason to believe, because it may be to their advantage so to pretend [the word 'pretend' is surely here redundant], they will not have reached the lowest depth of im-

morality." And that delicious *enfant terrible* Clifford writes: "Belief is desecrated when given to unproved and unquestioned statements for the solace and private pleasure of the believer. . . . Whoso would deserve well of his fellows in this matter will guard the purity of his belief with a very fanaticism of jealous care, lest at any time it should rest on an unworthy object, and catch a stain which can never be wiped away. . . . If [a] belief has been accepted on insufficient evidence [even though the belief be true, as Clifford on the same page explains] the pleasure is a stolen one. . . . It is sinful because it is stolen in defiance of our duty to mankind. That duty is to guard ourselves from such beliefs as from a pestilence which may shortly master our own body and then spread to the rest of the town. . . . It is wrong always, everywhere, and for every one, to believe anything upon insufficient evidence."

III

All this strikes one as healthy, even when expressed, as by Clifford, with somewhat too much of robustious pathos in the voice. Free will and simple wishing do seem, in the matter of our credences, to be only fifth wheels to the coach. Yet if any one should thereupon assume that intellectual insight is what remains after wish and will and sentimental preference have taken wing, or that pure reason is what then settles our opinions, he would fly quite as directly in the teeth of the facts.

It is only our already dead hypotheses that our willing nature is unable to bring to life again. But what has made them dead for us is for the most part a previous action of our willing nature of an antagonistic kind. When I say "willing nature," I do not mean only such deliberate volitions as may have set up habits of belief that we cannot now escape from—I mean all such factors of belief as fear and hope, prejudice and passion, imitation and partisanship, the circumpressure of our caste and set. As a matter of fact we find ourselves believing, we hardly know how or why. Mr. Balfour gives the name of "authority" to all those influences, born of the intellectual climate, that make hypotheses possible or impossible for us, alive or dead. Here in this room, we all of us believe in molecules and the conservation of energy, in democracy and necessary progress, in Protestant Christianity and the duty of fighting for "the doctrine of the immortal Monroe," all for no reasons worthy of the name. We see into these matters with no more inner clearness, and probably with much less, than any disbeliever in them might possess. His unconventionality would probably have some grounds to show for its conclusions; but for us, not insight, but the *prestige* of the opinions, is what makes the spark shoot from them and light up our sleeping magazines of faith. Our reason is quite satisfied, in nine hundred and ninety-nine cases out of every thousand of us, if it can find a few arguments that will do to recite in case our credulity is criticized by some one else. Our faith is faith in some one else's faith, and in the greatest matters this is most the case. Our belief in truth itself, for instance, that there is a truth, and that our minds and it are made for each other—what is it but a passionate affirmation of desire, in which our social system backs us up? We want to have a truth; we want to believe that our experiments and studies and discussions must put us in a continually better and better position towards it; and on this line we agree to fight out our thinking lives. But if a Pyrrhonistic sceptic asks us *how we know* all this, can our logic find a reply? No! certainly it cannot. It is just one volition against another—we willing to go in

for life upon a trust or assumption which he, for his part, does not care to make.

As a rule we disbelieve all facts and theories for which we have no use. Clifford's cosmic emotions find no use for Christian feelings. Huxley belabors the bishops because there is no use for sacerdotalism in his scheme of life. Newman, on the contrary, goes over to Romanism, and finds all sorts of reasons good for staying there, because a priestly system is for him an organic need and delight. Why do so few "scientists" even look at the evidence for telepathy, so called? Because they think, as a leading biologist, now dead, once said to me, that even if such a thing were true, scientists ought to band together to keep it suppressed and concealed. It would undo the uniformity of Nature and all sorts of other things without which scientists cannot carry on their pursuits. But if this very man had been shown something which as a scientist he might *do* with telepathy, he might not only have examined the evidence, but even have found it good enough. This very law which the logicians would impose upon us—if I may give the name of logicians to those who would rule out our willing nature here—is based on nothing but their own natural wish to exclude all elements for which they, in their professional quality of logicians, can find no use.

Evidently, then, our non-intellectual nature does influence our convictions. There are passional tendencies and volitions which run before and others which come after belief, and it is only the latter that are too late for the fair; and they are not too late when the previous passional work has been already in their own direction. Pascal's argument, instead of being powerless, then seems a regular clincher, and is the last stroke needed to make our faith in masses and holy water complete. The state of things is evidently far from simple; and pure insight and logic, whatever they might do ideally, are not the only things that really do produce our creeds.

IV

Our next duty, having recognized this mixed-up state of affairs, is to ask whether it be simply reprehensible and pathological, or whether, on the contrary, we must treat it as a moral element in making up our minds. The thesis I defend is, briefly stated, this: *Our passional nature not only lawfully may, but must, decide an option between propositions, whenever it is a genuine option that cannot by its nature be decided on intellectual grounds; for to say, under such circumstances, "Do not decide, but leave the question open," is itself a passional decision—just like deciding yes or no—and is attended with the same risk of losing the truth.* The thesis thus abstractly expressed will, I trust, soon become quite clear. . . .

VII

One more point, small but important, and our preliminaries are done. There are two ways of looking at our duty in the matter of opinion—ways entirely different, and yet ways about whose difference the theory of knowledge seems hitherto to have shown very little concern. *We must know the truth;* and *we must avoid error*—these are our first and great commandments as would-be knowers; but they are not two ways of stating an identical commandment, they are two separable laws. Although it may indeed happen that when we believe the truth *A,* we escape as an incidental consequence from believing the falsehood *B,* it hardly ever happens that by merely disbelieving *B* we necessarily believe *A.* We may in escaping *B* fall into believing other falsehoods, *C* or *D,* just as bad as *B;*

or we may escape *B* by not believing anything at all, not even *A.*

Believe truth! Shun error!—these, we see, are two materially different laws; and by choosing between them we may end by coloring differently our whole intellectual life. We may regard the chase for truth as paramount, and the avoidance of error as secondary; or we may, on the other hand, treat the avoidance of error as more imperative, and let truth take its chance. Clifford, in the instructive passage which I have quoted, exhorts us to the latter course. Believe nothing, he tells us, keep your mind in suspense for ever, rather than by closing it on insufficient evidence incur the awful risk of believing lies. You, on the other hand, may think that the risk of being in error is a very small matter when compared with the blessings of real knowledge, and be ready to be duped many times in your investigation rather than postpone indefinitely the chance of guessing true. I myself find it impossible to go with Clifford. We must remember that these feelings of our duty about either truth or error are in any case only expressions of our passional life. Biologically considered, our minds are as ready to grind out falsehood as veracity, and he who says, "Better go without belief forever than believe a lie!" merely shows his own preponderant private horror of becoming a dupe. He may be critical of many of his desires and fears, but this fear he slavishly obeys. He cannot imagine any one questioning its binding force. For my own part, I have also a horror of being duped; but I can believe that worse things than being duped may happen to a man in this world: so Clifford's exhortation has to my ears a thoroughly fantastic sound. It is like a general informing his soldiers that it is better to keep out of battle forever than to risk a single wound. Not so are victories either over enemies or over nature gained.

Our errors are surely not such awfully solemn things. In a world where we are so certain to incur them in spite of all our caution, a certain lightness of heart seems healthier than this excessive nervousness on their behalf. At any rate, it seems the fittest thing for the empiricist philosopher.

VIII

And now, after all this introduction, let us go straight at our question. I have said, and now repeat it, that not only as a matter of fact do we find our passional nature influencing us in our opinions, but that there are some options between opinions in which this influence must be regarded both as an inevitable and as a lawful determinant of our choice.

I fear here that some of you my hearers will begin to scent danger, and lend an inhospitable ear. Two first steps of passion you have indeed had to admit as necessary —we must think so as to avoid dupery, and we must think so as to gain truth; but the surest path to those ideal consummations, you will probably consider, is from now onwards to take no further passional step.

Well, of course, I agree as far as the facts will allow. Wherever the option between losing truth and gaining it is not momentous, we can throw the chance of *gaining truth* away, and at any rate save ourselves from any chance of *believing falsehood,* by not making up our minds at all till objective evidence has come. In scientific questions, this is almost always the case; and even in human affairs in general, the need of acting is seldom so urgent that a false belief to act on is better than no belief at all. Law courts, indeed, have to decide on the best evidence attainable for the moment, because a judge's duty is to make law as well as to ascertain it, and (as a learned judge once said to me) few cases are worth spending much time over: the great thing is to have them decided on *any* acceptable principle, and got out of the way. But in our dealings with objective nature we obviously are recorders, not makers, of the truth; and decisions for the mere sake of deciding promptly and getting on to the next business would be wholly out of place. Throughout the breadth of physical nature facts are what they are quite independently of us, and seldom is there any such hurry about them that the risks of being duped by believing a premature theory need be faced. The questions here are always trivial options, the hypotheses are hardly living (at any rate not living for us spectators), the choice between believing truth or falsehood is seldom forced. The attitude of sceptical balance is therefore the absolutely wise one if we would escape mistakes. What difference, indeed, does it make to most of us whether we have or have not a theory of the Röntgen rays, whether we believe or not in mind-stuff, or have a conviction about the causality of conscious states? It makes no difference. Such options are not forced on us. On every account it is better not to make them, but still keep weighing reasons *pro et contra* with an indifferent hand.

I speak, of course, here of the purely judging mind. For purposes of discovery such indifference is to be less highly recommended, and science would be far less advanced than she is if the passionate desires of individuals to get their own faiths confirmed had been kept out of the game. See for example the sagacity which Spencer and Weismann now display. On the other hand, if you want an absolute duffer in an investigation, you must, after all, take the man who has no interest whatever in its results: he is the warranted incapable, the positive fool. The most useful investigator, because the most sensitive observer, is always he whose eager interest in one side of the question is balanced by an equally keen nervousness lest he become deceived. Science has organized this nervousness into a regular *technique*, her so-called method of verification; and she has fallen so deeply in love with the method that one may even say she has ceased to care for truth by itself at all. It is only truth as technically verified that interests her. The truth of truths might come in merely affirmative form, and she would decline to touch it. Such truth as that, she might repeat with Clifford, would be stolen in defiance of her duty to mankind. Human passions, however, are stronger than technical rules. *"Le cœur a ses raisons,"* as Pascal says, *"que la raison ne connaît pas"* [The heart has its reasons which the reason does not know]; and however indifferent to all but the bare rules of the game the umpire, the abstract intellect, may be, the concrete players who furnish him the materials to judge of are usually, each one of them, in love with some pet "live hypothesis" of his own. Let us agree, however, that wherever there is no forced option, the dispassionately judicial intellect with no pet hypothesis, saving us, as it does, from dupery at any rate, ought to be our ideal.

The question next arises: Are there not somewhere forced options in our speculative questions, and can we (as men who may be interested at least as much in positively gaining truth as in merely escaping dupery) always wait with impunity till the coercive evidence shall have arrived? It seems *a priori* improbable that the truth should be so nicely adjusted to our needs and powers as that. In the great boarding-house of nature, the cakes and the butter and the syrup seldom come out so even and leave the plates so clean. Indeed, we should view them with scientific suspicion if they did.

IX

Moral questions immediately present themselves as questions whose solution cannot wait for sensible proof. A moral question is a question not of what sensibly exists, but of what is good, or would be good if it did exist. Science can tell us what exists; but to compare the *worths*, both of what exists and of what does not exist, we must consult not science, but what Pascal calls our heart. Science herself consults her heart when she lays it down that the infinite ascertainment of fact and correction of false belief are the supreme goods for man. Challenge the statement, and science can only repeat it oracularly, or else prove it by showing that such ascertainment and correction bring man all sorts of other goods which man's heart in turn declares. The question of having moral beliefs at all or not having them is decided by our will. Are our moral preferences true or false, or are they only odd biological phenomena, making things good or bad for *us*, but in themselves indifferent? How can your pure intellect decide? If your heart does not *want* a world of moral reality, your head will assuredly never make you believe in one. Mephistophelian scepticism, indeed, will satisfy the head's play-instincts much better than any rigorous idealism can. Some men (even at the student age) are so naturally cool-hearted that the moralistic hypothesis never has for them any pungent life, and in their supercilious presence the hot young moralist always feels strangely ill at ease. The appearance of knowingness is on their side, of *naïveté* and gullibility on his. Yet, in the inarticulate heart of him, he clings to it that he is not a dupe, and that there is a realm in which (as Emerson says) all their wit and intellectual superiority is no better than the cunning of a fox. Moral scepticism can no more be refuted or proved by logic than intellectual scepticism can. When we stick to it that there *is* truth (be it of either kind), we do so with our whole nature, and resolve to stand or fall by the results. The sceptic with his whole nature adopts the doubting attitude; but which of us is the wiser, Omniscience only knows.

Turn now from these wide questions of good to a certain class of questions of fact, questions concerning personal relations, states of mind between one man and another. *Do you like me or not?*—for example. Whether you do or not depends, in countless instances, on whether I meet you half-way, am willing to assume that you must like me, and show you trust and expectation. The previous faith on my part in your liking's existence is in such cases what makes your liking come. But if I stand aloof, and refuse to budge an inch until I have objective evidence, until you shall have done something apt, as the absolutists say, *ad extorquendum assensum meum* [to compel my assent], ten to one your liking never comes. How many women's hearts are vanquished by the mere sanguine insistence of some man that they *must* love him! he will not consent to the hypothesis that they cannot. The desire for a certain kind of truth here brings about that special truth's existence; and so it is in innumerable cases of other sorts. Who gains promotions, boons, appointments, but the man in whose life they are seen to play the part of live hypotheses, who discounts them, sacrifices other things for their sake before they have come, and takes risks for them in advance? His faith acts on the powers above him as a claim, and creates its own verification.

A social organism of any sort whatever, large or small, is what it is because each member proceeds to his own duty with a trust that the other members will simultaneously do theirs. Wherever a desired result is achieved by the cooperation of many independent persons, its existence as a fact is a pure consequence of the precursive faith in one another of those immediately concerned. A government, an army, a commercial system, a ship, a college, an athletic team, all exist on this condition, without which not only is nothing achieved, but nothing is even attempted. A whole train of passengers (individually brave enough) will be looted by a few highwaymen, simply because the latter can count on one another, while each passenger fears that if he makes a movement of resistance, he will be shot before any one else backs him up. If we believed that the whole car-full would rise at once with us, we should each severally rise, and train-robbing would never even be attempted. There are, then, cases where a fact cannot come at all unless a preliminary faith exists in its coming. *And where faith in a fact can help create the fact,* that would be an insane logic which should say that faith running ahead of scientific evidence is the "lowest kind of immorality" into which a thinking being can fall. Yet such is the logic by which our scientific absolutists pretend to regulate our lives!

X

In truths dependent on our personal action, then, faith based on desire is certainly a lawful and possibly an indispensable thing.

But now, it will be said, these are all childish human cases, and have nothing to do with great cosmical matters, like the question of religious faith. Let us then pass on to that. Religions differ so much in their accidents that in discussing the religious question we must make it very generic and broad. What then do we now mean by the religious hypothesis? Science says things are; morality says some things are better than other things; and religion says essentially two things.

First, she says that the best things are the more eternal things, the overlapping things, the things in the universe that throw the last stone, so to speak, and say the final word. "Perfection is eternal"—this phrase of Charles Secrétan seems a good way of putting this first affirmation of religion, an affirmation which obviously cannot yet be verified scientifically at all.

The second affirmation of religion is that we are better off even now if we believe her first affirmation to be true.

Now, let us consider what the logical elements of this situation are *in case the religious hypothesis in both its branches be really true.* (Of course, we must admit that possibility at the outset. If we are to discuss the question at all, it must involve a living option. If for any of you religion be a hypothesis that cannot, by any living possibility, be true, then you need go no farther. I speak to the "saving remnant" alone.) So proceeding, we see, first, that religion offers itself as a *momentous* option. We are supposed to gain, even now, by our belief, and to lose by our non-belief, a certain vital good. Secondly, religion is a *forced* option, so far as that good goes. We cannot escape the issue by remaining sceptical and waiting for more light, because, although we do avoid error in that way *if religion be untrue,* we lose the good, *if it be true,* just as certainly as if we positively chose to disbelieve. It is as if a man should hesitate indefinitely to ask a certain woman to marry him because he was not perfectly sure that she would prove an angel after he brought her home. Would he not cut

himself off from that particular angel-possibility as decisively as if he went and married some one else? Scepticism, then, is not avoidance of option; it is option of a certain particular kind of risk. *Better risk loss of truth than chance of error*—that is your faith-vetoer's exact position. He is actively playing his stake as much as the believer is; he is backing the field against the religious hypothesis, just as the believer is backing the religious hypothesis against the field. To preach scepticism to us as a duty until "sufficient evidence" for religion be found, is tantamount therefore to telling us, when in presence of the religious hypothesis, that to yield to our fear of its being error is wiser and better than to yield to our hope that it may be true. It is not intellect against all passions, then; it is only intellect with one passion laying down its law. And by what, forsooth, is the supreme wisdom of this passion warranted? Dupery for dupery, what proof is there that dupery through hope is so much worse than dupery through fear? I, for one, can see no proof; and I simply refuse obedience to the scientist's command to imitate his kind of option, in a case where my own stake is important enough to give me the right to choose my own form of risk. If religion be true and the evidence for it be still insufficient, I do not wish, by putting your extinguisher upon my nature (which feels to me as if it had after all some business in this matter), to forfeit my sole chance in life of getting upon the winning side—that chance depending, of course, on my willingness to run the risk of acting as if my passional need of taking the world religiously might be prophetic and right.

All this is on the supposition that it really may be prophetic and right, and that, even to us who are discussing the matter, religion is a live hypothesis which may be true. Now, to most of us religion comes in a still further way that makes a veto on our active faith even more illogical. The more perfect and more eternal aspect of the universe is represented in our religions as having personal form. The universe is no longer a mere *It* to us, but a *Thou*, if we are religious; and any relation that may be possible from person to person might be possible here. For instance, although in one sense we are passive portions of the universe, in another we show a curious autonomy, as if we were small active centers on our own account. We feel, too, as if the appeal of religion to us were made to our own active good-will, as if evidence might be forever withheld from us unless we met the hypothesis half-way. To take a trivial illustration: just as a man who in a company of gentlemen made no advances, asked a warrant for every concession, and believed no one's word without proof, would cut himself off by such churlishness from all the social rewards that a more trusting spirit would earn—so here, one who should shut himself up in snarling logicality and try to make the gods extort his recognition willy-nilly, or not get it at all, might cut himself off forever from his only opportunity of making the gods' acquaintance. This feeling, forced on us we know not whence, that by obstinately believing that there are gods (although not to do so would be so easy both for our logic and our life) we are doing the universe the deepest service we can, seems part of the living essence of the religious hypothesis. If the hypothesis *were* true in all its parts, including this one, then pure intellectualism, with its veto on our making willing advances, would be an absurdity; and some participation of our sympathetic nature would be logically required. I, therefore, for one, cannot see my way to accepting the agnostic rules for truth-seeking, or wilfully agree to keep my willing nature out of the game. I cannot

do so for this plain reason, that *a rule of thinking which would absolutely prevent me from acknowledging certain kinds of truth if those kinds of truth were really there, would be an irrational rule.* That for me is the long and short of the formal logic of the situation, no matter what the kinds of truth might materially be.

I confess I do not see how this logic can be escaped. But sad experience makes me fear that some of you may still shrink from radically saying with me, *in abstracto,* that we have the right to believe at our own risk any hypothesis that is live enough to tempt our will. I suspect, however, that if this is so, it is because you have got away from the abstract logical point of view altogether, and are thinking (perhaps without realizing it) of some particular religious hypothesis which for you is dead. The freedom to "believe what we will" you apply to the case of some patent superstition; and the faith you think of is the faith defined by the schoolboy when he said, "Faith is when you believe something that you know ain't true." I can only repeat that this is misapprehension. *In concreto,* the freedom to believe can only cover living options which the intellect of the individual cannot by itself resolve; and living options never seem absurdities to him who has them to consider. When I look at the religious question as it really puts itself to concrete men, and when I think of all the possibilities which both practically and theoretically it involves, then this command that we shall put a stopper on our heart, instincts, and courage, and *wait*—acting of course meanwhile more or less as if religion were *not* true [1]—till doomsday, or till such time as

---

[1] Since belief is measured by action, he who forbids us to believe religion to be true, necessarily also forbids us to act as we should if we did believe it to be true. The whole defense of religious faith

our intellect and senses working together may have raked in evidence enough—this command, I say, seems to me the queerest idol ever manufactured in the philosophic cave. Were we scholastic absolutists, there might be more excuse. If we had an infallible intellect with its objective certitudes, we might feel ourselves disloyal to such a perfect organ of knowledge in not trusting to it exclusively, in not waiting for its releasing word. But if we are empiricists, if we believe that no bell in us tolls to let us know for certain when truth is in our grasp, then it seems a piece of idle fantasticality to preach so solemnly our duty of waiting for the bell. Indeed we *may* wait if we will —I hope you do not think that I am denying that—but if we do so, we do so at our peril as much as if we believed. In either case we *act*, taking our life in our hands. No one of us ought to issue vetoes to the other, nor should we bandy words of abuse. We ought, on the contrary, delicately and profoundly to respect one another's mental freedom: then only shall we bring about the intellectual republic; then only shall we have that spirit of inner tolerance without which all our outer tolerance is soulless, and which is empiricism's glory; then only

hinges upon action. If the action required or inspired by the religious hypothesis is in no way different from that dictated by the naturalistic hypothesis, then religious faith is a pure superfluity, better pruned away, and controversy about its legitimacy is a piece of idle trifling, unworthy of serious minds. I myself believe, of course, that the religious hypothesis gives to the world an expression which specifically determines our reactions, and makes them in a large part unlike what they might be on a purely naturalistic scheme of belief.

shall we live and let live, in speculative as well as in practical things.

I began by a reference to Fitz-James Stephen; let me end by a quotation from him. "What do you think of yourself? What do you think of the world? . . . These are questions with which all must deal as it seems good to them. They are riddles of the Sphinx, and in some way or other we must deal with them. . . . In all important transactions of life we have to take a leap in the dark. . . . If we decide to leave the riddles unanswered, that is a choice; if we waver in our answer, that, too, is a choice: but whatever choice we make, we make it at our peril. If a man chooses to turn his back altogether on God and the future, no one can prevent him; no one can show beyond reasonable doubt that he is mistaken. If a man thinks otherwise and acts as he thinks, I do not see that any one can prove that *he* is mistaken. Each must act as he thinks best; and if he is wrong, so much the worse for him. We stand on a mountain pass in the midst of whirling snow and blinding mist, through which we get glimpses now and then of paths which may be deceptive. If we stand still we shall be frozen to death. If we take the wrong road we shall be dashed to pieces. We do not certainly know whether there is any right one. What must we do? 'Be strong and of a good courage.' Act for the best, hope for the best, and take what comes. . . . If death ends all, we cannot meet death better." [2]

[2] *Liberty, Equality, Fraternity,* p. 353, 2d edition. London, 1874.

COMMENT

The Meaning of Theism

For the theist, the key to reality lies in God and his design. This belief does not exclude several positions that we have already examined, since a theist can be a teleologist, a dualist, or an idealist; but he cannot be a complete materialist or an absolute sceptic.

God has been defined as "a being who is personal, supreme, and good." [1] This definition is in accord with what most people mean when they use the word "God." They think of Him as personal—that is, as conscious mind or spirit. Of course, God's mind is conceived as much larger or greater than any human mind, but still somewhat like mind or spirit as we know it. God is also thought of as supreme—if not omnipotent, at least immensely great and powerful—so powerful, indeed, that He can profoundly affect the whole world. Finally, a personal and supreme being would not be called God if He were not also good—perhaps not perfect, but at least good in a measure that far surpasses our poor human capacities.

If it be granted that the concept of God should be so defined, the question arises whether the belief in God is mature and defensible—whether it is consistent with the life of reason, which Socrates declared is alone worth living. Is faith in God, as Freud maintained, a mere illusory compensation for fear, repression, and catastrophe? Or is it an inalienable possession of man's spiritual life, as rational as it is emotionally satisfying? Can this faith withstand the criticism of philosophy? What *reasons* are there for believing in the existence of God, and how valid are these reasons?

We shall consider four arguments: (1) the ontological argument; (2) the argument for a first cause, which is often called the cosmological argument; (3) the argument from design, also called the teleological argument; and (4) the argument based on values. Not only are these arguments very interesting in themselves, but the question of their truth or falsity is of the greatest practical moment.

The Ontological Argument

The term *ontological* (which means "pertaining to the nature of being") was used by Kant to designate the argument first formulated by the great medieval theologian Saint Anselm, Archbishop of Canterbury (1033–1109). Although Anselm's own statement appears in this book, the extreme subtlety of his argument calls for some explication.

His "proof," which is intended to establish the existence of an utterly infinite and perfect deity, may be restated as follows: Anyone who uses the term "God" correctly, even a foolish atheist, has in mind "a being than which no greater can be conceived." Now, let us compare two beings that might be called God. The first has all the properties required to make him the very greatest of beings *except that he does not exist.* He is only an imaginary being. The second has all the properties of the first being but, *in addition,* exists.

[1] J. M. E. McTaggart, *Some Dogmas of Religion* (London: Edward Arnold, 1906), p. 186.

Clearly the second is greater than the first. Therefore, that being than which no greater can be conceived must be the second being—that is, a really existent being. Such a being is God; hence God exists.

The crux of the argument is that real existence is inseparable from the concept of deity. As Descartes phrased the argument, when I analyze the idea of God, I find that it includes existence; therefore, God exists.

This ingenious argument has had a chequered history. It was immediately criticized by an aged monk, Gaunilo, and was rejected by the greatest medieval philosopher, St. Thomas Aquinas. Then it was revived by Descartes, restated by Spinoza and Leibniz, and sharply criticized by Locke, Hume, and Kant. Relatively few philosophers in more recent times have accepted it.

The import of the argument is clarified by Gaunilo's objection and Anselm's reply. As interpreted by Gaunilo, the argument can be restated as follows: God is thought of as perfect; existence is necessary to perfection; therefore, God exists. This argument, said Gaunilo, is fallacious because by the same kind of reasoning I could "prove" the existence of a perfect island, to wit: If the island did not exist it would lack one of the elements of perfection, namely, real existence, and hence it would not be a perfect island. But the conclusion that a perfect island must exist is obviously absurd, and hence this type of argument is fallacious.

Anselm promptly replied to this attempted *reductio ad absurdum* by pointing out that a "perfect island" is perfect only in a weak and limited sense. By its very nature, an island is finite, and hence can be "perfect" only in a relative or inaccurate manner of speaking—it cannot be *infinitely* perfect. God, and not the hypothetical island, is that being than which no greater can be conceived—a being perfect in the sense of being incomparably greatest. Such absolute and infinite perfection applies to God and to God alone, and only such perfection requires existence.

Another objection was advanced by St. Thomas Aquinas. Going to the root of the argument, he questioned whether we really have in mind the concept of an utterly infinite or perfect being. He pointed out that we finite human beings have only an inadequate and indirect knowledge of God. Because of the infirmity of our understanding, we cannot discern God as He is in Himself, but only by the effects that He produces. If we could know God's essence absolutely, we would surely see that His essence involves His existence. But since we know God only relatively, His existence is not self-evident to us. We cannot leap from our imperfect idea of God to the conclusion that an absolutely perfect being exists.

Perhaps the most profound criticism of the ontological argument was advanced by Kant, whose objection turns on the meaning of the word "exists." Suppose I say that God exists. Am I making the same sort of statement as when I say that God is omnipotent? Kant would say no. The first statement asserts nothing about the *characteristics* of God; it merely tells me that God, whatever He is, exists, just as a rabbit, a cabbage, a stone, or a planet exists. This statement can be denied in only one way—namely, by denying that God exists. The second statement, that God is omnipotent, does tell me something about the *character* of God, and this statement, unlike the first, can be denied in *two* ways—either by denying that there is a God, or by denying that God is omnipotent.

Since the question of a thing's existence is thus *additional* to the question of its characteristics, we can grasp its characteristics without knowing whether it exists. Take the following illustration. As I sit at my desk I wonder whether there is a dollar bill in my pocket. Before I reach into my pocket to find out, I have in mind what the dollar bill would be like. The characteristics of the dollar bill which I have in mind are the same whether or not there really is a dollar bill in my pocket. Hence, I can grasp the characteristics of a dollar bill without knowing that it exists. Can we likewise grasp God's characteristics without knowing whether He exists? Yes, declares Kant. It is logically possible to think of an infinite and perfect Being without knowing that there *is* such a Being. But suppose we *mean* by God a necessarily existent God. It would still not follow that there really is such a Being. It would merely follow that *if* there is a God, then He is a necessarily existent Being—because that is what we mean. At best, Anselm's argument shows only that the thought of God implies the *thought* of God's existence. The thought of perfection implies the thought of existence, and real perfection implies real existence. But the *thought* of perfection does not imply *real* existence. This is the tenor of Kant's criticism.

But suppose, for the sake of argument, that Anselm's proof is sound. Just what would it prove? Would it prove the personal and transcendent God of Christian theology? Evidently not. As soon as we think of a being that is transcendent and hence does not include all things, we can immediately think of a greater being—namely, one that *does* include all things. Moreover, such a being would have to include all conceivable qualities that could be combined within a single being; otherwise we could conceive of a greater. On the basis of the ontological argument, Spinoza concluded that God must be all-inclusive and not only infinite but infinite in an infinite number of ways. And he also concluded that God could not be a person, because personality, in its very nature, involves limitation. It would appear that Spinoza's "God," rather than the God of orthodox theology, is in accord with Anselm's definition: "A Being than which no greater can be conceived." If we define God as *personal*, it seems that Anselm's argument, *even if valid*, would prove not the existence of God but the existence of another sort of Being.

The Cosmological Argument

The argument for a first cause, or cosmological argument, was formulated by Aristotle and has been supported by many famous philosophers, including St. Thomas Aquinas, Descartes, Spinoza, Leibniz, and Locke. In considering Descartes in Part Two, we have already examined one version, which involves a number of questionable assumptions. However, the argument can be stated in a less questionable form, and, indeed, at the present time there are many philosophers who regard it as valid.

The argument sometimes starts with the premise that "everything must have a cause" and concludes that God is a "first cause"—that is, an ultimate or uncaused cause. There is a glaring contradiction between the premise "Everything has a cause," and the conclusion "There must be a first cause." If everything must have a cause, why must not God also? Or if God can exist without a cause, why not nature or any part of it? These are surely difficulties, if not fatal objections, and it is important to see whether the argument can be stated in more tenable form.

Such a statement occurs in the argument of Aquinas that non-necessary things imply Necessary Being as their cause. The proof as so formulated does not imply that the Universe was created out of nothing (whatever that means!), or that it came into existence as the result of a temporal first cause. Aquinas is prepared to admit that the chains of causes and effects may run back into an infinite past with no beginning. What he denies is that we can have a *sufficient* explanation of nature in terms of such an infinite regress of causes. So long as we have merely series of causes of causes, however infinitely extended, we are explaining one dependent event by another dependent event by still another dependent event, and so on and on. This is unsatisfactory for two reasons. First, each event is dependent upon its antecedents, and hence no event is more than *conditionally* necessary. If everything is dependent upon something else, the whole process hangs upon nothing. An explanation that thus never gives us an *ultimate* necessity is incomplete, and hence is not a full and satisfactory explanation. Secondly, even if there is an infinite regress of causes, we can always ask why this chain occurs rather than some other chain. Or even if we consider the sum total of nature, we can ask why we have *this* totality rather than some quite different totality. The only *sufficient* explanation is that natural events, and even the whole of nature, must ultimately depend upon a necessary Being. Such a Being cannot have had an external cause, because it is an infinite and eternal Being—namely, God—whose essence is to exist.

This argument can be criticized in a number of ways. First, we can ask what is meant by saying that God is a necessary Being. The word "necessity" applies to *propositions* whose denial would be contradictory. "Two plus two equals four" is a necessary proposition, since it would be contradictory to deny it. But does "necessity" apply to *things* as well as to propositions? The character Cleanthes, in Hume's dialogue, answers: "Nothing is demonstrable unless the contrary implies a contradiction. Nothing that is distinctly conceivable implies a contradiction. Whatever we conceive as existent, we can also conceive as non-existent. There is no being, therefore, whose non-existence implies a contradiction." If necessity thus applies to logically necessitated propositions and not to things, nothing, not even God, is a necessary Being. To say that God necessitates himself seems to mean that God somehow argues himself into existence, and not even God can do that.

Defenders of the cosmological argument might reply, in the words of Hume, that if we knew God's "whole essence or nature, we should perceive it to be as impossible for him not to exist as for twice two not to be four." But the point is, replies Cleanthes, that we do *not* know God's whole essence or nature, and hence it is not clear to us how a Being could necessitate himself. If, in some mysterious way, a Being can be necessary, why might not the natural universe be this necessarily existent Being? If you reply that every natural event is seen to be non-necessary (in the sense that its absence involves no contradiction), it does not follow that the whole of nature is non-necessary. A whole need not have the character of its parts. It does not follow from the fact that every note in a musical composition is short that the whole composition is short. Similarly, it does not follow from the fact that every natural thing or event is non-necessary that the whole of nature is non-necessary. If we are to insist upon a necessity that we do not understand, this necessity would seem as applicable to nature as to supernature.

But should we demand such an ultimate necessity? Why not simply suppose that the causal series of linked events stretches back infinitely and that there is no other explanation? If each part is determined by its antecedents, is not the whole sufficiently determined? It would seem to be absurd to demand an external cause for an infinite regress without beginning, since the causal relation implies priority in time and hence a beginning of existence. Our whole experience of causal connections, moreover, lies *within* nature, and we have no sufficient basis for projecting this relation *outside* of nature. Can we assume that what is true of particular things in the world—namely, that *they* are caused—is true of the universe in its totality? Must the universe have a cause outside its own nature? Or must it have any cause at all? To a consistent empiricist, such as Hume, the extension of the concept of causation beyond the field of all actual or possible experience offers special difficulties. On the other hand, if we understand the "necessity" of a necessary Being as logical rather than causal, we are faced by the difficulty already mentioned—that the necessity here involved is mysterious and seems applicable to the whole of nature no less than to supernature.

To these objections of Hume may be added one further objection. The cosmological argument, even if valid, throws no light on the character of the absolutely necessary Being. We are simply left with the very abstract notion of a self-necessitated necessitator. There would seem to be nothing in this conclusion that compels us to suppose that the necessary Being is either personal or good, and hence the argument, even if valid, is not sufficient to prove the existence of God.

Is the argument, therefore, worthless? Many philosophers believe that it retains its cogency, and that the objections we have considered are invalid. It seems to such philosophers that the evident self-insufficiency of natural events requires an ultimate self-sufficient foundation. Nature as a composite whole, moreover, seems also self-insufficient, because any composite *could* be composed in a different way. Why should there be this total natural constellation rather than some other? Does not the existence of such dependent and conditioned being require the existence of independent and unconditioned Being? Only an infinite, eternal, and non-composite Being—a pure spirit— could be thus independent and unconditioned, the guarantor of its own existence and all else besides. We have to fall back upon other arguments to establish some of the attributes of God, but the cosmological argument at least proves that nature is dependent upon supernature, and this conclusion carries us a long way, or so the believer in the cosmological argument would continue to maintain.

The Teleological Argument

The teleological argument, or argument from design, is very ancient but still popular. It was first expressly formulated by Plato, in the *Laws*, and has been restated by innumerable philosophers, among them St. Augustine, St. Thomas Aquinas, Locke, and Rousseau. It was especially popular in the seventeenth and eighteenth centuries, when the astronomy and physics of Newton were interpreted as the disclosure of a wonderful natural order requiring God as its source.

The argument is frequently stated in the form of a mechanical analogy. A classic example is the watch analogy, suggested by the eighteenth-century theologian William Paley. If, stranded on an uninhabited desert island, we were to find a watch, we should surely conclude that some intelligent being must have made it, since it would be absurd to suppose that such an intricate and obviously useful mechanism could be the result of chance. So, likewise, the wondrous contrivances of nature—for example, the structure and functions of the human body—must be the work of a Supreme Intelligence rather than of blind chance. This conclusion can be reinforced by illustrations drawn from modern science, such as the remarkable fitness of the environment to sustain life, the amazingly intricate structure of living organisms, and the vast sweep of cosmic evolution from the amoeba to man. Although, in the light of contemporary science, we are less inclined than Paley to compare the things of nature to a machine, we may still insist that the emergence of organisms, especially organisms with the complexity and skill of the human mind and body, would be inexplicable in a merely mechanistic world, and that a cosmic Designer is alone adequate to explain them.

The criticisms of Hume, as set forth by the character Philo in *The Dialogues on Natural Religion,* still constitute a powerful attack upon the design argument. The following brief analysis must be filled in by careful study of the original selection.

First, Philo points out that the argument is based upon a faulty analogy. It maintains that *like effects imply like causes.* Just as a house implies a designer, so the universe, as a marvelously organized whole, implies a designer. This sort of argument is logically sound only if the things being compared are quite similar. But how much similarity is there between a house and the infinite universe? It is very questionable whether we can thus make a small finite part a model for interpreting the whole infinite universe.

Secondly, the principle upon which the argument is based—that like effects imply like causes—is cogent only if we have *experience* of the things being compared. When, over and over again, we experience a certain type of sequence, we can infer the same type of cause when we observe the same sort of effect. But the universe as a whole is unique, and this unique *whole* is unexperienced by man. Hence, repeated experience of some natural sequence—for example, human design producing a human contrivance, such as a watch—does not provide a sound experiential basis for determining the origin of the universe, which is single, individual, and far beyond the range of human experience.

Thirdly, the mental ideas and faculties in God's mind constitute an order that, like any natural order, requires an ultimate explanation. If we accept the principle that order requires a designer, there would have to be a Designer of the Designer, and by the same token, a Designer of the Designer of the Designer, and so on *ad infinitum.* If we reject this infinite regress and arbitrarily stop at some point, why not stop with this present world?

Fourthly, even if we admit that there is a natural order that requires some ultimate explanation, there are several alternative hypotheses as plausible as the orthodox notion that an infinite and perfect God is the designer. The apparent design in the universe can be explained by (1) a finite deity, (2) an imperfect deity, (3) plural deities, (4) an internal designer, (5) an unconscious designing force, such as an instinctive or vegetative process, and (6) a mechanical principle of selection and conservation, such as the "survival of the fittest" (incidentally, Hume here anticipates Darwin). Most of Hume's discussion is devoted to an explanation of these alternative hypotheses, which the reader should very carefully consider.

In arguing for the first two alternatives—a finite deity and an imperfect deity—Philo maintains that it is illogical to suppose that a perfect and omnipotent God would produce so imperfect and evil a universe as we know exists. As he tersely remarks elsewhere in the Dialogues: "The questions asked by Epicurus, of old, are yet unanswered. Is Deity willing to prevent evil, but not able? Then he is impotent. Is He able, but not willing? Then He is malevolent. Is He both able and willing? Then whence cometh evil? Is He neither able nor willing? Then why call Him Deity?" Many philosophers have held that orthodox theology, with its belief in a perfect and omnipotent God, cannot satisfactorily answer these questions.

Are these criticisms of the argument from design conclusive? Evidently Hume did not think so. The criticisms are not presented as his but are put in the mouth of Philo, one of the three characters in the *Dialogues*. Hume abstains from indicating his own sympathies except at the very end of the book, where he suggests that "the opinions" of Cleanthes, the proponent of the design argument, are nearer to the truth than those of Philo. In a letter to a friend, George Elliot (dated March 10, 1751), Hume refers to Cleanthes as the "hero" of the dialogues, and asks for any suggestions which will strengthen that side of the dispute. Even Philo, in a final passage not quoted here, is made to remark that the apparent design in nature proves that its cause bears an analogy, though somewhat remote, to the human mind. Probably Hume felt that Philo's criticisms were weighty but by no means decisive.

One thing to note about most of these criticisms is that they do not tend to prove the *absence* of a designing agency or agencies. They indicate limitations rather than fatal defects in the design argument. They show that the finite order and goodness of nature are an insufficient basis for inferring an infinite, perfect, unitary, external, and conscious designer. Kant later pointed out an additional limitation—that the design argument can prove only a kind of architect, but it cannot prove a creator who makes the world out of nothing. Just as a watchmaker uses materials already in existence to make a watch, so the designer of a natural order may use pre-existing materials to compose his design. But these considerations are consistent with some kind of teleological explanation of the goodness and higher levels of order to be found in nature. It is true that Philo's final point, that the natural order may be the result of mere natural selection, is opposed to a teleological hypothesis, but the further course of the dialogue suggests that neither Cleanthes nor Philo regarded natural selection as sufficient, in itself, to explain the whole order of nature. It is also noteworthy that John Stuart Mill and William James could not bring themselves to the view that the Darwinian hypothesis of natural selection was alone sufficient to explain the higher levels of evolution. They preferred to believe in a finite God, struggling against evil but not wholly able to eliminate it. Moreover, this finite God need not be thought of as an external, transcendent Deity but can be construed as the total society of natural forces that are pushing on toward the good. Admittedly, this concept alters the usual meaning of "God," but some modern philosophers nevertheless prefer it.

What is the evidence? Nature exhibits levels of increasing complexity and richer integration: electrons, atoms, molecules, simple cells, plants, animals, personalities, human communities. The higher levels succeed the lower in time; there appears to be an evolutionary upsurge in the world, an anti-entropic drive toward wider and greater organization. In instinctive animal behavior there is seeming purposiveness, and in human beings there is deliberate purpose. Even if nature is not itself purposive, it has proved itself *fit* to produce purposive beings and higher levels of value. As W. P. Montague has remarked, "Material nature makes altogether too many winning throws for us not to suspect that she is playing with dice that are loaded, loaded with life and mind and purpose." [2] It may be argued, however, that the creative force is *within* nature rather than outside it. From the standpoint of sound method, if both a natural and a supernatural explanation are possible, the former is to be preferred. But many philosophers believe that natural explanations are insufficient and that supernatural explanations are therefore required.

Any finite God, *élan vital,* or emerging purposiveness, moreover, would itself be contingent, and hence would not help us to solve the ultimate mystery of why there is something rather than nothing.

The Argument Based on Esthetic and Moral Values

An additional argument, not represented in the readings from Anselm, Aquinas, or Hume, is that esthetic and moral values imply the existence of God.[3] Let us first consider the esthetic side of the argument. Ugliness is common in the works of man but exceedingly uncommon in natural scenery, where beauty is scattered with immense prodigality over the face of the visible world. Believing that this natural beauty is no mere illusion or subjective human impression and that blind chance is quite inadequate to explain it, a theist may conclude that it is the expression of a cosmic Spirit.

This type of reasoning is ancient. Plotinus (204–269) maintained that natural loveliness is the divine spirituality shining through matter. Similar ideas have been expressed by innumerable philosophers, poets, pantheists,

[2] *Belief Unbound* (Yale University Press, 1930), pp. 73–74.
[3] For an excellent statement of this argument, see G. Dawes Hicks, *The Philosophical Bases of Theism* (London: G. Allen & Unwin, 1937), Chap. 7.

and nature-mystics. Indeed, when confronted by sublime natural scenery, almost everyone spontaneously feels a kind of spiritual presence

> Whose dwelling is the light of setting suns,
> And the round ocean and the living air,
> And the blue sky, and in the mind of man.

Or, if an immediate spirit is not felt, nature often appears to be the handiwork of a supreme Artist.

As a deep mystical sense of the conformity of the soul and nature, this sort of feeling will not readily yield to criticism. But many philosophers distrust such apparent intuitions. The view that nature is, as Sir Thomas Browne said, the "art of God" is a form of the argument from design, and it is liable to much the same criticism as Hume and others have leveled against the design argument. One may question, moreover, whether beauty is an objective quality of nature. An alternative interpretation is that it is merely a subjective feeling evoked by artistic or natural objects. George Santayana, in *The Sense of Beauty,* for example, defines beauty as "pleasure objectified": we feel pleasure in the presence of the object, but we are so absorbed in the outward sensuous qualities that we spontaneously impute the value to the object rather than to our own psychological state, in which the value really resides. Still another interpretation is formulated by Kant in *The Critique of Judgment.* He maintained that beauty is neither in the object alone nor in the appreciative mind alone but in a felt harmony between the two. The beauty is actualized when an object fit to be appreciated and a mind fit to appreciate are united at the moment of contemplation. On the basis of either Santayana's or Kant's interpretation, beauty depends upon an appreciative contemplator, and hence is not an objective characteristic of nature.

If the beauty of nature is thus relative to a perceiver, we could expect natural objects to appear more or less beautiful, or even more or less ugly, as mood and situation change. In fact, nature does not always appear beautiful. Lord Tweedsmuir, describing the scenery of northernmost Canada, speaks of "immense rivers, pouring billions of dirty gallons to the ocean, too much coarse vegetation, an infinity of mud, and everywhere a superfluity of obscene insect life." [4] Aldous Huxley, in a striking essay, has contrasted Europe, "so well gardened that it resembles a work of art," with the "hostile" and "profoundly sinister" atmosphere, "the damp and stifling darkness," and "the malevolently tangled rattan" of the tropical jungle.[5] One may question whether nature unambiguously connotes a divine artistry.

Turning from esthetic to moral values, the theist may argue that the nature

[4] "Canada's Far North," *Sunday Times,* London, 1937; quoted by John Laird, *Theism and Cosmology* (London: G. Allen & Unwin, 1940), pp. 279–280.
[5] "Wordsworth in the Tropics," in *Do What You Will* (Doubleday, Doran & Co., 1929).

of moral experience implies the existence of God. The premise of this argument is that duty is unconditional and absolute. If it is wrong for me to do a certain act, no idea or desire of mine can make it right; and if it is right, no belief or wish of mine to the contrary can make it wrong. I cannot validly plead the right to commit murder, for example, on the ground that it conforms to my purposes or inclinations: murder is objectively and absolutely wrong. But such absolute moral laws cannot be based upon limited, fallible, shifting human perspectives, or upon merely material things. A moral law or ideal can exist nowhere or nohow but in a mind; and an absolute moral law or ideal can exist only in a Mind that is eternal and absolute, the source of whatever is true in our moral ideas. The belief in God is thus the logical presupposition of an absolute morality. This type of argument, which was formulated long ago by St. Augustine (354–430), has been restated by many philosophers.

Kant advanced another moral argument for the existence of God. He maintained that virtue alone is unconditionally good and that it consists in conformity to absolute moral laws, even though happiness may thereby be sacrificed. But the whole and perfect good requires happiness also—virtue crowned with happiness is better than virtue alone or virtue combined with misery. In life as we find it, however, the virtuous are sometimes wretched and the vicious prosper. This is neither right nor rational. If the highest good is to be achieved, there must be a final rectification—there must be a God to guarantee an afterlife with appropriate rewards and punishments, so that virtue may finally receive its due reward and vice its appropriate punishment. Since our duty is unconditional and absolute, moreover, it commands us to seek the *summum bonum,* the highest good, which is manifestly unattainable in this life. And since "ought" implies "can," there must be an afterlife in which we can transcend our earthly limitations and attain those absolute goods which duty commands us to pursue. Only a God can guarantee an afterlife and a final reward for virtue. Hence the existence of God must be assumed as the basis of virtue and ultimate justice.

The premise of the arguments of both Augustine and Kant is that morality is absolute. If moral values are relative, the premise is invalid. The question of absolute and relative values will engage our attention in Part Four; and we shall not now try to anticipate the discussion. But even if values are shown to be absolute, it may not follow that God exists. If we should agree with Socrates, as depicted in Plato's dialogues, that there are objective and eternal universals having some kind of existence independent of mind, we could maintain the absoluteness of morality without recourse to an eternal deity.

Furthermore, Kant's assumption that there must exist a perfect harmony between virtue and happiness begs the question at issue. He reasons that it is altogether right and rational that virtue should be rewarded with happiness, and that God must therefore exist to guarantee this ideal state in an afterlife. But this is simply the old, old notion that somehow, somewhere, there *must* be a complete escape from evil, a release from all unmerited tragedy, an ultimate harmony. But there is no such harmony in the world as we observe it, and to assume that it must therefore exist supernaturally is to jump to the very conclusion that needs to be proved.

Also, to maintain, as Kant does, that we have a duty to pursue an unlimited good and that this duty implies an afterlife is again a subtle way of begging the question. We can agree with him that "I ought" implies "I can"—that it is never one's duty to do the impossible—but it does not follow that we have a duty to achieve a complete and perfect good and that consequently such a good must be attainable. On the contrary, it may simply be that such good *is* unattainable and that therefore we have no duty to attain it. Even if morality were to imply an afterlife, moreover, it is not obvious that there would have to be a God. Some philosophers, such as J. M. E. McTaggart, have believed in an afterlife without believing in God.

The Question of Faith

Even if the arguments for the existence of a deity are regarded as inconclusive, belief in God may be based upon faith. Are we ever justified in believing in doctrines which we cannot show to be true or even probable? Is faith a legitimate basis for belief?

Faith has been defended by such philosophers as St. Augustine, St. Thomas Aquinas, Pascal, Kant, and Kierkegaard, but perhaps the most interesting and cogent defense is to be found in William James' famous essay "The Will to Believe." Since this essay is written in an engaging and informal style which somewhat veils its logical structure, we shall here attempt to summarize the argument.

James' purpose is to defend not any and all kinds of faith but only belief entertained under the conditions that he specifies. He points out that we are often confronted by the problem of choosing between two mutually incompatible hypotheses. Such a choice he calls an "option," and he classifies options into three pairs of opposites: (1) *living* or *dead*, (2) *forced* or *avoidable*, and (3) *momentous* or *trivial*. A *living* option offers a choice sufficiently exciting to tempt our will; a *dead* option presents a choice that leaves us cold. A *forced* option cannot be escaped; an *avoidable* option can be indefinitely postponed or evaded. Finally, a *momentous* option makes an important difference; a *trivial* option has no significant consequences.

James cites many illustrations to clarify these distinctions, but we shall confine ourselves to a single example. Suppose you were critically ill and had to decide whether to risk a very dangerous operation. You would be confronted by two hypotheses: (1) that your chances of recovery would be better if you were to have the operation, and (2) that your chances would be better if you were to avoid the operation. Obviously, this option would be living, since you could not be indifferent to it; forced, since you could not delay or evade a decision (non-decision being equivalent to negative decision); and momentous, since it would be a life-and-death matter. James calls an option *genuine* when it is living, forced, and momentous.

He then distinguishes between three attitudes towards an hypothesis: belief, nonbelief, and disbelief. In terms of consequences, nonbelief and disbelief are sometimes identical. In the illustration cited above, the *failure* to decide (nonbelief) is practically equivalent to disbelief in the advisability of the operation. In either case, there would be no operation.

James also points out that whichever way a person may decide some risk is involved. By believing one runs the risk of falling into error; by disbelieving or nonbelieving one runs the risk of losing the benefit of the truth. For example, if you should believe in God and God does not exist, you would fall into error. But if you should not believe in God and God does exist, you would lose the benefit of a salutary truth. Sometimes it is better to believe in the hope of gaining the truth than to disbelieve in the hope of avoiding error.

Having thus defined his terms, James states three conditions which must be present in order for faith to be justified:

1. when we are confronted by a *genuine* option—living, forced, and momentous:

2. when we do not have enough reason or evidence to prove that one hypothesis (*e.g.*, that God exists) is more probable than the alternative hypothesis (that God does not exist); and

3. when the result of believing is to make life substantially better.

There is a final twist to the argument. James points out that belief in a proposition sometimes helps to make that proposition come true. He cites the example of a man's faith that his sweetheart really loves him. This faith helps to create a relation of confidence and intimacy that ensures, or helps to ensure, the very love which is the object of belief. In such case, faith is doubly justified.

James' argument is ingenious, and many people regard it as valid. It should not be used to justify credulity, however, and it should be hedged with qualifications. First, if we believe on the basis of faith, we should be clear-headed about what we are doing. We should recognize that it *is* faith and not reason. We should distinguish between *valuable* and *probable*, between *allurement* and *evidence*, between *wishful thinking* and *rational demonstration*. The mere fact that we desire a certain state to be the case is no evidence that it *is* the case. I may desire immortality, but my desire will not make me immortal. Believing in God may make me happier, but this has no bearing on the truth of my belief. "If wishes were horses, beggars would ride." If my wish or desire alone impels me to believe, I should not suppose that I have rational ground for belief.

Secondly, we should try to keep our unverified beliefs to a minimum. The more we assume without sufficient evidence, the more chances there are that we shall fall into error. The tendency to believe without good evidence, moreover, weakens the scientific temper, which is the main source of intellectual advance. Belief in these circumstances is not easy for a scientifically trained mind. It seems too much like "kidding" oneself. Perhaps the best of all faiths is the faith in inquiry, and this calls for the courage to abide by reason.

Thirdly, James speaks as if there were no intermediate shades of opinion between complete belief and complete disbelief. Actually there are many shades of belief and doubt. We rightly distinguish between probability and certainty, and we recognize that there are innumerable degrees of probability, depending upon the strength of the evidence. In a rational mind, the degree of credence is generally proportional to the degree of probability.

Fourthly, James is perhaps too much inclined to interpret nonbelief as practically equivalent to disbelief. In some situations, there is indeed no practical difference between them, but very often there is a difference. Moreover, the nonbelief of an agnostic is quite different from the nonbelief of an inquirist. There are five attitudes that we should distinguish:

Complete belief—"It is so."

Tentativity—"It may be so."

Complete disbelief—"It is not so."

Agnostic nonbelief—"We can never know."

Inquiristic nonbelief—"Let us try to find out."

Complete belief, complete disbelief, and agnostic nonbelief tend to cut off inquiry, whereas tentativity and inquiristic nonbelief tend to stimulate inquiry. Here is a practical difference of great importance—a difference which James seems to overlook.

Fifthly, his point that faith sometimes creates its own verification has limited validity. When the outcome of one's endeavors depends upon one's morale, faith in the venture may help to ensure success. A football team's faith that it will win may help to make it win; a man's faith that he will get well may help him to recover from a psychological or psychosomatic illness. No one will argue, however, that a man's faith in God will ensure, or even help to ensure, God's existence. The truth or falsity of most beliefs depends upon objective factors, independent of how one feels or thinks. Of course, *if* God exists and *if* he is a Being that enters into personal relations with individuals, the faith that one can commune with God may be very helpful in establishing the communion.

PART FOUR

The Basis of Morality

INTRODUCTORY NOTE

THERE ARE FEW words more common in the English language than *good, better, worse, right, wrong,* and *ought.* We use these words, or their synonyms, every day. "What a good piece of pie!" "You had better see that movie." "You ought to obey that traffic signal." "That is the wrong way to study for exams." And so on. Each of these utterances expresses a judgment, favorable or unfavorable. Although there are factual implications in each instance, the primary intention is to *evaluate* something rather than merely to state a fact. Purely descriptive sentences, such as "That man is six feet tall," stand in obvious contrast.

Corresponding to these two types of sentences, the evaluative and the descriptive, are two distinct fields of philosophy—*axiology,* or the theory of values, and *metaphysics,* or the theory of reality. In Part Three we have been concerned with metaphysics; in Part Four we shall turn to axiology—or, rather, to *ethics,* which is one of the principal parts of axiology. In its total scope, axiology is the theory of all types of value—not only the morally good or right, but the holy, the beautiful, the useful, or anything else prizeworthy. But we shall confine ourselves to moral values, which are the subject matter of ethics.

The function of ethics is not to tell you what men do, but to tell you what men *ought,* in a moral sense, to do. Its fundamental concepts are *good* and *bad* and *right* and *wrong.* How can we tell a good life from a bad one? How can we distinguish between right and wrong acts? These are the questions that ethics seeks to answer. Although such words as *good* and *right* can be used in a nonmoral sense, we shall be concerned with their moral usage.

The readers of this book have already been introduced to ethics in Part One. Socrates, in the *Apology* and *Crito,* was criticizing the ethics of custom and expediency and defending the ideal of wisdom. In Part Five, we shall again meet Socrates, this time as a character in Plato's *Republic.* In this dialogue, Socrates maintains that goodness is the harmonious development of all parts of the personality under the control of reason. Similarly, he defines the good of the state as the harmonious development of all classes under the control of wise men. Some readers of this book will prefer to consider the selections from the *Republic* in connection with the ethical problems of Part Four rather than the social problems of Part Five.

In an introductory book, it is impossible to survey the many types of ethics. We have confined our survey to the following:

1. *Aristotle's theory of rational development.* The good is the active exercise of those faculties distinctive of man, especially reason.

2. *Cicero's theory of natural law.* The good is the life according to nature —both the nature of man and the nature of his environment.

3. *Kant's theory of duty for duty's sake.* The only unqualified good is good will, which is based upon respect for duty. Our duty is to obey universal moral laws, regardless of the particular consequences.

4. *Mill's theory of happiness.* The good life excels in both quantity and quality of pleasure. Right acts are the most useful in achieving this goal.

5. *Dewey's theory of moral experiment.* The good life is experimental and has no final end or goal except growth.

6. *Stevenson's theory of limited scepticism.* Ethical judgments are in part statements about matters of fact and in part expressions of emotional attitudes. The former can be tested by evidence; the latter cannot.

These six theories exhibit a considerable variety of doctrine and introduce the most basic questions of ethics.

12

Morality Based on Reason

ARISTOTLE

(For biographical note see pages 181–182.)

From *The Nicomachean Ethics*[*]

1. [*The Nature of Happiness*]

[*Aristotle begins, in a way characteristic of his method, with a generalization which, if accepted, will lead to a more exact account of his subject. It is a generalization which is fundamental to his philosophy and in his own mind there is no doubt about the truth of it. Yet he is not at this point asserting its truth. He is content to state a position which he has found reason to hold. It may be defined in some such words as these.* The good is that at which all things aim. *If we are to understand this, we must form to ourselves a clear notion of what is meant by an aim or, in more technical language, an "end." The first chapter of the* Ethics *is concerned with making the notion clear.*]

It is thought that every activity, artistic or scientific, in fact every deliberate action or pursuit, has for its object the attainment of some good. We may therefore assent to the view which has been expressed that "the good" is "that at which all things aim." . . . Since modes of action involving the practiced hand and the instructed brain are numerous, the number of their ends is proportionately large. For instance, the end of medical science is health; of military science, victory; of economic science, wealth. All skills of that kind which come under a single "faculty"—a skill in making bridles or any other part of a horse's gear comes under the faculty or art of horsemanship, while horsemanship itself and every branch of military practice comes under the art of war, and in like manner other arts and techniques are subordinate to yet others—in all these the ends of the master arts are to be preferred to those of the subordinate skills, for it is the former that provide the motive for pursuing the latter. . . .

Now if there is an end which as moral agents we seek for its own sake, and which is the cause of our seeking all the other ends—if we are not to go on choosing one

* *The Ethics of Aristotle,* trans. by J. A. K. Thomson, George Allen and Unwin, London, 1953. Reprinted by permission. The sentences in italics are explanatory comments by the translator.

act for the sake of another, thus landing ourselves in an infinite progression with the result that desire will be frustrated and ineffectual—it is clear that this must be the good, that is the absolutely good. May we not then argue from this that a knowledge of the good is a great advantage to us in the conduct of our lives? Are we not more likely to hit the mark if we have a target? If this be true, we must do our best to get at least a rough idea of what the good really is, and which of the sciences, pure or applied, is concerned with the business of achieving it.

[*Ethics is a branch of politics. That is to say, it is the duty of the statesman to create for the citizen the best possible opportunity of living the good life. It will be seen that the effect of this injunction is not to degrade morality but to moralize politics. The modern view that "you cannot make men better by act of parliament" would have been repudiated by Aristotle as certainly as by Plato and indeed by ancient philosophers in general.*]

Now most people would regard the good as the end pursued by that study which has most authority and control over the rest. Need I say that this is the science of politics? It is political science that prescribes what subjects are to be taught in states, which of these the different sections of the population are to learn, and up to what point. We see also that the faculties which obtain most regard come under this science: for example, the art of war, the management of property, the ability to state a case. Since, therefore, politics makes use of the other practical sciences, and lays it down besides what we must do and what we must not do, its end must include theirs. And that end, in politics as well as in ethics, can only be the good for man. For even if the good of the community coincides with that of the individual, the good of the community is clearly a greater and more perfect good both to get and to keep. This is not to deny that the good of the individual is worth while. But what is good for a nation or a city has a higher, a diviner, quality.

Such being the matters we seek to investigate, the investigation may fairly be represented as the study of politics. . . .

[*. . . Let us consider what is the end of political science. For want of a better word we call it "Happiness." People are agreed on the word but not on its meaning.*]

. . . Since every activity involving some acquired skill or some moral decision aims at some good, what do we take to be the end of politics—what is the supreme good attainable in our actions? Well, so far as the name goes there is pretty general agreement. "It is happiness," say both intellectuals and the unsophisticated, meaning by "happiness" living well or faring well. But when it comes to saying in what happiness consists, opinions differ and the account given by the generality of mankind is not at all like that given by the philosophers. The masses take it to be something plain and tangible, like pleasure or money or social standing. Some maintain that it is one of these, some that it is another, and the same man will change his opinion about it more than once. When he has caught an illness he will say that it is health, and when he is hard up he will say that it is money. Conscious that they are out of their depths in such discussions, most people are impressed by anyone who pontificates and says something that is over their heads. Now it would no doubt be a waste of time to examine all these opinions; enough if we consider those which are most in evidence or have something to be said for them. Among these we shall have to discuss the view held by some that, over and above particular goods like those I have just mentioned, there is another which is good in itself and the cause of whatever goodness there is in all these others. . . .

[*A man's way of life may afford a clue to his genuine views upon the nature of happiness. It is therefore worth our while to glance at the different types of life.*]

. . . There is a general assumption that the manner of a man's life is a clue to what he on reflection regards as the good—in other words happiness. Persons of low tastes (always in the majority) hold that it is pleasure. Accordingly they ask for nothing better than the sort of life which consists in having a good time. (I have in mind the three well-known types of life—that just mentioned, that of the man of affairs, that of the philosophic student.) The utter vulgarity of the herd of men comes out in their preference for the sort of existence a cow leads. Their view would hardly get a respectful hearing, were it not that those who occupy great positions sympathize with a monster of sensuality like Sardanapalus. The gentleman, however, and the man of affairs identify the good with honor, which may fairly be described as the end which men pursue in political or public life. Yet honor is surely too superficial a thing to be the good we are seeking. Honor depends more on those who confer than on him who receives it, and we cannot but feel that the good is something personal and almost inseparable from its possessor. Again, why do men seek honor? Surely in order to confirm the favorable opinion they have formed of themselves. It is at all events by intelligent men who know them personally that they seek to be honored. And for what? For their moral qualities. The inference is clear; public men prefer virtue to honor. It might therefore seem reasonable to suppose that virtue rather than honor is the end pursued in the life of the public servant. But clearly even virtue cannot be

quite the end. It is possible, most people think, to possess virtue while you are asleep, to possess it without acting under its influence during any portion of one's life. Besides, the virtuous man may meet with the most atrocious luck or ill-treatment; and nobody, who was not arguing for argument's sake, would maintain that a man with an existence of that sort was "happy." . . . The third type of life is the "contemplative," and this we shall discuss later.

As for the life of the business man, it does not give him much freedom of action. Besides, wealth obviously is not the good we seek, for the sole purpose it serves is to provide the means of getting something else. So far as that goes, the ends we have already mentioned would have a better title to be considered the good, for they are desired on their own account. But in fact even their claim must be disallowed. We may say that they have furnished the ground for many arguments, and leave the matter at that. . . .

[*What then is the good? If it is what all men in the last resort aim at, it must be happiness. And that for two reasons: (1) happiness is everything it needs to be, (2) it has everything it needs to have.*]

. . . [The good] is one thing in medicine and another in strategy, and so in the other branches of human skill. We must inquire, then, what is the good which is the end common to all of them. Shall we say it is that for the sake of which everything else is done? In medicine this is health, in military science victory, in architecture a building, and so on—different ends in different arts; every consciously directed activity has an end for the sake of which everything that it does is done. This end may be described as its good. Consequently, if there be some one thing which is the end of all things consciously done, this will be the double good; or, if there be more than one end, then it will be all of these. . . .

In our actions we aim at more ends than one—that seems to be certain—but, since we choose some (wealth, for example, or flutes and tools or instruments generally) as means to something else, it is clear that not all of them are ends in the full sense of the word, whereas the good, that is the supreme good, is surely such an end. Assuming then that there is some one thing which alone is an end beyond which there are no further ends, we may call *that* the good of which we are in search. If there be more than one such final end, the good will be that end which has the highest degree of finality. An object pursued for its own sake possesses a higher degree of finality than one pursued with an eye to something else. A corollary to that is that a thing which is never chosen as a means to some remoter object has a higher degree of finality than things which are chosen both as ends in themselves and as means to such ends. We may conclude, then, that something which is always chosen for its own sake and never for the sake of something else is without qualification a final end.

Now happiness more than anything else appears to be just such an end, for we always choose it for its own sake and never for the sake of some other thing. It is different with honor, pleasure, intelligence and good qualities generally. We choose them indeed for their own sake in the sense that we should be glad to have them irrespective of any advantage which might accrue from them. But we also choose them for the sake of our happiness in the belief that they will be instrumental in promoting that. On the other hand nobody chooses happiness as a means of achieving them or anything else whatsoever than just happiness.

The same conclusion would seem to follow from another consideration. It is a generally accepted view that the final good is self-sufficient. By "self-sufficient" is meant not what is sufficient for oneself living the life of a solitary but includes parents, wife and children, friends and fellow-citizens in general. For man is a social animal. . . . A self-sufficient thing, then, we take to be one which on its own footing tends to make life desirable and lacking in nothing. And we regard happiness as such a thing. . . .

[*But we desire a clearer definition of happiness. The way to this may be prepared by a discussion of what is meant by the "function" of a man.*]

But no doubt people will say, "To call happiness the highest good is a truism. We want a more distinct account of what it is." We might arrive at this if we could grasp what is meant by the "function" of a human being. If we take a flutist or a sculptor or any craftsman—in fact any class of men at all who have some special job or profession—we find that his special talent and excellence comes out in that job, and this is his function. The same thing will be true of man simply as man—that is of course if "man" does have a function. But is it likely that joiners and shoemakers have certain functions or specialized activities, while man as such has none but has been left by Nature a functionless being? Seeing that eye and hand and foot and every one of our members has some obvious function, must we not believe that in like manner a human being has a function over and above these particular functions? Then what exactly is it? The mere act of living is not peculiar to man—we find it even in the vegetable kingdom—and what we are looking for is something peculiar to him. We must therefore exclude from our definition the life that manifests itself in mere nurture and growth. A step higher should come the life that is confined to experiencing sensations. But that we see is shared by horses, cows and the brute creation as a whole. We are left, then, with a life concerning which we can make two statements.

1. First, it belongs to the rational part of man.

2. Secondly, it finds expression in actions. The rational part may be either active or passive: passive in so far as it follows the dictates of reasoning. A similar distinction can be drawn within the rational life; that is to say, the reasonable element in it may be active or passive. Let us take it that what we are concerned with here is the reasoning power in action, for it will be generally allowed that when we speak of "reasoning" we really mean *exercising* our reasoning faculties. (This seems the more correct use of the word.)

Now let us assume for the moment the truth of the following propositions. (*a*) The function of a man is the exercise of his noncorporeal faculties or "soul" in accordance with, or at least not divorced from, a rational principle. (*b*) The function of an individual and of a *good* individual in the same class—a harp player, for example, and a good harp player, and so through the classes—is generically the same, except that we must add superiority in accomplishment to the function, the function of the harp player being merely to play on the harp, while the function of the good harp player is to play on it well. (*c*) The function of man is a certain form of life, namely an activity of the soul exercised in combination with a rational principle or reasonable ground of action. (*d*) The function of a good man is to exert such activity well. (*e*) A function is performed well when performed in accordance with the excellence proper to it.—If these assumptions are granted, we conclude that the good for man is "an activity of soul in accordance with goodness" or (on the supposition that there

may be more than one form of goodness) "in accordance with the best and most complete form of goodness."

[*Happiness is more than momentary bliss.*]

There is another condition of happiness; it cannot be achieved in less than a complete lifetime. One swallow does not make a summer; neither does one fine day. And one day, or indeed any brief period of felicity, does not make a man entirely and perfectly happy. . . .

[. . . *Our first principle—our definition of happiness—should be tested not only by the rules of logic but also by the application to it of current opinions on the subject.*]

So we must examine our first principle not only logically, that is as a conclusion from premises, but also in the light of what is currently said about it. For if a thing be true, the evidence will be found in harmony with it; and, if it be false, the evidence is quickly shown to be discordant with it.

But first a note about "goods." They have been classified as (*a*) external, (*b*) of the soul, (*c*) of the body. Of these we may express our belief that goods of the soul are the best and are most properly designated as "good." Now according to our definition happiness is an expression of the soul in considered actions, and that definition seems to be confirmed by this belief, which is not only an old popular notion but is accepted by philosophers. We are justified, too, in saying that the end consists in certain acts or activities, for this enables us to count it among goods of the soul and not among external goods. We may also claim that our description of the happy man as the man who lives or fares well chimes in with our definition. For happiness has pretty much been stated to be a form of such living or faring well. Again, our definition seems to include the elements detected in the various analyses of happiness —virtue, practical wisdom, speculative wisdom, or a combination of these, or one of them in more or less intimate association with pleasure. All these definitions have their supporters, while still others are for adding material prosperity to the conditions of a happy life. Some of these views are popular convictions of long standing; others are set forth by a distinguished minority. It is reasonable to think that neither the mass of men nor the sages are mistaken altogether, but that on this point or that, or indeed on most points, there is justice in what they say.

Now our definition of happiness as an activity in accordance with virtue is so far in agreement with that of those who say that it *is* virtue, that such an activity *involves* virtue. But of course it makes a great difference whether we think of the highest good as consisting in the *possession* or in the *exercise* of virtue. It is possible for a disposition to goodness to exist in a man without anything coming of it; he might be asleep or in some other way have ceased to exercise his function of a man. But that is not possible with the activity in our definition. For in "doing well" the happy man will of necessity *do*. Just as at the Olympic Games it is not the best-looking or the strongest men present who are crowned with victory but competitors —the successful competitors, so in the arena of human life the honors and rewards fall to those who show their good qualities in action.

Observe, moreover, that the life of the actively good is inherently pleasant. Pleasure is a psychological experience, and every man finds that pleasant for which he has a liking—"fond of" so and so is the expression people use. For example, a horse is a source of pleasure to a man who is fond of horses, a show to a man who is fond of

sight-seeing. In the same way just actions are a source of pleasure to a man who likes to see justice done, and good actions in general to one who likes goodness. Now the mass of men do not follow any consistent plan in the pursuit of their pleasures, because their pleasures are not inherently pleasurable. But men of more elevated tastes and sentiments find pleasure in things which are in their own nature pleasant, for instance virtuous actions, which are pleasant in themselves and not merely to such men. So their life does not need to have pleasure fastened about it like a necklace, but possesses it as a part of itself. We may go further and assert that he is no good man who does not find pleasure in noble deeds. Nobody would admit that a man is just, unless he takes pleasure in just actions; or liberal, unless he takes pleasure in acts of liberality; and so with the other virtues. Grant this, and you must grant that virtuous actions are a source of pleasure in themselves. And surely they are also both good and noble, and that always in the highest degree, if we are to accept, as accept we must, the judgment of the good man about them, he judging in the way I have described. Thus, happiness is the best, the noblest, the most delightful thing in the world, and in it meet all those qualities which are separately enumerated in the inscription upon the temple at Delos:

Justice is loveliest, and health is best,
And sweetest to obtain is heart's desire.

All these good qualities inhere in the activities of the virtuous soul, and it is these, or the best of them, which we say constitute happiness.

For all that those are clearly right who, as I remarked, maintain the necessity to a happy life of an addition in the form of material goods. It is difficult, if not impossible, to engage in noble enterprises without money to spend on them; many can only be performed through friends, or wealth, or political influence. There are also certain advantages, such as the possession of honored ancestors or children, or personal beauty, the absence of which takes the bloom from our felicity. For you cannot quite regard a man as happy if he be very ugly to look at, or of humble origin, or alone in the world and childless, or—what is probably worse—with children or friends who have not a single good quality. . . .

[*Our definition of happiness compels us to consider the nature of virtue. But before we can do this we must have some conception of how the human soul is constituted. It will serve our purpose to take over (for what it is worth) the current psychology which divides the soul into "parts."*]

Happiness, then, being an activity of the soul in conformity with perfect goodness, it follows that we must examine the nature of goodness. . . . The goodness we have to consider is human goodness. This—I mean human goodness or (if you prefer to put it that way) human happiness—was what we set out to find. By human goodness is meant not fineness of physique but a right condition of the soul, and by happiness a condition of the soul. That being so, it is evident that the statesman ought to have some inkling of psychology, just as the doctor who is to specialize in diseases of the eye must have a general knowledge of physiology. Indeed, such a general background is even more necessary for the statesman in view of the fact that his science is of a higher order than the doctor's. Now the best kind of doctor takes a good deal of trouble to acquire a knowledge of the human body as a whole. Therefore the statesman should also be a psychologist and study the soul with an eye to his profession. Yet he will do so only as far as his own problems make it necessary; to go into

greater detail on the subject would hardly be worth the labor spent on it.

Psychology has been studied elsewhere and some of the doctrines stated there may be accepted as adequate for our present purpose and used by us here. The soul is represented as consisting of two parts, a rational and an irrational. . . . As regards the irrational part there is one subdivision of it which appears to be common to all living things, and this we may designate as having a "vegetative" nature, by which I mean that it is the cause of nutrition and growth, since one must assume the existence of some such vital force in all things that assimilate food. . . . Now the excellence peculiar to this power is evidently common to the whole of animated nature and not confined to man. This view is supported by the admitted fact that the vegetative part of us is particularly active in sleep, when the good and the bad are hardest to distinguish. . . . Such a phenomenon would be only natural, for sleep is a cessation of that function on the operation of which depends the goodness or badness of the soul. . . . But enough of this, let us say no more about the nutritive part of the soul, since it forms no portion of goodness in the specifically *human* character.

But there would seem to be another constituent of the soul which, while irrational, contains an element of rationality. It may be observed in the types of men we call "continent" and "incontinent." They have a principle—a rational element in their souls—which we commend, because it encourages them to perform the best actions in the right way. But such natures appear at the same time to contain an irrational element in active opposition to the rational. In paralytic cases it often happens that when the patient wills to move his limbs to the right they swing instead to the left. Exactly the same thing may happen to the soul; the impulses of the incontinent man carry him in the opposite direction from that towards which he was aiming. The only difference is that, where the body is concerned, we see the uncontrolled limb, while the erratic impulse we do not see. Yet this should not prevent us from believing that besides the rational an irrational principle exists running opposite and counter to the other. . . . Yet, as I said, it is not altogether irrational; at all events it submits to direction in the continent man, and may be assumed to be still more amenable to reason in the "temperate" and in the brave man, in whose moral make-up there is nothing which is at variance with reason.

We have, then, this clear result. The irrational part of the soul, like the soul itself, consists of two parts. The first of these is the vegetative, which has nothing rational about it at all. The second is that from which spring the appetites and desire in general; and this does in a way participate in reason, seeing that it is submissive and obedient to it. . . . That the irrational element in us need not be heedless of the rational is proved by the fact that we find admonition, indeed every form of censure and exhortation, not ineffective. It may be, however, that we ought to speak of the appetitive part of the soul as rational, too. In that event it will rather be the rational part that is divided in two, one division rational in the proper sense of the word and in its nature, the other in the derivative sense in which we speak of a child as "listening to reason" in the person of its father.

These distinctions within the soul supply us with a classification of the virtues. Some are called "intellectual," as wisdom, intelligence, prudence. Others are "moral," as liberality and temperance. When we are speaking of a man's *character* we do not describe him as wise or intelligent but as gentle or temperate. Yet we praise a wise man, too, on the ground of his "disposition" or settled habit of acting wisely. The dispositions so praised are what we mean by "virtues."

2. [*Moral Goodness*]

[. . . *We have to ask what moral virtue or goodness is. It is a confirmed disposition to act rightly, the disposition being itself formed by a continuous series of right actions.*]

Virtue, then, is of two kinds, intellectual and moral. Of these the intellectual is in the main indebted to teaching for its production and growth, and this calls for time and experience. Moral goodness, on the other hand, is the child of habit, from which it has got its very name, ethics being derived from *ethos,* "habit." . . . This is an indication that none of the moral virtues is implanted in us by nature, since nothing that nature creates can be taught by habit to change the direction of its development. For instance a stone, the natural tendency of which is to fall down, could never, however often you threw it up in the air, be trained to go in that direction. No more can you train fire to burn downwards. Nothing in fact, if the law of its being is to behave in one way, can be habituated to behave in another. The moral virtues, then, are produced in us neither *by* Nature nor *against* Nature. Nature, indeed, prepares in us the ground for their reception, but their complete formation is the product of habit.

Consider again these powers or faculties with which Nature endows us. We acquire the ability to use them before we do use them. The senses provide us with a good illustration of this truth. We have not acquired the sense of sight from repeated acts of seeing, or the sense of hearing from repeated acts of hearing. It is the other way round. We had these senses before we used them, we did not acquire them as a result of using them. But the moral virtues we do acquire by first exercising them. The same is true of the arts and crafts in general. The craftsman has to learn how to make things, but he learns in the process of making them. So men become builders by building, harp players by playing the harp. By a similar process we become just by performing just actions, temperate by performing temperate actions, brave by performing brave actions. Look at what happens in political societies—it confirms our view. We find legislators seeking to make good men of their fellows by making good behavior habitual with them. . . .

We may sum it all up in the generalization, "Like activities produce like dispositions." This makes it our duty to see that our activities have the right character, since the differences of quality in them are repeated in the dispositions that follow in their train. So it is a matter of real importance whether our early education confirms us in one set of habits or another. It would be nearer the truth to say that it makes a very great difference indeed, in fact all the difference in the world. . . .

[*There is one way of discovering whether we are in full possession of a virtue or not. We possess it if we feel pleasure in its exercise; indeed, it is just with pleasures and pains that virtue is concerned.*]

We may use the pleasure (or pain) that accompanies the exercise of our dispositions as an index of how far they have established themselves. A man is temperate who abstaining from bodily pleasures finds this abstinence pleasant; if he finds it irksome, he is intemperate. Again, it is the man who encounters danger gladly, or at least without painful sensations, who is brave; the man who has these sensations is a coward. In a word, moral virtue has to do with pains

and pleasures. There are a number of reasons for believing this. (1) Pleasure has a way of making us do what is disgraceful; pain deters us from doing what is right and fine. Hence the importance—I quote Plato —of having been brought up to find pleasure and pain in the right things. True education is just such a training. (2) The virtues operate with actions and emotions, each of which is accompanied by pleasure or pain. This is only another way of saying that virtue has to do with pleasures and pains. (3) Pain is used as an instrument of punishment. For in her remedies Nature works by opposites, and pain can be remedial. (4) When any disposition finds its complete expression it is, as we noted, in dealing with just those things by which it is its nature to be made better or worse, and which constitute the sphere of its operations. Now when men become bad it is under the influence of pleasures and pains when they seek the wrong ones among them, or seek them at the wrong time, or in the wrong manner, or in any of the wrong forms which such offenses may take; and in seeking the wrong pleasures and pains they shun the right. . . .

So far, then, we have got this result. Moral goodness is a quality disposing us to act in the best way when we are dealing with pleasures and pains, while vice is one which leads us to act in the worst way when we deal with them. . . .

[*We have now to state the "differentia" of virtue. Virtue is a disposition; but how are we to distinguish it from other dispositions? We may say that it is such a disposition as enables the good man to perform his function well. And he performs it well when he avoids the extremes and chooses the mean in actions and feelings.*]

. . . Excellence of whatever kind affects that of which it is the excellence in two ways. (1) It produces a good state in it.

(2) It enables it to perform its function well. Take eyesight. The goodness of your eye is not only that which makes your eye good, it is also that which makes it function well. Or take the case of a horse. The goodness of a horse makes him a good horse, but it also makes him good at running, carrying a rider and facing the enemy. Our proposition, then, seems to be true, and it enables us to say that virtue in a man will be the disposition which (a) makes him a good man, (b) enables him to perform his function well. . . .

Every form . . . of applied knowledge, when it performs its function well, looks to the mean and works to the standard set by that. It is because people feel this that they apply the *cliché*, "You couldn't add anything to it or take anything from it" to an artistic masterpiece, the implication being that too much and too little alike destroy perfection, while the mean preserves it. Now if this be so, and if it be true, as we say, that good craftsmen work to the standard of the mean, then, since goodness like nature is more exact and of a higher character than any art, it follows that goodness is the quality that hits the mean. By "goodness" I mean goodness of moral character, since it is moral goodness that deals with feelings and actions, and it is in them that we find excess, deficiency and a mean. It is possible, for example, to experience fear, boldness, desire, anger, pity, and pleasures and pains generally, too much or too little or to the right amount. If we feel them too much or too little, we are wrong. But to have these feelings at the right times on the right occasions towards the right people for the right motive and in the right way is to have them in the right measure, that is somewhere between the extremes; and this is what characterizes goodness. The same may be said of the mean and extremes in actions. Now it is in the field of actions and

feelings that goodness operates; in them we find excess, deficiency and, between them, the mean, the first two being wrong, the mean right and praised as such. . . . Goodness, then, is a mean condition in the sense that it aims at and hits the mean. Consider, too, that it is possible to go wrong in more ways than one. (In Pythagorean terminology evil is a form of the Unlimited, good of the Limited.) But there is only one way of being right. That is why going wrong is easy, and going right difficult; it is easy to miss the bull's eye and difficult to hit it. Here, then, is another explanation of why the too much and the too little are connected with evil and the mean with good. As the poet says,

Goodness is one, evil is multiform.

[*We are now in a position to state our definition of virtue with more precision. Observe that the kind of virtue meant here is moral, not intellectual, and that Aristotle must not be taken as saying that the kind of virtue which he regards as the highest and truest is any sort of mean.*]

We may now define virtue as a disposition of the soul in which, when it has to choose among actions and feelings, it observes the mean relative to us, this being determined by such a rule or principle as would take shape in the mind of a man of sense or practical wisdom. We call it a mean condition as lying between two forms of badness, one being excess and the other deficiency; and also for this reason, that, whereas badness either falls short of or exceeds the right measure in feelings and actions, virtue discovers the mean and deliberately chooses it. Thus, looked at from the point of view of its essence as embodied in its definition, virtue no doubt is a mean; judged by the standard of what is right and best, it is an extreme.

[*Aristotle enters a caution. Though we have said that virtue observes the mean in actions and passions, we do not say this of all acts and all feelings. Some are essentially evil and, when these are involved, our rule of applying the mean cannot be brought into operation.*]

But choice of a mean is not possible in every action or every feeling. The very names of some have an immediate connotation of evil. Such are malice, shamelessness, envy among feelings, and among actions adultery, theft, murder. All these and more like them have a bad name as being evil in themselves; it is not merely the excess or deficiency of them that we censure. In their case, then, it is impossible to act rightly; whatever we do is wrong. . . .

[*Aristotle now suggests some rules for our guidance.*]

. . . We shall find it useful when aiming at the mean to observe these rules. (1) *Keep away from that extreme which is the more opposed to the mean.* It is Calypso's advice:

"Swing round the ship clear of this surf
and surge."

For one of the extremes is always a more dangerous error than the other; and—since it is hard to hit the bull's-eye—we must take the next best course and choose the least of the evils. And it will be easiest for us to do this if we follow the rule I have suggested. (2) *Note the errors into which we personally are most liable to fall.* (Each of us has his natural bias in one direction or another.) We shall find out what ours are by noting what gives us pleasure and pain. After that we must drag ourselves in the opposite direction. For our best way of reaching the middle is by giving a wide berth to our darling sin. It is the method used by a carpenter when he is straightening a warped board. (3) *Always be particularly on your guard against pleasure and pleasant things.* When

Pleasure is at the bar the jury is not impartial. So it will be best for us if we feel towards her as the Trojan elders felt towards Helen, and regularly apply their words to her. If we are for packing her off, as they were with Helen, we shall be the less likely to go wrong.

3. [*Intellectual Goodness*]

[. . . *Aristotle gives reasons for thinking that happiness in its highest and best manifestation is found in cultivating the "contemplative" life.*]

. . . If happiness is an activity in accordance with virtue, it is reasonable to assume that it will be in accordance with the highest virtue; and this can only be the virtue of the best part of us. Whether this be the intellect or something else—whatever it is that is held to have a natural right to govern and guide us, and to have an insight into what is noble and divine, either as being itself also divine or more divine than any other part of us—it is the activity of this part in accordance with the virtue proper to it that will be perfect happiness. Now we have seen already that this activity has a speculative or contemplative character. This is a conclusion which may be accepted as in harmony with our earlier arguments and with the truth. For "contemplation" is the highest form of activity, since the intellect is the highest thing in us and the objects which come within its range are the highest that can be known. But it is also the most continuous activity, for we can think about intellectual problems more continuously than we can keep up any sort of physical action. Again, we feel sure that a modicum of pleasure must be one of the ingredients of happiness. Now it is admitted that activity along the lines of "wisdom" is the pleasantest of all the good activities. At all events it is thought that philosophy ("the pursuit of wisdom") has pleasures marvelous in purity and duration, and it stands to reason that those who have knowledge pass their time more pleasantly than those who are engaged in its pursuit. Again, self-sufficiency will be found to belong in an exceptional degree to the exercise of the speculative intellect. The wise man, as much as the just man and everyone else, must have the necessaries of life. But, given an adequate supply of these, the just man also needs people with and towards whom he can put his justice into operation; and we can use similar language about the temperate man, the brave man, and so on. But the wise man can do more. He can speculate all by himself, and the wiser he is the better he can do it. Doubtless it helps to have fellow workers, but for all that he is the most self-sufficing of men. Finally it may well be thought that the activity of contemplation is the only one that is praised on its own account, because nothing comes of it beyond the act of contemplation, whereas from practical activities we count on gaining something more or less over and above the mere action. Again, it is commonly believed that, to have happiness, one must have leisure; we occupy ourselves in order that we may have leisure, just as we make war for the sake of peace. Now the practical virtues find opportunity for their exercise in politics and in war, but there are occupations which are supposed to leave no room for leisure. Certainly it is true of the trade of war, for no one deliberately chooses to make war for the sake of making it or tries to bring about a war. A man would be regarded as a bloodthirsty monster if he were to make war on a friendly state just to produce battles and slaughter. The business of the politician also makes leisure impossible. Besides the activity itself, politics aims at securing positions of power and honor or the happiness of the politician himself or his fellow citizens—a happiness obviously distinct from that which we are seeking.

We are now in a position to suggest the truth of the following statements. (a) Political and military activities, while preeminent among good activities in beauty and grandeur, are incompatible with leisure, and are not chosen for their own sake but with a view to some remoter end, whereas the activity of the intellect is felt to excel in the serious use of leisure, taking as it does the form of contemplation, and not to aim at any end beyond itself, and to own a pleasure peculiar to itself, thereby enhancing its activity. (b) In this activity we easily recognize self-sufficiency, the possibility of leisure and such freedom from fatigue as is humanly possible, together with all the other blessings of pure happiness. Now if these statements are received as true, it will follow that it is this intellectual activity which forms perfect happiness for a man—provided of course that it ensures a complete span of life, for nothing incomplete can be an element in happiness.

Yes, but such a life will be too high for *human* attainment. It will not be lived by us in our merely human capacity but in virtue of something divine within us, and so far as this divine particle is superior to man's composite nature, to that extent will its activity be superior to that of the other forms of excellence. If the intellect is divine compared with man, the life of the intellect must be divine compared with the life of a human creature. And we ought not to listen to those who counsel us *O man, think as man should* and *O mortal, remember your mortality*. Rather ought we, so far as in us lies, to put on immortality and to leave nothing unattempted in the effort to live in conformity with the highest thing within us. Small in bulk it may be, yet in power and preciousness it transcends all the rest. We may in fact believe that this is the true self of the individual, being the sovereign and better part of him. It would be strange, then, if a man should choose to live not his own life but another's. Moreover the rule, as I stated it a little before, will apply here —the rule that what is best and pleasantest for each creature is that which intimately belongs to it. Applying it, we shall conclude that the life of the intellect is the best and pleasantest for man, because the intellect more than anything else *is* the man. Thus it will be the happiest life as well.

COMMENT

The Basis of Aristotle's Ethics

Aristotle begins by noting that the goal of every action is some good, and that the good is what all things seek. He thus takes for granted as the basis of his ethics the teleological metaphysics which we reviewed in Chapter 7.

The acts of human beings, like those of other creatures, are undertaken for some purpose, either as means to some further ends or for their own sake. Human arts are differentiated by the ends toward which they are directed. "Art," in this connection, does not mean merely "fine" art; it means a skill, technique, or applied science—the physician's art of healing, for example. Some arts are instrumental to others, as bridle-making is instrumental to horsemanship, horsemanship to military strategy, and military strategy to politics. The highest and most inclusive art *is* politics; its function is to direct all the other arts so as to achieve the good for man. It is thus a kind of art of arts. (We shall return to this conception when we discuss Dewey's ethics in Chapter 16.) Since the end of politics is to achieve human wellbeing, politics is inseparable from ethics, which defines the goal of man. (Aristotle would frown upon the divorce of politics and ethics which, since the time of Machiavelli, has become altogether too characteristic of modern life.)

Good is that which all things seek, but each kind of thing seeks a different kind of good. Every thing tends to realize the form characteristic of its type. A puppy, for example, tends to realize the essential characteristics of a dog, just as a human infant tends to realize the essential characteristics of a human being. The good of each thing, or species, is the perfection of its form— the most complete expression of its fundamental characteristics. The good for a bear is to express its bear nature; the good for an alligator is to express its alligator nature; and the good for a human being is to express its human nature.

Aristotle notes that man's good is usually called "happiness," then suggests three criteria for recognizing happiness. First, happiness is an *end*, not a mere means. Secondly, it is sufficient in itself to satisfy us—we are looking for the whole and complete good. Thirdly, it is found in the life and work peculiar to man—a criterion which follows from Aristotle's metaphysical doctrine that each thing tends toward the fulfillment of its type.

In regard to this last criterion, Aristotle asks what it is that only man can do. In his treatise on psychology, he had distinguished three basic parts or aspects of man's nature: the vegetative, the appetitive, and the intellectual. The vegetative part, which man shares even with plants, is the capacity to take nourishment, grow, and reproduce. The appetitive, which man shares with animals, is the capacity for feeling, sensation, and impulse. The intellectual is the capacity to abstract, reflect, calculate—to live by rule instead of being swayed by appetite, to rise to knowledge of universal truths. This is the mark and chief glory of humankind. Man's proper function is the exercise and development of this distinctive part of his soul. We may define happiness as the excellent performance of this function, not just once in a while but throughout a life.

This definition embraces other common conceptions of happiness. Some say that happiness is virtue, others that it is pleasure, and still others that it is external prosperity. Now, according to Aristotle, virtue is the spring from which goodness flows, pleasure is its accompaniment, and prosperity is its normal precondition. The good thus inclusively conceived fulfills not only the third criterion but the other two as well—since it is an end-in-itself and all-sufficient.

Moral and Intellectual Goodness

There are two kinds of good, intellectual and moral, corresponding to the rational and irrational divisions of man's nature. Intellectual good consists in the virtues of the rational part of the soul—for example, prudence and wisdom. Moral good consists in the virtues of the irrational part when it is acting in obedience to reason—for example, temperance and courage.

In discussing the moral good, Aristotle asks whether it is the result of nature or of nurture; his answer is that both factors are contributory. Nature supplies man with the capacity for virtue, but this capacity must be perfected by habit. To be musical, a person must have some native talent, but he becomes musical by practicing music. To be virtuous, a person must likewise have native capacity, but he becomes virtuous by practicing virtue.

The maxim that should govern moral practice is this: "So act that you, a human being of a certain nature faced with a particular situation, may achieve the exact mean between excess and deficiency—a mean relative to you and the particular circumstances that you face." Aristotle insists that we should maintain a sense of proportion, avoiding the extremes that mar the harmony of life. He gives many examples: dignified self-respect is a mean between humility and vanity; courage, between cowardice and rashness; generosity, between stinginess and prodigality; temperance, between asceticism and licentiousness; friendliness, between quarrelsomeness and obsequiousness; and so on.

The mean is not a fixed point—it is adjustable to the time, the place, the circumstances, the nature of the agent and all those affected. It is as difficult to attain the mean as it is to hit a bull's eye. In trying to be generous, for example, it is relatively easy just to give money away—but to give it to the right person, to the right extent, at the right time, with the right motive, and in the right manner may be very difficult.

A comparison of Aristotle and Kant on this subject is instructive. Aristotle takes the view that, since virtue requires tact and the intuitive grasp of particulars, it cannot be formulated in invariable rules. Kant, on the contrary, holds that virtue consists in obedience to abstract universal rules, which are morally binding regardless of particular consequences. This contrast will become clear when we review Kant's ethics, in Chapter 14.

In discussing intellectual goodness, Aristotle classifies reason as theoretical, practical, and productive. The theoretical seeks to grasp truth for its own sake; the practical is concerned with useful actions; and the productive is directed toward making works of fine and useful art. Although Aristotle admits the value of practical and productive reason, he sings the praises of intellectual contemplation above all others. Nowhere else do his words kindle with such eloquence.

Some Critical Questions

In considering the merits and demerits of this theory, we should keep certain key questions in mind:

1. *Can we deduce good from the nature of things?* The presupposition of Aristotle's ethics is that each kind of thing has certain characteristic tendencies and that the good is the fulfillment of these tendencies. Man's good, accordingly, can be deduced from human nature. It may be objected that this implies an optimistic and undemonstrated premise (that developed reality is fully good) and allows the tendencies of the actual world to dictate our standards of value. Some philosophers, such as Kant, deny that the *ought* (good and right) can be derived from the *is* (matters of fact), and thus take fundamental issue with the basis of Aristotle's ethics. This issue is especially relevant to Cicero's theory of natural law, which we shall discuss in the next chapter, and hence we shall postpone its consideration.

2. *Is the wider definition of good correct?* We can distinguish, in Aristotle's theory, between a "wide" and a "narrow" definition of ultimate good. In its wide meaning, good is the actualization of potentialities. In its narrow meaning, it is the actualization of *human* potentialities, which are taken to be essentially rational.

Let us first consider the wider definition. It is very wide indeed, for it applies to animals, plants, and even inanimate things. Whether Aristotle would interpret it so broadly is not altogether clear. In his teleological metaphysics, he speaks of "end" or "final cause" in this very inclusive way, but he does not state explicitly that every end is good. If, however, the actualization of potentialities is taken to be the essence of good, there is no logical reason to stop short with conscious or even unconscious organisms.

This very wide definition, a critic might say, confuses an "end" in a temporal sense (the *finis* of a process) with an "end" in an ethical sense (good as an end rather than as a means). Another type of confusion may also be involved. We often say that something is a *good* example of its kind, and good in this sense, a biologist might claim, applies only to a fully developed animal, which clearly exhibits the powers and abilities of its species. But "good" in this sense does not imply positive value; a cancer specialist might speak of a perfectly good case of cancer, meaning a case so far developed that it clearly exhibits the generic characteristics of the malignancy. Has Aristotle confused good in this sense with good in its value import?

The attempt to extend the meaning of intrinsic goodness to include non-conscious things has often been challenged. If there were no feelings, no desires, no thoughts whatsoever—if all things in the universe were as unconscious as sticks and stones—would there be any value? Some philosophers maintain that a world without consciousness would be without value; if this were so, we should have to reject Aristotle's wider interpretation of good.

3. *Is the narrower definition of good correct?* Aristotle's interpretation of human goodness rests upon two premises: (*a*) the good is to be found in the life and work peculiar to man, and (*b*) rationality is the distinctive mark of the human creature. Both premises can be challenged.

(*a*) Why should we suppose that the human good is to be found in what is distinctive to man? That a certain factor is peculiar to a species does not necessarily imply any ethical superiority in that factor. If all human beings were just like other animals except that they alone had bowlegs, this would not prove that human good is bowleggedness. Perhaps Aristotle is taking it for granted that man *is* superior to other animals and that this superiority must lie in that which man alone possesses. But some philosophers would question this view. Hedonists, for example, would say that good is pleasure, and the fact that a dog can feel pleasure does not detract from human good. We may or may not believe that this view is mistaken and Aristotle's theory correct—but is there any way of supporting our conviction?

(b) *Is* reason the differentia of humankind? Certain psychologists, such as Wolfgang Köhler, have demonstrated that chimpanzees also have the capacity to reason. These clever animals can figure out ways of piling up and mounting boxes, for example, so as to reach a bunch of bananas hanging high from the top of their cage. Aristotle would no doubt reply that this is only *practical*, not *theoretical*, reason, but it may be that chimpanzees also have curiosity and enjoy satisfying it. At least it is not at all obvious that reason is *the* distinctive mark of human beings. What fundamentally distinguishes man is the whole remarkable development of human culture, including art and religion and spiritual love in addition to philosophy and science.

Perhaps Aristotle is correct in supposing that man's good is the actualization of his potentialities, but he may conceive these potentialities too narrowly. Our human good, one can argue, is the free functioning and full development of our many-sided nature, including emotion, imagination, and will. Aristotle's rather exclusive emphasis upon reason betrays the natural bias of a philosopher.

Still other questions might be posed. Is ethics inseparable from politics? Is virtue to be found in adherence to a mean? Does virtue consist in an intuitive response to particular circumstances, as Aristotle believed, or in obedience to universal rules, as Kant contended? Is pleasure merely contributory to the happy life, as Aristotle supposed, or is it the very essence of happiness, as Bentham maintained? Is the ideal of intellectual contemplation unrealizable by all but the aristocratic few, and, if so, should we favor the development of an intellectual élite rather than the cultivation of the masses? Other questions will probably occur to the reader.

In Chapter 13, we shall turn to a theory that is somewhat similar to that of Aristotle and yet markedly different in certain respects. It places less emphasis upon reason and the élite and more upon Nature's plan and universal humanity.

13

Morality Based on Nature

MARCUS TULLIUS CICERO (106–43 B.C.)

Statesman, philosopher, and man of letters, Cicero was one of the greatest intellectual figures during the last days of the Roman Republic. He won fame as a young lawyer for his successful defense of Sextus Roscius, the victim of a trumped-up murder charge and enemy of the powerful dictator, Sulla. In 75 B.C., Cicero was sent to Sicily as an administrator, and five years later acted as prosecutor of Verres, an unscrupulous governor whose cruel and corrupt rule had excited the hostility of the Sicilians. So powerful was the indictment that Verres, abandoning all hope of a defense, fled into exile.

In the year 66, Cicero, now a famous man, was elected a magistrate of Rome. Two years later he became Roman consul, at a time when the Republic was in a critical condition because of corruption and sedition. The courage and eloquence with which Cicero defeated the conspiracy of Catiline, whom he denounced before the Roman Senate in four famous orations, won him still greater celebrity. One of his enemies, Publius Clodius, a tribune, thereupon charged him with putting Catiline's fellow conspirators to death without public trial, and he was forced into exile. But he soon returned to public office and brilliantly defended the old forms of the Roman constitution against the encroachments of autocracy. After Caesar's murder, he denounced Mark Antony in a series of impassioned orations before the Senate. His death was then demanded by Antony, and he was assassinated.

Despite his tumultuous public career, Cicero found time to write various philosophical and literary works. He developed the Stoic doctrine that the only just government is that based upon law and that the moral foundation of law is the natural kinship and equality of all men.

From *The Laws*[*]

PERSONS OF THE DIALOGUE: *Marcus Tullius Cicero* himself; *Quintus Tullius Cicero,* his brother; and *Titus Pomponius Atticus,* his friend.

Marcus. . . . Out of all the material of the philosophers' discussions, surely there comes nothing more valuable than the full realization that we are born for Justice, and that right is based, not upon men's opinions, but upon Nature. This fact will immediately be plain if you once get a clear conception of man's fellowship and union with his fellow-men. For no single thing is so like another, so exactly its counterpart, as all of us are to one another. Nay, if bad habits and false beliefs did not twist the weaker minds and turn them in whatever direction they are inclined, no one would be so like his own self as all men would be like all others. And so, however we may define man, a single definition will apply to all. This is a sufficient proof that there is no difference in kind between man and man; for if there were, one definition could not be applicable to all men; and indeed reason, which alone raises us above the level of the beasts and enables us to draw inferences, to prove and disprove, to discuss and solve problems, and to come to conclusions, is certainly common to us all, and, though varying in what it learns, at least in the capacity to learn it is invariable. For the same things are invariably perceived by the senses, and those things which stimulate the senses, stimulate them in the same way in all men; and those rudimentary beginnings of intelligence to which I have referred, which are imprinted on our minds, are imprinted on all minds alike; and speech, the mind's interpreter, though differing in the choice of words, agrees in the sentiments expressed. In fact, there is no human being of any race who, if he finds a guide, cannot attain to virtue.

The similarity of the human race is clearly marked in its evil tendencies as well as in its goodness, for pleasure also attracts all men; and even though it is an enticement to vice, yet it has some likeness to what is naturally good. For it delights us by its lightness and agreeableness; and for this reason, by an error of thought, it is embraced as something wholesome. It is through a similar misconception that we shun death as though it were a dissolution of nature, and cling to life because it keeps us in the sphere in which we were born; and that we look upon pain as one of the greatest of evils, not only because of its cruelty, but also because it seems to lead to the destruction of nature. In the same way, on account of the similarity between moral worth and renown, those who are publicly honored are considered happy, while those who do not attain fame are thought miserable. Troubles, joys, desires, and fears haunt the minds of all men without distinction, and even if different men have different beliefs, that does not prove,

* The following excerpts from Books I and II of *The Laws* and Book III of *The Republic* are taken from *De Re Publica, De Legibus,* with an English translation by Clinton Walker Keyes (Loeb Classical Library), Harvard University Press, Cambridge, Mass., 1943. Reprinted by permission.

for example, that it is not the same quality of superstition that besets those races which worship dogs and cats as gods, as that which torments other races. But what nation does not love courtesy, kindliness, gratitude, and remembrance of favors bestowed? What people does not hate and despise the haughty, the wicked, the cruel, and the ungrateful? Inasmuch as these considerations prove to us that the whole human race is bound together in unity, it follows, finally, that knowledge of the principles of right living is what makes men better.

If you approve of what has been said, I will go on to what follows. But if there is anything that you care to have explained, we will take that up first.

Atticus. We have no questions, if I may speak for both of us.

Marcus. The next point, then, is that we are so constituted by Nature as to share the sense of Justice with one another and to pass it on to all men. And in this whole discussion I want it understood that what I shall call Nature is [that which is implanted in us by Nature]; that, however, the corruption caused by bad habits is so great that the sparks of fire, so to speak, which Nature has kindled in us are extinguished by this corruption, and the vices which are their opposites spring up and are established. But, if the judgments of men were in agreement with Nature, so that, as the poet says, they considered "nothing alien to them which concerns mankind," then Justice would be equally observed by all. For those creatures who have received the gift of reason from Nature have also received right reason, and therefore they have also received the gift of Law, which is right reason applied to command and prohibition. And if they have received Law, they have received Justice also. Now, all men have received reason; therefore, all

men have received Justice. Consequently, Socrates was right when he cursed, as he often did, the man who first separated utility from Justice; for this separation, he complained, is the source of all mischief. For what gave rise to Pythagoras' famous words about friendship? . . . From this it is clear that, when a wise man shows toward another endowed with equal virtue the kind of benevolence which is so widely diffused among men, that will then have come to pass which, unbelievable as it seems to some, is after all the inevitable result—namely, that he loves himself no whit more than he loves another. For what difference can there be among things which are all equal? But, if the least distinction should be made in friendship, then the very name of friendship would perish forthwith; for its essence is such that, as soon as either friend prefers anything for himself, friendship ceases to exist.

Now, all this is really a preface to what remains to be said in our discussion, and its purpose is to make it more easily understood that Justice is inherent in Nature. After I have said a few words more on this topic, I shall go on to the civil law, the subject which gives rise to all this discourse.

Quintus. You certainly need to say very little more on that head, for from what you have already said, Atticus is convinced, and certainly I am, that Nature is the source of Justice.

Atticus. How can I help being convinced, when it has just been proved to us, first, that we have been provided and equipped with what we may call the gifts of the gods; next, that there is only one principle by which men may live with one another, and that this is the same for all, and possessed equally by all; and, finally, that all men are bound together by a certain natural feeling of kindliness and good-will, and also by a partnership in Justice? Now that we have admitted the truth of these conclusions, and rightly, I think, how can we separate Law and Justice from Nature? . . .

Marcus. Once more, then, before we come to the individual laws, let us look at the character and nature of Law, for fear that, though it must be the standard to which we refer everything, we may now and then be led astray by an incorrect use of terms, and forget the rational principles on which our laws must be based.

Quintus. Quite so, that is the correct method of exposition.

Marcus. Well, then, I find that it has been the opinion of the wisest men that Law is not a product of human thought, nor is it any enactment of peoples, but something eternal which rules the whole universe by its wisdom in command and prohibition. Thus they have been accustomed to say that Law is the primal and ultimate mind of God, whose reason directs all things either by compulsion or restraint. Wherefore that Law which the gods have given to the human race has been justly praised; for it is the reason and mind of a wise lawgiver applied to command and prohibition.

Quintus. You have touched upon this subject several times before. But before you come to the laws of peoples, please make the character of this heavenly Law clear to us, so that the waves of habit may not carry us away and sweep us into the common mode of speech of such subjects.

Marcus. Ever since we were children, Quintus, we have learned to call, "If one summon another to court," [1] and other rules of the same kind, laws. But we must come to the true understanding of the matter, which is as follows: this and other commands and prohibitions of nations have the power to summon to righteousness and

away from wrongdoing; but this power is not merely older than the existence of nations and States, it is coeval with that God who guards and rules heaven and earth. For the divine mind cannot exist without reason, and divine reason cannot but have this power to establish right and wrong. No written law commanded that a man should take his stand on a bridge alone, against the full force of the enemy, and order the bridge broken down behind him; yet we shall not for that reason suppose that the heroic Cocles [2] was not obeying the law of bravery and following its decrees in doing so noble a deed. Even if there was no written law against rape at Rome in the reign of Lucius Tarquinius, we cannot say on that account that Sextus Tarquinius did not break that eternal Law by violating Lucretia, the daughter of Tricipitinus. For reason did exist, derived from the Nature of the universe, urging men to right conduct and diverting them from wrongdoing, and this reason did not first become Law when it was written down, but when it first came into existence; and it came into existence simultaneously with the divine mind. Wherefore the true and primal Law, applied to command and prohibition, is the right reason of supreme Jupiter.

Quintus. I agree with you, brother, that what is right and true is also eternal, and does not begin or end with written statutes.

Marcus. Therefore, just as that divine mind is the supreme Law, so, when [reason] is perfected in man, [that also is Law; and this perfected reason exists] in the mind of the wise man; but those rules which, in varying forms and for the need of the moment, have been formulated for the guidance of nations, bear the title of laws rather by favor than because they

[1] A familiar quotation from the Laws of the Twelve Tables, the earliest written code of Roman law.

[2] Horatius Cocles, who, with two companions, held the bridge over the Tiber against the Etruscan army.

are really such. For every law which really deserves that name is truly praiseworthy, as they prove by approximately the following arguments. It is agreed, of course, that laws were invented for the safety of citizens, the preservation of States, and the tranquillity and happiness of human life, and that those who first put statutes of this kind in force convinced their people that it was their intention to write down and put into effect such rules as, once accepted and adopted, would make possible for them an honorable and happy life; and when such rules were drawn up and put in force, it is clear that men called them "laws." From this point of view it can be readily understood that those who formulated wicked and unjust statutes for nations, thereby breaking their promises and agreements, put into effect anything but "laws." It may thus be clear that in the very definition of the term "law" there inheres the idea and principle of choosing what is just and true. I ask you then, Quintus, according to the custom of the philosophers: if there is a certain thing, the lack of which in a State compels us to consider it no State at all, must we consider this thing a good?

Quintus. One of the greatest goods, certainly.

Marcus. And if a State lacks Law, must it for that reason be considered no State at all?

Quintus. It cannot be denied.

Marcus. Then Law must necessarily be considered one of the greatest goods.

Quintus. I agree with you entirely.

Marcus. What of the many deadly, the many pestilential statutes which nations put in force? These no more deserve to be called laws than the rules a band of robbers might pass in their assembly. For if ignorant and unskilful men have prescribed deadly poisons instead of healing drugs, these cannot possibly be called physicians' prescriptions; neither in a nation can a statute of any sort be called a law, even though the nation, in spite of its being a ruinous regulation, has accepted it. Therefore Law is the distinction between things just and unjust, made in agreement with that primal and most ancient of all things, Nature; and in conformity to Nature's standard are framed those human laws which inflict punishment upon the wicked but defend and protect the good.

Quintus. I understand you completely, and believe that from now on we must not consider or even call anything else a law.

Marcus. Then you do not think the Titian or Apuleian Laws were really laws at all?

Quintus. No; nor the Livian Laws either.[3]

Marcus. And you are right, especially as the Senate repealed them in one sentence and in a single moment. But the Law whose nature I have explained can neither be repealed nor abrogated.

---

[3] Examples of laws passed in Rome. It is implied that these enacted laws are not laws in the profounder sense that applies to natural laws.

From *The Republic*

. . . True law is right reason in agreement with nature; it is of universal application, unchanging and everlasting; it summons to duty by its commands, and averts from wrongdoing by its prohibitions. And it does not lay its commands or prohibitions upon good men in vain, though neither have any effect on the wicked. It is a sin to try to alter this law, nor is it allowable to attempt to repeal any part of it, and it is impossible to abolish it entirely. We cannot be freed from its obligations by senate or people, and we need not look outside ourselves for an expounder or interpreter of it. And there will not be different laws at Rome and at Athens, or different laws now and in the future, but one eternal and unchangeable law will be valid for all nations and all times, and there will be one master and ruler, that is, God, over us all, for he is the author of this law, its promulgator, and its enforcing judge. Whoever is disobedient is fleeing from himself and denying his human nature, and by reason of this very fact he will suffer the worst penalties, even if he escapes what is commonly considered punishment. . . .

COMMENT

The "Ought-Is" Question and the Philosophy of Natural Law

One of the crucial questions of ethical theory is suggested by David Hume in a famous passage:

> In every system of morality, which I have hitherto met with, I have always remarked, that the author proceeds for some time in the ordinary way of reasoning, and establishes the being of a God, or makes observations concerning human affairs; when of a sudden I am surprized to find, that instead of the usual copulation of proposition, *is,* and *is not,* I meet with no proposition that is not connected with an *ought,* or an *ought not.* This change is imperceptible; but is, however, of the last consequence. For as this *ought,* or *ought not,* expresses some new relation or affirmation, 'tis necessary that it should be observed and explained; and at the same time that a reason should be given, for what seems altogether inconceivable, how this new relation can be a deduction from others, which are entirely different from it.[1]

The philosophy of natural law, as formulated by Cicero, is one of the classic answers to the problem posed by Hume. The advocates of this type of theory are seeking some touchstone for judging moral questions outside the individual whimsies of human beings and the enforced orthodoxies and blind

[1] *A Treatise of Human Nature,* ed. by L. A. Selby-Bigge (Oxford: Clarendon Press, 1886), p. 469.

prejudices of groups. The only reliable touchstone, they believe, is to be found in the *nature* of human beings and their cosmic environment. Valid statements about what ought to be (or ought to be done) are derivable from *what is*—from the nature of things.

Whatever may be our judgment as to the soundness of this type of philosophy, there can be no doubt about its historical importance. Among Greek philosophers, it is most explicit in the writings of the Stoics, such as Epictetus and Marcus Aurelius, and in philosophers strongly influenced by them, notably Cicero and Seneca. It represented the heritage of the ancient world that could be most readily adapted to Christian teaching, and in the writings of such Catholics as St. Thomas Aquinas and such Protestants as Thomas Hooker, it received an interpretation consonant with Christianity. John Locke and Hugo Grotius, among later thinkers, gave it a more individualistic and secular expression. Its explosive force was revealed in the natural-rights theories of the American and French revolutions. Although it suffered a decline in the nineteenth century, it has recently shown vigorous signs of revival. It figured prominently in the debates that led to the formulation and adoption of the United Nations Declaration of Human Rights—a document which stipulates the fundamental conditions of human dignity and well-being for all people everywhere. Thus, for more than two thousand years, the concept of *nature* as a basis for ethics has played an immense and continuing role.

The Ethics of Cicero

At the present time, Cicero is not generally considered to be one of the major figures in the history of philosophy. He is, however, certainly very important in the history of thought, for he wielded an immense influence upon medieval and Renaissance culture. Because of the typicality of his ideas and the clarity and eloquence of his style, we have selected the philosophy of Cicero as representative of the "natural law" tradition. His ethical philosophy may be summarized under three interrelated headings: (1) the concept of a cosmic order as the ground of objective moral laws, (2) the idea of natural law, and (3) the doctrine of the natural kinship of all human beings. Let us glance at each of these tenets.

1. *Cosmic order as the basis of objective moral law.* The metaphysical background of Cicero's theory is the Stoic conception of nature as rational and divine. "Nature" is the divine reason infused through the cosmos—the inner essence and animating force of all things—and human reason is the divine element in man. By means of reason, man can discover the fundamental laws of the universe and can direct his conduct in conformity with these laws. To live according to nature is to develop one's essential faculties and, at the same time, to be in harmony with the divine order of the cosmos.

2. *The law of nature.* Cicero's theory of natural law is based on the conception of natural harmony. Grounded in the innermost nature of man, society, and the universe, natural law is independent of convention, legislation, and all other institutional devices. Far from being an arbitrary construction based on human wish or decree, it is both a law of nature and a moral law, universal, irrevocable, and inalienable. It provides the ultimate standard of right conduct, whether of individuals or of states.

"Natural law" in this sense should be clearly distinguished from what modern science means by *a* natural law. Physicists speak of the law of gravity, but this is a law in a purely descriptive and non-moral sense. Everyone is subject to such a natural law and no one can disobey it, because it is imposed upon our bodies by physical necessity without the cooperation of our will or reason. It is just as binding upon a worm or a rock as it is upon a human being. But "natural law" in Cicero's sense is quite different. Man is obliged to obey it only by his reason and conscience: it is not automatically compulsory. The "natural law" that we should live in peace and friendship with our fellow men, for example, is frequently violated. It orders our conduct only to the extent that it is apprehended by our reason and imposed by our will.

Why, then, should such a thing be called a "law of nature"? Because the good for man depends upon the *nature* of man and his universe. Moral laws are not purely arbitrary. The *"ought,"* in Hume's terminology, is based upon what *"is."* Norms are founded on facts. Even when it is broken, the moral law remains a non-arbitrary standard, irrevocable in the sense that it is eternally valid. Those who violate it suffer evil and harm; those who live in harmony with it enjoy the highest blessedness. In this sense, it is enforced by natural sanctions.

This doctrine does not mean that there is a perfect identity between *what is* and *what ought to be.* Cicero does not deny that there are bad men and bad societies. But nature determines certain tendencies that require completion if good is to be achieved. Each individual entity possesses a nature which it shares with other members of the species. This essential nature determines its most fundamental tendencies. Good inheres in the fulfillment of these tendencies; evil, in their frustration. The good for a human being, therefore, differs from the good for a fox or a bear. Cicero agrees with Aristotle that reason is man's most distinctive faculty and that human virtue consists above all in the development of reason and in the rational direction of other human faculties to their natural fulfillment. Although each human life varies in many incidental ways, its fundamental good is to be found in the fulfillment of the essential tendencies of the species and, beyond this, in a harmonization with the basic forces of the universe. The general pattern of action required for the attainment of this good is the law of nature.

3. *The natural kinship of all human beings.* In Cicero's philosophy, the doctrine of natural law is combined with the doctrine of natural brotherhood and equality. All men by nature are kin. "No single thing is so like another . . . as all of us are to one another. . . . And so, however we may define man, a single definition will apply to all." This does not mean that all men are equal in learning or that they should be made equal in worldly goods, but, rather, that they all possess a similar psychological constitution and, should be treated with the dignity and respect that befits a human being. In opposition to all forms of relativism and parochialism—the bias of race, nation, class, or creed—Cicero asserts the great doctrine of human brotherhood.

One of the momentous implications of this doctrine is that the highest allegiance is not to the local state but to the universal fellowship. All men, as children of nature, are bound in conscience by the same laws and belong, in this sense, to the same "commonwealth." "Those who share Law must also share Justice; and those who share these are to be regarded as members of the same commonwealth. . . . Hence we must now conceive of this whole universe as one commonwealth of which both gods and men are members." Cicero does not deny that we should be citizens of the particular state in which we find ourselves; he even emphasizes the importance of civic duties. Local allegiance, however, is ethically subordinate to the wider allegiance to nature and man. If the laws of the state do not conform to the laws of nature, they no more deserve to be called laws than do the dictates of a robber band. Here is the ultimate source of the revolutionary doctrine that men owe a higher allegiance to nature and to nature's God than to any temporal ruler and hence have the inalienable right to revolt against an unjust and tyrannical state.

Cicero's emphasis is not upon natural *rights* but upon natural law; but the insistence upon rights, characteristic of the American Declaration of Independence and the French Declaration of the Rights of Man, is an easy deduction from the natural-law theory. A *right* is a justifiable claim. A *legal* right is a claim that can be legally justified; a *moral* right is a claim that can be morally justified. *Natural* rights are *moral*, not legal, rights. They are those claims that are derived not from the customs and enacted laws of society but from the law of nature—the claims that human beings can legitimately make in view of the essential characteristics of human nature and its natural environment.

Facts and Norms

The theory of natural law and rights is one answer, as we have said, to Hume's question as to the relation between "is" and "ought." It may be helpful in judging the validity of Cicero's philosophy to glance at various alternative answers to Hume's problem. Without attempting to give an exhaustive classification, we can distinguish between descriptivist, nondescriptivist, and intermediate theories.

1. *Descriptivist theories.* The descriptivist doctrine maintains that ethical norms—rules or standards for right action—are simply descriptive of, or immediately inferrable from, natural facts. For example, there is the sort of ethical naturalism that identifies normative principles with physical or biological laws (*e.g.*, survival of the fittest is "the law of life" and therefore a valid standard). In a less naïve form, this type of theory recognizes the distinction between the laws governing nonhuman nature and those governing human nature, and identifies valid norms with the biological, psychological, or sociological laws that apply specifically to human life. Another variation is to identify valid norms with existing norms—what ought to be with custom or positive law. There are also the two forms of ethical historicism: first, *futurism,* the identification of what ought to be with what will be ("the wave of the future"), and, second, *archaism,* the identification of what ought to be with what has been (the "golden age" of the past).

It is not difficult to show that such descriptivist theories involve a fundamental fallacy. Given the factual proposition, *X is* (or *was,* or *will be*) *the case,* we are asked to conclude that *X is good,* or *X ought to be.* But the fact that something is or was or will be the case is never a *sufficient* ground for asserting that it is valuable or obligatory, since the whole tragedy of existence is to be found in the disparity between *fact* and *value.*

2. *Nondescriptivist theories.* Nondescriptivist theories maintain that there is a wide and impassable gulf between norms and facts. An example is the "emotive theory," which its critics have dubbed the "boo-hurrah" interpretation of ethics. According to this view, ethical statements are like "boo" and "hurrah" in that they merely express emotional attitudes of favor or disfavor. As A. J. Ayer, one of the proponents of the theory, has written: "In saying that a certain type of action is right or wrong, I am not making any factual statement. . . . I am merely expressing certain moral sentiments. So that there is no sense in asking which of us is in the right." [2] No one is "in the right," because no ethical statements have an objective basis. If you say, "Cherry pie is delicious," and I reply, "No it isn't," there is no real contradiction, because each of us is merely expressing his own taste. So it is, according to Ayer, with ethical statements. This type of theory stands in obvious contrast to Cicero's theory of natural law.

The ethical philosophy of Kant, which we shall examine in the next chapter, is a nondescriptivist theory of a very different kind. Kant sharply distinguishes between "ought" and "is" and denies that the former can be derived from the latter. But unlike Ayer, he believes that duty is objective and absolute. The rules of morality, he contends, are based upon pure *a*

[2] *Language, Truth, and Logic* (London: V. Gollancz, 1936), p. 107.

priori reason rather than empirical science, and hence cannot be determined by the observation of facts. This theory resembles the emotive theory in one respect—the denial that ethical norms are descriptive of what is the case.

If the fallacy of descriptivist theories is to *identify* fact and value, perhaps the fallacy of nondescriptivist theories is to *separate* them. The effect is to limit unduly the province of empirical reason and thus to prevent the utilization of science and intelligence in ethics.

3. *Intermediate theories.* The so-called intermediate theories maintain that normative statements are neither purely descriptive nor, if valid, divorced from fact. An example is C. D. Broad's chapter on Bishop Butler in *Five Types of Ethical Theory*. Here Broad suggests that "virtue consists in acting in accordance with the *ideal nature* of man." This is not a descriptivist theory because "no man's actual nature is the ideal nature of man." But an ideal concept is derived from a consideration of actual entities—imperfect instances arranged in a series. Take the concept of a "perfect circle." "We see such things as cakes and biscuits and pennies. On reflection we see that they fall into a series—cake, biscuit, penny—in which a certain attribute is more and more fully realized. Finally we form the concept of a perfect circle as the ideal limit to such a series." Similarly, "By comparing and contrasting actual horses, all of which are defective in various respects and to various degrees, we can form the notion of an ideal horse." And in the same way, "If we arrange actual men, including ourselves, in a series, and reflect on it, we can detect a closer and closer approximation to an ideal which is not realized in any of them." [3] Such an ideal would not be arbitrary because it would be sustained by a grasp of actual human characteristics.

In the matter of health, for example, we compare various human beings, none of whom has perfect health but some of whom more closely approximate this limit than others. By imaginatively projecting the series, we arrive at the conception of an ideal or upper limit. An ordinary layman has a very hazy ideal of health, whereas a physician has a much clearer and more valid concept. The reason for the superiority of his concept is obvious: he has a far greater fund of relevant knowledge. So it is in many fields. The expert, with superior knowledge and insight, is able to formulate a more valid norm than the layman's. This implies that valid norms are not capricious but are sustained by genuine factual insights even though they *describe* no actual entities.

There are major premises here that should not be overlooked. If we compare particulars with respect to a certain quality, we must have some awareness of that quality. For example, if we compare more or less circular objects with respect to circularity, we must have in mind what is meant by cir-

[3] *Five Types of Ethical Theory* (Harcourt, Brace, 1930), pp. 57–59.

cularity. Otherwise we could not reach the concept of a perfect circle. Similarly, if we compare individuals with respect to worth, we must have some awareness of worth. The basic premises of this type of theory include the following: first, there *are* value properties, and in some way we can know them; and second, by comparing these properties, we can transcend mere facts and conceive ideal possibilities which serve as ethical norms.

One might judge from some of Cicero's pronouncements that his doctrine belongs to the first, or descriptivist, type; yet it seems that, on the whole, it belongs to the third, or intermediate, type. Right action is said to agree with nature, but by "nature" Cicero does not mean whatever happens to be the case. His ideal is the fulfillment of those tendencies that are most characteristic of human beings and that link them most harmoniously to their total environment. As a matter of fact, such tendencies are often obstructed, and hence fact and ideal are frequently far apart.

It may be questioned whether this theory entirely resolves the "ought-is" problem posed by Hume. It seems clear that *good*, in the sense of *what ought to be*, and *right*, in the sense of *what ought to be done*, are not natural characteristics, as are rectangularity or absent-mindedness. Many philosophers have concluded that these concepts have a distinctly *ethical* meaning—a meaning which must be grasped by intuition or *a priori* reason rather than by empirical science. In the next chapter we shall examine this contention.

Although the theory of natural law may not sufficiently account for "oughtness," or for the distinctively ethical meaning of right and good, it should not be dismissed as unimportant or fallacious. The idea that all human beings belong to a single moral "commonwealth"—that they should accordingly treat one another as friends rather than as enemies—has never been more important than in this age of atomic power. Such a commonwealth can be fully actualized only when men discover their common human nature and freely and intelligently seek to cultivate it. We can scarcely deny that human beings are a good deal alike the world over. We may amuse ourselves, if we choose, by imagining people who habitually prefer loneliness, anxiety, disease, hunger, cold, fatigue, ignorance, insanity, and other forms of misery, and whose moral attitudes are in all essential respects the reverse of our own; but such human beings do not seem to be the kind that occupies this planet. Not only is there a common human nature but, increasingly, there is a common human nurture. As modern technology becomes ever more pervasive, linking all human beings by modern instruments of production, transport, and communication and exposing all to the promises and threats of our "atomic age," there is an ever more imperative need for a moral universality to match a technological universality. Massively in the background, moreover, is the enduring and overarching environment of nature—the basic conditions of our planetary existence. Death comes to every man, and while he lives he must cope with the natural laws that govern the whole organic process of life and movement. A moral "commonwealth" is created when human beings, conscious of their common needs, their common environment, and their common destiny, seek by rational and responsible means to enrich their common life.

14

Morality Based on Duty

IMMANUEL KANT (1724–1804)

The fourth child of an humble saddle-maker, Kant was born in Königsberg, East Prussia. His parents belonged to the Pietists, a revivalist sect within the Lutheran Church, and the family life was characterized by simple religious devotion. Kant detested the mechanical discipline and narrow range of ideas of the Pietist school to which he was sent. At sixteen, he enrolled in the University of Königsberg, supporting himself mainly by tutoring well-to-do students. There his intellectual interests turned to physics and astronomy. After six years at the University, Kant became a private tutor in several homes in East Prussia, a profession which he followed for some nine years. Returning to the University in 1755, he obtained a higher degree and a subordinate post on the faculty. For the next fifteen years he lived in academic poverty, until, in 1770, he was finally appointed a full Professor. In his lectures, he enthralled his student audiences with his knowledge, eloquence, and wit. The popular form of his teaching was in marked contrast to the difficult and technical style of his writing.

He never married, and the clocklike regularity of his bachelor ways became proverbial. His servant awakened him at four forty-five every morning; he spent the next hour drinking tea, smoking his pipe, and planning the day's work; from six to seven he prepared his lectures; from seven to nine or ten he taught; then he wrote until half-past eleven; at twelve he ate a hearty dinner; in the afternoon, rain or shine, he took a regular walk; after that, he read or wrote until, at ten, he went to bed. The rigidity of his routine did not prevent him from enjoying the society of ladies and enlivening many social gatherings with his dry wit. He had many friends in the town and, until he was old, he always dined with friends. His gallantry never deserted him; even when he was so old and feeble that he lost his footing and fell in the street, he courteously presented one of the two unknown ladies who helped him to his feet with the rose that he happened to be carrying.

Although he never traveled far from Königsberg, he was fond of travel books and sympathetic with intellectual and political emancipation the world over. "Have the courage to use your own intelligence!" he advised. He applauded the American and French revolutions, but not the Reign of Terror. "It was a time in Königsberg," wrote one of his colleagues, "when anyone who judged the Revolution even mildly, let alone favorably, was put on a black list as a Jacobin. Kant did not allow himself by that fact to be deterred from speaking up for the Revolution even at the table of noblemen."

Except for a remarkable astronomical treatise (1755), in which he anticipated Laplace's nebular hypothesis, all of his more important works were published late in his life, after he was awakened by Hume from his "dogmatic slumber." In an amazing decade, from 1780 to 1790, there appeared a series of epoch-making books, including *The Critique of Pure Reason* (1781), *The Prolegomena to All Future Metaphysics* (1783), *The Foundations of the Metaphysic of Morals* (1785), *The Critique of Practical Reason* (1788), and *The Critique of Judgment* (1790). He subsequently published works on politics and religion, but his main task was done. After 1796, his health gradually declined, and he died in 1804, aged nearly eighty.

From *The Foundations of The Metaphysic of Morals**

Section I.—Transition from Ordinary Moral Conceptions to the Philosophical Conception of Morality

Nothing in the whole world, or even outside of the world, can possibly be regarded as good without limitation except a *good will*. No doubt it is a good and desirable thing to have intelligence, sagacity, judgment, and other intellectual gifts, by whatever name they may be called; it is also good and desirable in many respects to possess by nature such qualities as courage, resolution, and perseverance; but all these gifts of nature may be in the highest degree pernicious and hurtful, if the will which directs them, or what is called the *character*, is not itself good. The same thing applies to *gifts of fortune*. Power, wealth, honor, even good health, and that general well-being and contentment with one's lot which we call *happiness*, give rise to pride and not infrequently to insolence, if a man's will is not good; nor can a reflective and impartial spectator ever look with satisfaction upon the unbroken prosperity of

* *The Philosophy of Kant as Contained in Extracts from His Own Writings,* selected and translated by John Watson. Jackson, Wylie and Company, Glasgow, 1888, second edition, 1891. (In this version, the original is somewhat condensed.)

a man who is destitute of the ornament of a pure and good will. A good will would therefore seem to be the indispensable condition without which no one is even worthy to be happy.

A man's will is good, not because the consequences which flow from it are good, nor because it is capable of attaining the end which it seeks, but it is good in itself, or because it wills the good. By a good will is not meant mere well-wishing; it consists in a resolute employment of all the means within one's reach, and its intrinsic value is in no way increased by success or lessened by failure.

This idea of the absolute value of mere will seems so extraordinary that, although it is endorsed even by the popular judgment, we must subject it to careful scrutiny.

If nature had meant to provide simply for the maintenance, the well-being, in a word the happiness, of beings which have reason and will, it must be confessed that, in making use of their reason, it has hit upon a very poor way of attaining its end. As a matter of fact the very worst way a man of refinement and culture can take to secure enjoyment and happiness is to make use of his reason for that purpose. Hence there is apt to arise in his mind a certain degree of *misology*, or hatred of reason. Finding that the arts which minister to luxury, and even the sciences, instead of bringing him happiness, only lay a heavier yoke on his neck, he at length comes to envy, rather than to despise, men of less refinement, who follow more closely the promptings of their natural impulses, and pay little heed to what reason tells them to do or to leave undone. It must at least be admitted, that one may deny reason to have much or indeed any value in the production of happiness and contentment, without taking a morose or ungrateful view

of the goodness with which the world is governed. Such a judgment really means that life has another and a much nobler end than happiness, and that the true vocation of reason is to secure that end.

The true object of reason then, in so far as it is practical, or capable of influencing the will, must be to produce a will which is *good in itself,* and not merely good *as a means* to something else. This will is not the only or the whole good, but it is the highest good, and the condition of all other good, even of the desire for happiness itself. It is therefore not inconsistent with the wisdom of nature that the cultivation of reason which is essential to the furtherance of its first and unconditioned object, the production of a good will, should, in this life at least, in many ways limit, or even make impossible, the attainment of happiness, which is its second and conditioned object.

To bring to clear consciousness the conception of a will which is good in itself, a conception already familiar to the popular mind, let us examine the conception of *duty,* which involves the idea of a good will as manifested under certain subjective limitations and hindrances.

I pass over actions which are admittedly violations of duty, for these, however useful they may be in the attainment of this or that end, manifestly do not proceed *from* duty. I set aside also those actions which are not actually inconsistent with duty, but which yet are done under the impulse of some natural inclination, although *not a direct inclination* to do these particular actions; for in these it is easy to determine whether the action that is consistent with duty, is done *from duty* or with some selfish object in view. It is more difficult to make a clear distinction of motives when there is a *direct* inclination to do a certain action, which is itself in conformity with duty. The preservation of one's own life.

for instance, is a duty; but, as everyone has a natural inclination to preserve his life, the anxious care which most men usually devote to this object, has no intrinsic value, nor the maxim from which they act any moral import. They preserve their life *in accordance with* duty, but not *because of* duty. But, suppose adversity and hopeless sorrow to have taken away all desire for life; suppose that the wretched man would welcome death as a release, and yet takes means to prolong his life simply from a sense of duty: then his maxim has a genuine moral import.

But, secondly, an action that is done from duty gets its moral value, *not from the object* which it is intended to secure, but from the maxim by which it is determined. Accordingly, the action has the same moral value whether the object is attained or not, if only the *principle* by which the will is determined to act is independent of every object of sensuous desire. What was said above makes it clear, that it is not the object aimed at, or, in other words, the consequences which flow from an action when these are made the end and motive of the will, that can give to the action an unconditioned and moral value. In what, then, can the moral value of an action consist, if it does not lie in the will itself, as directed to the attainment of a certain object? It can lie only in the principle of the will, no matter whether the object sought can be attained by the action or not. For the will stands as it were at the parting of the ways, between its *a priori* principle, which is formal, and its *a posteriori* material motive. As so standing it must be determined by something, and, as no action which is done from duty can be determined by a material principle, it can be determined only by the formal principle of all volition.

From the two propositions just set forth a third directly follows, which may be thus stated: *Duty is the obligation to act from reverence for law.* Now, I may have a natural *inclination* for the object that I expect to follow from my action, but I can never have *reverence* for that which is not a spontaneous activity of my will, but merely an effect of it; neither can I have reverence for any natural inclination, whether it is my own or another's. If it is my own, I can at most only approve of it; if it is manifested by another, I may regard it as conducive to my own interest, and hence I may in certain cases even be said to have a love for it. But the only thing which I can reverence or which can lay me under an obligation to act, is the law which is connected with my will, not as a consequence, but as a principle; a principle which is not dependent upon natural inclination, but overmasters it, or at least allows it to have no influence whatever in determining my course of action. Now if an action which is done out of regard for duty sets entirely aside the influence of natural inclination and along with it every object of the will, nothing else is left by which the will can be determined but objectively the *law* itself, and subjectively *pure reverence* for the law as a principle of action. Thus there arises the maxim, to obey the moral law even at the sacrifice of all my natural inclinations.

The supreme good which we call moral can therefore be nothing but the *idea of the law* in itself, in so far as it is this idea which determines the will, and not any consequences that are expected to follow. Only a *rational* being can have such an idea, and hence a man who acts from the idea of the law is already morally good, no matter whether the consequences which he expects from his action follow or not.

Now what must be the nature of a law, the idea of which is to determine the will, even apart from the effects expected to follow, and which is therefore itself entitled to be called good absolutely and without qualification? As the will must not be moved to act from any desire for the results expected to follow from obedience to a certain law, the only principle of the will which remains is that of the conformity of actions to universal law. In all cases I must act in such a way *that I can at the same time will that my maxim should become a universal law*. This is what is meant by conformity to law pure and simple; and this is the principle which serves, and must serve, to determine the will, if the idea of duty is not to be regarded as empty and chimerical. As a matter of fact the judgments which we are wont to pass upon conduct perfectly agree with this principle, and in making them we always have it before our eyes.

May I, for instance, under the pressure of circumstances, make a promise which I have no intention of keeping? The question is not, whether it is prudent to make a false promise, but whether it is morally right. To enable me to answer this question shortly and conclusively, the best way is for me to ask myself whether it would satisfy me that the maxim to extricate myself from embarrassment by giving a false promise should have the force of a universal law, applying to others as well as to myself. And I see at once, that, while I can certainly will the lie, I cannot will that lying should be a universal law. If lying were universal, there would, properly speaking, be no promises whatever. I might say that I intended to do a certain thing at some future time, but nobody would believe me, or if he did at the moment trust to my promise, he would afterwards pay me back in my own coin. My maxim thus proves itself to be self-destructive, so soon as it is taken as a universal law.

Duty, then, consists in the obligation to act from *pure* reverence for the moral law.

To this motive all others must give way, for it is the condition of a will which is good *in itself*, and which has a value with which nothing else is comparable.

There is, however, in man a strong feeling of antagonism to the commands of duty, although his reason tells him that those commands are worthy of the highest reverence. For man not only possesses reason, but he has certain natural wants and inclinations, the complete satisfaction of which he calls happiness. These natural inclinations clamorously demand to have their seemingly reasonable claims respected; but reason issues its commands inflexibly, refusing to promise anything to the natural desires, and treating their claims with a sort of neglect and contempt. From this there arises a *natural dialectic,* that is, a disposition to explain away the strict laws of duty, to cast doubt upon their validity, or at least, upon their purity and stringency, and in this way to make them yield to the demands of the natural inclinations.

Thus men are forced to go beyond the narrow circle of ideas within which their reason ordinarily moves, and to take a step into the field of *moral philosophy,* not indeed from any perception of speculative difficulties, but simply on practical grounds. The practical reason of men cannot be long exercised any more than the theoretical, without falling insensibly into a dialectic, which compels it to call in the aid of philosophy; and in the one case as in the other, rest can be found only in a thorough criticism of human reason.

Section II.—Transition from Popular Moral Philosophy to the Metaphysic of Morality

So far, we have drawn our conception of duty from the manner in which men employ it in the ordinary exercise of their practical reason. The conception of duty, however, we must not suppose to be therefore derived from experience. On the contrary, we hear frequent complaints, the justice of which we cannot but admit, that no one can point to a single instance in which an action has undoubtedly been done purely from a regard for duty; that there are certainly many actions which are not *opposed* to duty, but none which are indisputably done *from* duty and therefore have a moral value. Nothing indeed can secure us against the complete loss of our ideas of duty, and maintain in the soul a well-grounded respect for the moral law, but the clear conviction, that reason issues its commands on its own authority, without caring in the least whether the actions of men have, as a matter of fact, been done purely from ideas of duty. For reason commands inflexibly that certain actions should be done, which perhaps never have been done; actions, the very possibility of which may seem doubtful to one who bases everything upon experience. Perfect disinterestedness in friendship, for instance, is demanded of every man, although there may never have been a sincere friend; for pure friendship is bound up with the idea of duty as duty, and belongs to the very idea of a reason which determines the will on *a priori* grounds, prior to all experience.

It is, moreover, beyond dispute, that unless we are to deny to morality all truth and all reference to a possible object, the moral law has so wide an application that it is binding, not merely upon man, but upon all *rational beings,* and not merely under certain contingent conditions, and with certain limitations, but absolutely and necessarily. . . .

Only a rational being has the faculty of acting in conformity with the *idea* of law, or from principles; only a rational being, in other words, has a will. And as without

reason actions cannot proceed from laws, will is simply practical reason. If the will is infallibly determined by reason, the actions of a rational being are subjectively as well as objectively necessary; that is, will must be regarded as a faculty of choosing *that only* which reason, independently of natural inclination, declares to be practically necessary or good. On the other hand, if the will is not invariably determined by reason alone, but is subject to certain subjective conditions or motives, which are not always in harmony with the objective conditions; if the will, as actually is the case with man, is not in perfect conformity with reason; actions which are recognized to be objectively necessary, are subjectively contingent. The determination of such a will according to objective laws is therefore called *obligation.* That is to say, if the will of a rational being is not absolutely good, we conceive of it as capable of being determined by objective laws of reason, but not as by its very nature necessarily obeying them.

The idea that a certain principle is objective, and binding upon the will, is a command of reason, and the statement of the command in a formula is an *imperative.*

All imperatives are expressed by the word *ought,* to indicate that the will upon which they are binding is not by its subjective constitution necessarily determined in conformity with the objective law of reason. An imperative says, that the doing, or leaving undone of a certain thing would be good, but it addresses a will which does not always do a thing simply because it is good. Now, that is practically *good* which determines the will by ideas of reason, in other words, that which determines it, not by subjective influences, but by principles which are objective, or apply to all rational beings as such. *Good* and *pleasure* are quite distinct. Pleasure results from the influence of purely subjective causes upon the will of the subject, and these vary with the susceptibility of this or that individual, while a principle of reason is valid for all.

A perfectly good will would, like the will of man, stand under objective laws, laws of the good, but it could not be said to be under an *obligation* to act in conformity with those laws. Such a will by its subjective constitution could be determined only by the idea of the good. In reference to the Divine will, or any other holy will, imperatives have no meaning; for here the will is by its very nature necessarily in harmony with the law, and therefore *ought* has no application to it. Imperatives are formulae, which express merely the relation of objective laws of volition in general to the imperfect will of this or that rational being, as for instance, the will of man.

Now, all imperatives command either *hypothetically* or *categorically*. A hypothetical imperative states that a certain thing must be done, if something else which is willed, or at least might be willed, is to be attained. The categorical imperative declares that an act is in itself or objectively necessary, without any reference to another end.

Every practical law represents a possible action as good, and therefore as obligatory for a subject that is capable of being determined to act by reason. Hence all imperatives are formulae for the determination of an action which is obligatory according to the principle of a will that is in some sense good. If the action is good only because it is a means to *something else*, the imperative is *hypothetical;* if the action is conceived to be good *in itself*, the imperative, as the necessary principle of a will that in itself conforms to reason, is *categorical*.

An imperative, then, states what possible action of mine would be good. It supplies the practical rule for a will which does not at once do an act simply because it is good, either because the subject does not know it to be good, or because, knowing it to be good, he is influenced by maxims which are opposed to the objective principles of a practical reason.

The hypothetical imperative says only that an action is good relatively to a certain *possible* end or to a certain *actual* end. In the former case it is *problematic*, in the latter case *assertoric*. The categorical imperative, which affirms that an action is in itself or objectively necessary without regard to an end, that is, without regard to any other end than itself, is an *apodictic* practical principle.

Whatever is within the power of a rational being may be conceived to be capable of being willed by some rational being, and hence the principles which determine what actions are necessary in the attainment of certain possible ends, are infinite in number.

Yet there is one thing which we may assume that all finite rational beings actually make their end, and there is therefore one object which may safely be regarded, not simply as something that they *may* seek, but as something that by a necessity of their nature they actually *do* seek. This object is *happiness*. The hypothetical imperative, which affirms the practical necessity of an action as the means of attaining happiness, is *assertoric*. We must not think of happiness as simply a possible and problematic end, but as an end that we may with confidence presuppose *a priori* to be sought by everyone, belonging as it does to the very nature of man. Now skill in the choice of means to his own greatest well-being may be called *prudence*, taking the word in its more restricted sense. An imperative, therefore, which relates merely to the choice of means to one's own happiness, that is, a maxim of prudence, must be hypothetical; it commands an action, not absolutely, but only as a means to another end.

Lastly, there is an imperative which directly commands an action, without presupposing as its condition that some other end is to be attained by means of that action. This imperative is *categorical*. It has to do, not with the matter of an action and the result expected to follow from it, but simply with the form and principle from which the action itself proceeds. The action is essentially good if the motive of the agent is good, let the consequences be what they may. This imperative may be called the imperative of *morality*.

How are all these imperatives possible? The question is not, How is an action which an imperative commands actually realized? but, How can we think of the will as placed under obligation by each of those imperatives? Very little need be said to show how an imperative of skill is possible. He who wills the end, wills also the means in his power which are indispensable to the attainment of the end. Looking simply at the act of will, we must say that this proposition is analytic. If a certain object is to follow as an effect from my volition, my causality must be conceived as active in the production of the effect, or as employing the means by which the effect will take place. The imperative, therefore, simply states that in the conception of the willing of this end there is directly implied the conception of actions necessary to this end. No doubt certain synthetic propositions are required to determine the particular means by which a given end may be attained, but these have nothing to do with the principle or act of the will, but merely state how the object may actually be realized.

Were it as easy to give a definite conception of happiness as of a particular end, the imperatives of prudence would be of exactly the same nature as the imperatives of skill, and would therefore be analytic. For, we should be able to say, that he who wills the end wills also the only means in his power for the attainment of the end. But, unfortunately, the conception of happiness is so indefinite, that, although every man desires to obtain it, he is unable to give a definite and self-consistent statement of what he actually desires and wills. The truth is, that, strictly speaking, the imperatives of prudence are not commands at all. They do not say that actions are objective or *necessary*, and hence they must be regarded as counsels, not as commands of reason. Still, the imperative of prudence would be an analytic proposition, if the means to happiness could only be known with certainty. For the only difference in the two cases is that in the imperative of skill the end is merely possible, in the imperative of prudence it is actually given; and as in both all that is commanded is the means to an end which is assumed to be willed, the imperative which commands that he who wills the end should also will the means, is in both cases analytic. There is therefore no real difficulty in seeing how an imperative of prudence is possible.

The only question which is difficult of solution, is, how the imperative of morality is possible. Here the imperative is not hypothetical, and hence we cannot derive its objective necessity from any presupposition. Nor must it for a moment be forgotten, that an imperative of this sort cannot be established by instances taken from experience. We must therefore find out by careful investigation, whether imperatives which seem to be categorical may not be simply hypothetical imperatives in disguise.

One thing is plain at the very outset, namely, that only a categorical imperative can have the dignity of a practical *law*, and that the other imperatives, while they may no doubt be called *principles* of the will, cannot be called laws. An action which is necessary merely as a means to an arbitrary end, may be regarded as itself contingent, and if the end is abandoned, the maxim which prescribes the action has no longer any force. An unconditioned command, on the other hand, does not permit the will to choose the opposite, and therefore it carries with it the necessity which is essential to a law.

It is, however, very hard to see how there can be a categorical imperative or law of morality at all. Such a law is an *a priori* synthetic proposition, and we cannot expect that there will be less difficulty in showing how a proposition of that sort is possible in the sphere of morality than we have found it to be in the sphere of knowledge.

In attempting to solve this problem, we shall first of all inquire, whether the mere conception of a categorical imperative may not perhaps supply us with a formula, which contains the only proposition that can possibly be a categorical imperative. . . .

If I take the mere conception of a hypothetical imperative, I cannot tell what it may contain until the condition under which it applies is presented to me. But I can tell at once from the very conception of a categorical imperative what it must contain. Viewed apart from the law, the imperative simply affirms that the maxim, or subjective principle of action, must conform to the objective principle or law. Now the law contains no condition to which it is restricted, and hence nothing remains but the statement, that the maxim ought to conform to the universality of the law as such. It is only this conformity to law that the imperative can be said to represent as necessary.

There is therefore but one categorical imperative, which may be thus stated: *Act in conformity with that maxim, and that maxim only, which you can at the same time will to be a universal law. . . .*

The universality of the law which governs the succession of events, is what we mean by *nature,* in the most general sense, that is, the existence of things, in so far as their existence is determined in conformity with universal laws. The universal imperative of duty might therefore be put in this way: *Act as if the maxim from which you act were to become through your will a universal law of nature.*

If we attend to what goes on in ourselves in every transgression of a duty, we find, that we do not will that our maxim should become a universal law. We find it in fact impossible to do so, and we really will that the opposite of our maxim should remain a universal law, at the same time that we assume the liberty of making an exception in favor of natural inclination in our own case, or perhaps only for this particular occasion. Hence, if we looked at all cases from the same point of view, that is, from the point of view of reason, we should see that there was here a contradiction in our will. The contradiction is, that a certain principle is admitted to be necessary objectively or as a universal law, and yet is held not to be universal subjectively, but to admit of exceptions. What we do is, to consider our action at one time from the point of view of a will that is in perfect conformity with reason, and at another time from the point of view of a will that is under the influence of natural inclination. There is, therefore, here no real contradiction, but merely an antagonism of inclination to the command of reason. The universality of the principle is changed into a mere generality, in order that the practical principle of reason may meet the maxim half way. Not only is this limitation condemned by our own impartial judgment, but it proves that we actually recognize the validity of the categorical imperative, and merely allow ourselves to make a few exceptions in our own favor which we try to consider as of no importance, or as a necessary concession to circumstances.

This much at least we have learned, that if the idea of duty is to have any meaning and to lay down the laws of our actions, it must be expressed in categorical and not in hypothetical imperatives. We have also obtained a clear and distinct conception (a very important thing), of what is implied in a categorical imperative which contains the principle of duty for all cases, granting such an imperative to be possible at all. But we have not yet been able to prove *a priori*, that there actually is such an imperative; that there is a practical law which commands absolutely on its own authority, and is independent of all sensuous impulses; and that duty consists in obedience to this law.

In seeking to reach this point, it is of the greatest importance to observe, that the reality of this principle cannot possibly be derived from the *peculiar constitution of human nature*. For by duty is meant the practically unconditioned necessity of an act, and hence we can show that duty is a law for the will of all human beings, only by showing that it is applicable to all rational beings, or rather to all rational beings to whom an imperative applies at all. . . .

Practical principles that abstract from all subjective ends are *formal;* those that presuppose subjective ends, and therefore natural inclinations, are *material*. The ends which a rational being arbitrarily sets before himself as material ends to be produced by his actions, are all merely relative; for that which gives to them their value is simply their relation to the peculiar susceptibility of the subject. They can therefore yield no universal and necessary principles, or practical laws, applicable to all rational beings, and binding upon every will. Upon such relative ends, therefore, only hypothetical imperatives can be based.

Suppose, however, that there is something the existence of which has in itself an absolute value, something which, *as an end in itself,* can be a ground of definite laws; then, there would lie in that, and only in that, the ground of a possible categorical imperative or practical law.

Now, I say, that man, and indeed every rational being as such, *exists* as an end in himself, *not merely as a means* to be made use of by this or that will, and therefore man in all his actions, whether these are directed towards himself or towards other rational beings, must always be regarded as an end. No object of natural desire has more than a conditioned value; for if the natural desires, and the wants to which they give rise, did not exist, the object to which they are directed would have no value at all. So far are the natural desires and wants from having an absolute value, so far are they from being sought simply for themselves, that every rational being must wish to be entirely free from their influence. The value of every object which human action is the means of obtaining, is, therefore, always conditioned. And even beings whose existence depends upon nature, not upon our will, if they are without reason, have only the relative value of means, and are therefore called *things*. Rational beings, on the other hand, are called *persons,* because their very nature shows them to be ends in themselves, that is, something which cannot be made use of simply as a means. A person being thus an object of respect, a certain limit is placed upon arbitrary will. Persons are not purely subjective ends, whose existence has a value *for us* as the effect of our actions, but they are *objective ends,* or beings whose existence is an end in itself, for which no other end can be substituted. If all value were conditioned, and therefore contingent, it would be impossible to show that there is any supreme practical principle whatever.

If, then, there is a supreme practical principle, a principle which in relation to the human will is a categorical imperative, it must be an *objective* principle of the will, and must be able to serve as a universal practical law. For, such a principle must be derived from the idea of that which is necessarily an end for every one because it is an *end in itself.* Its foundation is this, that *rational nature exists as an end in itself.* Man necessarily conceives of his own existence in this way, and so far this is a *subjective* principle of human action. But in this way also every other rational being conceives of his own existence, and for the very same reason; hence the principle is also *objective,* and from it, as the highest practical ground, all laws of the will must be capable of being derived. The practical imperative will therefore be this: *Act so as to use humanity, whether in your own person or in the person of another, always as an end, never as merely a means.*

The principle, that humanity and every rational nature is an end in itself, is not borrowed from experience. For, in the first place, because of its universality it applies to all rational beings, and no experience can apply so widely. In the second place, it does not regard humanity subjectively, as an end of man, that is, as an object which the subject of himself actually makes his end, but as an objective end, which ought to be regarded as a law

that constitutes the supreme limiting condition of all subjective ends, and which must therefore have its source in pure reason. The objective ground of all practical laws consists in the *rule* and the form of universality, which makes them capable of serving as laws, but their *subjective* ground consists in the *end* to which they are directed. Now, by the second principle, every rational being, as an end in himself, is the subject of all ends. From this follows the third practical principle of the will, which is the supreme condition of its harmony with universal practical reason, namely, the idea of *the will of every rational being as a will which lays down universal laws of action.* . . .

At the point we have now reached, it does not seem surprising that all previous attempts to find out the principle of morality should have ended in failure. It was seen that man is bound under law by duty, but it did not strike anyone, that the *universal* system of laws to which he is subject are laws which he *imposes upon himself,* and that he is only under obligation to act in conformity with his own will, a will which by the purpose of nature prescribes universal laws. Now so long as man is thought to be merely subject to law, no matter what the law may be, he must be regarded as stimulated or constrained to obey the law from interest of some kind; for as the law does not proceed from *his own* will, there must be *something external* to his will which compels him to act in conformity with it. This perfectly necessary conclusion frustrated every attempt to find a supreme principle of duty. Duty was never established, but merely the necessity of acting from some form of interest, private or public. The imperative was therefore necessarily always conditioned, and could not possibly have the force of a moral command. The supreme principle of morality I shall therefore call the principle of the *autonomy* of the will, to distinguish it from all other principles, which I call principles of *heteronomy*.

The conception that every rational being in all the maxims of his will must regard himself as prescribing universal laws, by reference to which himself and all his actions are to be judged, leads to a cognate and very fruitful conception, that of a *kingdom of ends*.

By *kingdom*, I mean the systematic combination of different rational beings through the medium of common laws. Now, laws determine certain ends as universal, and hence, if abstraction is made from the individual differences of rational beings, and from all that is peculiar to their private ends, we get the idea of a complete totality of ends combined in a system; in other words, we are able to conceive of a kingdom of ends, which conforms to the principles formulated above.

All rational beings stand under the law, that each should treat himself and others, *never simply as means*, but always as *at the same time ends in themselves.* Thus there arises a systematic combination of rational beings through the medium of common objective laws. This may well be called a kingdom of ends, because the object of those laws is just to relate all rational beings to one another as ends and means. Of course this kingdom of ends is merely an ideal.

Morality, then, consists in the relation of all action to the system of laws which alone makes possible a kingdom of ends. These laws must belong to the nature of every rational being, and must proceed from his own will. The principle of the will, therefore, is, that no action should be done from any other maxim than one which is consistent with a universal law. This may be expressed in the formula: *Act so that the will may regard itself as in its maxims laying down universal laws.* Now, if the maxims of rational beings are not by their very nature in harmony with this objective principle, the principle of a universal system of laws, the necessity of acting in conformity with that principle is called practical obligation or *duty. . . . Autonomy* is thus the foundation of the moral value of man and of every other rational being.

The three ways in which the principle of morality has been formulated are at bottom simply different statements of the same law, and each implies the other two.

COMMENT

The Background of Kant's Theory

When Kant died, something unprecedented happened in the Prussian town of Königsberg. His friends were planning a small private funeral, but when the report of his death spread, the townspeople flocked to his house, demanding to see his body. On the day of the funeral, the bells of all the churches tolled, and the ordinary life of the town came to a standstill while thousands followed his coffin to the grave. Few men are buried with such a spontaneous upsurge of popular feeling. Evidently the people must have felt that Kant was one of them—that he represented the freedom and dignity of all human beings, whatever their status.

This belief is well-founded, for Kant's books are devoted to the betterment of life for all men. Despite their technical jargon, they express ideas that have wide and fundamental import. Kant sought to free the human mind from superstition and to provide a firm intellectual foundation for the main forms of culture—art, religion, morality, science, philosophy, and politics. He not only discussed basic philosophical concepts—such as God, duty, freedom, causation, purposiveness, the nature of beauty, the character and limits of scientific method—but also tried to promote the fundamental human values —the rights of man, peace on earth, and the emancipation of the mind through critical knowledge.

His chief philosophical theme is the search for universal principles. He maintained that *all* perceiving, knowing, and thinking make use of general concepts, such as *substance* and *cause* and *effect*. These absolutely universal concepts he called "categories." He also distinguished what he called "forms of sensibility," the properties of being in space and time, which apply to every object. All experience, according to Kant, is a combination of empirical elements (particular data) and *"a priori"* elements (the general forms and categories). He termed the latter *"a priori"* because he believed them to be the frames wherein we perceive and conceive things rather than generalizations from experience. In ordering and interpreting sense data, we actively impress upon them the patterns of our own intellect and sensibility. Hence the world as we know it bears the stamp of our own nature.

There are real things outside minds—here Kant differs from Berkeley and the idealists—but they are not as we grasp them. We never know things as they are *in themselves* but only as they *appear* to us. Just as a man born with a pair of blue glasses permanently affixed to his nose would find that every object has a bluish tint, so our distinctive ways of perceiving and thinking about all objects that we know give to those objects certain forms. And these forms are no more inherent in the objects than is the blue quality imposed on things by the perception of our bespectacled friend. By emphasizing the role played by the observer, Kant introduced a new perspective in philosophy.

He tried to discover what justification we have for asserting that the *a priori* elements are necessary. In *The Critique of Pure Reason*, for example, he considered the possible reasons that could be adduced for saying that every object of experience must have a cause and must conform to the other categories. Similarly, in his ethical philosophy, he tried to justify *a priori* elements in moral experience. The detailed application of moral principles requires a great deal of empirical knowledge, but the principles themselves, he believed, cannot be *proved* by experience.

In *The Foundations of the Metaphysic of Morals*, Kant was concerned with *pure* rather than *applied* ethics. Hence he did not give in this book, any detailed account of the application of moral principles; rather, the book is an attempt to justify such principles *a priori*.

The Main Outline of the Argument

Nothing but good will is unqualifiedly and unconditionally good. Pleasure, for example, is ordinarily good, but the pleasure a fiend derives from torturing an innocent child is not good. Knowledge, health, economic goods, and all the talents of mind and body are good if they are combined with a good will but evil if used with a bad will. Good will alone has supreme and incomparable worth, although, through no fault of the agent, its consequences may be unfortunate.

If a person has good will, it is better for him to be happy than miserable. But happiness, unlike good will, is not *always* good. Kant's contribution to ethics is not to discuss the value of happiness. He was mainly concerned with good will and said little about happiness or other goods.

The essence of good will is respect for duty. A man shows moral worth in doing a good deed not from inclination but from a sense of duty. Duty and inclination *may* be in harmony, but an act has no moral worth if it is motivated *entirely* by inclination.

In developing the concept of duty, Kant drew a very important distinction between *hypothetical* and *categorical imperatives*. An "imperative" is a statement that something ought to be done. A *hypothetical* imperative depends for its validity upon inclination: I ought to do something *because I wish for something else*. There is an *if*, expressed or understood. "*If* I want to get to Boston, I ought to take the first road to my right." A *categorical* imperative, on the other hand, is independent of inclination: I ought to do so and so, *whether I wish or not*. "Tell the truth." "Do not murder." There are no "buts" or "ifs" attached. We cannot excuse a murder by pleading that the murderer was so inclined, or that murder was a means to some other goal. Hypothetical imperatives are non-moral; categorical imperatives are moral.

How can we determine what is categorically imperative? Not by the test of best results—Kant was unalterably opposed to such a utilitarian approach. Good will is a matter of inner attitude, not of outward consequences. If the ultimate basis of morality is *a priori*, moreover, it cannot depend upon consequences known through experience. *A priori* statements are commonly proved by showing that to deny them would be a contradiction. To deny that "two plus two equals four" is contradictory—hence the statement is true. Kant believed that this same method could be used in ethics. Suppose we are considering whether it is ever our duty to lie. If the principle manifest in this type of action is contradictory, it is wrong; otherwise, it is right. Now, when we try to conceive lying as an *a priori* principle (universal and necessary without exception), we *do* run into contradiction. If lying were universally practiced, there would be no truth to lie about, and lying would cease to be possible. But truth telling, since it is independent of lying, *can* be universalized. By Kant's test lying is immoral and truth telling is moral.

This test of right action is summed up in his first formula of the categorical imperative: *i.e.*, we should act only upon those maxims that we can will as universal laws. This formula rules out murder, promise-breaking, theft, etc. Murder cannot be a universal practice, for there would soon be no one to murder or be murdered. Promise-breaking cannot be universalized, for no one would believe a promise if promises were never kept. Theft cannot be universalized, for if no one ever respected private property there would be none to steal. But not all types of immorality would be self-eliminating if universalized. We can *imagine* a society in which unkindness, for example, is the rule. But we cannot *will* that there be universal unkindness, because we want to be treated fairly and decently. When we act in accordance with a principle that we cannot will to be universally applied, the act is immoral.

No man wants to be treated unkindly, because he has worth as a human being—he is an end-in-himself. Kant's second formula of the categorical imperative, in fact, is that we should regard every man as an end-in-himself, never merely as a means to our ends. This formula, which is similar to the Golden Rule, excludes all forms of selfishness, since the essence of selfishness is to use a person as a mere tool. It forbids slavery, prostitution, exploitation, the violation of individual rights, or any action that fails to respect the dignity and worth of human beings.

The characteristic that makes a person an end-in-himself is above all his freedom, and accordingly Kant puts a great deal of emphasis upon this attribute. Dare to be free, and respect the freedom of others—this is the spirit of his ethics. Everyone should act as a free moral agent, himself willing the moral law and freely accepting the responsibility to abide by it. This third formula is stated in a number of ways, but most briefly as follows: "Act as a member of a kingdom of ends." By this statement Kant means that all men should unite in a self-governing society of free and responsible agents, each of whom respects himself and everyone else as free, rational, and intrinsically precious.

Since freedom is indispensable to morality, we should believe in it as an article of moral faith, even though, according to Kant, we cannot justify it by theoretical proof. As we have seen in Chapter 11, on "Theism," Kant argues that faith in God and immortality is also justified on moral grounds.

Some Main Issues

Whatever our opinion of Kant's ethics—and there is much to admire as well as to criticize—we cannot deny that he presents issues of great importance. Some of these are as follows:

1. *Are ethical principles empirical or a priori?* The motive of Kant's philosophy is the discovery and justification of *a priori* forms, concepts, and principles. In ethics, he draws a sharp distinction between "is" and "ought" and contends that the moral *ought* must be formulated in *a priori* principles. Is he correct?

If empirical science is a knowledge of *existence,* and if an "ideal" or "norm" is what ought to be but *is not,* the conception of a "normative empirical science" is contradictory. And if so, ethics is either merely subjective —as the advocates of the emotive theory contend—or it is *a priori.* Modern philosophers have been deeply disturbed by the problem thus posed.

The proponents of natural law, such as Cicero, try to solve the problem by denying the sharp antithesis between *what is* and *what ought to be*—and on this point they receive support from utilitarians such as Mill and pragmatists such as Dewey. What ought to be, it can be argued, is what satisfies genuine needs. A need arises when there is an uncompleted tendency in human nature—a frustrated, or at least unconsummated, impulse or desire. These needs can be determined scientifically, and plans to satisfy them can be elaborated with due regard to facts. The objective of securing the greatest possible fulfillment should determine which needs are to receive preferential treatment, and here, too, there are facts to guide us.

Kant would reply that such an empirical procedure is a mere begging of the question. It *assumes* that morality consists in the fulfillment of our needs —but this assumption he would sharply challenge. If *need* is interpreted in a non-moral sense, it is not a moral concept and hence is irrelevant; but if it is interpreted in a moral sense, it must be connected with obligation—and obligation is not the sort of thing that empirical science can discover and justify. *Moral* objectivity is quite different from *scientific* objectivity, and an objective moral *ought* can never be determined scientifically. Rejecting the emotive view that morality is subjective, Kant concludes that moral objectivity must rest upon *a priori* foundations.

2. *Is good will, and good will alone, unconditionally good?* Let us consider Kant's contention that pleasure is good if combined with a good will but evil if combined with a bad will. A hedonist would agree that pleasure gained from wanton torture is bad, but he would say that it is bad not *in* and *of itself* but in its evil consequences. Its bad effects greatly outweigh its intrinsic goodness—but *as pleasure,* it is intrinsically good. The hedonist would add

that what makes good will "intrinsically good" is simply the pleasure that it involves, rather than the accompanying sense of duty.

This interpretation would imply that if the pleasure gained from tormenting somebody were great enough to outweigh any pain that the act entails, such an act would therefore be legitimate—and of course Kant would deny this. A non-hedonist might admit that good will is intrinsically good, but maintain that there are other intrinsic goods, such as truth and beauty, that are no less ultimate and unconditional. Kant's definition of "good will" as respect for duty can also be criticized. The consciousness of duty is cold unless kindled by love, but love is classified by Kant as an "inclination" without moral value *per se*. If good will were interpreted as inclusive of the great positive values of love, it would be more plausible to maintain that it is the pearl beyond all price and comparison.

3. *Does Kant's ethics provide a workable test of right?* Since the moral "ought" denotes not merely subjective but also objective rightness, there are categorical and not merely hypothetical imperatives. An opponent might concede this point and still find Kant's formulae for determining categorical imperatives unsatisfactory.

His first formula, the test of universality, does not take account of individual differences which may be ethically decisive. Consider Kant's dispute with the French philosopher Benjamin Constant. The moral duty to tell the truth, Constant argued, is not unconditional. It would be ethically right to lie to a would-be murderer in order to save his intended victim, for a man bent on murder has forfeited all right to a truth which would abet his plot. To this contention Kant replied, "The duty of truthfulness makes no distinction between persons to whom one has this duty and to whom one can exempt himself from this duty; rather, it is an unconditional duty which holds in all circumstances." [1] Hence, we are duty-bound to tell even a truth that would result in murder. This is an extreme position that very few thinkers, whether philosophers or laymen, would endorse. In the case cited by Constant, there is a conflict between two duties: the duty to tell the truth and the duty to save a life. In such instances, how can we decide which duty is paramount without a consideration of consequences?

We can agree with Kant up to a certain point: granted that an act is right for one person, it must be right *under the same conditions* for everybody. But when the conditions (physical or psychological) vary, a philanthropic exception to the general rule may be warranted. If this is so, if a moral rule can be set aside on account of empirical circumstances, morality is not *a priori* and universal, as Kant supposed.

It is difficult to see how we can carry out Kant's second formula—always

[1] "On a Supposed Right to Lie from Altruistic Motives," *Critique of Practical Reason and Other Writings in Moral Philosophy*, trans. by L. W. Beck (University of Chicago Press, 1949), p. 349.

treat a human being as an end-in-himself—unless we have a view to the effects of our actions. The sacrifice of a life—as when we tell a truth that aids a murderer—to abstract moral principle scarcely constitutes treating the victim as an end-in-himself! To carry out the formula, we must have some positive idea of the ends of man and how to achieve them—and this calls for a more empirical and teleological approach than Kant is prepared to admit.

In his third formula, he bids us to be free and responsible. The moral law, he contends, must be the subject's own free voice and is not a whit the less a universal law for being that. But every man is an *individual*—a concrete, particular, flesh-and-blood person—he is not the grammatical abstraction "mankind." There is always something about *you* that is never common to *us;* and your freedom, like mine, consists partly in expressing what is unique to you. Freedom does not consist merely in willing the dictates of universal abstract reason; it is more individual, it is warmer, more personal and creative.

As a giant of human thought, Kant had deep insights, but even the giants make mistakes. The reader of this book might well consider in what respects Kant was correct and in what respects he was mistaken.

15

Morality Based on Happiness

JOHN STUART MILL (1806–1873)

Mill was reared in London and was educated privately by his father, James Mill, a famous political philosopher. No child ever received a more prodigious education. Mill was reading Plato and Thucydides in the original Greek at an age when most children are reading nursery stories in their native language. His father set him to learn Greek at the age of three; Latin, algebra, and geometry at the age of eight; logic at twelve; and political economy at thirteen. Jeremy Bentham, the Utilitarian philosopher, was an intimate friend of the family, and young John was thoroughly indoctrinated in his philosophy.

When Mill reached the age of seventeen, he was appointed a clerk in the East India Company, in whose service he remained for thirty-five years, rising steadily to the highest post in his department, that of examiner of correspondence and dispatches to India. This position afforded him considerable leisure for his intense intellectual pursuits.

In his twenty-first year, he fell into a deep mental depression, evidently the result of his unnatural childhood and years of intellectual cramming. He gradually emerged from this illness, but with a new sense of the insufficiency of his father's doctrinaire philosophy and a keener appreciation of the value of poetry, especially Wordsworth's. Thereafter he sought to broaden his outlook and succeeded in becoming a much better rounded (though less consistent) philosopher than either Bentham or his father. An important influence upon Mill was Harriet Taylor, the beautiful and talented wife of a London merchant, who finally married him (in 1851) after her husband died. They lived happily together for seven years, until they were separated by her untimely death. It was through her, Mill said, that he came to be more of a democrat and socialist, and *On Liberty* was their joint work.

After his long service in the India Office, he retired on a pension at the age of fifty-two. The remaining fifteen years of his life, although marred by ill health, were packed with intellectual and political activity. In 1865, he consented to run for Parliament as a representative of the working man for the constituency of Westminster; and during his single term of office (1866–1868), he made a considerable impression by his vigorous championing of reform. In 1869, he retired with his stepdaughter, Helen Taylor, to a small white stone cottage near Avignon, in France, where he continued to write. In May 1873 he died, the victim of a local fever.

Among his important books were *Logic* (1843), *The Principles of Political Economy* (1848), *On Liberty* (1859), *Utilitarianism* (1863), *Examination of Sir William Hamilton's Philosophy* (1865), and *Autobiography* (published after his death, in 1873).

JOHN STUART MILL

From *Utilitarianism*

CHAPTER II

WHAT UTILITARIANISM IS

A passing remark is all that needs be given to the ignorant blunder of supposing that those who stand up for utility as the test of right and wrong use the term in that restricted and merely colloquial sense in which utility is opposed to pleasure. An apology is due to the philosophical opponents of utilitarianism, for even the momentary appearance of confounding them with anyone capable of so absurd a misconception; which is the more extraordinary, inasmuch as the contrary accusation, of referring everything to pleasure, and that, too, in its grossest form, is another of the common charges against utilitarianism: and, as has been pointedly remarked by an able writer, the same sort of persons, and often the very same persons, denounce the theory "as impracticably dry when the word 'utility' precedes the word

'pleasure,' and as too practicably voluptuous when the word 'pleasure' precedes the word 'utility'." Those who know anything about the matter are aware that every writer, from Epicurus to Bentham, who maintained the theory of utility, meant by it, not something to be contradistinguished from pleasure, but pleasure itself, together with exemption from pain; and instead of opposing the useful to the agreeable or the ornamental, have always declared that the useful means these, among other things. Yet the common herd, including the herd of writers, not only in newspapers and periodicals, but in books of weight and pretension, are perpetually falling into this shallow mistake. Having caught up the word "utilitarian," while knowing nothing whatever about it but its sound, they habitually express by it the rejection or the neglect of pleasure in some of its forms: of beauty, of ornament, or of amusement. Nor is the term thus ignorantly misapplied solely in disparagement, but occasionally in compliment, as though it implied superiority to frivolity and the mere pleasures of the moment. And this perverted use is the only one in which the word is popularly known, and the one from which the new generation are acquiring their sole notion of its meaning. Those who introduced the word, but who had for many years discontinued it as a distinctive appellation, may well feel themselves called upon to resume it if by doing so they can hope to contribute anything towards rescuing it from this utter degradation.

The creed which accepts as the foundation of morals "utility" or the "greatest happiness principle" holds that actions are right in proportion as they tend to promote happiness, wrong as they tend to produce the reverse of happiness. By happiness is intended pleasure, and the absence of pain; by unhappiness, pain, and the privation of pleasure. To give a clear view of the moral standard set up by the theory, much more requires to be said; in particular, what things it includes in the ideas of pain and pleasure; and to what extent this is left an open question. But these supplementary explanations do not affect the theory of life on which this theory of morality is grounded—namely, that pleasure and freedom from pain are the only things desirable as ends; and that all desirable things (which are as numerous in the utilitarian as in any other scheme) are desirable either for the pleasure inherent in themselves, or as means to the promotion of pleasure and the prevention of pain.

Now such a theory of life excites in many minds, and among them in some of the most estimable in feeling and purpose, inveterate dislike. To suppose that life has (as they express it) no higher end than pleasure—no better and nobler object of desire and pursuit—they designate as ut-

terly mean and groveling; as a doctrine worthy only of swine, to whom the followers of Epicurus were, at a very early period, contemptuously likened; and modern holders of the doctrine are occasionally made the subject of equally polite comparisons by its German, French, and English assailants.

When thus attacked, the Epicureans have always answered that it is not they, but their accusers, who represent human nature in a degrading light, since the accusation supposes human beings to be capable of no pleasures except those of which swine are capable. If this supposition were true, the charge could not be gainsaid, but would then be no longer an imputation; for if the sources of pleasure were precisely the same to human beings and to swine, the rule of life which is good enough for the one would be good enough for the other. The comparison of the Epicurean life to that of beasts is felt as degrading, precisely because a beast's pleasures do not satisfy a human being's conceptions of happiness. Human beings have faculties more elevated than the animal appetites and, when once made conscious of them, do not regard anything as happiness which does not include their gratification. I do not, indeed, consider the Epicureans to have been by any means faultless in drawing out their scheme of consequences from the utilitarian principle. To do this in any sufficient manner, many Stoic, as well as Christian, elements require to be included. But there is no known Epicurean theory of life which does not assign to the pleasures of the intellect, of the feelings and imagination, and of the moral sentiments, a much higher value as pleasures than to those of mere sensation. It must be admitted, however, that utilitarian writers in general have placed the superiority of mental over bodily pleasures chiefly in the greater permanency, safety, uncostliness, etc., of the former—that is, in their circumstantial advantages rather than in their intrinsic nature. And on all these points utilitarians have fully proved their case; but they might have taken the other and, as it may be called, higher ground with entire consistency. It is quite compatible with the principle of utility to recognize the fact that some kinds of pleasure are more desirable and more valuable than others. It would be absurd that, while, in estimating all other things, quality is considered as well as quantity, the estimation of pleasures should be supposed to depend on quantity alone.

If I am asked what I mean by difference of quality in pleasures, or what makes one pleasure more valuable than another, merely as a pleasure, except its being greater in amount, there is but one possible answer. Of two pleasures, if there be one to which all or almost all who have experience of both give a decided preference, irrespective of any feeling of moral obligation to prefer it, that is the more desirable pleasure. If one of the two is, by those who are competently acquainted with both, placed so far above the other that they prefer it, even though knowing it to be attended with a greater amount of discontent, and would not resign it for any quantity of the other pleasure which their nature is capable of, we are justified in ascribing to the preferred enjoyment a superiority in quality so far outweighing quantity as to render it, in comparison, of small account.

Now it is an unquestionable fact that those who are equally acquainted with and equally capable of appreciating and enjoying both, do give a most marked preference to the manner of existence which employs their higher faculties. Few human creatures would consent to be changed into any of the lower animals for a promise of the fullest allowance of a beast's pleasures; no intelligent human being would consent to be a fool, no instructed person would be an ignoramus, no person of feeling and conscience would be selfish and base, even though they should be persuaded that the fool, the dunce, or the rascal is better satisfied with his lot than they are with theirs. They would not resign what they possess more than he for the most complete satisfaction of all the desires which they have in common with him. If they ever fancy they would, it is only in cases of unhappiness so extreme that to escape from it they would exchange their lot for almost any other, however undesirable in their own eyes. A being of higher faculties requires more to make him happy, is capable probably of more acute suffering, and certainly accessible to it at more points, than one of an inferior type; but in spite of these liabilities, he can never really wish to sink into what he feels to be a lower grade of existence. We may give what explanation we please of this unwillingness; we may attribute it to pride, a name which is given indiscriminately to some of the most and to some of the least estimable feelings of which mankind are capable: we may refer it to the love of liberty and personal independence, an appeal to which was with the Stoics one of the most effective means for the inculcation of it; to the love of power or to the love of excitement, both of which do really enter into and contribute to it; but its most appropriate appellation is a sense of dignity, which all human beings possess in one form or other, and in some, though by no means in exact, proportion to their higher faculties, and which is so essential a part of the happiness of those in whom it is strong that nothing which conflicts with it could be otherwise than momentarily an object of desire to them. Whoever supposes that this preference takes place at a sacrifice of happiness—that the superior being, in anything like equal circumstances, is not happier than the inferior—confounds the two very different ideas of happiness and content. It is undisputable that the being whose capacities of enjoyment are low has the greatest chance of having them fully satisfied; and a highly endowed being will always feel that any happiness which he can look for, as the world is constituted, is imperfect. But he can learn to bear its imperfections, if they are at all bearable; and they will not make him envy the being who is indeed unconscious of the imperfections, but only because he feels not at all the good which those imperfections qualify. It is better to be a human being dissatisfied than a pig satisfied; better to be Socrates dissatisfied than a fool satisfied. And if the fool, or the pig, are of a different opinion, it is because they only know their own side of the question. The other party to the comparison knows both sides.

It may be objected that many who are capable of the higher pleasures occasionally, under the influence of temptation, postpone them to the lower. But this is quite compatible with a full appreciation of the intrinsic superiority of the higher. Men often, from infirmity of character, make their election for the nearer good, though they know it to be the less valuable; and this no less when the choice is between two bodily pleasures than when it is between bodily and mental. They pursue sensual indulgences to the injury of health, though perfectly aware that health is the greater good. It may be further objected that many who begin with youthful enthusiasm for everything noble, as they advance in years, sink into indolence and selfishness. But I do not believe that those who undergo this very common change voluntarily choose the lower description of pleasures in preference

to the higher. I believe that, before they devote themselves exclusively to the one, they have already become incapable of the other. Capacity for the nobler feelings is in most natures a very tender plant, easily killed, not only by hostile influences, but by mere want of sustenance; and in the majority of young persons it speedily dies away if the occupations to which their position in life has devoted them, and the society into which it has thrown them, are not favorable to keeping that higher capacity in exercise. Men lose their high aspirations as they lose their intellectual tastes, because they have not time or opportunity for indulging them; and they addict themselves to inferior pleasures, not because they deliberately prefer them, but because they are either the only ones to which they have access, or the only ones which they are any longer capable of enjoying. It may be questioned whether any one who has remained equally susceptible to both classes of pleasures, ever knowingly and calmly preferred the lower, though many, in all ages, have broken down in an ineffectual attempt to combine both.

From this verdict of the only competent judges, I apprehend there can be no appeal. On a question which is the best worth having of two pleasures, or which of two modes of existence is the most grateful to the feeling, apart from its moral attributes and from its consequences, the judgment of those who are qualified by knowledge of both, or, if they differ, that of the majority of them, must be admitted as final. And there needs be the less hesitation to accept this judgment respecting the quality of pleasures, since there is no other tribunal to be referred to even on the question of quantity. What means are there of determining which is the acutest of two pains, or the intensest of two pleasurable sensations, except the general suffrage of those who are familiar with both? Neither pains nor pleasures are homogeneous, and pain is always heterogeneous with pleasure. What is there to decide whether a particular pleasure is worth purchasing at the cost of a particular pain, except the feelings and judgment of the experienced? When, therefore, those feelings and judgment declare the pleasures derived from the higher faculties to be preferable *in kind,* apart from the question of intensity, to those of which the animal nature, disjointed from the higher faculties, is susceptible, they are entitled on this subject to the same regard.

I have dwelt on this point, as being a necessary part of a perfectly just conception of utility or happiness considered as the directive rule of human conduct. But it is by no means an indispensable condition to the acceptance of the utilitarian standard; for that standard is not the agent's own greatest happiness, but the greatest amount of happiness altogether; and if it may possibly be doubted whether a noble character is always the happier for its nobleness, there can be no doubt that it makes other people happier, and that the world in general is immensely a gainer by it. Utilitarianism, therefore, could only attain its end by the general cultivation of nobleness of character, even if each individual were only benefited by the nobleness of others, and his own, so far as happiness is concerned, were a sheer deduction from the benefit. But the bare enunciation of such an absurdity as this last renders refutation superfluous.

According to the greatest happiness principle, as above explained, the ultimate end, with reference to and for the sake of which all other things are desirable—whether we are considering our own good or that of other people—is an existence exempt as far as possible from pain, and as rich as possible in enjoyments, both in point of quan-

tity and quality; the test of quality and the rule for measuring it against quantity being the preference felt by those who, in their opportunities of experience, to which must be added their habits of self-consciousness and self-observation, are best furnished with the means of comparison. This, being, according to the utilitarian opinion, the end of human action, is necessarily also the standard of morality, which may accordingly be defined "the rules and precepts for human conduct," by the observance of which an existence such as has been described might be, to the greatest extent possible, secured to all mankind; and not to them only, but, so far as the nature of things admits, to the whole sentient creation.

Against this doctrine, however, arises another class of objectors who say that happiness, in any form, cannot be the rational purpose of human life and action; because, in the first place, it is unattainable; and they contemptuously ask, What right hast thou to be happy?—a question which Mr. Carlyle clenches by the addition, What right, a short time ago, hadst thou even *to be?* Next they say that men can do *without* happiness; that all noble human beings have felt this, and could not have become noble but by learning the lesson of *Entsagen,* or renunciation; which lesson, thoroughly learned and submitted to, they affirm to be the beginning and necessary condition of all virtue.

The first of these objections would go to the root of the matter were it well founded; for if no happiness is to be had at all by human beings, the attainment of it cannot be the end of morality or of any rational conduct. Though, even in that case, something might still be said for the utilitarian theory, since utility includes not solely the pursuit of happiness, but the prevention or mitigation of unhappiness; and if the former aim be chimerical, there will be all the greater scope and more imperative need for the latter, so long at least as mankind think fit to live, and do not take refuge in the simultaneous act of suicide recommended under certain condition by Novalis. When, however, it is thus positively asserted to be impossible that human life should be happy, the assertion, if not something like a verbal quibble, is at least an exaggeration. If by happiness be meant a continuity of highly pleasurable excitement, it is evident enough that this is impossible. A state of exalted pleasure lasts only moments or in some cases, and with some intermissions, hours or days, and is the occasional brilliant flash of enjoyment, not its permanent and steady flame. Of this the philosophers who have taught that happiness is the end of life were as fully aware as those who taunt them. The happiness which they meant was not a life of rapture; but moments of such, in an existence made up of few and transitory pains, many and various pleasures, with a decided predominance of the active over the passive, and having as the foundation of the whole not to expect more from life than it is capable of bestowing. A life thus composed, to those who have been fortunate enough to obtain it, has always appeared worthy of the name of happiness. And such an existence is even now the lot of many, during some considerable portion of their lives. The present wretched education and wretched social arrangements are the only real hindrance to its being attainable by almost all.

The objectors perhaps may doubt whether human beings, if taught to consider happiness as the end of life, would be satisfied with such a moderate share of it. But great numbers of mankind have been satisfied with much less. The main constituents of a satisfied life appear to be two, either of which by itself is often found sufficient for the purpose: tranquillity and excitement. With much tranquillity, many find that they can be content with very little pleasure; with much excitement, many can reconcile themselves to a considerable quantity of pain. There is assuredly no inherent impossibility of enabling even the mass of mankind to unite both, since the two are so far from being incompatible that they are in natural alliance, the prolongation of either being a preparation for, and exciting a wish for, the other. It is only those in whom indolence amounts to a vice that do not desire excitement after an interval of repose; it is only those in whom the need of excitement is a disease that feel the tranquillity which follows excitement dull and insipid, instead of pleasurable in direct proportion to the excitement which preceded it. When people who are tolerably fortunate in their outward lot do not find in life sufficient enjoyment to make it valuable to them, the cause generally is caring for nobody but themselves. To those who have neither public nor private affections, the excitements of life are much curtailed, and in any case dwindle in value as the time approaches when all selfish interests must be terminated by death; while those who leave after them objects of personal affection, and especially those who have also cultivated a fellow-feeling with the collective interests of mankind, retain as lively an interest in life on the eve of death as in the vigor of youth and health. Next to selfishness, the principal cause which makes life unsatisfactory is want of mental cultivation. A cultivated mind—I do not mean that of a philosopher, but any mind to which the fountains of knowledge have been opened, and which has been taught, in any tolerable degree, to exercise its faculties —finds sources of inexhaustible interest in all that surrounds it: in the objects of nature, the achievements of art, the imaginations of poetry, the incidents of history, the ways of mankind, past and present, and their prospects in the future. It is possible, indeed, to become indifferent to all this, and that too without having exhausted a thousandth part of it, but only when one has had from the beginning no moral or human interest in these things, and has sought in them only the gratification of curiosity.

Now there is absolutely no reason in the nature of things why an amount of mental culture sufficient to give an intelligent interest in these objects of contemplation should not be the inheritance of every one born in a civilized country. As little is there an inherent necessity that any human being should be a selfish egotist, devoid of every feeling or care but those which center in his own miserable individuality. Something far superior to this is sufficiently common even now, to give ample earnest of what the human species may be made. Genuine private affections and a sincere interest in the public good are possible, though in unequal degrees, to every rightly brought up human being. In a world in which there is so much to interest, so much to enjoy, and so much also to correct and improve, every one who has this moderate amount of moral and intellectual requisites is capable of an existence which may be called enviable; and unless such a person, through bad laws or subjection to the will of others, is denied the liberty to use the sources of happiness within his reach, he will not fail to find this enviable existence, if he escape the positive evils of life, the great sources of physical and mental suffering—such as indigence, disease, and the unkindness, worthlessness, or premature loss of objects of affection. The main stress of the problem lies, therefore, in the contest with these calamities from which it is a rare good fortune entirely to escape; which, as things now are, cannot be obviated, and often cannot be in any material degree mitigated. Yet no one whose opinion deserves a moment's consideration can doubt that most of the great positive evils of the world are in themselves removable, and will, if human affairs continue to improve, be in the end reduced within narrow limits. Poverty, in any sense implying suffering, may be completely extinguished by the wisdom of society combined with the good sense and providence of individuals. Even that most intractible of enemies, disease, may be indefinitely reduced in dimensions by good physical and moral education and proper control of noxious influences, while the progress of science holds out a promise for the future of still more direct conquests over this detestable foe. And every advance in that direction relieves us from some, not only of the chances which cut short our own lives, but, what concerns us still more, which deprive us of those in whom our happiness is wrapped up. As for vicissitudes of fortune and other disappointments connected with worldly circumstances, these are principally the effect either of gross imprudence, of ill-regulated desires, or of bad or imperfect social institutions. All the grand sources, in short, of human suffering are in a great degree, many of them almost entirely, conquerable by human care and effort; and though their removal is grievously slow—though a long succession of generations will perish in the breach before the conquest is completed, and this world becomes all that, if will and knowledge were not wanting, it might easily be made —yet every mind sufficiently intelligent and generous to bear a part, however small and inconspicuous, in the endeavor will draw a noble enjoyment from the contest itself, which he would not for any bribe in the form of selfish indulgence consent to be without.

And this leads to the true estimation of what is said by the objectors concerning the possibility and the obligation of learning to do without happiness. Unquestionably it is possible to do without happiness; it is done involuntarily by nineteen-twentieths of mankind, even in those parts of our present world which are least deep in barbarism; and it often has to be done voluntarily by the hero or the martyr, for the sake of something which he prizes more than his individual happiness. But this something, what is it, unless the happiness of others or some of the requisites of happiness? It is noble to be capable of resigning entirely one's own portion of happiness, or chances of it; but, after all, this self-sacrifice must be for some end; it is not its own end; and if we are told that its end is not happiness but virtue, which is better than happiness, I ask, would the sacrifice be made if the hero or martyr did not believe that it would earn for others immunity from similar sacrifices? Would it be made if he thought that his renunciation of happiness for himself would produce no fruit for any of his fellow creatures, but to make their lot like his, and place them also in the condition of persons who have renounced happiness? All honor to those who can abnegate for themselves the personal enjoyment of life when by such renunciation they contribute worthily to increase the amount of happiness in the world; but he who does it or professes to do it for any other purpose is no more deserving of admiration than the ascetic mounted on his pillar. He may be an inspiriting proof of what men *can* do, but assuredly not an example of what they *should*.

Though it is only in a very imperfect state of the world's arrangements that any one can best serve the happiness of others by the absolute sacrifice of his own, yet, so long as the world is in that imperfect state,

I fully acknowledge that the readiness to make such a sacrifice is the highest virtue which can be found in man. I will add that in this condition of the world, paradoxical as the assertion may be, the conscious ability to do without happiness gives the best prospect of realizing such happiness as is attainable. For nothing except that consciousness can raise a person above the chances of life, by making him feel that, let fate and fortune do their worst, they have not power to subdue him; which, once felt, frees him from excess of anxiety concerning the evils of life, and enables him, like many a Stoic in the worst times of the Roman Empire, to cultivate in tranquillity the sources of satisfaction accessible to him, without concerning himself about the uncertainty of their duration any more than about their inevitable end.

Meanwhile, let utilitarians never cease to claim the morality of self-devotion as a possession which belongs by as good a right to them as either to the Stoic or to the Transcendentalist. The utilitarian morality does recognize in human beings the power of sacrificing their own greatest good for the good of others. It only refuses to admit that the sacrifice is itself a good. A sacrifice which does not increase or tend to increase the sum total of happiness, it considers as wasted. The only self-renunciation which it applauds is devotion to the happiness, or to some of the means of happiness, of others, either of mankind collectively or of individuals within the limits imposed by the collective interests of mankind.

I must again repeat what the assailants of utilitarianism seldom have the justice to acknowledge, that the happiness which forms the utilitarian standard of what is right in conduct is not the agent's own happiness but that of all concerned. As between his own happiness and that of others, utilitarianism requires him to be as strictly impartial as a disinterested and benevolent spectator. In the golden rule of Jesus of Nazareth, we read the complete spirit of the ethics of utility. "To do as you would be done by," and "to love your neighbor as yourself," constitute the ideal perfection of utilitarian morality. As the means of making the nearest approach to this ideal, utility would enjoin, first, that laws and social arrangements should place the happiness or (as, speaking practically, it may be called) the interest of every individual as nearly as possible in harmony with the interest of the whole; and, secondly, that education and opinion, which have so vast a power over human character, should so use that power as to establish in the mind of every individual an indissoluble association between his own happiness and the good of the whole, especially between his own happiness and the practice of such modes of conduct, negative and positive, as regard for the universal happiness prescribes; so that not only he may be unable to conceive the possibility of happiness to himself, consistently with conduct opposed to the general good, but also that a direct impulse to promote the general good may be in every individual one of the habitual motives of action, and the sentiments connected therewith may fill a large and prominent place in every human being's sentient existence. If the impugners of the utilitarian morality represented it to their own minds in this its true character, I know not what recommendation possessed by any other morality they could possibly affirm to be wanting to it; what more beautiful or more exalted developments of human nature any other ethical system can be supposed to foster, or what springs of action, not accessible to the utilitarian, such systems rely on for giving effect to their mandates.

The objectors to utilitarianism cannot always be charged with representing it in a discreditable light. On the contrary, those among them who entertain anything like a just idea of its disinterested character sometimes find fault with its standard as being too high for humanity. They say it is exacting too much to require that people shall always act from the inducement of promoting the general interests of society. But this is to mistake the very meaning of a standard of morals, and confound the rule of action with the motive of it. It is the business of ethics to tell us what are our duties, or by what test we may know them; but no system of ethics requires that the sole motive of all we do shall be a feeling of duty; on the contrary, ninety-nine hundredths of all our actions are done from other motives, and rightly so done if the rule of duty does not condemn them. It is the more unjust to utilitarianism that this particular misapprehension should be made a ground of objection to it, inasmuch as utilitarian moralists have gone beyond almost all others in affirming that the motive has nothing to do with the morality of the action, though much with the worth of the agent. He who saves a fellow creature from drowning does what is morally right, whether his motive be duty or the hope of being paid for his trouble; he who betrays the friend that trusts him is guilty of a crime, even if his object be to serve another friend to whom he is under greater obligations. But to speak only of actions done from the motive of duty, and in direct obedience to principle: it is a misapprehension to the utilitarian mode of thought to conceive it as implying that people should fix their minds upon so wide a generality as the world, or society at large. The great majority of good actions are intended not for the benefit of the world, but for that of individuals, of which the good of the world is made up; and the thoughts of the most virtuous man need not on these occasions travel beyond the particular persons concerned, except so far as is necessary to assure himself that in benefiting them he is not violating the rights, that is, the legitimate and authorized expectations, of any one else. The multiplication of happiness is, according to the utilitarian ethics, the object of virtue: the occasions on which any person (except one in a thousand) has it in his power to do this on an extended scale, in other words, to be a public benefactor, are but exceptional; and on these occasions alone is he called on to consider public utility; in every other case, private utility, the interest or happiness of some few persons, is all he has to attend to. Those alone the influence of whose actions extends to society in general need concern themselves habitually about so large an object. In the case of abstinences indeed—of things which people forbear to do from moral considerations, though the consequences in the particular case might be beneficial—it would be unworthy of an intelligent agent not to be consciously aware that the action is of a class which, if practiced generally, would be generally injurious, and that this is the ground of the obligation to abstain from it. The amount of regard for the public interest implied in this recognition is no greater than is demanded by every system of morals, for they all enjoin to abstain from whatever is manifestly pernicious to society.

The same considerations dispose of another reproach against the doctrine of utility, founded on a still grosser misconception of the purpose of a standard of morality, and of the very meaning of the words "right" and "wrong." It is often affirmed that utilitarianism renders men cold and unsympathizing; that it chills their moral feelings towards individuals; that it makes them regard only the dry and hard consideration of the consequences of actions, not taking into their moral estimate the qualities from which those actions emanate. If the assertion means that they do not allow their judgment respecting the rightness or wrongness of an action to be influenced by their opinion of the qualities of the person who does it, this is a complaint not against utilitarianism, but against any standard of morality at all; for certainly no known ethical standard decides an action to be good or bad because it is done by a good or a bad man, still less because done by an amiable, a brave, or a benevolent man, or the contrary. These considerations are relevant, not to the estimation of actions, but of persons; and there is nothing in the utilitarian theory inconsistent with the fact that there are other things which interest us in persons besides the rightness and wrongness of their actions. The Stoics, indeed, with the paradoxical misuse of language which was part of their system, and by which they strove to raise themselves above all concern about anything but virtue, were fond of saying that he who has that has everything; that he, and only he, is rich, is beautiful, is a king. But no claim of this description is made for the virtuous man by the utilitarian doctrine. Utilitarians are quite aware that there are other desirable possessions and qualities besides virtue, and are perfectly willing to allow to all of them their full worth. They are also aware that a right action does not necessarily indicate a virtuous character, and that actions which are blamable often proceed from qualities entitled to praise. When this is apparent in any particular case, it modifies their estimation, not certainly of the act, but of the agent. I grant that they are, notwithstanding, of opinion that in the long run the best proof of a good character is good actions; and resolutely refuse to consider any mental disposition as good of which the predominant tendency is to produce bad conduct. This makes them unpopular with many people; but it is an unpopularity which they must share with every one who regards the distinction between right and wrong in a serious light; and the reproach is not one which a conscientious utilitarian need be anxious to repel.

If no more be meant by the objection than that many utilitarians look on the morality of actions, as measured by the utilitarian standards, with too exclusive a regard, and do not lay sufficient stress upon the other beauties of character which go towards making a human being lovable or admirable, this may be admitted. Utilitarians who have cultivated their moral feelings, but not their sympathies, nor their artistic perceptions, do fall into this mistake; and so do all other moralists under the same conditions. What can be said in excuse for other moralists is equally available for them, namely, that, if there is to be any error, it is better that it should be on that side. As a matter of fact, we may affirm that among utilitarians, as among adherents of other systems, there is every imaginable degree of rigidity and of laxity in the application of their standard; some are even puritanically rigorous, while others are as indulgent as can possibly be desired by sinner or by sentimentalist. But on the whole, a doctrine which brings prominently forward the interest that mankind have in the repression and prevention of conduct which violates the moral law, is likely to be inferior to no other in turning the sanctions of opinion against such violations. It is true, the question, "What does violate the moral law?" is one on which those who recognize different standards of morality are likely now and then to differ. But difference of opinion on moral questions was not first introduced into the world by utilitarianism,

while that doctrine does supply, if not always an easy, at all events a tangible and intelligible, mode of deciding such differences.

It may not be superfluous to notice a few more of the common misapprehensions of utilitarian ethics, even those which are so obvious and gross that it might appear impossible for any person of candor and intelligence to fall into them; since persons, even of considerable mental endowment, often give themselves so little trouble to understand the bearings of any opinion against which they entertain a prejudice, and men are in general so little conscious of this voluntary ignorance as a defect, that the vulgarest misunderstandings of ethical doctrines are continually met with in the deliberate writings of persons of the greatest pretensions both to high principle and to philosophy. We not uncommonly hear the doctrine of utility inveighed against as a *godless* doctrine. If it be necessary to say anything at all against so mere an assumption, we may say that the question depends upon what idea we have formed of the moral character of the Deity. If it be a true belief that God desires, above all things, the happiness of his creatures, and that this was his purpose in their creation, utility is not only not a godless doctrine, but more profoundly religious than any other. If it be meant that utilitarianism does not recognize the revealed will of God as the supreme law of morals, I answer that a utilitarian who believes in the perfect goodness and wisdom of God necessarily believes that whatever God has thought fit to reveal on the subject of morals must fulfill the requirements of utility in a supreme degree. But others besides utilitarians have been of opinion that the Christian revelation was intended, and is fitted, to inform the hearts and minds of mankind with a spirit which should enable them to find for themselves what is right, and incline them to do it when found, rather than to tell them, except in a very general way, what it is; and that we need a doctrine of ethics, carefully followed out, to *interpret* to us the will of God. Whether this opinion is correct or not, it is superfluous here to discuss; since whatever aid religion, either natural or revealed, can afford to ethical investigation, is as open to the utilitarian moralist as to any other. He can use it as the testimony of God to the usefulness or hurtfulness of any given course of action, by as good a right as others can use it for the indication of a transcendental law, having no connection with usefulness or with happiness.

Again, utility is often summarily stigmatized as an immoral doctrine by giving it the name of "expediency," and taking advantage of the popular use of that term to contrast it with principle. But the expedient, in the sense in which it is opposed to the right, generally means that which is expedient for the particular interest of the agent himself; as when a minister sacrifices the interests of his country to keep himself in place. When it means anything better than this, it means that which is expedient for some immediate object, some temporary purpose, but which violates a rule whose observance is expedient in a much higher degree. The expedient, in this sense, instead of being the same thing with the useful, is a branch of the hurtful. Thus it would often be expedient, for the purpose of getting over some momentary embarrassment, or attaining some object immediately useful to ourselves or others, to tell a lie. But inasmuch as the cultivation in ourselves of a sensitive feeling on the subject of veracity is one of the most useful, and the enfeeblement of that feeling one of the most hurtful, things to which our conduct can be instrumental; and inasmuch

as any, even unintentional, deviation from truth does that much towards weakening the trustworthiness of human assertion, which is not only the principal support of all present social well-being, but the insufficiency of which does more than any one thing that can be named to keep back civilization, virtue, everything on which human happiness on the largest scale depends—we feel that the violation, for a present advantage, of a rule of such transcendent expediency is not expedient, and that he who, for the sake of convenience to himself or to some other individual, does what depends on him to deprive mankind of the good, and inflict upon them the evil, involved in the greater or less reliance which they can place in each other's word, acts the part of one of their worst enemies. Yet that even this rule, sacred as it is, admits of possible exceptions is acknowledged by all moralists; the chief of which is when the withholding of some fact (as of information from a malefactor, or of bad news from a person dangerously ill) would save an individual (especially an individual other than oneself) from great and unmerited evil, and when the withholding can only be effected by denial. But in order that the exception may not extend itself beyond the need, and may have the least possible effect in weakening reliance on veracity, it ought to be recognized and, if possible, its limits defined; and, if the principle of utility is good for anything, it must be good for weighing these conflicting utilities against one another, and marking out the region within which one or the other preponderates.

Again, defenders of utility often find themselves called upon to reply to such objections as this—that there is not time, previous to action, for calculating and weighing the effects of any line of conduct on the general happiness. This is exactly as if any one were to say that it is impossible to guide our conduct by Christianity because there is not time, on every occasion on which anything has to be done, to read through the Old and New Testaments. The answer to the objection is that there has been ample time, namely, the whole past duration of the human species. During all that time, mankind have been learning by experience the tendencies of actions; on which experience all the prudence, as well as all the morality, of life are dependent. People talk as if the commencement of this course of experience had hitherto been put off, and as if, at the moment when some man feels tempted to meddle with the property or life of another, he had to begin considering for the first time whether murder and theft are injurious to human happiness. Even then I do not think that he would find the question very puzzling; but, at all events, the matter is now done to his hand. It is truly a whimsical supposition that, if mankind were agreed in considering utility to be the test of morality, they would remain without any agreement as to what *is* useful, and would take no measures for having their notions on the subject taught to the young, and enforced by law and opinion. There is no difficulty in proving any ethical standard whatever to work ill if we suppose universal idiocy to be conjoined with it; but on any hypothesis short of that, mankind must by this time have acquired positive beliefs as to the effects of some actions on their happiness; and the beliefs which have thus come down are the rules of morality for the multitude, and for the philosopher until he has succeeded in finding better. That philosophers might easily do this, even now, on many subjects; that the received code of ethics is by no means of divine right; and that mankind have still much to learn as to the effects of actions on the general happiness, I admit or rather earnestly maintain. The corollaries from the principle of utility, like the precepts of every practical art, admit of indefinite improvement, and, in a progressive state of the human mind, their improvement is perpetually going on. But to consider the rules of morality as improvable is one thing; to pass over the intermediate generalization entirely and endeavor to test each individual action directly by the first principle is another. It is a strange notion that the acknowledgment of a first principle is inconsistent with the admission of secondary ones. To inform a traveler respecting the place of his ultimate destination is not to forbid the use of landmarks and direction-posts on the way. The proposition that happiness is the end and aim of morality does not mean that no road ought to be laid down to that goal, or that persons going thither should not be advised to take one direction rather than another. Men really ought to leave off talking a kind of nonsense on this subject, which they would neither talk nor listen to on other matters of practical concernment. Nobody argues that the art of navigation is not founded on astronomy because sailors cannot wait to calculate the Nautical Almanac. Being rational creatures, they go to sea with it ready calculated; and all rational creatures go out upon the sea of life with their minds made up on the common questions of right and wrong, as well as on many of the far more difficult questions of wise and foolish. And this, as long as foresight is a human quality, it is to be presumed they will continue to do. Whatever we adopt as the fundamental principle of morality, we require subordinate principles to apply it by; the impossibility of doing without them, being common to all systems, can afford no argument against any one in particular; but gravely to argue as if no such secondary principles could be had, and as if mankind had remained till now, and always must remain, without drawing any general conclusions from the experience of human life, is as high a pitch, I think, as absurdity has ever reached in philosophical controversy.

The remainder of the stock arguments against utilitarianism mostly consist in laying to its charge the common infirmities of human nature, and the general difficulties which embarrass conscientious persons in shaping their course through life. We are told that a utilitarian will be apt to make his own particular case an exception to moral rules, and, when under temptation, will see a utility in the breach of a rule, greater than he will see in its observance. But is utility the only creed which is able to furnish us with excuses for evil doing, and means of cheating our own conscience? They are afforded in abundance by all doctrines which recognize as a fact in morals the existence of conflicting considerations, which all doctrines do that have been believed by sane persons. It is not the fault of any creed, but of the complicated nature of human affairs, that rules of conduct cannot be so framed as to require no exceptions, and that hardly any kind of action can safely be laid down as either always obligatory or always condemnable. There is no ethical creed which does not temper the rigidity of its laws by giving a certain latitude, under the moral responsibility of the agent, for accommodation to peculiarities of circumstances; and under every creed, at the opening thus made, self-deception and dishonest casuistry get in. There exists no moral system under which there do not arise unequivocal cases of conflicting obligation. These are the real difficulties, the knotty points both in the theory of ethics and in the conscientious guidance of personal conduct. They are overcome practically, with greater or with less success, according to the intellect and virtue of the individual; but it can hardly be pretended that anyone will be the less qualified for dealing with them, from possessing an ultimate standard to which conflicting rights and duties can be referred. If utility is the ultimate source of moral obligations, utility may be invoked to decide between them when their demands are incompatible. Though the application of the standard may be difficult, it is better than none at all; while in other systems the moral laws all claiming independent authority, there is no common umpire entitled to interfere between them; their claims to precedence one over another rest on little better than sophistry, and, unless determined, as they generally are, by the unacknowledged influence of consideration of utility, afford a free scope for the action of personal desires and partialities. We must remember that only in these cases of conflict between secondary principles is it requisite that first principles should be appealed to. There is no case of moral obligation in which some secondary principle is not involved; and if only one, there can seldom be any real doubt which one it is, in the mind of any person by whom the principle itself is recognized.

CHAPTER IV

Of What Sort of Proof the Principle of Utility Is Susceptible

It has already been remarked that questions of ultimate ends do not admit of proof, in the ordinary acceptation of the term. To be incapable of proof by reasoning is common to all first principles, to the first premises of our knowledge, as well as to those of our conduct. But the former, being matters of fact, may be the subject of a direct appeal to the faculties which judge of fact—namely, our senses and our internal consciousness. Can an appeal be made to the same faculties on questions of practical ends? Or by what other faculty is cognizance taken of them?

Questions about ends are, in other words, questions what things are desirable. The utilitarian doctrine is that happiness is desirable, and the only thing desirable, as an end; all other things being only desirable as means to that end. What ought to be required of this doctrine, what conditions is it requisite that the doctrine should fulfill— to make good its claim to be believed?

The only proof capable of being given that an object is visible is that people actually see it. The only proof that a sound is audible is that people hear it; and so of the other sources of our experience. In like manner, I apprehend, the sole evidence it is possible to produce that anything is desirable is that people do actually desire it. If the end which the utilitarian doctrine proposes to itself were not, in theory and in practice, acknowledged to be an end, nothing could ever convince any person that it was so. No reason can be given why the general happiness is desirable, except that each person, so far as he believes it to be attainable, desires his own happiness. This, however, being a fact, we have not only all the proof which the case admits of, but all which it is possible to require, that happiness is a good; that each person's happiness is a good to that person, and the general happiness, therefore, a good to the aggregate of all persons. Happiness has made out its title as *one* of the ends of conduct, and consequently one of the criteria of morality.

But it has not, by this alone, proved itself to be the sole criterion. To do that, it would seem, by the same rule, necessary to show, not only that people desire happiness, but that they never desire anything else. Now it is palpable that they do desire things which, in common language, are decidedly distinguished from happiness. They desire, for example, virtue and the absence of vice, no less really than pleasure and the absence of pain. The desire of virtue is not as universal, but it is as authentic a fact as the desire of happiness. And hence the opponents of the utilitarian standard deem that they have a right to infer that there are other ends of human action besides happiness, and that happiness is not the standard of approbation and disapprobation.

But does the utilitarian doctrine deny that people desire virtue, or maintain that virtue is not a thing to be desired? The very reverse. It maintains not only that virtue is to be desired, but that it is to be desired disinterestedly, for itself. Whatever may be the opinion of utilitarian moralists as to the original conditions by which virtue is made virtue, however they may believe (as they do) that actions and dispositions are only virtuous because they promote another end than virtue, yet this being granted, and it having been decided, from considerations of this description, what *is* virtuous, they not only place virtue at the very head of the things which are good as means to the ultimate end, but they also recognize as a psychological fact the possibility of its being, to the individual, a good in itself, without looking to any end beyond it; and hold that the mind is not in a right state, not in a state conformable to utility, not in the state most conducive to the general happiness, unless it does love virtue in this manner—as a thing desirable in itself, even although, in the individual instance, it should not produce those other desirable consequences which it tends to produce, and on account of which it is held to be virtue. This opinion is not, in the smallest degree, a departure from the happiness principle. The ingredients of happiness are very various, and each of them is desirable in itself, and not merely when considered as swelling an aggregate. The principle of utility does not mean that any given pleasure, as music, for instance, or any given exemption from pain, as for example health, is to be looked upon as means to a collective something termed happiness, and to be desired on that account. They are desired and desirable in and for themselves; besides being means, they are a part of the end. Virtue, according to the utilitarian doctrine, is not naturally and originally part of the end, but it is capable of becoming so; and in those who love it disinterestedly it has become so, and is desired and cherished, not as a means to happiness, but as a part of their happiness.

To illustrate this further, we may remember that virtue is not the only thing originally a means, and which if it were not a means to anything else would be and remain indifferent, but which by association with what it is a means to comes to be desired for itself, and that too with the utmost intensity. What, for example, shall we say of the love of money? There is nothing originally more desirable about money than about any heap of glittering pebbles. Its worth is solely that of the things which it will buy; the desires for other things than itself, which it is a means of gratifying. Yet the love of money is not only one of the strongest moving forces of human life, but money is, in many cases, desired in and for itself; the desire to possess it is often stronger than the desire to use it, and goes on increasing when all the desires which point to ends beyond it, to be compassed by it, are falling off. It may, then, be said truly that money is desired not for the sake of an end, but as part of the end. From being a means to happiness, it has come to be itself a principal ingredient of the individual's conception of happiness. The same may be said of the majority of the great objects of human life: power, for example,

or fame, except that to each of these there is a certain amount of immediate pleasure annexed, which has at least the semblance of being naturally inherent in them—a thing which cannot be said of money. Still, however, the strongest natural attraction, both of power and of fame, is the immense aid they give to the attainment of our other wishes; and it is the strong association thus generated between them and all our objects of desire which gives to the direct desire of them the intensity it often assumes, so as in some characters to surpass in strength all other desires. In these cases the means have become a part of the end, and a more important part of it than any of the things which they are means to. What was once desired as an instrument for the attainment of happiness has come to be desired for its own sake. In being desired for its own sake it is, however, desired as *part* of happiness. The person is made, or thinks he would be made, happy by its mere possession; and is made unhappy by failure to obtain it. The desire of it is not a different thing from the desire of happiness any more than the love of music or the desire of health. They are included in happiness. They are some of the elements of which the desire of happiness is made up. Happiness is not an abstract idea but a concrete whole; and these are some of its parts. And the utilitarian standard sanctions and approves their being so. Life would be a poor thing, very ill provided with sources of happiness, if there were not this provision of nature by which things originally indifferent, but conducive to, or otherwise associated with, the satisfaction of our primitive desires, become in themselves sources of pleasure more valuable than the primitive pleasures, both in permanency, in the space of human existence that they are capable of covering, and even in intensity.

Virtue, according to the utilitarian conception, is a good of this description. There was no original desire of it, or motive to it, save its conduciveness to pleasure, and especially to protection from pain. But through the association thus formed it may be felt a good in itself, and desired as such with as great intensity as any other good; and with this difference between it and the love of money, of power, or of fame, that all of these may, and often do, render the individual noxious to the other members of the society to which he belongs, whereas there is nothing which makes him so much a blessing to them as the cultivation of the disinterested love of virtue. And consequently, the utilitarian standard, while it tolerates and approves those other acquired desires, up to the point beyond which they would be more injurious to the general happiness than promotive of it, enjoins and requires the cultivation of the love of virtue up to the greatest strength possible, as being above all things important to the general happiness.

It results from the preceding considerations that there is in reality nothing desired except happiness. Whatever is desired otherwise than as a means to some end beyond itself, and ultimately to happiness, is desired as itself a part of happiness, and is not desired for itself until it has become so. Those who desire virtue for its own sake desire it either because the consciousness of it is a pleasure, or because the consciousness of being without it is a pain, or for both reasons united; as in truth the pleasure and pain seldom exist separately, but almost always together—the same person feeling pleasure in the degree of virtue attained, and pain in not having attained more. If one of these gave him no pleasure, and the other no pain, he would not love or desire virtue, or would desire it only for the other benefits which it might produce to himself or to persons whom he cared for.

We have now, then, an answer to the question, of what sort of proof the principle of utility is susceptible. If the opinion which I have now stated is psychologically true—if human nature is so constituted as to desire nothing which is not either a part of happiness or a means of happiness, we can have no other proof, and we require no other, that these are the only things desirable. If so, happiness is the sole end of human action, and the promotion of it the test by which to judge of all human conduct; from whence it necessarily follows that it must be the criterion of morality, since a part is included in the whole.

And now to decide whether this is really so, whether mankind do desire nothing for itself but that which is a pleasure to them, or of which the absence is a pain, we have evidently arrived at a question of fact and experience, dependent, like all similar questions, upon evidence. It can only be determined by practised self-consciousness and self-observation, assisted by observation of others. I believe that these sources of evidence, impartially consulted, will declare that desiring a thing and finding it pleasant, aversion to it and thinking of it as painful, are phenomena entirely inseparable or rather two parts of the same phenomenon; in strictness of language, two different modes of naming the same psychological fact; that to think of an object as desirable (unless for the sake of its consequences) and to think of it as pleasant are one and the same thing; and that to desire anything except in proportion as the idea of it is pleasant, is a physical and metaphysical impossibility.

So obvious does this appear to me that I expect it will hardly be disputed; and the objection made will be, not that desire can possibly be directed to anything ultimately except pleasure and exemption from pain, but that the will is a different thing from desire; that a person of confirmed virtue or any other person whose purposes are fixed carries out his purposes without any thought of the pleasure he has in contemplating them or expects to derive from their fulfilment, and persists in acting on them, even though these pleasures are much diminished by changes in his character or decay of his passive sensibilities, or are outweighed by the pains which the pursuit of the purposes may bring upon him. All this I fully admit and have stated it elsewhere as positively and emphatically as anyone. Will, the active phenomenon, is a different thing from desire, the state of passive sensibility, and, though originally an offshoot from it, may in time take root and detach itself from the parent stock, so much so that in the case of an habitual purpose, instead of willing the thing because we desire it, we often desire it only because we will it. This, however, is but an instance of that familiar fact, the power of habit, and is nowise confined to the case of virtuous actions. Many indifferent things which men originally did from a motive of some sort, they continue to do from habit. Sometimes this is done unconsciously; the consciousness coming only after the action; at other times with conscious volition, but volition which has become habitual and is put in operation by the force of habit, in opposition perhaps to the deliberate preference, as often happens with those who have contracted habits of vicious or hurtful indulgence. Third and last comes the case in which the habitual act of will in the individual instance is not in contradiction to the general intention prevailing at other times, but in fulfilment of it; as in the case of the person of confirmed virtue and of all who pursue deliberately and consistently any determinate end. The distinction between will and desire thus understood is an authentic and highly important psychological fact; but the fact consists solely in this— that will, like all other parts of our constitution, is amenable to habit, and that we may will from habit what we no longer desire for itself, or desire only because we will it. It is not the less true that will, in the beginning, is entirely produced by desire; including in that term the repelling influence of pain as well as the attractive one of pleasure. Let us take into consideration no longer the person who has a confirmed will to do right, but him in whom that virtuous will is still feeble, conquerable by temptation, and not to be fully relied on; by what means can it be strengthened? How can the will to be virtuous, where it does not exist in sufficient force, be implanted or awakened? Only by making the person *desire* virtue—by making him think of it in a pleasurable light, or of its absence in a painful one. It is by associating the doing right with pleasure, or the doing wrong with pain, or by eliciting and impressing and bringing home to the person's experience the pleasure naturally involved in the one or the pain in the other, that it is possible to call forth that will to be virtuous which, when confirmed, acts without any thought of either pleasure or pain. Will is the child of desire, and passes out of the dominion of its parent only to come under that of habit. That which is the result of habit affords no presumption of being intrinsically good; and there would be no reason for wishing that the purpose of virtue should become independent of pleasure and pain were it not that the influence of the pleasurable and painful associations which prompt to virtue is not sufficiently to be depended on for unerring constancy of action until it has acquired the support of habit. Both in feeling and in conduct, habit is the only thing which imparts certainty; and it is because of the importance to others of being able to rely absolutely on one's feelings and conduct, and to oneself of being able to rely on one's own, that the will to do right ought to be cultivated into this habitual independence. In other words, this state of the will is a means to good, not intrinsically a good; and does not contradict the doctrine that nothing is a good to human beings but in so far as it is either itself pleasurable or a means of attaining pleasure or averting pain.

But if this doctrine be true, the principle of utility is proved. Whether it is so or not, must now be left to the consideration of the thoughtful reader.

COMMENT

Mill's Utilitarian Heritage

"What good is happiness? It won't buy money." This witticism reverses the true relation between means and ends. Money is a means, and happiness is an end. Money is important because it contributes to happiness, and happiness is good for its own sake. It is illogical—and hence amusing—to speak as if money were the end and happiness only the means.

The ethical theory known as utilitarianism maintains that right action, like money, is valuable essentially as a means. Unlike Kant, the Utilitarians make *consequences* the test of right and wrong. An action is right if it brings about the best results.

But what are the *best results?* "The greatest happiness of the greatest number," declared Jeremy Bentham, a typical Utilitarian. By happiness he meant the surplus of pleasure over pain; and the proper end of moral action, he maintained, is to bring about this surplus in the lives of as many people as possible. Acts should be judged right in proportion as they tend to increase pleasure or decrease pain among the maximum number of people. The intrinsic value of the pleasure or disvalue of the pain is to be judged quantitatively, not qualitatively. What matters is that we get as much pleasure as possible, not that we get a certain kind. "Quantity of pleasure being equal," Bentham taught, "pushpin [a very simple game] is as good as poetry." The quantity has two dimensions—intensity and duration. The *more* intense and durable a pleasure is, and the *less* intense and durable a pain, the better— apart from future consequences. The pain of a toothache, for example, is worse the longer and more intense it is; the pleasure of a happy friendship is better the more intense and prolonged it is.

Bentham did not deny that there are, in a sense, *bad* pleasures and *good* pains. The pleasures of cruelty or intemperance produce, in the long run, an overbalance of pain—they are good in themselves but bad in their consequences, and their instrumental badness outweighs their intrinsic goodness. Similarly, there are pains with pleasant consequences. But nothing but pleasure is *intrinsically* good, and nothing but pain is *intrinsically* bad. The art of living well is to calculate the worth of actions in terms of all the plus values of pleasure and the minus values of pain, subtracting the latter from the former. Bentham exercised a great deal of ingenuity in working out the details of this "moral arithmetic."

So far he was expressing an *ethical* theory. In addition, he advanced the *psychological* doctrine that every man is naturally selfish and hence almost invariably seeks pleasure or the avoidance of pain for himself. This egoistic doctrine is inconsistent with the contention that everyone ought to seek "the greatest happiness of the greatest number." What sense is there in saying that man ought to aim at the greatest social good if his nature is inescapably selfish? Bentham tried to avoid contradiction by arguing that governments should establish a system of rewards and punishments which would induce individuals, on the very basis of their egoism, to further the maximum social happiness.

James Mill, as a close friend and colleague of Bentham, saw to it that these ideas were impressed upon the adolescent mind of his son John Stuart Mill. He put into John's hands Dumont's *Traites de Legislation,* an exposition by a sympathetic Frenchman of Bentham's ethical and political philosophy. The effect was akin to a religious conversion. "The reading of this book," John Stuart Mill remarked in his *Autobiography,* "was an epoch in my life; one of the turning points in my mental history. . . . When I laid down the last volume I had become a different being. The 'principle of utility' gave unity to my conception of things. I now had a creed, a doctrine, a philosophy; in one of the best senses of the word, a religion." The fifteen-year-old boy straightway resolved to become a disciple of Bentham and "a reformer of the world."

His mind, however, could not permanently rest in this allegiance. In his twenty-first year he suffered a severe mental crisis, and as he emerged from this illness, it seemed to him that the philosophy of his father and Bentham had unduly slighted "the internal culture of the individual," especially the cultivation of feeling and imagination. When he turned many years later to the composition of *Utilitarianism,* he was trying to defend the ethical philosophy of his father and Bentham from the attacks made upon it, but he was too divided in mind to make a good defense. The conflict between his loyalty to Bentham and his deep independent convictions produced many strains and inconsistencies. His book is, nevertheless, worth very careful study, because even his confusions and errors are highly instructive.

Although Mill begins his discussion of Utilitarianism with remarks that appear to be in perfect agreement with Bentham's theory, he soon exhibits his independence. This divergence gives rise to some of the most fundamental issues in the whole field of ethics. Let us now consider some of these issues.

The Question of Qualities of Pleasure

In estimating the intrinsic value of pleasures, Mill subordinates Bentham's quantitative standards—intensity and duration—to a standard of quality. The pleasures of the cultivated life, he maintains, are superior in *kind* to the pleasures of the uncultivated. Hence the pleasures of a human being are qualitatively superior to the pleasures of a pig, and the pleasures of a Socrates are qualitatively superior to the pleasures of an uncultivated fool. This is a radical break with Bentham's quantitative hedonism, which maintains that the pleasure of a dolt is no better or worse than the quantitatively equal pleasure of a highly developed person.

Is Mill correct in supposing that there are different kinds of pleasure? At first glance, the facts seem to bear out his view. The pleasure of reading a good philosophical book, for example, apparently differs qualitatively from the pleasure of playing a brisk game of handball. But is the qualitative difference in the *pleasures,* or is it in the differing *accompaniments* of the pleasures? If we consider pleasant *experiences,* and not bare pleasures, there *are* genuine qualitative differences; but these differences may be not in the pleasures but in the very different *contents* of experience that have the common property of pleasing. In the case of reading, the experience is quiet, meditative, and relaxed; in the case of playing handball, it is exciting, kinesthetic, and strenuous. Some psychologists, such as Edward Titchener, in his *Textbook on Psychology,* have maintained that the pleasures in such diverse experiences differ only in intensity and duration, and that the only qualitative differences are in such accompaniments as we have just pointed out. Mill inadvertently lends support to this interpretation, since he speaks of the "nobility," "dignity," "intellectuality," etc. of the "pleasures" that he prefers. It would seem that he is talking not about bare pleasures, abstracted from any content, but, rather, about *experiences* which contain not only pleasure but various intellectual, moral, and esthetic qualities.

It is theoretically possible to maintain that there are qualitative differences in pure pleasures and that these differences are ethically important. Just as there are different kinds of colors—red, blue, green, etc.—so there might be different kinds of pleasures. And just as one might hold that warm colors, let us say, are qualitatively superior to cool colors, so one might contend that certain kinds of pleasures are qualitatively superior to others. One difficulty with this view is that we do not find such indisputable qualitative differences in pleasures. Even if we did, we might still be unable to tell whether some kinds of pleasure are really better than others.

This sort of qualitative hedonism, in any event, is not Mill's view. He *appears* to be advocating hedonism, but he is really maintaining, albeit unclearly and inconsistently, that the good is the pleasant *development* of the personality. This is a kind of synthesis of hedonism and self-realizationism rather than hedonism pure and simple.

The contrast between Bentham and Mill emphasizes the question of the nature of intrinsic goodness. Does the ultimate good of life consist solely in pleasure? Or does it consist in enjoyments that contain more than pleasure? It is a widely held belief that the joys of art, intellectual achievement, and spiritual love are qualitatively superior to joys of a purely physical or sensual nature. Is Mill correct in thinking this is true—or is Bentham correct in thinking it false? These are questions for the reader to ponder.

The Question of Moral Arithmetic

Bentham maintained that the business of the legislator or moralist is to calculate the probable effects of alternative acts with a view to maximizing pleasure and minimizing pain. This entails the quantitative assessment of pleasures and pains. That there are great difficulties in comparing intensities with durations, adding up pleasures and pains, and subtracting pains from pleasures has often been pointed out. Bentham might reply that such calculation, although difficult, should be carried out as best we can, and that at least a rough estimation of the hedonic consequences of acts is indispensable to any rational direction of our lives.

By introducing questions of quality, Mill greatly restricts the applicability of Bentham's moral arithmetic. His qualitative test is *preference*—not the preference of the average man but that of the moral connoisseur. He tells us that wise persons, such as Socrates, are more competent than the unwise to compare pleasures, to judge which are qualitatively superior, and to decide whether, in a particular instance, considerations of quantity should be sacrificed to considerations of quality. "From this verdict of the only competent judges," he declares, "I apprehend there can be no appeal."

In practice, he accepts another test—which again is not quantitative. Replying to the objection that there is insufficient time previous to action in which to calculate the probable consequences of acts, he asserts that the past experience of mankind, formulated in moral rules, provides a generally acceptable guide. The question of obligation, he believes, must be answered in terms of the utility of the general practice and not simply in terms of the utility of the particular act. The common moral rules sum up the funded experience of the race—that certain practices, such as truth-telling, have good results, and that their opposites, such as lying, have bad results. The long duration of a moral rule, he implies, is virtual proof of its adaptation to the ethical needs of mankind.

The difference between the approaches of Bentham and of Mill gives rise to a number of questions: To what extent does Utilitarianism entail the measurement of pleasures and pains? Are intensities commensurable with durations, and pains with pleasures? Is the preference of the wise a better guide than quantitative assessment? Is the concept of a moral connoisseur sound? To what extent is the legitimacy of particular acts to be decided by reference to the general practices formulated in moral rules?

The Question of the Social Distribution of Good

Bentham purposes that the morality of acts be determined by their contribution to "the greatest happiness of the greatest number"—and Mill, at times, employs the same phrase. But does this formula mean the greatest amount of happiness among men, or the greatest number of men who are happy? And, supposing that there is a conflict between greatest happiness and greatest number, should we sacrifice the greatest number to the greatest happiness, or the greatest happiness to the greatest number? Mill's ambiguous formula provides us with no answer.

There are indications, however, that Bentham is more democratic and equalitarian in his approach to the problem of distribution than Mill. Each person, he declared, should count for one, and no one for more than one. This tenet could be interpreted as meaning that the pleasure of any man is as intrinsically good as the quantitatively equal pleasure of any other man. But it could also be interpreted to mean that a smaller amount of pleasure *equally* distributed is morally preferable (at least on occasion) to a greater amount *unequally* distributed. If this was Bentham's real conviction, he was not a strict utilitarian and hedonist—for the principle of equality so interpreted is based upon a sense of distributive justice rather than upon the utilitarian principle of maximizing pleasure and minimizing pain.

Mill's position, in any event, is comparatively aristocratic. Although he verbally subscribes to Bentham's phrases, his emphasis upon quality, wisdom, and self-cultivation implies a very different standard than the greatest possible pleasure of the greatest possible number. The word "greatest" indicates a quantitative criterion—whether it be number of people or amount of pleasure. Mill's criterion, on the other hand, is qualitative. In effect, he favors an intellectual aristocracy—though it is worth noting that he does not identify the intellectually superior with the rich and powerful of the earth.

The differences between Bentham and Mill again serve to emphasize an important set of problems. What is a fair and just distribution of good? Can it be reconciled with a quantitative hedonism? Should the controlling consideration be the number of people receiving the good, or the amount of the good? Or should both amount and number be subordinated, as in Mill, to considerations of quality?

The Question of Ultimate Principles

The ethical philosophy of Mill, like that of Bentham, falls into two main parts. The first part is a theory about the nature of right—the doctrine that the proper standard for judging right is best results. This theory is logically independent of hedonism, or of any other particular interpretation of goodness. It simply states that the right must be determined in the light of good consequences—whatever the good may be. The good might be pleasure, or satisfaction of desire, or actualization of potentialities—or almost anything else. Bentham and Mill speak as if the test of consequences is necessarily linked to one and only one end—namely, "happiness" as each conceives it. But this is manifestly not the case.

The question of the validity of utilitarianism—in the wide sense of the term—turns largely upon whether it can satisfactorily explain our many and varied duties. The non-utilitarian will argue that there are kinds of moral rectitude that cannot be interpreted as utilitarian rightness. He would say, for example, that having made a solemn promise, we have a duty to keep it *even if no more good is thereby to be achieved*. The utilitarian, in contrast, would maintain that there is no valid test of right and wrong except welfare. Our duty is to help people and not to hurt them—and the more we help them and the less we hurt them the better. If it becomes clear that, in the long run, keeping a promise will have bad rather than good results, or results less good than some other alternative, our moral obligation is not to keep the promise but to choose whatever alternative yields the best results. This clash between the utilitarians and the non-utilitarians is one of the crucial issues in ethics— and the reader of this book should consider very carefully where the truth lies.

The second part of the ethical philosophy of Bentham and the two Mills is a theory about the nature of ultimate good and evil. Here again, as we have seen, there is disagreement between John Stuart Mill, who embraced a kind of hedonic self-realizationism, and Bentham, who clung to pure quantitative hedonism. The issue is extremely important, but it is not one that can be decided by any conclusive proof. Mill (not realizing the extent of his divergence from Bentham) undertook to "prove" that pleasure alone is ultimately good, but his so-called proof (he admits that *strict* or *conclusive* proof is impossible) contains some of the most widely advertised fallacies in the history of philosophy. We shall refrain from pointing out these fallacies, leaving to the reader the exercise of discovering them.

The anti-hedonistic view might be stated somewhat as follows. What the wise man approves of, as Aristotle pointed out, is the fullest actualization of human potentialities. Hence the atrophy of any essential part of the human personality would be a loss, even if the amount of pleasure were to remain the same. If some drug should put to sleep all man's faculties except the capacity to feel pleasure, and if life should nonetheless continue under these conditions, this loss of human capacities would not be a matter of sheer ethical indifference even if the amount of pleasure and pain in the world should remain the same. Or, again, if we imagine a world of men and a world of lower animals, *equal in the amount of pleasure they contain,* it would not follow that the two worlds are equal in ultimate goodness—because the men, in addition to experiencing pleasure, have insight into truth, love, imagination, excellence of character, enjoyment of beauty, etc. The reply of the hedonist, that all these things are good as means because they *give* pleasure, would not seem to the anti-hedonist an adequate answer. He would say that it is important not merely to feel pleasure, but to feel pleasure in certain ways, with certain accompaniments rather than others. *Real* happiness embraces the great goods of beauty and truth and nobility of character as having intrinsic and not merely instrumental value.

In deciding between hedonism and alternative ethical theories, we must summon up whatever insight we can muster—not the insight of each one of us individually but of all of us cooperatively. In ethical as in scientific matters, individual insight is deepened and steadied by being submitted to a "community of interpretation."

16

Morality Based on Experimental Logic

JOHN DEWEY
(For biographical note see pages 134–135.)

The impact of the alteration in methods of scientific thinking upon moral ideas is, in general, obvious. Goods, ends are multiplied. Rules are softened into principles, and principles are modified into methods of understanding. Ethical theory began among the Greeks as an attempt to find a regulation for the conduct of life which should have a rational basis and purpose instead of being derived from custom. But reason as a substitute for custom was under the obligation of supplying objects and laws as fixed as those of custom had been. Ethical theory ever since has been singularly hypnotized by the notion that its business is to discover some final end or good or some ultimate and supreme law. This is the common element among the diversity of theories. Some have held that the end is loyalty or obedience to a higher power or authority; and they have variously found this higher principle in Divine Will, the will of the secular ruler, the maintenance of institutions in which the purpose of superiors is embodied, and the rational consciousness of duty. But they have differed from one another because there was one point in which they were agreed: a single and final source of law. Others have asserted that it is impossible to locate morality in conformity to law-giving power, and that it must be sought in ends that are goods. And some have sought the good in self-realization, some in holiness, some in happiness, some in the greatest possible aggregate of pleasures. And yet these schools have agreed in the assumption that there is a single, fixed and final good. They have been able to dispute with one another only because of their common premise.

The question arises whether the way out of the confusion and conflict is not to go to the root of the matter by questioning this common element. Is not the belief in the single, final and ultimate (whether conceived as good or as authoritative law) an intellectual product of that feudal organization which is disappearing historically and of that belief in a bounded, ordered cosmos, wherein rest is higher than motion, which has disappeared from natural sci-

* From *Reconstruction in Philosophy* (originally given as lectures in Japan), New York: Henry Holt and Company, 1920; enlarged edition, Boston: Beacon Press, 1948. Reprinted by permission of the Beacon Press.

ence? It has been repeatedly suggested that the present limit of intellectual reconstruction lies in the fact that it has not as yet been seriously applied in the moral and social disciplines. Would not this further application demand precisely that we advance to a belief in a plurality of changing, moving, individualized goods and ends, and to a belief that principles, criteria, laws are intellectual instruments for analyzing individual or unique situations?

The blunt assertion that every moral situation is a unique situation having its own irreplaceable good may seem not merely blunt but preposterous. For the established tradition teaches that it is precisely the irregularity of special cases which makes necessary the guidance of conduct by universals, and that the essence of the virtuous disposition is willingness to subordinate every particular case to adjudication by a fixed principle. It would then follow that submission of a generic end and law to determination by the concrete situation entails complete confusion and unrestrained licentiousness. Let us, however, follow the pragmatic rule, and in order to discover the meaning of the idea ask for its consequences. Then it surprisingly turns out that the primary significance of the unique and morally ultimate character of the concrete situation is to transfer the weight and burden of morality to intelligence. It does not destroy responsibility; it only locates it. A moral situation is one in which judgment and choice are required antecedently to overt action. The practical meaning of the situation—that is to say the action needed to satisfy it—is not self-evident. It has to be searched for. There are conflicting desires and alternative apparent goods. What is needed is to find the right course of action, the right good. Hence, inquiry is exacted: observation of the detailed makeup of the situation; anal-

ysis into its diverse factors; clarification of what is obscure; discounting the more insistent and vivid traits; tracing the consequences of the various modes of action that suggest themselves; regarding the decision reached as hypothetical and tentative until the anticipated or supposed consequences which led to its adoption have been squared with actual consequences. This inquiry is intelligence. Our moral failures go back to some weakness of disposition, some absence of sympathy, some onesided bias that makes us perform the judgment of the concrete case carelessly or perversely. Wide sympathy, keen sensitiveness, persistence in the face of the disagreeable, balance of interests enabling us to undertake the work of analysis and decision intelligently are the distinctively moral traits—the virtues or moral excellencies.

It is worth noting once more that the underlying issue is, after all, only the same as that which has been already threshed out in physical inquiry. There too it long seemed as if rational assurance and demonstration could be attained only if we began with universal conceptions and subsumed particular cases under them. The men who initiated the methods of inquiry that are now everywhere adopted were denounced in their day (and sincerely) as subverters of truth and foes of science. If they have won in the end, it is because, as has already been pointed out, the method of universals confirmed prejudices and sanctioned ideas that had gained currency irrespective of evidence for them; while placing the initial and final weight upon the individual case, stimulated painstaking inquiry into facts and examination of principles. In the end, loss of eternal truths was more than compensated for in the accession of quotidian facts. The loss of the system of superior and fixed definitions and kinds was more than made up for by the growing system of hypotheses and laws used in classifying facts. After all, then, we are only pleading for the adoption in moral reflection of the logic that has been proved to make for security, stringency and fertility in passing judgment upon physical phenomena. And the reason is the same. The old method in spite of its nominal and esthetic worship of reason discouraged reason, because it hindered the operation of scrupulous and unremitting inquiry.

More definitely, the transfer of the burden of the moral life from following rules or pursuing fixed ends over to the detection of the ills that need remedy in a special case and the formation of plans and methods for dealing with them, eliminates the causes which have kept moral theory controversial, and which have also kept it remote from helpful contact with the exigencies of practice. The theory of fixed ends inevitably leads thought into the bog of disputes that cannot be settled. If there is one *summum bonum,* one supreme end, what is it? To consider this problem is to place ourselves in the midst of controversies that are as acute now as they were two thousand years ago. Suppose we take a seemingly more empirical view, and say that while there is not a single end, there also are not as many as there are specific situations that require amelioration; but there are a number of such natural goods as health, wealth, honor or good name, friendship, esthetic appreciation, learning and such moral goods as justice, temperance, benevolence, etc. What or who is to decide the right of way when these ends conflict with one another, as they are sure to do? Shall we resort to the method that once brought such disrepute upon the whole business of ethics: Casuistry? Or shall we have recourse to what Bentham well called the *ipse dixit* method: the arbitrary preference of this or that person for

this or that end? Or shall we be forced to arrange them all in an order of degrees from the highest good down to the least precious? Again we find ourselves in the middle of unreconciled disputes with no indication of the way out.

Meantime, the special moral perplexities where the aid of intelligence is required go unenlightened. We cannot seek or attain health, wealth, learning, justice or kindness in general. Action is always specific, concrete, individualized, unique. And consequently judgments as to acts to be performed must be similarly specific. To say that a man seeks health or justice is only to say that he seeks to live healthily or justly. These things, like truth, are adverbial. They are modifiers of action in special cases. How to live healthily or justly is a matter which differs with every person. It varies with his past experience, his opportunities, his temperamental and acquired weaknesses and abilities. Not man in general but a particular man suffering from some particular disability aims to live healthily, and consequently health cannot mean for him exactly what it means for any other mortal. Healthy living is not something to be attained by itself apart from other ways of living. A man needs to be healthy *in* his life, not apart from it, and what does life mean except the aggregate of his pursuits and activities? A man who aims at health as a distinct end becomes a valetudinarian, or a fanatic, or a mechanical performer of exercises, or an athlete so onesided that his pursuit of bodily development injures his heart. When the endeavor to realize a so-called end does not temper and color all other activities, life is portioned out into strips and fractions. Certain acts and times are devoted to getting health, others to cultivating religion, others to seeking learning, to being a good citizen, a devotee of fine art and so on. This is the only logical alternative to subordinating all aims to the accomplishment of one alone—fanaticism. This is out of fashion at present, but who can say how much of distraction and dissipation in life, and how much of its hard and narrow rigidity is the outcome of men's failure to realize that each situation has its own unique end and that the whole personality should be concerned with it? Surely, once more, what a man needs is to live healthily, and this result so affects all the activities of his life that it cannot be set up as a separate and independent good.

Nevertheless the general notions of health, disease, justice, artistic culture are of great importance: Not, however, because this or that case may be brought exhaustively under a single head and its specific traits shut out, but because generalized science provides a man as physician and artist and citizen, with questions to ask, investigations to make, and enables him to understand the meaning of what he sees. Just in the degree in which a physician is an artist in his work he uses his science, no matter how extensive and accurate, to furnish him with tools of inquiry into the individual case, and with methods of forecasting a method of dealing with it. Just in the degree in which, no matter how great his learning, he subordinates the individual case to some classification of diseases and some generic rule of treatment, he sinks to the level of the routine mechanic. His intelligence and his action become rigid, dogmatic, instead of free and flexible.

Moral goods and ends exist only when something has to be done. The fact that something has to be done proves that there are deficiencies, evils in the existent situation. This ill is just the specific ill that it is. It never is an exact duplicate of anything else. Consequently the good of the situation has to be discovered, projected and attained on the basis of the exact defect and

trouble to be rectified. It cannot intelligently be injected into the situation from without. Yet it is the part of wisdom to compare different cases, to gather together the ills from which humanity suffers, and to generalize the corresponding goods into classes. Health, wealth, industry, temperance, amiability, courtesy, learning, esthetic capacity, initiative, courage, patience, enterprise, thoroughness and a multitude of other generalized ends are acknowledged as goods. But the *value* of this systematization is intellectual or analytic. Classifications *suggest* possible traits to be on the lookout for in studying a particular case; they suggest methods of action to be tried in removing the inferred causes of ill. They are tools of insight; their value is in promoting an individualized response in the individual situation.

Morals is not a catalogue of acts nor a set of rules to be applied like drugstore prescriptions or cook-book recipes. The need in morals is for specific methods of inquiry and of contrivance: Methods of inquiry to locate difficulties and evils; methods of contrivance to form plans to be used as working hypotheses in dealing with them. And the pragmatic import of the logic of individualized situations, each having its own irreplaceable good and principle, is to transfer the attention of theory from preoccupation with general conceptions to the problem of developing effective methods of inquiry.

Two ethical consequences of great moment should be remarked. The belief in fixed values has bred a division of ends into intrinsic and instrumental, of those that are really worth while in themselves and those that are of importance only as means to intrinsic goods. Indeed, it is often thought to be the very beginning of wisdom, of moral discrimination, to make this distinction. Dialectically, the distinction is interesting and seems harmless. But carried into practice it has an import that is tragic. Historically, it has been the source and justification of a hard and fast difference between ideal goods on one side and material goods on the other. At present those who would be liberal conceive intrinsic goods as esthetic in nature rather than as exclusively religious or as intellectually contemplative. But the effect is the same. So-called intrinsic goods, whether religious or esthetic, are divorced from those interests of daily life which because of their constancy and urgency form the preoccupation of the great mass. Aristotle used this distinction to declare that slaves and the working class though they are necessary *for* the state—the commonweal—are not constituents *of* it. That which is regarded as *merely* instrumental must approach drudgery; it cannot command either intellectual, artistic or moral attention and respect. Anything becomes *unworthy* whenever it is thought of as intrinsically lacking worth. So men of "ideal" interests have chosen for the most part the way of neglect and escape. The urgency and pressure of "lower" ends have been covered up by polite conventions. Or, they have been relegated to a baser class of mortals in order that the few might be free to attend to the goods that are really or intrinsically worth while. This withdrawal, in the name of higher ends, has left, for mankind at large and especially for energetic "practical" people, the lower activities in complete command.

No one can possibly estimate how much of the obnoxious materialism and brutality of our economic life is due to the fact that economic ends have been regarded as *merely* instrumental. When they are recognized to be as intrinsic and final in their place as any others, then it will be seen that they are capable of idealization, and that if life is to be worth while, they must acquire ideal and intrinsic value. Esthetic, religious and other "ideal" ends are now thin and meager or else idle and luxurious because of the separation from "instrumental" or economic ends. Only in connection with the latter can they be woven into the texture of daily life and made substantial and pervasive. The vanity and irresponsibility of values that are merely final and not also in turn means to the enrichment of other occupations of life ought to be obvious. But now the doctrine of "higher" ends gives aid, comfort and support to every socially isolated and socially irresponsible scholar, specialist, esthete and religionist. It protects the vanity and irresponsibility of his calling from observation by others and by himself. The moral deficiency of the calling is transformed into a cause of admiration and gratulation.

The other generic change lies in doing away once for all with the traditional distinction between moral goods, like the virtues, and natural goods like health, economic security, art, science and the like. The point of view under discussion is not the only one which has deplored this rigid distinction and endeavored to abolish it. Some schools have even gone so far as to regard moral excellencies, qualities of character as of value only because they promote natural goods. But the experimental logic when carried into morals makes every quality that is judged to be good according as it contributes to amelioration of existing ills. And in so doing, it enforces the moral meaning of natural science. When all is said and done in criticism of present social deficiencies, one may well wonder whether the root difficulty does not lie in the separation of natural and moral science. When physics, chemistry, biology, medicine, contribute to the detection of concrete human woes and to the development of plans for remedying them and relieving the human estate, they become moral; they become part of the apparatus of moral inquiry or science. The latter then loses its peculiar flavor of the didactic and pedantic; its ultra-moralistic and hortatory tone. It loses its thinness and shrillness as well as its vagueness. It gains agencies that are efficacious. But the gain is not confined to the side of moral science. Natural science loses its divorce from humanity; it becomes itself humanistic in quality. It is something to be pursued not in a technical and specialized way for what is called truth for its own sake, but with the sense of its social bearing, its intellectual indispensableness. It is technical only in the sense that it provides the technique of social and moral engineering.

When the consciousness of science is fully impregnated with the consciousness of human value, the greatest dualism which now weighs humanity down, the split between the material, the mechanical, the scientific and the moral and ideal will be destroyed. Human forces that now waver because of this division will be unified and reinforced. As long as ends are not thought of as individualized according to specific needs and opportunities, the mind will be content with abstractions, and the adequate stimulus to the moral or social use of natural science and historical data will be lacking. But when attention is concentrated upon the diversified concretes, recourse to all intellectual materials needed to clear up the special cases will be imperative. At the same time that morals are made to focus in intelligence, things intellectual are moralized. The vexatious and wasteful conflict between naturalism and humanism is terminated.

These general considerations may be amplified. First: Inquiry, discovery take the same place in morals that they have come to occupy in sciences of nature. Validation, demonstration become experimental, a matter of consequences. Reason, always an honorific term in ethics, becomes actualized in the methods by which the needs and conditions, the obstacles and resources, of situations are scrutinized in detail, and intelligent plans of improvement are worked out. Remote and abstract generalities promote jumping at conclusions, "anticipations of nature." Bad consequences are then deplored as due to natural perversity and untoward fate. But shifting the issue to analysis of a specific situation makes inquiry obligatory and alert observation of consequences imperative. No past decision nor old principle can ever be wholly relied upon to justify a course of action. No amount of pains taken in forming a purpose in a definite case is final; the consequences of its adoption must be carefully noted, and a purpose held only as a working hypothesis until results confirm its rightness. Mistakes are no longer either mere unavoidable accidents to be mourned or moral sins to be expiated and forgiven. They are lessons in wrong methods of using intelligence and instructions as to a better course in the future. They are indications of the need of revision, development, readjustment. Ends grow, standards of judgment are improved. Man is under just as much obligation to develop his most advanced standards and ideals as to use conscientiously those which he already possesses. Moral life is protected from falling into formalism and rigid repetition. It is rendered flexible, vital, growing.

In the second place, every case where moral action is required becomes of equal moral importance and urgency with every other. If the need and deficiencies of a specific situation indicate improvement of health as the end and good, then for that situation health is the ultimate and supreme good. It is no means to something else. It is a final and intrinsic value. The same thing is true of improvement of economic status, of making a living, of attending to business and family demands—all of the things which under the sanction of fixed ends have been rendered of secondary and merely instrumental value, and so relatively base and unimportant. Anything that in a given situation is an end and good at all is of equal worth, rank and dignity with every other good of any other situation, and deserves the same intelligent attention.

We note thirdly the effect in destroying the roots of Phariseeism. We are so accustomed to thinking of this as deliberate hypocrisy that we overlook its intellectual premises. The conception which looks for the end of action within the circumstances of the actual situation will not have the same measure of judgment for all cases. When one factor of the situation is a person of trained mind and large resources, more will be expected than with a person of backward mind and uncultured experience. The absurdity of applying the same standard of moral judgment to savage peoples that is used with civilized will be apparent. No individual or group will be judged by whether they come up to or fall short of some fixed result, but by the direction in which they are moving. The bad man is the man who no matter how good he *has* been is beginning to deteriorate, to grow less good. The good man is the man who no matter how morally unworthy he *has* been is moving to become better. Such a conception makes one severe in judging himself and humane in judging others. It excludes that arrogance which always accompanies judgment based on degree of approximation to fixed ends.

In the fourth place, the process of growth, of improvement and progress, rather than the static outcome and result,

becomes the significant thing. Not health as an end fixed once and for all, but the needed improvement in health—a continual process—is the end and good. The end is no longer a terminus or limit to be reached. It is the active process of transforming the existent situation. Not perfection as a final goal, but the ever-enduring process of perfecting, maturing, refining is the aim in living. Honesty, industry, temperance, justice, like health, wealth and learning, are not goods to be possessed as they would be if they expressed fixed ends to be attained. They are directions of change in the quality of experience. Growth itself is the only moral "end."

Although the bearing of this idea upon the problem of evil and the controversy between optimism and pessimism is too vast to be here discussed, it may be worth while to touch upon it superficially. The problem of evil ceases to be a theological and metaphysical one, and is perceived to be the practical problem of reducing, alleviating, as far as may be removing, the evils of life. Philosophy is no longer under obligation to find ingenious methods of proving that evils are only apparent, not real, or to elaborate schemes for explaining them away or, worse yet, for justifying them. It assumes another obligation:— That of contributing in however humble a way to methods that will assist us in discovering the causes of humanity's ills. Pessimism is a paralyzing doctrine. In declaring that the world is evil wholesale, it makes futile all efforts to discover the remedial causes of specific evils and thereby destroys at the root every attempt to make the world better and happier. Wholesale optimism, which has been the consequence of the attempt to explain evil away, is, however, equally an incubus.

After all, the optimism that says that the world is already the best possible of all worlds might be regarded as the most cynical of pessimisms. If this is the best possible, what would a world which was fundamentally bad be like? Meliorism is the belief that the specific conditions which exist at one moment, be they comparatively bad or comparatively good, in any event may be bettered. It encourages intelligence to study the positive means of good and the obstructions to their realization, and to put forth endeavor for the improvement of conditions. It arouses confidence and a reasonable hopefulness as optimism does not. For the latter in declaring that good is already realized in ultimate reality tends to make us gloss over the evils that concretely exist. It becomes too readily the creed of those who live at ease, in comfort, of those who have been successful in obtaining this world's rewards. Too readily optimism makes the men who hold it callous and blind to the sufferings of the less fortunate, or ready to find the cause of troubles of others in their personal viciousness. It thus co-operates with pessimism, in spite of the extreme nominal differences between the two, in benumbing sympathetic insight and intelligent effort in reform. It beckons men away from the world of relativity and change into the calm of the absolute and eternal.

The import of many of these changes in moral attitude focuses in the idea of happiness. Happiness has often been made the object of the moralists' contempt. Yet the most ascetic moralist has usually restored the idea of happiness under some other name, such as bliss. Goodness without happiness, valor and virtue without satisfaction, ends without conscious enjoyment— these things are as intolerable practically as they are self-contradictory in conception. Happiness is not, however, a bare possession; it is not a fixed attainment. Such a happiness is either the unworthy selfishness which moralists have so bitterly condemned, or it is, even if labeled bliss, an insipid tedium, a millennium of ease in relief from all struggle and labor. It could satisfy only the most delicate of mollycoddles. Happiness is found only in success; but success means succeeding, getting forward, moving in advance. It is an active process, not a passive outcome. Accordingly it includes the overcoming of obstacles, the elimination of sources of defect and ill. Esthetic sensitiveness and enjoyment are a large constituent in any worthy happiness. But the esthetic appreciation which is totally separated from renewal of spirit, from re-creation of mind and purification of emotion is a weak and sickly thing, destined to speedy death from starvation. That the renewal and re-creation come unconsciously, not by set intention, but makes them the more genuine.

Upon the whole, utilitarianism has marked the best in the transition from the classic theory of ends and goods to that which is now possible. It had definite merits. It insisted upon getting away from vague generalities, and down to the specific and concrete. It subordinated law to human achievement instead of subordinating humanity to external law. It taught that institutions are made for man and not man for institutions; it actively promoted all issues of reform. It made moral good natural, humane, in touch with the natural goods of life. It opposed unearthly and otherworldly morality. Above all, it acclimatized in human imagination the idea of social welfare as a supreme test. But it was still profoundly affected in fundamental points by old ways of thinking. It never questioned the idea of a fixed, final and supreme end. It only questioned the current notions as to the nature of this end; and then inserted pleasure and the greatest possible aggregate of pleasures in the position of the fixed end.

Such a point of view treats concrete activities and specific interests not as worth while in themselves, or as constituents of happiness, but as mere external means to getting pleasures. The upholders of the old tradition could therefore easily accuse utilitarianism of making not only virtue but art, poetry, religion and the state into mere servile means of attaining sensuous enjoyment. Since pleasure was an outcome, a result valuable on its own account independently of the active processes that achieve it, happiness was a thing to be possessed and held onto. The acquisitive instincts of man were exaggerated at the expense of the creative. Production was of importance not because of the intrinsic worth of invention and reshaping the world, but because its external results feed pleasure. Like every theory that sets up fixed and final aims, in making the end passive and possessive, it made all active operations mere tools. Labor was an unavoidable evil to be minimized. Security in possession was the chief thing practically. Material comfort and ease was magnified in contrast with the pains and risk of experimental creation. . . . The idea of a fixed and single end lying beyond the diversity of human needs and acts rendered utilitarianism incapable of being an adequate representative of the modern spirit. It has to be reconstructed through emancipation from its inherited elements.

If a few words are added upon the topic of education, it is only for the sake of suggesting that the educative process is all one with the moral process, since the latter is a continuous passage of experience from worse to better. Education has been traditionally thought of as preparation: as learning, acquiring certain things because they will later be useful. The end is remote, and education is getting ready, is a preliminary to something more important to happen later on. Childhood is only a preparation for adult life, and adult life for another life. Always the future, not the present, has been the significant thing in education: Acquisition of knowledge and skill for future use and enjoyment; formation of habits required later in life in business, good citizenship and pursuit of science. Education is thought of also as something needed by some human beings merely because of their dependence upon others. We are born ignorant, unversed, unskilled, immature, and consequently in a state of social dependence. Instruction, training, moral discipline are processes by which the mature, the adult, gradually raise the helpless to the point where they can look out for themselves. The business of childhood is to grow into the independence of adulthood by means of the guidance of those who have already attained it. Thus the process of education as the main business of life ends when the young have arrived at emancipation from social dependence.

These two ideas, generally assumed but rarely explicitly reasoned out, contravene the conception that growing, or the continuous reconstruction of experience, is the only end. If at whatever period we choose to take a person, he is still in process of growth, then education is not, save as a by-product, a preparation for something coming later. Getting from the present the degree and kind of growth there is in it is education. This is a constant function, independent of age. The best thing that can be said about any special process of education, like that of the formal school period, is that it renders its subject capable of further education: more sensitive to conditions of growth and more able to take advantage of them. Acquisition of skill, possession of knowledge, attainment of culture are not ends: they are marks of growth and means to its continuing.

The contrast usually assumed between the period of education as one of social dependence and of maturity as one of social independence does harm. We repeat over and over that man is a social animal, and then confine the significance of this statement to the sphere in which sociality usually seems least evident, politics. The heart of the sociality of man is in education. The idea of education as preparation and of adulthood as a fixed limit of growth are two sides of the same obnoxious untruth. If the moral business of the adult as well as the young is a growing and developing experience, then the instruction that comes from social dependencies and interdependencies is as important for the adult as for the child. Moral independence for the adult means arrest of growth, isolation means induration. We exaggerate the intellectual dependence of childhood so that children are too much kept in leading strings, and then we exaggerate the independence of adult life from intimacy of contacts and communication with others. When the identity of the moral process with the processes of specific growth is realized, the more conscious and formal education of childhood will be seen to be the most economical and efficient means of social advance and reorganization, and it will also be evident that the test of all the institutions of adult life is their effect in furthering continued education. Government, business, art, religion, all social institutions have a meaning, a purpose. That purpose is to set free and to develop the capacities of human individuals without respect to race, sex, class or economic status. And this is all one with saying that the test of their value is the extent to which they educate every individual into the full stature of his possibility. Democracy has many meanings, but if it has a moral meaning, it is found in resolving that the supreme test of all political institutions and industrial arrangements shall be the contribution they make to the all-around growth of every member of society.

COMMENT

Main Emphases in Dewey's Ethics

Since the pragmatism of Dewey has been illustrated and discussed in Chapter 5, our comments in this chapter can be brief.

When Dewey takes up the subject of ethics, he shifts his emphasis from *value* to *valuation*, being more concerned with the process of appraisal than with the qualities appraised. Valuation, he maintains, should be in accordance with the methods of experimental logic. No one has insisted more strenuously than Dewey upon scientific study of the actual needs of human beings and the concrete, experimental means of satisfying these needs. "Not all who say Ideals, Ideals," he remarks, "shall enter into the kingdom of the ideal, but those who know and respect the roads that conduct to the kingdom." [1]

[1] "The Pragmatic Acquiescence," *New Republic,* Vol. 49 (Jan. 5, 1927), p. 189.

His main contribution to ethical theory has been to explore the roads rather than to describe the destination. Indeed, he does not believe in a fixed destination but rather, in a never-ending and exploratory journey. Since conditions are constantly changing, rules cannot be made nor goals ascertained in advance. Living well is an experiment, and there should be flexible reappraisal and reorientation as the experiment progresses.

Valuation is stimulated by tension, conflict, unsatisfactoriness; and successful valuation points to ways of resolving the tensions and releasing the pent-up energies. In regard to ethics, as in pragmatist theory in general, inquiry is conceived to be instrumentalist—a tool for controlling experience. Values are not passively "given," without intelligent effort, but are actively constructed. There is a fundamental difference between what is merely "liked" and what is genuinely "likable," merely "desired" and really "desirable," merely "admired" and truly "admirable," merely "satisfying" and dependably "satisfactory." Only the latter are *values* in the sense that they have been *validated*. They can be achieved only if we know the conditions and consequences of our desires, affections, and enjoyments, and if we learn intelligently to coordinate and control them. The idea of a *good* should be treated as a hypothesis, to be tested like any other.

In the testing, we must see ends and means as "continuous"—the ends as means to future satisfactions, and the means as not merely instrumentally but intrinsically valuable or disvaluable. Kant, for example, was fundamentally mistaken in exalting virtue as an end apart from being a means, for the very qualities that make it good as end make it good as means also. Dewey believes that experience is most satisfactory when the instrumental and the consummatory are closely linked—when action and contemplation fructify each other. We should neither subordinate growth and spontaneity to static contemplation nor concentrate merely upon activity to the neglect of rational goals. Life should combine both repose and stimulation—the sense of achievement and the sense of adventure. In thus insisting upon "the continuity of means and ends," Dewey is exhibiting the anti-dualistic tendency that pervades his entire philosophy. He protests strongly against the inveterate tendency to think in terms of hard-and-fast distinctions between, for example, facts and values, experience and nature, freedom and organization, learning and doing; and he seeks to resolve all such sharp dualisms by insisting upon the continuity and interpenetration of "opposites." Values are to be studied as natural facts, and facts are to be evaluated; experience is to be regarded as inseparable from nature, and nature is to be interpreted in terms of experience; freedom is to be secured by organization, and organization is to be liberalized by freedom; learning is to be achieved by doing, and doing is to be directed by learning. His whole philosophy can thus be regarded as a "revolt against dualism," of almost every kind and description. The fruit of this philosophy is the perfecting of experience by the elimination of conflicts.

There is no sense, according to Dewey, in talking about *the* end of life—as if there were a single end or final consummation. Life is simply an on-going process, with a plurality of ends which function also as means. His stress is upon the dynamic rather than the static, the specific rather than the general, the concrete and plural rather than the abstract and monistic. "Faith in the varied possibilities of diversified experience," he declares, "is attended with the joy of constant discovery and constant growing." [2] Growth provides its own sufficient criterion, and it is a mistake to seek anything more fixed and constant.

On the Distinction Between Science, Technology, and Morals

According to some critics, Dewey's ethical philosophy is strong in method but weak in vision; strong in delineating the variety of experience but weak in revealing the unity of life; strong in its awareness of novelty but weak in its blindness to universal and enduring values; strong in opposing static absolutism but weak in yielding to mercurial relativism; strong in realizing the need for growth but weak in criticizing the direction of growth; strong in relating science, technology, and morals, weak in failing to distinguish them. Whether this estimate is justified we shall leave to the readers of this book to decide. The last point of criticism, however, calls for more detailed comment.

The heart of Dewey's ethical philosophy is the attempt to link science, technology, and morals, and it is therefore important to consider their interrelations. We can begin by noting three realms of discourse, as illustrated by the following sentences:

"That is a strong poison."

"You ought to use a strong poison" (said to a would-be murderer).

"You ought not to murder."

The first sentence is *descriptive;* it simply indicates a matter of fact, with no commendation or disparagement. The second sentence is *evaluative,* but in what Kant would call a *hypothetical* rather than a categorical sense. The "ought" here simply means that, *if* you want to murder this man, you ought to use a poison strong enough to accomplish your purpose. It does not express a *duty* to use a strong poison. The third sentence is also *evaluative,* but in what Kant would call a *categorical* rather than a hypothetical sense. It expresses a duty to refrain from murdering. Sentences of the first type are characteristic of pure science; sentences of the second type are characteristic of technology; and sentences of the third type are characteristic of morals. (To

[2] "What I Believe," *Forum* (March 1930), p. 179.

accept these distinctions, we would not have to agree with Kant's formulae for determining categorical imperatives. If we were utilitarians, for example, our formula might read: "So act that in every case there shall be no better results." If our duty is to achieve the best results possible, it is still our *duty*.)

The charge that can be made against Dewey is that he has failed to distinguish clearly among science, technology, and morals. In his laudable effort to relate them, he has obscured their differences. We shall not discuss the adequacy of his distinction between pure science and technology—this question is relevant to the issues presented in Chapter 5 and might well be debated in that connection. At present, we are concerned only with the relation between morals and science and between morals and technology.

1. *Morals and science.* "Experience," Dewey notes, "actually presents esthetic and moral traits." [3] These stand on "the same level" as the redness of a rose or the absentmindedness of a professor—they are matters of fact which can be studied like any other. There is a valid point here that should not be denied. Human beings do exhibit esthetic and moral traits and experience satisfactions and enjoyments. These can be described like any other natural facts. Moral theories that try to exclude consideration of human nature and its environment are hopelessly unrealistic. If this is all that Dewey means, we need not disagree with him. But it is still the case that a psychologist bent upon *describing* human nature has a different task than the moralist bent upon *evaluating* moral alternatives. Such words as "good," "right," "ought," as used by the moralist, are nouns and adjectives of commendation, not of description. How can we make the leap from description to evaluation? How can we get, for example, from "desired" to *ethically* "desirable"? The latter does not mean *psychologically* desirable, in the sense that someone *can* desire it. It means *worth* desiring—desiring in the sense that it *ought* to be desired. A naturalistic theory of ethics, such as that of Dewey, seems to overlook the nondescriptive, purely ethical character of the moral *ought*.

Dewey could reply that "desirable" means that which one desires *after* one has seen all its conditions and consequences. But this does not solve the problem, because it is perfectly possible for a malevolent person to desire something that is morally evil after he has thoroughly understood its connections with other things. Dewey could also reply that the ethically desirable is that which is desired by a fair and impartial judge. But this definition is circular; it amounts to saying that something is ethically desirable (good or right) when it is approved by somebody who approves only what *is* ethically desirable. The only solution, Dewey's critics would say, is to admit a clearcut distinction between facts and norms, morals and science—and this he fails to do.

2. *Morals and technology.* Dewey often appears to be identifying morality

[3] *Experience and Nature* (Chicago: Open Court, 1929), p. 2.

with technology, or to be thinking of it as a kind of super-technology. There would seem to be much to support this point of view. The language of technological discourse, as we have already noted, is distinguished by normative terms, such as "ought" or "ought not," or by imperatives, such as "do this" or "do not do that." Such language is intended to direct choice among alternative possibilities. There are different kinds of norms and normative statements belonging to different levels of technological discourse. Many technological imperatives are mere counsels of skill, as when a carpenter says to his helper, "You ought to sharpen the teeth of that saw." He means, "*If* you want to use your saw effectively for the purpose at hand, you ought to sharpen its teeth." At a somewhat higher and more general level, the norms have a quasi-ethical or esthetic character, as in the case of the artistic norm of "beauty," the legal norm of "justice," the medical norm of "health," and the economic norm of "prosperity." Finally, there are highest level norms that pertain to a total economy of values. They are invoked when there is a conflict between lower-level oughts, and may be thought of as decidedly ethical. Morality will then be conceived as a technology of technologies, the function of which is to coordinate all the various techniques that a society has at its disposal.

This view of morality is by no means new. Aristotle had a similar conception of the art of arts, the technology of technologies. In the opening paragraphs of his *Ethics,* as we have seen, he pointed out that the arts are to be distinguished by the ends which they serve. Health is the aim of medicine, vessels of shipbuilding, victory of military strategy, and wealth of economics. The ends and the corresponding arts form a hierarchy, some being subservient to others. Bridle-making is subservient to horsemanship, horsemanship to strategy, and so on. Finally we arrive at some ultimate end and the art corresponding to it. This is the art of arts—the art whose function it is to harmonize and control all the other arts and whose end, therefore, is not this or that particular good but the good for man. Aristotle calls this highest art the art of politics, of which ethics, since it defines the ultimate good, is an integral part. Here the word "art" is being used in the same sense as we intend by "technology," and Aristotle's conception of politics as an "art of arts" is analogous to the conception of morality as a "technology of technologies."

Up to a point, this way of looking at morality seems sound, but there are important qualifications that need to be made. It is important to recognize that morality, as a kind of supreme technology, is fundamentally different from ordinary technology—so different, indeed, that we should perhaps not call it a technology at all. An ordinary technological norm is an *instrument* of a decision-maker, not a *control* over him; and, therefore, to interpret moral norms as ordinary technological norms would imply that technology needs no control or is somehow self-regulating. Such a view is exceedingly mischievous, especially in this age of nuclear fission, when bombs threaten to blow all of us, even the technologists and all their works, to smithereens. Consequently, there must be norms controlling the decision-maker rather than norms which are merely his instruments. The right use of instrumental norms presupposes some non-instrumental criteria.

In the case of ordinary technology, in other words, it is not the right motivation of the agent that is in question but the skill to be used in carrying out a motivation that is taken for granted. In the case of morality, on the other hand, it is precisely the motivation that is most in question, and the problem of finding the right means is secondary. The norms of ordinary technology usually prescribe how to perform some action. The moral question, on the other hand, is not simply *how* to do something, but *what* to do.

Pragmatists, such as John Dewey, are prone to exaggerate the similarity between ordinary technology and morality. They are so intent upon the fluidity and instrumentality of norms that they neglect or even deny the question of *ultimate* motivation. They are inclined to take "the problematic situation" as it arises and to interpret right action as "problem-solving" within the context of this situation. The problem, as they see it, is "solved" when the diverse competing interests in the situation are brought into some kind of moving equilibrium, which leads to new "problematic situations" and thus to new and revised norms. So understood, morality is closely akin to ordinary technology. But morality cannot afford merely to implement and reconcile interests that are taken for granted. Its task is more radical. It criticizes interests in the light of ultimate norms; and, in exercising this sort of stubborn and very radical criticism, it differentiates itself from technology.

The question that we have posed is whether Dewey has sufficiently realized this fact, and whether he has also realized the clear-cut difference between morality (or ethics, as its theoretical basis) and natural science.

17

Morality Based on Limited Scepticism

CHARLES LESLIE STEVENSON (1908–)

An American contributor to the international movement known as logical empiricism, Stevenson was educated at Yale, Cambridge, and Harvard, receiving his doctorate at Harvard in 1935. He has taught at Yale and Harvard, and is currently Professor of Philosophy at the University of Michigan. He is best known for his *Ethics and Language* (1944) and for his articles on the analysis of ethical concepts.

*The Nature of Ethical Disagreement**

When people disagree about the value of something—one saying that it is good or right, and another that it is bad or wrong—by what methods of argument or inquiry can their disagreement be resolved? Can it be resolved by the methods of science, or does it require methods of some other kind, or is it open to no rational solution at all?

The question must be clarified before it can be answered. And the word that is particularly in need of clarification, as we shall see, is the word "disagreement."

Let us begin by noting that "disagreement" has two broad senses: In the first

sense it refers to what I shall call "disagreement in belief." This occurs when Mr. A believes *p,* when Mr. B believes *not-p,* or something incompatible with *p,* and when neither is content to let the belief of the other remain unchallenged. Thus doctors may disagree in belief about the causes of an illness; and friends may disagree in belief about the exact date on which they last met.

In the second sense, the word refers to what I shall call "disagreement in attitude." This occurs when Mr. A has a favorable attitude to something, when Mr. B has

* Originally published by the Centro di Metodologia e Analisi del Linguaggio, Milan, Italy. Reprinted by permission of the author and the Centro di Metodologia.

an unfavorable or less favorable attitude to it, and when neither is content to let the other's attitude remain unchanged. The term "attitude" is here used in much the same sense that R. B. Perry uses "interest"; it designates any psychological disposition of being *for* or *against* something. Hence love and hate are relatively specific kinds of attitudes, as are approval and disapproval, and so on.

This second sense can be illustrated in this way: Two men are planning to have dinner together. One is particularly anxious to eat at a certain restaurant, but the other doesn't like it. Temporarily, then, the men cannot "agree" on where to dine. Their argument may be trivial, and perhaps only half serious; but in any case it represents a disagreement *in attitude*. The men have divergent preferences, and each is trying to redirect the preference of the other.

Further examples are readily found. Mrs. Smith wishes to cultivate only the four hundred; Mr. Smith is loyal to his old poker-playing friends. They accordingly disagree, in attitude, about whom to invite to their party. The progressive mayor wants modern school-buildings and large parks; the older citizens are against these "new-fangled" ways; so they disagree on civic policy. These cases differ from the one about the restaurant only in that the clash of attitudes is more serious, and may lead to more vigorous argument.

The difference between the two senses of "disagreement" is essentially this: the first involves an opposition of beliefs, both of which cannot be true, and the second involves an opposition of attitudes, both of which cannot be satisfied.

Let us apply this distinction to a case that will sharpen it. Mr. A believes that most voters will favor a proposed tax, and Mr. B disagrees with him. The disagreement concerns attitudes—those of the voters—but note that A and B are *not* disagreeing in attitude. Their disagreement is *in belief about* attitudes. It is simply a special kind of disagreement in belief, differing from disagreement in belief about head colds only with regard to subject matter. It implies not an opposition of the actual attitudes of the speakers, but only of their beliefs about certain attitudes. Disagreement *in* attitude, on the other hand, implies that the very attitudes of the speakers are opposed. A and B may have opposed beliefs about attitudes without having opposed attitudes, just as they may have opposed beliefs about head colds without having opposed head colds. Hence we must not, from the fact that an argument is concerned with attitudes, infer that it necessarily involves disagreement *in* attitude.

We may now turn more directly to disagreement about values, with particular reference to normative ethics. When people argue about what is good, do they disagree in belief, or do they disagree in attitude? A long tradition of ethical theorists strongly suggests, whether they always intend to or not, that the disagreement is one *in belief*. Naturalistic theorists, for instance, identify an ethical judgment with some sort of scientific statement, and so make normative ethics a branch of science. Now a scientific argument typically exemplifies disagreement in belief, and if an ethical argument is simply a scientific one, then it too exemplifies disagreement in belief. The usual naturalistic theories of ethics that stress attitudes—such as those of Hume, Westermarck, Perry, Richards, and so many others—stress disagreement in belief no less than the rest. They imply, of course, that disagreement about what is good is disagreement *in belief* about attitudes; but we have seen that that is simply one sort of disagreement in belief, and by no means the same as disagreement *in* attitude. Analyses that stress disagreement *in* attitude are extremely rare.

If ethical arguments, as we encounter them in everyday life, involved disagreement in belief exclusively—whether the beliefs were about attitudes or about something else—then I should have no quarrel with the ordinary sort of naturalistic analysis. Normative judgments could be taken as scientific statements, and amenable to the usual scientific proof. But a moment's attention will readily show the disagreement in belief has not the exclusive role that theory has so repeatedly ascribed to it. It must be readily granted that ethical arguments usually involve disagreement in belief; but they *also* involve disagreement in attitude. And the conspicuous role of disagreement in attitude is what we usually take, whether we realize it or not, as the distinguishing feature of ethical arguments. For example: suppose that the representative of a union urges that the wage level in a given company ought to be higher—that it is only right that the workers receive more pay. The company representative urges in reply that the workers ought to receive no more than they get. Such an argument clearly represents a disagreement in attitude. The union is *for* higher wages; the company is *against* them, and neither is content to let the other's attitude remain unchanged. *In addition* to this disagreement in attitude, of course, the argument may represent no little disagreement in belief. Perhaps the parties disagree about how much the cost of living has risen, and how much the workers are suffering under the present wage scale. Or perhaps they disagree about the company's earnings, and the extent to which the company could raise wages and still operate at a profit. Like any typical ethical argument, then, this argument involves both disagreement in attitude and disagreement in belief.

It is easy to see, however, that the disagreement in attitude plays a unifying and predominating role in the argument. This is so in two ways:

In the first place, disagreement in attitude determines what beliefs are *relevant* to the argument. Suppose that the company affirms that the wage scale of fifty years ago was far lower than it is now. The union will immediately urge that this contention, even though true, is irrelevant. And it is irrelevant simply because information about the wage level of fifty years ago, maintained under totally different circumstances, is not likely to affect the present attitudes of either party. To be relevant, any belief that is introduced into the argument must be one that is likely to lead one side or the other to have a different attitude, and so reconcile disagreement in attitude. Attitudes are often functions of beliefs. We often change our attitudes to something when we change our beliefs about it; just as a child ceases to *want* to touch a live coal when he comes to *believe* that it will burn him. Thus in the present argument, any beliefs that are at all likely to alter attitudes, such as those about the increasing cost of living or the financial state of the company, will be considered by both sides to be relevant to the argument. Agreement in belief on these matters may lead to agreement in attitude toward the wage scale. But beliefs that are likely to alter the attitudes of neither side will be declared irrelevant. They will have no bearing on the disagreement in attitude, with which both parties are primarily concerned.

In the second place, ethical argument usually terminates when disagreement in attitude terminates, even though a certain amount of disagreement in belief remains. Suppose, for instance, that the company and the union continue to disagree in belief about the increasing cost of living, but that the company, even so, ends by favoring the higher wage scale. The union will then be content to end the argument, and will cease to press its point about living costs. It may bring up that point again, in some future argument of the same sort, or in urging the righteousness of its victory to the newspaper columnists; but for the moment the fact that the company has agreed in attitude is sufficient to terminate the argument. On the other hand: suppose that both parties agreed on all beliefs that were introduced into the argument, but even so continued to disagree in attitude. In that case neither party would feel that their dispute had been successfully terminated. They might look for other beliefs that could be introduced into the argument. They might use words to play on each other's emotions. They might agree (in attitude) to submit the case to arbitration, both feeling that a decision, even if strongly adverse to one party or the other, would be preferable to a continued impasse. Or, perhaps, they might abandon hope of settling their dispute by any peaceable means.

In many other cases, of course, men discuss ethical topics without having the strong, uncompromising attitudes that the present example has illustrated. They are often as much concerned with redirecting their own attitudes, in the light of greater knowledge, as with redirecting the attitudes of others. And the attitudes involved are often altruistic, rather than selfish. Yet the above example will serve, so long as that is understood, to suggest the nature of ethical disagreement. Both disagreement in attitude and disagreement in belief are involved, but the former predominates in that (1) it determines what sort of disagreement in belief is relevantly disputed in a given ethical argument, and (2) it determines, by its continued presence or its resolution, whether or not the argument has

been settled. We may see further how intimately the two sorts of disagreement are related: since attitudes are often functions of beliefs, an agreement in belief may lead people, as a matter of psychological fact, to agree in attitude.

Having discussed disagreement, we may turn to the broad question that was first mentioned, namely: By what methods or argument or inquiry may disagreement about matters of value be resolved?

It will be obvious that to whatever extent an argument involves disagreement in belief, it is open to the usual methods of the sciences. If these methods are the *only* rational methods for supporting beliefs— as I believe to be so, but cannot now take time to discuss—then scientific methods are the only rational methods for resolving the disagreement in *belief* that arguments about values may include.

But if science is granted an undisputed sway in reconciling beliefs, it does not thereby acquire, without qualification, an undisputed sway in reconciling attitudes. We have seen that arguments about values include disagreement in attitude, no less than disagreement in belief, and that in certain ways the disagreement in attitude predominates. By what methods shall the latter sort of disagreement be resolved?

The methods of science are still available for that purpose, but only in an indirect way. Initially, these methods have only to do with establishing agreement in belief. If they serve further to establish agreement in attitude, that will be due simply to the psychological fact that altered beliefs may cause altered attitudes. Hence scientific methods are conclusive in ending arguments about values only to the extent that their success in obtaining agreement in belief will in turn lead to agreement in attitude.

In other words: the extent to which

scientific methods can bring about agreement on values depends on the extent to which a commonly accepted body of scientific beliefs would cause us to have a commonly accepted set of attitudes.

How much is the development of science likely to achieve, then, with regard to values? To what extent *would* common beliefs lead to common attitudes? It is, perhaps, a pardonable enthusiasm to *hope* that science will do everything—to hope that in some rosy future, when all men know the consequences of their acts, they will all have common aspirations, and live peaceably in complete moral accord. But if we speak not from our enthusiastic hopes, but from our present knowledge, the answer must be far less exciting. We usually *do not know,* at the beginning of any argument about values, whether an agreement in belief, scientifically established, will lead to an agreement in attitude or not. It is logically possible, at least, that two men should continue to disagree in attitude even though they had all their beliefs in common, and even though neither had made any logical or inductive error, or omitted any relevant evidence. Differences in temperament, or in early training, or in social status, might make the men retain different attitudes even though both were possessed of the complete scientific truth. Whether this logical possibility is an empirical likelihood I shall not presume to say; but it is unquestionably a possibility that must not be left out of account.

To say that science can always settle arguments about value, we have seen, is to make this assumption: Agreement in attitude will always be consequent upon complete agreement in belief, and science can always bring about the latter. Taken as purely heuristic, this assumption has its usefulness. It leads people to discover the discrepancies in their beliefs, and to prolong enlightening argument that *may* lead, as a matter of fact, from commonly accepted beliefs to commonly accepted attitudes. It leads people to reconcile their attitudes in a rational, permanent way, rather than by rhapsody or exhortation. But the assumption is *nothing more,* for present knowledge, than a heuristic maxim. It is wholly without any proper foundation of probability. I conclude, therefore, that scientific methods cannot be guaranteed the definite role in the so-called "normative sciences" that they may have in the natural sciences. Apart from a heuristic assumption to the contrary, it is possible that the growth of scientific knowledge may leave many disputes about values permanently unsolved. Should these disputes persist, there are non-rational methods for dealing with them, of course, such as impassioned, moving oratory. But the purely intellectual methods of science, and, indeed, *all* methods of reasoning, may be insufficient to settle disputes about values, even though they may greatly help to do so.

For the same reasons, I conclude that normative ethics is not a branch of any science. It deliberately deals with a type of disagreement that science deliberately avoids. Ethics is not psychology, for instance; for although psychologists may, of course, agree or disagree in belief about attitudes, they need not, as psychologists, be concerned with whether they agree or disagree with one another *in* attitude. Insofar as normative ethics draws from the sciences, in order to change attitudes *via* changing people's beliefs, it *draws* from *all* the sciences; but a moralist's peculiar aim —that of *redirecting* attitudes—is a type of activity, rather than knowledge, and falls within no science. Science may study that activity, and may help indirectly to forward it; but it is not *identical* with that activity.

I have only a moment to explain why the ethical terms, such as "good," "wrong," "ought," and so on, are so habitually used to deal with disagreement in attitude. On account of their repeated occurrence in emotional situations they have acquired a strong emotive meaning. This emotive meaning makes them serviceable in initiating changes in a hearer's attitudes. Sheer emotive impact is not likely, under many circumstances, to change attitudes in any permanent way; but it *begins* a process that can then be supported by other means.

There is no occasion for saying that the meaning of ethical terms is *purely* emotive, like that of "alas" or "hurrah." We have seen that ethical *arguments* include many expressions of *belief;* and the rough rules of ordinary language permit us to say that some of these beliefs are expressed by an ethical judgment itself. But the beliefs so expressed are by no means always the same. Ethical terms are notable for their ambiguity, and opponents in an argument may use them in different senses. Sometimes this leads to artificial issues; but it usually does not. So long as one person says "This is good" with emotive praise, and another says "No, it is bad," with emotive condemnation, a disagreement in attitude is manifest. Whether or not the beliefs that these statements express are logically incompatible may not be discovered until later in the argument; but even if they are

actually compatible, disagreement in attitude will be preserved by emotive meaning; and this disagreement, so central to ethics, may lead to an argument that is certainly not artificial in its issues, so long as it is taken for what it is.

The many theorists who have refused to identify ethical statements with scientific ones have much to be said in their favor. They have seen that ethical judgments mold or alter attitudes, rather than describe them, and they have seen that ethical judgments can be guaranteed no definitive scientific support. But one need not, on that account, provide ethics with any extramundane, sui generis *subject matter.* The distinguishing features of an ethical judgment can be preserved by a recognition of emotive meaning and disagreement in attitude, rather than by some non-natural quality—and with far greater intelligibility. If an unique subject matter is *postulated,* as it usually is, to preserve the important distinction between normative ethics, and science, it serves no purpose that is not served by the very simple analysis I have here suggested. Unless non-natural qualities can be defended by positive arguments, rather than as an "only resort" from the acknowledged weakness of ordinary forms of naturalism, they would seem nothing more than the invisible shadows cast by emotive meaning.

COMMENT

The Background and Character of Stevenson's Theory

The foregoing essay is so clear that an analytical summary is unnecessary. It will be helpful, however, to relate the essay to logical empiricism, which is one of the most vigorous movements in contemporary philosophy.

One of the main tenets of this movement, as we pointed out in Chapter 6, is the employment of verifiability as the criterion of meaning. Like Charles Peirce, the logical empiricists have maintained that a factual statement is clear if, and only if, it is verifiable or disverifiable. If we cannot possibly conceive how a statement can be confirmed or disconfirmed by experiment or observation, then the statement is factually meaningless. In the case of some statements—for example, a statement of conjecture as to what is on the other side of the moon—it may be impossible to verify the statements either directly or indirectly, but they are still verifiable *in principle*. We can imagine space travel which would permit observation of the other side of the moon, and hence a statement that there are mountains on that side is, in principle, verifiable. In addition, *logical* propositions (the propositions of pure mathematics and formal logic) have meaning because they, too, are testable. In this case, however, the testing consists in finding out whether they are consistent or contradictory within themselves or with their premises. "Two plus two equals four" is consistent and therefore logically "true"; "two plus two equals five" is contradictory and therefore logically "false."

If a proposition is neither logically nor empirically testable, it is said to have no real meaning and to be neither true nor false. Alfred J. Ayer maintains, for example, that the statement, "There is a supernatural God," cannot be tested by any conceivable observation and consequently is nonsensical. The atheist's assertion that there is no such God is said to be equally nonsensical, since it is only a significant proposition that can be significantly contradicted.[1]

On the basis of this general theory of meaning, the logical empiricists have advanced a doctrine of ethical scepticism. The argument, in its bald form, runs as follows. Ethical statements cannot be verified in any sort of non-subjective experience. Therefore they are meaningless. They affirm nothing; they make no assertions; it is impossible to advance good reasons either for or against them; they can be neither true nor false. All they do is evince subjective attitudes, such as desire or sentiment. They do not even state any facts about feelings; they merely express feelings, as when one says "Ouch!"

The interpretation of ethics advanced by Stevenson is somewhat more subtle and complex. Like other logical empiricists, he approaches philosophy from the point of view of the analysis of language. When we examine sentences, we find that some of them, such as the propositions of pure mathematics, are logical; some of them, such as the propositions of natural science, are descriptive; and some of them, such as the propositions that express our inner feelings, are "emotive." The only sentences that can be properly called true or false are the purely logical (*true* in the sense of being consistent, *false* in the sense of being contradictory) or the empirical (*true* in the sense of being verifiable, *false* in the sense of being disverifiable). Emotive

[1] *Cf.* Ayer's *Language, Truth, and Logic*, second edition (New York: Dover, 1946), p. 115.

utterances do not present testable assertions and hence are not true or false. Nevertheless, they play a very important role in human life and are worthy of careful consideration.

Many ethical sentences, Stevenson believes, contain verifiable or disverifiable references to matters of fact, and to this extent they are true or false. What is really distinctive about them, however, is that they involve norms and ideals ("the ought") which have not been actualized and so cannot be described; and these normative factors, in some irreducible degree, involve nonrational emotions and dispositions rather than rational beliefs. To this extent they cannot be called true or false. This ultimate nonrationality, Stevenson argues, is the Achilles' heel that dooms all descriptive theories of ethics.

It follows that disagreements in ethics, if they exist, may involve either conflicts in beliefs or conflicts in emotional attitudes. The former can be resolved insofar as the beliefs can be verified or disverified. The latter cannot be thus resolved unless the differences in attitude depend upon differences in belief. If we could be sure that all disagreements in attitude are rooted in disagreements in belief, we could hope to resolve our ethical differences. But of this we cannot be sure; indeed, the contrary often seems to be the case.

Is the Theory Satisfactory?

The question as to whether this theory is philosophically sound can best be left to the users of this book to consider. Perhaps a few remarks, however, will clarify the issue.

There is no doubt that Stevenson is correct about many matters. He has correctly indicated that moral utterances are frequently "emotive." When we make ethical statements, we are often simply expressing favorable attitudes or trying to create such attitudes in others through the use of emotionally persuasive language. Stevenson has made a further important contribution in perspicaciously exploring the causal relationship between factual beliefs and value-attitudes. Much of what he has to say about the nature of ethical disagreements rings true.

To a person who believes that there are objective moral judgments, however, his theory will appear unsatisfactory. Let us consider again the "ought-is" problem posed in our comment on Cicero in Chapter 13. The question is: How are normative judgments related to factual descriptions? Can we derive norms from descriptions? What kind of substantial validation may ethical norms and judgments receive?

Stevenson's answer is that "ethical judgments" are in part statements about matters of fact and in part expressions of emotional attitudes. The former can be validated, at least in principle, and the latter cannot. But believers in the objectivity of ethical judgments would reject this answer as quite unsatisfactory. Neither the statements of fact nor the expressions of attitude, they would say, are properly speaking ethical judgments at all, and it does not help to combine them. For the factual statements remain factual statements and therefore not ethical (being concerned with the "is" rather than the "ought"), and the expressions of attitude remain expressions of attitude and therefore not objective, as a real *judgment* must be. Since an emotive expression merely expresses an emotional disposition or appeals emotionally to certain dispositions in the party being addressed, it leaves us without any objective moral standard. Stevenson's interpretation amounts to saying that no *moral* conviction is really any better or truer than any other. Can we really believe that our profoundest moral convictions are thus baseless? Do we not *know*, as a result of ethical insight, that love is better than murder? Do we not know that it is wrong to torture human beings for torture's sake? If we have no such insights, what real basis have we for living a decent life? So the critics of Stevenson's theory might argue.

The real question, then, is whether or not there is an objective basis for ethical judgments, and, if there is, whether Stevenson's theory adequately accounts for this objectivity.

It should be noted that all the ethical theories that we have considered in previous chapters—the theories of Aristotle, Cicero, Kant, Mill, and Dewey—seek to provide an objective basis for ethics. Hence they all stand in contrast with the ethical theory of logical empiricism, as do many other types of theory which we have not had the space to review. An example is the sort of "intuitionism" represented by G. E. Moore, who believes that we "intuit" the goodness of certain objects (love, knowledge, virtue, happiness, and beauty) and by Sir David Ross, who believes that we "intuit" the rightness of certain acts (promise-keeping, truth-telling, etc.).[2] To say that someone knows something intuitively is to say that he knows it otherwise than by reasoning or generalizing from experience—that he knows it by direct and immediate insight.

Logical empiricists, such as Stevenson, reply that they have no such intuitions, and that even the intuitionists do not agree among themselves. They maintain that the so-called ethical intuitions are not really self-evident, and that they are not supported by a sufficient "consensus of experts" to warrant our confidence that they are genuine. Many philosophers, unlike the logical empiricists, believe that *some* intuitions are sound. This difference in point of view has far-reaching implications which, regrettably, we do not have space to explore.

[2] *Cf.* Moore's *Principia Ethica*, 1903, and *Ethics*, 1912, and Ross's *The Right and the Good*, 1930, and *Foundations of Ethics*, 1939.

Toward a Suggested Answer

By way of conclusion, we might try to suggest an answer, or at least an approach to an answer, to the ought-is question. What we ought to do, it would seem, is to help people and not hurt them. We help them when we increase their enjoyments and decrease their sufferings. Enjoyments and sufferings, or tendencies to increase or diminish them, are thus the natural grounds for moral judgments. These grounds are subject to empirical observation, and an ethically responsible person is not disdainful of knowledge thus gleaned. He does not wildly cruise in the seas of possibility with no regard for the shores of fact. A poet may enjoy such reckless adventure but a sober moralist charts his course with a view to reaching port.

Good, bad, right, and *wrong,* however, involve *oughtness.* Enjoyment is good in the sense that it ought to exist; suffering is bad in the sense that it ought not to exist. An act is right if it ought to be done; wrong if it ought not to be done. The specifically ethical factor in good and right comes in with the "ought" and only with it. To treat right and good as natural properties, disregarding this ethical factor, is a fallacy. Sound moral judgments involve an "ought," but they are sustained by ascertainable facts and thus have an objective basis. The further analysis of the meaning of "ought" would lead us into very difficult ethical theory, but perhaps we have already said enough to suggest the tenor of a reasonable answer to the ought-is problem.

We have now reached the end of Part Four, and we shall turn to social philosophy in Part Five. We have not, however, finished with ethics, since the social ideals that we shall examine involve ethical questions.

PART FIVE

Social Ideals

INTRODUCTORY NOTE

SOCIAL PHILOSOPHY IS not a sharply distinct and separate field. The fundamental issues that divide social philosophers are ultimately metaphysical, epistemological, or ethical. Among the questions debated are the following: What is the basis of political obligation? What is the nature of a good social order? What is right social action? Is the state an organism? Are the actions of government to be justified by reference to the ends of the individual or of society? Does history have a pattern that can be known and predicted? All these questions involve metaphysical, epistemological, or ethical issues.

An example may help to make clear the nature of social philosophy. In his *Discourse on Political Economy*, Rousseau declares:

> The body politic . . . is also a moral being possessed of a will; and this general will, which tends always to the preservation and welfare of the whole and of every part, and is the source of the laws, constitutes for all the members of the State, in their relations to one another and to it, the rule of what is just or unjust.[1]

This sentence is replete with philosophical notions: that the body politic is a moral being; that it possesses a "general will" distinct from the individual wills of its members; that the general will is a *good* will; and that it defines, through the medium of law, what is just and what is unjust in the relations of citizens to one another and to the state. Philosophers, and not social scientists, are best fitted to clarify and criticize such ideas.

The philosophers represented in the following four chapters—Plato, Hobbes, Mill, Marx, and Whitehead—discuss questions of great interest to all students of human affairs. Other important social philosophers, such as Aristotle, Locke, Rousseau, and Hegel, are omitted for lack of space. Each of the philosophers chosen represents a social ideal—in the case of Plato,

[1] *The Social Contract* (Everyman's Edition, Dutton, 1913), p. 253.

wisdom; of Hobbes, security; of Mill, liberty; of Marx, fraternity (a "class-less" communism); of Whitehead, art as socially valuable.

It may be helpful to indicate in advance some of the issues that will arise in studying these thinkers:

1. Plato maintains that values are absolute, not relative; that genuine knowledge—especially the knowledge of absolute values—is restricted to the few; that these few, when thoroughly educated, should rule the state; that the choice goods are to be preferred to the common goods; and that the fore-most of all virtues, in the state or in the individual, is wisdom.

2. Hobbes contends that values are relative, not absolute; that men, being naturally egoistic, tend to prey upon one another; that consequently the pre-civil condition of mankind is intolerable anarchy; that the state is brought into existence to eliminate this anarchy and to attain peace and security; and that it is rational for citizens to obey their sovereign so long as he protects them.

3. Mill believes that the ultimate good is the happiness and self-realization of individuals; that actions are right to the extent that they promote indi-vidual welfare; that virtually all opinions are liable to error; that it is wrong to suppress dissident opinions; and that the progress of society depends upon the cultivation of a rich variety among individuals.

4. Marx argues that it is possible to know and to predict accurately the course of history; that the most fundamental factor in determining the his-tory of any society is economic development; that human rights and values are relative to the stages of historical evolution; that conflict, especially class struggle, is the basic mode of revolutionary change; that mankind, after passing through various stages of class society—slavery, feudalism, capital-ism—will finally attain a free, just, and classless social order; and that it is right and rational to assist the historical process by whatever means—even violent and dictatorial—that may be found necessary.

5. Whitehead believes that modern civilization has become tragically lop-sided. We are suffering because the understanding of human relations and the cultivation of values have not kept pace with the rapid tempo of scientific and technological advancement. One requisite for correcting this unbalance is greater emphasis upon art and esthetic education.

To some extent these theories involve questions of fact that social scientists are best prepared to answer, but to a great extent they involve questions of ethics, epistemology, or metaphysics that philosophers are best qualified to discuss. Such questions are too momentous, however, to be left to experts, whether philosophers or social scientists. All of us should ponder them.

The readings for this Part are confined to selections from the original philosophers except in the case of Marx. In this instance, we have included an excerpt from Carr's *The Soviet Impact on the Western World,* which presents the challenge of Marxian and Soviet ideology in a form that has the most meaning for present-day Americans. It may be that the readers of this book will wish to study in addition the *Communist Manifesto,* which is obtainable in many editions. Although it is one of the outstanding political documents of all time, it is omitted here because it is so readily available and because it is not so much a philosophical essay as a passionate call to revolutionary action.

18

Aristocracy

PLATO (428/7–348/7 B.C.)

As a member of one of the most distinguished families in Athens, Plato was in touch with political and social developments from his early childhood. He grew to manhood during the long, turbulent period of the Peloponnesian War, and his mind must have been deeply disturbed by war and revolution. Athens was finally defeated by Sparta when Plato was twenty-three, and he watched the ensuing oligarchical dictatorship, of which his uncle Charmides and his cousin Critias were leaders, with hope which soon turned to horror. His anger was most deeply aroused when his old friend Socrates was eventually tried and executed by the restored democratic faction. The shock of this event, which occurred when he was just twenty-eight, was the decisive influence upon his entire career. He concluded that good government depends upon the rare union of power and wisdom, and resolved to emulate and so far as possible complete the work of Socrates. Retiring from Athens to Megara, he began to write his famous dialogues, which lovingly portray his old master.

He is said to have spent the next ten years traveling in Greece, Italy, Egypt, and Asia Minor. For a time he lived at the court of Dionysius I, the tyrant of Syracuse, whose son-in-law, Dion, became Plato's friend and ardent admirer. At the age of forty he returned to Athens to found the Academy, a school for philosophers, mathematicians, and statesmen. This school was the main center of his interest for the remainder of his long life. In addition to teaching, he continued to write dialogues, which became more technical as he grew older. This quiet, academic life was interrupted in 367 B.C., when he was close on sixty. Dion, his old friend, persuaded him to return to Syracuse as tutor to Dionysius II, a young man of thirty, who had succeeded to the throne. The venture turned out badly. Dionysius and Dion eventually quarreled and Plato went back to Athens. Not easily daunted, he returned to Syracuse six years later in the hope of remedying the situation—and once again met with broken promises and barely escaped with his life. Then he settled down in the Academy to spend the last years of his life teaching and writing. He died at the age of eighty or eighty-one and, according to Cicero, was hard at work at the very end. Generally considered the greatest of the Greek philosophers, he has exercised an immense influence on the thought and literature of the world ever since his death.

From *The Republic**

Scene: The home of Cephalus, a retired manufacturer living at Piraeus, the harbor town about five miles from Athens.

Characters (in the following sections of the dialogue): Glaucon, Adeimantus, and Socrates, who narrates the entire conversation to an unspecified audience.

THE VIRTUES IN THE STATE

[*Plato's original aim in constructing an ideal state was to find in it justice exemplified on a larger scale than in the individual. Assuming that four cardinal qualities make up the whole of virtue, he now asks wherein consist the wisdom, courage, temperance, and justice of the state, or, in other words, of the individuals composing the state in their public capacity as citizens.*

Wisdom in the conduct of state affairs will be the practical prudence or good counsel of the deliberative body. Only the philosophic Rulers will possess the necessary insight into what is good for the community as a whole. They will have "right belief" grounded on immediate knowledge of the meaning of goodness in all its forms. The

Auxiliaries will have only a right belief accepted on the authority of the Rulers. Their functions will be executive, not deliberative.

The Courage of the state will obviously be manifested in the fighting force. Socrates had defined courage as knowledge of what really is, or is not, to be feared, and he had regarded it as an inseparable part of all virtue, which consists in knowing what things are really good or evil. If the only real evil is moral evil, then poverty, suffering, and all the so-called evils that others can inflict on us, including death itself, are not to be feared, since, if they are met in the right spirit, they cannot make us worse men. This knowledge only the philosophic Rulers will possess to the full. The courage of the Auxiliaries will consist in the power of holding fast to the conviction implanted by their education.

Temperance is not, as we might expect, the peculiar virtue of the lowest order in the state. As self-mastery, it means the subordination of the lower elements to the higher; but government must be with the willing consent of the governed, and temperance will include the unanimous agree-

* Translated with Introduction and Notes by Francis MacDonald Cornford, Oxford University Press, London, 1941; New York, 1945. Reprinted by permission. Some of Cornford's footnotes have here been omitted.

ment of all classes as to who should rule and who obey.[1] *It is consequently like a harmony pervading and uniting all parts of the whole, a principle of solidarity. In the* Laws, *which stresses the harmonious union of different and complementary elements, this virtue overshadows even Justice.*

Justice is the complementary principle of differentiation, keeping the parts distinct. It has been before us all through the construction of the state since it first appeared on the economic level as the division of labor based on natural aptitudes. "Doing one's own work" now has the larger sense of a concentration on one's peculiar duty or function in the community. This conception of "doing and possessing what properly belongs to one" is wide enough to cover the justice of the law-courts, assuring to each man his due rights. Injustice will mean invasion and encroachment upon the rights and duties of others.

The virtue described in this chapter is what Plato calls "civic" or "popular" virtue. Except in the Rulers, it is not directly based on that ultimate knowledge of good and evil which is wisdom, to be attained only at the end of the higher education of the philosopher.]

So now at last, son of Ariston, said I, your commonwealth is established. The next thing is to bring to bear upon it all the light you can get from any quarter, with the help of your brother and Polemarchus and all the rest, in the hope that we may see where justice is to be found in it and where injustice, how they differ, and which of the two will bring happiness to its possessor, no matter whether gods and men see that he has it or not.

Nonsense, said Glaucon; you promised

to conduct the search yourself, because it would be a sin not to uphold justice by every means in your power.

That is true; I must do as you say, but you must all help.

We will.

I suspect, then, we may find what we are looking for in this way. I take it that our state, having been founded and built up on the right lines, is good in the complete sense of the word.

It must be.

Obviously, then, it is wise, brave, temperate, and just.

Obviously.

Then if we find some of these qualities in it, the remainder will be the one we have not found. It is as if we were looking somewhere for one of any four things: if we detected that one immediately, we should be satisfied; whereas if we recognized the other three first, that would be enough to indicate the thing we wanted; it could only be the remaining one. So here we have four qualities. Had we not better follow that method in looking for the one we want?

Surely.

To begin then: the first quality to come into view in our state seems to be its wisdom; and there appears to be something odd about this quality.[2]

What is there odd about it?

I think the state we have described really has wisdom; for it will be prudent in counsel, won't it?

Yes.

And prudence in counsel is clearly a form of knowledge; good counsel cannot be due to ignorance and stupidity.

Clearly.

But there are many and various kinds of knowledge in our commonwealth. There is

[1] At *Statesman* 276 E the true king is distinguished from the despot by the voluntary submission of his subjects to his rule.

[2] Because the wisdom of the whole resides in the smallest part, as explained below.

the knowledge possessed by the carpenters or the smiths, and the knowledge how to raise crops. Are we to call the state wise and prudent on the strength of these forms of skill?

No; they would only make it good at furniture-making or working in copper or agriculture.

Well then, is there any form of knowledge, possessed by some among the citizens of our new-founded commonwealth, which will enable it to take thought, not for some particular interest, but for the best possible conduct of the state as a whole in its internal and external relations?

Yes, there is.

What is it, and where does it reside?

It is precisely that art of guardianship which resides in those Rulers whom we just now called Guardians in the full sense.

And what would you call the state on the strength of that knowledge?

Prudent and truly wise.

And do you think there will be more or fewer of these genuine Guardians in our state than there will be smiths?

Far fewer.

Fewer, in fact, than any of those other groups who are called after the kind of skill they possess?

Much fewer.

So, if a state is constituted on natural principles, the wisdom it possesses as a whole will be due to the knowledge residing in the smallest part, the one which takes the lead and governs the rest. Such knowledge is the only kind that deserves the name of wisdom, and it appears to be ordained by nature that the class privileged to possess it should be the smallest of all.

Quite true.

Here then we have more or less made out one of our four qualities and its seat in the structure of the commonwealth.

To my satisfaction, at any rate.

Next there is courage. It is not hard to discern that quality or the part of the community in which it resides so as to entitle the whole to be called brave.

Why do you say so?

Because anyone who speaks of a state as either brave or cowardly can only be thinking of that part of it which takes the field and fights in its defence; the reason being, I imagine, that the character of the state is not determined by the bravery or cowardice of the other parts.

No.

Courage, then, is another quality which a community owes to a certain part of itself. And its being brave will mean that, in this part, it possesses the power of preserving, in all circumstances, a conviction about the sort of things that it is right to be afraid of—the conviction implanted by the education which the law-giver has established. Is not that what you mean by courage?

I do not quite understand. Will you say it again?

I am saying that courage means preserving something.

Yes, but what?

The conviction, inculcated by lawfully established education, about the sort of things which may rightly be feared. When I added "in all circumstances," I meant preserving it always and never abandoning it, whether under the influence of pain or of pleasure, of desire or of fear. If you like, I will give an illustration.

Please do.

You know how dyers who want wool to take a purple dye, first select the white wool from among all the other colors, next treat it very carefully to make it take the dye in its full brilliance, and only then dip it in the vat. Dyed in that way, wool gets a fast color, which no washing, even with soap, will rob of its brilliance; whereas if they choose wool of any color but white, or if they neglect to prepare it, you know what happens.

Yes, it looks washed-out and ridiculous.

That illustrates the result we were doing our best to achieve when we were choosing our fighting men and training their minds and bodies. Our only purpose was to contrive influences whereby they might take the color of our institutions like a dye, so that, in virtue of having both the right temperament and the right education, their convictions about what ought to be feared and on all other subjects might be indelibly fixed, never to be washed out by pleasure and pain, desire and fear, solvents more terribly effective than all the soap and fuller's earth in the world. Such a power of constantly preserving, in accordance with our institutions, the right conviction about the things which ought, or ought not, to be feared, is what I call courage. That is my position, unless you have some objection to make.

None at all, he replied; if the belief were such as might be found in a slave or an animal—correct, but not produced by education—you would hardly describe it as in accordance with our institutions, and you would give it some other name than courage.

Quite true.

Then I accept your account of courage.

You will do well to accept it, at any rate as applying to the courage of the ordinary citizen; [3] if you like we will go into it more fully some other time. At present we are in search of justice, rather than of courage; and for that purpose we have said enough.

I quite agree.

Two qualities, I went on, still remain to be made out in our state, temperance and

[3] As distinct from the perfect courage of the philosophic Ruler, based on immediate knowledge of values.

the object of our whole inquiry, justice. Can we discover justice without troubling ourselves further about temperance?

I do not know, and I would rather not have justice come to light first, if that means that we should not go on to consider temperance. So if you want to please me, take temperance first.

Of course I have every wish to please you.

Do go on then.

I will. At first sight, temperance seems more like some sort of concord or harmony than the other qualities did.

How so?

Temperance surely means a kind of orderliness, a control of certain pleasures and appetites. People use the expression, "master of oneself," whatever that means, and various other phrases that point the same way.

Quite true.

Is not "master of oneself" an absurd expression? A man who was master of himself would presumably be also subject to himself, and the subject would be master; for all these terms apply to the same person.

No doubt.

I think, however, the phrase means that within the man himself, in his soul, there is a better part and a worse; and that he is his own master when the part which is better by nature has the worse under its control. It is certainly a term of praise; whereas it is considered a disgrace, when, through bad breeding or bad company, the better part is overwhelmed by the worse, like a small force outnumbered by a multitude. A man in that condition is called a slave to himself and intemperate.

Probably that is what is meant.

Then now look at our newly founded state and you will find one of these two conditions realized there. You will agree that it deserves to be called master of itself, if temperance and self-mastery exist where the better part rules the worse.

Yes, I can see that is true.

It is also true that the great mass of multifarious appetites and pleasures and pains will be found to occur chiefly in children and women and slaves, and, among free men so called, in the inferior multitude; whereas the simple and moderate desires which, with the aid of reason and right belief, are guided by reflection, you will find only in a few, and those with the best inborn dispositions and the best educated.

Yes, certainly.

Do you see that this state of things will exist in your commonwealth, where the desires of the inferior multitude will be controlled by the desires and wisdom of the superior few? Hence, if any society can be called master of itself and in control of pleasures and desires, it will be ours.

Quite so.

On all these grounds, then, we may describe it as temperate. Furthermore, in our state, if anywhere, the governors and the governed will share the same conviction on the question who ought to rule.[4] Don't you think so?

I am quite sure of it.

Then, if that is their state of mind, in which of the two classes of citizens will temperance reside—in the governors or in the governed?

In both, I suppose.

So we were not wrong in divining a resemblance between temperance and some kind of harmony. Temperance is not like courage and wisdom, which made the state wise and brave by residing each in one particular part. Temperance works in a differ-

ent way; it extends throughout the whole gamut of the state, producing a consonance of all its elements from the weakest to the strongest as measured by any standard you like to take—wisdom, bodily strength, numbers, or wealth. So we are entirely justified in identifying with temperance this unanimity or harmonious agreement between the naturally superior and inferior elements on the question which of the two should govern, whether in the state or in the individual.

I fully agree.

Good, said I. We have discovered in our commonwealth three out of our four qualities, to the best of our present judgment. What is the remaining one, required to make up its full complement of goodness? For clearly this will be justice.

Clearly.

Now is the moment, then, Glaucon, for us to keep the closest watch, like huntsmen standing round a covert, to make sure that justice does not slip through and vanish undetected. It must certainly be somewhere hereabouts; so keep your eyes open for a view of the quarry, and if you see it first, give me the alert.

I wish I could, he answered; but you will do better to give me a lead and not count on me for more than eyes to see what you show me.

Pray for luck, then, and follow me.

I will, if you will lead on.

The thicket looks rather impenetrable, said I; too dark for it to be easy to start up the game. However, we must push on.

Of course we must.

Here I gave the view halloo. Glaucon, I exclaimed, I believe we are on the track and the quarry is not going to escape us altogether.

That is good news.

Really, I said, we have been extremely

---

[4] This principle of freedom—government with consent of the governed—is thus recognized. The "democratic" freedom to "do whatever you like" is condemned in later chapters.

stupid. All this time the thing has been under our very noses from the start, and we never saw it. We have been as absurd as a person who hunts for something he has all the time got in his hand. Instead of looking at the thing, we have been staring into the distance. No doubt that is why it escaped us.

What do you mean?

I believe we have been talking about the thing all this while without ever understanding that we were giving some sort of account of it.

Do come to the point. I am all ears.

Listen, then, and judge whether I am right. You remember how, when we first began to establish our commonwealth and several times since, we have laid down, as a universal principle, that everyone ought to perform the one function in the community for which his nature best suited him. Well, I believe that that principle, or some form of it, is justice.

We certainly laid that down.

Yes, and surely we have often heard people say that justice means minding one's own business and not meddling with other men's concerns; and we have often said so ourselves.

We have.

Well, my friend, it may be that this minding of one's own business, when it takes a certain form, is actually the same thing as justice. Do you know what makes me think so?

No, tell me.

I think that this quality which makes it possible for the three we have already considered, wisdom, courage, and temperance, to take their place in the commonwealth, and so long as it remains present secures their continuance, must be the remaining one. And we said that, when three of the four were found, the one left over would be justice.

It must be so.

Well now, if we had to decide which of these qualities will contribute most to the excellence of our commonwealth, it would be hard to say whether it was the unanimity of rulers and subjects, or the soldier's fidelity to the established conviction about what is, or is not, to be feared, or the watchful intelligence of the Rulers; or whether its excellence were not above all due to the observance by everyone, child or woman, slave or freeman or artisan, ruler or ruled, of this principle that each one should do his own proper work without interfering with others.

It would be hard to decide, no doubt.

It seems, then, that this principle can at any rate claim to rival wisdom, temperance, and courage as conducing to the excellence of a state. And would you not say that the only possible competitor of these qualities must be justice?

Yes, undoubtedly.

Here is another thing which points to the same conclusion. The judging of law-suits is a duty that you will lay upon your Rulers, isn't it?

Of course.

And the chief aim of their decisions will be that neither party shall have what belongs to another or be deprived of what is his own.

Yes.

Because that is just?

Yes.

So here again justice admittedly means that a man should possess and concern himself with what properly belongs to him.[5]

True.

Again, do you agree with me that no great harm would be done to the community by a general interchange of most forms of work, the carpenter and the cob-

[5] Here the legal conception of justice is connected with its moral significance.

bler exchanging their positions and their tools and taking on each other's jobs, or even the same man undertaking both?

Yes, there would not be much harm in that.

But I think you will also agree that another kind of interchange would be disastrous. Suppose, for instance, someone whom nature designed to be an artisan or tradesman should be emboldened by some advantage, such as wealth or command of votes or bodily strength, to try to enter the order of fighting men; or some member of that order should aspire, beyond his merits, to a seat in the council-chamber of the Guardians. Such interference and exchange of social positions and tools, or the attempt to combine all these forms of work in the same person, would be fatal to the commonwealth.

Most certainly.

Where there are three orders, then, any plurality of functions or shifting from one order to another is not merely utterly harmful to the community, but one might fairly call it the extreme of wrongdoing. And you will agree that to do the greatest of wrongs to one's own community is injustice.

Surely.

This, then, is injustice. And, conversely, let us repeat that when each order—tradesman, Auxiliary, Guardian—keeps to its own proper business in the commonwealth and does its own work, that is justice and what makes a just society.

I entirely agree.

THE THREE PARTS OF THE SOUL

[*It has been shown that justice in the state means that the three chief social functions—deliberative and governing, executive, and productive—are kept distinct and rightly performed. Since the qualities of a community are those of the component in-*

dividuals, we may expect to find three corresponding elements in the individual soul. All three will be present in every soul; but the structure of society is based on the fact that they are developed to different degrees in different types of character.

The existence of three elements or "parts" of the soul is established by an analysis of the conflict of motives. A simple case is the thirsty man's appetite for drink, held in check by the rational reflection that to drink will be bad for him. That two distinct elements must be at work here follows from the general principle that the same thing cannot act or be affected in two opposite ways at the same time. By "thirst" is meant simply the bare craving for drink; it must not be confused with a desire for some good (e.g., health or pleasure) expected as a consequence of drinking. This simple craving says, "Drink"; Reason says, "Do not drink": the contradiction shows that two elements are at work.

A third factor is the "spirited" element, akin to our "sense of honor," manifested in indignation, which takes the side of reason against appetite, but cannot be identified with reason, since it is found in children and animals and it may be rebuked by reason.

This analysis is not intended as a complete outline of psychology; that could be reached only by following "a longer road." It is concerned with the factors involved in moral behavior. . . .]

THE VIRTUES IN THE INDIVIDUAL

[*The virtues in the state were the qualities of the citizen, as such, considered as playing the special part in society for which he was qualified by the predominance in his nature of the philosophic, the pugnacious, or the commercial spirit. But all three ele-*

ments exist in every individual, who is thus a replica of society in miniature. In the perfect man reason will rule, with the spirited element as its auxiliary, over the bodily appetites. Self-control or temperance will be a condition of internal harmony, all the parts being content with their legitimate satisfactions. Justice finally appears, no longer only as a matter of external behavior toward others, but as an internal order of the soul, from which right behavior will necessarily follow. Injustice is the opposite state of internal discord and faction. To ask whether justice or injustice pays the better is now seen to be as absurd as to ask whether health is preferable to disease.]

And so, after a stormy passage, we have reached the land. We are fairly agreed that the same three elements exist alike in the state and in the individual soul.

That is so.

Does it not follow at once that state and individual will be wise or brave by virtue of the same element in each and in the same way? Both will possess in the same manner any quality that makes for excellence.

That must be true.

Then it applies to justice: we shall conclude that a man is just in the same way that a state was just. And we have surely not forgotten that justice in the state meant that each of the three orders in it was doing its own proper work. So we may henceforth bear in mind that each one of us likewise will be a just person, fulfilling his proper function, only if the several parts of our nature fulfill theirs.

Certainly.

And it will be the business of reason to rule with wisdom and forethought on behalf of the entire soul; while the spirited element ought to act as its subordinate and ally. The two will be brought into accord, as we said earlier, by that combination of mental and bodily training which will tune up one string of the instrument and relax the other, nourishing the reasoning part on the study of noble literature and allaying the other's wildness by harmony and rhythm. When both have been thus nurtured and trained to know their own true functions, they must be set in command over the appetites, which form the greater part of each man's soul and are by nature insatiably covetous. They must keep watch lest this part, by battening on the pleasures that are called bodily, should grow so great and powerful that it will no longer keep to its own work, but will try to enslave the others and usurp a dominion to which it has no right, thus turning the whole of life upside down. At the same time, those two together will be the best of guardians for the entire soul and for the body against all enemies from without: the one will take counsel, while the other will do battle, following its ruler's commands and by its own bravery giving effect to the ruler's designs.

Yes, that is all true.

And so we call an individual brave in virtue of this spirited part of his nature, when, in spite of pain or pleasure, it holds fast to the injunctions of reason about what he ought or ought not to be afraid of.

True.

And wise in virtue of that small part which rules and issues these injunctions, possessing as it does the knowledge of what is good for each of the three elements and for all of them in common.

Certainly.

And, again, temperate by reason of the unanimity and concord of all three, when there is no internal conflict between the ruling element and its two subjects, but all are agreed that reason should be ruler.

Yes, that is an exact account of temperance, whether in the state or in the individual.

Finally, a man will be just by observing the principle we have so often stated.

Necessarily.

Now is there any indistinctness in our vision of justice, that might make it seem somehow different from what we found it to be in the state?

I don't think so.

Because, if we have any lingering doubt, we might make sure by comparing it with some commonplace notions. Suppose, for instance, that a sum of money were entrusted to our state or to an individual of corresponding character and training, would anyone imagine that such a person would be specially likely to embezzle it?

No.

And would he not be incapable of sacrilege and theft, or of treachery to friend or country; never false to an oath or any other compact; the last to be guilty of adultery or of neglecting parents or the due service of the gods?

Yes.

And the reason for all this is that each part of his nature is exercising its proper function, of ruling or of being ruled.

Yes, exactly.

Are you satisfied, then, that justice is the power which produces states or individuals of whom that is true, or must we look further?

There is no need; I am quite satisfied.

And so our dream has come true—I mean the inkling we had that, by some happy chance, we had lighted upon a rudimentary form of justice from the very moment when we set about founding our commonwealth. Our principle that the born shoemaker or carpenter had better stick to his trade turns out to have been an adumbration of justice; and that is why it has helped us. But in reality justice, though

evidently analogous to this principle, is not a matter of external behavior, but of the inward self and of attending to all that is, in the fullest sense, a man's proper concern. The just man does not allow the several elements in his soul to usurp one another's functions; he is indeed one who sets his house in order, by self-mastery and discipline coming to be at peace with himself, and bringing into tune those three parts, like the terms in the proportion of a musical scale, the highest and lowest notes and the mean between them, with all the intermediate intervals. Only when he has linked these parts together in well-tempered harmony and has made himself one man instead of many, will he be ready to go about whatever he may have to do, whether it be making money and satisfying bodily wants, or business transactions, or the affairs of state. In all these fields when he speaks of just and honorable conduct, he will mean the behavior that helps to produce and to preserve this habit of mind; and by wisdom he will mean the knowledge which presides over such conduct. Any action which tends to break down this habit will be for him unjust; and the notions governing it he will call ignorance and folly.

That is perfectly true, Socrates.

Good, said I. I believe we should not be thought altogether mistaken, if we claimed to have discovered the just man and the just state, and wherein their justice consists.

Indeed we should not.

Shall we make that claim, then?

Yes, we will.

So be it, said I. Next, I suppose, we have to consider injustice.

Evidently.

This must surely be a sort of civil strife among the three elements, whereby they usurp and encroach upon one another's functions and some one part of the soul rises up in rebellion against the whole, claiming a supremacy to which it has no right because its nature fits it only to be the servant of the ruling principle. Such turmoil and aberration we shall, I think, identify with injustice, intemperance, cowardice, ignorance, and in a word with all wickedness.

Exactly.

And now that we know the nature of justice and injustice, we can be equally clear about what is meant by acting justly and again by unjust action and wrongdoing.

How do you mean?

Plainly, they are exactly analogous to those wholesome and unwholesome activities which respectively produce a healthy or unhealthy condition in the body; in the same way just and unjust conduct produce a just or unjust character. Justice is produced in the soul, like health in the body, by establishing the elements concerned in their natural relations of control and subordination, whereas injustice is like disease and means that this natural order is inverted.

Quite so.

It appears, then, that virtue is as it were the health and comeliness and well-being of the soul, as wickedness is disease, deformity, and weakness.

True.

And also that virtue and wickedness are brought about by one's way of life, honorable or disgraceful.

That follows.

So now it only remains to consider which is the more profitable course: to do right and live honorably and be just, whether or not anyone knows what manner of man you are, or to do wrong and be unjust, provided that you can escape the chastisement which might make you a better man.

But really, Socrates, it seems to me ridiculous to ask that question now that the nature of justice and injustice has been brought to light. People think that all the luxury and wealth and power in the world cannot make life worth living when the bodily constitution is going to rack and ruin; and are we to believe that, when the very principle whereby we live is deranged and corrupted, life will be worth living so long as a man can do as he will, and wills to do anything rather than to free himself from vice and wrong-doing and to win justice and virtue?

Yes, I replied, it is a ridiculous question. . . .

THE PARADOX: PHILOSOPHERS MUST BE KINGS

[Challenged to show that the ideal state can exist, Socrates first claims that an ideal is none the worse for not being realizable on earth. The assertion that theory comes closer than practice to truth or reality is characteristically Platonic. The ideal state or man is the true state or man; for if men, who are in fact always imperfect, could reach perfection, they would only be realizing all that their nature aims at being and might conceivably be. Further, the realm of ideals is the real world, unchanging and eternal, which can be known by thought. The visible and tangible things commonly called real are only a realm of fleeting appearance, where the ideal is imperfectly manifested in various degrees of approximation. . . .

An ideal has an indispensable value for practice, in that thought thereby gives to action its right aim. So, instead of proving that the ideal state or man can exist here, it is enough to discover the least change, within the bounds of possibility, that would bring the actual state nearest to the ideal. This change would be the union, in the

same persons, of political power and the
love of wisdom, so as to close the gulf,
which had been growing wider since the age
of Pericles, between the men of thought
and the men of action. The corresponding
change in the individual is the supremacy
of the reason, the divine element in man,
over the rest of our nature.]

But really, Socrates, Glaucon continued, if
you are allowed to go on like this, I am
afraid you will forget all about the question
you thrust aside some time ago: whether a
society so constituted can ever come into
existence, and if so, how. No doubt, if it
did exist, all manner of good things would
come about. I can even add some that you
have passed over. Men who acknowledged
one another as fathers, sons, or brothers
and always used those names among themselves would never desert one another; so
they would fight with unequalled bravery.
And if their womenfolk went out with them
to war, either in the ranks or drawn up in
the rear to intimidate the enemy and act
as a reserve in case of need, I am sure all
this would make them invincible. At home,
too, I can see many advantages you have
not mentioned. But, since I admit that our
commonwealth would have all these merits
and any number more, if once it came into
existence, you need not describe it in further detail. All we have now to do is to
convince ourselves that it can be brought
into being and how.

This is a very sudden onslaught, said I;
you have no mercy on my shilly-shallying.
Perhaps you do not realize that, after I
have barely escaped the first two waves,[6]
the third, which you are now bringing
down upon me, is the most formidable of
all. When you have seen what it is like and

heard my reply, you will be ready to excuse
the very natural fears which made me
shrink from putting forward such a paradox for discussion.

The more you talk like that, he said, the
less we shall be willing to let you off from
telling us how this constitution can come
into existence; so you had better waste
no more time.

Well, said I, let me begin by reminding
you that what brought us to this point was
our inquiry into the nature of justice and
injustice.

True; but what of that?

Merely this: suppose we do find out
what justice is,[7] are we going to demand
that a man who is just shall have a character which exactly corresponds in every
respect to the ideal of justice? Or shall we
be satisfied if he comes as near to the ideal
as possible and has in him a larger measure
of that quality than the rest of the world?

That will satisfy me.

If so, when we set out to discover the essential nature of justice and injustice and
what a perfectly just and a perfectly unjust
man would be like, supposing them to exist,
our purpose was to use them as ideal patterns: we were to observe the degree of
happiness or unhappiness that each exhibited, and to draw the necessary inference that our own destiny would be like
that of the one we most resembled. We did
not set out to show that these ideals could
exist in fact.

That is true.

Then suppose a painter had drawn an
ideally beautiful figure complete to the last
touch, would you think any the worse of
him, if he could not show that a person as
beautiful as that could exist?

No, I should not.

---

[6] The equality of women and the abolition of the
family. [These concepts have been spoken of as
waves, and the wave metaphor is now continued.]

[7] Justice, as a "civic" virtue, has been defined
. . . ; but the wise man's virtue, based on knowledge, has still to be described.

Well, we have been constructing in discourse the pattern of an ideal state. Is our theory any the worse, if we cannot prove it possible that a state so organized should be actually founded?

Surely not.

That, then, is the truth of the matter. But if, for your satisfaction, I am to do my best to show under what conditions our ideal would have the best chance of being realized, I must ask you once more to admit that the same principle applies here. Can theory ever be fully realized in practice? Is it not in the nature of things that action should come less close to truth than thought? People may not think so; but do you agree or not?

I do.

Then you must not insist upon my showing that this construction we have traced in thought could be reproduced in fact down to the last detail. You must admit that we shall have found a way to meet your demand for realization, if we can discover how a state might be constituted in the closest accordance with our description. Will not that content you? It would be enough for me.

And for me too.

Then our next attempt, it seems, must be to point out what defect in the working of existing states prevents them from being so organized, and what is the least change that would effect a transformation into this type of government—a single change if possible, or perhaps two; at any rate let us make the changes as few and insignificant as may be.

By all means.

Well, there is one change which, as I believe we can show, would bring about this revolution—not a small change, certainly, nor an easy one, but possible.

What is it?

I have now to confront what we called the third and greatest wave. But I must state my paradox, even though the wave should break in laughter over my head and drown me in ignominy. Now mark what I am going to say.

Go on.

Unless either philosophers become kings in their countries or those who are now called kings and rulers come to be sufficiently inspired with a genuine desire for wisdom; unless, that is to say, political power and philosophy meet together, while the many natures who now go their several ways in the one or the other direction are forcibly debarred from doing so, there can be no rest from troubles, my dear Glaucon, for states, nor yet, as I believe, for all mankind; nor can this commonwealth which we have imagined ever till then see the light of day and grow to its full stature. This it was that I have so long hung back from saying; I knew what a paradox it would be, because it is hard to see that there is no other way of happiness either for the state or for the individual. . . .

COMMENT

Relative and Absolute Morality

The *Republic* is formed of many diverse strands. Plato interweaves ethics, art, religion, politics, education, and philosophy to form a rich and variegated pattern. Seizing upon different facets of his social philosophy, critics have denounced him as an arch-totalitarian or praised him as an inspired liberal.

Actually, he is neither—although his vision of the ideal city includes both liberal and totalitarian elements.

In the section of the *Republic* preceding our selections, Plato set forth some of the essential premises of his thought. He begins by a refutation of the Sophist theory that moral principles are purely relative; on the contrary, he maintains, they have a rational and absolute basis. Thrasymachus, a Sophist, is introduced as a rather cynical advocate of the theory that "just or right means nothing but what is to the interest of the stronger party." This doctrine is similar to Karl Marx's declaration, in the *Communist Manifesto,* that "the ruling ideas of every age are the ideas of the ruling class." But Marx looked forward to an all-human morality based upon the eventual achievement of a classless society, whereas Thrasymachus champions the doctrine that right means nothing but the interest of the dominant political force. Through the character of Socrates, Plato advances a number of objections to this theory. He argues that any statesman deserving of the name cares above all for the good of his subjects. The thirst for power results in uncontrolled competition; the wise ruler puts a limit to his personal ambitions. Unbridled power produces strife; true justice promotes harmony and concord. The human soul has its characteristic function, which is not the lust for power or sensual gratification but the subordination of impulse to rational principles of conduct. Plato thus maintains that there are objective principles of morality and justice.

When Thrasymachus, worsted in the argument, sullenly withdraws, Glaucon and Adeimantus—Plato's elder brothers—step into the discussion. They ask Socrates to criticize a theory which they find both plausible and disturbing—that people prefer a just to an unjust life for reasons of mere expediency. A person, they are inclined to think, would be quite ready to commit injustice if he could escape the penalties. Glaucon cites the legend of a certain Gyges who possessed a magic ring which made him invisible at will and who was thus able to commit crime without fear of detection. If we had such power, Glaucon asks, would we continue to behave virtuously? Would we not use our immunity from punishment to gain unfair personal and social advantages? Individual and political morality, it would seem, is a kind of compromise brought about by the necessities of social life and dictated by self-interest. Socrates, as the principal speaker in the dialogue, vehemently rejects this doctrine, as he had earlier rejected the theory of Thrasymachus. He maintains that there is a real objective distinction between right and wrong acts and between good and bad ends, and that it is possible for philosophers to discern this distinction. Here is one of the main premises of Plato's social theory.

Virtues in the State and in the Individual

Socrates, in the dialogue, sees no way of immediately refuting the theory described by Glaucon and Adeimantus and suggests that an answer can best be found if the argument is projected from the level of the individual to that of the community. He proposes to study the origin and nature of the state, in the hope of thereby discovering the nature of justice and other virtues.

No man is self-sufficient; if he is to live and prosper he must cooperate with his fellows. Basic economic needs, such as those for food, shelter, and clothing, can best be supplied if the members of a community minister to one another's wants through a division of labor. Thus appear tailors, shoemakers, carpenters, smiths, shepherds, and other specialized workers. After the basic necessities are supplied, the demand for luxuries becomes insistent, and new occupations, catering to this demand, spring into being. Thus expanding, the state will enter into keen commercial and imperialistic rivalry with other states, and this will likely involve it in war. Hence there will be need of a standing army. Finally, there must be some body to formulate the laws and direct the government's policies. There will thus be three classes of citizens, namely (1) the producers—farmers, artisans, traders, and professional workers—who supply the material wealth of the community and constitute the bulk of the population; (2) the army and police ("Auxiliaries"), who safeguard the society against enemies from within and without; and (3) the governing class ("Guardians"), who are responsible for the tasks of statesmanship.

Having sketched the origin and composition of the state, Socrates goes on to consider its ideal structure. Each class exhibits its proper and characteristic virtue: the Guardians, wisdom; the Auxiliaries, courage; the workers, temperance (which is also present in the other two classes). The fourth virtue, justice, is the result of the right allocation and performance of functions throughout the entire state. Socrates similarly analyzes the three main parts of the human personality—reason, spirit, and appetite—and the virtues of wisdom, courage, temperance, and justice within the individual soul. Since this analysis, with Cornford's commentary, is reproduced in the foregoing excerpts, there is no need to enlarge upon it here.

Plato is leading up to the supreme principle of his social philosophy—that government by the best—the wise—is the solution for social ills. The welfare and righteousness of the state can be ensured only if it is governed rationally. Consequently, the Auxiliaries and producers, who fall short of genuine wisdom, must be excluded from the government, and the Guardians must be intensively trained to become true philosopher-kings.

The Means of Achieving the Ideal

If the Guardians are to be wise, they must be very carefully bred, selected, reared, and educated. The biological fitness of the ruling class should be guaranteed by a comprehensive program of eugenics; the most select parents should be induced to have the greatest number of children. Even more important is education, which Plato regards as the main foundation of the state.

He conceives education as a journey of the mind from the concrete practicalities of sensory experience to the eternal and abstract realities of the intellect. It begins with the arts and gymnastics and mounts upward through mathematics, astronomy, and harmonics (the mathematical theory of musical form) to philosophy. The preliminary education continues until about the age of eighteen; then follows two years of military training, for males and females alike. The Guardians are then provisionally selected by "ordeals of toil and pain," and only those who manifest the proper character and intelligence will receive the highest training. The program of mathematical and scientific training will occupy the prospective Guardians from the age of twenty to thirty, and they will then have intensive training in philosophy ("dialectics") for five additional years, or until they have "grasped by pure intelligence the very nature of Goodness itself." The students who have distinguished themselves throughout this long and arduous training will serve a political apprenticeship for about fifteen years, discharging the subordinate functions "suitable to the young." Finally, those who have fully proved their mettle, both men and women, will be selected at the age of fifty to fulfill the high function of philosopher-kings. Others, fit to be soldiers but incapable of the highest intellectual flights, remain Auxiliaries; and the great mass of the people, as members of the producing class, receive the lesser education appropriate to their station.

Every precaution should be taken to ward off temptations and keep the Guardians and Auxiliaries faithful to the state. The chief temptations arise from private interests. The competitive struggle for property, Plato believes, is incompatible with full devotion to the social good. Hence he proposes that the Guardians and Auxiliaries should have no private possessions or acquisitive occupations and that they should receive their maintenance from the state. This proposal is not the same as modern communism, since it applies only to the Auxiliaries and Guardians and not to the producers who constitute the bulk of the population.

Plato also believes that normal marriage and family life are incompatible with a wholehearted devotion to the state, since there is always a temptation to prefer family interests to community welfare. Hence he proposes to abolish private homes and monogamous marriage among the Guardians and Auxiliaries. They should live and share their meals together, realizing the principle that "friends have all things in common." Sexual intercourse should be strictly controlled in the interests of the eugenics program.

Such is the pattern of the aristocratic state. But even the "best" of states may decay, and Plato imaginatively sketches, in a section here omitted, the decline of the state through successive stages of timocracy—the rule of the military class; oligarchy—the rule of the wealthy; democracy the rule of the many; and tyranny—the rule of the irresponsible dictator. Finally, he discusses art and rewards and punishments after death, but these topics do not now concern us.

Some Main Issues

No one will agree with all the details of Plato's argument, but even when we least agree we can find his ideas challenging. Among the principal issues that he presents are the following:

1. *Force* versus *morality*. In Books I and II of the *Republic,* Plato raises one of the basic issues in political philosophy—the question as to whether force or morality is the foundation of the state. Against Thrasymachus, Socrates (as a character in the dialogue) argues that the authority of the ruler is morally based on right rather than might. In reply to Glaucon and Adeimantus, he maintains that social obligation is based on duty rather than selfish expediency. The policies of the state, he insists, should conform to the pattern of the Good, which wise men, long disciplined by education, can alone discern. He distinguishes between *opinion* and *knowledge* about goodness, and maintains that genuine knowledge requires an intellectual grasp of *"forms."* The form is the universal essence that is somehow exemplified in particular instances. All beautiful things, for example, exemplify the form of beauty, and all just acts and institutions exemplify the form of justice.

According to Plato, these forms or universals are real, but they exist in their full and essential reality apart from particular things. The perfection, unity, and eternality of the forms separates them from the imperfection, multiplicity, and impermanence of particular things. The sensible nature of the thing declares itself as relative and contingent and points to the imperishable essence which is connected with it and yet independent of it—a form free from limitation, change, defilement. The nature of this super-reality is hard to define—Plato appears to have struggled with the problem throughout his whole philosophical career. In the *Phaedo,* the particulars are said to "participate" in the forms, or the forms are said to be "present" in the particulars. Elsewhere in Plato's dialogues the individual things are said to "imitate" the forms, or to be related as an imperfect "copy" to a pattern or archetype. But all such language is metaphorical, and the essential truth is that the universal somehow transcends the particulars. In the *Republic,* this is taken to mean that the pattern of the ideal state is eternal and hence exempt from the relativities of power politics and shifting expediency.

Whether Plato's theory—or any doctrine of eternal and objective universals—is sound has been one of the principal questions of philosophy from his day until the present. It is possible to agree with him that universals are real, and yet to differ from him in holding that they are immanent in particulars rather than separate and transcendent. "Justice" really exists, but in particular instances—not in "a heaven above the heavens" or as a separate, eternal essence. The "form," in this sense, is simply the characteristic common to all members of the class of things (in this case, the class of just things). The human mind has the power to notice resemblances and to abstract (*i.e.,* mentally to extricate) the common characteristics. Thus, universals can be said to consist, on the one hand, of *common properties* in things, and on the other hand, of *concepts* which represent these properties. This theory of real but immanent universals is the doctrine of Aristotle, and it serves as well as Plato's theory as an alternative to moral relativism. What is required is that moral concepts must conform to real objective distinctions, and on this point Plato and Aristotle agree.

2. *The "closed" versus the "open" society.* With his vision fixed upon eternal forms, Plato wishes, after a fundamental revolution in human affairs, to arrest history and preserve the ideal state in its static perfection. As means to this end, he proposes rigorous censorship of the arts and religion, the use of myths and "noble lies" to reconcile the lower classes to their subordinate status, and the regulation of all details of social life, including marriage and the ownership of property, among the Guardians and Auxiliaries. In effect, he insists upon a tight, "closed" unity of the body politic.

This emphasis upon a static unity is related to his organic theory of the state. Plato maintains that the state is the human soul "writ large," just as the soul is the state "writ small." There is some question as to how literally we should understand this doctrine, but it seems to imply that the state, like the individual personality, is an organism—*i.e.,* a living being with a life and worth of its own. Individuals appear mainly to derive their character and value from their relation to this organic whole. This sort of ethical organicism receives its most express and elaborate expression in the social philosophy of Hegel, but it is foreshadowed in the *Republic.*

The contrasting ideal of an "open" society—in which the freedom and intrinsic value of the individual are primarily emphasized—was eloquently formulated by John Stuart Mill in *On Liberty* (see Chap. 20). Both Mill and Plato, in a sense, maintain an ethics of self-realization, but Plato contends that the private interest of the individual is at one with the interest of the state, whereas Mill is distrustful of the state and believes that self-realization lies in the cultivation of individuality.

We can roughly divide political philosophers into two schools of thought corresponding to their positions on this issue. In one "camp" are the organic theorists—Plato, Rousseau, Hegel, and Marx—who stress the importance of the general will and the value and significance of collective processes. In the other group are the individualistic theorists—Hume, Bentham, Mill, and Jefferson—who disbelieve in the organic nature of society and regard social institutions as means to the happiness of individuals. The dispute between these two schools of thought is perhaps the most important conflict in the whole of political philosophy.

3. *Aristocracy* versus *democracy*. The basic tenet of Plato's social philosophy, as we have seen, is that philosopher-kings should rule. This conviction is consistent with his general attitude toward life: he habitually prefers the choice goods to the common goods. Hence he ranks democracy, whose slogan is "equality," as fourth in his classification of five types of government, superior only to tyranny and inferior to aristocracy, timocracy, and oligarchy. The typical democrat seems to him an ill-educated and superficial fellow who wishes to drag all excellent things down to the mediocre level of the average.

The democrat might reply that philosopher-kings are difficult to find or to produce and that a government *of* the few is almost certain to be a government *for* the few. No one can be trusted with irresponsible power, not even the so-called wise. It is the wearer of the shoe who knows where it pinches, and consequently he cannot allow the few aristocrats to choose his shoes for him. If the state exacts duties of its citizens, moreover, it should grant them rights—for responsibility implies freedom. It is only by living as free men—by participating in government and exercising self-rule—that we cease to be mere imitators and become fully developed human beings. With such arguments, the democrat might answer Plato.

If we democrats and liberals are sensible, however, we will not indiscriminately reject the whole of Plato's social philosophy. We need experts in our government and wisdom in our lives. We should adapt to our own ends Plato's great ideal of a state based upon education, and we should seek to reconcile the aristocratic ideal of excellence with the democratic ideal of sharing. Our goal should be a culture both high in attainment and broad in terms of democratic participation.

19

Peace and Security

THOMAS HOBBES (1588–1679)

Hobbes was the son of a poor and ignorant country parson who could scarcely read the church prayers. A precocious lad, he attracted the attention of his schoolmaster by translating the Greek text of Euripedes' *Medea* into Latin verse. At fifteen he entered Oxford, the cost of his education being paid by his uncle, a prosperous tradesman. He found the University instruction still dominated by medieval logic and Aristotelian philosophy, and most of the students "debauched to drunkenness, wantonness, gaming, and other vices." After taking his degree, he became tutor and then secretary to William Cavendish, later the second Earl of Devonshire. This connection with the influential Cavendish family was to last, with some interruptions, for the remainder of his life. It opened the door to cultivated society, and Hobbes became acquainted with Bacon, Harvey, and other distinguished men. His secretarial duties were light, and he found ample leisure for scholarly pursuits, which included a translation of Thucydides, published in 1628. He also accompanied his master on trips to the Continent, where he met Galileo in Florence and Mersenne, Gassendi, and other French philosophers in Paris.

In 1637 he returned to England, resolved to write philosophy and study politics. At the ripe age of fifty-two he published his first original book, a volume entitled *The Elements of Law Natural and Politic.* Meanwhile the civil wars were brewing, and Hobbes, finding his ideas sharply attacked, took alarm and fled to France. He spent the next eleven years in Paris, while insurrection and civil war raged in England. During this period he engaged in controversy with Descartes, wrote a second political treatise, *De Cive,* and served briefly as tutor to the Prince of Wales, later Charles II. In 1651, he published his greatest work, *Leviathan,* a plea for materialism and political absolutism. This book offended the Republicans for its defense of absolutism, the Royalists for its scorn of the divine right of kings, and the clergy for its championship of the state over the church. Finding himself unpopular among the exiles in Paris, Hobbes returned to England and submitted to Cromwell.

Hobbes now devoted himself to philosophy, expounding his materialistic metaphysics in *De Corpore* (1655). He also engaged in furious controversy with his critics, not always creditably. In 1660 the Stuarts were restored, with Hobbes' former student and friend, now Charles II, on the throne. Despite his friendship with the king, however, his public reputation was that of an atheist and blasphemer, and the House of Commons considered the advisability of ordering a public burning of his books. Since he could not obtain leave in England to publish works on controversial subjects, his *Behemoth: the History of the Causes of the Civil Wars of England* (1688) had to be published abroad. By this time he was old in years but indefatigable in spirit, singing by night and playing tennis by day, as intellectually keen as he was physically vigorous. At eighty-four he wrote an autobiography in Latin verse, and in the next few years translated the whole of Homer's *Iliad* and *Odyssey*. He died in his boots at the age of ninety-one, struck by apoplexy.

From *Leviathan*

CHAPTER XIII

OF THE NATURAL CONDITION OF MANKIND AS CONCERNING THEIR FELICITY, AND MISERY

Nature hath made men so equal, in the faculties of the body and mind; as that, though there be found one man sometimes manifestly stronger in body or of quicker mind than another, yet when all is reckoned together, the difference between man and man is not so considerable, as that one man can thereupon claim to himself any benefit, to which another may not pretend as well as he. For as to the strength of body, the weakest has strength enough to kill the strongest, either by secret machination, or by confederacy with others that are in the same danger with himself.

And as to the faculties of the mind—setting aside the arts grounded upon words, and especially that skill of proceeding upon general and infallible rules, called science; which very few have, and but in few things; as being not a native faculty, born with us; nor attained, as prudence, while we look after somewhat else—I find yet a greater equality amongst men, than that of strength. For prudence is but experience, which equal time equally bestows on all men, in those things they equally apply themselves unto. That which may perhaps make such equality incredible, is but a vain conceit of one's own wisdom, which almost all men think they have in a greater degree than the vulgar; that is, than all men but themselves, and a few others, whom by fame, or for concurring with themselves, they approve. For such is the nature of men, that howsoever they may acknowledge many others to be more witty, or more eloquent, or more learned, yet they will hardly believe there be many so wise as themselves; for they see their own wit at hand, and other men's at a distance. But this proveth rather that men are in that point equal, than unequal. For there is not ordinarily a greater sign of the equal distribution of anything, than that every man is contented with his share.

From this equality of ability, ariseth equality of hope in the attaining of our ends. And therefore if any two men desire the same thing, which nevertheless they cannot both enjoy, they become enemies; and in the way to their end, which is principally their own conservation, and sometimes their delectation only, endeavor to destroy, or subdue one another. And from hence it comes to pass that where an invader hath no more to fear than another man's single power; if one plant, sow, build, or possess a convenient seat, others may probably be expected to come prepared with forces united, to dispossess and deprive him, not only of the fruit of his labor, but also of his life or liberty. And the invader again is in the like danger of another.

And from this diffidence of one another, there is no way for any man to secure himself so reasonable as anticipation; that is, by force or wiles to master the persons of all men he can, so long, till he see no other power great enough to endanger him: and this is no more than his own conservation requireth, and is generally allowed. Also because there be some, that taking pleasure in contemplating their own power in the acts of conquest, which they pursue farther than their security requires; if others, that otherwise would be glad to be at ease within modest bounds, should not by invasion increase their power, they would not be able long time, by standing only on their defence, to subsist. And by consequence, such augmentation of domin-

ion over men being necessary to a man's conservation, it ought to be allowed him.

Again, men have no pleasure, but on the contrary a great deal of grief, in keeping company, where there is no power able to overawe them all. For every man looketh that his companion should value him at the same rate he sets upon himself; and upon all signs of contempt, or undervaluing, naturally endeavors, as far as he dares (which amongst them that have no common power to keep them in quiet, is far enough to make them destroy each other), to extort a greater value from his contemners by damage, and from others by the example.

So that in the nature of man, we find three principal causes of quarrel. First, competition; second, diffidence; thirdly, glory.

The first maketh men invade for gain; the second, for safety; and the third, for reputation. The first use violence to make themselves masters of other men's persons, wives, children, and cattle; the second, to defend them; the third, for trifles, as a word, a smile, a different opinion, and any other sign of undervalue, either direct in their persons, or by reflection in their kindred, their friends, their nation, their profession, or their name.

Hereby it is manifest that during the time men live without a common power to keep them all in awe, they are in that condition which is called war; and such a war as is of every man against every man. For *war* consisteth not in battle only, or the act of fighting, but in a tract of time wherein the will to contend by battle is sufficiently known, and therefore the notion of *time* is to be considered in the nature of war, as it is in the nature of weather. For as the nature of foul weather lieth not in a shower or two of rain, but in an inclination thereto of many days together; so the nature of war consisteth not in actual fighting, but in the known disposition thereto, during all the time there is no assurance to the contrary. All other time is *peace*.

Whatsoever therefore is consequent to a time of war, where every man is enemy to every man; the same is consequent to the time, wherein men live without other security than what their own strength and their own invention shall furnish them withal. In such condition there is no place for industry, because the fruit thereof is uncertain: and consequently no culture of the earth; no navigation, nor use of the commodities that may be imported by sea; no commodious building; no instruments of moving, and removing, such things as require much force; no knowledge of the face of the earth; no account of time; no arts; no letters; no society; and which is worst of all, continual fear, and danger of violent death; and the life of man, solitary, poor, nasty, brutish, and short.

It may seem strange to some man that has not well weighed these things, that nature should thus dissociate, and render men apt to invade and destroy one another; and he may therefore, not trusting to this inference, made from the passions, desire perhaps to have the same confirmed by experience. Let him therefore consider with himself, when taking a journey, he arms himself and seeks to go well accompanied; when going to sleep, he locks his doors; when even in his house he locks his chests; and this when he knows there be laws, and public officers, armed, to revenge all injuries shall be done him: what opinion he has of his fellow-subjects, when he rides armed; of his fellow citizens, when he locks his doors; and of his children, and servants, when he locks his chests. Does he not there as much accuse mankind by his actions, as I do by my words? But neither

of us accuse man's nature in it. The desires, and other passions of man, are in themselves no sin. No more are the actions that proceed from those passions, till they know a law that forbids them: which till laws be made they cannot know; nor can any law be made, till they have agreed upon the person that shall make it.

It may preadventure be thought, there was never such a time nor condition of war as this; and I believe it was never generally so, over all the world: but there are many places where they live so now. For the savage people in many places of America, except the government of small families, the concord whereof dependeth on natural lust, have no government at all; and live at this day in that brutish manner, as I said before. Howsoever, it may be perceived what manner of life there would be, where there were no common power to fear; by the manner of life which men that have formerly lived under a peaceful government, use to degenerate into in a civil war.

But though there had never been any time wherein particular men were in a condition of war one against another; yet in all times, kings, and persons of sovereign authority, because of their independency, are in continual jealousies, and in the state and posture of gladiators; having their weapons pointing, and their eyes fixed on one another; that is, their forts, garrisons, and guns upon the frontiers of their kingdoms; and continual spies upon their neighbors; which is a posture of war. But because they uphold thereby the industry of their subjects, there does not follow from it that misery which accompanies the liberty of particular men.

To this war of every man against every man, this also is consequent: *that nothing can be unjust*. The notions of right and wrong, justice and injustice, have there no place. Where there is no common power, there is no law; where no law, no injustice. Force and fraud are in war the two cardinal virtues. Justice and injustice are none of the faculties neither of the body nor mind. If they were, they might be in a man that were alone in the world, as well as his senses and passions. They are qualities that relate to men in society, not in solitude. It is consequent also to the same condition, that there be no propriety, no dominion, no *mine* and *thine* distinct; but only that to be every man's, that he can get; and for so long as he can keep it. And thus much for the ill condition which man by mere nature is actually placed in; though with a possibility to come out of it, consisting partly in the passions, partly in his reason.

The passions that incline men to peace are fear of death, desire of such things as are necessary to commodious living, and a hope by their industry to obtain them. And reason suggesteth convenient articles of peace, upon which men may be drawn to agreement. These articles are they which otherwise are called the Laws of Nature; whereof I shall speak more particularly in the two following chapters.

CHAPTER XIV

OF THE FIRST AND SECOND NATURAL LAWS, AND OF CONTRACTS

The right of nature, which writers commonly call *jus naturale,* is the liberty each man hath to use his own power, as he will himself, for the preservation of his own nature; that is to say, of his own life; and consequently, of doing anything, which in his own judgment and reason, he shall conceive to be the aptest means thereunto.

By *liberty,* is understood, according to the proper signification of the word, the absence of external impediments: which

impediments, may oft take away part of a man's power to do what he would; but cannot hinder him from using the power left him, according as his judgment, and reason shall dictate to him.

A *law of nature, lex naturalis,* is a precept or general rule, found out by reason, by which a man is forbidden to do that which is destructive of his life, or taketh away the means of preserving the same; and to omit that by which he thinketh it may be best preserved. For though they that speak of this subject, use to confound *jus* and *lex, right* and *law;* yet they ought to be distinguished: because *right* consisteth in liberty to do or to forbear, whereas *law* determineth and bindeth to one of them; so that law, and right differ as much as obligation and liberty; which in one and the same matter are inconsistent.

And because the condition of man, as hath been declared in the precedent chapter, is a condition of war of everyone against everyone; in which case everyone is governed by his own reason, and there is nothing he can make use of that may not be a help unto him in preserving his life against his enemies: it followeth, that in such a condition every man has a right to everything; even to one another's body. And therefore, as long as this natural right of every man to everything endureth, there can be no security to any man, how strong or wise soever he be, of living out the time which nature ordinarily alloweth men to live. And consequently it is a precept, or general rule of reason, *that every man ought to endeavor peace, as far as he has hope of obtaining it; and when he cannot obtain it, that he may seek and use all helps and advantages of war.* The first branch of which rule containeth the first and fundamental law of nature; which is, *to seek peace and follow it.* The second, the sum of the right of nature; which is, *by all means we can, to defend ourselves.*

From this fundamental law of nature, by which men are commanded to endeavor peace, is derived this second law: *that a man be willing, when others are so too, as far forth as for peace and defence of himself he shall think it necessary, to lay down this right to all things; and be contented with so much liberty against other men, as he would allow other men against himself.* For as long as every man holdeth this right, of doing anything he liketh, so long are all men in the condition of war. But if other men will not lay down their right, as well as he, then there is no reason for anyone to divest himself of his: for that were to expose himself to prey, which no man is bound to, rather than to dispose himself to peace. . . .

Whensoever a man transferreth his right, or renounceth it; it is either in consideration of some right reciprocally transferred to himself, or for some other good he hopeth for thereby. For it is a voluntary act; and of the voluntary acts of every man, the object is some *good to himself.* And therefore there be some rights which no man can be understood by any words, or other signs, to have abandoned or transferred. As first a man cannot lay down the right of resisting them that assault him by force, to take away his life; because he cannot be understood to aim thereby, at any good to himself. The same may be said of wounds, and chains, and imprisonment: both because there is no benefit consequent to such patience, as there is to the patience of suffering another to be wounded or imprisoned; as also because a man cannot tell, when he seeth men proceed against him by violence, whether they intend his death or not. And lastly the motive, an end for which this renouncing and transferring of right is introduced, is nothing else

but the security of a man's person, in his life, and in the means of so preserving life as not to be weary of it. And therefore if a man by words, or other signs, seem to despoil himself of the end for which those signs were intended, he is not to be understood as if he meant it, or that it was his will, but that he was ignorant of how such words and actions were to be interpreted.

The mutual transferring of right, is that which men call *contract.*

CHAPTER XV
OF OTHER LAWS OF NATURE

From that law of nature by which we are obliged to transfer to another such rights as, being retained, hinder the peace of mankind, there followeth a third; which is this, *that men perform their covenants made:* without which, covenants are in vain, and but empty words; and the right of all men to all things remaining, we are still in the condition of war.

And in this law of nature, consisteth the fountain and original of *justice.* For where no covenant hath preceded, there hath no right been transferred, and every man has right to everything; and consequently, no action can be unjust. But when a covenant is made, then to break it is *unjust;* and the definition of *injustice* is no other than *the not performance of covenant.* And whatsoever is not unjust, is *just.*

But because covenants of mutual trust, where there is a fear of not performance on either part, as hath been said in the former chapter, are invalid; though the original of justice be the making of covenants; yet injustice actually there can be none, till the cause of such fear be taken away; which while men are in the natural condition of war, cannot be done. Therefore before the names of just and unjust can have place, there must be some coercive power, to compel men equally to the performance of their covenants, by the terror of some punishment greater than the benefit they expect by the breach of their covenant; and to make good that propriety which by mutual contract men acquire, in recompense of the universal right they abandon: and such power there is none before the erection of a commonwealth. And this is also to be gathered out of the ordinary definition of justice in the Schools; for they say, that *justice is the constant will of giving to every man his own.* And therefore where there is no *own,* that is no propriety, there is no injustice; and where is no coercive power erected, that is, where there is no commonwealth, there is no propriety; all men having right to all things: therefore where there is no commonwealth, there nothing is unjust. So that the nature of justice consisteth in keeping of valid covenants; but the validity of covenants begins not but with the constitution of a civil power sufficient to compel men to keep them, and then it is also that propriety begins. . . .

CHAPTER XVII

OF THE CAUSES, GENERATION, AND DEFINITION OF A COMMONWEALTH

The final cause, end, or design of men who naturally love liberty and dominion over others, in the introduction of that restraint upon themselves in which we see them live in commonwealths, is the foresight of their own preservation, and of a more contented life thereby; that is to say, of getting themselves out from that miserable condition of war, which is necessarily consequent, as hath been shown in Chapter XIII, to the natural passions of men, when there is no visible power to keep them in awe, and tie them by fear of punishment to the performance of their covenants and observation of those laws of nature set down in the fourteenth and fifteenth chapters.

For the laws of nature, as justice, equity, modesty, mercy, and, in sum, *doing to others as we would be done to,* of themselves, without the terror of some power to cause them to be observed, are contrary to our natural passions, that carry us to partiality, pride, revenge, and the like. And covenants, without the sword, are but words, and of no strength to secure a man at all. Therefore notwithstanding the laws of nature, which everyone hath then kept, when he has the will to keep them when he can do it safely; if there be no power erected, or not great enough for our security, every man will, and may, lawfully rely on his own strength and art, for caution against all other men. And in all places where men have lived by small families, to rob and spoil one another has been a trade, and so far from being reputed against the law of nature, that the greater spoils they gained, the greater was their honor; and men observed no other laws therein but the laws of honor; that is, to abstain from cruelty, leaving to men their lives, and instruments of husbandry. And as small families did then; so now do cities and kingdoms, which are but greater families, for their own security enlarge their dominions, upon all pretences of danger and fear of invasion, or assistance that may be given to invaders, and endeavor as much as they can to subdue or weaken their neighbors, by open force and secret arts, for want of other caution, justly; and are remembered for it in after ages with honor.

Nor is it the joining together of a small number of men, that gives them this security; because in small numbers, small additions on the one side or the other make the advantage of strength so great, as is sufficient to carry the victory, and therefore gives encouragement to an invasion. The multitude sufficient to confide in for our security, is not determined by any certain number, but by comparison with the enemy we fear; and is then sufficient, when the odds of the enemy is not of so visible and conspicuous moment, to determine the event of war, as to move him to attempt.

And be there never so great a multitude, yet if their actions be directed according to their particular judgments and particular appetites, they can expect thereby no defence nor protection, neither against a common enemy nor against the injuries of one another. For being distracted in opinions concerning the best use and application of their strength, they do not help but hinder one another; and reduce their strength by mutual opposition to nothing: whereby they are easily, not only subdued by a very few that agree together; but also when there is no common enemy, they make war upon each other, for their particular interests. For if we could suppose a great multitude of men to consent in the observation of justice, and other laws of nature, without a common power to keep them all in awe, we might as well suppose all mankind to do the same; and then there neither would be, nor need to be any civil government or commonwealth at all, because there would be peace without subjection.

Nor is it enough for the security, which men desire should last all the time of their life, that they be governed and directed by one judgment for a limited time, as in one battle or one war. For though they obtain a victory by their unanimous endeavor against a foreign enemy; yet afterwards, when either they have no common enemy, or he that by one part is held for an enemy, is by another part held for a friend, they must needs by the difference of their interests dissolve, and fall again into a war amongst themselves.

It is true that certain living creatures, as bees and ants, live sociably one with another, which are therefore by Aristotle numbered amongst political creatures; and yet have no other direction than their particular judgments and appetites; nor speech, whereby one of them can signify to another what he thinks expedient for the common benefit: and therefore some man may perhaps desire to know why mankind cannot do the same. To which I answer:

First, that men are continually in competition for honor and dignity, which these creatures are not; and consequently amongst men there ariseth on that ground, envy and hatred, and finally war; but amongst these not so.

Secondly, that amongst these creatures, the common good differeth not from the private; and being by nature inclined to their private, they procure thereby the common benefit. But man, whose joy consisteth in comparing himself with other men, can relish nothing but what is eminent.

Thirdly, that these creatures, having not, as man, the use of reason, do not see, nor think they see, any fault in the administration of their common business; whereas amongst men, there are very many that think themselves wiser, and able to govern the public better, than the rest; and these strive to reform and innovate, one this way, another that way; and thereby bring it into distraction and civil war.

Fourthly, that these creatures, though they have some use of voice in making known to one another their desires and other affections; yet they want that art of words by which some men can represent to others, that which is good in the likeness of evil, and evil in the likeness of good, and augment or diminish the apparent greatness of good and evil; discontenting men and troubling their peace at their pleasure.

Fifthly, irrational creatures cannot distinguish between *injury* and *damage;* and therefore as long as they be at ease, they are not offended with their fellows: whereas man is then most troublesome when he is most at ease; for then it is that he loves to show his wisdom, and control the actions of them that govern the commonwealth.

Lastly, the agreement of these creatures is natural; that of men is by covenant only, which is artificial: and therefore it is no wonder if there be somewhat else required, besides covenant, to make their agreement constant and lasting; which is a common power, to keep them in awe, and to direct their actions to the common benefit.

The only way to erect such a common power, as may be able to defend them from the invasion of foreigners and the injuries of one another, and thereby to secure them in such sort as that, by their own industry, and by the fruits of the earth, they may nourish themselves and live contentedly; is, to confer all their power and strength upon one man, or upon one assembly of men, that may reduce all their wills, by plurality of voices, unto one will: which is as much as to say, to appoint one man, or assembly of men, to bear their person; and everyone to own and acknowledge himself to be author of whatsoever he that so beareth their person, shall act or cause to be acted in those things which concern the common peace and safety; and therein to submit their wills, everyone to his will, and their judgments, to his judgment. This is more than consent, or concord; it is a real unity of them all, in one and the same person, made by covenant of every man with every man, in such manner as if every man should say to every man, *"I authorize and give up my right of governing myself to this man, or to this assembly of men, on this condition, that thou give up thy right to him, and authorize all his actions in like manner."* This done, the multitude so united in one person, is called a *commonwealth,* in Latin *civitas.* This is the generation of that great LEVIATHAN, or rather, to speak more reverently, of that *mortal god,* to which we owe under the *immortal God,* our peace and defence. For by this authority, given him by every particular man in the commonwealth, he hath the use of so much power and strength conferred on him, that by terror thereof he is enabled to perform the wills of them all, to peace at home and mutual aid against their enemies abroad. And in him consisteth the essence of the commonwealth; which, to define it, is *one person, of whose acts a great multitude, by mutual covenants one with another, have made themselves every one the author, to the end he may use the strength and means of them all, as he shall think expedient, for their peace and common defence.*

And he that carrieth this person, is called *sovereign,* and said to have sovereign power; and everyone besides, his *subject. . . .*

COMMENT

The Premises of Hobbes' Argument

Hobbes was born prematurely, as the story goes, because his mother took fright at the near approach of the Spanish Armada. In commenting on the circumstances of his birth, he said, "Fear and I were twins." This remark, made in his old age, expresses his realization that fear had been a dominant motive in his life. His social philosophy is concerned primarily with the need for security.

He lived during the most unstable period of English history. Among the shifts and disturbances which occurred during his lifetime were the First Civil War between King and Parliament (1642–1645), the Second Civil War (1648), the rule of the "Rump Parliament" (1649–1653), Cromwell's dictatorship (1654–1658), and the Restoration of the Stuarts (1660). Hobbes' emphasis on security was a natural reaction to a period so unsettled.

This emphasis rested upon several premises: (1) an interpretation of human nature, (2) an analysis of moral experience, and (3) a conception of the pre-civil condition of man.

1. *An interpretation of human nature.* Hobbes believed that man is a kind of elaborate machine, whose "vital motions" are determined by outward stimuli. If a stimulus is favorable to the machine's operations, it evokes *desire* or motion toward; if unfavorable, it evokes *aversion* or motion away from. More complex motives and emotions are all derived from these elementary reactions of advance or retreat. The emotions springing from desire, such as love and hope, are generally pleasant; the emotions springing from aversion, such as hate and fear, are unpleasant. If the effect is pleasant, the organism seeks to continue or renew the stimulus; if unpleasant, to avoid it. "The object of man's desire is not to enjoy once only, and for one instant of time; but to assure for ever the way of his future desire." [1] There is no lasting repose, no final breathing space, but only ceaseless pursuit of power. Power is defined as the "present means to obtain future, apparent good." Since the means are precarious, there is no limit to the power which men seek. "I put for a general inclination of all mankind," declares Hobbes, "a perpetual and restless desire of power after power, which ceases only in death." [2]

Motivated by egoistic concern for his own power, each person tends to conflict with others. "If any two men desire the same thing, which they nevertheless cannot both enjoy, they become enemies and . . . endeavor to destroy or subdue one another." [3] The result would be a constant and intolerable war of each against all if it were not for the faculty of reason. By means of this faculty, men "acquire the knowledge of consequences, and dependence of one fact upon another." [4] Reason does not select the ends of action—these are determined by desire and aversion—but it reflects upon the consequences of acts and judges how the ends can be most fully achieved. By its

---

[1] *Leviathan*, XI.
[2] *Ibid.*
[3] *Ibid.*, XIII.
[4] *Ibid.*, V.

means, men escape from the suicidal anarchy which their predatory natures would force upon them.

2. *An analysis of moral experience.* At the most primitive and pre-social level of human life, "good" simply means "whatsoever is the object of any man's appetite or desire," and "evil" means "the object of his hate and aversion." [5] Values are derived from human drives, and since the drives are invariably egoistic, good and evil are always relative to the individual.

> These words of good, evil, and contemptible are ever used with relation to the person that useth them: there being nothing simply and absolutely so; nor any common rule of good and evil to be taken from the nature of the objects themselves; but from the person of the man, where there is no commonwealth; or, in a commonwealth, from the person that representeth it; or from an arbitrator or judge, whom men disagreeing shall by consent set up, and make his sentence rule thereof. [6]

This quotation points to two levels of moral experience: the level *before* and the level *after* the creation of the commonwealth. *Before* there is no moral authority except the desires and aversions of the individual, whoever he be. But *after* the creation of the state, the ultimate moral authority is the sovereign or judicial arbitrator. The social concepts of law and justice arise only within the state.

In speaking of a pre-civil level of morality, Hobbes did not mean that he actually *finds* men at this level. He was pointing out the kind of morality men would have if they lacked civil institutions, and he was saying that the second or higher level of morality requires an organized political state.

3. *The pre-civil condition of man.* That "the state of nature" is a nasty condition of anarchy follows from Hobbes' analysis of human nature. Since everyone naturally preys upon his fellows, the consequence is "such a war as is of every man against every man." It is easy to misunderstand Hobbes' meaning. "The state of nature" may never have existed; and whether it did or not does not really affect his argument. This is the state that *would* exist if men were wholly dominated by passions, without the restraint of reason and civil society. It is an analytical, not a historical, concept. Hobbes, in effect, was saying that we must permanently be on guard, because the brutish state of nature would be our lot if we should abandon reason and destroy political sovereignty. It is an emphatic way of saying that the civil state is extremely necessary.

Natural Law and the Social Contract

The state of nature is haunted by "continual fear and danger of violent death," and reason therefore impels human beings to set up the coercive

[5] *Ibid.*, VI.
[6] *Ibid.*

power of a central government, which alone can establish peace and security. The contrast between the condition of man *outside* and *in* a duly constituted state is sharply drawn.

> Out of it, any man may rightly spoil or kill another; in it, none but one. Out of it, we are protected by our own forces; in it, by the power of all. Out of it, no man is sure of the fruit of his labors; in it, all men are. Lastly, out of it, there is a dominion of passions, war, fear, poverty, slovenliness, solitude, barbarism, ignorance, cruelty; in it, the dominion of reason, peace, security, riches, decency, society, elegancy, sciences and benevolence.[7]

What is required to pass from the natural to the civil state is determined by "the laws of nature." These laws are the dictates of reason defining what needs to be done to safeguard life. They are "natural" in the sense that they are based upon the instinct of self-preservation aided by reason. In substance these laws state that peace, cooperation, and the keeping of covenants are essential to survival, but that, if these be lacking, it is rational to defend oneself with the most effective means available.

In conformity to natural law, reason impels men to escape from the lethal anarchy of the state of nature, and to set up, by mutual agreement, the civil state. Every man must agree to live in peace in consideration of the like agreement of others. But human nature being what it is, mere agreement to live peaceably together is insufficient. For this reason, men must form a contract with one another to set up a common power "to keep them in awe, and to direct their actions to the Common Benefit." [8]

The idea of a "social contract" was not original with Hobbes. Its roots are to be found in ancient Greek philosophy, and it had become a commonplace in political theory by the time Hobbes wrote *Leviathan*. His account is distinguished by its sharp insistence that the conferring of absolute power upon a sovereign is the only refuge from chronic war, which would break out again if ever the civil power should crumble. The power of the sovereign *is* absolute, since no limiting conditions were stipulated when he received his power. Indeed, no effective condition could have been stipulated, since covenants are but words without the power of enforcement until the sovereign is established. According to this interpretation, the contract is not between citizen and ruler but between citizen and citizen—every citizen covenanting with every other to form a civil society *and to obey the government*.

The government is not necessarily a monarchy. Hobbes personally thought monarchy the safest and best type of government, but he recognized that the sovereign *might* be an assembly. There is nothing in his theory that presupposes a king or single ruler, provided that the sovereign group is sufficiently united to maintain authority.

---

[7] *De Cive*, ed. by Sterling P. Lamprecht (Appleton-Century-Crofts, 1949), p. 114.
[8] *Op. cit.*, XVII.

It is sometimes said that the power conferred upon the sovereign is irrevocable. This is a misinterpretation of Hobbes' theory. He insisted that the sovereign power must be undisputed so long as it is effective in keeping the peace; but if the government does not in fact govern, if anarchy breaks out afresh, there is no longer reason for submission. The citizens are then thrown back upon their natural resources for self-preservation and may rightly set up a new sovereign who can protect them.

The social contract, like the state of nature, should not be interpreted historically. Only in special circumstances do states originate by deliberate contract. The "social contract" is the *logical* basis of the state, which, so far as men are governed by reason, remains operative as a continuing tacit agreement. The function of this type of theory is to emphasize the activity of reason in devising, and the activity of will in instituting, the political community. Among democratic theorists, such as Locke, it is a way of insisting that legitimate government rests upon the consent of the governed.

Application to International Politics

The clearest example of "the state of nature" is the relation of sovereign states to one another:

> . . . In all times, kings, and persons of sovereign authority, because of their independency, are in continual jealousies, and in the state and posture of gladiators; having their weapons pointing, and their eyes fixed on one another; that is, their forts, garrisons, and guns upon the frontiers of their kingdoms; and continual spies upon their neighbors; which is a posture of war.[9]

Hobbes remarked that this international anarchy does not occasion as much misery as anarchy among individuals.

Living in the seventeenth century, Hobbes could not foresee how powerfully his social philosophy would apply to international affairs in the second half of the twentieth century. We now know that a hydrogen bomb can obliterate a city like Moscow or New York in a trice, and that the fall-out from such a bomb can destroy life over a vastly wider area. Competent authorities have declared that an atomic world war might so poison the earth's atmosphere as to cause universal death. Here is danger on a scale that Hobbes never even dreamed of.

The remedy for anarchy, as he clearly perceived, is the creation of government with power to enforce its decisions. It is not sufficient for nations to promise not to go to war with one another, for "covenants, without the sword, are but words." [10] A binding covenant must be a surrender of sovereignty, whether of individuals or of nations, to some effective central authority.

[9] *Ibid.,* XIII.
[10] *Ibid.,* XVII.

The establishment of the United Nations Organization was a step toward world government. The supreme question is whether this beginning can be transformed into an international authority with power to enforce the peace. The human race has now reached the point at which it must either abandon war and the dogma of unlimited national sovereignty or accept the possibility of universal annihilation. Hobbes' argument that we should obey the dictates of self-preservation applies today with terrific force.

Some Critical Remarks

The main defect of Hobbes' social philosophy is fairly obvious. His insistence upon the necessity of coercive government is excessive because his account of human nature is too grim. Having described human beings as essentially selfish and predatory, he concluded that only fear and coercion could hold them in check. There is a vein of realism in this argument that should not be overlooked, but it does scant justice to the fraternal aspects of human life. The impulse to cooperate is as real as the impulse to compete; sympathy is as real as selfishness. Hobbes speaks as if rational self-interest alone impels men to unite in a political order, but it is at least as true to say, with Aristotle, that man is naturally a political animal.

Hobbes' one-sided characterization of human nature leads to a paradoxical theory of the state. At the same time that Hobbes demands unlimited power for his sovereign, he virtually limits the sovereign's functions to the safeguarding of life and limb. Thus his state is maximal in powers but minimal in functions. It may be instructive to compare Hobbes' view with that of Lincoln, who also lived during a period of civil strife. "The legitimate object of government," declared Lincoln, "is 'to do for the people what needs to be done, but which they cannot, by individual effort, do at all, or do so well, for themselves.' " [11] The emphasis is positive rather than negative—on the promotion of welfare rather than the suppression of anti-social impulses. Lincoln would limit the powers of the state but not its functions; Hobbes would limit its functions but not its powers.

He was so insistent upon the unfettered power of the sovereign that he had no sympathy for a Bill of Rights or a system of constitutional checks. He did not recognize, as did Locke and Jefferson, that irresponsible absolute power corrupts absolutely, or that the social contract should be a democratic instrument, based on the will and participation of the governed. He conceived of law as the mere command of the rulers rather than as a body of principles limiting their arbitrary power and applying to sovereign and subjects alike.

The social-contract theory, as he developed it, is inadequate to explain the inner cohesion of society. Purely selfish interests, even though enlightened by

[11] Michael D. Oakeshott, *The Social and Political Doctrines of Contemporary Europe* (Cambridge University Press, 1939), p. 19.

reason, cannot provide social unity or generate a binding social contract. In opposition to Hobbes, Rousseau pointed out that there is a great difference between a real community of interests and a mere sum of selfish interests. He maintained that society must be "a moral, collective body," which essentially binds men together, their wills merged and transformed in a corporate will. His theory has defects of its own, but it lacks the particular defects of Hobbes' egoistic theory.

The strength of Hobbes' argument is most evident when we consider its application to international affairs. In the atomic age, the simple dictates of self-preservation demand an international authority with power to maintain peace. But even here the argument can easily be oversimplified—there are many causes of war besides political anarchy among nations. Poverty, imperialism, racial antagonism, and the conflict of ideologies—to mention but a few factors—are also productive of international strife. There is no single cause of war and no single remedy. We must act in many fields at once—political, economic, moral, religious, and philosophical—creating a real world community to give force and substance to international peace.

20

Liberty

JOHN STUART MILL
(For biographical note see pages 395–396.)

From *On Liberty*

CHAPTER I

INTRODUCTORY

. . . The object of this Essay is to assert one very simple principle, as entitled to govern absolutely the dealings of society with the individual in the way of compulsion and control, whether the means used be physical force in the form of legal penalties, or the moral coercion of public opinion. That principle is, that the sole end for which mankind are warranted, individually or collectively, in interfering with the liberty of action of any of their number, is self-protection. That the only purpose for which power can be rightfully exercised over any member of a civilized community, against his will, is to prevent harm to others. His own good, either physical or moral, is not a sufficient warrant. He cannot rightfully be compelled to do or forbear because it will be better for him to do so, because it will make him happier, because, in the opinions of others, to do so would be wise, or even right. These are good reasons for remonstrating with him, or reasoning with him, or persuading him, or entreating him, but not for compelling him, or visiting him with any evil in case he do otherwise. To justify that, the conduct from which it is desired to deter him must be calculated to produce evil to some one else. The only part of the conduct of anyone, for which he is amenable to society, is that which concerns others. In the part which merely concerns himself, his independence is, of right, absolute. Over himself, over his own body and mind, the individual is sovereign.

It is perhaps hardly necessary to say that this doctrine is meant to apply only to human beings in the maturity of their faculties. We are not speaking of children, or of young persons below the age which the law may fix as that of manhood or womanhood. Those who are still in a state to require being taken care of by others, must be protected against their own actions as well as against external injury. For the same reason, we may leave out of consideration those backward states of society in which the race itself may be considered as in its nonage. The early difficulties in the way of spontaneous progress are so great, and there is seldom any choice of means for overcoming them; and a ruler full of the spirit of improvement is warranted in the use of any expedients that will attain an end, perhaps otherwise unattainable. Despotism is a legitimate mode of government in dealing with barbarians, provided the end be their improvement, and the means justified by actually effecting that end. Liberty, as a principle, has no application to any state of things anterior to the time when mankind have become capable of being improved by free and equal discussion. Until then, there is nothing for them but implicit obedience to an Akbar or a Charlemagne, if they are so fortunate as to find one. But as soon as mankind have attained the capacity of being guided to their own improvement by conviction or persuasion (a period long since reached in all nations with whom we need here concern ourselves), compulsion, either in the direct form or in that of pains and penalties for noncompliance, is no longer admissible as a means to their own good, and justifiable only for the security of others.

It is proper to state that I forego any advantage which could be derived to my argument from the idea of abstract right, as a thing independent of utility. I regard utility as the ultimate appeal on all ethical questions; but it must be utility in the largest sense, grounded on the permanent interests of a man as a progressive being. Those interests, I contend, authorized the subjection of individual spontaneity to external control, only in respect to those actions of each which concern the interest of other people. If anyone does an act hurtful to others, there is a *prima facie* case for punishing him, by law, or, where legal penalties are not safely applicable, by general disapprobation. There are also many positive acts for the benefit of others, which he may rightfully be compelled to perform: such as to give evidence in a court of justice; to bear his fair share in the common defense, or in any other joint work necessary to the interest of the society of which he enjoys the protection; and to perform certain acts of individual beneficence, such as saving a fellow-creature's life, or interposing to protect the defenseless against ill-usage, things which whenever it is obviously a man's duty to do, he may rightfully be made responsible to society for not doing. A person may cause evil to others not only by his actions but by his inaction, and in either case he is justly accountable to them for the injury. The latter case, it is true, requires a much more cautious exercise of compulsion than the former. To make anyone answerable for doing evil to others is the rule; to make him answerable for not preventing evil is, comparatively speaking, the exception. Yet there are many cases clear enough and grave enough to justify that exception. In all things which regard the external relations of the individual, he is *de jure* amenable to those whose interests are concerned, and, if need be, to society as their protector. There are often good reasons for not holding him to the responsibility; but these reasons must arise from the special expediencies of the case: either because it is a kind of case in which he is on the whole likely to act better, when left to his own discretion, than when controlled in any way in which society have it in their power to control him; or because the attempt to exercise control would produce other evils, greater than those which it would prevent. When such reasons as these preclude the enforcement of responsibility, the conscience of the agent himself should step into the vacant judgment seat, and protect those interests of others which have no external protection; judging himself all the more rigidly, because the case does not admit of his being made accountable to the judgment of his fellow-creatures.

But there is a sphere of action in which society, as distinguished from the individual, has, if any, only an indirect interest; comprehending all that portion of a person's life and conduct which affects only himself, or if it also affects others, only with their free, voluntary, and undeceived consent and participation. When I say only himself, I mean directly, and in the first instance; for whatever affects himself, may affect others through himself; and the objection which may be grounded on this contingency, will receive consideration in the sequel. This, then, is the appropriate region of human liberty. It comprises, *first,* the inward domain of consciousness; demanding liberty of conscience in the most comprehensive sense; liberty of thought and feeling; absolute freedom of opinion and sentiment on all subjects, practical or speculative, scientific, moral, or theological. The liberty of expressing and publishing opinions may seem to fall under a different principle, since it belongs to that part of the conduct of an individual which concerns other people; but, being almost of as much importance as the liberty of thought itself, and resting in great part on the same reasons, is practically inseparable from it. *Secondly,* the principle requires liberty of tastes and pursuits; of framing the plan of our life to suit our own character; of doing as we like, subject to such consequences as may follow: without impediment from our fellow-creatures, so long as what we do does not harm them, even though they should think our conduct fool-

ish, perverse, or wrong. *Thirdly,* from this liberty of each individual, follows the liberty, within the same limits, of combination among individuals; freedom to unite, for any purpose not involving harm to others: the persons combining being supposed to be of full age, and not forced or deceived.

No society in which these liberties are not, on the whole, respected, is free, whatever may be its form of government; and none is completely free in which they do not exist absolute and unqualified. The only freedom which deserves the name, is that of pursuing our own good in our own way, so long as we do not attempt to deprive others of theirs, or impede their efforts to obtain it. Each is the proper guardian of his own health, whether bodily, or mental and spiritual. Mankind are greater gainers by suffering each other to live as seems good to themselves, than by compelling each to live as seems good to the rest.

Though this doctrine is anything but new, and, to some persons, may have the air of a truism, there is no doctrine which stands more directly opposed to the general tendency of existing opinion and practice. . . . There is . . . an increasing inclination to stretch unduly the powers of society over the individual, both by the force of opinion and even by that of legislation; and as the tendency of all the changes taking place in the world is to strengthen society, and diminish the power of the individual, this encroachment is not one of the evils which tend spontaneously to disappear, but, on the contrary, to grow more and more formidable. The disposition of mankind, whether as rulers or as fellow-citizens, to impose their own opinions and inclinations as a rule of conduct on others, is so energetically supported by some of the best and by some of the worst feelings incident to human nature, that it is hardly ever kept under restraint by anything but want of power; and as the power is not declining, but growing, unless a strong barrier of moral conviction can be raised against the mischief, we must expect, in the present circumstances of the world, to see it increase. . . .

CHAPTER II

OF THE LIBERTY OF THOUGHT AND DISCUSSION

The time, it is to be hoped, is gone by, when any defence would be necessary of the "liberty of the press" as one of the securities against corrupt or tyrannical government. . . . Speaking generally, it is not, in constitutional countries, to be apprehended that the government, whether completely responsible to the people or not, will often attempt to control the expression of opinion, except when in doing so it makes itself the organ of the general intolerance of the public. Let us suppose, therefore, that the government is entirely at one with the people, and never thinks of exerting any power of coercion unless in agreement with what it conceives to be their voice. But I deny the right of the people to exercise such coercion, either by themselves or by their government. The power itself is illegitimate. The best government has no more title to it than the worst. It is as noxious, or more noxious, when exerted in accordance with public opinion, than when in opposition to it. If all mankind minus one were of one opinion, and only one person were of the contrary opinion, mankind would be no more justified in silencing that one person, than he, if he had the power, would be justified in silencing mankind. Were an opinion a personal possession of no value except to the

owner; if to be obstructed in the enjoyment of it were simply a private injury, it would make some difference whether the injury was inflicted only on a few persons or on many. But the peculiar evil of silencing the expression of an opinion is, that it is robbing the human race: posterity as well as the existing generation; those who dissent from the opinion, still more than those who hold it. If the opinion is right, they are deprived of the opportunity of exchanging error for truth; if wrong, they lose, what is almost as great a benefit, the clearer perception and livelier impression of truth, produced by its collision with error.

It is necessary to consider separately these two hypotheses, each of which has a distinct branch of the argument corresponding to it. We can never be sure that the opinion we are endeavoring to stifle is a false opinion; and if we were sure, stifling it would be an evil still.

First: the opinion which it is attempted to suppress by authority may possibly be true. Those who desire to suppress it, of course deny its truth; but they are not infallible. They have no authority to decide the question for all mankind, and exclude every other person from the means of judging. To refuse a hearing to an opinion, because they are sure that it is false, is to assume that *their* certainty is the same thing as *absolute* certainty. All silencing of discussion is an assumption of infallibility. Its condemnation may be allowed to rest on this common argument, not the worse for being common.

Unfortunately for the good sense of mankind, the fact of their fallibility is far from carrying the weight in their practical judgment which is always allowed to it in theory; for while everyone well knows himself to be fallible, few think it necessary to take any precautions against their own fallibility, or admit the supposition that any opinion of which they feel very certain, may be one of the examples of the error to which they acknowledge themselves to be liable. Absolute princes, or others who are accustomed to unlimited deference, usually feel this complete confidence in their own opinions on nearly all subjects. People more happily situated, who sometimes hear their opinions disputed, and are not wholly unused to be set right when they are wrong, place the same unbounded reliance only on such of their opinions as are shared by all who surround them, or to whom they habitually defer; for in proportion to a man's want of confidence in his own solitary judgment, does he usually repose, with implicit trust, on the infallibility of "the world" in general. And the world, to each individual, means the part of it with which he comes in contact—his party, his sect, his church, his class of society; the man may be called, by comparison, almost liberal and large-minded to whom it means anything so comprehensive as his own country or his own age. Nor is his faith in this collective authority at all shaken by his being aware that other ages, countries, sects, churches, classes, and parties have thought, and even now think, the exact reverse. He devolves upon his own world the responsibility of being in the right against the dissentient worlds of other people; and it never troubles him that mere accident has decided which of these numerous worlds is the object of his reliance, and that the same causes which make him a Churchman in London, would have made him a Buddhist or a Confucian in Pekin. Yet it is as evident in itself as any amount of argument can make it, that ages are no more infallible than individuals; every age having held many opinions which subsequent ages have deemed not only false but absurd; and it is as certain that many opinions now general will be rejected by future ages, as it is that many, once general, are rejected by the present.

The objection likely to be made to this argument would probably take some such form as the following. There is no greater assumption of infallibility in forbidding the propagation of error, than in any other thing which is done by public authority on its own judgment and responsibility. Judgment is given to men that they may use it. Because it may be used erroneously, are men to be told that they ought not to use it at all? To prohibit what they think pernicious, is not claiming exemption from error, but fulfilling the duty incumbent on them, although fallible, of acting on their conscientious conviction. If we were never to act on our opinions, because those opinions may be wrong, we should leave all our interests uncared for, and all our duties unperformed. An objection which applies to all conduct can be no valid objection to any conduct in particular. It is the duty of governments, and of individuals, to form the truest opinions they can; to form them carefully, and never impose them upon others unless they are quite sure of being right. But when they are sure (such reasoners may say), it is not conscientiousness but cowardice to shrink from acting on their opinions, and allow doctrines which they honestly think dangerous to the welfare of mankind, either in this life or in another, to be scattered abroad without restraint, because other people, in less enlightened times, have persecuted opinions now believed to be true. Let us take care, it may be said, not to make the same mistake; but governments and nations have made mistakes in other things, which are not denied to be fit subjects for the exercise of authority: they have laid on bad taxes, made unjust wars. Ought we therefore to lay on no taxes, and, under whatever provocation, make no wars? Men, and governments, must act to the best of their ability. There is no such thing as absolute certainty, but there is assurance sufficient for the purposes of human life. We may, and must, assume our opinion to be true for the guidance of our own conduct: and it is assuming no more when we forbid bad men to pervert society by the propagation of opinions which we regard as false and pernicious.

I answer that it is assuming very much more. There is the greatest difference between presuming an opinion to be true because, with every opportunity for contesting it, it has not been refuted, and assuming its truth for the purpose of not permitting its refutation. Complete liberty of contradicting and disproving our opinion is the very condition which justifies us in assuming its truth for purposes of action; and on no other terms can a being with human faculties have any rational assurance of being right.

When we consider either the history of opinion, or the ordinary conduct of human life, to what is it to be ascribed that the one and the other are no worse than they are? Not certainly to the inherent force of the human understanding; for, on any matter not self-evident, there are ninety-nine persons totally incapable of judging of it for one who is capable; and the capacity of the hundredth person is only comparative: for the majority of the eminent men of every past generation held many opinions now known to be erroneous, and did or approved numerous things which no one will now justify. Why is it, then, that there is on the whole a preponderance among mankind of rational opinions and rational conduct? If there really is this preponder-

ance—which there must be unless human affairs are, and have always been, in an almost desperate state—it is owing to a quality of the human mind, the source of everything respectable in man either as an intellectual or as a moral being, namely, that his errors are corrigible. He is capable of rectifying his mistakes, by discussion and experience. Not by experience alone. There must be discussion, to show how experience is to be interpreted. Wrong opinions and practices gradually yield to fact and argument; but facts and arguments, to produce any effect on the mind, must be brought before it. Very few facts are able to tell their own story, without comments to bring out their meaning. The whole strength and value, then, of human judgment, depending on the one property, that it can be set right when it is wrong, reliance can be placed on it only when the means of setting it right are kept constantly at hand. In the case of any person whose judgment is really deserving of confidence, how has it become so? Because he has kept his mind open to criticism of his opinions and conduct. Because it has been his practice to listen to all that could be said against him; to profit by as much of it as was just, and expound to himself, and upon occasion to others, the fallacy of what was fallacious. Because he has felt that the only way in which a human being can make some approach to knowing the whole of a subject, is by hearing what can be said about it by persons of every variety of opinion, and studying all modes in which it can be looked at by every character of mind. No wise man ever acquired his wisdom in any mode but this; nor is it in the nature of human intellect to become wise in any other manner. The steady habit of correcting and completing his own opinion by collating it with those of others, so far from causing doubt and hesitation in carrying it into practice, is the only stable foundation for a just reliance on it: for, being cognizant of all that can, at least obviously, be said against him, and having taken up his position against all gainsayers—knowing that he has sought for objections and difficulties, instead of avoiding them, and has shut out no light which can be thrown upon the subject from any quarter—he has a right to think his judgment better than that of any person, or any multitude, who have not gone through a similar process.

It is not too much to require that what the wisest of mankind, those who are best entitled to trust their own judgment, find necessary to warrant their relying on it, should be submitted to by that miscellaneous collection of a few wise and many foolish individuals, called the public. The most intolerant of churches, the Roman Catholic Church, even at the canonization of a saint, admits, and listens patiently to, a "devil's advocate." The holiest of men, it appears, cannot be admitted to posthumous honors, until all that the devil could say against him is known and weighed. If even the Newtonian philosophy were not permitted to be questioned, mankind could not feel as complete assurance of its truth as they now do. The beliefs which we have most warrant for, have no safeguard to rest on but a standing invitation to the whole world to prove them unfounded. If the challenge is not accepted, or is accepted and the attempt fails, we are far enough from certainty still; but we have done the best that the existing state of human reason admits of; we have neglected nothing that could give the truth a chance of reaching us: if the lists are kept open, we may hope that if there be a better truth, it will be found when the human mind is capable of receiving it; and in the meantime we may rely on having attained such approach to truth as is possible in our own day. This is the amount of certainty attainable by a fallible being, and this the sole way of attaining it.

Strange it is that men should admit the validity of the arguments for free discussion, but object to their being "pushed to an extreme"; not seeing that unless the reasons are good for an extreme case, they are not good for any case. Strange that they should imagine that they are not assuming infallibility, when they acknowledge that there should be free discussion on all subjects which can possibly be *doubtful,* but think that some particular principle or doctrine should be forbidden to be questioned because it is so *certain,* that is, because *they are certain* that it is certain. To call any proposition certain while there is anyone who would deny its certainty if permitted, but who is not permitted, is to assume that we ourselves, and those who agree with us, are the judges of certainty, and judges without hearing the other side.

In the present age—which has been described as "destitute of faith, but terrified at scepticism"—in which people feel sure, not so much that their opinions are true, as that they should not know what to do without them—the claims of an opinion to be protected from public attack are rested not so much on its truth, as on its importance to society. There are, it is alleged, certain beliefs so useful, not to say indispensable, to well-being that it is as much the duty of governments to uphold those beliefs, as to protect any other of the interests of society. In a case of such necessity, and so directly in the line of their duty, something less than infallibility may, it is maintained, warrant, and even bind, governments to act on their own opinion, confirmed by the general opinion of mankind. It is also often argued, and still oftener thought, that none but bad men would desire to weaken these salutary beliefs; and there can be nothing wrong, it is thought, in restraining bad men, and prohibiting what only such men would wish to practice. This mode of thinking makes the justification of restraints on discussion not a question of the truth of doctrines, but of their usefulness; and flatters itself by that means to escape the responsibility of claiming to be an infallible judge of opinions. But those who thus satisfy themselves, do not perceive that the assumption of infallibility is merely shifted from one point to another. The usefulness of an opinion is itself matter of opinion: as disputable, as open to discussion, and requiring discussion as much as the opinion itself. There is the same need of an infallible judge of opinions to decide an opinion to be noxious, as to decide it to be false, unless the opinion condemned has full opportunity of defending itself. And it will not do to say that the heretic may be allowed to maintain the utility or harmlessness of his opinion, though forbidden to maintain its truth. The truth of an opinion is part of its utility. If we would know whether or not it is desirable that a proposition should be believed, is it possible to exclude the consideration of whether or not it is true? In the opinion, not of bad men, but of the best men, no belief which is contrary to truth can be really useful; and can you prevent such men from urging that plea, when they are charged with culpability for denying some doctrine which they are told is useful, but which they believe to be false? Those who are on the side of received opinions never fail to take all possible advantage of this plea: you do not find *them* handling the question of utility as if it could be completely abstracted from that of truth; on the contrary, it is, above all, because their doctrine is "the truth," that the knowledge or the belief of it is held to be so indispensable. There can be no fair discussion of the question of usefulness when

an argument so vital may be employed on one side, but not on the other. And in point of fact, when law or public feeling do not permit the truth of an opinion to be disputed, they are just as little tolerant of a denial of its usefulness. The utmost they allow is an extenuation of its absolute necessity, or of the positive guilt of rejecting it.

In order more fully to illustrate the mischief of denying a hearing to opinions because we, in our own judgment, have condemned them, it will be desirable to fix down the discussion to a concrete case; and I choose, by preference, the cases which are least favorable to me—in which the argument against freedom of opinion, both on the score of truth and on that of utility, is considered the strongest. Let the opinions impugned be the belief in a God and in a future state, or any of the commonly received doctrines of morality. To fight the battle on such ground gives a great advantage to an unfair antagonist; since he will be sure to say (and many who have no desire to be unfair will say it internally), "Are these the doctrines which you do not deem sufficiently certain to be taken under the protection of law? Is the belief in a God one of the opinions to feel sure of which you hold to be assuming infallibility?" But I must be permitted to observe that it is not the feeling sure of a doctrine (be it what it may) which I call an assumption of infallibility. It is the undertaking to decide that question *for others*, without allowing them to hear what can be said on the contrary side. And I denounce and reprobate this pretension not the less if put forth on the side of my most solemn convictions. However positive anyone's persuasion may be, not only of the falsity but of the pernicious consequences—not only of the pernicious consequences, but (to adopt expressions which I altogether condemn) the immorality and impiety of an opinion; yet if, in pursuance of that private judgment, though backed by the public judgment of his country or his contemporaries, he prevents the opinion from being heard in its defense, he assumes infallibility. And so far from the assumption being less objectionable or less dangerous because the opinion is called immoral or impious, this is the case of all others in which it is most fatal. These are exactly the occasions on which the men of one generation commit those dreadful mistakes which excite the astonishment and horror of posterity. It is among such that we find the instances memorable in history, when the arm of the law has been employed to root out the best men and the noblest doctrines; with deplorable success as to the men, though some of the doctrines have survived to be (as if in mockery) invoked in defense of similar conduct toward those who dissent from *them,* or from their received interpretation.

Mankind can hardly be too often reminded, that there was once a man named Socrates, between whom and the legal authorities and public opinion of his time there took place a memorable collision. Born in an age and country abounding in individual greatness, this man has been handed down to us by those who best knew both him and the age, as the most virtuous man in it; while *we* know him as the head and prototype of all subsequent teachers of virtue, the source equally of the lofty inspiration of Plato and the judicious utilitarianism of Aristotle, . . . the two headsprings of ethical as of all other philosophy. This acknowledged master of all the eminent thinkers who have since lived—whose fame, still growing after more than two thousand years, all but outweighs the whole remainder of the names which make his native city illustrious—was put to death by his countrymen, after a judicial conviction, for impiety and immorality. Impiety, in

denying the gods recognized by the State; indeed his accuser asserted (see the *Apologia*) that he believed in no gods at all. Immorality, in being, by his doctrines and instructions, a "corruptor of youth." Of these charges the tribunal, there is every ground for believing, honestly found him guilty, and condemned the man who probably of all then born had deserved best of mankind to be put to death as a criminal.

To pass from this to the only other instance of judicial iniquity, the mention of which, after the condemnation of Socrates, would not be an anti-climax: the event which took place on Calvary rather more than eighteen hundred years ago. The man who left on the memory of those who witnessed his life and conversation such an impression of his moral grandeur that eighteen subsequent centuries have done homage to him as the Almighty in person, was ignominiously put to death, as what? As a blasphemer. Men did not merely mistake their benefactor; they mistook him for the exact contrary of what he was, and treated him as that prodigy of impiety which they themselves are now held to be for their treatment of him. The feelings with which mankind now regard these lamentable transactions, especially the later of the two, render them extremely unjust in their judgment of the unhappy actors. These were, to all appearance, not bad men—not worse than men commonly are, but rather the contrary; men who possessed in a full, or somewhat more than a full measure, the religious, moral, and patriotic feelings of their time and people: the very kind of men who, in all times, our own included, have every chance of passing through life blameless and respected. The high-priest who rent his garments when the words were pronounced which, according to all the ideas of his country, constituted the blackest guilt, was in all probability quite as sincere in his horror and indignation as the generality of respectable and pious men now are in the religious and moral sentiments they profess; and most of those who now shudder at his conduct, if they had lived in his time, and been born Jews, would have acted precisely as he did. Orthodox Christians who are tempted to think that those who stoned to death the first martyrs must have been worse men than they themselves are, ought to remember that one of those persecutors was Saint Paul.

Let us add one more example, the most striking of all, if the impressiveness of an error is measured by the wisdom and virtue of him who falls into it. If ever anyone possessed of power had grounds for thinking himself the best and most enlightened among his contemporaries, it was the Emperor Marcus Aurelius. Absolute monarch of the whole civilized world, he preserved through life not only the most unblemished justice, but what was less to be expected from his Stoical breeding, the tenderest heart. The few failings which are attributed to him were all on the side of indulgence; while his writings, the highest ethical product of the ancient mind, differ scarcely perceptibly, if they differ at all, from the most characteristic teachings of Christ. This man, a better Christian in all but the dogmatic sense of the word than almost any of the ostensibly Christian sovereigns who have since reigned, persecuted Christianity. Placed at the summit of all the previous attainments of humanity, with an open, unfettered intellect, and a character which led him of himself to embody in his moral writings the Christian ideal, he yet failed to see that Christianity was to be a good and not an evil to the world, with his duties to which he was so deeply penetrated. Existing society he knew to be in a deplorable state. But such as it was, he saw, or thought he saw, that it was held together, and prevented from being worse, by belief and reverence of the received divinities. As a ruler of mankind, he deemed it his duty not to suffer society to fall in pieces; and saw not how, if its existing ties were removed, any others could be formed which could again knit it together. The new religion openly aimed at dissolving these ties: unless, therefore, it was his duty to adopt that religion, it seemed to be his duty to put it down. Inasmuch then as the theology of Christianity did not appear to him true or of divine origin; inasmuch as this strange history of a crucified God was not credible to him, and a system which purported to rest entirely upon a foundation to him so wholly unbelievable, could not be foreseen by him to be that renovating agency which, after all abatements, it has in fact proved to be; the gentlest and most amiable of philosophers and rulers, under a solemn sense of duty, authorized the persecution of Christianity. To my mind this is one of the most tragical facts in all history. It is a bitter thought, how different a thing the Christianity of the world might have been, if the Christian faith had been adopted as the religion of the empire under the auspices of Marcus Aurelius instead of those of Constantine. But it would be equally unjust to him and false to truth to deny that no one plea which can be urged for punishing anti-Christian teaching was wanting to Marcus Aurelius for punishing as he did the propagation of Christianity. No Christian more firmly believes that atheism is false, and tends to the dissolution of society, than Marcus Aurelius believed the same things of Christianity; he who, of all men then living, might have been thought the most capable of appreciating it. Unless anyone who approves of punishment for the promulgation of opinions, flatters himself that he is a wiser and better man than Marcus Aurelius—more deeply versed in the wisdom of his time, more elevated in his intellect above it—more earnest in his search for truth, or more single-minded in his devotion to it when found; let him abstain from that assumption of the joint infallibility of himself and the multitude, which the great Antoninus made with so unfortunate a result.

Aware of the impossibility of defending the use of punishment for restraining irreligious opinions by any argument which will not justify Marcus Antoninus, the enemies of religious freedom, when hard pressed, occasionally accept this consequence, and say, with Dr. Johnson, that the persecutors of Christianity were in the right; that persecution is an ordeal through which truth ought to pass, and always passes successfully, legal penalties being, in the end, powerless against truth, though sometimes beneficially effective against mischievous errors. This is a form of the argument for religious intolerance sufficiently remarkable not to be passed without notice.

A theory which maintains that truth may justifiably be persecuted because persecution cannot possibly do it any harm, cannot be charged with being intentionally hostile to the reception of new truths; but we cannot commend the generosity of its dealing with the persons to whom mankind are indebted for them. To discover to the world something which deeply concerns it, and of which it was previously ignorant; to prove to it that it had been mistaken on some vital point of temporal or spiritual interest, is as important a service as a human being can render to his fellow-creatures, and in certain cases, as in those of the early Christians and of the Reformers, those who think with Dr. Johnson believe it to have been the most precious gift which could be bestowed on mankind. That the authors of such splendid benefits should be requited by martyrdom, that their reward should be to be dealt with as the vilest of criminals, is not, upon this theory, a deplorable error and misfortune, for which humanity should mourn in sackcloth and ashes, but the normal and justifiable state of things. The propounder of a new truth, according to this doctrine, should stand, as stood, in the legislation of the Locrians, the proposer of a new law, with a halter round his neck, to be instantly tightened if the public assembly did not, on hearing his reasons, then and there adopt his proposition. People who defend this mode of treating benefactors cannot be supposed to set much value on the benefit; and I believe this view of the subject is mostly confined to the sort of persons who think that new truths may have been desirable once, but that we have had enough of them now.

But, indeed, the dictum that truth always triumphs over persecution is one of those pleasant falsehoods which men repeat after one another till they pass into commonplaces, but which all experience refutes. History teems with instances of truth put down by persecution. If not suppressed forever, it may be thrown back for centuries. To speak only of religious opinions: the Reformation broke out at least twenty times before Luther, and was put down. Arnold of Brescia was put down. Fra Dolcino was put down. Savonarola was put down. The Albigeois were put down. The Vaudois were put down. The Lollards were put down. The Hussites were put down. Even after the era of Luther, wherever persecution was persisted in, it was successful. In Spain, Italy, Flanders, the Austrian Empire, Protestantism was rooted out; and, most likely, would have been so in England, had Queen Mary lived, or Queen Elizabeth died. Persecution has always succeeded, save where the heretics were too strong a party to be effectually persecuted.

No reasonable person can doubt that Christianity might have been extirpated in the Roman Empire. It spread, and became predominant, because the persecutions were only occasional, lasting but a short time, and separated by long intervals of almost undisturbed propagandism. It is a piece of idle sentimentality that truth, merely as truth, has any inherent power denied to error of prevailing against the dungeon and the stake. Men are not more zealous for truth than they often are for error, and a sufficient application of legal or even of social penalties will generally succeed in stopping the propagation of either. The real advantage which truth has, consists in this, that when an opinion is true, it may be extinguished once, twice, or many times, but in the course of ages there will generally be found persons to rediscover it, until some one of its reappearances falls on a time when from favorable circumstances it escapes persecution until it has made such head as to withstand all subsequent attempts to suppress it.

It will be said that we do not now put to death the introducers of new opinions: we are not like our fathers who slew the prophets, we even build sepulchres to them. It is true we no longer put heretics to death; and the amount of penal infliction which modern feeling would probably tolerate, even against the most obnoxious opinions, is not sufficient to extirpate them. . . . But though we do not now inflict so much evil on those who think differently from us as it was formerly our custom to do, it may be that we do ourselves as much evil as ever by our treatment of them. Socrates was put to death, but the Socratic philosophy rose like the sun in heaven, and spread its illumination over the whole intellectual firmament. Christians were cast to the lions, but the Christian church grew up a stately and spreading tree, overtopping the older and less vigorous growths, and stifling them by its shade. Our merely social intolerance kills no one, roots out no opinions, but induces men to disguise them, or to abstain from any active effort for their diffusion. With us, heretical opinions do not perceptibly gain, or even lose, ground in each decade or generation; they never blaze out far and wide, but continue to smolder in the narrow circles of thinking and studious persons among whom they originate, without ever lighting up the general affairs of mankind with either a true or a deceptive light. And thus is kept up a state of things very satisfactory to some minds, because, without the unpleasant process of fining or imprisoning anybody, it maintains all prevailing opinions outwardly undisturbed, while it does not absolutely interdict the exercise of reason by dissentients afflicted with the malady of thought. A convenient plan for having peace in the intellectual world, and keeping all things going on therein very much as they do already! But the price paid for this sort of intellectual pacification is the sacrifice of the entire moral courage of the human mind. A state of things in which a large portion of the most active and inquiring intellects find it advisable to keep the general principles and grounds of their convictions within their own breasts, and attempt, in what they address to the public, to fit as much as they can of their own conclusions to premises which they have internally renounced, cannot send forth the open, fearless characters, and logical, consistent intellects who once adorned the thinking world. The sort of men who can be looked for under it, are either mere conformers to commonplace, or time-servers for truth, whose arguments on all great subjects are meant for their hearers, and are not those which have convinced themselves. Those who avoid this alternative, do so by narrowing their thoughts and interest to things which can be spoken of without venturing within the region of principles—that is, to small practical matters which would come right of themselves if but the minds of mankind were strengthened and enlarged, and which will never be made effectually right until then; while that which would strengthen and enlarge men's minds, free and daring speculation on the highest subjects, is abandoned.

Those in whose eyes this reticence on the part of heretics is no evil should consider, in the first place, that in consequence of it there is never any fair and thorough discussion of heretical opinions; and that such of them as could not stand such a discussion, though they may be prevented from spreading, do not disappear. But it is not the minds of heretics that are deteriorated most by the ban placed on all inquiry which does not end in the orthodox conclusions. The greatest harm done is to those who are not heretics, and whose whole mental development is cramped, and their reason cowed, by the fear of heresy. Who can compute what the world loses in the multitude of promising intellects combined with timid characters, who dare not follow out any bold, vigorous, independent train of thought, lest it should land them in something which would admit of being considered irreligious or immoral? Among them we may occasionally see some man of deep conscientiousness, and subtle and refined understanding, who spends a life in sophisticating with an intellect which he cannot silence, and exhausts the resources of ingenuity in attempting to reconcile the promptings of his conscience and reason with orthodoxy, which yet he does not, perhaps, to the end succeed in doing. No one can be a great thinker who does not recognize that as a thinker it is his first duty to follow his intellect to whatever conclusions it may lead. Truth gains more even by the errors of one who, with due study and preparation, thinks for himself, than by the true opinions of those who only hold them because they do not suffer themselves to think. Not that it is solely, or chiefly, to form great thinkers, that freedom of thinking is required. On the contrary, it is as much and even more indispensable to enable average human beings to attain the mental stature which they are capable of. There have been, and may again be, great individual thinkers in a general atmosphere of mental slavery. But there never has been, nor ever will be, in that atmosphere an intellectually active people. Where any people has made a temporary approach to such a character, it has been because the dread of heterodox speculation was for a time suspended. Where there is a tacit convention that principles are not to be disputed; where the discussion of the greatest questions which can occupy humanity is considered to be closed, we cannot hope to find that generally high scale of mental activity which has made some periods of history so remarkable. Never when controversy avoided the subjects which are large and important enough to kindle enthusiasm, was the mind of a people stirred up from its foundations, and the impulse given which raised even persons of the most ordinary intellect to something of the dignity of thinking beings. Of such we have had an example in the condition of Europe during the times immediately following the Reformation; another, though limited to the Continent and to a more cultivated class, in the speculative movement of the latter half of the eighteenth century; and a third, of still briefer duration, in the intellectual fermentation of Germany during the Goethean and Fichtean period. These periods differed widely in the particular opinions which they developed; but were alike in this, that during all three the yoke of authority was broken. In each, an old mental despotism had been thrown off, and no new one had yet taken its place. The impulse given at these three periods has made Europe what it now is. Every single improvement which has taken place either in the human mind or in institutions, may be traced distinctly to one or other of them. Appearances have for some time indicated that all three impulses are well nigh spent; and we can expect no fresh start until we again assert our mental freedom.

Let us now pass to the second division of the argument, and dismissing the supposition that any of the received opinions may be false, let us assume them to be true, and examine into the worth of the manner in which they are likely to be held, when their truth is not freely and openly canvassed. However unwillingly a person who has a strong opinion may admit the possibility that his opinion may be false, he ought to be moved by the consideration that, however true it may be, if it is not fully, frequently, and fearlessly discussed, it will be held as a dead dogma, not a living truth.

There is a class of persons (happily not quite so numerous as formerly) who think it enough if a person assents undoubtingly to what they think true, though he has no knowledge whatever of the grounds of the opinion, and could not make a tenable defense of it against the most superficial objections. Such persons, if they can once get their creed taught from authority, naturally think that no good, and some harm, comes of its being allowed to be questioned. Where their influence prevails, they make it nearly impossible for the received opinion to be rejected wisely and considerately, though it may still be rejected rashly and ignorantly; for to shut out discussion entirely is seldom possible, and when it once gets in, beliefs not grounded on conviction

are apt to give way before the slightest semblance of an argument. Waiving, however, this possibility—assuming that the true opinion abides in the mind, but abides as a prejudice, a belief independent of, and proof against, argument—this is not the way in which truth ought to be held by a rational being. This is not knowing the truth. Truth, thus held, is but one superstition the more, accidentally clinging to the words which enunciate a truth.

If the intellect and judgment of mankind ought to be cultivated, a thing which Protestants at least do not deny, on what can these faculties be more appropriately exercised by anyone, than on the things which concern him so much that it is considered necessary for him to hold opinions on them? If the cultivation of the understanding consists in one thing more than in another, it is surely in learning the grounds of one's own opinions. Whatever people believe, on subjects on which it is of the first importance to believe rightly, they ought to be able to defend against at least the common objections. But, some one may say, "Let them be *taught* the grounds of their opinions. It does not follow that opinions must be merely parroted because they are never heard controverted. Persons who learn geometry do not simply commit the theorems to memory, but understand and learn likewise the demonstrations; and it would be absurd to say that they remain ignorant of the grounds of geometrical truths, because they never hear any one deny, and attempt to disprove them." Undoubtedly: and such teaching suffices on a subject like mathematics, where there is nothing at all to be said on the wrong side of the question. The peculiarity of the evidence of mathematical truths is that all the argument is on one side. There are no objections, and no answers to objections. But on every subject on which difference of opinion is possible, the truth depends on a balance to be struck between two sets of conflicting reasons. Even in natural philosophy, there is always some other explanation possible of the same facts—some geocentric theory instead of heliocentric, some phlogiston instead of oxygen—and it has to be shown why that other theory cannot be the true one; and until this is shown, and until we know how it is shown, we do not understand the grounds of our opinion. But when we turn to subjects infinitely more complicated, to morals, religion, politics, social relations, and the business of life, three-fourths of the arguments for every disputed opinion consist in dispelling the appearances which favor some opinion different from it. The greatest orator, save one, of antiquity, has left it on record that he always studied his adversary's case with as great, if not still greater, intensity than even his own. What Cicero practiced as the means of forensic success requires to be imitated by all who study any subject in order to arrive at the truth. He who knows only his own side of the case, knows little of that. His reasons may be good, and no one may have been able to refute them. But if he is equally unable to refute the reasons on the opposite side; if he does not so much as know what they are, he has no ground for preferring either opinion. The rational position for him would be suspension of judgment, and unless he contents himself with that, he is either led by authority, or adopts, like the generality of the world, the side to which he feels most inclination. Nor is it enough that he should hear the arguments of adversaries from his own teachers, presented as they state them, and accompanied by what they offer as refutations. That is not the way to do justice to the arguments, or bring them into real contact with his own mind. He must be able to hear them from persons who actually believe them; who

defend them in earnest, and do their very utmost for them. He must know them in their most plausible and persuasive form; he must feel the whole force of the difficulty which the true view of the subject has to encounter and dispose of; else he will never really possess himself of the portion of truth which meets and removes that difficulty. Ninety-nine in a hundred of what are called educated men are in this condition; even of those who can argue fluently for their opinions. Their conclusion may be true, but it might be false for anything they know: they have never thrown themselves into the mental position of those who think differently from them, and considered what such persons may have to say; and consequently they do not, in any proper sense of the word, know the doctrine which they themselves profess. They do not know those parts of it which explain and justify the remainder; the considerations which show that a fact which seemingly conflicts with another is reconcilable with it, or that, of two apparently strong reasons, one and not the other ought to be preferred. All that part of the truth which turns the scale, and decides the judgment of a completely informed mind, they are strangers to; nor is it ever really known but to those who have attended equally and impartially to both sides, and endeavored to see the reasons of both in the strongest light. So essential is this discipline to a real understanding of moral and human subjects, that if opponents of all important truths do not exist, it is indispensable to imagine them, and supply them with the strongest arguments which the most skilful devil's advocate can conjure up. . . .

If, however, the mischievous operation of the absence of free discussion, when the received opinions are true, were confined to leaving men ignorant of the grounds of those opinions, it might be thought that this, if an intellectual, is no moral evil, and does not affect the worth of the opinions, regarded in their influence on the character. The fact, however, is that not only the grounds of the opinion are forgotten in the absence of discussion, but too often the meaning of the opinion itself. The words which convey it cease to suggest ideas, or suggest only a small portion of those they were originally employed to communicate. Instead of a vivid conception and a living belief, there remain only a few phrases retained by rote; or, if any part, the shell and husk only of the meaning is retained, the finer essence being lost. The great chapter in human history which this fact occupies and fills, cannot be too earnestly studied and meditated on.

It is illustrated in the experience of almost all ethical doctrines and religious creeds. They are full of meaning and vitality to those who originate them, and to the direct disciples of the originators. Their meaning continues to be felt in undiminished strength, and is perhaps brought out into even fuller consciousness, so long as the struggle lasts to give the doctrine or creed an ascendancy over other creeds. At last it either prevails, and becomes the general opinion, or its progress stops; it keeps possession of the ground it has gained, but ceases to spread further. When either of these results has become apparent, controversy on the subject flags, and gradually dies away. The doctrine has taken its place, if not as a received opinion, as one of the admitted sects or divisions of opinion: those who hold it have generally inherited, not adopted it; and conversion from one of these doctrines to another, being now an exceptional fact, occupies little place in the thoughts of their professors. Instead of being, as at first, constantly on the alert either to defend themselves against the world, or to bring the world over to them, they have subsided into acquiescence, and neither listen, when they can help it, to arguments against their creed, nor trouble dissentients (if there be such) with arguments in its favor. From this time may usually be dated the decline in the living power of the doctrine. We often hear the teachers of all creeds lamenting the difficulty of keeping up in the minds of believers a lively apprehension of the truth which they nominally recognize, so that it may penetrate the feelings, and acquire a real mastery over the conduct. No such difficulty is complained of while the creed is still fighting for its existence: even the weaker combatants then know and feel what they are fighting for, and the difference between it and other doctrines; and in that period of every creed's existence, not a few persons may be found, who have realized its fundamental principles in all the forms of thought, have weighed and considered them in all their important bearings, and have experienced the full effect on the character which belief in that creed ought to produce in a mind thoroughly imbued with it. But when it has come to be an hereditary creed, and to be received passively, not actively; when the mind is no longer compelled, in the same degree as at first, to exercise its vital powers on the questions which its belief presents to it: there is a progressive tendency to forget all of the belief except the formularies, or to give it a dull and torpid assent, as if accepting it on trust dispensed with the necessity of realizing it in consciousness, or testing it by personal experience, until it almost ceases to connect itself at all with the inner life of the human being. Then are seen the cases, so frequent in this age of the world as almost to form the majority, in which the creed remains as it were outside the mind, incrusting and petrifying it against all other influences addressed to the higher parts of our nature; manifesting its power by not suffering any fresh and living conviction to get in, but itself doing nothing for the mind or heart, except standing sentinel over them to keep them vacant.

To what an extent doctrines intrinsically fitted to make the deepest impression upon the mind may remain in it as dead beliefs, without being ever realized in the imagination, the feelings, or the understanding, is exemplified by the manner in which the majority of believers hold the doctrines of Christianity. By Christianity I here mean what is accounted such by all churches and sects—the maxims and precepts contained in the New Testament. These are considered sacred, and accepted as laws, by all professing Christians. Yet it is scarcely too much to say that not one Christian in a thousand guides or tests his individual conduct by reference to those laws. The standard to which he does refer it, is the custom of his nation, his class, or his religious profession. He has thus, on the one hand, a collection of ethical maxims, which he believes to have been vouchsafed to him by infallible wisdom as rules for his government; and on the other a set of every-day judgments and practices, which go a certain length with some of those maxims, not so great a length with others, stand in direct opposition to some, and are, on the whole, a compromise between the Christian creed and the interests and suggestions of worldly life. To the first of these standards he gives his homage; to the other his real allegiance. . . .

The same thing holds true, generally speaking, of all traditional doctrines—those of prudence and knowledge of life, as well as of morals or religion. All languages and literatures are full of general observations on life, both as to what it is, and how to conduct oneself in it; observations which everybody knows, which everybody repeats, or hears with acquiescence, which are received as truisms, yet of which most people first truly learn the meaning when experience, generally of a painful kind, has made it a reality to them. How often, when smarting under some unforeseen misfortune or disappointment, does a person call to mind some proverb or common saying, familiar to him all his life, the meaning of which, if he had ever before felt it as he does now, would have saved him from the calamity. There are indeed reasons for this, other than the absence of discussion; there are many truths of which the full meaning *cannot* be realized until personal experience has brought it home. But much more of the meaning even of these would have been understood, and what was understood would have been far more deeply impressed on the mind, if the man had been accustomed to hear it argued *pro* and *con* by people who did understand it. The fatal tendency of mankind to leave off thinking about a thing when it is no longer doubtful, is the cause of half their errors. A contemporary author has well spoken of "the deep slumber of a decided opinion."

But what! (it may be asked) Is the absence of unanimity an indispensable condition of true knowledge? Is it necessary that some part of mankind should persist in error to enable any to realize the truth? Does a belief cease to be real and vital as soon as it is generally received; and is a proposition never thoroughly understood and felt unless some doubt of it remains? As soon as mankind have unanimously accepted a truth, does the truth perish within them? The highest aim and best result of improved intelligence, it has hitherto been thought, is to unite mankind more and more in the acknowledgment of all important truths; and does the intelligence only last as long as it has not achieved its object? Do the fruits of conquest perish by the very completeness of the victory?

I affirm no such thing. As mankind improve, the number of doctrines which are no longer disputed or doubted will be constantly on the increase: and the well-being of mankind may almost be measured by the number and gravity of the truths which have reached the point of being uncontested. The cessation, on one question after another, of serious controversy, is one of the necessary incidents of the consolidation of opinion; a consolidation as salutary in the case of true opinions, as it is dangerous and noxious when the opinions are erroneous. But though this gradual narrowing of the bounds of diversity of opinion is necessary in both senses of the term, being at once inevitable and indispensable, we are not therefore obliged to conclude that all its consequences must be beneficial. The loss of so important an aid to the intelligent and living apprehension of a truth, as is afforded by the necessity of explaining it to, or defending it against, opponents, though not sufficient to outweigh, is no trifling drawback from, the benefit of its universal recognition. Where this advantage can no longer be had, I confess I should like to see the teachers of mankind endeavoring to provide a substitute for it; some contrivance for making the difficulties of the question as present to the learner's consciousness, as if they were pressed upon him by a dissentient champion, eager for his conversion. . . .

It is the fashion of the present time to disparage negative logic—that which points out weaknesses in theory or errors in practice, without establishing positive truths. Such negative criticism would indeed be poor enough as an ultimate result; but as a means to attaining any positive knowledge or conviction worthy the name, it cannot be valued too highly; and until people are again systematically trained to it, there will be few great thinkers, and a low general average of intellect, in any but the mathematical and physical departments of speculation. On any other subject no one's opinions deserve the name of knowledge, except so far as he has either had forced upon him by others, or gone through of himself, the same mental process which would have been required of him in carrying on an active controversy with opponents. That, therefore, which when absent, it is so indispensable, but so difficult, to create, how worse than absurd it is to forego, when spontaneously offering itself! If there are any persons who contest a received opinion, or who will do so if law or opinion will let them, let us thank them for it, open our minds to listen to them, and rejoice that there is some one to do for us what we otherwise ought, if we have any regard for either the certainty or the vitality of our convictions, to do with much greater labor for ourselves.

It still remains to speak of one of the principal causes which make diversity of opinion advantageous, and will continue to do so until mankind shall have entered a stage of intellectual advancement which at present seems at an incalculable distance. We have hitherto considered only two possibilities: that the received opinion may be false, and some other opinion consequently true; or that, the received opinion being true, a conflict with the opposite error is essential to a clear apprehension and deep feeling of its truth. But there is a commoner case than either of these: when the conflicting doctrines, instead of being one true and the other false, share the truth between them; and the nonconforming opinion is needed to supply the remainder of the truth, of which the received doctrine embodies only a part. Popular opinions, on subjects not palpable to sense, are often true, but seldom or never the whole truth. They are a part of the truth; sometimes a greater, sometimes a smaller part, but exaggerated, distorted, and disjointed from the truths by which they ought to be accompanied and limited. Heretical opinions, on the other hand, are generally some of these suppressed and neglected truths, bursting the bonds which kept them down, and neither seeking reconciliation with the truth contained in the common opinion, or fronting it as enemies, and setting themselves up, with similar exclusiveness, as the whole truth. The latter case is hitherto the most frequent, as, in the human mind, one-sidedness has always been the rule, and many-sidedness the exception. Hence, even in revolutions of opinion, one part of the truth usually sets while another rises. Even progress, which ought to superadd, for the most part only substitutes, one partial and incomplete truth for another; improvement consisting chiefly in this, that the new fragment of truth is more wanted, more adapted to the needs of the time, than that which it displaces. Such being the partial character of prevailing opinions, even when resting on a true foundation, every opinion which embodies somewhat of the portion of truth which the common opinion omits, ought to be considered precious, with whatever amount of error and confusion that truth may be blended. No sober judge of human affairs will feel bound to be indignant because those who force on our notice truths which we should otherwise have overlooked, overlook some of those which we see. Rather, he will think that so long as popular truth is one-sided, it is more desirable than otherwise that un-

popular truth should have one-sided assertors too; such being usually the most energetic, and the most likely to compel reluctant attention to the fragment of wisdom which they proclaim as if it were the whole.

Thus, in the eighteenth century, when nearly all the instructed, and all those of the uninstructed who were led by them, were lost in admiration of what is called civilization, and of the marvels of modern science, literature, and philosophy, and while greatly overrating the amount of unlikeness between the men of modern and those of ancient times, indulged the belief that the whole of the difference was in their own favor; with what a salutary shock did the paradoxes of Rousseau explode like bombshells in the midst, dislocating the compact mass of one-sided opinion, and forcing its elements to recombine in a better form and with additional ingredients. Not that the current opinions were on the whole farther from the truth than Rousseau's were: on the contrary, they were nearer to it: they contained more of positive truth, and very much less of error. Nevertheless there lay in Rousseau's doctrine, and has floated down the stream of opinion along with it, a considerable amount of exactly those truths which the popular opinion wanted; and these are the deposit which was left behind when the flood subsided. The superior worth of simplicity of life, the enervating and demoralizing effect of the trammels and hypocrisies of artificial society, are ideas which have never been entirely absent from cultivated minds since Rousseau wrote; and they will in time produce their due effect, though at present needing to be asserted as much as ever, and to be asserted by deeds, for words, on this subject, have nearly exhausted their power.

In politics, again, it is almost a commonplace, that a party of order or stability, and a party of progress or reform, are both necessary elements of a healthy state of political life; until the one or the other shall have so enlarged its mental grasp as to be a party equally of order and of progress, knowing and distinguishing what is fit to be preserved from what ought to be swept away. Each of these modes of thinking derives its utility from the deficiencies of the other; but it is in a great measure the opposition of the other that keeps each within the limits of reason and sanity. Unless opinions favorable to democracy and to aristocracy, to property and to equality, to coöperation and to competition, to luxury and to abstinence, to sociality and individuality, to liberty and discipline, and all the other standing antagonisms of practical life, are expressed with equal freedom, and enforced and defended with equal talent and energy, there is no chance of both elements obtaining their due: one scale is sure to go up, and the other down. Truth, in the great practical concerns of life, is so much a question of the reconciling and combining of opposites, that very few have minds sufficiently capacious and impartial to make the adjustment with an approach to correctness, and it has to be made by the rough process of a struggle between combatants fighting under hostile banners. On any of the great open questions just enumerated, if either of the two opinions has a better claim than the other, not merely to be tolerated, but to be encouraged and countenanced, it is the one which happens at the particular time and place to be in a minority. That is the opinion which, for the time being, represents the neglected interests, the side of human well-being which is in danger of obtaining less than its share. I am aware that there is not, in this country, any intolerance of differences of opinion on most of these topics. They are adduced to show, by admitted and multiplied examples, the universality of the fact that only through diversity of opinion is there, in the existing state of human intellect, a chance of fair play to all sides of the truth. When there are persons to be found who form an exception to the apparent unanimity of the world on any subject, even if the world is in the right, it is always probable that dissentients have something worth hearing to say for themselves, and that truth would lose something by their silence. . . .

We have now recognized the necessity to the mental well-being of mankind (on which all their other well-being depends) of freedom of opinion, and freedom of the expression of opinion, on four distinct grounds; which we will now briefly recapitulate.

First, if any opinion is compelled to silence, that opinion may, for aught we can certainly know, be true. To deny this is to assume our own infallibility.

Secondly, though the silenced opinion be an error, it may, and very commonly does, contain a portion of truth; and since the general or prevailing opinion on any subject is rarely or never the whole truth, it is only by the collision of adverse opinions that the remainder of the truth has any chance of being supplied.

Thirdly, even if the received opinion be not only true, but the whole truth; unless it is suffered to be, and actually is, vigorously and earnestly contested, it will, by most of those who receive it, be held in the manner of a prejudice, with little comprehension or feeling of its rational grounds. And not only this, but, fourthly, the meaning of the doctrine itself will be in danger of being lost, or enfeebled, and deprived of its vital effect on the character and conduct: the dogma becoming a mere formal profession, inefficacious for good, but cumbering the ground, and preventing the growth of any real and heartfelt conviction, from reason or personal experience. . . .

CHAPTER III

Of Individuality, as One of the Elements of Well-being

Such being the reasons which make it imperative that human beings should be free to form opinions, and to express their opinions without reserve; and such the baneful consequences to the intellectual, and through that to the moral nature of man, unless this liberty is either conceded, or asserted in spite of prohibition; let us next examine whether the same reasons do not require that men should be free to act upon their opinions—to carry these out in their lives, without hindrance, either physical or moral, from their fellow-men, so long as it is at their own risk and peril. This last proviso is of course indispensable. No one pretends that actions should be as free as opinions. On the contrary, even opinions lose their immunity when the circumstances in which they are expressed are such as to constitute their expression a positive instigation to some mischievous act. An opinion that corn-dealers are starvers of the poor, or that private property is robbery, ought to be unmolested when simply circulated through the press, but may justly incur punishment when delivered orally to an excited mob assembled before the house of a corn-dealer, or when handed about among the same mob in the form of a placard. Acts, of whatever kind, which without justifiable cause do harm to others, may be, and in the more important cases absolutely require to be, controlled by the unfavorable sentiments, and, when needful, by the active interference of man-

kind. The liberty of the individual must be thus far limited; he must not make himself a nuisance to other people. But if he refrains from molesting others in what concerns them, and merely acts according to his own inclination and judgment in things which concern himself, the same reasons which show that opinion should be free, prove also that he should be allowed, without molestation, to carry his opinions into practice at his own cost. That mankind are not infallible; that their truths, for the most part, are only half-truths; that unity of opinion, unless resulting from the fullest and freest comparison of opposite opinions, is not desirable, and diversity not an evil, but a good, until mankind are much more capable than at present of recognizing all sides of the truth, are principles applicable to men's modes of action, not less than to their opinions. As it is useful that while mankind are imperfect there should be different opinions, so it is that there should be different experiments of living; that free scope should be given to varieties of character, short of injury to others; and that the worth of different modes of life should be proved practically, when any one thinks fit to try them. It is desirable, in short, that in things which do not primarily concern others, individuality should assert itself. Where not the person's own character, but the traditions or customs of other people are the rule of conduct, there is wanting one of the principal ingredients of human happiness, and quite the chief ingredient of individual and social progress.

In maintaining this principle, the greatest difficulty to be encountered does not lie in the appreciation of means toward an acknowledged end, but in the indifference of persons in general to the end in itself. If it were felt that the free development of individuality is one of the leading essentials of well-being; that it is not only a coördinate element with all that is designated by the terms civilization, instruction, education, culture, but is itself a necessary part and condition of all those things; there would be no danger that liberty should be undervalued, and the adjustment of the boundaries between it and social control would present no extraordinary difficulty. But the evil is, that individual spontaneity is hardly recognized by the common modes of thinking as having any intrinsic worth, or deserving any regard on its own account. The majority, being satisfied with the ways of mankind as they now are (for it is they who make them what they are), cannot comprehend why those ways should not be good enough for everybody; and what is more, spontaneity forms no part of the ideal of the majority of moral and social reformers, but is rather looked on with jealousy, as a troublesome and perhaps rebellious obstruction to the general acceptance of what these reformers, in their own judgment, think would be best for mankind. Few persons, out of Germany, even comprehend the meaning of the doctrine which Wilhelm von Humboldt, so eminent both as a *savant* and as a politician, made the text of a treatise—that "the end of man, or that which is prescribed by the eternal or immutable dictates of reason, and not suggested by vague and transient desires, is the highest and most harmonious development of his powers to a complete and consistent whole"; that, therefore, the object "towards which every human being must ceaselessly direct his efforts, and on which especially those who design to influence their fellow-men must ever keep their eyes, is the individuality of power and development"; that for this there are two requisites, "freedom, and variety of situations"; and that from the union of these arise

"individual vigor and manifold diversity," which combine themselves in "originality." [1]

Little, however, as people are accustomed to a doctrine like that of Von Humboldt, and surprising as it may be to them to find so high a value attached to individuality, the question, one must nevertheless think, can only be one of degree. No one's idea of excellence in conduct is that people should do absolutely nothing but copy one another. No one would assert that people ought not to put into their mode of life, and into the conduct of their concerns, any impress whatever of their own judgment, or of their own individual character. On the other hand, it would be absurd to pretend that people ought to live as if nothing whatever had been known in the world before they came into it; as if experience had as yet done nothing toward showing that one mode of existence, or of conduct, is preferable to another. Nobody denies that people should be so taught and trained in youth as to know and benefit by the ascertained results of human experience. But it is the privilege and proper condition of a human being, arrived at the maturity of his faculties, to use and interpret experience in his own way. It is for him to find out what part of recorded experience is properly applicable to his own circumstances and character. The traditions and customs of other people are, to a certain extent, evidence of what their experience has taught *them:* presumptive evidence, and as such, have a claim to his deference. But in the first place, their experience may be too narrow, or they may not have interpreted it rightly. Secondly, their interpretation of experience may be correct, but unsuitable to him. Customs

[1] *The Sphere and Duties of Government,* from the German of Baron Wilhelm von Humboldt, pp. 11–13.

are made for customary circumstances and customary characters, and his circumstances or his character may be uncustomary. Thirdly, though the customs be both good as customs, and suitable to him, yet to conform to custom, merely *as* custom, does not educate or develop in him any of the qualities which are the distinctive endowment of a human being. The human faculties of perception, judgment, discriminative feeling, mental activity, and even moral preference, are exercised only in making a choice. He who does anything because it is the custom makes no choice. He gains no practice either in discerning or in desiring what is best. The mental and moral, like the muscular powers, are improved only by being used. The faculties are called into no exercise by doing a thing merely because others do it, no more than by believing a thing only because others believe it. If the grounds of an opinion are not conclusive to the person's own reason, his reason cannot be strengthened, but is likely to be weakened, by his adopting it; and if the inducements to an act are not such as are consentaneous to his own feelings and character (where affection, or the rights of others, are not concerned) it is so much done toward rendering his feelings and character inert and torpid, instead of active and energetic.

He who lets the world, or his own portion of it, choose his plan of life for him, has no need of any other faculty than the ape-like one of imitation. He who chooses his plan for himself, employs all his faculties. He must use observation to see, reasoning and judgment to foresee, activity to gather materials for decision, discrimination to decide, and when he has decided, firmness and self-control to hold to his deliberate decision. And these qualities he requires and exercises exactly in proportion as the part of his conduct which he

determines according to his own judgment and feelings is a large one. It is possible that he might be guided in some good path, and kept out of harm's way, without any of these things. But what will be his comparative worth as a human being? It really is of importance, not only what men do, but also what manner of men they are that do it. Among the works of man which human life is rightly employed in perfecting and beautifying, the first in importance surely is man himself. Supposing it were possible to get houses built, corn grown, battles fought, causes tried, and even churches erected and prayers said, by machinery—by automatons in human form —it would be a considerable loss to exchange for these automatons even the men and women who at present inhabit the more civilized parts of the world, and who assuredly are but starved specimens of what nature can and will produce. Human nature is not a machine to be built after a model, and set to do exactly the work prescribed for it, but a tree, which requires to grow and develop itself on all sides, according to the tendency of the inward forces which make it a living thing.

It will probably be conceded that it is desirable people shall exercise their understandings, and that an intelligent following of custom, or even occasionally an intelligent deviation from custom, is better than a blind and simply mechanical adhesion to it. To a certain extent it is admitted that our understanding should be our own: but there is not the same willingness to admit that our desires and impulses should be our own likewise; or that to possess impulses of our own, and of any strength, is anything but a peril and a snare. Yet desires and impulses are as much a part of a perfect human being as beliefs and restraints; and strong impulses are only perilous when not properly balanced—when one set of aims and inclinations is developed into strength, while others, which ought to coexist with them, remain weak and inactive. It is not because men's desires are strong that they act ill; it is because their consciences are weak. There is no natural connection between strong impulses and a weak conscience. The natural connection is the other way. To say that one person's desires and feelings are stronger and more various than those of another, is merely to say that he has more of the raw material of human nature, and is therefore capable, perhaps of more evil, but certainly of more good. Strong impulses are but another name for energy. Energy may be turned to bad uses; but more good may always be made of an energetic nature than of an indolent and impassive one. Those who have most natural feeling are always those whose cultivated feelings may be made the strongest. The same strong susceptibilities which make the personal impulses vivid and powerful, are also the source from whence are generated the most passionate love of virtue, and the sternest self-control. It is through the cultivation of these that society both does its duty and protects its interests; not by rejecting the stuff of which heroes are made because it knows not how to make them. A person whose desires and impulses are his own—are the expression of his own nature, as it has been developed and modified by his own culture—is said to have a character. One whose desires and impulses are not his own, has no character, no more than a steam-engine has a character. If, in addition to being his own, his impulses are strong, and are under the government of a strong will, he has an energetic character. Whoever thinks that individuality of desires and impulses should not be encouraged to unfold itself, must maintain that society has no need of strong natures—is

not the better for containing many persons who have much character—and that a high general average of energy is not desirable. . . .

It is not by wearing down into uniformity all that is individual in themselves, but by cultivating it, and calling it forth, within the limits imposed by the rights and interests of others, that human beings become a noble and beautiful object of contemplation; and as the works partake the character of those who do them, by the same process human life also becomes rich, diversified, and animating, furnishing more abundant aliment to high thoughts and elevating feelings, and strengthening the tie which binds every individual to the race, by making the race infinitely better worth belonging to. In proportion to the development of his individuality, each person becomes more valuable to himself, and is therefore capable of being more valuable to others. There is a greater fullness of life about his own existence, and when there is more life in the units there is more in the mass which is composed of them. As much compression as is necessary to prevent the stronger specimens of human nature from encroaching on the rights of others cannot be dispensed with; but for this there is ample compensation even in the point of view of human development. The means of development which the individual loses by being prevented from gratifying his inclinations to the injury of others, are chiefly obtained at the expense of the development of other people. And even to himself there is a full equivalent in the better development of the social part of his nature, rendered possible by the restraint put upon the selfish part. To be held to rigid rules of justice for the sake of others, develops the feelings and capacities which have the good of others for their object. But to be restrained in things not affecting their good, by their mere displeasure, develops nothing valuable, except such force of character as may unfold itself in resisting the restraint. If acquiesced in, it dulls and blunts the whole nature. To give any fair play to the nature of each, it is essential that different persons should be allowed to lead different lives. In proportion as this latitude has been exercised in any age, has that age been noteworthy to posterity. Even despotism does not produce its worst effects, so long as individuality exists under it; and whatever crushes individuality is despotism, by whatever name it may be called, and whether it professes to be enforcing the will of God or the injunctions of men.

Having said that the individuality is the same thing with development, and that it is only the cultivation of individuality which produces, or can produce, well-developed human beings, I might here close the argument: for what more or better can be said of any condition of human affairs than that it brings human beings themselves nearer to the best thing they can be? or what worse can be said of any obstruction to good than that it prevents this? Doubtless, however, these considerations will not suffice to convince those who most need convincing; and it is necessary further to show that these developed human beings are of some use to the undeveloped—to point out to those who do not desire liberty, and would not avail themselves of it, that they may be in some intelligible manner rewarded for allowing other people to make use of it without hindrance.

In the first place, then, I would suggest that they might possibly learn something from them. It will not be denied by anybody that originality is a valuable element in human affairs. There is always need of persons not only to discover new truths, and point out when what were once truths are true no longer, but also to commence new practices, and set the example of more enlightened conduct, and better taste and sense in human life. This cannot well be gainsaid by anybody who does not believe that the world has already attained perfection in all its ways and practices. It is true that this benefit is not capable of being rendered by everybody alike: there are but few persons, in comparison with the whole of mankind, whose experiments, if adopted by others, would be likely to be any improvement on established practice. But these few are the salt of the earth; without them, human life would become a stagnant pool. Not only is it they who introduce good things which did not before exist; it is they who keep the life in those which already exist. If there were nothing new to be done, would human intellect cease to be necessary? Would it be a reason why those who do the old things should forget why they are done, and do them like cattle, not like human beings? There is only too great a tendency in the best beliefs and practices to degenerate into the mechanical; and unless there were a succession of persons whose everrecurring originality prevents the grounds of those beliefs and practices from becoming merely traditional, such dead matter would not resist the smallest shock from anything really alive, and there would be no reason why civilization should not die out, as in the Byzantine Empire. Persons of genius, it is true, are, and are always likely to be, a small minority; but in order to have them, it is necessary to preserve the soil in which they grow. Genius can only breathe freely in an *atmosphere* of freedom. Persons of genius are, *ex vi termini* [by the force of the phraseology], more individual than any other people—

less capable, consequently, of fitting themselves, without hurtful compression, into any of the small number of molds which society provides in order to save its members the trouble of forming their own character. If from timidity they consent to be forced into one of these molds, and to let all that part of themselves which cannot expand under the pressure remain unexpanded, society will be little the better for their genius. If they are of a strong character, and break their fetters, they become a mark for the society which has not succeeded in reducing them to commonplace, to point out with solemn warning as "wild," "erratic," and the like; much as if one should complain of the Niagara river for not flowing smoothly between its banks like a Dutch canal.

I insist thus emphatically on the importance of genius, and the necessity of allowing it to unfold itself freely both in thought and in practice, being well aware that no one will deny the position in theory, but knowing also that almost everyone, in reality, is totally indifferent to it. People think genius a fine thing if it enables a man to write an exciting poem, or paint a picture. But in its true sense, that of originality in thought and action, though no one says that it is not a thing to be admired, nearly all, at heart, think that they can do very well without it. Unhappily this is too natural to be wondered at. Originality is the one thing which unoriginal minds cannot feel the use of. They cannot see what it is to do for them: how should they? If they could see what it would do for them, it would not be originality. The first service which originality has to render them, is that of opening their eyes: which being once fully done, they would have a chance of being themselves original. Meanwhile, recollecting that nothing was ever yet done which

someone was not the first to do, and that all good things which exist are the fruits of originality, let them be modest enough to believe that there is something still left for it to accomplish, and assure themselves that they are more in need of originality, the less they are conscious of the want.

In sober truth, whatever homage may be professed, or even paid, to real or supposed mental superiority, the general tendency of things throughout the world is to render mediocrity the ascendant power among mankind. In ancient history, in the Middle Ages, and in a diminishing degree through the long transition from feudality to the present time, the individual was a power in himself; and if he had either great talents or a high social position, he was a considerable power. At present individuals are lost in the crowd. In politics it is almost a triviality to say that public opinion now rules the world. The only power deserving the name is that of masses, and of governments while they make themselves the organ of the tendencies and instincts of masses. This is as true in the moral and social relations of private life as in public transactions. Those whose opinions go by the name of public opinion are not always the same sort of public: in America they are the whole white population; in England, chiefly the middle class. But they are always a mass, that is to say, collective mediocrity. And what is a still greater novelty, the mass do not now take their opinions from dignitaries in Church or State, from ostensible leaders, or from books. Their thinking is done for them by men much like themselves, addressing them or speaking in their name, on the spur of the moment, through the newspapers. I am not complaining of all this. I do not assert that anything better is compatible, as a general rule, with the present low state of the human mind. But that does not hinder the government of mediocrity from being mediocre government. No government by a democracy or a numerous aristocracy, either in its political acts or in the opinions, qualities, and tone of mind which it fosters, ever did or could rise above mediocrity, except in so far as the sovereign Many have let themselves be guided (which in their best times they always have done) by the counsels and influence of a more highly gifted and instructed One or Few. The initiation of all wise or noble things comes and must come from individuals; generally at first from some one individual. The honor and glory of the average man is that he is capable of following that initiative; that he can respond internally to wise and noble things, and be led to them with his eyes open. I am not countenancing the sort of "hero-worship" which applauds the strong man of genius for forcibly seizing on the government of the world and making it do his bidding in spite of itself. All he can claim is, freedom to point out the way. The power of compelling others into it is not only inconsistent with the freedom and development of all the rest, but corrupting to the strong man himself. It does seem, however, that when the opinions of masses of merely average men are everywhere become or becoming the dominant power, the counterpoise and corrective to that tendency would be the more and more pronounced individuality of those who stand on the higher eminences of thought. It is in these circumstances most especially, that exceptional individuals, instead of being deterred, should be encouraged in acting differently from the mass. In other times there was no advantage in their doing so, unless they acted not only differently but better. In this age, the mere example of nonconformity, the mere refusal

to bend the knee to custom, is itself a service. Precisely because the tyranny of opinion is such as to make eccentricity a reproach, it is desirable, in order to break through that tyranny, that people should be eccentric. Eccentricity has always abounded when and where strength of character has abounded; and the amount of eccentricity in a society has generally been proportional to the amount of genius, mental vigor, and moral courage it contained. That so few now dare to be eccentric marks the chief danger of the time.

I have said that it is important to give the freest scope possible to uncustomary things, in order that it may in time appear which of these are fit to be converted into customs. But independence of action, and disregard of custom, are not solely deserving of encouragement for the chance they afford that better modes of action, and customs more worthy of general adoption, may be struck out; nor is it only persons of decided mental superiority who have a just claim to carry on their lives in their own way. There is no reason that all human existence should be constructed on some one or some small number of patterns. If a person possesses any tolerable amount of common sense and experience, his own mode of laying out his existence is the best, not because it is the best in itself, but because it is his own mode. Human beings are not like sheep; and even sheep are not undistinguishably alike. A man cannot get a coat or a pair of boots to fit him unless they are either made to his measure, or he has a whole warehouseful to choose from: and is it easier to fit him with a life than with a coat, or are human beings more like one another in their whole physical and spiritual conformation than in the shape of their feet? If it were only that people have diversities of taste, that is reason enough for not attempting to shape them all after one model. But different persons also require different conditions for their spiritual development; and can no more exist healthily in the same moral, than all the variety of plants can in the same physical, atmosphere and climate. The same things which are helps to one person towards the cultivation of his higher nature are hindrances to another. The same mode of life is a healthy excitement to one, keeping all his faculties of action and enjoyment in their best order, while to another it is a distracting burthen, which suspends or crushes all internal life. Such are the differences among human beings in their sources of pleasure, their susceptibilities of pain, and the operation on them of different physical and moral agencies, that unless there is a corresponding diversity in their modes of life, they neither obtain their fair share of happiness, nor grow up to the mental, moral, and æsthetic stature of which their nature is capable. . . .

There is one characteristic of the present direction of public opinion peculiarly calculated to make it intolerant of any marked demonstration of individuality. The general average of mankind are not only moderate in intellect, but also moderate in inclinations: they have no tastes or wishes strong enough to incline them to do anything unusual, and they consequently do not understand those who have, and class all such with the wild and intemperate whom they are accustomed to look down upon. Now, in addition to this fact which is general, we have only to suppose that a strong movement has set in towards the improvement of morals, and it is evident what we have to expect. In these days such a movement has set in; much has actually been effected in the way of increased regularity of conduct and discouragement of excesses; and there is a philanthropic spirit abroad, for the exercise of which there is no more inviting field than the moral and prudential improvement of our fellow-creatures. These tendencies of the times cause the public to be more disposed than at most former periods to prescribe general rules of conduct, and endeavor to make every one conform to the approved standard. And that standard, express or tacit, is to desire nothing strongly. Its ideal of character is to be without any marked character; to maim by compression, like a Chinese lady's foot, every part of human nature which stands out prominently, and tends to make the person markedly dissimilar in outline to commonplace humanity.

As is usually the case with ideals which exclude one-half of what is desirable, the present standard of approbation produces only an inferior imitation of the other half. Instead of great energies guided by vigorous reason, and strong feelings strongly controlled by a conscientious will, its result is weak feelings and weak energies, which therefore can be kept in outward conformity to rule without any strength either of will or of reason. Already energetic characters on any large scale are becoming merely traditional. There is now scarcely any outlet for energy in this country except business. The energy expended in this may still be regarded as considerable. What little is left from that employment is expended on some hobby; which may be a useful, even a philanthropic hobby, but is always some one thing, and generally a thing of small dimensions. The greatness of England is now all collective; individually small, we only appear capable of anything great by our habit of combining; and with this our moral and religious philanthropists are perfectly contented. But it was men of another stamp than this that made England what it has been; and men of another stamp will be needed to prevent its decline.

The despotism of custom is everywhere the standing hindrance to human advancement, being in unceasing antagonism to that disposition to aim at something better than customary, which is called, according to circumstances, the spirit of liberty, or that of progress or improvement. The spirit of improvement is not always a spirit of liberty, for it may aim at forcing improvements on an unwilling people; and the spirit of liberty, in so far as it resists such attempts, may ally itself locally and temporarily with the opponents of improvement; but the only unfailing and permanent source of improvement is liberty, since by it there are as many possible independent centers of improvement as there are individuals. The progressive principle, however, in either shape, whether as the love of liberty or of improvement, is antagonistic to the sway of custom, involving at least emancipation from that yoke; and the contest between the two constitutes the chief interest of the history of mankind. . . .

What has made the European family of nations an improving, instead of a stationary portion of mankind? Not any superior excellence in them, which, when it exists, exists as the effect not as the cause; but their remarkable diversity of character and culture. Individuals, classes, nations, have been extremely unlike one another: they have struck out a great variety of paths, each leading to something valuable; and although at every period those who traveled in different paths have been intolerant of one another, and each would have thought it an excellent thing if all the rest could have been compelled to travel his road, their attempts to thwart each other's development have rarely had any permanent success, and each has in time endured to receive the good which the others have offered. Europe is, in my judgment, wholly indebted to this plurality of paths for its progressive and many-sided development. But it already begins to possess this benefit in a considerably less degree. M. de Tocqueville, in his last important work, remarks how much more the Frenchmen of the present day resemble one another than did those even of the last generation. The same remark might be made of Englishmen in a far greater degree. In a passage already quoted from Wilhelm von Humboldt, he points out two things as necessary conditions of human development, because necessary to render people unlike one another: namely, freedom, and variety of situations. The second of these two conditions is in this country every day diminishing. The circumstances which surround different classes and individuals, and shape their characters, are daily becoming more assimilated. Formerly, different ranks, different neighborhoods, different trades and professions, lived in what might be called different worlds; at present to a great degree in the same. Comparatively speaking, they now read the same things, listen to the same things, see the same things, go to the same places, have their hopes and fears directed to the same objects, have the same rights and liberties, and the same means of asserting them. Great as are the differences of position which remain, they are nothing to those which have ceased. And the assimilation is still proceeding. All the political changes of the age promote it, since they all tend to raise the low and to lower the high. Every extension of education promotes it, because education brings people under common influences, and gives them access to the general stock of facts and sentiments. Improvement in the means of communication promotes it, by bringing the inhabitants of distant places into personal contact, and keeping up a rapid flow of changes of residence between one place and another. The increase of commerce and manufactures promotes it, by diffusing more widely the advantages of easy circumstances, and opening all objects of ambition, even the highest, to general competition, whereby the desire of rising becomes no longer the character of a particular class, but of all classes. A more powerful agency than even all these, in bringing about a general similarity among mankind, is the complete establishment, in this and other free countries, of the ascendancy of public opinion in the State. As the various social eminences which enabled persons entrenched on them to disregard the opinion of the multitude gradually become leveled; as the very idea of resisting the will of the public, when it is positively known that they have a will, disappears more and more from the minds of practical politicians: there ceases to be any social support for nonconformity—any substantive power in society which, itself opposed to the ascendancy of numbers, is interested in taking under its protection opinions and tendencies at variance with those of the public.

The combination of all these causes forms so great a mass of influences hostile to individuality, that it is not easy to see how it can stand its ground. It will do so with increasing difficulty, unless the intelligent part of the public can be made to feel its value—to see that it is good there should be differences, even though not for the better, even though, as it may appear to them, some should be for the worse. If the claims of individuality are ever to be asserted, the time is now, while much is still wanting to complete the enforced assimilation. It is only in the earlier stages that any stand can be successfully made against the encroachment. The demand that all other people shall resemble ourselves grows by what it feeds on. If resistance waits till life is reduced *nearly* to one uniform type, all deviations from that type will come to be considered impious, immoral, even monstrous and contrary to nature. Mankind speedily become unable to conceive diversity, when they have been for some time unaccustomed to see it.

COMMENT

The Basis of Mill's Argument

The older liberals, especially Locke and Jefferson, espoused liberty as an inalienable natural right. Mill, in contrast, avowedly based his argument upon "utility, in the largest sense." Progress, he maintained, is desirable for human welfare, and free thought and action are necessary for that end. The ultimate standard for judging social institutions is their contribution to happiness. Mill thus began by running up the banner of utilitarianism.

The real premise of his argument, however, is not the calculation of pleasure and pain but the inner value of character and unhampered individuality. In Chapter III of *On Liberty*, he mentions with approval the doctrine of "self-realization" advocated by Wilhelm von Humboldt. "The end of man," according to this German writer, "is the highest and most harmonious development of his powers to a complete and consistent whole," and for this there are two requisites, "freedom and variety of situations." This theory of self-realization is the focus of Mill's teaching. It underlies his decided preference for highly developed individuals rather than "ape-like imitators." Liberty enables a man to be a man—to attain the full use and development of his powers. To live freely is to unfold one's individual human capacities; to live servilely—by custom, imitation, social pressure, or repressive political rule—is to be less than a man. Liberty is the acknowledgment of the peculiar dignity of man as man—and of *each* man in his matchless individuality. There is slight trace in this essay of the earlier teaching of the Utilitarians that it does not matter what men are like provided that they have as much pleasure and as little pain as possible.

Mill had become convinced that the modern enemy of liberty is the tyranny of the majority. No longer is the problem that of overthrowing a tyrannical king or the oligarchy of a few. It is the much more difficult problem of freeing dissident individuals and minorities from the pressure of a mass-society. Mill had been shocked by Alexis de Tocqueville's classic study, *Democracy in America* (1835–1840), which maintained that the ultimate triumph of democracy is inevitable and that its tendency is to reduce all men to a level of equal mediocrity. Sharing de Tocqueville's alarm, Mill believed that a truly liberal society must be created as a safeguard against mass illiberalism. Such a society would be deeply respectful of human freedom. His argument, therefore, is primarily a defense of individuality against the conventionalities of society, the despotism of social custom, and the overweening powers of government.

Kinds of Freedom

The liberties that Mill believed to be most important are the freedoms of thought, of expression, of association, and of action.

1. *Freedom of thought.* Freedom of thought requires that every man feel free to think independently. He must not be afraid of "dangerous thoughts" or intellectually subservient to the powers-that-be. To objections that man has a duty to the community, Mill would reply that this duty can be fulfilled not by enforced or credulous orthodoxy but only by free inquiry and the loyalty of a critical mind.

Freedom of thought implies the right to privacy in one's opinions—the right not to be hostilely interrogated by one's neighbors, by state authorities, or by other agencies, such as the Church. The state should be used to protect the individual or minorities against the multitude rather than as a repressive or inquisitorial body. Also, the *mores* of the populace should be changed by education, so that people will become more tolerant. To attain full mental freedom, we must not merely tolerate but enjoy and cultivate our intellectual differences.

2. *Freedom of expression.* Freedom of thought, as Mill remarked, is practically inseparable from freedom of expression. No man can possibly feel free in his thoughts if he does not dare to express them. There is no liberty of thought if facts are withheld, if censorship or propaganda is substituted for open debate, and if there is no opportunity to explore controversial issues without fear of penalties. The most effective way of enslaving the human mind is to control the stimuli to thought.

Mill's plea for free expression—the liberty of speech, press, and publishing—speaks eloquently for itself: there is no need to summarize it here. If summary be required, his own words serve very well:

> The peculiar error of silencing the expression of an opinion is that it is robbing the human race; posterity as well as the existing generation; those who dissent from the opinion, still more than those who hold it. If the opinion is right, they are deprived of the opportunity of exchanging error for truth: if wrong, they lose, what is almost as great a benefit, the clear perception and livelier impression of truth, produced by its collision with error.

This position is supported by detailed arguments which the reader should ferret out for himself.

3. *Freedom of association.* Freedom of association involves the right of human beings to associate with whom they please and to join such organizations as they prefer. It is not discussed in detail in *On Liberty* but it is taken up in other works of Mill. In *The Subjection of Women,* he protests against the tendency of males to tyrannize over females and to limit the political and social associations of women. In *Representative Government,* he argues that a people can express themselves adequately only when minorities have a right to associate and, as minority groups, to discuss the pros and cons of social policy. He deplores the tendency of political parties to force out independents and wishes to make it relatively easy for a political minority to air its views and to win the status of a majority. In *The Principles of Political Economy,* he defends the right of workers to form trade unions and applauds the spontaneous organization of workers' and consumers' cooperatives. Even in *On Liberty,* his argument for the freedom of individuals applies, by implication, to any body of individuals who unite, by free choice, for some end or purpose.

His position, however, would have been strengthened if he had more explicitly defended the freedom of association in *On Liberty.* The tyranny of public opinion is weakened if there is a rich variety of associations and if the state has many formidable rivals. Human beings, moreover, are social creatures, and their free development requires many and varied ties. Mill overemphasizes the individual and underemphasizes the autonomous organization.

4. *Freedom of action.* Mill defends the "liberty of tastes and pursuits; of

framing the plan of our life to suit our own character; of doing as we like
. . . without impediment from our fellow-creatures, so long as what we do
does not harm them, even though they should think our conduct foolish, perverse, or wrong." Human beings are more valuable to themselves and to
others if they fully and freely develop their own natures. They must therefore be protected against the fear of being different.

Mill points out the importance of distinguishing between speech and action,
allowing more liberty to the former than to the latter. He is prepared to
tolerate almost unlimited discussion so long as it does not directly incite to
seditious or criminal activity. Only by the collision between opinions, he
argues, will the whole truth be brought out; and without controversy, even a
true doctrine degenerates into a lifeless dogma. But overt action, as distinguished from advocacy, requires more social control. If others in addition to
the agent are primarily affected by the action, society has the right and perhaps the duty to interfere. Even so, Mill advocates great forbearance, on the
ground that variety and experimentation are, in general, far more conducive
to progress than conformity.

Individualistic and Social Conceptions of Liberty

Mill's treatise *On Liberty* was begun as an essay in 1854 and was published
as a book in 1859. During the remainder of his life, his thinking on the subject of liberty gradually took on a more social emphasis. He recognized increasingly that poverty and private economic tyranny enormously limit freedom, and that genuine freedom involves more than the right to be left alone.
In *Utilitarianism* (1863), he pointed out that there is a great deal of unnecessary squalor. In his *Autobiography* (1873), the last edition of *Political Economy,* and *Socialism* (published after his death), he moved far in the direction
of a liberal socialism, expressing the belief that society should take vigorous
steps to provide universal education, remove the inequities of wealth, and
raise the living standards of the poorer classes. But he still saw great danger
in centralizing power in government and favored a diversified social system
with ample opportunity for nonconformity. In these later works, he was feeling his way toward a broader social philosophy.

The main limitation of his argument in *On Liberty* was his excessive individualism. He was still under the strong influence of the older liberal idea that
man is born free but has enslaved himself in a network of social relations—
that freedom will be regained by striking off the ties and coercions of society.
Among the many thinkers who expressed this negative, individualistic conception of liberty were James Mill, father of John Stuart, and Jeremy Bentham, an intimate friend of the family. "Every law is contrary to liberty,"
Bentham baldly stated, and "all government is only a tissue of sacrifices." [1]

[1] *Works* (Edinburgh, 1843), I, pp. 301, 313.

James Mill's ideas about liberty and government differed in no essential respect from those of Bentham: his basic premise is that if each man intelligently seeks his own interests, the greatest happiness for the greatest number will result. John Stuart Mill was thoroughly indoctrinated in these ideas and found it difficult to break away from them. In *On Liberty,* he was intent upon defending the individual in his independence, even in his eccentricity, as against government, public opinion, and "collective mediocrity."

This individualistic doctrine, which stemmed from Locke and earlier thinkers, was extremely valuable as a protest against feudal and monarchical fetters, as support to a rising capitalistic order, and as a basis for asserting the civil rights of the individual; but as a theory of liberty it is inadequate. It does not sufficiently take into account the difference between *being allowed* and *being able,* a distinction essential to Mill's own purpose. "Being allowed" implies the *absence* of external restraint—and this negative condition of freedom Mill and his predecessors emphasized. But "being able" implies the *presence* of opportunity and adequate resources—and these positive conditions, such as education, health, economic security, and an adequate supply of tools and resources, were insufficiently recognized by the traditional liberals. No man is really free if he lives in the kingdom of necessity—if he is insecure, hungry, diseased, ignorant, or consumed with hate and prejudice. "Liberty" of the merely negative sort paradoxically leads to a very great constraint, since it leaves the bully free to subdue the weak and makes no provision for those positive goods without which freedom is chimerical.

The very conception of the individual as self-sufficient and self-regarding—the basis of the individualistic liberal theory—is false. "I am not my brother's keeper" is the cry of a murderer. Truer is the insight of John Donne: "No man is an Iland, intire to it selfe; every man is a peece of the Continent, a part of the maine. . . ." Mill, by the time he wrote *On Liberty,* had partly repudiated the "island theory" of individual personality, so prominent in the writings of Bentham. For example, he stated: "No person is an entirely isolated being; it is impossible for a person to do anything seriously or permanently hurtful to himself, without mischief reaching at least to his near connections, and often far beyond them." [2] Mill realized that the freedom of each must be limited by the like freedom of all; yet he continued to assert that "the only freedom which deserves the name is that of pursuing our own good in our own way." He had not fully grasped the extent of human interdependence and the fact that genuine freedom is to be found in self-transcendence and fraternity.

A positive and social conception of freedom is well expressed by another great Victorian social theorist, Thomas Hill Green (1836–1882), in the following characteristic passage:

[2] *On Liberty,* Chap. IV, fifth paragraph.

We shall probably all agree that freedom, rightly understood, is the greatest of blessings. . . . But when we thus speak of freedom, we should consider carefully what we mean by it. We do not mean merely freedom from restraint or compulsion. We do not mean merely freedom to do as we like irrespectively of what it is that we like. We do not mean a freedom that can be enjoyed by one man or one set of men at the cost of a loss of freedom to others. When we speak of freedom as something to be so highly prized, we mean a positive power or capacity of doing or enjoying something worth doing or enjoying, and that, too, something that we do or enjoy in common with others. We mean by it a power which each man exercises through the help or security given him by his fellow-men, and which he in turn helps to secure for them.[3]

Mill never fully attained to such an affirmative and social conception of freedom. His essay *On Liberty* represents a transition from Bentham's extreme individualism to the more social point of view expressed by Green.

But if his theory is too individualistic, this defect should not blind us to its great merits. Nowhere in English literature, unless it be in Milton's *Areopagitica,* can we find so eloquent a plea for free inquiry, courageous speech, and unintimidated action. In this age of fear and totalitarianism, when there have been so many forces even in democratic America to suppress the critical and creative mind, the ringing words of Mill are peculiarly relevant. He wrote for our age as few writers of the past have done.

[3] "Liberal Legislation and Freedom of Contract" (lecture), 1880.

21

Communism and Western Ideals

KARL MARX (1818–1883)

Born in Treves in the German Rhineland, Marx was the son of well-to-do
Jewish parents who had been converted to Christianity. He studied law, history, and philosophy at the Universities of Bonn and Berlin, imbibing the
doctrines of Hegel, then at the height of his fame. His Doctor's thesis was on
the materialism of Democritus and Epicurus. In 1842–1843, he edited a
newspaper at Cologne, which was suppressed by the Prussian government
because of its advanced ideas. After marrying Jennie von Westphalen, a
beautiful young woman of aristocratic lineage, he went to Paris, where he
studied the socialist movement. There he met Friedrich Engels, the German
manager of a textile factory in Manchester. On the basis of the socialist convictions which they shared, the two young men formed a friendship that
endured throughout their lives.

In 1845, the Prussian government, incensed by Marx's continued attacks,
persuaded the French authorities to deport him. He then went with Engels
to live in Brussels, where he continued his political and journalistic activities.
During this period he wrote, singly or in collaboration with Engels, a number
of socialist works, the most famous of which was the *Communist Manifesto,*
published on the eve of the revolutionary disturbances of 1848. Expelled in
turn from Belgium, Marx returned to Cologne, where he founded a radical
newspaper and participated in the revolutionary uprisings of 1848–1849. The
ensuing political reaction compelled him to seek refuge in England.

With his family, he spent the remainder of his life in London. There he
worked for years in the British Museum, accumulating the research materials
for his indictment of capitalist society. Having only a small income as a correspondent for the New York *Tribune,* he lived with his wife and children
in a squalid attic, often without sufficient food, decent clothing, or other basic
necessities. His later years were saddened by ill health and the death of several of his children, but nothing could divert him from unremitting service to

his ideals. In 1864, he helped to organize the First International, a radical political organization which continued under his direction until 1872. His major work was *Capital,* a detailed historical and economic analysis of capitalist society, which he referred to as "the task to which I have sacrificed my health, my happiness in life, and my family." Volume One was published in 1867 and the two remaining volumes after his death.

Judged by worldly standards, Marx's life would scarcely be called a success, but he became posthumously one of the chief makers of the modern world. The essay by Edward Hallett Carr gives an indication of Marx's enormous influence, and the Speech which immediately follows is a brief, pungent example of his revolutionary thought.

Speech at the Anniversary of the *People's Paper*[*]

The so-called Revolutions of 1848 were but poor incidents—small fractures and fissures in the dry crust of European society. However, they denounced the abyss. Beneath the apparently solid surface, they betrayed oceans of liquid matter, only needing expansion to rend into fragments continents of hard rock. Noisedly and confusedly they proclaimed the emancipation of the proletarian, *i.e.,* the secret of the nineteenth century, and of the revolution of that century. That social revolution, it is true, was no novelty invented in 1848. Steam, electricity, and the self-acting mule were revolutionists of a rather more dangerous character than even citizens Barbès, Raspail and Blanqui. But, although the atmosphere in which we live weighs upon everyone with a 20,000 pound force, do you feel it? No more than European society before 1848 felt the revolutionary atmosphere enveloping and pressing it from all sides.

There is one great fact, characteristic of this, our nineteenth century, a fact which no party dares deny. On the one hand, there have started into life industrial and scientific forces, which no epoch of the former human history had ever suspected. On the other hand, there exist symptoms of decay, far surpassing the horrors recorded of the latter times of the Roman empire. In our days everything seems pregnant with its contrary; machinery gifted with the wonderful power of shortening and fructifying human labor, we behold starving and overworking it. The new-fangled sources of wealth, by some strange weird spell, are turned into sources of want. The victories of art seem bought by the loss of character. At the same pace that mankind masters nature,

[*] Delivered by Marx at the anniversary celebration of the *People's Paper,* a Chartist organ, in April 1856.

man seems to become enslaved to other men or to his own infamy. Even the pure light of science seems unable to shine but on the dark background of ignorance. All our inventions and progress seem to result in endowing material forces with intellectual life, and in stultifying human life into a material force. This antagonism between modern industry and science on the one hand, modern misery and dissolution on the other hand; this antagonism between the productive powers and the social relations of our epoch, is a fact, palpable, overwhelming, and not to be controverted. Some parties may wail over it; others may wish to get rid of modern arts in order to get rid of modern conflicts. Or they may imagine that so signal a progress in industry wants to be completed by as signal a regress in politics.

On our part, we do not mistake the shape of the shrewd spirit that continues to mark all these contradictions. We know that to work well the new-fangled forces of society, they only want to be mastered by new-fangled men—and such are the working men. They are as much the invention of modern times as machinery itself. In the signs that bewilder the middle class, the aristocracy and the poor prophets of regression, we do recognize our brave friend, Robin Goodfellow, the old mole that can work in the earth so fast, that worthy pioneer—the revolution. The English working men are the first born sons of modern industry. They will then, certainly, not be the last in aiding the social revolution produced by that industry, a revolution, which means the emancipation of their own class all over the world, which is as universal as capital-rule and wages-slavery. I know the heroic struggles the English working class have gone through since the middle of the last century—struggles less glorious because they are shrouded in obscurity and burked by the middle class historians to revenge the misdeeds of the ruling class.

There existed in the middle ages in Germany a secret tribunal, called the "Vehmgericht." If a red cross was seen marked on a house people knew that its owner was doomed by the "Vehm." All the houses of Europe are now marked with the mysterious red cross. History is the judge—its executioner, the proletarian.

EDWARD HALLETT CARR (1892–   )

A graduate of Cambridge University, Carr was a member of the British Delegation to the Versailles Peace Conference (1919) and has held various positions in the Foreign Office, including that of Assistant Advisor on League of Nations Affairs and First Secretary. In 1936 he became Professor of International Politics at University College in Wales. In addition to his teaching, he has served as Director of Foreign Publicity in the British Ministry of Information and as a leader in the cultural activities of the United Nations. His numerous publications on international politics and Soviet theory have been widely read.

The Ideological Impact *

. . . Bolshevism, like Christianity or like any other doctrine which has made a powerful impact on the world, has two aspects: the destructive or revolutionary, and the constructive or positive. Broadly speaking the tendency in any great movement is for the revolutionary aspect to predominate in the earlier stages, the positive aspect in the later. Primitive Christianity was revolutionary until it had disrupted the old Roman civilization; then it created a new and positive world order of its own, and underwent a corresponding modification of its outlook. The Reformation began by being revolutionary and destructive, and ended by becoming the basis of a new social order. Bolshevism has passed, or is passing, through the same two phases; and both have had their impact on the western world. The revolutionary element of Marxist ideology may be considered under three heads—its materialism, its dialectical character, and its relativism.

Materialism, though its metaphysical implications are politically neutral, has been associated in modern times with the tradition of revolution. Materialism, combined with the absolute or static rationalism of the 18th century, was the philosophy of the French revolution. Materialism, combined with the dialectical and relativist rationalism of Hegel, gave birth to Marxism which provided the philosophical background of the Russian revolution. Revolutionary materialism was a revolt both against Christianity and against a metaphysical idealism which believed in spiritual values and pure ideas as the ultimate reality behind the material universe. Translated into political terms, it attacked the privileged classes by alleging that their preoccupation with men's souls masked a convenient and profitable neglect of the needs of men's bodies—when the men concerned belonged to the unprivileged class. Hence Marxism taught that the ultimate reality was material and, above all, economic.

Men make their own history [wrote Engels, summarizing the doctrine in the last year of his life], but in a given environment in which they live, upon the foundation of extant relations. Among these relations, economic relations, however great may be the influence exercised on them by other relations of a political and ideological order, are those whose action is ultimately decisive, forming a red thread which runs through all the other relations and enables us to understand them.

No one can doubt the enormously increased popularity and influence of such conceptions in the modern world. To improve the material standards of living of the masses is today a mission commanding the same kind of moral fervor as formerly went into the task of winning their souls. We have traveled far from primitive Christian conceptions of the wickedness of the material world and of the importance of avoiding and resisting its temptations. The social functions of the church have received a new and revolutionary emphasis. The kind of theology popular in the 19th century

* From *The Soviet Impact on the Western World,* Macmillan Company, New York, 1947. Reprinted by permission of Macmillan and Company, Ltd., London, and The Macmillan Company, New York.

which promised rewards hereafter as compensation for the sufferings of this world—what came to be derisively dubbed "pie in the sky"—fell into disrepute. Modern churchmen have been known to argue that the cure of men's souls cannot be successfully undertaken in isolation from the cure of their bodies; and a well-known free church weekly describes itself as a "Journal of Social and Christian Progress." In the academic sphere the immense expansion of economic studies in the last thirty years, and the corresponding decline of philosophy and the humanities, are minor signs of the times. Whether the result be attributed to the impact of Marxism, or of the Soviet Union, or to the rising political consciousness of the unprivileged class, or merely to the increasing stringency of material conditions, greater prominence is given in contemporary life and thought than ever before to the economic foundations of the social order.

The Marxist philosophy was not only materialistic, but dialectical. This character it derived from Hegel's dialectical idealism. According to this doctrine the world moves forward through a continuous interplay and conflict of ideas; one idea, or thesis, is contradicted and assailed by its antithesis, and out of this struggle comes not the victory either of thesis or of antithesis, but a new synthesis; the synthesis is thus established as a thesis, and the process of contradiction begins once more. This state of flux, or historical process, is the ultimate reality: it is also rational, since it is moving forward along certain lines which can be determined by rational investigation. This was what Hegel called the dialectic, and Marx, in substituting the conflict of classes and their material interest for the Hegelian conflict of ideas, preserved the rest of the Hegelian structure intact. Indeed the principles of conflict and flux oc-

cupy in the Marxist system a more central place than the materialism. Whether directly from Hegel, or through Marx, or through other channels, the dialectical conception has deeply penetrated western thought since the latter part of the 19th century. Among its symptoms are the belief in perpetual conflict substituted for the belief in a natural harmony of interests; the recognition that social phenomena are not static, but dynamic, and must be studied not as fixed states, but as processes; and the emphasis on history as the key to reality. In the 18th century, philosophy took over from religion the function of explaining the nature of reality. In the 19th century this role was passed on from philosophy to history.

Belief in the historical process, in never-ceasing flux, as the ultimate reality should logically preclude belief in any absolute outside it. The course of history being predetermined by laws of its own is an absolute in its own right, and all that man has to do is to conform to those laws and to help to fulfill them. Hegel, the real inventor of what came to be known to German philosophers as *Historismus,* preached that freedom consisted in the recognition and voluntary acceptance of necessity. This form of historical determinism is the basis of what may be called the "scientific" side of Marx's teaching: the contradictions of capitalism made socialism demonstrably inevitable. "When Marxists organize the communist party and lead it into battle," wrote Bukharin, "this action is also an expression of historical necessity which finds its form precisely through the will and the actions of men."[1] It has sometimes been suggested that to portray history as a chain of events developing one out of the other by an inevitable process is to deprive hu-

[1] N. Bukharin, *Historical Materialism* (English trans.), p. 51.

man beings of all incentive to action. This is good logic but poor psychology. Men like to work for a cause which they think certain to win; conversely, there is no surer way of sapping an adversary's morale than to persuade him that he is bound to lose. Marxism has derived an enormous accretion of strength from the belief that the realization of its predictions is historically inevitable. To have history on one's side is the modern equivalent of being on the side of the angels.

This belief in history is a fundamental tenet of Bolshevism. Both Lenin and Trotsky frequently personified—not to say, deified—history. "History will not forgive us," wrote Lenin on the eve of the Bolshevik revolution, "if we do not seize power now." What is right is to assist the historical process to develop along its predestined lines: what is wrong is to oppose or impede that process. The victory of the proletariat, being scientifically inevitable, is also morally right. The French revolutionaries had adopted the slogan *salus populi suprema lex* [the welfare of the people is the supreme law]; Plekhanov, the Russian Marxist, was logical and consistent when he translated this into *salus revolutiae* [sic] *suprema lex* [the welfare of the revolution is the supreme law].[2] The revolution was the fulfillment of the historical process: everything that aided history to fulfill itself was right. Ethics could have no other basis and no other meaning. Like other totalitarian philosophies and religions, Bolshevism inevitably tends to justify the means by the end. If the end is absolute, nothing that serves that end can be morally condemned.

The emphasis on history leads on to the third revolutionary element in Marxism, its relativism. The laws of nature are absolute

[2] G. V. Plekhanov, *Works*, XII (in Russian), pp. 418–19.

and timeless—or were until recently regarded as such. The laws of the social sciences are embedded in history and conditioned by it: what is true of one period is obviously not true of another. There is no such thing as democracy in the abstract: the nature of democracy depends on the historical development of the society in which it is established, and the application of the same formal rules will yield different results in different social environments. No laws of economics are universally true without regard to time or place. There are classical economics based on the broad presuppositions of *laissez-faire*, the economics of "imperfect competition" or monopoly capitalism, and the economics of socialism or the planned society; and different principles will apply to each. Conceptions like "freedom" and "justice" remain abstract and formal until we are able to place them in a concrete historical setting, and bring them to earth by answering the questions "freedom for whom, and from what" or "justice for whom and at whose expense." Not only every social or political institution, but every social and political idea changes with the historical context, or, more specifically, with changes in the relations of productive forces. Reality is never static, everything is relative to a given stage in the historical process.

This thorough-going relativism is ideologically the most destructive weapon in the Marxist armory. It can be used to dissolve all the absolute ideas on which the existing order seeks to base its moral superiority. Law is not law in the abstract, but a set of concrete rules enacted by an economically dominant class for the maintenance of its privileges and authority. *Bourgeois* law is largely concerned with the protection of the property rights of the *bourgeoisie:* "law and order," though good things in the abstract, become a traditional slogan by which those in possession seek to discredit strikers, revolutionaries and other rebels against the existing social order, however oppressive that order may be. Equality in the abstract is purely formal. "One man, one vote" does not ensure actual equality in a society where one voter may be a millionaire and another a pauper; even equality before the law may be a mockery when the law is framed and administered by the members of a privileged class. Freedom itself can be equally formal. Freedom to choose or refuse a job is unreal if freedom to refuse is merely tantamount to freedom to starve. Freedom of opinion is nullified if social or professional pressures render the holding of some opinions lucrative and expose the holders of other opinions to an economic boycott. Freedom of the press and of public meeting are illusory if the principal organs of the press and the principal meeting-places are, as is inevitable in capitalist society, controlled by the moneyed class. Thus the supposed absolute values of liberal democracy are undermined by the corrosive power of the Marxist critique: what was thought of as absolute turns out to be relative to a given social structure and to possess validity only as an adjunct to that structure. These views have made enormous headway in the last twenty-five years. To discuss history in constitutional terms, or in terms of a struggle for liberty, democracy or some other abstract ideal, is today almost as old-fashioned as to discuss it in terms of kings and battles. Under the impact of Marxism the study of history has everywhere been placed on sociological foundations. If the 18th century rationalists substituted philosophy for religion, and Hegel substituted history for philosophy, Marx carried the process one stage further by substituting sociology for history.

But the inroads of relativism go deeper still. If the institutional pattern of society and the ideals which animate it are conditioned by the material—or specifically by the economic—foundations on which the society rests, so also are the thought and action of its individual members. Marxism finally deprived the individual of his individuality and made him, first and foremost, the member of a class. What the individual *bourgeois* thought and believed and did was not—or at any rate not merely—the product of his own thinking and volition, but of the conditions imposed on him by his membership of the *bourgeoisie*. Relativism thus becomes the vehicle of a complete scepticism. It is the culmination—or, perhaps, the *reductio ad absurdum*—of the great movement of human thought initiated by Descartes, who made the thinking individual the fixed starting point of his system: *cogito ergo sum*. The achievement of the Enlightenment is thus brought to nought. "Dare to be wise! Dare to use your own intelligence! That is the motto of the Enlightenment." [3] But now human reason, having challenged and destroyed all other values, ends by turning the same weapons against itself. Individualism, having challenged and destroyed the authority of other sources of value and set up the individual judgment as the ultimate source, carries the argument to its logical conclusion and proves that this source also is tainted. The process of debunking is pursued to the point where the debunker is himself debunked. The reason of the individual can have no independent validity. His thinking is conditioned by his social situation, and that situation is in turn determined by the stage reached in the historical process.

This weapon can be wielded with devastating force. If pressed home, it would lead

[3] Kant, *Werke* (ed. Cassirer), IV, p. 169.

to a rejection of all absolute truth or at any rate of all human capacity to know it. Nothing would be true except in relation to a particular situation or a particular purpose, and nothing could be known except from an angle of approach which inevitably makes all knowledge purely subjective. Marxist and Soviet criticism has, however, not been concerned to pursue the matter to this extreme and logical conclusion, but rather to use relativism as a weapon to discredit and dissolve the theories and values of *bourgeois* civilization. The sting of the theory of "conditioned thinking" is that it is so largely true. Obviously few individuals in fact think for themselves; obviously, too, their thinking is in large measure unconsciously conditioned by their social and national background and by their desire to find justification in theory for the practice which the pursuit of their interests demands. It requires no great skill to demonstrate that the political and economic theories which have been fashionable at different periods of history and in different countries reflect the views and the interests of the dominant group at the time and place in question. "Intellectual production," as the *Communist Manifesto* brutally puts it, "changes with material production"; and "the ruling ideas of any particular age have always been merely the ideas of its ruling class." Perhaps the extreme self-confidence and self-satisfaction characteristic of the period of *bourgeois* supremacy, especially in the English-speaking world, made it peculiarly vulnerable to attack. More certainly, the decline in that supremacy, and the challenge presented to it by the first world war and by its consequences, of which the Bolshevik revolution was the most significant, spread the impression that there were hitherto undetected chinks in the armor of *bourgeois* theory. There can be no doubt

that the Marxist critique, and the weapon of relativism which it released, was a powerful factor in that wave of general debunking of *bourgeois* values which reached its climax between the two world wars. Few intelligent democrats today deny the validity of some aspects of the Marxist onslaught. The impact of the Soviet Union in the last twenty-five years has helped to drive it home; and Soviet prestige has in turn been increased by the recognition of its validity.

This then is the essence of the revolutionary or destructive impact of Marxism on the western world. A true revolution is never content merely to expose the abuses of the existing order, the cases in which its practice falls short of its precept, but attacks at their root the values on which the moral authority of the existing order is based. Thus Christianity was not so much concerned to denounce the cruelties or injustices of Roman rule as to challenge the principle of authority represented by it. The Reformation did not merely denounce ecclesiastical abuses and misdeeds; it attacked the principle which found the ultimate source of authority in a visible church and its head. The French revolution was not content to arraign individual kings and ministers as wicked; it struck at the principle of royal sovereignty. The gravamen of the Marxist revolution is not that it has exposed the failures and shortcomings of western democracy, but that it has called in question the moral authority of the ideals and principles of western democracy by declaring them to be a reflection of the interests of a privileged class. The serious thing about the contemporary revolution is not that Marxism has kindled and inflamed the resentments of the under-privileged against the existing order and helped to make them articulate: the serious thing is that it has undermined the self-confidence of the privileged by sapping their own faith in the sincerity and efficacy of the principles on which their moral authority rested.

.   .   .   .   .

All this is the negative or destructive side of the impact of the Marxist and Soviet ideologies on the western world. Such criticism successfully undermines the adversary's position, but does nothing to establish one's own. Indeed consistent relativism, by attacking every absolute, renders any position untenable. It is true that some 19th century thinkers, following the impulsive example of Proudhon, who wrote "I deny all absolutes, I believe in progress," attempted to make progress itself their absolute. Moreover this attempt drew a certain scientific coloring from some of the cruder interpretations of Darwinian evolution. But progress itself is meaningless in the absence of some absolute standard—there is nothing to distinguish progress from regression; and most 19th century believers in progress consciously or unconsciously postulated Tennyson's "far-off divine event, to which the whole creation moves." Marx, for all his belief in the historical process and in the scientific quality of his predictions, made no pretence of being neutral. He had a robust constitution which indulged freely in the luxury of moral judgments. Though the thoughts and actions of individuals were conditioned by their social situation, he was fully prepared to censure or praise them on what were in all seeming moral grounds. Though the victory of the proletariat was scientifically inevitable, Marx implicitly encouraged men to work for it on the ground that it was morally right. The moral undertones, which are never far beneath the surface in Marx, became overtones in the current Soviet ideology. The change is significant for the evolution of

Bolshevism from a destructive and revolutionary force into a positive and constructive force. The charge of inconsistency, of a departure from original Marxist orthodoxy, is paralleled in the history of all revolutions which "settle down" and become the basis of a new social order. Every established social order needs its absolutes.

The absolute value which Marxist and Soviet ideology have to offer and to which all else is subordinated is the emancipation of the proletariat, the establishment of its supremacy at the expense of other classes and the ultimate attainment of classless society. The word "proletarian" by its derivation means no more than the unclassed, the under-privileged or the underdog, in whose name all revolutions are made. But it was a stroke of insight which enabled Marx to perceive that the industrial worker, the "wage-slave," was the characteristic "proletarian" of the industrial age, and must be the bearer and the eponymous hero of the next revolution. Just as Hegel abandoned relativism in order to find an absolute in the Prussian nation, so Marx abandoned relativism in order, with better reason, to find his absolute in the proletariat. At the very outset of his career, in 1843, Marx had written that "there is only one class whose wrongs are not specific but are those of the whole society—the proletariat." [4] In the *Communist Manifesto* he implicitly answers the charge that, in becoming the champion of the proletariat, he was merely supporting the cause of one class against another:

All previous movements were movements of minorities or in the interest of minorities. The proletarian movement is the conscious movement of the immense majority in the interest of the immense majority.

The victory of the proletariat, he explained elsewhere in the *Manifesto*, meant not the

[4] Quoted in I. Berlin, *Karl Marx*, p. 87.

domination of the proletariat as a class but the end of all class antagonism and the introduction of the classless society. On the tenth anniversary of the Bolshevik revolution Stalin proclaimed the same doctrine:

A revolution in the past generally ended by the replacement at the seat of administration of one group of exploiters by another group of exploiters. The exploiters were changed, the exploitation remained. So it was at the time of the movement for the liberation of the slaves. So it was at the period of the peasant rising. So it was in the period of the well-known "great" revolutions in England, in France, in Germany. . . . The October revolution is different *in principle* from these revolutions. It sets as its goal not the replacement of one form of exploitation by another form of exploitation, of one group of exploiters by another group of exploiters, but the annihilation of every form of exploitation of man by man, the annihilation of every kind of exploiting group, the establishment of the dictatorship of the proletariat, the establishment of the power of the most revolutionary class of all the hitherto existing oppressed classes, and the organization of a new classless socialist society. This is why the *victory* of the October revolution means a radical break in the history of mankind.

The contemporary western ideology of the "common man" doubtless has traditional roots in Christianity and in other revolutionary movements of the past. But it owes its revival and current popularity largely to the impact of Marxism and of the Soviet Union. This is the positive side of the bad conscience generated by the Marxist critique among the *bourgeois* ruling class of the last hundred years. It is the conscience-stricken *bourgeoisie* itself which has shown most eagerness to proclaim "the century of the common man." The "common man" has become an absolute in his own right.

The specific character of the ideal associated with the cult of the proletariat or the common man is social or "socialist"—not using the word in a party sense—in two connotations. It is primarily social as opposed to primarily political in its aims; and it is primarily social as opposed to primarily individual in its values.

In the first place, then, the Bolshevik revolution is primarily social where the French revolution was primarily political. Its concept of social justice is not exhausted by the political ideals of liberty and equality. Of the three ideals of the French revolution, liberty has been tarnished by the discovery that, in default of equality, it remains the privilege of the few; equality by the discovery that, unless it remains purely formal, it can only be achieved through the sacrifice of liberty; and fraternity alone remains, perhaps because little attempt has hitherto been made to give it concrete form. It has been said with more than a grain of truth that the specific ideal of the proletarian revolution is neither liberty nor equality but fraternity. The universality of the Bolshevik appeal, its claim to speak in the name of oppressed groups and classes, both national groups and exploited classes, all over the world, has been a large element in its strength. Even where there has been a retreat in Soviet policy and in Soviet ideology from the unbridled internationalism of the first revolutionary years, the retreat has not been into nationalism of the old-fashioned kind. Soviet nationalism has always claimed to be something different on the ground that it is built up on the brotherhood of the many nations and races composing the Soviet Union.

The strength of Soviet patriotism [said Stalin in one of his war-time speeches] lies in the fact that it is based not on racial or nationalist prejudices but . . . on the fraternal partnership of the working people of all the nations of our country.[5]

[5] Speech of November 6, 1944.

It is not wholly unfair to contrast this new Soviet ideology with the kind of nationalism which, in the western world, has almost always meant the supremacy of a certain national group or groups. It would be difficult to deny that the social and political ideas of the English-speaking world rested until recently, and in some measure still rest, on the unspoken assumption of the superior right of the white man in general, and even of certain sections of the white race in particular. This assumption, which reflects the privileges won by English-speaking countries and a few closely allied nations in the prosperous days of *bourgeois* civilization, is reflected in all the relations of the English-speaking world with the "colored peoples" and renders those relations peculiarly vulnerable to the Soviet attack. The English-speaking countries have perhaps not been sufficiently sensitive to the threat to their world-wide position implicit in the Soviet appeal to the brotherhood of man; in so far as they have recently become more sensitive to it and have overcome some of the traditional prejudice of race and color, this is due in large part, directly or indirectly, to the impact of the Soviet Union.

The second and more significant effect of the impact of the Bolshevik ideology has been to hasten the disappearance of the individualist values of *bourgeois* society and the substitution for them of the social values of mass civilization. The age of *bourgeois* capitalism emancipated the individual from his predetermined place in the social and economic order, replaced status by contract, and left the individual free to choose his calling and to rely on his own judgment and his own efforts. The *bourgeois* order brought prosperity and privilege to the capable and enterprising few. Individualism really meant the claim of outstanding individuals to be different,

to distinguish themselves by their attainments, and by the enjoyment of corresponding privileges, from the undifferentiated mass of common men. But for the ordinary worker individual freedom to choose his job seemed largely illusory when its complement was freedom to starve. To have no social obligation to work might seem a boon; but it might be purchased at too high a price if society in its turn had no obligation to provide for the workless. The advantages of individualism perhaps never impressed themselves at all deeply on the consciousness of the masses. At any rate by the end of the 19th century the retreat from individualism had begun; the benefits of an assured status once more seemed more alluring than the combination of a partly fictitious independence with a real and intolerable risk. Trade unions, collective bargaining, social insurance and the ever-growing volume of social legislation were symptoms, or perhaps contributory causes, of the retreat from individualism towards the new values of mass civilization. The modern cult of the common man is both broader and bolder in its universality than any previous social program; for it asserts the social rights not of members of a select society or group but of individual men and women everywhere and without discrimination.

Yet this is not pure gain. The cult of the proletariat, of the common man, by insisting on the equality of social rights common to all, has confirmed the emphasis, already implicit in modern techniques of production, on similarity and standardization. It treats society as a conglomeration of undifferentiated individuals, just as science treats matter as a conglomeration of undifferentiated atoms. The social unit displays a growing determination to "condition" the individuals composing it in uniform ways and for uniform purposes and a growing ability to make this determination effective. The view that the exclusive or primary aim of education is to make the individual think for himself is outmoded; few people any longer contest the thesis that the child should be educated "in" the official ideology of his country. The standardization of production makes it necessary for large numbers of individuals to spend their working hours doing exactly the same thing in exactly the same way. Press and radio ensure that they are inoculated with the same ideas or with a few simple variants of them; commercial advertising strives to make them want the same things to eat, drink and wear, and the same amusements to distract them. The individual becomes depersonalized; the machine and the organization are more and more his masters. The contemporary problem of individualism in a mass civilization has no precedent anywhere in history.

All this has often been described and analyzed, and is quite independent of anything that has happened in Russia in the last thirty years. The strong point about the Soviet ideology is that it has been framed in response to the new conditions of mass civilization, and that it has arisen in a country where the sense of community has always been more active than the sense of individual rights. It is therefore far more of a piece than the confused and conflicting beliefs which arise in the west from the attempt to reconcile past and present. The trend towards mass civilization seems irresistible and irreversible; the alternatives are to accept it or to let contemporary civilization perish altogether. But how much of the individualism of the past can be embodied in the collective forms of the present is an unsolved problem. It looks as if the western world will have to develop a stronger sense of the duty of the individual to society, and the Soviet Union a stronger

sense of the obligations of society to the individual. Even in the early 1920's Lenin recognized the impracticability of collective management in industry and insisted on a return to one-man management and one-man responsibility. In the 1930's Stalin spoke on several occasions of the dangers of "depersonalization" and the importance of individual initiative—once, significantly enough, in a much-quoted speech of 1935 at the Red Army Academy at a time when strenuous efforts were being made to increase the prestige and efficiency of the officer corps. In the previous year in his interview with Mr. H. G. Wells he had denied the existence of any "irreconcilable contrast between the individual and the collective, between the particular personality and the interest of the collective." He went on:

Socialism does not deny individual interests but reconciles them with the interests of the collectivity. . . . The fullest satisfaction can be given to these individual interests only by a socialist society. Moreover a socialist society alone presents a solid guarantee for the protection of the interests of the individual.[6]

These generalizations do not carry us far. But they show the Soviet leaders increasingly aware of the problems of mass civilization in its relation to the individual. In the western world, and particularly in Great Britain, the individualist tradition is so strong and ingrained that the phenomena of mass civilization are often approached not merely without sympathy, but with mistrust and dislike. This does not help; and it has still to be proved that individual enterprise and individual distinction are necessarily crushed out of existence by the far-reaching organization, the external standardization and, perhaps, external drabness which go with mass civilization. Cer-

6 Stalin, *Leninism* (10th Russian edition), p. 602.

tainly the Soviet Union has gone some way to maintain and develop these qualities even within the framework of a discipline far more rigid than the western world is likely to require or accept. The age-long problem of the place of the individual in society and of the relation of society to the individual is once more on the agenda; and it will have to be worked out in the west, as well as in the Soviet Union, in terms of the mass civilization of the contemporary world.

COMMENT

The Marxian Theory of History

In his Speech at the Anniversary of the People's Paper, Marx pointed out the paradoxical character of modern civilization:

> At the same pace that mankind masters nature, man seems to become enslaved to other men or to his own infamy. Even the pure light of science seems unable to shine but on the dark background of ignorance. All our invention and progress seem to result in endowing material forces with intellectual life, and in stultifying human life into a material force.

If Marx could have witnessed the upheavals of the twentieth century—the World Wars, the Depression, the Fascist movement, the titanic struggle between Communism and anti-Communism, the rapid piling up of atomic weapons—he would have regarded them as striking evidence of the truth of his assertions. "Everything," as he said, "seems pregnant with its contrary." The most amazing advances have led to the most terrible retrogressions.

Why have progress and regress thus gone hand in hand? Marx's philosophy of history is an attempt to answer this question. In a preface written in 1883 to a German edition of the *Communist Manifesto,* Engels summed up the tenor of this philosophy:

> That in every historical epoch, the prevailing mode of economic production and exchange, and the social organization necessarily following from it, form the basis upon which is built up, and from which alone can be explained, the political and intellectual history of that epoch; that consequently the whole history of mankind . . . has been a history of class struggles, contests between exploiting and exploited, ruling and oppressed classes; that the history of these class struggles form a series of evolutions in which a stage has [now] been reached where the exploited and oppressed class—the proletariat—cannot attain its emancipation from the sway of the exploiting and ruling class—the bourgeoisie—without at the same time, and once for all, emancipating society at large from exploitation, oppression, class distinctions and class struggles.

In accordance with this theory, our age of crisis must be explained primarily in economic terms.

The fundamental difficulty in the modern world, Marx believed, is the "antagonism between the productive powers and the social relations" of capitalist society. The "productive powers" are the factors immediately operative in the factory or field—the labor power, raw materials, tools, and techniques used in turning out commodities. The "social relations" are the class structure and institutions of property, involving the contrast between rich and poor, capitalists and workers, landowners and farm-hands. (In the societies of the past, there were similar divisions between freemen and slaves, patricians and plebeians, lords and serfs, guild-masters and journeymen.) As an economy matures, the productive powers tend to change more rapidly than the social relations. The most dynamic factor, technology, is the main cause of this relatively fast transformation and expansion of the productive forces. "Steam, electricity, and the self-acting mule were revolutionists of a rather more dangerous character than . . . Barbès, Raspail, and Blanqui." The social relations, since they are so involved with vested interests, are relatively slow to adapt themselves to the expanding productive forces. The greatest crises of history, Marx believed, are primarily the result of the incongruity between rapidly changing techniques and slowly changing class stratifications.

Marx tried to prove that the conflict between the productive powers and the social relations is bound to become more intense as capitalism matures. Profit-motivated employers spend less and less on wages in proportion to their expenditure on plant, machinery, and raw materials. The small employer cannot afford this heavy machinery and cannot compete with the more efficient methods of large-scale production. Hence large companies destroy or absorb small companies. Wealth becomes increasingly concentrated in the hands of the few, and a vast army of the unemployed, displaced by machines, is created. These developments mean a shrinking of the power to consume accompanied by an expansion of the power to produce—overproduction in relation to the number of full purses and underproduction in relation to the number of empty bellies. Since these trends tend to cause business depression, there is a feverish attempt to maintain profits by finding cheaper sources of labor and raw materials and by capturing foreign markets. The nations dominated by capitalistic interests are driven into imperialism, commercial rivalry, and war.

Marx had no doubt that the crises of capitalism would deepen and that the workers would ultimately revolt. He predicted that the proletariat, after winning their revolution, will reorganize the economic system on the basis of planned production for social use. Step by step, they will create a new social order which will put an end to the exploitation of men by men, of class by class, of nation by nation, of blacks by whites, of females by males. Not only human beings but science, art, and morality as well will be freed from economic oppression. The minute division of labor, which stunts and distorts human growth, will be limited in the interests of the wholeness and all-sided development of personality. The state, with its coercive functions, will gradually "wither away" and be replaced by voluntary and cooperative institutions. Mankind will pass from the kingdom of necessity into the kingdom of freedom.

The main emphasis of this philosophy was "materialistic": the basic conflict is between the dynamic forces of production and the static class relations, and this conflict expresses itself socially in the intense struggle of economic classes. Although Marx was thus an economic "materialist" in his theory of history, he was remarkably idealistic in his prophecies. He maintained that mankind will ultimately escape from war, starvation, hate, and coercion.

But the *means* which he envisaged were quite different from the ends. One of his root-ideas is the necessity for the complete and ruthless power of the proletariat in its march toward a free, classless state. He failed to take account of the corrupting influence of absolute power and the tendency of dictatorship to perpetuate itself. He did not foresee that the Communist Revolution would occur mainly in politically backward states, such as Russia, in which the autocratic tradition of the old order would persist and accentuate the severity of "proletarian" dictatorship. What is ostensibly the dictatorship of the proletariat has become the dictatorship of a single party or even of a small cabal within this party.

In Lenin, the contradiction between ends and means reached its apogee. Lenin referred again and again to the objective of a cooperative and decentralized social order, but this ideal was made the excuse for ruthless party dictatorship. The end was so great that dissent became damnable. Any means, however repressive, were justifiable to preserve the true faith. In the name of a free and just society, he and his party undertook the extreme persecution of heretics. This is one of the saddest ironies of history.

Criticism and Conclusion

The Soviet ideological impact upon the Western world is lucidly discussed by Edward Hallett Carr, and we need not enlarge upon his excellent account. It may be helpful, however, to add a few final words of criticism.

It is not very difficult to detect errors and misreckonings in Marx's social theory. He underestimated the historical role of the peasantry and the strength of the middle class; he did not realize to what extent the workers under capitalism could better their lot by collective bargaining and political action; he did not appreciate the possibilities of a middle way, such as democratic social planning in a welfare state, as in Denmark; he did not anticipate the fact that insurance and social security could provide protection against unemployment, poverty, and the other vicissitudes of life; he did not understand that a new, undemocratic social differentiation would arise within the victorious "proletariat" in Communist-dominated states; he did not grasp the extent to which evil means, such as violence and dictatorship, would pervert and contaminate noble ends; he could not foresee that new total weapons of destruction, such as the hydrogen bomb, would require men to think in a radically new way. He was not a crystal-gazer; he could envisage the future only in broad and uncertain outlines.

We have already noted the tendency of Marxism to turn into a fixed set of dogmas. This is the fault not so much of Marx himself as of his followers. Expressing the critical temper of Marx's philosophy, Engels declared: "Everything that is real within the realm of the history of mankind is bound to become unreasonable after a while; hence it is already by definition unreasonable, is afflicted with unreasonableness from the very beginning. . . . Everything that exists deserves to perish." [1] This radically critical approach implies that Marxism itself must be revised and ultimately superseded. Untrue to this critical spirit, the Soviet theoreticians have fiercely denounced the revisionists who have dared to depart from the letter of the Marxist creed.

For lack of space, we have passed over the larger questions of social philosophy—whether Marx's ideal of a classless society is sound; whether the state is an instrument of class rule and is destined to wither away; whether Marx exaggerated the role of economic forces in history; whether he overemphasized class struggle and underemphasized mutual aid as a factor in historical development; whether it is possible to predict the course of history even in its broad, fundamental stages. These are questions of great import that we all would do well to ponder.

We are more likely to avoid prejudice if we remember that there are liberal and democratic elements in Marxism and that much of what Marx recommended has already come to pass in democratic countries. In the *Communist Manifesto,* for example, he advocated a graduated income tax, governmental control of credit by means of a national bank, public ownership of the means of transportation, extension of factories and instruments of production owned by the state, improvement of the soil in accordance with a common plan, free education for all children in public schools, and abolition of child labor. These objectives either have been realized or are near to realization in many democratic countries. In Britain, for example, the coal, gas, and electricity industries, a considerable section of the inland transport industry, the radio industry, and a large proportion of the medical services have been brought under social ownership, and steep inheritance and income taxes, public fiscal

[1] *Ludwig Feuerbach and the Outcome of Classical German Philosophy* (New York: International Publishers, 1941), p. 11.

policies, and various public-welfare measures have substantially reduced inequalities in privilege. To a large extent, Marx's "revolution" has already been achieved under democratic auspices.

The greatness of Western civilization, many of us believe, lies primarily in its liberal and democratic creed. It is this creed that has nourished the dignity of man and that has inspired our boldest venture: the attempt to achieve a community in which all men shall be kings over themselves. If we can be true to this faith, so long as we avoid blind prejudice and the insanity of war, the future of mankind will be bright. We shall then be able to link our immense new scientific and technological resources to the arts of life rather than to the techniques of death. As years of peace bring tolerance, the Communists may become more appreciative of civil rights and the anti-Communists more appreciative of social and economic rights. Then both can join in mankind's ancient war against poverty, ignorance, disease, and oppression.

22

Art and Esthetic Education

ALFRED NORTH WHITEHEAD (1861–1947)

The son of a vicar in the Anglican Church, Whitehead was born at Ramsgate, a village near Canterbury Cathedral. He was educated at Sherborne, one of England's oldest boarding schools, and at Trinity College, Cambridge. He remained in the college for a quarter of a century as a teacher of mathematics, and then taught for an additional thirteen years at the University of London.

Meanwhile he had married Evelyn Wade, who bore him a daughter and two sons. "Her vivid life," he wrote in an autobiographical sketch, "has taught me that beauty, moral and esthetic, is the aim of existence; and that kindness, and love, and artistic satisfaction are among its modes of attainment." [1]

In 1924, at the age of sixty-three, he joined the Philosophy Department at Harvard, where he taught until his retirement in 1937. Although he had collaborated with Bertrand Russell in writing the great *Principia Mathematica* (1910–1913), it was not until his later life that he turned to speculative philosophy, writing a brilliant series of books, including *The Concept of Nature* (1920), *Science and the Modern World* (1925), *Process and Reality* (1929), and *Adventures of Ideas* (1933). These works established his reputation as one of the towering figures in modern thought. He died in his eighty-seventh year in his small apartment near Harvard Yard.

[1] Paul Arthur Schilpp, *The Philosophy of Alfred North Whitehead*, Northwestern University, Evanston, 1941, p. 8.

Art and Esthetic Education*

There is no easy single solution of the practical difficulties of education. We can, however, guide ourselves by a certain simplicity in its general theory. The student should concentrate within a limited field. Such concentration should include all practical and intellectual acquirements requisite for that concentration. This is the ordinary procedure; and, in respect to it, I should be inclined even to increase the facilities for concentration rather than to diminish them. With the concentration there are associated certain subsidiary studies, such as languages for science. Such a scheme of professional training should be directed to a clear end congenial to the student. It is not necessary to elaborate the qualifications of these statements. Such a training must, of course, have the width requisite for its end. But its design should not be complicated by the consideration of other ends. This professional training can only touch one side of education. Its center of gravity lies in the intellect, and its chief tool is the printed book. The center of gravity of the other side of training should lie in intuition without an analytical divorce from the total environment. Its object is immediate apprehension with the minimum of eviscerating analysis. The type of generality, which above all is wanted, is the appreciation of variety of value. I mean an esthetic growth. There is something between the gross specialized values of the mere practical man, and the thin specialized values of the mere scholar. Both types have missed something;

and if you add together the two sets of values, you do not obtain the missing elements. What is wanted is an appreciation of the infinite variety of vivid values achieved by an organism in its proper environment. When you understand all about the sun and all about the atmosphere and all about the rotation of the earth, you may still miss the radiance of the sunset. There is no substitute for the direct perception of the concrete fact with a high light thrown on what is relevant to its preciousness.

What I mean is art (and esthetic education). It is, however, art in such a general sense of the term that I hardly like to call it by that name. Art is a special example. What we want is to draw out habits of esthetic apprehension. According to the metaphysical doctrine which I have been developing, to do so is to increase the depth of individuality. The analysis of reality indicates the two factors, activity emerging into individualized esthetic value. Also the emergent value is the measure of the individualization of the activity. We must foster the creative initiative towards the maintenance of objective values. You will not obtain the apprehension without the initiative, or the initiative without the apprehension. As soon as you get towards the concrete, you cannot exclude action. Sensitiveness without impulse spells decadence, and impulse without sensitiveness spells brutality. I am using the word "sensitiveness" in its most general significance, so as to include apprehension of what lies

* From *Science and the Modern World*, Macmillan, New York, 1925. Reprinted by permission of The Macmillan Company and Cambridge University Press.

beyond oneself; that is to say, sensitiveness to all the facts of the case. Thus "art" in the general sense which I require is any selection by which the concrete facts are so arranged as to elicit attention to particular values which are realizable by them. For example, the mere disposing of the human body and the eyesight so as to get a good view of a sunset is a simple form of artistic selection. The habit of art is the habit of enjoying vivid values.

But, in this sense, art concerns more than sunsets. A factory, with its machinery, its community of operatives, its social service to the general population, its dependence upon organizing and designing genius, its potentialities as a source of wealth to the holders of its stock is an organism exhibiting a variety of vivid values. What we want to train is the habit of apprehending such an organism in its completeness. It is very arguable that the science of political economy, as studied in its first period after the death of Adam Smith (1790), did more harm than good. It destroyed many economic fallacies, and taught how to think about the economic revolution then in progress. But it riveted on men a certain set of abstractions which were disastrous in their influence on modern mentality. It dehumanized industry. This is only one example of a general danger inherent in modern science. Its methodological procedure is exclusive and intolerant, and rightly so. It fixes attention on a definite group of abstractions, neglects everything else, and elicits every scrap of information and theory which is relevant to what it has retained. This method is triumphant, provided that the abstractions are judicious. But, however triumphant, the triumph is within limits. The neglect of these limits leads to disastrous oversights. The anti-rationalism of science is partly justified, as a preservation of its useful methodology;

it is partly mere irrational prejudice. Modern professionalism is the training of minds to conform to the methodology. The historical revolt of the seventeenth century, and the earlier reaction towards naturalism, were examples of transcending the abstractions which fascinated educated society in the Middle Ages. These early ages had an ideal of rationalism, but they failed in its pursuit. For they neglected to note that the methodology of reasoning requires the limitations involved in the abstract. Accordingly, the true rationalism must always transcend itself by recurrence to the concrete in search of inspiration. A self-satisfied rationalism is in effect a form of anti-rationalism. It means an arbitrary halt at a particular set of abstractions. This was the case with science.

There are two principles inherent in the very nature of things, recurring in some particular embodiments whatever field we explore—the spirit of change, and the spirit of conservation. There can be nothing real without both. Mere change without conservation is a passage from nothing to nothing. Its final integration yields mere transient nonentity. Mere conservation without change cannot conserve. For after all, there is a flux of circumstance, and the freshness of being evaporates under mere repetition. The character of existent reality is composed of organisms enduring through the flux of things. The low type of organisms have achieved a self-identity dominating their whole physical life. Electrons, molecules, crystals, belong to this type. They exhibit a massive and complete sameness. In the higher types, where life appears, there is greater complexity. Thus, though there is a complex, enduring pattern, it has retreated into deeper recesses of the total fact. In a sense, the self-identity of a human being is more abstract than that of a crystal. It is the life of the spirit. It relates rather to the individualization of the creative activity; so that the changing circumstances received from the environment, are differentiated from the living personality, and are thought of as forming its perceived field. In truth, the field of perception and the perceiving mind are abstractions which, in the concrete, combine into the successive bodily events. The psychological field, as restricted to sense-objects and passing emotions, is the minor permanence, barely rescued from the nonentity of mere change; and the mind is the major permanence, permeating that complete field, whose endurance is the living soul. But the soul would wither without fertilization from its transient experiences. The secret of the higher organisms lies in their two grades of permanences. By this means the freshness of the environment is absorbed into the permanence of the soul. The changing environment is no longer, by reason of its variety, an enemy to the endurance of the organism. The pattern of the higher organism has retreated into the recesses of the individualized activity. It has become a uniform way of dealing with circumstances; and this way is only strengthened by having a proper variety of circumstances to deal with.

This fertilization of the soul is the reason for the necessity of art. A static value, however serious and important, becomes unendurable by its appalling monotony of endurance. The soul cries aloud for release into change. It suffers the agonies of claustrophobia. The transitions of humor, wit, irreverence, play, sleep, and—above all—of art are necessary for it. Great art is the arrangement of the environment so as to provide for the soul vivid, but transient, values. Human beings require something which absorbs them for a time, something out of the routine which they can stare at. But you cannot subdivide life, except in the abstract analysis of thought. Accord-

ingly, the great art is more than a transient refreshment. It is something which adds to the permanent richness of the soul's self-attainment. It justifies itself both by its immediate enjoyment, and also by its discipline of the inmost being. Its discipline is not distinct from enjoyment, but by reason of it. It transforms the soul into the permanent realization of values extending beyond its former self. This element of transition in art is shown by the restlessness exhibited in its history. An epoch gets saturated by the masterpieces of any one style. Something new must be discovered. The human being wanders on. Yet there is a balance in things. Mere change before the attainment of adequacy of achievement, either in quality or output, is destructive of greatness. But the importance of a living art, which moves on and yet leaves its permanent mark, can hardly be exaggerated.

In regard to the esthetic needs of civilized society the reactions of science have so far been unfortunate. Its materialistic basis has directed attention to *things*, as opposed to *values*. The antithesis is a false one, if taken in a concrete sense. But it is valid at the abstract level of ordinary thought. This misplaced emphasis coalesced with the abstractions of political economy, which are in fact the abstractions in terms of which commercial affairs are carried on. Thus all thought concerned with social organization expressed itself in terms of material things and of capital. Ultimate values were excluded. They were politely bowed to, and then handed over to the clergy to be kept for Sundays. A creed of competitive business morality was evolved, in some respects curiously high; but entirely devoid of consideration for the value of human life. The workmen were conceived as mere hands, drawn from the pool of labor. To God's question, men gave the answer of

Cain—"Am I my brother's keeper?"; and they incurred Cain's guilt. This was the atmosphere in which the industrial revolution was accomplished in England, and to a large extent elsewhere. The internal history of England during the last half century has been an endeavor slowly and painfully to undo the evils wrought in the first stage of the new epoch. It may be that civilization will never recover from the bad climate which enveloped the introduction of machinery. This climate pervaded the whole commercial system of the progressive northern European races. It was partly the result of the esthetic errors of Protestantism and partly the result of scientific materialism, and partly the result of the abstractions of political economy. An illustration of my point is to be found in Macaulay's essay criticizing Southey's *Colloquies on Society*. It was written in 1830. Now Macaulay was a very favorable example of men living at that date, or at any date. He had genius; he was kind-hearted, honorable, and a reformer. This is the extract: "We are told,

that our age has invented atrocities beyond the imagination of our fathers; that society has been brought into a state compared with which extermination would be a blessing; and all because the dwellings of cotton-spinners are naked and rectangular. Mr. Southey has found out a way he tells us, in which the effects of manufactures and agriculture may be compared. And what is this way? To stand on a hill, to look at a cottage and a factory, and to see which is the prettier."

Southey seems to have said many silly things in his book; but, so far as this extract is concerned, he could make a good case for himself if he returned to earth after the lapse of nearly a century. The evils of the early industrial system are now a commonplace of knowledge. The point which I am insisting on is the stone-blind eye with which even the best men of that time regarded the importance of esthetics in a nation's life. I do not believe that we have as yet nearly achieved the right estimate.

COMMENT

Unbalanced Cultural Development

The theme of *Science and the Modern World* is the influence of the scientific mentality upon Western civilization during the past three centuries. Science has probed some of the deepest mysteries of the universe and invented the most fecund machines. These achievements, however, have not been matched by a comparable moral, religious, and esthetic advance. We have not learned how to relate human beings happily and creatively to one another. In philosophy, the remedy is to recognize more fully the role of values in existence; in industry, to put more stress upon quality and human costs; in education, to foster wide humanistic sympathies and the appreciation of beauty and art.

Whereas the older materialists, with their assumption of the bare valuelessness of matter, conceived of goodness and beauty as accidental appearances, Whitehead has sketched a metaphysics which has different implications. The history of the universe, as he envisages it, is the evolution of organisms from the simple to the complex. Electrons, atoms, molecules, cells, plants, animals, men, and human communities form a series of mounting complexity and inclusiveness, the higher organisms embracing innumerable lower ones. Even matter at its lowest level is "organic," and every organism is essentially influenced by others; each higher level exhibits its own emergent qualities; and values, such as beauty, are as real and fundamental as any other aspect of nature. This is a far cry from the reductive materialism characteristic of so much thought in the modern age.

Whitehead concludes his argument with a discussion of the requisites of social betterment, maintaining that progress depends upon the restoration of balance in our civilization. We should cease to sacrifice wisdom to knowledge, well-rounded development to specialized skill, concrete appreciation to abstract understanding, synthesis to analysis, quality to quantity. If we are to obtain a proper balance, art and esthetic education must become much more pervasive in our society.

By art Whitehead means not merely poems and paintings and statues and musical compositions, but fondly made tools and comely attire and attractive gardens and dwellings and the pleasing appearance of highways and towns and cultivated fields. Whenever we enjoy vivid qualities for their own sake, our experience is esthetic, and art is the control and creation of these qualities so as to elicit an appreciation of values. In this sense, art and esthetic experience are as necessary to civilization as are science and technology.

Art and Science

To understand the force of Whitehead's contention, it will be useful to compare science and art. They are alike, as against the shallower perceptions of common sense, in grasping the interrelations of things, science tracing connections between causes and effects, art revealing connections among our perceptions and feelings. A master of poetic metaphor, for example, must have a keen eye for hitherto unsuspected correlations and identities. But science yields an abstract set of laws descriptive of nature, whereas art produces a concrete pattern expressive of values.

The prime mark of science is its objective and verifiable character. A scientist is never satisfied until his description is confirmed by other scientists. If a table were to be thus scientifically described, its weight, measure, and atomic structure would be recorded in exact verifiable terms. The scientist would thus reduce the concrete appearance to a set of abstractions which are "the same" for all qualified observers. An object for science is a combination of abstract properties, something to be analyzed into elements (the more measurable the better), something which is the effect of something else, something to be verified by the agreement of experts.

Art is an individual, subjective, and personal affair, and yet it too is not merely private. Several artists may choose to paint the same table, but each will wait for an individual vision to come to him. He will brood upon the scene until the thing beheld is soaked with emotional significance and transformed by his distinctive imagination. A table painted by Chardin, Van Gogh, or Cézanne is always unique, bearing the peculiar mark of the painter. Art expresses subjective states in a form palpable to others; it communicates the least communicable aspects of experience.

What is most precious and distinctive about any human being is his inner life, his appreciations, his sense of values. Art objectifies this subjective core of life. It conveys the sense of a living presence rather than a dead set of abstractions. Science, with its abstract descriptions and causal laws, can provide no substitute for this experience of vivid and dynamic values. A civilization that neglects art for the sake of specialized education, competitive business, or scientific and technological advancement, is cutting the roots of its spiritual powers.

The Social Functions of Art

Esthetic experience is an exercise and training in the intuition of relations. Deeply ingrained by esthetic cultivation, the habit of seeing things in their togetherness becomes second nature and extends to much besides art. Without this habit, we would not be able to sense so keenly the interconnections in our environment or the concrete relations of human beings to one another.

By means of art, we transcend the incommunicability of our appreciative experiences. We make contact with the inner heart of life, and transmit what we thus discover to others. Art simultaneously trains us to be more spontaneous and more receptive. It enhances our free creativeness, while it brings us into contact with the individuality, the concrete value of actual objects, actual people. There could scarcely be any real social cohesion, any genuine spiritual integration within a society, without the personal spontaneity, the intuitive sense of relations, and the imaginative sympathy that art and esthetic experience cultivate.

One of the outstanding qualities of art is that it is a universal language—a way of communicating across all boundaries of class, creed, nationality, and race. It reflects regional peculiarities, but at the same time it is and should be the language of all humanity. "Give me the right word and the right accent," wrote Joseph Conrad, "and I will move the world." Every great artist can make a similar claim. Art can help immensely to cultivate that community of feeling without which peace and world understanding are impossible.

There is every reason to hope that fine craftsmanship and art will play a more important role in the future. As we make the transition from an economy of scarcity to an economy of relative abundance, we can afford to clean up the filth and ugliness of our slums and devote more attention to the quality of production. Shoddy things, however numerous, are hardly worth making. The work of an artist impresses by virtue of its quality rather than its quantity. If Americans would turn increasingly to the creation and enjoyment of things of fine quality, and if education were designed to evoke the creative and appreciative capacities of the whole population, our civilization would be greatly enhanced, and, incidentally, the problem of future unmanageable surpluses would be happily averted.

Some readers of this book may feel that Whitehead exaggerates the importance of art and esthetic education in human development and of beauty in the cosmic scheme of things. Few thoughtful readers, however, will deny the need to attain a better balance in our civilization and to heal the rift between mechanization and humanization. Art is required to attain these objectives.

BIBLIOGRAPHY

Suggestions for Further Reading

Titles marked by an asterisk are recommended for beginners in philosophy. The older classics are listed in the chronological order of their initial publication; other titles are listed alphabetically. In some instances, when there are many editions of a classic, only the author and title are listed.

PART ONE—WHAT IS PHILOSOPHY?

On the Nature of Philosophy

Blanshard, Brand, *On Philosophical Style.* Manchester University Press, 1954.

Blanshard, Brand, Ducasse, Curt J., Hendel, Charles W., Murphy, Arthur E., and Otto, Max C., *Philosophy in American Education.* New York: Harper, 1945.

Bronstein, Daniel J., Krikorian, Yervant H., and Wiener, Philip P., *Basic Problems of Philosophy,* rev. ed. New York: Prentice-Hall, 1955. Ch. 9.

Cohen, Morris R., *The Faith of a Liberal.* New York: Holt, 1946. Chs. 42 and 46.

Ducasse, Curt J., *Philosophy as a Science.* New York: Oskar Piest, 1941.

Edman, Irwin, *Four Ways of Philosophy.* New York: Holt, 1937.

*James, William, *Some Problems of Philosophy.* New York: Longmans, Green, 1911. Ch. 1.

*Montague, William P., *Great Visions of Philosophy.* La Salle: Open Court Publishing Company, 1950. Prologue.

*Muirhead, John H., *The Use of Philosophy.* London: G. Allen and Unwin, 1928.

*Perry, Ralph Barton, *A Defence of Philosophy.* Cambridge: Harvard University Press, 1931.

Schlick, Moritz, "The Future of Philosophy" in *Publications in Philosophy.* Stockton: College of the Pacific, 1932.

On Socrates as a Philosopher

Cross, Robert N., *Socrates: The Man and His Mission.* London: Methuen, 1914.

*Guardini, Romano, *The Death of Socrates: An Interpretation of the Platonic Dialogues: Euthyphro, Apology, Crito and Phaedo.* New York: Sheed and Ward, 1948.

*Jaeger, Werner, *Paideia: The Idea of Greek Culture,* Vol. II. Oxford: Basil Blackwell, 1946–1947.

*Taylor, A. E., *Socrates.* New York: Appleton, 1933.

PART TWO—THE WAYS OF KNOWING

Classics

Plato, *The Theaetetus and the Sophist,* trans. with a commentary by F. M. Cornford. London: Routledge and K. Paul, 1935.

Bacon, Francis, *Selections,* ed. by Matthew T. McClure. New York: Scribner, 1928.

Galilei, Galileo, *Dialogues Concerning Two New Sciences.* Evanston: Northwestern University Press, 1946.

Descartes, René, *The Philosophical Works of Descartes,* trans. by Elizabeth S. Haldane and G. R. T. Ross. Cambridge University Press, 1912.

———, *Philosophical Writings,* trans. by Nor-

man Kemp Smith. London: Macmillan, 1952.

Spinoza, Benedict, *On the Improvement of the Understanding.* New York: Hafner, 1949.

Locke, John, *An Essay Concerning Human Understanding,* ed. by A. S. Pringle-Pattison. Oxford: Clarendon Press, 1924.

Leibniz, Gottfried W., *New Essays Concerning Human Understanding.* Chicago: Open Court Publishing Company, 1916.

Hume, David, *A Treatise of Human Nature,* ed. by L. A. Selby-Bigge. Oxford: Clarendon Press, 1949.

———, *Enquiry Concerning Human Under-*

standing, ed. by L. A. Selby-Bigge. Oxford: Clarendon Press, 1936.

Kant, Immanuel, *Critique of Pure Reason,* trans. by Norman Kemp Smith. London: Macmillan, 1929.

———, *Prolegomena to Any Future Metaphysics.* Manchester University Press, 1953.

Comte, Auguste, *The Positive Philosophy.* London: Trübner, 1875.

Mill, John Stuart, *A System of Logic.* New York: Harper, 1904. Books III, VI.

———, *Philosophy of Scientific Method,* ed. by Ernest Nagel. New York: Hafner, 1950.

On Descartes and Rationalism

Balz, A. G. A., *Descartes and the Modern Mind.* New Haven: Yale University Press, 1952.

Beck, Leslie J., *The Method of Descartes.* Oxford: Clarendon Press, 1952.

Gibson, A. Boyce, *The Philosophy of Descartes.* London: Methuen, 1932.

Keeling, Stanley V., *Descartes.* London: E. Benn, 1934.

*Mellone, Sydney, *The Dawn of Modern Thought: Descartes, Spinoza, Leibniz.* New York: Oxford University Press, 1930.

On Peirce and Empiricism

Buchler, Justus, *Charles Peirce's Empiricism.* New York: Harcourt, Brace, 1939.

Feibleman, James, *An Introduction to Peirce's Philosophy.* New York: Harper, 1946.

Gallie, W. B., *Peirce and Pragmatism.* Harmondsworth, Middlesex: Pelican Books, 1952.

Goudge, Thomas A., *The Thought of C. S. Peirce.* University of Toronto Press, 1950.

Peirce, Charles Sanders, *Collected Papers of Charles Sanders Peirce,* Cambridge: Harvard University Press, 1931–1935.

Wiener, Philip P. and Young, Frederick H. (editors), *Studies in the Philosophy of Charles Sanders Peirce.* Cambridge: Harvard University Press, 1952.

On James and Pragmatism

Bergson, Henri, "On the Pragmatism of William James" in *Creative Mind.* New York: Philosophical Library, 1946.

*Hocking, William E., *Types of Philosophy.* New York: Scribner, 1929. Chs. 9 and 10.

James, William, *The Meaning of Truth.* New York: Longmans, Green, 1914.

———, *Pragmatism.* New York: Longmans, Green, 1907.

Moore, G. E., "William James' 'Pragmatism'" in *Philosophical Studies.* London: K. Paul, 1922.

Perry, Ralph Barton, *Present Philosophical Tendencies.* New York: Longmans, Green, 1912.

*———, *The Thought and Character of William James.* Cambridge: Harvard University Press, 1948. New York: Tudor, 1955.

Russell, Bertrand, "William James' Conception of Truth" in *Philosophical Essays.* London: Longmans, Green, 1910.

Santayana, George, *Character and Opinion in the United States.* New York: Scribner, 1924. Tudor, 1955.

On Dewey and Pragmatism

Dewey, John, *Essays in Experimental Logic.* University of Chicago Press, 1916.

———, *Experience and Nature,* rev. ed. New York: Norton, 1929.

———, *How We Think.* Boston: Heath, 1933.

———, *Logic: The Theory of Inquiry.* New York: Holt, 1938.

———, *The Quest for Certainty.* New York: Minton, Balch, 1929.

———, *Reconstruction in Philosophy.* Boston: Beacon Press, 1948.

Feldman, William T., *The Philosophy of John Dewey.* Baltimore: Johns Hopkins University Press, 1934.

Hook, Sidney, *John Dewey.* New York: John Day, 1939.

Kallen, Horace M., and others, *The Philosopher of the Common Man.* New York: Putnam, 1940.

Schilpp, Paul Arthur (editor), *The Philosophy of John Dewey.* Evanston: Northwestern University Press, 1939. New York: Tudor, 1951.

Thayer, Horace, *The Logic of Pragmatism.* New York: Humanities Press, 1952.

White, Morton G., *The Origin of Dewey's Instrumentalism.* New York: Columbia University Press, 1943.

On Russell and the Correspondence Theory

Dorward, Alan, *Bertrand Russell.* London: Longmans, Green, 1951.

Fritz, Charles A., *Bertrand Russell's Construction of the External World.* London: Routledge and K. Paul, 1952.

*Joad, C. E. M., *Introduction to Modern Philosophy*. Oxford: Clarendon Press, 1941.

Russell, Bertrand, *An Inquiry into Meaning and Truth*. New York: Norton, 1940.

——, "The Monistic Theory of Truth" in *Philosophical Essays*. London: Longmans, Green, 1910.

——, *Our Knowledge of the External World*. Chicago: Open Court Publishing Company, 1914.

On the Coherence Theory

Blanshard, Brand, *The Nature of Thought*. London: G. Allen and Unwin, 1940.

Ewing, Alfred C., *Idealism: A Critical Survey*. London: Methuen, 1934. Ch. 5.

Joachim, Harold H., *The Nature of Truth*. Oxford: Clarendon Press, 1906.

Recent Epistemological Theory

Ayer, Alfred J., *The Foundations of Empirical Knowledge*. New York: Macmillan, 1940.

——, *Language, Truth and Logic*, 2nd ed., revised. London: Gollancz, 1948.

——, *Philosophical Essays*. London: Macmillan, 1954.

Bridgman, P. W., *The Logic of Modern Physics*. New York: Macmillan, 1927.

——, *The Nature of Physical Theory*. Princeton University Press, 1936.

Carnap, Rudolf, *The Unity of Science*. London: K. Paul, 1934.

Cohen, Morris R., *Reason and Nature*. New York: Harcourt, Brace, 1931.

Hobhouse, L. T., *The Theory of Knowledge*. New York: Macmillan, 1895.

Lewis, Clarence I., *An Analysis of Knowledge and Valuation*. La Salle: Open Court Publishing Company, 1946.

——, *Mind and the World Order*. New York: Scribner, 1929.

Lovejoy, Arthur O., *The Revolt Against Dualism*. Chicago: Open Court Publishing Company, 1930.

Mead, George Herbert, *The Philosophy of the Act*. University of Chicago Press, 1938.

——, *The Philosophy of the Present*. Chicago: Open Court Publishing Company, 1932.

Montague, William P., *The Ways of Knowing*. London: George Allen, 1925.

Nagel, Ernest, *Sovereign Reason*. Glencoe: Free Press, 1954.

Poincaré, Henri, *The Foundations of Science*. New York: Science Press, 1913.

Price, Henry H., *Perception*. London: Methuen, 1950.

——, *Thinking and Experience*. Cambridge: Harvard University Press, 1955.

Reichenbach, Hans, *Experience and Prediction*. University of Chicago Press, 1938.

——, *The Rise of Scientific Philosophy*. Berkeley: University of California Press, 1951.

Santayana, George, *Scepticism and Animal Faith*. New York: Scribner, 1924.

Stace, Walter T., *The Theory of Knowledge and Existence*. Oxford: Clarendon Press, 1932.

Urmson, J. O., *Philosophical Analysis: Its Development from 1919 to 1939*. New York: Oxford University Press, 1955.

Whitehead, Alfred North, *The Organization of Thought*. London: Williams, 1917.

Wood, Ledger, *The Analysis of Knowledge*. Princeton University Press, 1941.

PART THREE—THE NATURE OF REALITY

Classics

Plato, *Timaeus*, ed. by Glenn R. Morrow. New York: Liberal Arts Press, 1949.

Aristotle, *The Basic Works of Aristotle*, ed. by Richard McKeon. New York: Random House, 1941.

Lucretius, *On the Nature of the Universe*, trans. by R. E. Latham. Baltimore: Penguin Books, 1951. (A very readable translation.)

Plotinus, *Enneads*, trans. by Stephen MacKenna. London: Warner, 1917–1930.

Augustine, Saint, *Basic Writings*. New York: Random House, 1948.

Aquinas, Saint Thomas, *Basic Writings*. New York: Random House, 1945.

Descartes, René, *Philosophical Writings*, trans. by Norman Kemp Smith. London: Macmillan, 1952.

Hobbes, Thomas, *Selections*, ed. by F. J. E. Woodbridge. New York: Scribner, 1930.

Spinoza, Benedict, *Selections*, ed. by John Wild. New York: Scribner. 1930.

Locke, John, *An Essay Concerning Human Understanding*, ed. by A. S. Pringle-Pattison. Oxford: Clarendon Press, 1924.

Leibniz, Gottfried W., *The Monadology and Other Philosophical Writings*. London: Oxford University Press, 1925.

Berkeley, George, *Philosophical Writings*, ed. by T. E. Jessop. Edinburgh: Nelson, 1952.

Hume, David, *A Treatise of Human Nature*, ed. by L. A. Selby-Bigge. Oxford: Clarendon Press, 1949.

———, *Enquiry Concerning Human Understanding*, ed. by Selby-Bigge. Oxford: Clarendon Press, 1936.

———, *Dialogues Concerning Natural Religion*, ed. by Norman Kemp Smith. Oxford: Clarendon Press, 1935.

Kant, Immanuel, *Critique of Pure Reason*. London: Macmillan, 1929.

———, *Critique of Judgment*. London: Macmillan, 1914.

Hegel, G. W. F., *Selections*, ed. by J. Loewenberg. New York: Scribner, 1929.

Kierkegaard, Soren, *Concluding Unscientific Postscript*. Princeton University Press, 1941.

On Aristotle and Teleology

Allan, Donald J., *The Philosophy of Aristotle*. New York: Oxford University Press, 1952.

Henderson, L. J., *The Fitness of the Environment*. New York: Macmillan, 1927.

Hobhouse, L. T., *Development and Purpose*. London: Macmillan, 1913.

Mure, G. R. G., *Aristotle*. London: Benn, 1932.

Ross, William D., *Aristotle*. New York: Scribner, 1924.

Sinnott, Edmund, *Biology of the Spirit*. New York: Viking Press, 1955.

———, *Cell and Psyche: The Biology of Purpose*. Chapel Hill: University of North Carolina Press, 1950.

*Stocks, J. L., *Aristotelianism*. New York: Longmans, Green, 1922.

*Taylor, A. E., *Aristotle*. London: Jack, 1919.

Thomson, J. Arthur, *The System of Animate Nature*. New York: Holt. 1920.

Wild, John, *Introduction to Realistic Philosophy*. New York: Harper, 1948.

On Materialism, Naturalism, and Emergent Evolution

Broad, C. D., *The Mind and Its Place in Nature*. New York: Harcourt, Brace, 1925. Chs. 2, 14.

Haldane, J. S., *Mechanism, Life, and Personality*. London: J. Murray, 1914.

*Hocking, William E., *Types of Philosophy*. New York: Scribner, 1929. Chs. 3–7.

Krikorian, Y. H. (editor), *Naturalism and the Human Spirit*. New York: Columbia University Press, 1944.

Lange, F. A., *The History of Materialism*. New York: Harcourt, Brace, 1925.

McDougall, William, *Modern Materialism and Emergent Evolution*, New York: Van Nostrand, 1929.

Morgan, C. Lloyd, *Emergent Evolution*. New York: Holt, 1923.

———, *Life, Mind and Spirit*. New York: Holt, 1925.

Perry, Ralph Barton, *Present Philosophical Tendencies*. New York: Longmans, Green, 1912. Part II.

*Pratt, James B., *Naturalism*. New Haven: Yale University Press, 1939.

*———, *Matter and Spirit*. New York: Macmillan, 1922.

Sellars, R. W.; McGill, V. J.; Farber, M., *Philosophy for the Future: The Quest of Modern Materialism*. New York: Macmillan, 1949.

Smuts, J. C., *Holism and Evolution*. New York: Macmillan, 1926.

Stout, G. F., *Mind and Matter*. Cambridge University Press, 1931. Book Two.

Woodbridge, F. J. E., *An Essay on Nature*. New York: Columbia University Press, 1940.

On Idealism

*Adams, George P., *Idealism and the Modern Age*. New Haven: Yale University Press, 1919.

———, *Man and Metaphysics*. New York: Columbia University Press, 1948.

Bradley, F. H., *Appearance and Reality*. Oxford: Clarendon Press, 1930.

Bosanquet, Bernard, *The Meeting of Extremes in Contemporary Philosophy*. London: Macmillan, 1924.

———, *The Principle of Individuality and Value*. London: Macmillan, 1912.

———, *The Value and Destiny of the Individual*. London: Macmillan, 1913.

Cunningham, G. W., *The Idealistic Argument in Recent British and American Philosophy*. New York: Century, 1933.

Ewing, A. C., *Idealism*. London: Methuen, 1934.

Hocking, William E., *The Self, Its Body and Freedom*. New Haven: Yale University Press, 1928.

*———, *Types of Philosophy*. New York: Scribner, 1929. Chs. 19–26.

*Hoernle, R. F. A., *Idealism as a Philosophy*. New York: Doran, 1927.

McTaggart, J. M. E., *The Nature of Existence*. Cambridge University Press, 1921.

Moore, G. E., "The Refutation of Idealism" in *Philosophical Studies*. London: K. Paul, 1922.

Perry, Ralph Barton, *Present Philosophical Tendencies*. New York: Longmans, Green, 1912. Chs. 6–8.

*Royce, Josiah, *The Spirit of Modern Philosophy*. Boston: Houghton, Mifflin, 1892. New York: Tudor, 1955.

———, *The World and the Individual*. London: Macmillan, 1904.

Sinclair, May, *The New Idealism*. New York: Macmillan, 1917.

On Hume and Scepticism

Laird, John, *Hume's Philosophy of Human Nature*. London: Methuen, 1932.

Montague, William P., "The Method of Scepticism" in *The Ways of Knowing*. London: George Allen, 1925.

*Morris, Charles R., *Locke, Berkeley, Hume*. Oxford: Clarendon Press, 1931.

Santayana, George, *Scepticism and Animal Faith*. New York: Scribner, 1924.

Smith, Norman Kemp, *The Philosophy of David Hume*. London: Macmillan, 1941.

Vaihinger, Hans, *The Philosophy of "As If."* New York: Harcourt, Brace, 1935.

On Theism and Religious Philosophy

Bergson, Henri, *The Two Sources of Morality and Religion*. New York: Holt, 1935.

Brightman, Edgar, *A Philosophy of Religion*. New York: Prentice-Hall, 1940.

Buber, Martin, *I and Thou*. Edinburgh: Clark, 1937.

———, *Between Man and Man*. London: K. Paul, 1947.

*Dewey, John, *A Common Faith*. New Haven: Yale University Press, 1934.

*Hicks, G. Dawes, *The Philosophical Bases of Theism*. London: G. Allen and Unwin, 1937.

Hocking, William E., *The Meaning of God in Human Experience*. New Haven: Yale University Press, 1912.

*James, William, *The Varieties of Religious Experience*. New York: Longmans, Green, 1902.

Laird, John, *Mind and Deity*. London: G. Allen and Unwin, 1941.

MacMurray, John, *The Structure of Religious Experience*. New Haven: Yale University Press, 1936.

McTaggart, J. M. E., *Some Dogmas of Religion*. London: Arnold, 1906.

Mill, John Stuart, *Three Essays on Religion*. London: Longmans, Green, 1885.

*Montague, William P., *Belief Unbound*. New Haven: Yale University Press, 1931.

*Pratt, James B., *Eternal Values in Religion*. New York: Macmillan, 1950.

Santayana, George, *Interpretations of Poetry and Religion*. New York: Scribner, 1927.

*———, *Reason in Religion* (Vol. III of *The Life of Reason*). New York: Scribner, 1948.

*Stace, Walter T., *Religion and the Modern Mind*. Philadelphia: Lippincott, 1952.

———, *Time and Eternity*. Princeton University Press, 1952.

*Taylor, A. E., *Does God Exist?* New York: Macmillan, 1947.

Temple, William, *Nature, Man and God*. London: Macmillan, 1934.

Tennant, F. R., *Philosophical Theology*. Cambridge University Press, 1928, 1930.

*Whitehead, Alfred North, *Religion in the Making*. New York: Macmillan, 1926.

Recent Metaphysical Theory

Alexander, Samuel, *Space, Time and Deity*. London: Macmillan, 1934.

Bergson, Henri, *Creative Evolution*. New York: Holt, 1911.

Gotshalk, D. W., *Structure and Reality*. New York: Dial, 1937.

James, William, *A Pluralistic Universe*. London: Longmans, Green, 1909.

———, *Some Problems of Philosophy*. New York: Longmans, Green, 1911.

*Russell, Bertrand, *Philosophy*. New York: Norton, 1927.

———, *Mysticism and Logic*. New York: Longmans, Green, 1918.

Ryle, Gilbert, *The Concept of Mind*. London: Hutchinson, 1949.

Santayana, George, *Realms of Being*. New York: Scribner, 1942.

Wahl, Jean, *A Short History of Existentialism.* New York: Philosophical Library, 1949.

*Whitehead, Alfred North, *Nature and Life.* Cambridge University Press, 1934. (The simplest introduction to Whitehead's difficult system.)

PART FOUR—THE BASIS OF MORALITY

Classics

Plato, *Dialogues.* Especially the *Gorgias, Protagoras,* and *Philebus.*

Aristotle, *Nichomachean Ethics.*

Oates, W. J. (editor), *The Stoic and Epicurean Philosophers.* (Epicurus, Lucretius, Epictetus, Marcus Aurelius.) New York: Random House, 1940.

Spinoza, Benedict, *Ethics.* London: Oxford University Press, 1930.

Butler, Joseph, *Works,* Vols. I and II. Oxford: Clarendon Press, 1897.

Hume, David, *A Treatise of Human Nature,* Book III, and *An Enquiry Concerning the Principles of Morals.*

Kant, Immanuel, *Critique of Practical Reason and Other Writings in Moral Philosophy,* trans. by Lewis White Beck. University of Chicago Press, 1949.

Bentham, Jeremy, *An Introduction to the Principles of Morals and Politics.* New York: Hafner, 1948.

Mill, John Stuart, *Utilitarianism.*

Green, Thomas H., *Prolegomena to Ethics.* Oxford: Clarendon Press, 1890.

Nietzsche, Friedrich, *The Philosophy of Nietzsche* (Contains *Thus Spake Zarathustra, Beyond Good and Evil,* and *The Genealogy of Morals*). New York: Modern Library, n.d.

Melden, A. I., *Ethical Theories,* rev. ed. New York: Prentice-Hall, 1955. (An excellent anthology of classical theories.)

On Aristotle and Ethics of Reason

Mure, G. R. G., *Aristotle.* New York: Oxford University Press, 1939. Ch. 7.

*Pratt, J. B., *Reason in the Art of Living.* New York: Macmillan, 1949. Ch. 9.

Ross, W. D., *Aristotle.* New York: Scribner, 1924.

Santayana, George, *Reason in Science* (Vol. V of *The Life of Reason*), New York: Scribner, 1928. Chs. 8–10.

*Wild, John, *Introduction to Realistic Philosophy.* New York: Harper, 1948. Part I.

On the Ethics of Natural Law and Natural Rights

Gierke, Otto, *Natural Law and the Theory of Society.* London: Cambridge University Press, 1934.

*Huxley, Thomas Henry and Julian, *Touchstone for Ethics.* New York: Harper, 1947.

Kluckhohn, Clyde, *Mirror for Man.* New York: Whittlesey House, 1949.

*Maritain, Jacques, *The Rights of Man and Natural Law.* New York: Scribner, 1945.

*Mill, John Stuart, "Nature" in *Three Essays on Religion.* London: Longmans, Green, 1885.

Needham, Joseph, *Human Law and the Laws of Nature in China and the West.* New York: Oxford University Press, 1951.

Ritchie, David G., *Natural Rights.* London: Allen, 1916.

*Wild, John, *Plato's Modern Enemies and the Theory of Natural Law.* University of Chicago Press, 1953.

On the Ethics of Kant

Broad, C. D., *Five Types of Ethical Theory.* New York: Harcourt, Brace, 1930.

Körner, S., *Kant.* Baltimore: Penguin Books, 1955.

Paton, H. J., *The Categorical Imperative.* London: Hutchinson, 1947.

Scott, John W., *Kant on the Moral Life.* London: A. & C. Black, 1924.

Schroeder, H. H., "Some Common Misinterpretations of the Kantian Ethics" in *Philosophical Review,* July 1940.

Teale, Alfred E., *Kantian Ethics.* London: Oxford University Press, 1951.

Mill and Utilitarianism

*Anschutz, Richard P., *The Philosophy of John Stuart Mill.* Oxford: Clarendon Press, 1953.

Ewing, A. C., "Utilitarianism" in *Ethics,* January 1948.

Moore, G. E., *Ethics.* New York: Holt, 1912. Chs. 1 and 2.

Plamenatz, John, *Mill's Utilitarianism.* Oxford: Blackwell, 1949.

Sidgwick, Henry, *The Methods of Ethics.* London: Macmillan, 1922.

Stephen, Leslie, *The English Utilitarians.* London: Duckworth, 1900.

Dewey and Pragmatic Ethics

Dewey, John, and Tufts, J. H., *Ethics,* rev. ed. New York: Holt, 1932.

*Dewey, John, *Human Nature and Conduct.* New York: Holt, 1922.

———, *The Quest for Certainty.* New York: Minton, Balch, 1929. Ch. 10.

*James, William, "The Moral Philosopher and the Moral Life" in *The Will to Believe and Other Essays in Popular Philosophy.* New York: Longmans, Green, 1897.

Otto, Max, *The Human Enterprise.* New York: Appleton-Century, 1940.

———, *Things and Ideals.* New York: Holt, 1924.

Stevenson and the Ethics of Logical Empiricism

*Ayer, A. J., *Language, Truth and Logic,* 2nd ed. London: Gollanz, 1948. Ch. 6.

Carnap, Rudolf, *Philosophy and Logical Syntax.* London: K. Paul, Trench, Trübner, 1935. Pp. 22–26.

Pap, Arthur, *Elements of Analytic Philosophy.* New York: Macmillan, 1949.

Schlick, Moritz, *Problems of Ethics.* New York: Prentice-Hall, 1939.

Stevenson, C. L., *Ethics and Language.* New Haven: Yale University Press, 1945.

Stroll, Avrum, *The Emotive Theory of Ethics. University of California Publications in Philosophy,* Vol. 28. Berkeley: University of California Press, 1954.

Recent Ethical Theory

Bradley, F. H., *Ethical Studies.* Oxford: Clarendon Press, 1927.

Ewing, A. C., *The Definition of Good.* New York: Macmillan, 1947.

*———, *Ethics.* New York: Macmillan, 1953.

Hartmann, Nicolai, *Ethics.* New York: Macmillan, 1932.

Lewis, C. I., *An Analysis of Knowledge and Valuation.* La Salle: Open Court Publishing Company, 1946.

———, *The Ground and Nature of the Right.* New York: Columbia University Press, 1955.

Maritain, Jacques, *The Person and the Common Good.* New York: Longmans, Green, 1930.

Mumford, Lewis, *The Conduct of Life.* New York: Harcourt, Brace, 1951.

Moore, G. E., *Ethics.* London: Oxford University Press, 1911.

———, *Principia Ethica.* Cambridge University Press, 1903.

Niebuhr, Reinhold, *Moral Man and Immoral Society.* New York: Scribner, 1932.

Perry, Ralph Barton, *General Theory of Value.* New York: Longmans, Green, 1926.

*———, *The Moral Economy.* New York: Scribner, 1909.

———, *Realms of Value.* Cambridge: Harvard University Press, 1954.

Prichard, H. A., *Duty and Interest.* New York: Oxford University Press, 1928.

———, *Moral Obligation.* New York: Oxford University Press, 1950.

Rashdall, Hastings, *The Theory of Good and Evil.* Oxford: Clarendon Press, 1907.

Rice, Philip Blair, *On the Knowledge of Good and Evil.* New York: Random House, 1955.

Ross, David, *Foundations of Ethics.* London: Oxford University Press, 1939.

———, *The Right and the Good.* Oxford: Clarendon Press, 1930.

*Royce, Josiah, *The Philosophy of Loyalty.* New York: Macmillan, 1908.

*Russell, Bertrand, *Human Society in Ethics and Politics.* London: Allen and Unwin, 1954.

Toulmin, S., *Reason in Ethics.* Cambridge University Press, 1937.

Westermarck, Edward, *Origin and Development of the Moral Ideas.* London: Macmillan, 1906.

———, *Ethical Relativity.* New York: Harcourt, Brace, 1932.

PART FIVE—SOCIAL IDEALS

Classics

Plato, *Republic, Statesman, Laws.*

Aristotle, *Politics.*

Machiavelli, Niccolò, *The Prince.*

Hobbes, Thomas, *Leviathan.* Oxford: Blackwell, 1946.

Hobbes, Thomas, *De Cive, or the Citizen*. New York: Appleton-Century-Crofts, 1949.

Locke, John, *Second Treatise of Civil Government*.

———, *A Letter Concerning Toleration*.

Rousseau, Jean Jacques, *The Social Contract*.

Kant, Immanuel, *Perpetual Peace*. London: Allen and Unwin, 1917.

Hegel, G. W. F., *Lectures on the Philosophy of History*. London: Bell, 1902.

———, *The Philosophy of Right*. Oxford: Clarendon Press, 1942.

Mill, John Stuart, *Utilitarianism, Liberty, and Representative Government*. London: Dent, 1931.

Marx, Karl, *Selected Works*. New York: International Publishers, 1933.

———, *A Handbook of Marxism*, ed. by Emile Burns. New York: International Publishers, 1935.

Plato and the Aristocratic Ideal

Barker, Ernest, *Greek Political Theory: Plato and His Predecessors*. London: Methuen, 1918.

*Crossman, R. H. S., *Plato Today*. London: G. Allen and Unwin, 1937.

Gould, John, *The Development of Plato's Ethics*. New York: Cambridge University Press, 1955.

Grene, David, *Man in His Pride*. University of Chicago, 1950.

Jaeger, Werner, *Paideia*, Vol. II. Oxford: Basil Blackwell, 1946–1947.

*Koyre, Alexander, *Discovering Plato*. New York: Columbia University Press, 1945.

Levinson, Ronald, *In Defense of Plato*. Cambridge: Harvard University Press, 1953.

Murphy, Neville, *The Interpretation of Plato's Republic*. Oxford: Clarendon Press, 1951.

Popper, Karl R., *The Open Society and Its Enemies*. Princeton University Press, 1950.

*Wild, John, *Plato's Theory of Man*. Cambridge: Harvard University Press, 1946.

The Political Philosophy of Hobbes

Gooch, G. P., *Hobbes*. London: H. Milford, 1940.

———, *Political Thought in England: Bacon to Halifax*. London: Oxford University Press, 1944.

Graham, William, *English Political Thought: Hobbes to Maine*. London: E. Arnold, 1907.

Laird, John, *Hobbes*. London: Benn, 1934.

Stephen, Leslie, *Hobbes*. New York: Macmillan, 1904.

Strauss, Leo, *The Political Philosophy of Hobbes*. Oxford: Clarendon Press, 1936.

Mill and Liberalism

Anschutz, Richard P., *The Philosophy of John Stuart Mill*. Oxford: Clarendon Press, 1953.

Croce, Benedetto, *History as the Story of Liberty*. London: G. Allen and Unwin, 1941.

Dewey, John, *Freedom and Culture*. New York: Minton, Balch, 1939.

*———, *Liberalism and Social Action*. New York: Putnam, 1935.

*Dickinson, G. Lowes, *Justice and Liberty*. New York: Doubleday, 1908.

Halévy, Élie, *The Growth of Philosophical Radicalism*. New York: Macmillan, 1928.

*Hobhouse, Leonard T., *Liberalism*. New York: Holt, 1911.

*Laski, Harold, *The Rise of Liberalism*. New York: Harper, 1936.

Packe, Michael St. John, *The Life of John Stuart Mill*. London: Secker and Warburg, 1954.

*Russell, Bertrand, *Authority and the Individual*. New York: Simon and Schuster, 1949.

*———, *Freedom versus Organization, 1814–1914*. New York: Norton, 1934.

Wooton, Barbara, *Freedom Under Planning*. Chapel Hill: University of North Carolina Press, 1945.

Marxism

*Adams, H. P., *Karl Marx in His Earlier Writings*. London: G. Allen and Unwin, 1940.

*Buber, Martin, *Paths in Utopia*. London: Routledge and K. Paul, 1949.

Carr, Edward H., *The Soviet Impact on the Western World*. New York: Macmillan, 1946.

Cole, G. D. H., *A History of Socialist Thought*, Vols. I and II. London: Macmillan, 1953–1954.

———, *What Marx Really Meant*. New York: Knopf, 1934.

Federn, Karl, *The Materialistic Conception of History*. London: Macmillan, 1939.

Hook, Sidney, *From Hegel to Marx*. New York: Reynal and Hitchcock, 1936.

———, *Towards the Understanding of Karl Marx*. New York: John Day, 1933.

Meyer, Alfred G., *Marxism*. Cambridge: Harvard University Press, 1954.

*Popper, Karl R., *The Open Society and Its Enemies*. Princeton University Press, 1950.

Somerville, John, *Soviet Philosophy*. New York: Philosophical Library, 1946.

*Venable, Vernon, *Human Nature: The Marxian View*. New York: Knopf, 1945.

Art in the Social Order

Dewey, John, *Art as Experience*. New York: Minton, Balch, 1934.

Gotshalk, D. W., *Art and the Social Order*. University of Chicago Press, 1947.

*Morris, William, *Hopes and Fears for Art*. London: Longmans, Green, 1903.

*Mumford, Lewis, *Art and Technics*. New York: Columbia University Press, 1952.

———, *Technics and Civilization*. New York: Harcourt, Brace, 1934.

Neutra, Richard, *Survival Through Design*. New York: Oxford University Press, 1954.

Plekhanov, G. V., *Art and Social Life*. London: Lawrence and Wishart, 1953.

*Read, Herbert, *Art and Society*, 2nd ed. New York: Pantheon Books, 1945.

———, *Education Through Art*. London: Faber, 1943.

*———, *The Grass Roots of Art*. New York: Wittenburn, 1947.

———, *Icon and Idea: The Function of Art in the Development of Human Consciousness*. Cambridge: Harvard University Press, 1953.

Recent Social Philosophy

Bosanquet, Bernard, *Philosophical Theory of the State*. London: Macmillan, 1920.

Dewey, John, *Individualism, Old and New*. New York: Minton, Balch, 1930.

———, *The Public and Its Problems*. New York: Holt, 1927.

*Fromm, Erich, *Escape from Freedom*. New York: Farrar and Rinehart, 1942.

*———, *Man for Himself*. New York: Rinehart, 1947.

*———, *The Sane Society*. New York: Rinehart, 1955.

Hobhouse, L. T., *The Metaphysical Theory of the State*. London: Macmillan, 1918.

Laski, Harold, *The State in Theory and Practice*. New York: Viking Press, 1935.

Mannheim, Karl, *Diagnosis of Our Time*. New York: Oxford University Press, 1944.

———, *Ideology and Utopia*. New York: Harcourt, Brace, 1936.

———, *Man and Society in an Age of Reconstruction*. New York: Harcourt, Brace, 1940.

Mumford, Lewis, *The Condition of Man*. New York: Harcourt, Brace, 1944.

———, *The Culture of Cities*. New York: Harcourt, Brace, 1938.

*———, *Technics and Civilization*. New York: Harcourt, Brace, 1934.

Northrop, F. C. S., *The Meeting of East and West*. New York: Macmillan, 1946.

Pareto, Vilfredo, *The Mind and Society*. New York: Harcourt, Brace, 1935.

*Perry, Ralph Barton, *Puritanism and Democracy*. New York: Vanguard Press, 1944.

Popper, Karl R., *The Open Society and Its Enemies*. Princeton University Press, 1950.

Sabine, George, *History of Political Theory*. New York: Holt, 1950.

Spengler, Oswald, *The Decline of the West*. New York: Knopf, 1932.

*Stace, Walter T., *The Destiny of Western Man*. New York: Reynal and Hitchcock, 1944.

Tawney, R. H., *The Acquisitive Society*. New York: Harcourt, Brace, 1946.

*———, *Equality*. New York: Harcourt, Brace, 1931.

———, *Religion and the Rise of Capitalism*. New York: Harcourt, Brace, 1926.

Toynbee, Arnold J., *Civilization on Trial*. New York: Oxford University Press, 1948.

———, *A Study of History*. New York: Oxford University Press, 1934–1954.

Veblen, Thorstein, *What Veblen Taught*, ed. by Wesley C. Mitchell. New York: Viking Press, 1936.

Weber, Max, *The Protestant Ethic and the Rise of Capitalism*. London: G. Allen and Unwin, 1930.

INDEX

Index

(Topics and names mentioned only casually are omitted.)

559